Amsterdam

timeout.com/amsterdam

Penguin Books

PENGUIN BOOKS

Published by the Penguin Group
Penguin Books Ltd, 80 Strand, London WC2R ORL, England
Penguin Books USA Inc., 375 Hudson Street, New York, New York 10014, USA
Penguin Books Australia Ltd, 250 Camberwell Road, Camberwell, Victoria 3124, Australia
Penguin Books Canada Ltd, 10 Alcorn Avenue, Toronto, Ontario, Canada M4V 3B2
Penguin Books (NZ) Ltd, cnr Rosedale and Airborne Roads, Albany, Auckland, New Zealand

Penguin Books Ltd, Registered Offices: Harmondsworth, Middlesex, England

First published 1991
Second edition 1993
Third edition 1995
Fourth edition 1996
Fifth edition 1998
Sixth edition 2000
Seventh edition 2002

Eighth edition 2004
10 9 8 7 6 5 4 3 2 1

Copyright © Time Out Group Ltd 1991, 1993, 1995, 1996, 1998, 2000, 2002, 2004
All rights reserved

Colour reprographics by Icon, Crowne House, 56-58 Southwark Street, London SE1 1UN
Printed and bound by Cayfosa-Quebecor, Ctra. de Caldes, Km 3 08 130 Sta, Perpètua de Mogoda, Barcelona, Spain

Edited and designed by
Time Out Guides Limited
Universal House
251 Tottenham Court Road
London W1T 7AB
Tel + 44 (0)20 7813 3000
Fax + 44 (0)20 7813 6001
Email guides@timeout.com
www.timeout.com

Editorial

Editor Steve Korver
Deputy Editor Simon Cropper
Listings Checker Nevena Bajalica
Proofreader Edoardo Albert
Indexer Jonathan Cox

Editorial/Managing Director Peter Fiennes
Series Editor Ruth Jarvis
Deputy Series Editor Lesley McCave
Guides Co-ordinator Anna Norman
Accountant Sarah Bostock

Design

Art Director Mandy Martin
Acting Art Director Scott Moore
Acting Art Editor Tracey Ridgewell
Senior Designer Averil Sinnott
Designers Astrid Kogler, Sam Lands
Digital Imaging Dan Conway
Ad Make-up Charlotte Blythe

Picture Desk

Picture Editor Jael Marschner
Deputy Picture Editor Kit Burnet
Picture Researcher Alex Ortiz

Advertising

Sales Director Mark Phillips
International Sales Manager Ross Canadé
International Sales Executive James Tuson
Advertising Sales (Amsterdam) Boom Chicago
Advertising Assistant Sabrina Ancilleri

Marketing

Marketing Manager Mandy Martinez
US Publicity & Marketing Associate Rosella Albanese

Production

Guides Production Director Mark Lamond
Production Controller Samantha Furniss

Time Out Group

Chairman Tony Elliott
Managing Director Mike Hardwick
Group Financial Director Richard Waterlow
Group Commercial Director Lesley Gill
Group Marketing Director Christine Cort
Group General Manager Nichola Coulthard
Group Art Director John Oakey
Online Managing Director David Pepper

Contributors

Introduction Steve Korver. **History** Steve Korver (*If the cap fits…* Kim Renfrew). **Amsterdam Today** Willem de Blaaw.
Architecture Steve Korver. **Art** Steve Korver. **Sex & Drugs** Steve Korver, Petra Timmerman (*Ask a silly question* Petra
Timmerman). **Water** Steve Korver. **Where to Stay** Laura Martz (*Cultural cooking with Lloyd* Steve Korver). **Sightseeing** Steve
Korver (*Camouflage made easy, Authenti-city or Amst-ersatz?* Serge van Wijngaarden). **Restaurants** Steve Korver. **Bars** Pip
Farquharson (*Food for drinking* Steve Korver). **Coffeeshops** Pip Farquharson (*High-tech tokes* Steve Korver). **Shops & Services**
Kate Holder (*Mode in the Netherlands* Kim Renfrew; *From cut-price to cutting-edge* Steve Korver). **Festivals & Events** Steve
Korver. **Children** Tim Muentzer. **Film** Willem de Blaauw (*Lights! Camera! Clog action!* Steve Korver). **Galleries** Steve Korver.
Gay & Lesbian Willem de Blaauw, Kim Renfrew. **Music** Alex Tobin (*Handy André, It's a gas, Poptastic-scholastic* Steve Korver).
Nightclubs Erin Tasmania (*Hope springs nocturnal* Steve Korver). **Sport & Fitness** Tim Muentzer (*The word of the Redeemer*
Steve Korver; *Amsterdam Arena vs Mount Zion* Serge van Wijngaarden). **Theatre, Comedy & Dance** Tim Muentzer (*Over the
edge* Steve Korver). **Trips Out of Town** Steve Korver. **Directory** Steve Korver, Nevena Bajalica.

Maps Mapworld, 71 Blandy Road, Henley on Thames, Oxon RG9 1QB. **Amsterdam transport map** Studio Olykan.

Photography by Heloise Bergman, except: pages 6, 16, 17, 21 Hulton Archive; page 7 Mary Evans Picture Library;
page 18 Koen Wessing/Hollandse Hoogte; page 19 Steye Raviez/Hollandse Hoogte; page 35 Rijksmuseum Amsterdam;
page 36 Muiderslot; page 37 Museum Boijmans Van Beuningen; page 38 (top) Bijbelsmuseum; page 38 (bottom)
Amsterdam Historical Museum; page 39 (top) Van Gogh Museum; page 39 (bottom) Stedelijk Museum of Modern Art;
pages 179, 184 Corbis; page 227 Hadley Kinkade. The following images were provided by the featured
establishments/artist: pages 33, 104, 123, 183, 219, 246, 249.

The Editor would like to thank: Nevena Bajalica, Will Fulford-Jones, Cath Phillips, Jaro Renout, Nel and Klaas, Rene Nuijens,
Pip@underwateramsterdam.com, Nepco, Mr and Mrs Cameron, Andy, Onno, and all contributors from previous editions,
whose work formed the basis for parts of this book.

Contents

Introduction

While Amsterdam's impressive gabled houses reflect past Golden Age glories, their distorted reflection in the canal waters below them perhaps tell us more: this is one happily twisted town. And like the slippery eels under the surface, Amsterdam's true essence always seems to slither away just when you think you've put your finger on it.

As with any city, there's far more to Amsterdam than chocolate-box stereotypes. Finding what this 'more' might be inevitably draws you first to the Red Light District near the geographical centre, with its always freshly fleshed windows. The way the city radiates out from this (certainly not charmless) ancient inner pit led a visiting Albert Camus to note that the circumscribing Canal Ring resembles the circles of Hell. So we'd like to take this opportunity to welcome you to one hell of a town.

It's also a hell of a convenient town, in fact, very much like this guidebook: almost pocket-sized. Almost everything of interest is within easy walking distance. The chaos of the centre soon gives way to the more rarefied walking opportunities of the Canal Ring, which in turn gives way to the more funky streetlife neighbourhoods like the Jordaan and the Pijp. Between these two lies Museumplein where, in a mere square kilometre, you can indulge in an almost endless cakewalk through the history of western art. This area – along with the Eastern Docklands and a city-bisecting line where an underground Metro line is being laid – is undergoing massive redevelopment: Amsterdam is currently in an intense state of flux. But hey, fluxing is what this city does best.

Happily, the city's famously laid-back character seems eternal: there's still plenty of chillage to be found in this most global of villages. In the summer, when the terraces open, the city has an almost Mediterranean feel. The locals like to be out in the open. In fact, Amsterdam's chequered reputation of the past derives largely from their tolerant, upfront attitude, which now happily translates to offering its endless stream of visitors a full spectrum of diversions between the mellow and the chaotic, the chocolate-box and the eel-infested...

ABOUT THE TIME OUT CITY GUIDES

The *Time Out Amsterdam Guide* is one of an expanding series of Time Out City Guides, now numbering 45, produced by the people behind London and New York's successful listings magazines. Our guides are all written and updated by resident experts who have striven to provide you with all the most up-to-date information you'll need to explore the city or read up on its background, whether you're a local or a first-time visitor.

THE LOWDOWN ON THE LISTINGS

Above all, we've tried to make this book as useful as possible. Addresses, telephone numbers, websites, transport information, opening times, admission prices and credit card details have all been included in the listings. And, as far as possible, we've given details of facilities, services and events, all checked and correct as we went to press. However, owners and managers can change their arrangements at any time, and they often do. Before you go out of your way, we'd advise you to telephone and check opening times, ticket prices and other particulars. While every effort has been made to ensure the accuracy of the information contained in this guide, the publishers cannot accept responsibility for any errors it may contain.

PRICES AND PAYMENT

We have noted where venues such as shops, hotels, restaurants, museums, attractions and the like accept the following credit cards: American Express (AmEx), Diners Club (DC), MasterCard (MC) and Visa (V). Many will also accept travellers' cheques, along with other, less widely held credit cards.

As this book was being completed in late 2003, many European countries – including the Netherlands – are still experiencing more fluctuations in prices than usual as a result from the introduction of the euro in 2002.

In other words, the prices we've supplied should be treated as guidelines, not gospel. However, if they vary wildly from those we've quoted, please write and let us know. We aim to give the best and most up-to-date advice, so we always want to know if you've been badly treated or overcharged.

THE LIE OF THE LAND

Central Amsterdam divides fairly neatly into separate neighbourhoods. The Old Centre is

split down the middle into the Old Side and the New Side, and is bordered by a ring of canals known as the grachtengordel. Outside these canals lie a number of smaller, primarily residential neighbourhoods, such as the Pijp, the Museum Quarter and the Jordaan. Each of these areas has its own section within the Sightseeing chapter, and these area designations have been used consistently throughout the book.

TELEPHONE NUMBERS
The area code for Amsterdam is 020. All phone numbers in this guide take this code unless otherwise stated. We have stipulated where phone numbers are charged at non-standard rates – such as 0800 numbers, which are free, and 0900, which are billed at premium rate. For more details on telephone codes and charges, *see p288.*

Advertisers

We would like to stress that no establishment has been included in this book because it has advertised in any of our publications and no payment of any kind has influenced any review. The opinions given in this book are those of Time Out writers and entirely independent.

ESSENTIAL INFORMATION
For all the practical information you might need for visiting the city – on such topics as visas, facilities and access for the disabled, emergency numbers, Dutch vocabulary and local transport – turn to the Directory chapter at the back of the guide. It starts on page 274.

MAPS
Wherever possible, map references have been provided for every venue in the guide, indicating the page and grid reference at which it can be found on our street maps of Amsterdam. There are also overview maps of the city and of the Netherlands, and a map of Amsterdam's tram network. The maps start on page 302.

LET US KNOW WHAT YOU THINK
We hope you enjoy the *Time Out Amsterdam Guide*, and we'd like to know what you think of it. We welcome tips for places that you consider we should include in future editions and take note of your criticism of our choices. There's a reader's reply card at the back of this book for your feedback, or you can email us at amsterdamguide@timeout.com.

There is an online version of this book, along with guides to 45 international cities, at **www.timeout.com**.

In Context

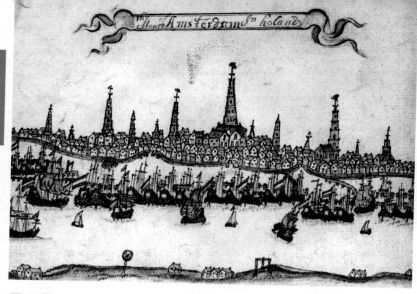

History

Copious amounts of religious strife, countless wars and near-infinite protests: Amsterdam's history was never dull.

According to legend, Amsterdam was founded by two lost fishermen who promised they'd build a town where they finally hit land. They reached terra firma, and their seasick dog was quick to annoint the patch with vomit.

The reality, sadly, is more mundane. Although the Romans occupied other parts of Holland, they didn't reach the north. Soggy bog was not the stuff on which empires were built, so the legions moved on. Archaeologists have found no evidence of settlement at Amsterdam before AD 1000, though there are prehistoric remains further east in Drenthe. Amsterdam's site, in fact, was partially under water for years, and the River Amstel had no fixed course until enterprising farmers from around Utrecht built dykes during the 11th century. Once the peasants had done the work, the nobility took over.

During the 13th century, the most important place in the newly reclaimed area was the tiny hamlet of Oudekerk aan de Amstel. In 1204, the Lord of Amstel built a castle nearby on what is now the outskirts of Amsterdam. After the Amstel was dammed in about 1270, a village grew up on the site of what is now Dam Square, acquiring the name Aemstelledamme.

The Lord of Amstel at this time was Gijsbrecht, a pugnacious man often in trouble with his liege lord, the Bishop of Utrecht, and with his nearest neighbour, Count Floris V of Holland. Tension increased when Floris bestowed toll rights – and some independence – on the young town in 1275. Events culminated with Gijsbrecht murdering Floris at Muiden (where Floris's castle, Muiderslot, can still be seen). Gijsbrecht's estates were confiscated by the Bishop of Utrecht and given to the Counts of Holland, and Amsterdam has remained part of the province of North Holland ever since.

In 1323, the Count of Holland, Floris VI, made Amsterdam one of only two toll points in the province for the import of brews. This was no trivial matter at a time when most people drank beer; drinking the local water, in fact, was practically suicidal. Hamburg had the largest brewing capacity in northern Europe, and within 50 years a third of that city's production was flowing through Amsterdam. Thanks to its position between the Atlantic and Hanseatic ports, and by pouring its beer profits into other ventures, the city increased its trade in an assortment of essential goods.

Yet Amsterdam remained small. As late as 1425, the 'city' consisted only of a few blocks of houses with kitchen gardens and two churches, arranged along the final 1,000-metre (0.62-mile) stretch of the River Amstel and bordered by what are now known as Geldersekade, Singel and Kloveniersburgwal. Virtually all these old buildings – such as the Houtenhuis, still standing in the Begijnhof – were wooden, so fire was a constant threat; in the great fire of May 1452, three quarters of the town were razed. Structures built after the fire had to be faced with stone and roofed with tiles or slates. These new architectural developments coincided with urban expansion, as – most notably – foreign commerce led to improvements in shipbuilding.

> **'In the great fire of May 1452, three quarters of the town were razed.'**

WAR AND REFORMATION

None of the wealth and glory of Amsterdam's Golden Age would have been possible without the turbulence that preceded it. During the 16th century, Amsterdam's population increased from about 10,000 (low even by medieval standards) to 50,000 by 1600. The city's first big expansion accommodated this growth, but people coming to the booming city found poverty, disease and squalor in the hastily built workers' quarters. Local merchants, however, weren't complaining: during the 1500s, the city started to emerge as one of the world's major trading powers.

Amsterdam may have been almost autonomous as a chartered city, but on paper it was still under the thumbs of absentee rulers. Through the intricate and exclusive marriage bureau known as the European aristocracy, the Low Countries (the Netherlands and Belgium) had passed into the hands of the Catholic Austro-Spanish House of Habsburg. The Habsburgs were the mightiest monarchs in Europe and Amsterdam was a comparative backwater among their European possessions, but events soon gave the city a new prominence.

Amsterdam's status as a trade centre attracted all kinds of radical religious ideas that were flourishing across northern Europe, encouraged by Martin Luther's audacious condemnation of the all-powerful Catholic Church in 1517. Though Luther's beliefs failed to catch on with locals, many people were drawn to the austere creeds of the Anabaptists and, later, Calvin. When they first arrived from Germany in about 1530, the Catholic city fathers tolerated the Anabaptists. But when they started to run around naked and even seized the Town Hall

in 1534 during an attempt to establish a 'New Jerusalem' on the River Amstel, the leaders were arrested and executed, signalling an unparalleled period of religious repression: 'heretics' were burned at the stake on the Dam.

After the Anabaptists were culled, Calvinist preachers arrived from Geneva, where the movement started, and via France. The arrival of the sober Calvinists caused a transformation. In 1566, religious discontent erupted into what became known as the Iconoclastic Fury. This spontaneous uprising led to the sacking of many churches and monasteries, and Philip II of Spain sent an army to suppress the heresy.

ALTERED STATES

The Eighty Years' War (1568-1648) between the Habsburgs and the Dutch is often seen as a struggle for religious freedom, but there was more to it than that. The Dutch were, after all, looking for political autonomy from an absentee king who represented a continual drain on their coffers. By the last quarter of the 16th century, Philip II of Spain was fighting wars against England and France, in the East against the Ottoman Turks, and in the New World for control of his colonies. The last thing he needed was a revolt in the Low Countries.

Amsterdam toed the Catholic line during the revolt, supporting Philip II until it became clear he was losing. Only in 1578 did the city patricians side with the rebels, led by the first William of Orange. The city and William then

Floris V: old king toll. *See p6.*

combined to expel the Catholics and dismantle their institutions in what came to be called the Alteration. A year later, the Protestant states of the Low Countries united in opposition to Philip when the first modern-day European Republic was born at the Union of Utrecht. The Republic of Seven United Provinces was made up of Friesland, Gelderland, Groningen, Overijssel, Utrecht, Zeeland and Holland. Though lauded as the forerunner of the modern Netherlands, it wasn't the unitary state that William of Orange had wanted, but rather a loose federation with an impotent States General assembly.

Each province appointed a Stadhouder (or viceroy), who commanded the Republic's armed forces and had the right to appoint some of the cities' regents or governors. The Stadhouder of each province sent delegates to the assembly, held at the Binnenhof in the Hague. While fitted with clauses to hinder Catholicism from ever suppressing the Reformed religion again, the Union of Utrecht also enshrined freedom of conscience and religion (at least until the Republic's demise in 1795), thus providing the blueprint that made Amsterdam a safe haven for future political and religious refugees.

CALVIN CLEAN

From its earliest beginnings, Amsterdam had been governed by four Burgomasters – mayors, basically – and a council representing citizens' interests. By 1500, though, city government had become an incestuous business: the city council's

36 members were appointed for life, 'electing' the mayors from their own ranks. Selective intermarriage meant that the city was, in effect, governed by a handful of families. When Amsterdam joined the rebels in 1578, the only change in civic administration was that the Catholic elite was replaced by a Calvinist faction comprising equally wealthy families.

However, social welfare was transformed. Formerly the concern of the Catholic Church, welfare under the Calvinists was incorporated into government. The Regents, as the Calvinist elite became known, took over the convents and monasteries, starting charitable organisations such as orphanages. But the Regents' work ethic and abstemious way of life would not tolerate any kind of excess: crime, drunkenness and immorality were all punishable offences.

During the two centuries before the Eighty Years' War, Amsterdam had developed a powerful maritime force. Even so, it remained overshadowed by Antwerp until 1589, when that city fell to the Spanish. In Belgium, the Habsburg Spanish had adopted siege tactics, leaving Amsterdam unaffected by the hostilities and free to benefit from the blockades suffered by rival ports. Thousands of refugees fled north, among them some of Antwerp's most prosperous merchants, who were mostly Protestant and Jewish (specifically Sephardic Jews who had earlier fled their original homes in Spain and Portugal to escape the Inquisition). These refugees brought the skills, the gold and,

Eejit-prop

Hostility in the Anglo-Dutch Wars of the 17th century was as much a verbal business as a job for projectiles. For sheer lexicographic whallop, the Anglo camp probably had the edge: British propagandists displayed the sort of talent that these days only finds employment in advertising. Not content with cutting to the meat of the matter by, say, dubbing the Dutch 'a bad thing', Britannia's fevered wordsmiths wound themselves up in pejorative pirouettes, describing the enemy as 'crab lice of Europe who would stick until they have drained Britain dry', 'usurpers that deprive fish of their dwelling places', 'sons of mud who worship Mammon' and – oh so sweetly – 'dunghill souls'.

It's hard for the latter-day reader to keep both eyebrows on an even keel when faced by a killer couplet like 'Sprung out of Mire and Slime/And like a Mushroom, Ripen'd in Small Time', or by a tight, evocative one-liner

like 'A Dutchman is a lusty, fat, two-legged cheese worm' – but they presumably went down well enough at the time. Still, a pamphlet title like *The Dutch-men's Pedigree as a Relation, Showing how They Were First Bred and Descended from a Horse-Turd which Was Enclosed in a Butter-Box* bursts through the frontier of effective propaganda into the no-man's-land of screaming silliness. It's like something out of Monty Python.

Perhaps Albion's propagandists would have been better off absorbing the larger lessons of history – and then perhaps the two warring nations would have saved themselves centuries of bitch-slapping over spice routes. Still, all's well that ends well. 21st-century Anglo-Dutch relations are harmonious and even-handed: the Dutch supply the dope and the Brits supply the hordes of drunken weekend travellers. What ever would the pamphleteers have made of that?

famously, the diamond industry that would soon help make Amsterdam one of the greatest trading cities in the world.

THE GOLDEN AGE

European history seems to be littered with Golden Ages, but in Amsterdam's case the first six decades of the 17th century genuinely deserve the label. The small city on the Amstel came to dominate world trade and set up major colonies, resulting in a population explosion and a frenzy of urban expansion in Amsterdam. Its girdle of canals was one of the great engineering feats of the time. This all happened while the country was at war with Spain and presided over not by kings, but by businessmen.

The East India Company doesn't have much of a ring to it, but Verenigde Oost Indische Compagnie (VOC), the world's first transnational company, loses something in translation. The VOC was created by a States General charter in 1602 to finance the wildly expensive and hellishly dangerous voyages to the East. Drawn by the potential fortunes to be made out of trade in spices and silk, the shrewd Dutch saw sense in sending out merchant fleets, but they also knew that one disaster could leave an individual investor penniless. As a result, the main cities set up trading 'chambers', which evaluated the feasibility (and profitability) of ventures then sent ships eastwards. The power of the VOC was far-reaching: it had the capacity to found colonies, establish its own army, declare war and sign treaties. With 1,450 ships, the VOC managed to make over 4,700 profitable journeys.

The story of Isaac Lemaire illustrates just how powerful the VOC became. Lemaire fled to Amsterdam from Antwerp in 1589 and became a founder member of the VOC, buying a ƒ90,000 stake in the company (over €40 million in today's money). Later, after being accused of embezzlement, he quit and cast around for ways to set up on his own. However, the VOC had a monopoly on trade with the East via the Cape of Good Hope; at the time, there was no alternative route. Lemaire was not easily beaten, and heard Portuguese seamen claiming the Cape route was not the only passage to the East: they believed the fabulous spice islands of Java, the Moluccas and Malaya could also be reached by sailing to the tip of South America, where a strait would lead into the Pacific. In 1615, Lemaire financed a voyage, led by his son, that discovered the strait that bears his name.

While the VOC concentrated on the spice trade, a new company received its charter from the Dutch Republic in 1621. The Dutch West India Company (West Indische Compagnie), while not as successful as its sister, dominated trade with Spanish and Portuguese territories

in Africa and America, and in 1623 began to colonise Manhattan Island. The settlement was laid out on a grid similar to Amsterdam's, and adopted the Dutch city's name. But although it flourished to begin with, New Amsterdam didn't last. After the Duke of York's invasion in 1664, the peace treaty between England and the Netherlands determined that New Amsterdam would change its name to New York and come under British control. The Dutch got Surinam as a feeble consolation prize.

Though commerce with the Indies became extensive, it never surpassed Amsterdam's European business: the city had become the major European centre for distribution and trade. Grain from Russia, Poland and Prussia, salt and wine from France, cloth from Leiden and tiles from Delft all passed through the port. Whales were hunted by Amsterdam's fleets, generating a flourishing soap trade, and sugar and spices from Dutch colonies were distributed to ports throughout Scandinavia and the north of Europe. All this activity was financed by the Bank of Amsterdam, which had been set up in the cellars of the City Hall by the municipal council as early as 1609. It was a unique initiative and led to the city being considered the money vault of Europe, its notes readily exchangeable throughout the trading world.

A QUESTION OF WILL POWER

The political structure of the young Dutch Republic was complex. When the Union of Utrecht was signed in 1579, no suitable monarch or head of state was found, so the existing system was adapted to fit new needs. The seven provinces were represented by a 'national' council, the States General. In addition, the provinces appointed a Stadhouder.

The obvious choice for Stadhouder after the union was William of Orange, the wealthy Dutchman who had led the rebellion against Philip II of Spain. William was then succeeded by his son, Maurits of Nassau, who was as successful against the Spanish as his father had been, eventually securing the Twelve Years' Truce (1609-21). Though each province could, in theory, elect a different Stadhouder, in practice they usually chose the same person. After William's popular tenure, it became a tradition to elect an Orange as Stadhouder. By 1641 the family had become sufficiently powerful for William II to marry a British princess, Mary Stuart. It was their son, William III, who set sail in 1688 to accept the throne of England in the so-called Glorious Revolution.

But the Oranges were not popular with everyone. The provinces' representatives at the States General were known as regents, and Holland's – and therefore Amsterdam's – regent was in a powerful enough position to challenge the authority and decisions of the Stadhouder. This power was exercised in 1650, in a crisis precipitated by Holland's decision to disband its militia after the Eighty Years' War against Spain. Stadhouder William II wanted the militia to be maintained – and, importantly, paid for – by Holland, and in response to the disbandment, he had kinsman William Frederick launch a surprise attack on Amsterdam.

When William II died three months later, the leaders of the States of Holland called a Great Assembly of the provinces. Even though there was no outward resistance to the Williams' earlier attack on the city, the provinces – with the exception of Friesland and Groningen, which remained loyal to William Frederick – decided that there should be no Stadhouders, and Johan de Witt, Holland's powerful regent, swore no prince of Orange would ever become Stadhouder again. This became law in the Act of Seclusion of 1653.

During this era, Amsterdam's ruling assembly, the Heren XLVIII (a sheriff, four mayors, a 36-member council and seven jurists), kept a firm grip on all that went on both within and without the city walls. Though this system was self-perpetuating, with the mayors and the council coming from a handful of prominent families, these people were merchants rather than aristocrats, and anyone who made enough money could, in theory, become a member.

The less elevated folk – the craftsmen, artisans and shopkeepers – were equally active in maintaining their position. A guild system had developed in earlier centuries, linked to the Catholic Church, but under the new order, guilds were independent organisations run by their members. The original Amsterdammers – known as *poorters* from the Dutch for 'gate', as they originally lived within the gated walls of the city – began to see their livelihoods being threatened by an influx of newcomers who were prepared to work for lower wages.

Things came to a head when the shipwrights began to lose their trade to competitors in the nearby Zaan region and protested. The shipwrights' lobby was so strong that the city regents decreed Amsterdam ships had to be repaired in Amsterdam yards. This kind of protectionism extended to almost all industrial sectors in the city and effectively meant most crafts became closed shops. Only poorters, or those who had married poorters' daughters, were allowed to join a guild, thereby protecting Amsterdammers' livelihoods and, essentially, barring outsiders from joining their trades.

GROWING PAINS
Though Amsterdam's population had grown to 50,000 by 1600, this was nothing compared with the next 50 years, when it ballooned fourfold. Naturally, the city was obliged to expand to fit its new residents. The most elegant of the major

If the cap fits…

Dutch auction. Dutch oven. Dutch uncle. Dutch fuck. The origin of these concepts may be doubtful, but there's no uncertainty about the name of the pioneering feminist we have to thank for the Dutch cap: Aletta Jacobs. One of 11 children, she was born into a liberal-intellectual Jewish family in Sappermeer in 1854. She left school at 13, but education beckoned again, and after starting studies at the University of Groningen she transferred to Amsterdam in 1876, later graduating as the Netherlands' first female doctor. (To mark the 50th anniversary of her achievement, a plaque – still in place – was unveiled in her presence at the corner of Roemer Visschersraat and Tesselsschadestraat, near the Vondelpark.)

In 1880, her clinic for poor women brought her into contact with many who were ruined through childbirth, so she began dispensing family-planning advice – so beginning the first free service of its kind in the world. Around this time she read about the somewhat unsnappily named Mensinga Pessary. Her vociferous campaigning for its use led to it being known throughout the world by the much catchier moniker 'Dutch cap'.

But it wasn't all sex, sex, sex: Aletta was a devoted suffragette, becoming president first of the Amsterdam branch in 1895, then – in 1903 – of the entire Dutch Association for Woman's Suffrage. This passion was born from her attempt in 1883 to become the first woman to vote in a Dutch election. She was predictably barred from doing so, and so began a battle that she waged until universal voting rights were granted in 1919 by Jacob's Law, named after her.

After this victory, she dedicated her later years to the international suffrage movement, and also travelled across the world with pacifist organisations. She died in Baarn in 1929, although her personal and political legacy survives at the Aletta Jacobs Archive (www.alettajacobs.org).

canals circling the city centre was Herengracht (Lords' Canal): begun in 1613, this was where many of the Heren XLVIII had their homes. So there would be no misunderstanding about relative status, Herengracht was followed further out by Keizersgracht (Emperors' Canal) and Prinsengracht (Princes' Canal). Immigrants were housed much more modestly in the Jordaan.

For all the city's wealth, famine hit Amsterdam with dreary regularity in the 17th century. Guilds had benevolent funds set aside for their members in times of need, but social welfare was primarily in the hands of the ruling merchant class. Amsterdam's elite was noted for its philanthropy, but only poorters were eligible for assistance: even they had to fall into a specific category, described as 'deserving poor'. Those seen as undeserving were sent to houses of correction. The initial philosophy behind these had been idealistic: hard work would produce useful citizens. But soon, the institutions became little more than prisons.

Religious freedom was still not what it might have been, either. As a result of the Alteration of 1578, open Catholic worship was banned in the city during the 17th century, and Catholics were forced to practise in secret. Some Catholics started attic churches, which are exactly what their name suggests: of those set up during the 1600s, the Museum Amstelkring has preserved Amsterdam's only surviving example – Our Lord in the Attic – in its entirety.

DECLINE AND FALL

Though Amsterdam remained one of the wealthiest cities in Europe until the early 19th century, its dominant trading position was lost to England and France after 1660. The United Provinces then spent a couple of centuries bickering about trade and politics with Britain and the other main powers. Wars were frequent: major sea conflicts included battles against the Swedes and no fewer than four Anglo-Dutch wars, from which the Dutch came off worse. It wasn't that they didn't win any battles; more that the small country ran out of men and money.

Despite – or perhaps because of – its history with the Orange family, Amsterdam became the most vocal opponent of the family's attempt to acquire kingdoms, though it supported William III when he crossed the sea to become King of England in 1688. The city fathers believed a Dutchman on their rival's throne could only be an advantage, and for a while they were proved right. However, William was soon back in Amsterdam looking for more money to fight more wars, this time against France.

The admirals who led the wars against Britain are Dutch heroes, and the Nieuwe Kerk has monuments to admirals Van Kinsbergen

(1735-1819), Bentinck (1745-1831) and, most celebrated of all, Michiel de Ruyter (1607-76). The most famous incident, although not prominent in British history books, occurred during the Second English War (1664-7), when de Ruyter sailed up the rivers Thames and Medway to Chatham, stormed the dockyards and burnt the *Royal Charles*, the British flagship, as it lay at anchor. The *Royal Charles*'s coat of arms was stolen, and is now displayed in the Rijksmuseum.

Despite diminished maritime prowess, Amsterdam retained the highest standard of living of all Europe until well into the 18th century. The Plantage district was a direct result of the city's prosperity, and tradesmen and artisans flourished: their role in society can still be gauged by the intricate shapes and carvings on gablestones.

The Dutch Republic also began to lag behind the major European powers in the 18th century. The Agricultural and Industrial Revolutions didn't get off the ground in the Netherlands until later: Amsterdam was nudged out of the shipbuilding market by England, and its lucrative textile industry was lost to other provinces. However, the city managed to exploit its position as the financial centre of the world until the final, devastating Anglo-Dutch War (1780-84). The British hammered the Dutch merchant and naval fleets, crippling the profitable trade with their Far Eastern colonies.

The closest the Dutch came to the Republican movements of France and the United States was with the Patriots. During the 1780s, the Patriots managed to shake off the influence of the Stadhouders in many smaller towns, but in 1787 they were foiled in Amsterdam by the intervention of the Prince of Orange and his brother-in-law, Frederick William II, King of Prussia. Hundreds of Patriots then fled to exile in France, where their welcome convinced them that Napoleon's intentions towards the Dutch Republic were benign. In 1795, they returned, backed by a French army of 'advisers'. With massive support from Amsterdam, they celebrated the new Batavian Republic.

It sounded too good to be true, and it was. According to one contemporary, 'the French moved over the land like locusts'. Over ƒ100 million (about €50 million today) was extracted from the Dutch, and the French also sent an army, 25,000 of whom had to be fed, equipped and housed by their Dutch 'hosts'. Republican ideals seemed hollow when Napoleon installed his brother Louis as King of the Netherlands in 1806, and the symbol of Amsterdam's mercantile ascendancy and civic pride, the City Hall of the Dam, was requisitioned as the royal palace. Even Louis was disturbed by the impoverishment of a nation that had been Europe's most prosperous. However, after Louis had allowed Dutch smugglers to break Napoleon's blockade of Britain, he was forced to abdicate in 1810 and the Low Countries were absorbed into the French Empire.

Even so, government by the French wasn't an unmitigated disaster for the Dutch. The foundations of the modern state were laid in the Napoleonic period, and a civil code introduced – not to mention a broadening of culinary possibilities. However, trade with Britain ceased, and the cost of Napoleon's wars prompted the Dutch to join the revolt against France. After Napoleon's defeat, Amsterdam became the capital of a constitutional monarchy, incorporating what is now Belgium; William VI of Orange was crowned King William I in 1815. But though the Oranges still reigned in the northern provinces, the United Kingdom of the Netherlands, as it then existed, lasted only until 1830.

BETWEEN THE OCCUPATIONS

When the French were finally defeated and left Dutch soil in 1813, Amsterdam emerged as the capital of the new kingdom of the Netherlands but very little else. With its coffers depleted and its colonies occupied by the British, Amsterdam faced a hard fight for recovery.

The fight was made tougher by two huge obstacles. For a start, Dutch colonial assets had been reduced to present-day Indonesia, Surinam and the odd island in the Caribbean. Just as important, though, was the fact that the Dutch were slow to join the Industrial Revolution. The Netherlands had few natural resources to exploit, and business preferred sail power to steam. Add to this the fact that Amsterdam's opening to the sea, the Zuider Zee, was too shallow for the new steamships, and it's easy to see why the Dutch were forced to struggle.

Prosperity, though, returned to Amsterdam after the 1860s. The city adjusted its economy, and its trading position was improved by the building of two canals. The opening of the Suez Canal in 1869 sped up the passage to the Orient and led to an increase in commerce, while the discovery of diamonds in South Africa revitalised the diamond industry. But what the city needed most was easy access to the major shipping lanes of northern Europe. When it was opened in 1876, the Noordzee Kanaal (North Sea Canal) let Amsterdam take advantage of German industrial trade and it became the Netherlands' greatest shipbuilding port again, at least temporarily. Industrial machinery was introduced late to Amsterdam. However, by the late 19th century, the city had begun to modernise production of the luxury

goods for which it would become famous: beer, chocolates, cigars and cut diamonds.

Of course, not all of Amsterdam's trade was conducted on water, and the city finally got a major rail link and a new landmark in 1889. Centraal Station was designed by PJH Cuypers in 1876, and was initially intended to be in the Pijp. When it was decided that the track should instead run along the Zuider Zee, separating the city from the lifeblood of its seafront, a deluge of objections – ultimately overridden – ensued.

There was also dispute when the Rijksmuseum was situated at what was then the fringe of the city, and about the selection of Cuypers as its architect. The result was, like Centraal Station, uniquely eclectic and led to the museum attracting ridicule as a 'cathedral of the arts'. Still, the city's powers consolidated Amsterdam's position at the forefront of Europe with the building of a number of landmark structures such as the Stadsschouwburg (in 1894), the Stedelijk Museum (1895) and the Tropen Institute (1926). The city's international standing had soon improved to such a point that, in 1928, it hosted the Olympics.

NEW DEVELOPMENTS

Amsterdam's population had stagnated at 250,000 for two centuries after the Golden Age, but between 1850 and 1900 it more than doubled. Extra labour was needed to meet the demands of a revitalised economy, but the major problem was how to house the new workers. Today the old inner city quarters are desirable addresses, but they used to be the homes of Amsterdam's poor. The picturesque Jordaan, where regular riots broke out in the 1930s, was occupied primarily by the lowest-paid workers, its canals were used as cesspits and the mortality rate was high. Around the centre, new developments – the Pijp, Dapper and Staatslieden quarters – were built: they weren't luxurious, but at least they had simple lavatory facilities. Wealthier city-dwellers, meanwhile, found elegance and space in homes constructed around Vondelpark and in the south of the city.

The city didn't fare badly in the first two decades of the 20th century, but Dutch neutrality during World War I brought problems to parts of the population. While the elite lined their pockets selling arms, the poor were confronted with food shortages. In 1917, with food riots erupting (especially in the Jordaan), the city had to open soup kitchens and introduce rationing. The army was called in to suppress another outbreak of civil unrest in the Jordaan in 1934. This time the cause was unemployment, endemic throughout the industrialised world after the Wall Street Crash of 1929.

Made (and unmade) in Amsterdam

Amsterdam has always been a magnet for foreigners craving freedom. But freedom is a double-edged sword: freedom of thought can lead to freedom of excess. Here are some tales of the inspiring and cautionary kind...

REASONS TO BE CHEERFUL

Comenius This theologian and pedagogue (1592-1670) – the 'Czech Father of Education' and the first person to put illustrations in textbooks – settled in Amsterdam for the same reasons as Descartes. He lived, wrote and printed his own books at Prinsengracht 415 until his death 16 years later.

Descartes The great French philosopher (1596-1650) lived in Amsterdam for 16 years (*see p88*), drawn by the freedom it afforded him to write and publish his works. His most famous and influential line was, of course, 'I think, therefore I Amsterdam'.

Peter the Great OK, there were rumours of excess (*see p91*), but during his visits to Amsterdam the Russian monarch (1672-1725) found the means and techniques not only to drag his rotting corpse of an Empire into the modern world, but also to build a city – St Petersburg – on a bog.

Skunk This American import (c.1989) took the world by storm after an auspicious Amsterdam debut, and went on to become the basis for all Nederweeds.

Máxima Zorreguieta From daughter (b.1971) of a big noise in an Argentinian dictatorship to (probably) the next Queen of the Netherlands: it's the stuff of fairy tales.

REASONS TO BE TEARFUL

Chet Baker The crooning, trumpet-playing pretty boy (1929-88) collapsed his face while feeding his heroin habit here, right up until his final moody decrescendo – from a hotel window (*see p78*).

Derek Dunne The former Irish football star (1967-2000) set out to expand his horizons, and became one of the Netherlands' biggest heroin traffickers. He was killed during a row about debts.

Louis Napoleon Amsterdam lost its long held freedom to Napoleon at the dawn of the 19th century who set up his brother Louis (1778-1846) as ruler. On a whim, Louis re-zoned City Hall as a personal palace, but thanks to his insane wife and general unpopularity it became more of a personal prison.

Unfortunately, the humiliation of means testing for unemployment benefit meant that many families suffered in hungry silence. Many Dutch workers even moved to Germany, where National Socialism was creating new jobs. At home, Amsterdam initiated extensive public works under the 1934 General Extension Plan, whereby the city's southern outskirts were developed for public housing. The city was just emerging from the Depression by the time the Nazis invaded in May 1940.

WORLD WAR II

Amsterdam endured World War II without being flattened by bombs, but nonetheless its buildings, infrastructure, inhabitants and morale were reduced to a terrible state by the occupying Nazi forces. The Holocaust also left an indelible scar on a city whose population in 1940 was ten per cent Jewish.

Early in the morning of 10 May 1940, German bombers mounted a surprise attack on Dutch airfields and military barracks. The government and people had hoped that the Netherlands could remain neutral, as they were in World War I, so the armed forces were unprepared for war. Though the Dutch aimed to hold off the Germans until the British and French could come to their assistance, their plan failed. Queen Wilhelmina fled to London to form a government in exile, leaving Supreme Commander Winkelman in charge. After

Rotterdam was destroyed by bombing and the Germans threatened other cities with the same treatment, Winkelman surrendered on 14 May. The Dutch colonies of Indonesia and New Guinea were invaded by the Japanese in January 1942. After their capitulation on 8 March, Dutch colonials were imprisoned in Japanese concentration camps.

During the war, Hitler appointed Austrian Nazi Arthur Seyss-Inquart as Rijkskommissaris (State Commissioner) of the Netherlands, and asked him to tie the Dutch economy to the German one and to Nazify Dutch society. Though it won less than five per cent of the votes in the 1939 elections, the National Socialist Movement (NSB) was the largest fascist political party in the Netherlands, and was the only Dutch party not prohibited during the occupation. Its doctrine resembled German Nazism, but the NSB wanted to maintain Dutch autonomy under the direction of Germany.

During the first years of the war, the Nazis let most people live relatively unmolested. Rationing, however, made the Dutch vulnerable to the black market, while cinemas and theatres eventually closed because of curfews and censorship. Later, the Nazis adopted more aggressive measures: Dutch men were forced to work in German industry, and economic exploitation assumed appalling forms. In April 1943, all Dutch soldiers, who had been captured

Dark days: the Nazis roll in.

Salesmanship, 1946: 'May look like a dishcloth, madam, but this incomparable fish...'

during the invasion and then released in the summer of 1940, were ordered to give themselves up as prisoners of war. In an atmosphere of deep shock and outrage, strikes broke out, but were violently suppressed.

To begin with, ordinary citizens, as well as the political and economic elite, had no real reason to make a choice between collaboration and resistance. But as Nazi policies became more virulent, opposition to them swelled, and a growing minority of people were confronted with the difficult choice of whether to obey German measures or to resist. There were several patterns of collaboration. Some people joined the NSB, while others intimidated Jews, got involved in economic collaboration or betrayed people in hiding or members of the Resistance. Amazingly, a small number even signed up for German military service.

The most shocking institutional collaboration involved the police, who dragged Jews out of their houses for deportation, and Dutch Railways, which was paid for transporting Jews to their deaths. When the war was over, 450,000 people were arrested for collaborating – although most were quickly released. Mitigating circumstances – NSB members who helped the Resistance, for example – made judgments complicated, but 14,500 were convicted and sentenced; 39 were executed.

The Resistance was made up chiefly of Communists and, to a lesser extent, Calvinists. Anti-Nazi activities took several forms, with illegal newspapers keeping the population informed and urging them to resist the Nazi dictators. Underground groups took many shapes and sizes. Some spied for the Allies, others fought an armed struggle against the Germans through assassination and sabotage, and others falsified identity cards and food vouchers. A national organisation took care of people who wanted to hide, and aided the railway strikers, Dutch soldiers and illegal workers being sought by the Germans, with other groups helping Jews into hiding. By 1945, more than 300,000 people had gone underground in the Netherlands.

Worse was to follow towards the end of the war. In 1944, the Netherlands plunged into Hongerwinter – the Hunger Winter. Supplies of coal vanished after the liberation of the south and a railway strike, called by the Dutch government in exile in order to hasten German defeat, was disastrous for the supply of food. In retaliation for the strike, the Germans damaged Schiphol Airport and the harbours of Rotterdam and Amsterdam – foiling any attempts to bring in supplies – and grabbed everything they could. Walking became the only means of transport, domestic refuse was no longer collected, sewers overflowed and the population became vulnerable to disease.

To survive, people stole fuel: more than 20,000 trees were cut down and 4,600 buildings were demolished. Floors, staircases, joists and rafters were plundered, causing the collapse of

Bike risers: the **Provos** hoist their egalitarian symbol, 1966. *See p20.*

many houses, particularly those left by deported Jews. Supplies were scarce and many couldn't afford to buy their rationing allowance, let alone the expensive produce on the black market. By the end of the winter, 20,000 people had died of starvation and disease, and much of the city was seriously damaged.

But hope was around the corner. The Allies had liberated the south of the Netherlands on 5 September 1944, Dolle Dinsdag (Mad Tuesday), and complete liberation came on 5 May 1945, when it became apparent that the Netherlands was the worst hit country in western Europe.

In spite of the destruction and the loss of so many lives, there were effusive celebrations. But more blood was shed on 7 May, when German soldiers opened fire on a crowd who had gathered in Dam Square to welcome their Canadian liberators. 22 people were killed.

THE HOLOCAUST

'I see how the world is slowly becoming a desert, I hear more and more clearly the approaching thunder that will kill us,' wrote Anne Frank in her diary on 15 July 1944. Though her words obviously applied to the Jews, they were relevant to all those who were persecuted during the war. Granted, anti-Semitism in Holland had not been as virulent as in Germany, France or Austria. But even so, most – though not all – of the Dutch population closed its eyes to the persecution, and there's still a feeling of national guilt as a result.

The Holocaust happened in three stages. First came measures to enforce the isolation of the Jews: the ritual slaughter of animals was prohibited, Jewish government employees were dismissed, Jews were banned from public

places and, eventually, all Jews were forced to wear a yellow Star of David. (Some non-Jews wore the badge as a mark of solidarity.) Concentration was the second stage. From early 1942, all Dutch Jews were obliged to move to three areas in Amsterdam, isolated by signs, drawbridges and barbed wire. The final stage was deportation. Between July 1942 and September 1943, most of the 140,000 Dutch Jews were deported, via Kamp Westerbork. Public outrage at the deportations was foreshadowed by the most dramatic protest against the anti-Semitic terror, the February Strike of 1941.

The Nazis also wanted to eliminate Dutch Gypsies: more than 200,000 European Gypsies, including many Dutch, were exterminated in concentration camps. Homosexuals, too, were threatened with extermination, but their persecution was less systematic: public morality acts prohibited homosexual behaviour, and gay pressure groups ceased their activities. In addition, men arrested for other activities were punished more severely if they were found to be gay. In Dutch educational textbooks, the extermination of Gypsies and homosexuals is still often omitted, but Amsterdam has the worlds first memorial to persecuted gays – the Homomonument, which incorporates pink triangles in its design, turning the Nazi badge of persecution into a symbol of pride.

THE POST-WAR ERA

The country was scarred by the occupation, losing ten per cent of its housing, 30 per cent of its industry and 40 per cent of its production capacity. Though Amsterdam escaped the bombing raids that devastated Rotterdam, it bore the brunt of deportations: only 5,000 Jews,

The world of Amsterdam interiors, '60s hippy style.

out of a pre-war Jewish population of 80,000, remained. Despite intense poverty and drastic shortages of food, fuel and building materials, the Dutch tackled the task of post-war recovery with a strong sense of optimism. In 1948, people threw street parties, firstly to celebrate the inauguration of Queen Juliana, and, later, the four gold medals won by Amsterdam athlete Fanny Blankers-Koen at the London Olympics.

Some Dutch flirted briefly with communism after the war, but in 1948 a compromise was struck between the Catholic KVP and the newly created Labour party PvdA, and the two proceeded to govern in successive coalitions until 1958. Led by Prime Minister Willem Drees, the government resuscitated social programmes and laid the basis for a welfare state. The Dutch now reverted to the virtues of a conservative, provincial society: decency, hard work and thrift. The country's first priority, though, was economic recovery. The city council concentrated on reviving the two motors of its economy: Schiphol Airport and the Port of Amsterdam, the latter of which was boosted by the opening of the Amsterdam-Rhine Canal in 1952. Joining Belgium and Luxembourg in the Benelux also brought the country trade benefits, and the Netherlands was the first to repay its Marshall Plan loans. The authorities dusted off their pre-war development plans and embarked on rapid urban expansion. But as people moved to new suburbs, businesses moved into the centre, worsening congestion on the already cramped roads. After the war, the Dutch colonies of New Guinea and Indonesia were liberated from the Japanese and pushed for independence. With Indonesia accounting for 20 per cent of their pre-war economy, the

Dutch launched military interventions in 1947 and 1948. But these did not prevent the transfer of sovereignty to Indonesia on 27 December 1949, while the dispute with New Guinea dragged on until 1962 and did much to damage the Netherlands' reputation abroad. Colonial immigrants to the Netherlands – including the later arrival of Surinamese (about half the population of that country) – and Turkish and Moroccan 'guest workers' now comprise 16 per cent of the population. Though poorer jobs and housing have usually been their lot, racial tensions were low until the mid-1990s, which also saw the brief rise of the neo-fascist CD party.

'Foreign hippies flocked to the city.'

Although the economy and welfare state revived in the 1950s, there was still civil unrest. Strikes flared at the port and council workers defied a ban on industrial action. In 1951, protesters clashed with police outside the Concertgebouw, angered by the appointment of a pro-Nazi conductor. In 1956 demonstrators besieged the Felix Meritis Building, home of the Dutch Communist Party from 1946 until the late '70s, outraged by the Soviet invasion of Hungary.

In the late '40s and '50s, Amsterdammers returned to pre-war pursuits: fashion and celebrity interviews filled the newspapers and cultural events mushroomed. In 1947, the city launched the prestigious Holland Festival, while the elite held the Boekenbal, an annual event where writers met royalty and other dignitaries. New avant-garde movements emerged, notable among them the CoBrA art group, whose 1949 exhibition at the Stedelijk Museum of Modern Art caused an uproar, and the *vijftigers*, a group of experimental poets led by Lucebert. Many of these artists met in brown cafés around Leidseplein.

FAREWELL TO WELFARE

The '60s proved to be one of the most colourful decades in Amsterdam's history. There were genuine official attempts to improve society. The IJ Tunnel eased communications to north Amsterdam just as the national economy took off. There were high hopes for rehousing developments such as the Bijlmermeer, and influential new architecture from the likes of Aldo van Eyck and Herman Herzberger.

Yet the generous hand of the welfare state was being bitten. Discontent began on a variety of issues, among them the nuclear threat, urban expansion and industrialisation, the consumer society and authority in general. Popular movements similar to those in other west European cities were formed, but with a zaniness all their own. Protest and dissent have always been a vital part of the Netherlands' democratic process, yet the Dutch have a habit of keeping things in proportion; so, popular demonstrations took a playful form.

Discontent gained focus in 1964, when pranks around 't Lieverdje statue, highlighting political or social problems, kickstarted a new radical subculture. Founded by anarchist philosophy student Roel van Duyn and 'anti-smoke magician' Robert Jasper Grootveld, the Provos – their name inspired by their gameplan: to provoke – numbered only about two dozen, but were enormously influential. Their style influenced the anti-Vietnam demos in the US and the Situationist antics in 1969 Paris, and set the tone for Amsterdam's love of liberal politics and absurdist theatre. Their finest hour came in March 1966, when protests about Princess Beatrix's controversial wedding to the German Claus van Amsberg, turned nasty after the Provos let off a smoke bomb on the carriage route, and a riot ensued.

Foreign hippies flocked to the city, attracted by its tolerant attitude to soft drugs. Though the possession of up to 30 grams (one ounce) of hash wasn't decriminalised until 1976, the authorities turned a blind eye, preferring to prosecute dealers who also pushed hard drugs. But the focal points of hippie culture at the dawn of the 1970s were the Melkweg and Paradiso, both of which emitted such a pungent aroma of marijuana that tokers could be smelt way over in Leidseplein. The city soon became a haven for drop-outs and hippies from all over Europe until the end of the decade, when the Dam and Vondelpark turned into unruly

campsites and public tolerance of the hippies waned. In the '70s, Amsterdam's popular culture shifted towards a tougher expression of disaffected urban youth. Yet Vondelpark, the Melkweg and the Dam remain a magnet for ageing and New Age hippies, even today.

Perhaps the most significant catalyst for discontent in the '70s – which exploded into civil conflict by the '80s – was housing. Amsterdam's small size and historic city centre had always been a nightmare for its urban planners. The city's population increased in the '60s, reaching its peak (nearly 870,000) by 1964. Swelling the numbers further were immigrants from the Netherlands' last major colony, Surinam, many of whom were dumped in the Bijlmermeer. It degenerated into a ghetto and, when a 747 crashed there in October 1992, the number of fatalities was impossible to ascertain: many victims were unregistered residents.

'Amsterdam became the first city to send an official anti-Olympics delegation.'

The Metro link to the Bijlmermeer is itself a landmark to some of Amsterdam's most violent protests. Passionate opposition erupted against the proposed clearance in February 1975 of the Jewish quarter of the Nieuwmarkt. Civil unrest culminated in 'Blue Monday', 24 March 1975, when police sparked clashes with residents and supporters. Police fired tear gas into the homes of those who refused to move out and battered down doors. Despite further violence, the first Metro line opened in 1977, with the Centraal Station link following in 1980, though only one of the four planned lines was completed.

City planners were shocked by the fervent opposition to their schemes for large, airy suburbs. It was not what people wanted: they cherished the narrow streets, the small squares and the cosy cafés. The public felt the council was selling out to big business, complaining that the centre was becoming unaffordable for ordinary people. In 1978, the council decided to improve housing through small-scale development, renovating houses street by street. But with an estimated 90,000 people still on the housing list in 1980, public concern grew.

Speculators who left property empty caused justifiable, acute resentment, which was soon mobilised into direct action: vacant buildings were occupied illegally by squatters. In March 1980, police turned against them for the first time and used tanks to evict them from a former office building in Vondelstraat. Riots ensued, but the squatters were victorious. In 1982, as Amsterdam's squatting movement reached its

Here's lookin' at you, hon: **Claus** and **Beatrix** tie the knot. *See p20.*

peak, clashes with police escalated: a state of emergency was called after one eviction battle. Soon, though, the city – led by new mayor Ed van Thijn – had gained the upper hand over the movement, and one of the last of the city's big squats, Wyers, fell amid tear gas in February 1984 to make way for a Holiday Inn. Squatters were no longer a force to be reckoned with, though their ideas of small-scale regeneration have since been absorbed into official planning.

BACK TO BASICS

Born and bred in Amsterdam, Ed van Thijn embodied a new strand in Dutch politics. Though a socialist, he took tough action against 'unsavoury elements' – petty criminals, squatters, dealers in hard drugs – and upgraded facilities to attract new businesses and tourists. A new national political era also emerged, with the election in 1982 of Rotterdam millionaire Ruud Lubbers as leader of the then centre-right coalition government of Christian Democrats and right-wing Liberals. He saw to it that the welfare system and government subsidies were trimmed to ease the country's large budget deficit, and aimed to revitalise the economy

with more businesslike policies. The price of Amsterdam's new affluence (among most groups, except the poorest) has been a swing towards commercialism, with the hordes of squatters largely supplanted by well-groomed yuppies. Flashy cafés, galleries and nouvelle cuisine restaurants replaced the alternative scene and a mood of calm settled on the city. Still, a classic example of Dutch free expression was provoked by the city's mid-'80s campaign to host the 1992 Olympics. Amsterdam became the first city ever to send an (ultimately successful) official anti-Olympics delegation.

Current mayor Job Cohen stills holds to a course that hopes to see Amsterdam completely re-invented as 'Business Gateway to Europe', where future visitors will be more prone to point their cameras towards the arising Eastern Docklands than towards the ever-photogenic Red Light District. But with the current economic decline, the advantages – both for business and the general atmosphere – of nurturing Amsterdam's long-held reputation as a hotbed for edgy creativity are becoming more apparent. So worry not: the city isn't ready to relinquish its rebel status just yet.

Key events

EARLY HISTORY

1204 Gijsbrecht van Amstel builds a castle in the coastal settlement that eventually becomes Amsterdam.
1270 The Amstel is dammed at Dam Square.
1300 Amsterdam is granted city rights by the Bishop of Utrecht.
1306 Work begins on the Oude Kerk.
1313 The Bishop of Utrecht grants Aemstelledamme full municipal rights and leaves it to William III of Holland.
1342 The city walls (*burgwallen*) are built.
1421 The St Elizabeth's Day Flood occurs, as does Amsterdam's first great fire.
1452 Fire destroys most wooden houses.
1489 Maximilian grants Amsterdam the right to add the imperial crown to its coat of arms.

WAR AND REFORMATION

1534 Anabaptists try to seize City Hall but fail. A period of anti-Protestant repression begins.
1565 William the Silent organises a Protestant revolt against Spanish rule.
1566 The Beeldenstorm (Iconoclastic Fury) is unleashed. Protestant worship is made legal.
1568 The Eighty Years War with Spain begins.
1577 The Prince of Orange annexes the city.
1578 Catholic Burgomasters are replaced by Protestants in a coup known as the Alteration.
1579 The Union of Utrecht is signed, allowing freedom of religious belief but not of worship.
1589 Antwerp falls to Spain; there is a mass exodus to the north.

THE GOLDEN AGE

1602 The Verenigde Oost Indische Compagnie (VOC) is founded.
1606 Rembrandt van Rijn is born.
1611 The Zuiderkerk is completed.
1613 Work starts on the western stretches of Herengracht, Keizersgracht and Prinsengracht.
1623 WIC colonises Manhattan Island; Peter Stuyvesant founds New Amsterdam in 1625.
1642 Rembrandt completes the *Night Watch*.
1648 The Treaty of Munster is signed, ending the Eighty Years War with Spain.
1654 England declares war on the United Provinces.
1667 England and the Netherlands sign the Peace of Breda.

DECLINE AND FALL

1672 England and the Netherlands go to war; Louis XIV of France invades.
1675 The Portuguese Synagogue is built.

1685 French Protestants take refuge after the revocation of the Edict of Nantes.
1689 William of Orange becomes King William III of England.
1696 Undertakers riot against funeral tax.
1787 Frederick William II, King of Prussia, occupies Amsterdam.
1795 French Revolutionaries are welcomed to Amsterdam by the Patriots. The Batavian Republic is set up and run from Amsterdam.
1806 Napoleon's brother is made King.
1810 King Louis is removed from the throne.
1813 Unification of the Netherlands. Amsterdam is no longer a self-governing city.
1815 Amsterdam becomes capital of Holland.

BETWEEN THE OCCUPATIONS

1848 The city's ramparts are pulled down.
1876 Noordzee Kanaal links Amsterdam with the North Sea.
1880s Oil is discovered in Sumatra. The Royal Dutch Company (Shell Oil) is founded.
1883 Amsterdam holds the World Exhibition.
1887 The Rijksmuseum is completed.
1889 Centraal Station opens.
1922 Women are granted the vote.
1928 The Olympics are held in Amsterdam.
1934 Amsterdam's population is 800,000.

World War II

1940 German troops invade Amsterdam.
1941 The February Strike ensues, in protest against the deportation of Jews.
1944-5 20,000 die in the Hunger Winter.
1945 Canadian soldiers free Amsterdam.
1947 Anne Frank's diary is published.

THE POST-WAR ERA

1966 The wedding of Princess Beatrix and Prince Claus ends in riots.
1968 The IJ Tunnel opens.
1976 Cannabis is decriminalised.
1977 First Metrolijn (underground) opens.
1980 Riots take place on Queen Beatrix's Coronation Day (30 April). The date becomes National Squatters' Day.
1986 The controversial 'Stopera' civic-headquarters-cum-opera-house is built.
1992 A Boeing 747 crashes into a block of flats in Bijlmermeer.
1997 The euro is approved as a European currency in the Treaty of Amsterdam.
1999 Prostitution is made legal after years of decriminalisation.
2002 The guilder is dead; long live the euro.

Amsterdam Today

Europe's most liberal and compact capital might be maturing, but it still knows how to deliver the goods.

Many Amsterdammers refer to the capital as a village. Not just because of its diminutive size but also because it doesn't have the big city problems other European capitals, like Paris or London, have to deal with. But while it's still an easy place to live, work and spend time in, the past few years have seen Amsterdam grow up and change very fast. Some of the changes are visible; others have more to do with rules and regulations that are not so apparent. The Dutch capital is now arguably almost as 'sensible' as its opposite numbers abroad – and yet (thank goodness) it still serves up a feast of fun for both tourists and inhabitants.

THE BUILDERS COME TO TOWN
The first thing you'll notice on arrival is that the city looks like a huge building site. In 2001 the council finally started work on the Noord-Zuidlijn, the new Metro line that will run from Amsterdam North, via Centraal Station, to the World Trade Center in the south of the city – and later all the way to Schiphol. It's due to open in 2011. The council and government

believe the new line is vital for the economic health of the city: it should attract much-needed new business, and the project itself will create 10,000 local jobs. But the citizens themselves? Many are against it. They think the current trams, buses and metro lines do a perfectly good job, and they shudder to think of the millions the prestigious new line will cost – money they feel could be better spent on crime prevention or housing. In any case, the financial side of the project is still not tied up, so it's unclear how – and when – the story will end.

CHANGING ROOMS
As a knock-on effect of the Noord-Zuidlijn work, Centraal Station is also getting a major revamp. Apart from expanding the station to accommodate the new Metro line, it's also being re-designed to make it safer, to pack in more shops and to provide links to the different types of public transport. It will also be home to the IJtram, a new tram that will run from the centre to IJburg, one of the new residential areas built on artificial islands east of Centraal Station (*see*

Ever get the feeling...

p101 **Smisle!**). For years Amsterdam has tried to solve its housing crisis by developing new residential areas in the east. After the aesthetic blunders of years past – the high-rise eyesores in south-east Bijlmermeer are truly brutal – the authorities were determined to make the blocks on Javakade and KNSM Eiland easy on the eye. And they've largely succeeded: the new buildings are often architecturally striking, especially when seen in their waterfront context. On the down side, the apartments they contain are costly to rent or buy, particularly when compared to more centrally-located council flats and apartments which go for €400 for 50 or 60 square metres (60 or 70 square feet). Tenants who have such cheap little pads tend to hang on to them long after their careers give them the chance to move up the property ladder, which makes it nearly impossible for newcomers to find affordable accommodation. Not surprisingly, talks about introducing a new rent law for council houses – the more you earn, the more you pay – was met with much criticism and will probably die a quiet death.

A NEW, CLEAN CUT IMAGE

Amsterdam's main attraction, its liberal and liberated atmosphere, has also been at the root of its main sources of concern over the past few years. Thanks to the relaxed laws, Amsterdam attracts many people who think that they can get away with almost anything. But the overall feeling among locals is that because a great deal of recent illegal activities were left unpunished

by police, morals and values drained away – with a large increase in petty crime and anti-social behaviour as the result. Since taking office at the beginning of 2001, Mayor Job Cohen has continued the clean-up work begun by his predecessor, Schelto Patijn, who started by banning explicit window displays in sex shops in the centre. A project called Streetwise ensures that, every weekend, portable toilets are set up around Leidseplein and Rembrandtplein to avoid partygoers relieving themselves against buildings. Those who still piss up walls get a huge fine if caught (as, incidentally, do cyclists who bike through a red traffic light or ride down the pedestrian Leidsestraat). Drinking alcohol on the street is now forbidden in areas such as Waterlooplein, Albert Cuypstraat, Leidseplein and – despite being named after the niece of late brewer Freddy Heineken – Marie Heinekenplein. And since many problems and fights are alcohol-related, there's also been talk of banning happy hours throughout the city.

TICKET TO SAFETY

Though Amsterdam is growing up fast, it's still a very safe city. Even areas like the Red Light District are much safer than run-down areas in other big cities. In fact, crime figures from the Amsterdam Police show that in 2002 street crime dropped by 18.1 per cent, drug-related crimes went down 33.2 per cent, and 'only' 23 people were offed. Still, mayor Cohen would like more government money to spend on making Amsterdam safer still. Aggression on public

... bikes are popular? **Floating park** in front of Centraal Station. *See p252.*

transport is a particular cause for concern: many Amsterdammers, notably the elderly, no longer like to travel by public transport. To address this issue, ticket inspectors have returned to a number of trams, more CCTVs have been wired up, self-defence skills have been taught to drivers, and stronger policing is in evidence at high-risk stations like Lelylaan.

NIGHT WATCHERS

This all sounds sensible enough, but it's a funny state of affairs when a city that earns a huge amount of money from sex and prides itself on being liberal then bans pole dancing – as happened at a new Amsterdam club in 2003. The council doesn't want more sex businesses to open, and has stopped issuing licences and permits to newcomers. Not that pole dancing is such a disgracefully wicked activity, and in any case much sleazier things take place in nearby establishments. But that, apparently, ain't the point: it's the 'principle' that counts. Club promoters and bar owners, though, were not amused, and who can blame them: they fear that if the trend continues, Amsterdam will end up about as sexy as Disneyland and lose its appeal for both the Dutch and the tourists. So the council invited them to come up with other ideas to make the city hipper, and the result, taking its name from the famous Rembrandt painting, was the Nachtwacht committee (*see p228* **Hope springs nocturnal**). Mission: to come up with ideas to spice up Amsterdam's nightlife – in the best possible taste, of course.

The famous coffeeshops are also under threat. Amsterdam's masters don't want any more of them. No new permits are granted, and whenever a coffeeshop closes down, its premises are obliged to be used for other purposes.

A STEP TO THE RIGHT

Another sign of the times was the roller-coaster career of Pim Fortuyn, the gay, right-wing, anti-Islamic politician who was murdered in 2002. His views raised many an eyebrow, but plenty of people approved – and he was nothing if not frank. On being asked if he actually knew any members of the Islamic community he bad-mouthed so vigorously, his reply was, 'Do I know them? I sleep with them!'

Fortuyn is dead, but his views live on. His attitude opened the eyes of other politicians, and now even the most left-wing exponents – those who used to sidestep certain issues for fear of being called racists – have incorporated watered-down versions of his views in their party programmes. The 'Islamic question' has had so much air time largely because tension between a small part of the Moroccan community and the police has been a fact of Amsterdam life since the late '90s. It began with a huge riot on August Allebéplein in the west, an area with a high immigrant population. Early in 2000, the Sloterparkbad swimming pool – renovated at a cost of €7 million – was forced to close for months because the police couldn't prevent a small group of Moroccan riff-raff intimidating staff and visitors, raiding

Where there's a **Whale**. *See p101.*

lockers and trashing toilets. Things got really nasty in mid 2003, when a policeman shot dead a Moroccan man who threatened him with a long knife. The demonstration that followed this incident culminated in another riot, which only fuelled anti-foreigner sentiment. It's all very sad in a city that has a long history of welcoming people from all over the world.

Meanwhile, segregation is on the up. Many areas in the west of the city, the Bijlmer and Amsterdam East are getting poorer, while the south and centre have priced out all but the rich. This unhealthy state of affairs is reflected in the educational system, too: schools in poor, immigrant communities have a hard time finding teachers. The council is aware of this, did lots of research and would like to change things – but hasn't yet come up with a solution. Having said that, most of the time the 100-plus nationalities in Amsterdam live together happily. The city's diversity is also seen in cross-cultural events, clothing styles and – remarkably – in the opening of Habibi Ana, Amsterdam's first gay bar aimed exclusively at Arabs.

THE PLEASURE PRINCIPLE

Still, it's not all gloom and doom in the Dutch capital – far from it. Amsterdam is still a fun and fab city to live in or spend a holiday in. The Dutch work to live, rather than the other way round, and there's still a big underground and squat scene which organises the most inventive events. The canals are beautiful and so are the different styles of architecture, from the old-fashioned canal-houses to the hippest office in town – the ING House in the Zuid, a glass building that resembles a large shoe. Most places of interest are within walking distance or easy accessible by bicycle.

Then there are the locals. Amsterdammers are friendly, albeit sometimes a trifle blunt, and always happy to show off their command of the English language. The arts are thriving, and there are many interesting bars, clubs and theatres. Oh, and then there's the Red Light District and, of course, the coffeeshops. The city is also super gay- and lesbian-friendly, with a vibrant scene and the world's first homosexual monument. And when it gets too crowded for your liking, a 25-minute train ride gets you to the countryside. Mix all these aspects up, add the fact that it's cheap both to live here and to visit when compared to the likes of London and Paris, and it's not hard to see why visitors and inhabitants can't get enough of it.

> ▶ For more on Amsterdam transport, *see p274.*

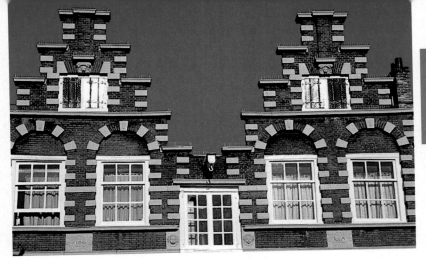

Architecture

From gabled Golden Age houses to the artificial islands of IJburg, Amsterdam is a tantalising brick tease.

'The colours are strong and sad, the forms symmetric, the façades kept new,' wrote Eugène Fromentin, the 19th-century art critic, of Amsterdam. 'We feel that it belongs to a people eager to take possession of the conquered mud.' The treacherous blubbery soil on which the merchants' town of Amsterdam is built meant that most attempts at monumental display were never going to get off the ground. Thanks to the make-up of the land – combined with the Protestant restraint that characterised the city's early developments and the fact that there were no royals keen to project their monstrous egos – it's not palaces and castles that are the architectural high points but, rather, warehouses, residential architecture, the stock exchange and the former City Hall.

Amsterdam's architectural epochs have followed the pulse of the city's prosperity. The decorative façades of wealthy 17th- and 18th-century merchants' houses still line the canals. A splurge of public spending in the affluent 1880s gave the city two of its most notable landmarks – **Centraal Station** and the **Rijksmuseum**. Conversely, social housing projects in the early 20th century stimulated the innovative work of the Amsterdam School, while Amsterdam's late-'80s resurgence as a financial centre and transport hub led to

an economic upturn and to thickets of bravura modern architecture on the outskirts of town and along the Eastern Docklands.

Prime viewing time for Amsterdam architecture is late on a summer's afternoon, as the sun gently picks out the varying colours and patterns of the brickwork. Then, as twilight falls, the canal houses – most of them more window than wall – light up like strings of lanterns, and you get a glimpse of the beautifully preserved, frequently opulent interiors that lie behind the façades.

MUD, GLORIOUS MUD

Amsterdam is built on reclaimed marshland, with a thick, soft layer of clay and peat beneath the topsoil. About 12 metres (39 feet) down is a hard band of sand, deposited 10,000 years ago during the Little Ice Age, and below that, after about five metres (16 feet) of fine sand, there is another firm layer, this one left by melting glacial ice after the Great Ice Age. A further 25 metres (82 feet) down, through shell-filled clay and past the bones of mammoths, is a third hard layer, deposited by glaciers over 180,000 years ago.

The first Amsterdammers built their homes on muddy mounds, making the foundations from tightly packed peat. Later, they dug trenches, filled them with fascines (thin, upright alder trunks) and built on those. But still the fruits of their labours sank slowly into the swamp. By the 17th century, builders were using longer underground posts and were rewarded with more stable structures, but it wasn't until around 1700 that piles were driven deep enough to hit the first hard sand layer.

The method of constructing foundations that subsequently developed has remained more or less the same ever since, though nowadays most piles reach the second sand level and some make the full 50-metre (164-foot) journey to the third hard layer. To begin, a double row of piles is sunk along the line of a proposed wall (since World War II, concrete has been used instead of wood). Then, a crossbeam is laid across each pair of posts, planks are fastened longitudinally on to the beams, and the wall is built on top. From time to time, piles break or rot, which is why Amsterdam is full of buildings that teeter precariously over the street, tilt lopsidedly or prop each other up in higgledy-piggledy rows.

STICKS AND STONES
Early constructions in Amsterdam were timber-framed, built mainly from oak with roofs of rushes or straw. Wooden houses were relatively light and less likely to sink into the mire, but after two devastating fires (in 1421 and 1452), the authorities began stipulating that outer walls be built of brick, though wooden front gables were still permitted. In a bid to blend in,

the first brick gables were shaped in imitation of their spout-shaped wooden predecessors.

Amsterdammers took to brick with relish. Granted, some grander 17th-century buildings were built of sandstone, while plastered façades were first seen a century later and reinforced concrete made its inevitable inroads in the 20th century. But Amsterdam is still essentially a city of brick: red brick from Leiden, yellow from Utrecht and grey from Gouda, all laid in curious formations and arranged in complicated patterns. Local architects' attachment to – and flair with – brick reached a zenith in the fantastical, billowing façades designed by the Amsterdam School early in the 20th century.

TOUCH WOOD
Only two wooden buildings remain in central Amsterdam: one (built in 1460) in the quiet courtyard of **Begijnhof** (No.34, known as the **Houtenhuis**), and the other on Zeedijk. The latter, **In't Aepjen** (Zeedijk 1; *see p78 and p138*), was built in the 16th century as a lodging house, getting its name from the monkeys that impecunious sailors used to leave behind as payment. Though the ground floor dates from the 19th century, the upper floors provide a clear example of how, in medieval times, each wooden storey protruded a little beyond the one below it, allowing rainwater to drip on to the street rather than run back into the body of the building. Early brick gables had to be built at an angle over the street for the same reason, though it also allowed objects to

be winched to the top floors without crashing against the windows of the lower ones.

Amsterdam's oldest building, though, is the **Oude Kerk** ('Old Church', Oude Kerksplein 23; *see p82*). It was begun in 1300, though only the base of the tower dates from then: over the ensuing 300 years the church developed a barnacle crust of additional buildings, mostly in a Renaissance style with a few Gothic additions. Surprisingly, nearly all the buildings retain their original medieval roofs, making the church unique in the Netherlands. The only full Gothic building in town – in the style of towering French and German churches – is the **Nieuwe Kerk** (at Dam and Nieuwezijds Voorburgwal; *see p75*), still called the 'New Church' even though building work on it began at the end of the 14th century.

When gunpowder arrived in Europe in the 15th century, Amsterdammers realised that the wooden palisade that surrounded their settlement would offer scant defence, and so set about building a new wall. Watchtowers and gates left over from it make up a significant proportion of the city's surviving pre 17th-century architecture, though most have been altered over the years. The **Schreierstoren** (Prins Hendrikkade 94-95; *see p78*) of 1480, however, has kept its original shape, with the addition of doors, windows and a pixie-hat roof. The base of the **Munttoren** (Muntplein; *see p84*) originally formed part of the Regulierspoort, a city gate built in 1490. Another city gate from the previous decade,

the **St Antoniespoort** (Nieuwmarkt 4), was converted into a public weighhouse (or 'Waag') in 1617, then further refashioned to become a Guild House. It's now **In de Waag**, a café-restaurant (*see p79 and p138*).

DUTCH RENAISSANCE

A favourite 16th-century amendment to these somewhat stolid defence towers was the addition of a sprightly steeple. Hendrick de Keyser (1565-1621) delighted in designing such spires, and it is largely his work that gives Amsterdam's present skyline a faintly oriental appearance. He added a lantern-shaped tower with an openwork orb to the Munttoren, and a spire that resembled the Oude Kerk steeple to the **Montelbaanstoren** (Oudeschans 2), a sea-defence tower that had been built outside the city wall. His **Zuiderkerk** (Zuiderkerkhof 72; *see p95*), built in 1603, sports a decorative spire said to have been much admired by Christopher Wren. The appointment of De Keyser as city mason and sculptor in 1595 had given him free reign, and his buildings represent the pinnacle of the Dutch Renaissance style (also known as Dutch Mannerist) – the greatest perhaps being **Westerkerk** (Prinsengracht 279; *see p89*), completed in 1631 as the biggest Protestant church in the world.

Since the beginning of the 17th century, Dutch architects had been gleaning inspiration from translations of Italian pattern books, adding lavish ornament to the classical system

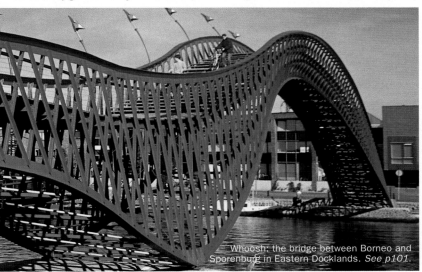
Whoosh: the bridge between Borneo and Sporenburg in Eastern Docklands. *See p101.*

of proportion they found there. Brick façades were decorated with stone strapwork (scrolls and curls derived from picture frames and leather work). Walls were built with alternating layers of red brick and white sandstone, a style that came to be called 'bacon coursing'. The old spout-shaped gables were replaced with cascading step-gables, often embellished with vases, escutcheons and masks (before house numbers were introduced in Amsterdam in the 18th century, ornate gables and wall plaques were a means of identifying houses).

The façade of the **Vergulde Dolphijn** (Singel 140-42), designed by De Keyser in 1600 for Captain Banning Cocq (the commander of Rembrandt's *Night Watch*), is a lively mix of red brick and sandstone, while the **Gecroonde Raep** (Oudezijds Voorburgwal 57) has a neat step-gable, with truly riotous decoration featuring busts, escutcheons, shells, scrolls and volutes. However, De Keyser's magnificent 1617 construction that followed the curve of a canal, the **Huis Bartolotti** (Herengracht 170-72, now part of the Theatre Instituut; *see p87*), is the finest example of the style.

This decorative step-gabled style was to last well into the 17th century. But gradually a stricter use of classical elements came into play; the façade of the Bartolotti house features rows of Ionic pilasters, and it wasn't long before others followed where De Keyser had led. The Italian pattern books that had inspired the Dutch Renaissance were full of the less ornamented designs of Greek and Roman antiquity. This appealed to many young architects who followed De Keyser, and who were to develop a more restrained, classical style. Many, such as Jacob van Campen (1595-1657), went on study tours of Italy, and returned fired with enthusiasm for the symmetric designs, simple proportions and austerity of Roman architecture. The buildings they constructed during the Golden Age are among the finest Amsterdam has to offer.

THE GOLDEN AGE

The 1600s were a boom time for builders as well as for businessmen. There was no way it could have been otherwise, as Amsterdam's population more than quadrupled during the first half of the century. Grand new canals were constructed, and wealthy merchants lined them with mansions and warehouses. Van Campen, along with fellow architects Philips Vingboons (1607-78) and his brother Justus (1620-98), were given the freedom to try out their ideas on a flood of new commissions.

Stately façades constructed of sandstone began to appear around Amsterdam, but brick still remained the most popular material.

Philips Vingboons's **Witte Huis** (Herengracht 168, now part of the Theatre Instituut) has a white sandstone façade with virtually no decoration: the regular rhythm of the windows is the governing principle of the design. The house he built in 1648 at **Oude Turfmarkt 145** has a brick façade adorned with three tiers of classical pilasters – Tuscan, Ionic and Doric – and festoons that were characteristic of the style. However, the crowning achievement of the period was Amsterdam's boast to the world of its mercantile supremacy and civic might: namely, the Stadhuis (City Hall) on the Dam, designed by Van Campen in 1648 and now known as the **Koninklijk Paleis** (*see p74*).

There was, however, one fundamental point of conflict between classical architecture and the requirements of northern Europe. For practical reasons, wet northern climes required steep roofs, yet low Roman pediments and flat cornices looked odd with a steep, pointed roof behind them. The architects solved the problem by adapting the Renaissance gable, with its multiple steps, into a tall, central gable with just two steps. Later, neck-gables were built with just a tall central oblong and no steps. The right angles formed at the base of neck-gables – and again at the step of elevated neck-gables – were often filled in with decorative sandstone carvings called claw-pieces.

On very wide houses, it was possible to build a roof parallel to the street rather than end-on, making a more attractive backdrop for a classical straight cornice. The giant **Trippenhuis** (Kloveniersburgwal 29; *see p79*), built by Justus Vingboons in 1662, has such a design, with a classical pediment, a frieze of cherubs and arabesques, and eight enormous Corinthian pilasters. It wasn't until the 19th century, when zinc cladding became cheaper, that flat and really low-pitched roofs became feasible.

THE 18TH CENTURY

Working towards the end of the 17th century, Adriaan Dortsman (1625-82) had been a strong proponent of the straight cornice. His stark designs – such as for the Van Loon house at **Keizersgracht 672-4** – ushered in a style that came to be known as Restrained Dutch Classicism (or the 'Tight Style' as it would translate directly from the Dutch description: *Strakke Stijl*). It was a timely entrance. Ornament was costly and, by the beginning of the 18th century, the economic boom was over.

The merchant families were prosperous, but little new building went on. Instead, the families gave their old mansions a facelift or revamped the interiors. A number of 17th-century houses got new sandstone façades (or plastered brick ones, which were cheaper), and French taste –

said to have been introduced by Daniel Marot, a French architect living in Amsterdam – became hip. As the century wore on, ornamentation regained popularity. Gables were festooned with scrolls and acanthus leaves (Louis XIV), embellished with asymmetrical rococo fripperies (Louis XV) or strung with disciplined lines of garlands (Louis XVI). The baroque grandeur of **Keizersgracht 444-6**, for example, hardly seems Dutch at all. Straight cornices appeared even on narrow buildings, and became extraordinarily ornate: a distinct advantage, this, as it hid the steep roof that lay behind, with decorative balustrades adding to the deception. The lavish cornice at **Oudezijds Voorburgwal 215-17** is a prime example.

ONE FOOT IN THE PAST

Fortunes slumped further after 1800, and during the first part of the century more buildings were demolished than constructed. When things picked up after 1860, architects raided past eras for inspiration. Neo-classical, neo-Gothic and neo-Renaissance features were sometimes lumped together in mix-and-match eclectic style. The **Krijtberg Church** (Singel 446) from 1881 has a soaring neo-Gothic façade and a high, vaulted basilica, while the interior of AL van Gendt's **Hollandse Manege** (Vondelstraat 140; see p109), also 1881, combines the classicism of the Spanish Riding School in Vienna with a state-of-the-art iron and glass roof.

On the other hand, the **Concertgebouw** (Van Baerlestraat 98; see p217), a Van Gendt construction from 1888, borrows from the late Renaissance, with 1892's **City Archive** (Amsteldijk 67) little more than De Keyser revisited. But the period's most adventurous building is the **Adventskerk** (Keizersgracht 676), which crams in a classical rusticated base, Romanesque arches, Lombardian moulding and fake 17th-century lanterns.

The star architect of the period was PJH Cuypers (1827-1921), who landed the commissions for both the **Rijksmuseum** (Stadhouderskade 41; see p106) of 1877-85 and **Centraal Station** (Stationsplein), built from 1882 to 1889. Both are in traditional red brick, adorned with Renaissance-style decoration in sandstone and gold leaf. Responding to those who thought his tastes too catholic, Cuypers – while still slipping in some of his excesses later during their construction – decided to organise each building according to a single coherent principle. This idea became the basis for modern Dutch architecture.

THIS IS THE MODERN WORLD

Brick and wood – good, honest, indigenous materials – appealed to Hendrik Petrus Berlage (1856-1934), as did the possibilities offered by industrial developments in the use of steel and glass. A rationalist, he took Cuypers' ideas a step further in his belief that a building should openly express its basic structure, with a modest amount of ornament in a supportive role. Notable also was the way he collaborated with sculptors, painters and even poets throughout construction. His **Beurs van Berlage** (Beursplein; see p74), built between 1898 and 1903 – all clean lines and functional shapes, with the mildest patterning in the brickwork – was startling at the time, and earned him the reputation of being the father of modern Dutch architecture.

Apart from the odd shopfront and some well-designed café interiors, the art nouveau and art deco movements had little direct impact on Amsterdam, though they did draw a few wild flourishes: HL de Jong's **Tuschinski** cinema (Reguliersbreestraat 26; see p192) of 1918-21, for example, is a delightful and seductive piece of high-camp fantasy. Instead, Amsterdam architects developed a style of their own, an idiosyncratic mix of art nouveau and Old Dutch using their favourite materials: wood and brick.

This movement, which became known as the Amsterdam School (see below), reacted against Berlage's sobriety by producing whimsical buildings with waving, almost sculptural brickwork. Built over a reinforced concrete frame, the brick outer walls go through a complex series of pleats, bulges, folds and curls that earned the work the nickname 'Schortjesarchitectuur' ('apron architecture'). Windows can be trapezoid or parabolic; doors are carved in strong, angular shapes; brickwork is decorative and often polychromatic; and brick and stone sculptures are in abundance.

The driving force behind the school came from ztwo young architects, Michel de Klerk (1884-1923) and Piet Kramer (1881-1961). Commissions for social housing projects – one for the **Dageraad** (constructed around PL Takstraat, 1921-23), one for **Eigen Haard** (in the Spaarndammerbuurt, 1913-20) – allowed them to treat entire blocks as single units. Just as importantly, the pair's adventurous clients gave them freedom to express their ideas. The school also produced more rural variants suggestive of village life such as the BT Boeyinga-designed 'garden village' Tuindorp Nieuwendam (Purmerplein, Purmerweg).

In the early 1920s, a new movement emerged that was the antithesis of the Amsterdam School – although certain 'cross-over' aspects can be observed in JF Staal's 1930-completed **Wolkenkrabbber** (Victorieplein), the first residential high-rise in the country. Developing rather than reacting against Berlage's ideas,

Back to school

Amsterdam is not really renowned for the monuments and palaces of past rulers and the ruling classes. Its Golden Age gabled houses were mere merchants' residences, while its other great architectural legacies were built for the working classes. The Amsterdam School, which peaked by 1925 and whose swoopy expressiveness is akin to a gentler version of Gaudí, worked with socialist vision in a time of prosperity.

While due credit can be given to the stonemasons who had practised non-geometrical brickwork when repairing the canals' sinking houses, it was Hendrik Berlage who formed the nexus of the movement. Not only did his work strip things down, rejecting all the neo-styles that had defined most 19th-century Dutch architecture, but he also provided the opportunity to experiment with new forms by coming up with Plan Zuid, an urban plan meant to provide housing for the working classes whose population had grown in the city since the Industrial Revolution.

Although the school was short-lived – it was forced to simplify within a decade when the money ran out, the Functionalism-obsessed De Stijl school started to diss the school's more self-indulgent tendencies, and its greatest proponent, Michel de Klerk, died – examples of the school's work remain. The Rivierenbuurt, Spaarndammerbuurt and Concertgebouwbuurt, plus the area around Mercantorplein, all offer ample gazing opportunity; what follows, though, are some of the school's highlights.

Located along the waterfront, the eerie and epic **Scheepsvaarthuis** (Prins Hendrikkade 108-114) is generally considered to be the school's first work. Completed in 1916, it was the work of three big names: JM van der Mey, Piet Kramer and de Klerk. Among the school's hallmarks on show are obsessively complex brickwork, infinite and allegorical decorations (reflecting its use as offices for shipping companies), sculptures and wrought-iron railings fused as one with the building.

Behind Westerpark lies the Spaarndammer neighbourhood, which sports the school's most frolicsome and bizarre work. The **Ship** (pictured), as locals like to call it, takes up a whole block bound by Zaanstraat, Hembrugstraat and Oostzaanstraat. Completed in 1919, it was commissioned by the Eigen Haard housing association and includes 102 homes and a school. Be sure to pop your head through the archway at Oostzaan 1-21, where you can see the courtyard and its central meeting hall, before visiting **Poste Restante** next door (Spaarndammerplantsoen 140, 475 0924/ www.posterestante.nl; open 2-5pm Wed, Thur, Sun). This former post office organises Amsterdam School walking tours and is also an exhibition space with videos and computers that tell the tale of the school.

the Functionalists believed that new building materials such as concrete and steel should not be concealed, but that the basic structure of a building should be visible. Function was supreme, ornament anathema. Their hard-edged concrete and glass boxes have much in common with the work of Frank Lloyd Wright in the USA, Le Corbusier in France and the Bauhaus in Germany.

Unsurprisingly, such radical views were not shared by everyone, and the period was a turbulent one in Amsterdam's architectural history. Early Functionalist work, such as 1930's **Openluchtschool** ('Open-air School', Cliostraat 40), 1934's **Cineac Cinema** (Reguliersbreestraat 31) and the **Round Blue Teahouse** (in Vondelpark; see p107), has a clean-cut elegance, and the Functionalist garden suburb of **Betondorp** (literally, 'Concrete Town'), built between 1921 and 1926, is more attractive than the name might suggest.

But after World War II, Functionalist ideology became an excuse for dreary, derivative, prefabricated eyesores. The urgent need for housing, coupled with town-planning theories that favoured residential satellite suburbs, led to the appearance of soulless, high-rise horrors on the edge of town, much the same as those put up elsewhere in Europe.

A change of heart during the 1970s refocused attention on making the city centre a pleasant jumble of residences, shops and offices. At the same time, a quirkier, more imaginative trend began to show itself in building design. The **ING Bank** (Bijlmerplein 888), inspired by anthroposophy and built in 1987 of brick, has hardly a right angle in sight. A use of bright colour, and a return to a human-sized scale, is splendidly evident in Aldo van Eyck's **Moederhuis** (Plantage Middenlaan 33) from 1981. New façades – daringly modern, yet built to scale – began to appear between the

However, the school's heartland is in Plan Zuid district, at the border of the Pijp and the Rivierenbuurt. The Josef Israelkade, betweeen 2e Van der Helststraat and Van Woustraat, is a pleasant stretch along the Amstelkanaal; enter PL Takstraat and circle Burg Tellegenstraat without forgetting to pop into the courtyard of **Cooperatiehof**. Socialist housing association de Dageraad ('the Dawn') allowed de Klerk and Kramer to do their hallucinatory best and employ their favourite sculptor, Hildo Krop. Kramer, incidentally, went on to design over 200 bridges; after visiting this area, you shouldn't have any problem recognising his work elsewhere in the city.

It's a different story elsewhere, though. Backtrack and cross the Amstelkanaal, and then walk down Waalstraat; here you'll find later examples of the school's work where tightening purse-strings resulted in more restraint. Nearby, on Vrijheidslaan and its side-streets, are some more classic school buildings, all freshly scrubbed and renovated. Conclude your tour by proceeding to Roelof Hartplein, where a window seat at **Wildschut** (*see p146*) affords a panorama of goodies. Look out for House Lydia (across the street at No.2), which served as home to Catholic girls; finished in 1927, it stands as one of the school's last constructs in which wacky window shapes and odd forms were still allowed.

old houses along the canals. The 1980s also saw, amid an enormous amount of controversy, the construction of what became known as the **Stopera**, a combined city hall (Stadhuis) and opera house on Waterlooplein (*see 220*). The eye-catching brick and marble coliseum of the **Muziektheater** is more successful than the dull oblongs that make up the City Hall.

Housing projects of the 1980s and 1990s have provided Amsterdam with some imaginative modern architecture. The conversion of a 19th-century army barracks, the **Oranje Nassau Kazerne** (Sarphatistraat and Mauritskade), into studios and flats, with the addition of a row of rather zanily designed apartment blocks, is one of the more successful examples. Building on the KNSM Eiland and other islands in the derelict Eastern Docklands has combined an intelligent conversion of existing structures with some inventive new architecture.

THE FUTURE

At the municipal information centre for planning and housing in **Zuiderkerk**, visitors can admire models of current and future developments set to transform the city in the near future. Those interested should pay a visit to **ARCAM** – the Architecture Centrum Amsterdam (*see p198*) – or pick up a copy of their excellent publication *25 Buildings You Should Have Seen, Amsterdam*. **Bureau Monumentenzorg Amsterdam**, meanwhile, provides an obsessive overview of the city's architecture from its origins to 1940 at www.bmz.amsterdam.nl.

Architectural travesties of the past have politicised the populace, who now keep a sharp eye on development. As such, referendums are now held prior to many new developments. Though 130,000 votes against the construction of IJburg (*see p46 and p101*) – a residential community currently being built on a series of man-made islands in the IJ-meer, just east

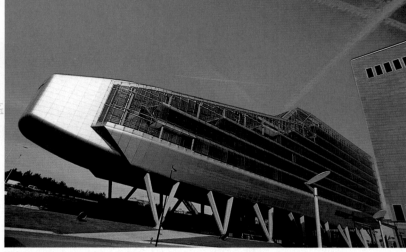

ING House: vision of the future. *See p34.*

of Amsterdam – was not enough to stop development around this ecologically sensitive area, it did inspire the promise that ƒ15 million (now around €7 million) would be invested in 'nature-development'. Parts of the area will also be a showcase for the recently hyped Dutch concept of *wilde wonen* – 'wild living', as it were – where residents themselves get to design and build their own houses.

Similarly, the referendum result against the laying of the new Noord-Zuidlijn (*see p23*) on the Metro network didn't halt the project but it did establish that the city needed to be considerably more diligent in its thinking. The powers that be, after all, apparently skimmed over such significant details as financing, loss of revenue for shopkeepers and the potential for all this digging to cause the speedier sinking of above-lying historical buildings when planning the line, none of which endeared them to voters.

Now that the facelift of **Museumplein** (*see p106*) has long been completed, all eyes are on the Eastern Docklands (*see p100*). It's hoped that redevelopments will turn it into a stunning photogenic harbourfront not unlike that in Sydney, Australia. Similarly, construction around the **ArenA** stadium in the South-East will hopefully pump some economic life into the nearby architectural prison known as the Bijlmermeer. This boulevard, due to be completed in 2006 but already sporting a huge Pathé cinema (*see p192*), mega shopping centre Villa ArenA, a couple of concert halls (*see p212 and p214*) and rows of lighting poles by Philippe Starck, should become home to many businesses and – thanks to the recent leaps and bounds made in building vertically on bog – the largest residential tower in the country.

In 2004 a futuristic building called Living Tomorrow (www.livingtomorrow.com) will also publicly open here as a joint project of interested organisations and companies who 'each in their own field of expertise, [show] how social and technological developments will affect our lifestyles, housing and work'.

Another building hotspot currently roping in a proper who's who of cutting-edge architects is **Zuidas** (www.zuidas.nl) in the South. Zuidas is grouped around the World Trade Center, near the wacky, shoe-shaped silver transparency **ING House** (Amstelveenseweg 500) that houses the ING HQ: the latter undoubtedly caught your eye on your ride in from Schiphol airport.

Currently, Dutch architecture – thanks in part to exponents like Rem Koolhaas – is very much in vogue. International periodicals, no longer casting LA and Hong Kong as the primary visionaries, now see the 'Dutch Model' – where boundaries between building, city and landscape planning have blurred beyond recognition – as both pragmatic and futuristic. After all, ecological degradation is now a worldwide phenomenon, and the space-constrained Netherlands has long seen nature as a construct that needs to be nurtured. Expect this principle to define some of the Dutch architecture of the future – although knowing what's gone before, it'll likely be incorporated in unexpected, eyebrow-raising fashion.

► For more on the **Oude Kerk**, *see p82*.
► For more on the **Eastern Docklands**, *see p100*.
► For more on **IJburg**, *see p101*.

Art

A profusion of colour, character and cabbages:
Dutch painters never rested on their laurels.

Ah, the Golden Age. Those six decades or so, whose boundary stones were the launch of the Verenigde Oost-Indische Compagnie (East India Company) in 1602 and the acquisition by the English of what is now New York in 1664, were sweet times indeed. Not only did the economic benefits of becoming the world's leading trading power allow for the building of Amsterdam's image-defining ring of canals to deal with a quadrupling of the population, but they also ushered in a never-before-seen flourishing of the arts.

While this era was preceded by rich medieval artistic achievements – particularly under the sponsorship of the Church and later through the more 'individual' inspiration of Flemish masters like Bosch and Brueghel – and was followed by an artist-friendly atmosphere that still prevails today, the Golden Age saw not only the affluent but also the aspirant middle classes get hungry for art. Of all the many artists who could make a decent living in this period, Rembrandt remains the most famous name and his *Night Watch* (on display at the Rijksmuseum) remains Amsterdam's most famous painting. But also the likes of Frans Hals, Jan Vermeer, Ferdinand Bol, Jan Steen and Jacob van Ruisdael could thrive both creatively and economically in these free and easy times.

It was all too good to last, but art continued to develop long after the Golden Age began to lose its gilt edge. The 18th century brought forward Jacob de Wit and Monet's great inspiration Johan Jongkind; the 19th century offered George Breitner, Isaac Israëls and Vincent van Gogh; while the 20th century produced such intensely varied talents as MC Escher, Piet Mondriaan and Karel Appel.

With all these names coming from such a tiny country, you can't help wondering if the Netherlands' battle with the sea is really all about creating extra wall space on which to hang their rich legacy.

In Amsterdam, the best of five centuries is waiting for you to marvel at: from the more traditional treasures on display at the Rijksmuseum (*see p106*), Museum Van Loon (*see p92*) and Museum Amstelkring (*see p81*) to the zanily modern best experienced at the Stedelijk Museum (*see p107*) – or by just keeping your eyes open as you walk around. To miss out on Amsterdam's art offerings is like skipping the Guinness on a visit to Dublin – and the following pages show but a few of the many, many highlights awaiting you.

Jacob Cornelisz. van Oostsanen ①

Van Oostsanen (c1470-1533), aka Jacob van Amsterdam, represents the beginning of the city's artistic tradition, and his sharpness of observation became a trademark for all Dutch art that was to follow. Thought to have been a student of Geertgen tot Sint Jans, he also betrays the influence of Bosch and Brueghel.

Saul and the Witch of Endor – one of only a few of his paintings that survived the Iconoclastic Fury – tells the whole biblical story in one panoramic, almost comic-book swoop. It begins on the left, where Saul seeks advice from a witch about his impending battle with the Philistines, and ends in the distance, behind the central witches' sabbath, with the 'poetic justice' of suicide in the face of defeat. Indeed, this dates from a time when witches could have used some better PR.
On display: Rijksmuseum (*see p106*).

Cornelis van Dalem & Jan van Wechelen ②

The Baker of Eeklo hangs in the castle built for Count Floris V (*see p6*). Painted in the second half of the 16th century by two rather obscure painters, the depicted tableaux of cabbage heads can probably only make sense to a people weaned on medieval stories of magic windmills that could grind old people up and then churn them out all young again. In this similar story, bakers are slicing the heads off clients to rebake them to specification. A cabbage – a symbol for the empty and idle head

— was used to keep the spewing of blood to a minimum. Sometimes, though, people's heads came out as 'half-baked' or 'misfired'. Whoops!
On display: Muiderslot (*see p259*).

Jan Steen

Leiden's Jan Steen (c1625-1679) has always had a bad rep. While he did run a tavern in his own home, his rowdy reputation is probably based on the drunken folk that inhabit his 'genre' paintings of everyday life. In fact, if you look carefully at *The Merry Family* (1668), Steen's view seems highly moralistic. With the inscription over the mantelpiece ('As the old sing, so pipe the young') putting literally what the painting reflects figuratively in a plethora of symbols: the emptiness of a life spent smoking, drinking and talking shit. The painting offers a lesson as valid today as the day it was painted. Steen cameos as the puffy-cheeked bagpiper.
On display: Rijksmuseum (*see p106*).

Hans van Meegeren

Dial F for Fake! Forgery is big business (weighed up by an entire museum in Drenthe; *see p264*) – an estimated 30 per cent of art on the market is fake. It's amazing anyone could mistake van Meegeren's heavy-handed **De Emmaüsgangers** as a Vermeer, but that's what happened in 1938: even the Rijksmuseum – home to real Vermeers like *The Kitchen Maid* – tried to bid for it. The phoney finally sold for the astronomical sum of 550,000 guilders, and it was only in 1945, when Hans van Meegeren (1889-1947) was facing the death penalty for selling another 'Vermeer' to the Nazis, did he own up to the 1938 coup. His motivation, it seems, was to avenge the bad reviews given his own paintings by a Vermeer expert – one who saw the fakes as bona fide. Van Meegeren died in 1947 while serving a one-year jail sentence.
On display: Museum Boijmans Van Beuningen, Rotterdam (*see p269*).

Jacob de Wit ④

Long before the invention of self-adhesive glow-in-the-dark stars, the Jordaan-born decorative artist Jacob de Wit (1695-1754) made a name for himself in the sphere of ceiling decoration. Initially influenced by Ruben's altar work in Antwerp, De Wit developed a much more delicate and sympathetic touch, which he applied to marvellous Rococo effect in a number of Amsterdam buildings, among them the Theater Instituut (*see p87*), the attic church at the Museum Amstelkring (*see p81*), the Rijksmuseum (*see p106*) and the Pintohuis (which is now a library; *see p94*). However, his celebrated mastery of trompe l'oeil illusion – later named *witjes* after him – is probably

best appreciated at the Bijbels Museum. One ceiling was painted for wealthy local merchant Jacob Cromhout, while the other, entitled *Apollo and the Four Seasons*, was salvaged in the 1950s from a nearby property on Herengracht. Both paintings have recently been superbly restored.

On display: Bijbels Museum (*see p87*).

Vincent van Gogh ⑤

The career of everyone's favourite one-eared genius, Vincent van Gogh (1853-90), can be mapped out in full in Amsterdam. Here you can marvel at the fact that the creator of the dark shadows of **The Potato Eaters** went on to paint the almost kinetic **Bedroom** (1888) a mere four years later. By then he had settled in France's clearer light and had abandoned the Vermeer-inspired, subdued colouring of his earlier work to embrace the expressionist style that would make him famous. Typical of his restless nature, this painting – made during a summer of long, hard work – depicts the bed he would have perhaps been better off just sleeping in. Two months later he had his first breakdown, and two years later he committed suicide.

On display: Van Gogh Museum (*see p107*).

George H Breitner ⑥

Like Van Gogh, Breitner (1857-1923) sought to re-invent painting's relevance in a post-photographic age. However, Breitner chose to

embrace this new technology. His vistas of Amsterdam cityscapes are essential documents of his heady times.

In **Dam Square** (c.1895), he used photos – note the snapshot feel and 'out of focus' areas – to paint a quintessentially impressionist view. Eminently conscientious documentalist that he was, Breitner returned to this painting in 1898 to add on the New Church's brand new stained glass window, which had been installed to commemorate that year's investiture of Queen Wilhelmina.
On display: Amsterdams Historisch Museum (*see p85*).

Piet Mondriaan

Piet Mondriaan (1872-1944), one of the founders of De Stijl (*see p195*), can be used as a handy summary of the history of art: he moved through realism, impressionism and cubism, before embracing the purely abstract. His use of nothing but lines and primary colour blocks earned him accusations of sterility, but

in fact it represented a very personal and subjective quest for essence and harmony. He was also something of a wag: note how his late, ultra-minimal canvas, **Composition with Two Lines** (1931), has been tilted by 45 degrees.
On display: Stedelijk Museum of Modern Art (*see p107*).

Karel Appel

Karel Appel (b.1920) once said, 'I just mess around' – and most people nod when they see his childish forms, bright colours and heavy strokes. But an art that favoured instinct over intellect was, its proponents argued, just what the world needed after World War II, when CoBrA (*see p195*) was launched. Today this long-time New York resident is arguably the best-known living Dutch artist. His rate of production is vast, and ex-forger Geert Jan Jansen claims Appel indentified several Jansen works as his own.
On display: CoBrA Museum (*see p111*).

Sex & Drugs

Welcome to an orchard of forbidden fruit.

It's pragmatism at its finest: what better way to stamp out crime than by legalising it? Granted, the story of Amsterdam's liberal attitudes ain't quite so finger-snappingly straightforward, but here's a fact known the world over: this city does sex and drugs with fewer hang-ups than anywhere else on the planet. It's little wonder that the visitors keep sliding in like iron filings to a magnet: Amsterdam lays on ways to fuck and to get fucked up that are so much more troublesome to arrange back home.

Some elements of the local authorities would prefer to re-invent Amsterdam as a business capital and attract a higher-minded breed of tourist (read: people turned on by nothing more seedy than art, canals and the town's easy-going vibe). However, if you ask most non-residents the first words that come into their minds when they hear the word 'Amsterdam', more often than not their answers will be 'Red Light District' and/or 'coffeeshops'. And since the city has such forward-thinking policies on sex and drugs, who can really blame them?

Of course, we wouldn't want you to forget the other 95 per cent of our guide to this most multi-faceted city – but we'd be shirking our duty if we didn't titillate you with the history behind the hundreds of nubile and naked ladies in their neon-framed windows, and the availability of joints the size of Oklahoma. The fun starts here.

SEX

What is it about travel that makes people so frisky? Even if you've never had a one night stand with a hotel bartender nor applied for membership of the Mile High Club, you can't deny that there's something about strange places and new faces that kindles an appetite for adventure. However, the legal consequences of, say, making a date with a prostitute vary from country to country: most governments prohibit prostitution but then selectively police only the more public levels of the sex industry, or hand out licences to escort agencies and erotic dance clubs, or create 'special zones' where men can let off steam without getting busted. The Netherlands has chosen a more honest approach.

The recorded history of prostitution in Amsterdam dates from the city's 13th century roots. As an industry it has always resisted all efforts to banish it, and eventually the Dutch came to accept the advantages of a more pragmatic approach. Although working as a prostitute has been completely legal since 1911, it was not until 2000 that the ban on brothels was lifted, thus formally permitting window and brothel sex-work. With the legalisation of brothels came the requirement that sex-workers carry an EU passport; and a 200-page rule book was introduced to govern the business of selling sexual services, covering everything from fire escapes to the appropriate length of a prostitute's fingernails.

By the 15th century, Amsterdam was a bustling port attracting money, merchants and sailors – or, more specifically, merchants and sailors with money – which in turn increased the amount of sex for sale. But it wasn't only randy men who influenced the industry's growth, but also the fact that many local women, separated from their seafaring husbands for months on end, were left with little or no means to sustain themselves or their children. Prostitution was one of the few money-making options available.

In the Middle Ages prostitutes had been permitted to work in one of the brothels located on what is now Damstraat. Keeping a whorehouse was then the exclusive privilege of the city's sheriff, and women found working elsewhere in the city were forcibly marched back to *chez* sheriff to the 'sound of drums and flutes.' But in the 15th century prostitutes began working the area around Zeedijk; and by the 17th century, some were walking through the Old Side with red lanterns to advertise their profession. Soon after, enterprising women turned to advertising themselves in the windows of their own homes, or from front-facing rooms rented from other homeowners; it's from this practice that today's rather more garish window trade is descended.

More 'traditional' methods of conducting business still apply, but it's the red-lit windows that have earned Amsterdam notoriety as a major sex capital. And no matter how prepared you think you are, you'll be taken aback the first time you see street after street of huge picture windows, each decorated with red velvet-effect soft furnishings, each sparingly lit, and each dominated by a nearly-naked woman. The women are in your face, obliging you to notice them, daring you to part with your money for a pleasurable 20 minutes or so. They come in all shapes, sizes, skin tones and ages. Not all of them look terribly excited to be there, but neither would you if your job involved standing up for hours and answering a string of stupid questions. Many of the women pass the time between clients by gossiping with colleagues, dancing and cavorting or teasing

Ask a silly question

Founded in 1994 by ex-prostitute Mariska Majoor, the **Prostitution Information Centre** (PIC; 'pic', conveniently enough, is Dutch for dick) sits right by the Oude Kerk – handy for repentance – in the heart of the Red Light District, and is open to anyone who wants a greater understanding of prostitutes and prostitution. Staff will do their best to answer all your questions, however frank or outlandish; see opposite for a range of queries both frequent and unusual, but all genuine. PIC supports its efforts through the sale of print information and books related to prostitution, PIC and Red Light souvenirs, and donations. Interested groups can also have a lecture session arranged.

Prostitution Information Centre

Enge Kerk Steeg 3 (420 7328/ www.pic-amsterdam.com). Tram 4, 9, 16, 24, 25, 26. **Open** noon-7pm Tue, Wed, Fri, Sat. **Map** p306 D2.

COMMON QUERIES
1. How do I go about negotiating a session with a prostitute?
2. How much will it cost?
3. Are all the prostitutes legally required to have medical checks for STDs?
4. Why do women become prostitutes?
5. Has legalisation made working conditions better for prostitutes?'

QUEERER QUERIES
1. Where can I find a prostitute willing to blow up a large balloon and then burst it for me?
2. Is it true that all Amsterdam prostitutes shave off all their pubic hair?
3. I've been masturbating to fantasies about visiting a prostitute and have chafed myself. Will I be refused service?
4. Doesn't all that sex hurt?
5. Where will I find the best one?

For the answers, *see p300*.

passers-by. When you eventually see someone who takes your fancy, talk to her politely and you'll be behind the curtain before you can say, 'I love Amsterdam'.

Amsterdam's best-known Red Light District spreads out around the Oudezijds Voorburgwal and Oudezijds Achterburgwal canals, and the famous windows alternate with the butcher, the baker and the candlestick maker. Two smaller, less heralded Red Light areas sit on the New Side (between Kattengat and Lijnbaanssteeg) and in the Pijp (Ruysdaelkade, from Albert Cuypstraat to 1e Jan Steenstraat).

'In the game of commercial sex, the big losers are female customers.'

What you see is not all you get; there are loads of other sexy options to choose from. A quick scan of the internet or the *Gouden Gids* (yellow pages) will lead you to escort services, professional S&M services, sex clubs, striptease clubs, swingers' clubs, brothels, live sex shows, sex services for gay men, peep shows, sex cinemas and more. The only thing that is not openly permitted is street prostitution. Although a *tippelzone* (tolerated 'walking zone') was set up on Theemsweg to resemble a street area, complete with private parking stalls, police security, and prostitute support services, the city looks likely to close it, since the prostitutes it was intended for are using it less. Some street prostitution does occur in the centre, most notoriously in the area behind Centraal Station.

In the game of commercial sex, the big losers are female customers. Sorry, gals: your options are limited. There are a few escort services that supply male prostitutes, and you may find a window prostitute who is happy to get busy with a woman – though this is more likely to happen if you visit her with your male partner. You could also make a point of visiting the most female friendly sex shop in Amsterdam, **Female and Partners** (*see p174*), to pick up a little consolation gift for yourself (though remember, batteries are rarely included). For visitors who are happy to look but reluctant to touch, a visit to a live sex show, at **Casa Rosso** (*see p80*) for instance, might inspire an evening of private fun elsewhere.

The most unique quality about the Red Light District is its integration into the Old Centre neighbourhood (for more, *see p77*). Police patrol the area with just enough visibility to dissuade most troublemakers. CCTV cameras placed strategically around the district keep a close eye on street activity and every window

is equipped with an emergency alarm system that the person behind it can activate if necessary. While the majority of clients, almost half of whom are locals, have no interest in harming a prostitute, these safeguards give workers a feeling of reassurance. One misdemeanour that's guaranteed to cause trouble is taking a photo of a window prostitute. If you get the urge, try to imagine yourself in their place and remember that they're not zoo animals. If you really need a picture of an Amsterdam window gal, some of the tourist shops sell suitable postcards.

The subject of prostitution always raises concerns about STDs. Sex workers take their healthcare seriously and will insist on using a condom – and clients should do likewise. There are no laws requiring prostitutes to have regular medical check-ups but there's an STD clinic in the Old Side's Red Light District where sex workers can go anonymously for free check-ups and information. There's also a prostitute rights organisation, De Rode Draad (the Red Thread); a sex workers' union, Vakwerk; and prostitution research institute Mr A de Graaf Stichting. You can find out about all three, and more, at the Prostitution Information Centre in the Red Light District (*see p41* **Ask a silly question**).

That said, the situation is by no means perfect. 2000's legal reforms were aimed in part at reducing the number of illegal immigrants working in prostitution, but in actual fact only a minority of prostitutes have no legal status. There are still exploitative situations involving coercion, parasitic and controlling 'boyfriends', and problems related to substance abuse. The most positive effect of the legal changes has been to legitimise prostitution as a profession, which means that sex workers have access to social services and can legitimately band together to improve their working conditions. However, the stigma remains. Even in the most ideal circumstances it's still difficult for prostitutes to balance their work and private lives. Further, prostitutes have problems when trying to get bank accounts, mortgages and insurance, despite being liable for taxes and generating an estimated €450 million a year.

Certainly, the locals' liberal, grown-up attitudes merit applause, and the methods they've employed to deal with the inevitability of a sex industry have arguably resulted in a better deal for both customer and sex worker. It's true, too, that the Dutch method for dealing with prostitution might prove to be the way forward for many of its European neighbours. Visit with an open mind, but don't be surprised if Amsterdam's fabled Red Light District falls short of at least some of the hype.

Come on in, it's legal.

DRUGS

You strut in through the front door of the coffeeshop, engage in a simple transaction and then smoke the sweet smoke. You strut out through the front door, wiggly, wasted and – most importantly, for you have done no wrong – free of paranoia. Welcome to the Netherlands.

A large part of the country's image abroad has been defined by its apparently lax attitude towards drugs. But this is misleading: soft drugs are still only semi-legal. Simply put, the famously pragmatic Dutch began back in the early 1970s to put drug laws into much-needed perspective. Swamped with heroin by Chinese gangs and repeatedly reminded by the ex-Provos and hippies then entering mainstream politics of the relatively benign and non-addictive nature of pot, the fight against wimpy drugs came to be seen as a ludicrous waste of time and money.

And so, in 1976, a vaguely worded law was passed to make a distinction between hard and soft drugs, effectively separating their markets from each other's influence and allowing the use and sale of small amounts of soft drugs – under 30 grams (one ounce). The 'front door' of the then embryonic 'coffeeshop' was now legal, although the 'back door', where produce arrived by the kilo, looked out on an illegal distribution system. While the coffeeshop owner deals on the condoned side of this economy and can fearlessly redirect his profits into other legal ventures (as many do, investing in hotels and nightclubs), and while suppliers experience the profitability of being illegal, the couriers who provide the link and run the risks without high returns remain in a legal limbo where such clichés as 'Kafkaesque' or 'Catch 22' are very real.

And yet the wobbly system has somehow worked. Time passed without the increase in soft drug use that the doomsayers expected. The coffeeshop became a permanent part of the Amsterdam streetscape. And the concerted efforts against hard-drug use – less through law enforcement and more via education, methadone programmes, needle exchanges, drop-in shoot-up centres and counselling – have resulted in one of the lowest junkie populations in the world. Junkies may have more street visibility here than in other European cities, but that's more to do with an openness that lets junkies dare to be seen.

Moves towards complete legalisation of soft drugs have always been thwarted by a variety of factors: misguided pressure from fellow EU members (mainly France – which, funnily enough, is Holland's pipeline for heroin – and more recently Germany); tension between the government and coffeeshop owners (who have come to enjoy testing the boundaries of the vague laws); and the lack of a local supply. This last factor, though, was weakened by the 'green wave' of the early '90s, when the US-designed skunk blew over and was found to grow very nicely under artificial light; its descendants are the basis for the near-infinite variety of Nederweeds. Technology has even gone so far as to produce viable hash from the local harvest: foreign markets and suppliers need no longer be involved.

> **'Some visitors show up on Friday, spend three days getting wasted on spliffs, spacecake and Amstel, then go home again.'**

After years of derision, many countries are now waking up to the advantages of the Dutch policies. So you might think now would be a good time for the Netherlands to fully legalise the growth, distribution and use of soft drugs. But as it turns out, the opposite seems to be happening. A conservative stream in government began a few years ago to crack down on home-growing, allowing only the cultivation of four plants at a time and banning the use of artificial light. Tighter restrictions also caused a decline in the number of coffeeshops: from 1,200 in 1997 to 782 in 2002. Amsterdam, home to about 20 per cent of these, now won't let any new coffeeshops open, and is also busy forcing coffeeshops that sell alcohol to choose between dope and booze.

In 2003 – the same year that saw the appearance of (albeit overpriced) prescription marijuana in the nation's pharmacies – coffeeshops narrowly avoided demise threatened by new anti-smoking legislation for smoke-free workplaces. Ever pragmatic, the authorities soon realised that non-smokers are unlikely to look for a job in a coffeeshop. And international shock and horror greeted the much-publicised suggestion later in the same year by the Christian Democrat Justice Minister that drug tourism could be eradicated by letting only Dutch residents buy from coffeeshops. But the municipalities – the level of government that he wanted to take responsibility for the mind-boggling logistics – turned the idea down.

There's an obvious difference between how the locals treat the easy availability of soft drugs and how visitors behave. The majority of smokin' locals treat soft drugs as just something else to do. Dope tourists, though, hit the coffeeshops with wide-eyed, giggling greed, then face a painful comedown when they belatedly realise that Dutch drugs are far stronger than those they're used to at home. (Perhaps that third spacecake might have been two too many…)

The easy availability of soft drugs has produced a new breed of tourist: those who come to the city merely to get so stoned they can't remember a thing about it. And it's this new breed that has led the tourist authorities to look upon their city's most famous law with pronounced ambivalence. On the one hand, the very presence of the coffeeshops attracts many visitors to the city. On the other, the kind of visitors the law attracts are, not to put too fine a point on it, hardly the kind of tourists the authorities welcome with open arms.

Although many of Amsterdam's weekend funseekers only blight certain areas of the city with their stag-party antics – the Red Light District chief among them – the authorities' displeasure is less a matter of high principle than a simple question of economics. Such visitors show up on Friday, spend three days getting wasted on spliffs, spacecake and Amstel, then go home again on Monday having made a negligible contribution to the Dutch GDP.

Then there's the thorny, under-publicised issue of organised crime. Every country has it in some form, of course, but the gangs in the Netherlands are able to go about their drug-running businesses with considerably more ease than the government would like. Worse still, many Dutch gangs are believed to be freely trafficking drugs both hard and soft all over Europe, a fact that hasn't exactly endeared the Netherlands to its neighbours.

And yet, and yet, and yet… The policy still works. And it's one that has long been taken for granted here: despite the goggle-eyed, slack-jawed amazement with which the rest of the world eyes the Dutch drugs policy, the locals barely give it a second thought. They've moved on. Long before the rest of the world has even caught up. So you might want to put a bit of that attitude in your pipe before you start to smoke it.

► For more on **prostitution**, see p77.
► For more on **coffeeshops**, see p147.
► For more on **sex shops**, see p176.

Water

Amsterdam wouldn't be what it is without stubborn farmers, beer – and an awful lot of water.

In 1652, during a downturn in Anglo-Dutch relations (*see p9* **Eejit-prop**), Owen Felltham described the Low Countries as 'the buttock of the world, full of veins and blood but no bones in it.' And sure, boggy Amsterdam does ride low enough to be ranked as one of Satan's near neighbours, but its soggy nature is in fact the foundation of its historical successes and go-with-the-flow reputation.

Originating as a village that subsisted on a bit of fishing and some small-town frolicking, Amsterdam fostered some of the first cheerleaders of democracy: stubborn farmers, who set themselves to build dikes to keep the sea and the mighty Amstel river at bay. The teamwork needed to fulfil such a massive task formed the basis for today's famed 'polder model', where all conflicts are resolved at endless meetings fuelled by coffee and the thirst for consensus. Of course, since flexibility and compromise also made good business sense, the approach turned out to be highly profitable.

Amsterdam was only properly set up as a centre of pragmatic trade and lusty sin in the 14th century, when it was granted beer tax exemption status. This opened the floodgates to a river of the stuff (flowing from Hamburg) and to lots of beer-drinking settlers. After beer profits other profits were born – from sea travels to both the East and the West – and before long Amsterdam became the richest and most powerful port on the planet. The resulting Golden Age saw the construction of the image-defining canal girdle (*see p86*), and these and the more ancient ones of the Old Centre formed a full circulatory system – and er, sewage system – in which goods and people from all over the world could flow in and out.

Besides developing a knack for building canals, dikes, windmills and ships, the Dutch came up with a whole bevy of other water-worthy inventions during the Golden Age. The inventor Cornelis Drebbel (1572-1634) came up with the first submarine prototype (basically a rowing boat fitted with rawhide and tubes), and local genius Jan van der Heyden (1637-1712) invented the first pump-action fire hose. More curious were the 'Tobacco-Smoke-Enema-Applicators', developed to attempt the reanimation of the drowners who were regularly pulled from the canals. This ancient technique – also applied with reversed 30-centimetre (12-inch) Gouda pipes – was standard practice and all part of the canalside scenery in Amsterdam until the 1850s, when the less dramatic but more effective mouth-to-mouth technique gained prominence. Talk about progress.

The fine-tuning of technologies at the end of the 19th century allowed the building of the North Sea Channel, thus giving Amsterdam a more direct route to the open sea and triggering a second Golden Age of sorts. The 1990s can be seen in a similar light, thanks to the huge influx of global corporations seeking a central location for their European headquarters. The Eastern Docklands (*see p100*) began transforming into a showcase for modern architecture that sought to seamlessly blend both private and public spaces with its watery surrounds. The arising artificial islands of IJburg further east continue this trend, as do ambitious plans to build vast windmill parks in the North Sea and create a floating runway for Schiphol airport. (While acceptance of this last idea is still very far off, it's not as ridiculous as it sounds: Schiphol itself used to be five metres (16 feet) under water. What's more, the fuel of the future, hydrogen – the mighty H in H_2O – is being taken very seriously, as proved by the 2004 debut of hydrogen-powered buses in 'Dam.

That water is of national importance in a country where two thirds of the land is reclaimed was shown recently, when Crown Prince Willem Alexander decided to slough off his image of rather doltish young manhood and embrace water as a personal crusade. 'Water is fantastically beautiful. It's essential to life. It's about health, environment, and transport. There's the fight against water and the fight against too little water. You can actually do everything with it, and it's primordially Dutch.'

Anything you say, Crown Prince.

Still, water does play a fundamental of the recreational lives of more regular folk. While eel-pulling (*see p103*) is no longer practiced as a canal sport, boating remains the most popular of calm pastimes. (Sadly its winter counterpart, ice-skating, has suffered greatly from global warming.) The opening of the city's first bonafide beach in IJburg was the news story of summer 2003 (and a worthy one at that: *see p101* **Smisle!**). And while the concept of making Prinsengracht swimmable remains a ploy by fringe political parties to get headline space, the more realistic plan to re-dig out canals – like Elandsgracht and Lindengracht – that were filled in to cope with motor traffic might actually happen in the short term, since Amsterdam is keenly aware that its waters remain one of its strongest tourist magnets.

For boys, a common form of recreation is urinating into a canal – though these days they risk a fine. This age-old tradition has been lumped in with *wildplassen* – 'wild pissing', or passing water willy-nilly. (As the local population's main 'petty grievance' along with canine excreta, the former cited by politicians

A typical Amsterdam houseboat.

as an example of the 'watering down' of civilisation's norms.) 'Wild Pissing Symposiums' – no shit – have been convened, and consensus-building pow-wows even came up with 'A Plan of Action: Wild Pissing'. Still, while it makes total sense to prevent historic buildings being slashed away by urine erosion, for boys discreetly seeking ritual oneness with the canals – and hence with the city's past, present and future – a €40 fine seems a tad harsh. The canal waters are essentially flushed daily anyway, ever since a hi-tech alternating sluice system was implemented – so what's the problem?

When compared to the original Venice, the waters of the 'Venice of the North' are essentially stench-free. In fact, here you can meditate on the wiggly reflections in the canals from up close without fear of succumbing to fumes. Not merely trippy, they act as a constant reminder that Amsterdam is a happily twisted and distorted town – and also a remarkably user-friendly town where you can throw your cares overboard and just go with the flow. Just don't take that last part too literally.

Where to Stay

Where to Stay

Need a bed? Book well ahead.

Amsterdam's chocolate-box smallness creates an intimacy that makes for memorable public encounters and backstreet discoveries – and scores of small hotels that can be charming and cosy or crowded and claustrophobic. The big ones tend to be chain-run and full of hordes of package tourists. They might be more likely to have vacant rooms, air-conditioning and well-lit hallways, but they're less likely to have anything memorable about them, for better or for worse.

The trick with lodging in Amsterdam is getting in (and we don't just mean squeezing up those narrow stairs). Book well in advance, especially if you want something special. In 2003, continuing hard times for hoteliers meant there were more empty rooms than usual, and deals could be snapped up on all price levels; you could well beat the prices listed here. Many hotels also post offers on their websites.

Hotels in Amsterdam cluster around clearly demarcated consumer zones; each is lined with dozens of anonymous small places. The sleazy Red Light District and slightly more salubrious Centraal Station area, the neon-lit entertainment quarters around Rembrandtplein and Leidseplein, the elegant canal zone between the station and Leidseplein, and the stately museum district are the main hotel areas, in ascending order of poshness, peacefulness and price.

Wherever you stay, the typical room might feel a bit cramped. Try to see it as cosy, and leave the 24-piece luggage set at home – Amsterdam isn't a dressing-up town anyway. If you need things like a lift or wide doorways, always ask: much of this wiggly city is not very disabled-friendly, and hotels are no exception. And when that promised king-size bed turns out to be two small ones pushed together, bear in mind that this is standard even in expensive hotels, what with windows being furniture's usual way into the city's old skinny buildings.

In lieu of bigness, Amsterdam's hoteliers seem to have gone for the 'small but perfectly formed' approach. 'Design hotels' are catching on at all but the lowest price levels, and even there, themed rooms abound. Other places around town emphasise art or literature, in-hotel bike rental, or being on a boat. Whatever you find, enjoy. The local wish to be unique will make your stay that much funkier and perhaps add a bit of poetry to your life. We'd expect nothing less from this self-expressive city.

RESERVATIONS

Aside from making contact well in advance with a hotels or arranging a travel-and-hotel package with your travel agent, there are other ways to make a booking. The **Nederlands Reserverings Centrum** (aka the Dutch Reservation Centre) makes bookings across the whole country for individuals and groups – by phone and online. The **Amsterdam Tourist Board** books rooms in and around the capital by phone and internet and from offices at Centraal Station and Schiphol Airport (*see p290*). Contacting one of these might be your best bet if you're stuck at the last minute; big hotels that don't fill up often let their last rooms go here cheap. Online bookings can also be made at **www.bookings.nl** and **www.hotels.nl**. The tourist board also produces a comprehensive guide (€3.50) to hotels in the city.

The best Hotels

For international chic
Blakes. See p55.

For hidden treasures
717. See p59.

For your first book tour when you want to be recognised
Ambassade Hotel. See p56.

For inspired awakenings
Hotel de Filosoof. See p65.

For plugging into the art and club scene
Winston Hotel. See p53.

For a hit of the hip new Pijp
Cake Under My Pillow. See p68.

For those backpacker nights you'll never remember
Young Budget Hotel Kabul. See p55.

For those backpacker nights you'll never remember (with air-conditioning)
Bulldog Budget Hotel. See p55.

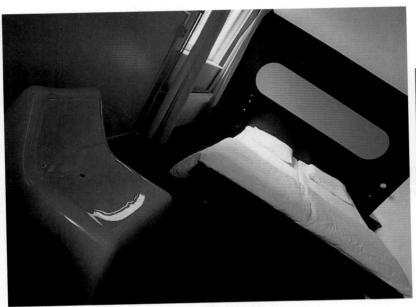

Winston Hotel: accommodation or installation? *See p53.*

Nederlands Reserverings Centrum
Nieuwe Gouw 1, 1442 LE Purmerend (0299 689144/ www.hotelres.nl). **Open** 8.30am-5.30pm Mon-Fri.
Book online or by phone: cancellations and changes to prior reservations must be made in whichever medium you made the booking. There's a round-the-clock phone message service in English.

Hotels

The Old Centre

Deluxe

Barbizon Palace
Prins Hendrikkade 59-72, 1012 AD (556 4564/fax 624 3353/www.nh-hotels.com). Tram 1, 2, 4, 5, 7, 9, 13, 17, 24, 25/Metro Centraal Station. **Rates** €278-€341 single/double; €446-€892 suite. **Credit** AmEx, DC, MC, V. **Map** p306 D2.
The lavishness of the surroundings is apparent as you walk into the black-and-white marble hall. Leading off it are amenities including a swanky fitness centre with sauna, Turkish bath and solarium, and the Michelin two-star French-Dutch Vermeer restaurant (*see p119*). Across the road from Centraal Station, the hotel even has its own landing stage for canal boats. Breakfast is €20.

Hotel services *Air-conditioning. Babysitting. Bar. Beauty services. Concierge. Disabled: adapted room. Gym. Limousine service. No-smoking floor. Parking. Restaurants.* **Room services** *Dataport. Minibar. Room service (24hrs). TV: satellite/pay movies/VCR (by request).*

The Grand
Oudezijds Voorburgwal 197, 1012 EX (555 3111/ fax 555 3222/www.thegrand.nl). Tram 4, 9, 14, 16, 24, 25. **Rates** €420-€465 single/double; €560-€1,495 suite. **Credit** AmEx, DC, MC, V. **Map** p306 D3.
The five-star Grand makes its luxurious mark by – among other things – offering some of the biggest hotel rooms in this tightly packed town. A whiff of privilege hits as soon as you enter the spacious courtyard, and carries through to the 182 rooms, suites and apartments, distinguished by their high ceilings, wide and tall windows, light wood furnishing and a signature potpourri wafting through the air. The Grand has been pampering the elite ever since it opened as an inn way back in the late 16th century, and had none other than Prince William of Orange as one of its first guests. It's also home to Café Roux (*see p119*). Breakfast is €22.
Hotel services *Air-conditioning. Babysitting. Bar. Business services. Concierge. Garden. Gym. Limousine service. No-smoking rooms. Parking. Restaurant. Swimming pool.* **Room services** *Dataport. Minibar. Room service (24hrs). TV: cable/pay movies/VCR (by request).*

Grand Hotel Krasnapolsky

Dam 9, 1012 JS (554 9111/fax 622 8607/www.nh-hotels.com). Tram 1, 2, 4, 5, 9, 13, 14, 16, 17, 24, 25. **Rates** €290-€320 single/double; €450-€700 suites; €60 extra bed. **Credit** AmEx, DC, MC, V. **Map** p306 D3.

Slightly re-worked by new owners NH Hotels, the feel remains corporate and the place bustles with business and package-tour guests. The 468 rooms include 36 fully furnished apartments. Guests can still breakfast (€21) and lunch orangerie-style in the glass-ceilinged Winter Garden and later choose to dine in one of the eight different restaurants that cover the cuisines of the world. After a meeting in one of the 22 convention rooms, business types can sit in the Lounge and watch the hordes on Dam Square – or keep working via the wireless internet connection in the lobby.
Hotel services *Air-conditioning. Babysitting. Bar. Beauty salon. Business services. Concierge. Disabled: adapted rooms. Garden. Gym. No-smoking floors. Parking. Restaurants.* **Room services** *Dataport. Minibar. Room service (24hrs). TV: satellite/pay movies.*

Hôtel de l'Europe

Nieuwe Doelenstraat 2-8, 1012 CP (531 1777/fax 531 1778/www.leurope.nl). Tram 4, 9, 14, 16, 24, 25. **Rates** €285-€345 single; €350-€390 double; €455-€960 double. **Credit** AmEx, DC, MC, V. **Map** p306 D3.

Looking out from one of the 100 individually decorated, Victorian-style rooms, you'd be forgiven for thinking this five-star hotel has a moat. It doesn't; but its location gives it a front-row view of the city's defining waterway, the Amstel. Its grandeur is further enhanced by the Excelsior restaurant (jacket required), which serves haute cuisine and champagne on its river-level terrace. With a Victorian-period lounge and foyer, this is truly an elegant place, catering for everyone from business types to just-married (the bridal suite comes complete with jacuzzi). Breakfast is €25.
Hotel services *Air-conditioning. Babysitting. Bar. Business services. Concierge. Gym. Limousine service. No-smoking rooms. Parking. Restaurants. Swimming pool.* **Room services** *Dataport. Minibar. Room service (24hrs). TV: cable/pay movies/VCR (by request).*

Sofitel Amsterdam

Nieuwezijds Voorburgwal 67, 1012 RE (627 5900/fax 623 8932/www.sofitel.nl). Tram 1, 2, 5, 13, 17. **Rates** €304-€345 single/double; €351-€424 triple; €499-€620 suite. **Credit** AmEx, DC, MC, V. **Map** p306 C2.

On a site where a monastery once stood, the Sofitel's location is certainly convenient but is anything but secluded these days. It stands near Centraal Station, between Kalverstraat and the canals and close to the DJ bars of the Nieuwezijds. Its 148 rooms are subtly decorated, and boast understated, attractive classical furnishings; the Duke of Windsor bar is fitted out with authentic lamps and panelling from the Orient Express. Breakfast is €17.50.

Hotel services *Air-conditioning. Babysitting. Bar. Concierge. Disabled: adapted room. Gym. No-smoking rooms. Parking (paid). Restaurant.* **Room services** *Dataport. Minibar. Room service (24hrs). TV: cable/pay movies.*

Victoria Hotel Amsterdam

Damrak 1-5, 1012 LG (623 4255/fax 625 2997/www.parkplaza.com). Tram 1, 2, 4, 5, 9, 13, 14, 16, 17, 24, 25. **Rates** €298-€310 single; €325-€345 double; €477-€525 suite; €52 extra bed. **Credit** AmEx, DC, MC, V. **Map** p306 D2.

This four-star establishment near Centraal Station is on an unlovely street overrun by trashy tourist shops and gaming parlours, but the Jordaan and the canals are an easy walk away. Comforts for the weary traveller include an indoor pool, a gym, a sauna and a steam room. Or you could just relax with a drink on Vic's Terrace and look down on the Damrak's tourist hordes. Breakfast is €20.
Hotel services *Air-conditioning. Babysitting. Bar. Beauty salon. Business services. Concierge. Disabled: adapted rooms. Gym. No-smoking rooms. Parking nearby (paid). Restaurants. Swimming pool (indoor).* **Room services** *Dataport (suites). Minibar. Room service (6.30am-11pm). TV: satellite/pay movies.*

Expensive

Hotel Inntel

Nieuwezijds Kolk 19, 1012 PV (530 1818/fax 422 1919/www.hotelinntel.com). Tram 1, 2, 5, 13, 17. **Rates** €285 single; €295-€325 double; €345 suite. **Credit** AmEx, DC, MC, V. **Map** p306 D2.

On a small pedestrian square, Inntel is quiet enough to ensure a good night's rest but central enough to be within walking distance from all the action. The 236 rooms are simple but tasteful, with a designer-cool edge. The conservatory-style breakfast room overlooks a terrace. Guests can eat at two neighbouring restaurants – Humphrey's (French) and Bon Ton (international) – and put the food on the hotel bill. Breakfast is €16.
Hotel services *Air-conditioning. Bar. Disabled: adapted rooms. Limousine service. No-smoking floors. Parking (paid).* **Room services** *Dataport. Minibar. Room service (6.30-10am Mon-Fri; 7-11am Sat, Sun). TV: satellite/pay movies.*

Moderate

Hotel Citadel

Nieuwezijds Voorburgwal 98-100, 1012 SG (627 3882/fax 627 4684/www.hotelcitadel.nl). Tram 1, 2, 4, 5, 9, 13, 14, 16, 17, 24, 25. **Rates** €85-€110 single; €120-€155 double; €160-€190 triple. **Credit** AmEx, DC, MC, V. **Map** p306 C2.

This bright, modern three-star hotel is a two-minute walk from the station, and near the Royal Palace on Dam Square. It's very handy for strolls along the canals into the Jordaan and, in the opposite direction, the Kalverstraat shopping area. All of the 38 rooms are comfortable and clean, in a generic hotel

Water beds

Amsterdam is best seen from the water, and many locals are so adamant about this that they live, at some inconvenience, on boats. But visitors don't have to repaint hulls, and can happily sample a houseboat's wendy-house atmosphere without the hassle. Still, floating hotels remain rarer than you might think and seem to appear and disappear like migratory water fowl. So we'll blow the horn on a few, but leave much of the investigating to you. And be warned: gangplanks can be dangerous after a few drinks.

Starting at the bottom, as it were, where you can expect to pay about €50 per person, **Frederic Rentabike** (Brouwersgracht 78, 624 5509/www.frederic.nl), as well as renting out bikes and more traditional rooms, lets out two houseboats by the night. Both are moored on the northern Jordaan's peaceful Brouwersgracht; the bigger one can hold three people in one long room and has nice touches like an antique wooden seat and fake-fur pillows. Similarly located and priced, the super-basic **Hotel Acacia** (Lindengracht 251, 622 1460/fax 638 0748/www.acacia hotel.nl) has two houseboats moored just outside on the Lijnbaansgracht. One is a plain white box, the other a peeling brown classic; each has two twin rooms.

Amsterdam House ('s Gravelandseveer 3-4, 626 2577/www.amsterdamhouse.com) rents rooms on ten houseboats, most moored by their office at the top of the Amstel. They come in a range of sizes – from a quarter of a small boat to all of a bigger one – and prices.

If it hasn't sailed for other shores, you'll find the **Sailing Home** (Steiger 3, Oosterdok, 627 4098/www.floating-tulip.com) moored by the Nemo (see p102), across a long footbridge east of Centraal Station, in the low season. Used for chartered trips in summer, the boat has 13 cabins, a bar and a breakfast buffet. Think of it as a gentler version of its massive neighbour, **Amstel Botel** (see p53). Doubles range from €80-€100 per night (though the price drops for weekdays and extended stays).

In the redeveloped Eastern Docklands (see p100), **Captain's Place** (Levantkade 184, 419 8119/www.meesvof.nl; pictured) is a beautifully refurbished ship, complete with banana tree garden and two guest rooms, each with an en suite bathroom and tub. It's ideal for a family: you can rent the whole boat (€250 for four people, €35 per extra person up to eight). It's open all year round and requires a minimum four-day stay.

In the same neighbourhood and representing the height of luxury, the **Ideaal II** (Levantkade, 419 7255/www.houseboats.nl) is a Dutch cargo barge that can fit up to five in its light and bright interior. It's kitted out with all imaginable comforts: waterbed, jacuzzi and gourmet kitchen – hell, you can even dive off the sundeck for a quick swim. The minimum stay is a week and its priced about €80-€100 per person, depending on the season.

If you take to life on a watery bed, then you might want to use **www.houseboat.nl** as a springboard to houseboat accommodation throughout the Netherlands.

kind of way (the quietest rooms at the back are a little on the dark side), and most have baths. They also have a nearby sister establishment, Singel Hotel (Singel 15, 626 3108/fax 620 3777).
Hotel services *Bar.* **Room services** *TV: cable/pay movies.*

Zosa
Kloveniersburgwal 20, 1012 CV (330 6241/fax 330 6242/www.zosa-online.com). Tram 4, 9, 17, 24, 25/Metro Nieuwmarkt. **Rates** €120 single; €145 double; €23 extra bed. **Credit** AmEx, MC, V. **Map** p306 D3.
Just off the happening Nieuwmarkt, where the red lights shade off into a desirable old urban neighbourhood, Zosa no longer does full service at its ground-floor restaurant, but still cooks up breakfasts and 24-hour room service snacks. Six modestly proportioned rooms take up three storeys (sorry, no lift). Each has its own whimsical theme – Wonders is decorated in Asian style; Retro has a glittery '70s feel – and overlooks the canal or the neighbours' fetching (but, alas, off-limits) garden. The cool young staff do a fine job of making you feel part of the scene. In mid-2003 Zosa was in the process of being bought, but the only likely change will be the restaurant's re-opening.
Hotel services *Bar. Restaurant.* **Room services** *Telephone. TV: cable.*

Budget

Amstel Botel
Oosterdokskade 2-4, 1011 AE (626 4247/fax 639 1952). Tram 1, 2, 5, 9, 13, 17, 24, 25. **Rates** €84 (rear side)-€89(water side) single/double/twin; €93-€95 triple. **Credit** AmEx, DC, MC, V. **Map** p307 E1.
The three-star, 176-room Amstel Botel is on a boat. It sounds more exciting than it is: if you're on the land side all you'll see is a construction site. The watery side is better(and worth the extra cost), with houses and boats visible across the old harbour. With the look of a decommissioned cruise ship, complete with clean-cut staff and geriatric guests, it does have its advantages – the price is right and with an air-conditioned bar surrounded by windows, it's refreshingly light and salubrious compared to most comparably priced hotels in the nearby Red Light District and around Centraal Station. Breakfast (buffet) is an extra €9.
Hotel services *Bar.* **Room services** *TV: cable.*

Greenhouse Effect
Warmoesstraat 55, 1012 HW (624 4974/fax 489 0850/www.the-greenhouse-effect.com). Tram 4, 9, 17, 24, 25. **Rates** €60 (shared facilities), €75 (private facilities) single; €90-€105 double/twin; €120-€130 triple; €120-€180 apartments. **Credit** AmEx, MC, V. **Map** p306 D2.
The Greenhouse Effect's 17 rooms are spread over two buildings across the street from each other in the heart of the party zone. The feel is basic and lived-in, but vastly improved by the rooms' various decorating themes, which include Red Light and Outer Space. Enhance your stay with the guest-discounted offerings at its bar and coffeeshop downstairs (*see p149*). Most rooms have private baths. There are also two self-catering apartments a few minutes' walk away.
Hotel services *Bar.* **Room services** *TV: cable.*

Hotel Vijaya
Oudezijds Voorburgwal 44 (638 0102/626 9406/fax 620 5277/www.hotelvijaya.com). Tram 4 ,5, 16, 24, 25. **Rates** €45-€75 single; €70-€105 double; €90-€145 triple; €110-€175 quad; €120-€195 quint. **Credit** AmEx, DC, MC, V. **Map** p306 D2.
The Vijaya, which calls itself a 'two-star budget hotel', is reassuringly friendly and unsleazy for the Red Light District, while charging lower prices than many of its less appealing neighbours. The 30 rooms have en suite facilities, the first-floor breakfast and reception area is roomy, and stays of more than one night get a free dinner in the owners' Indian restaurant a couple of canals away. The interior could use a coat or two of paint, and the lack of air-conditioning can make things sticky in summer, but just think of it as part of the price to pay for staying in two listed 18th-century buildings.
Hotel services *Bar. Breakfast room.* **Room services** *TV.*

Winston Hotel
Warmoestraat 129, 1012 JA (623 1380/fax 639 2308/www.winston.nl). Tram 4, 9, 14, 16, 24, 25. **Rates** €63-€69 single; €83-€92 double; €113-€123 triple; €121-€142 quad; €142-€158 quint; €166-€188 6-person room. **Credit** AmEx, DC, MC, V. **Map** p306 D2.
Be different: stay in a work of art at this gallery-hotel on the edge of the Red Light District. Twenty-six of its rooms have been painted and/or turned into installations by artists (viewable on website). They range from François Gervais' Matisse-inspired Durex Room to Monique Voudon's Green Room, a comment on media culture; Exes, by painter Suzanne Lanfermeijer, was completed as recently as 2003. The 24-hour bar for guests and interesting club nights (*see p214 and p223*) add to the fun.
Hotel services *Bar. Disabled: adapted room.*

Hostels

Bob's Youth Hostel
Nieuwezijds Voorburgwal 92, 1012 SG (623 0063/fax 675 6446/www.bobsyouthhostel.nl). Tram 1, 2, 5, 13, 17. **Rates** €18 dorm bed; €70 double. **No credit cards. Map** p306 D3.
This longtime slacker-backpacker favourite is a great place at which to meet fellow travellers, share smokes, and perhaps be a beneficiary when others offload their less exportable Amsterdam purchases. There are dorms, each with between four and 16 beds, as well as apartments for two people sharing. Most dorms are mixed, but one is women-only.
Hotel services *Bar. TV room: cable.*

Bulldog Budget Hotel

Oudezijds Voorburgwal 220, 1012 GJ (620 3822/fax 627 1612/www.bulldog.nl). Tram 4, 9, 14, 16, 24, 25/Metro Nieuwmarkt. **Rates** *€19-€26 dorm bed; €61.50 single; €61-€82 double; €96-€105 triple; €112-€122 quad.* **Credit** *AmEx, MC, V.* **Map** *p306 D3.*
This hotel, above a branch of the infamous bar and coffeeshop chain smack in the Red Light District, should have finished its overhaul by early 2004. It will have around 200 beds, a couple of dozen private rooms, and air-conditioning on three of the four floors. The new look is less stoner-style and more snazzy, with plenty of bright red paint, but some rooms are as pitch-dark as before – so get one canal-side if possible. The spiffy big ground-floor bar is fully equipped with sofas, TV, DVDs, internet terminals, and vegetating young guests. Nearby there are also six luxury apartments for rent. Dorms are no-smoking. One private room is fully accessible to disabled guests.
Hotel services *Internet. Parking (street).* **Room services** *TV: cable (selected rooms only).*

Flying Pig Hostels

Flying Pig Downtown *Nieuwendijk 100, 1012 MR (420 6822/group bookings 421 0583/fax 428 0802/www.flyingpig.nl). Tram 1, 2, 3, 5, 13, 17.* **Flying Pig Palace** *Vossiusstraat 46-7, 1071 AJ (400 4187/group reservations 421 0583/fax 421 0802/www.flyingpig.nl). Tram 2, 5, 20.* **Rates** *Downtown €19.50-€23.50 dorm bed; €57.50-€68 single/twin. Palace €19.50-€25.50 dorm bed; €54.50-€56 single; €56.50-€64 twin; €67.50 triple.* **Credit** *both MC, V.* **Map** *Downtown p306 D2. Palace p310 C6.*
The fun-loving Pigs pull in the backpackers with fully equipped kitchens, tourist information and lively guests-only bars. They're clean and laid-back, with no curfew, and most rooms have showers and loos. The Downtown branch will suit coffeeshop-hoppers; the Palace is in the far more dignified Museum Quarter, beside the Vondelpark. Bookings must generally be made online, or by phone on the morning of the night you want to stay. In summer, consider a night at the Pig's seaside outpost in Noordwijk, reachable for a small charge via shuttle; outdoor activities include kite-surfing.
Hotel services *Bar.*

Stayokay Hostels

Stadsdoelen *Kloveniersburgwal 97, 1011 KB (624 6832/fax 639 1035/www.stayokay.com). Tram 4, 9, 14, 16, 24, 25.* **City Hostel Vondelpark** *Zandpad 5, 1054 GA (589 8996/fax 589 8955/www.stayokay.com). Tram 1, 2, 5, 6, 7, 10.* **Rates** *Stadsdoelen €18.50-€22.50 dorm bed. City Hostel Vondelpark €20.50-€23 dorm/quad bed; €65-€77 single/twin; €104-€112 quad. Both hostels* HI members €2.50 reduction. **Credit** MC, V. **Map** *Stadsdoelen p306 D3. City Hostel Vondelpark p310 C6.*
The former NJHC (Dutch youth hostel organisation) has changed its name to reflect a long established lack of age limits, but the song remains the same. Its hostels are wholesome and filled with happy

wanderers of all ages and have rooms for larger groups (see the website for further information). The Stadsdoelen branch is on a stately canal in the city's heart. Its bar serves snacks and dinner, and sells €1 beers during happy hour. The huge Vondelpark branch is on the edge of Amsterdammers' favourite leafy retreat, best enjoyed at the terraced brasserie. It also has Internet access, a TV room, laundry facilities and a pool table. Both are clean, friendly and open round the clock.
Hotel services *Bar (both). Courtyard (Stadsdoelen only). Disabled: adapted rooms (Vondelpark only). No-smoking rooms (both). Restaurant (both).*

Young Budget Hotel Kabul

Warmoesstraat 38-42, 1012 JE (623 7158/fax 620 0869). Tram 4, 9, 14, 16, 24, 25. **Rates** *€17-€21 dorm bed; €45-€52 single; €65-€95 double; €85-€113 triple; €95 suite.* **Credit** *AmEx, DC, MC, V.* **Map** *p306 D2.*
Don't be put off by the Kabul's somewhat daunting exterior: the staff here are friendly and the aroma of cannabis smacks of the classic backpacker experience. Some big rooms (as well as the breakfast area) hang out over the water of the Damrak and let in loads of light – get one of these if you can; others in this no-frills labyrinth can be a tad gloomy. Some of the furniture shows the stains and graffiti of a million young travellers; better are the internet room and lack of curfew.
Hotel services *Bar.*

Western Canal Belt

Deluxe

Amsterdam Marriott Hotel

Stadhouderskade 12, 1054 ES (607 5555/fax 607 5511/www.marriotthotels.com). Tram 1, 2, 5, 6, 7, 10. **Rates** *€140-€278 room (for 1-4 people); €478-€525 suite (for 1-4 people).* **Credit** *AmEx, DC, MC, V.* **Map** *p310 C5.*
This five-star hotel caters to business travellers. It's housed beside Vondelpark in a hunk of late-20th-century brown brick that may offend some aesthetes, since it dominates the view south from Leidseplein; it also exudes an institutional American feel with its Pizza Hut and muzak. Still, the 392 rooms and suites – all at least doubles – are comfortable and spacious, and the health club is fully equipped. Breakfast costs an extra €12.50-€17.50.
Hotel services *Air-conditioning. Babysitting. Bars. Business services. Concierge. Disabled: adapted rooms. Gym. No-smoking floors. Parking (€25/day). Restaurants.* **Room services** *Dataport. Minibar. Room service (24hrs). TV: satellite/pay movies.*

Blakes

Keizersgracht 384, 1016 GB (530 2010/fax 530 2030/www.blakesamsterdam.com). Tram 1, 2, 5. **Rates** *€250-€320 single; €390-€490 double; €890-€990 duplex; €1,090-€1,490 suite.* **Credit** *AmEx, DC, MC, V.* **Map** *p310 C4.*

The personal touch: **Greenhouse Effect.** *See p53.*

Blakes has been a byword for boutique-hotel luxury in Amsterdam as well as London, ever since hotelier Anouska Hempel opened her outpost here in 1999. It sits partly in what's left of a theatre dating from 1617, in a desirable neighbourhood between the Jordaan and the 'Nine Streets'; in 2002 it expanded to a second building. There, the decor resembles that of Hempel's transcendentally minimalist eponymous hotel in London; the original is done up largely in the sumptuous colours and stripes of the London Blakes. The dramatic, elegant decor is complemented by sensational service, and the restaurant (*see p122*) is equally winning. Breakfast costs €24. **Hotel services** *Air-conditioning. Babysitting. Bar. Concierge. Garden. Limousine service. Parking (valet). Restaurant.* **Room services** *Dataport. Minibar. Room service (24hrs). TV: cable/VCR.*

Hotel Pulitzer

Prinsengracht 315-31, 1016 GZ (523 5235/ fax 627 6753/www.sheraton.nl). Tram 13, 14, 17. **Rates** €385 single; €410-€475 double; €750-€1,000 suite; €47 extra bed. **Credit** AmEx, DC, MC, V. **Map** p306 C3.

The 230 guest rooms of the five-star Pulitzer are enviably sited in a king's ransom of canal houses – 25 in total, situated around central courtyard gardens. Many of the traditionally decorated rooms have water views. A gallery holds changing exhibitions of contemporary Dutch art, and an annual classical concert is held on barges in front of the hotel. All in all, very classy. Breakfast is €25 extra. Check for deals at www.luxurycollection.com/pulitzer.

Hotel services *Air-conditioning. Babysitting. Bar. Business services. Concierge. Garden. Limousine service. No-smoking rooms. Parking (valet). Restaurant.* **Room services** *Dataport. Minibar. Room service (24hrs). TV: cable/pay movies/VCR (by request).*

Expensive

Ambassade Hotel

Herengracht 341, 1016 AZ (555 0222/fax 555 0277/www.ambassade-hotel.nl). Tram 1, 2, 5. **Rates** €158 single; €188 double; €220 triple; €260-€325 suite; €295 apartment; €32 extra bed. **Credit** AmEx, DC, MC, V. **Map** p310 C4.

This literary retreat draws publishers and authors – recent guests include Donna Tartt and Nicci French – and part of the appeal is surely the library of 1,000 or so signed books. The rooms in the ten lovely old canalside houses that make up the hotel are individually and exquisitely decorated in historic style. If that doesn't inspire you, soak away writer's block at the nearby hotel-owned Koan Float, a floatation and massage centre. Breakfast costs €15. **Hotel services** *Babysitting. Business services. Concierge. Limousine service. No-smoking rooms.* **Room services** *Internet. Room service (24hrs). TV: cable/VCR.*

Canal House Hotel

Keizersgracht 148, 1015 CX (622 5182/622 9987/ fax 624 1317/www.canalhouse.nl). Tram 13, 14, 17. **Rates** €140-€190 single/double. **Credit** DC, MC, V. **Map** p306 C3.

With its breakable ornaments and tricky stairways, the Canal House doesn't encourage visitors with young children – a relief if you don't have any – and the serenity is carried over with the absence of any TVs. The Irish owners have snapped up a treasure in this gorgeous 17th-century building, with ornate ceilings, antiques liberally sprinkled throughout the 26 rooms, and a breakfast room looking on to a garden. Stay here and you'll feel as if you're inhabiting the set of a costume drama.
Hotel services *Bar. Garden.* **Room services** *Dataport. Telephone.*

Estheréa

Singel 303-9, 1012 WJ (624 5146/fax 623 9001/ www.estherea.nl). Tram 1, 2, 5. **Rates** €145-€205 single; €154-€260 double; €216-€290 triple; €245-€315 quad. **Credit** AmEx, DC, MC, V. **Map** p306 C3.
It's worth paying extra for the canal view afforded by the 20 deluxe rooms at the Estheréa, but if they're all taken you'll still find individual traditional decor and meticulous attention to detail and service in whichever of the 71 rooms you stay in. Estheréa is a charming four-star hotel, just off the Spui, and still owned and run by the descendants of the woman who founded it on this spot after losing her husband in World War II. The luxurious breakfast room partly overlooks the canal; free tea and coffee are available all day. Breakfast costs €14.
Hotel services *Babysitting. Bar. Concierge. No-smoking rooms.* **Room services** *Dataport. Minibar. Room service (7.30am-10pm). TV: cable.*

Toren

Keizersgracht 164, 1015 CZ (622 6352/fax 626 9705/www.hoteltoren.nl). Tram 13, 14, 17. **Rates** €115-€150 single; €125-€215 double; €195 triple; €240 suite. **Credit** AmEx, DC, MC, V. **Map** p306 C3.
Around the corner from the Westerkerk, the Toren is in fact named not after the church's famed tower but, coincidentally enough, after the family that runs it. With over 30 members of staff to look after the 40 rooms, the four-star hotel maintains its ultra-high standards with ease. The Free University was founded in the 1618 canal house the hotel occupies; later, the building successfully hid 20 people from the Nazis. While its historic features have been preserved, the place has all mod cons, combining 17th-century atmosphere with 21st-century comfort. The garden suites open out onto a green oasis; the nine rooms overlooking the canal have jacuzzis. A terrific hotel, and great value. Breakfast is €12.
Hotel services *Air-conditioning (selected rooms). Babysitting. Bar. Garden. Parking (paid). Restaurant.* **Room services** *Minibar. TV: cable/pay movies.*

Moderate

Amsterdam Wiechmann

Prinsengracht 328-32, 1016 HX (626 3321/fax 626 8962/www.hotelwiechmann.nl). Tram 1, 2, 5, 7, 17. **Rates** €75-€95 single; €120-€140 double; €180-€230 triple/quad. **Credit** MC, V. **Map** p310 C4.

The owner of Amsterdam Wiechmann prides himself on his antiques and the wooden beams and panelling of the three restored canal houses that make up the hotel. Accommodation here is basic, but the prices are perfectly reasonable – and, by way of convenience, the place is located in a charming part of Amsterdam not far from Leidseplein. Look out for the collection of teapots in the window – just a sample of the curios to be found within.
Hotel services *Babysitting. Bar.* **Room services** *TV: cable.*

Southern Canal Belt

Deluxe

American Hotel

Leidsekade 97, 1017 PN (556 3000/fax 556 3001/ www.amsterdam-american.crowneplaza.com). Tram 1, 2, 5, 6, 7, 10. **Rates** €320-€373 single; €346-€399 double; €26 extra bed. **Credit** AmEx, DC, MC, V. **Map** p310 C5.
Its marvellous 1900 art nouveau exterior is listed, but inside the only traces of this landmark building's original appearance are the stained-glass windows in many rooms and the arching brick ceiling of the ground-floor Café Américain (*see p122*). Its glitzy new lobby feels as if it belongs to another hotel entirely. Some of the plush modern rooms have balconies or canal views. The café's big terrace at the edge of bustling Leidseplein is good for people-watching. Rock star sightings are even possible, as the hotel is handy for Leidseplein's various venues. Breakfast is €21.50.
Hotel services *Air-conditioning. Babysitting (by request). Bars. Business services. Concierge. Disabled: adapted room. Gym. Limousine service (by request). No-smoking floors. Parking (paid). Restaurants.* **Room services** *Dataport. Minibar. Room service (24hrs). TV: cable/pay movies.*

Inter-Continental Amstel Amsterdam

Professor Tulpplein 1, 1018 GX (622 6060/fax 622 5808/www.interconti.com). Tram 6, 7, 10. **Rates** €490-€540 single/double; €640-€2,470 suite. **Credit** AmEx, DC, MC, V. **Map** p311 F4.
The grand foyer gives a hint of what lies beyond in the city's most luxurious, most formal five-star hotel. With a ratio of two staff to each of the 79 antique- and Delft-adorned rooms and suites, you can expect to be pampered. Guests' high expectations seem to be met, too, given the number of returning celebs and royals – in 2003 they included Robbie Williams and later the Stones, who took almost every room. Superb cuisine can be enjoyed either in sumptuous La Rive (*see p125*) – or on the riverside terraces. Breakfast is €29.
Hotel services *Air-conditioning. Bars. Business services. Concierge. Gym. Limousine service. No-smoking rooms. Parking. Restaurants. Swimming pool.* **Room services** *Dataport. Minibar. Room service (24hrs). TV: cable/pay movies/VCR.*

Schiller Hotel

Rembrandtplein 26-36, 1017 CV (554 0700/fax 624 0098/www.nh-hotels.com). Tram 4, 9, 14. **Rates** €190-€240 single; €230-€280 double; €270 triple. **Credit** AmEx, DC, MC, V. **Map** p311 E4.

Amid the touristy tat of Rembrandtplein lies the refined covered terrace of the Schiller, a four-star hotel that's been faithfully restored to its former art deco style. New owners NH Hoteles have fortunately left the lobby as it was, with dim lighting, club chairs, paintings and '30s-style fixtures. The Schiller was originally renowned for the artists and poets who hung out here, and some artistic types still prop up the bar downstairs (worth a visit even if you're not staying here; *see p144*) – though in the hotel they've mostly given way to business visitors and tourists. The restaurant serves French cuisine. Breakfast is €16.

Hotel services *Babysitting (by request). Bar. Business services. No-smoking rooms. Restaurant.* **Room services** *Minibar (selected rooms). Room service (7am-11pm). TV: cable/pay movies.*

717

Prinsengracht 717, 1017 JW (427 0717/fax 423 0717/www.717hotel.nl). Tram 1, 2, 5. **Rates** €365 single; €390 double; €415-€640 suites; extra bed €50; small dogs €25. **Credit** AmEx, DC, MC, V. **Map** p310 D4.

Discreet could be the watchword for this early 19th-century canal house's exterior, but the refurbished interior yields something of a timeless romanticism. The original owner, Dutch designer and decorator Kees van der Valk, carefully arranged beautiful classical, primitive and contemporary objets d'art from all over Europe throughout its eight suites and the inviting sitting room and library. Breakfast, afternoon tea and glasses of wine can be savoured on a secluded maple-shaded patio and are included in your bill. An impressive place.

Hotel services *Air-conditioning (suites only). Business services. Garden. No-smoking rooms. Parking (paid).* **Room services** *Dataport. Minibar. Room service (7.30am-1am). TV: cable/ pay movies/VCR.*

Expensive

Eden Hotel

Amstel 144, 1017 AE (530 7878/fax 623 3267/www.bestwestern.nl). Tram 4, 9, 14. **Rates** €116-€160 single; €135-€205 twin/double; €180-€230 triple; €205-€255 quad; €140-€220 apartments. **Credit** AmEx, DC, MC, V. **Map** p307 C3.

This, with 340 rooms, is Amsterdam's largest three-star hotel, and it offers gratifying stacks of variety. Talented students from the Rietveld Art Academy have even designed three special rooms, all of which have river views (for a €17.50 supplement). There are also 13 apartments available for stays longer than a week. Located on the banks of the Amstel, Eden is an easy jump to virtually anywhere in the city. Breakfast costs €14.

Hotel services *Babysitting. Bar. Business services. Concierge. Disabled: adapted room. No-smoking rooms. Parking nearby. Restaurant.* **Room services** *Dataport (selected rooms). Minibar (selected rooms). TV: cable/pay movies.*

Hotel Dikker & Thijs La Fenice

Prinsengracht 444, 1017 KE (620 1212/fax 625 8986/www.dikkerenthijsfenice.nl). Tram 1, 2, 5. **Rates** €115-€195 single; €160-€245 double; €225-€345 suite. **Credit** AmEx, DC, MC, V. **Map** p310 C5.

This elegant little four-star hotel near Leidseplein is handy for central pursuits. Many of its 42 rooms, decorated in classic Italian style, have a canal vista over the Prinsengracht, and those in the 1737 building 'De Prins' have beamed ceilings. The small sixth-floor penthouse has both, plus a breathtaking bird's-eye view over the city and pictures of famous guests including Norman Mailer and Griel Marcus – though no bathtub or air-conditioning. The adjacent restaurant, De Prinsenkelder, serves French and Italian cuisine in the evenings in a listed interior.

Hotel services *Babysitting. Bar. Business services. Concierge. Parking (paid). Restaurant.* **Room services** *Dataport. Minibar. Room service (during restaurant hrs). TV: cable/pay movies.*

Moderate

Bridge Hotel

Amstel 107-11, 1018 EM (623 7068/fax 624 1565/www.thebridgehotel.nl). Tram 4, 6, 7, 9, 10. **Rates** €65 single; €65-€130 double; €90-€130 triple; €140-€195 apartment/quad.* **Credit** AmEx, DC, MC, V. **Map** p307 E3.

Located on the Amstel with a view of the city's locks and nearly next door to the Carré Theatre, the 36-room Bridge Hotel is ideal for romantic walks. Friendly staff make a stay here pleasant and, for the cheery country-pine rooms, prices are reasonable (although at some times, the hotel cheekily insists that weekend bookings run for three nights). The top-floor apartment (with two to be added by late 2003) offers a spacious home from home – but only after a long climb up the stairs.

Hotel services *Bar.* **Room services** *TV: cable.*

Hotel Agora

Singel 462, 1017 AW (627 2200/fax 627 2202/www.hotelagora.nl). Tram 1, 2, 5. **Rates** €67-€98 single; €83-€130 double; €150 triple; €175 quad. **Credit** AmEx, DC, MC, V. **Map** p310 D4.

It's easy to see why this cosy two-star hotel usually has a full house: its owners are personable, the location terrific (near the Bloemenmarkt; *see p164*), and the 18th-century canal house itself is a lovely historic treasure (though there isn't a lift). Of the 16 rooms, five look out over Singel: four of the five have private bathrooms with pretty tilework, and one has a shower off the hall; guests in other rooms share bathrooms. Breakfast in bed is gratis; guests can also take it in the convivial lounge and garden area.

Hotel services *Garden.* **Room services** *Room service (8am-10.30pm). TV: cable.*

STAYOKAY HOSTELS

Stayokay is a chain of 30 hostels located throughout the Netherlands. You will find our hostels at surprisingly lovely places: in the dunes, the woods, along the waterside and in the city. The Stayokay hostels are housed in different unique buildings, ranging from modern facilities to castles or country houses. The same informal, relaxed atmosphere can be found at all Stayokay hostels, where friendly, helpful staff awaits your arrival!

WE OFFER YOU...

• beds on comfortable 2-, 4-, 6- and 8- bedded rooms and dormitories, most with private sanitary facilities • comfortable double bunks, bedside lights, table and chairs and private cupboards • breakfast included • bedsheets included • restaurant • TV lounge • internet facilities • luggage lockers • laundry facilities (at most hostels) • discounted tickets for local attractions • and more...

HOSTELLING INTERNATIONAL

Stayokay is part of the Hostelling International network, comprising over 4.000 hostels worldwide. HI members receive € 2,50 discount per night.

RESERVATIONS

You can reserve directly at the hostel or at **www.stayokay.com**. Alternatively you can make a reservation via the Hostelling International IBN network.

OUR HOSTELS IN THE CENTRE OF AMSTERDAM

Stayokay Amsterdam Vondelpark

Zandpad 5
1054 GA Amsterdam
tel +31 (0)20 589 89 96
fax +31 (0)20 589 89 55

Stayokay Amsterdam Stadsdoelen

Kloveniersburgwal 97
1011 KB Amsterdam
tel +31 (0)20 624 68 32
fax +31 (0)20 639 10 35

Diverse, exciting and comfortable Stayokay Amsterdam Vondelpark is one of Europe's largest and most modern hostels. Located in the centre of Amsterdam, in the beautiful Vondelpark.

Downtown Amsterdam, international, exciting Stayokay Amsterdam Stadsdoelen is located in a stately canal house in the city centre.

EXPERIENCE HOLLAND, AMSTERDAM INCLUDED!
Visit our website at **www.stayokay.com** to find out more information about our other hostels. Some of them are at very short distance from Amsterdam and are in interesting areas with easy access by public transport. This way you allow yourself to see much more of Holland!

The summit of luxury: **Inter-Continental Amstel Amsterdam**. *See p57.*

Seven Bridges

Reguliersgracht 31, 1017 LK (623 1329). Tram 16, 24, 25. **Rates** €90-€150 single; €100-€190 double. **Credit** AmEx, MC, V. **Map** p311 E4.
Seven Bridges has enough lightly coloured antique furnishings to dispel the myth that old-fashioned means sombre tones and dark wood. Both proprietors take great pride in their small hotel, and the eight rooms contain some charming pieces: how about preening in a Napoleonic mirror as your toes sink into a handwoven carpet? Breakfast is served in the rooms. **Hotel services** *No-smoking rooms.* **Room services** *TV: cable.*

Budget

Euphemia Hotel

Fokke Simonszstraat 1-9, 1017 TD (622 9045/fax 638 9673/www.euphemiahotel.com). Tram 16, 24, 25. **Rates** €65-€90 double; €69-€100 triple; €92-€140 quad. **Credit** AmEx, DC, MC, V. **Map** p311 E5.
Located on a quiet side street handy for museum-hopping, this former monastery now has 30 cheap and comfy rooms, including a few dorm-style three- and four-bed rooms. Fortunately, you don't have to behave like a monk: the attitude towards visitors out to sample coffeeshops or gay nightlife is relaxed. Most bathrooms are en suite and there's a communal sitting room with TV. Two inconveniences are a two-night minimum at weekends and limited car access. **Hotel services** *Internet (not in rooms). No-smoking rooms.*

Hans Brinker Budget Hotel

Kerkstraat 136-8, 1017 GR (622 0687/fax 638 2060/ www.hans-brinker.com). Tram 1, 2, 5, 16, 24, 25. **Rates** €21-€24 dorm bed; €52 single; €70 double; €90 triple. **Credit** MC, V. **Map** p311 E4.
A sizeable presence on Kerkstraat, this centrally located hostel with a sure gift for self-promotion has – wait for it – over 530 beds. One of its clever ad campaigns pointed out that it's 'close to the best hospitals in Amsterdam' – not exactly the most reassuring statement and not the sort of 'feature' on the average tourist's wish-list, but a good indication that it won't be dull staying here. There's a large bar, cantina and disco, staff are friendly, and everything is clean and looked after. The main drag? No advance bookings during the summer. **Hotel services** *Bar. Restaurant.*

Hotel Prinsenhof

Prinsengracht 810, 1017 JL (623 1772/fax 638 3368/www.hotelprinsenhof.com). Tram 4. **Rates** €40-€75 single; €60-€80 double; €85-€100 triple; €100-€135 quad. **Credit** AmEx, MC, V. **Map** p311 E4.
This pretty canal house, a stone's throw from Rembrandtplein, has beamed ceilings, wood furnishings and some water views. Facilities are basic: there's no lift – though a motorised hook in the central stairway makes hoisting your luggage up almost fun – and only three of the 11 rooms have en suite toilet and shower. Staff are friendly and the place is incredibly clean to boot. Good value. **Hotel services** *Dataport. Telephone.*

Hotel Quentin

Leidsekade 89, 1017 PN (626 2187/fax 622 0121/
www.quentinhotel.com). Tram 1, 2, 5. **Rates** €40-
€65 single; €65-€100 double; €110-€125 triple; €113
quad. **Credit** AmEx, DC, MC, V. **Map** p310 C5.
Quentin Crisp once stayed in this small laid-back
hotel, and his visit has been honoured in its name.
Something of his eccentric spirit seems to live on
here, attracting touring rock bands, artsy types,
gays and lesbians. The 32 rooms are clean with
decent furnishings, and many are quite spacious.
There's a friendly lounge with a vending machine
for quelling hunger round the clock, and the canal-
side location is a winner. Breakfast is €5.
Hotel services *Bar/lounge.* **Room services** *TV:*
cable.

Hostels

International Budget Hostel

Leidsegracht 76, 1016 CR (624 2784/fax 772 4825).
Tram 1, 2, 5. **Rates** €72-€75 twin; €24-€28 dorm
bed in quad. **Credit** AmEx, MC, V. **Map** p310 C4.
International Budget Hostel is the only inexpensive
youth hostel to offer rooms with a canal view. Most
rooms are quads with shared facilities (the exceptions are two twin rooms with private baths) and
dorms are mixed, although if they're not too busy
they try to oblige requests for single-sex rooms.
There's no curfew. Breakfast is €1-€4.
Hotel services *TV room: cable.*

Jodenbuurt, the Plantage & the Oost

Moderate

Arena

's Gravesandestraat 51, 1092 AA (850 2400/850
2420/fax 850 2425/www.hotelarena.nl). Tram 3,
6, 9, 10, 14. **Rates** €100-€125 single; €125-€175
double; €140-€165 triple. **Credit** AmEx, DC, MC, V.
Map p312 G3.
Once an orphanage, then a youth hostel, this landmark building has been converted into a modish
hotel, with airy rooms that are minimally kitted out
with hardwood floors and designer furniture. It's not
centrally situated, but the standard of the facilities
means you may not want to leave: the swanky
restaurant serves fine international food, and the
café lounge has a terrace in front and a large garden
behind. Some say it's more mouth than trousers: we
once heard someone mutter, 'The best thing about
this place is the marketing'. Guests get a discount to
the nightclub (*see p227*) unless it's closed for private
parties. For uninterrupted sleep, avoid guest rooms
facing the entrance.
Hotel services *Bar. Café. Concierge. Disabled:*
adapted rooms. Garden. Parking (paid). Restaurant.
Room services *Telephone. TV:*
cable/DVD/Playstation.

The Jordaan

Budget

Hotel van Onna

Bloemgracht 102-5108, 1015 TN (626 5801/
www.vanonna.nl). Tram 13, 17. **Rates** €40 single;
€80 double; €120 triple. **No credit cards**.
Map p305 B3.
This hotel's charm comes from its pleasant setting
overlooking a quiet Jordaan canal and the delightfully informal feel created by the eponymous and
laid-back owner. The 41 rooms, housed in three 17th-
century houses, are basic but modern, clean and
warm. All rooms have an en suite bathroom and the
price includes a Dutch breakfast.
Hotel services *No-smoking rooms.*

The Museum Quarter, Vondelpark & the South

Deluxe

Hilton Amsterdam

Apollolaan 138, 1077 BG (710 6000/fax 710 9000/
www.hilton.com). Tram 5, 24. **Rates** €360-€438
single; €380-€458 double; €485-€505 suite. **Credit**
AmEx, DC, MC, V.
Despite being famed for John and Yoko's 'bed-in' of
1969 and as the final leaping point of legendary local
rocker Herman Brood, the huge five-star Hilton
looks pretty unexciting. However, it does offer 271
air-conditioned rooms and its own Italian restaurant.
The John and Yoko suite can be hired for weddings
or for accommodation; it's especially popular with
honeymooners. The hotel's location – waaaay south
– is not ideal, but it does have room for a yacht club
and marina (docking must be pre-arranged).
Breakfast is €23.50.
Hotel services *Air-conditioning. Babysitting. Bar.*
Beauty salon. Business services. Concierge. Disabled:
adapted rooms. Garden. Gym. Limousine service.
No-smoking floors. Parking. Restaurant. **Room**
services *Dataport. Minibar. Refrigerator (suites*
only). Room service (24hrs). TV: cable/pay
movies/web TV.

Hotel Okura Amsterdam

Ferdinand Bolstraat 333, 1072 LH (678 7111/fax
671 2344/www.okura.nl). Tram 12, 25. **Rates** €340-
€410 single; €375-€445 double; €845-€1,775 suite;
€73 extra bed. **Credit** AmEx, DC, MC, V.
Perfectly situated – it's a short walk to the RAI congress centre and the World Trade Centre – and
equipped for business, the luxury five-star Okura
boasts 321 rooms, 49 suites and 16 banqueting/con-
ference rooms. There are two bars and four restaurants; one of each has an incredible panoramic view
of the city. Of the restaurants, the Japanese Yamazato
(*see p134*) just won a Michelin star, and new wun-
derkind chef Onno Kokmeijer is aiming for a second

at the renowned French Le Ciel Bleu. The privileged few can breakfast, drink and check out the vista in the new executive lounge. The swish health club has a new jet lag programme. Breakfast is an extra €25. **Hotel services** *Air-conditioning. Babysitting. Bars. Beauty salon. Business services. Concierge. Disabled: adapted rooms. Gym. Limousine service. No-smoking rooms. Parking (paid). Restaurants. Swimming pool (indoor).* **Room services** *Dataport. Minibar. Room service (24hrs). TV: satellite/pay movies/VCR (suites only). Wireless internet.*

Hotel Vondel

Vondelstraat 28-30, 1054 GE (612 0120/fax 685 4321/www.srs-worldhotels.com). Tram 1, 3, 6, 12. **Rates** €220 single/double; €415 suite. **Credit** AmEx, DC, MC, V. **Map** p310 C5.

This stylish four-star hotel, located in a quiet area, takes its name from Joost van den Vondel (1587-1679), the 'Prince among Poets' and the Netherlands' most acclaimed playwright. The interior is lovely: lots of the 70 rooms are sumptuously decorated in crimson and cream, with detailing in walnut, and the lobby is filled with contemporary paintings and soft sofas. Many of the rooms that look out over the Vondelstraat have balconies. Breakfast is €16.50. **Hotel services** *Bar. Business services. Concierge. Garden.* **Room services** *Dataport. Minibar. TV: cable/pay movies/VCR.*

Bilderberg Hotel Jan Luyken

Jan Luijkenstraat 58, 1071 CS (573 0730/fax 676 3841/www.janluyken.nl). Tram 2, 3, 5, 12. **Rates** €190 single; €220-€305 double; €40 extra bed. **Credit** AmEx, DC, MC, V, JCB. **Map** p310 D6.

On a quiet street between the Vondelpark and the museums, the boutique hotel Jan Luyken has an intimate and friendly feel. While its rooms are now in designer style, it's held on to the antique chandeliers and panelling and a general traditional-formal feel. At the new bar, Wines & Bites, guests can sample a lengthy list of half-bottles, snacks and light meals. Rooms have inviting beds with multi-textured linens in warm colours; some have balconies. The little spa room, with jacuzzi and champagne-stocked fridge, is a perfect place to unwind (but costs extra). Breakfast is €16.50. **Hotel services** *Air-conditioning. Babysitting. Bar. Business services. Garden. No-smoking floors.* **Room services** *Dataport. Minibar. Refrigerator. Room service (7am-midnight). TV: cable/pay movies.*

AMS Omega Hotel

Jacob Obrechtstraat 33, 1071 KG (664 5182/fax 664 0809/www.omegahotel.nl). Tram 2, 3, 5, 12. **Rates** €135-€179 single; €145-€189 double; €185-€229 triple. **Credit** AmEx, DC, MC, V. **Map** p310 C6.

The four-star Omega, situated on a quiet square in the well-to-do Old South, now belongs to a chain but thankfully has held on to its individual character. The interior is a rich array of reds and dark wood tones, with a smattering of antiques in the lobby and bedrooms that are decorated in a clean but classic style. Breakfast (around €12) is served until 11am. In summer, enjoy drinks in the garden or on the terrific panoramic rooftop. **Hotel services** *Air-conditioning (selected rooms). Bar. Business services. Concierge. Garden. No-smoking rooms.* **Room services** *Dataport. Minibar. Room service (24hrs). TV: cable.*

Affordable class and fab facilities:
Arena. See p63.

Le Meridien Park Hotel

Stadhouderskade 25, 1071 ZD (671 1222/fax 664 9455/www.lemeridien.com). Tram 1, 2, 5. **Rates** €280 twin; €315 triple; €400 suite; €35 extra bed. **Credit** AmEx, DC, MC, V. **Map** p310 D5.
This four-star hotel is perfectly positioned for both local nightlife – with a casino and Leidseplein a moment away – and the gentler, more cultural daytime attractions of Museumplein. The hotel offers wide-ranging facilities, especially for business travellers, with five small boutiques including a hair salon and an upmarket gift shop. Rooms are decorated in English style, and many offer a city or canal view; all suites are split level and overlook the canal. Breakfast costs €19.50.
Hotel services *Air-conditioning (selected rooms). Babysitting. Bar. Business services. Limousine service. No-smoking floors. Parking (paid). Restaurant.* **Room services** *Dataport (selected rooms). Minibar (selected rooms). Room service (24hrs). TV: satellite/pay movies.*

Hotel de Filosoof

Anna van den Vondelstraat 6, 1054 GZ (683 3013/ fax 685 3750/www.hotelfilosoof.nl). Tram 1. **Rates** €98-€108 single; €115-€135 double; €160-€195 triple. **Credit** AmEx, MC, V. **Map** p309 B6.
Thoughtful types will be absorbed by this themed hotel, which has added a new building, making for a total of 38 rooms. Each is dedicated to a philosopher or philosophy; choices include Marx, new additions Wittgenstein and Sartre, and Zen and Egypt for spiritual types. The place is filled with cosy spaces to sit in, including the spacious bar in the reception area, and everywhere you look there are

quotes by philosophers. The pretty garden has been enlarged via a merger with the garden of a nearby retirement home. A delight.
Hotel services *Babysitting. Bar. Garden.* **Room services** *TV: cable.*

Hotel V

Victorieplein 42, 1078 PH (662 3233/fax 676 6398/ www.hotelv.nl). Tram 4, 12, 25. **Rates** €75-€85 single; €110-€130 double; €155 triple. **Credit** AmEx, DC, MC, V.
Part of Amsterdam's new wave of hip design hotels, Hotel V prides itself on 'design without attitude'. Each of its 24 rooms sports an upbeat slogan on the wall featuring the letter V ('Love don't hate', 'Have fun') amid an otherwise simple, IKEA-type look. The clubby-looking breakfast room boasts cow-print stools and a long white banquette. The staff are pleased to point you toward the hottest new clubs and restaurants, and they'll rent you a bike to get there; the only disadvantage to the place being their non-central location, south of the Pijp.
Hotel services *Bar. Garden. Parking (street).* **Room services** *TV: cable.*

Hotel van de Kasteelen

Frans van Mierisstraat 34, 1071 RT (679 8995/fax 670 6604/www.hotelvandekasteelen.com). Tram 3, 5, 12, 16. **Rates** €75-€170 single; €85-€229 double; €30 extra bed. **Credit** AmEx, MC, V. **Map** p310 D6.
On a quiet, tree-lined street close to Museumplein, this small, friendly hotel is popular with visitors who aim to spend a good amount of their time at the cultural epicentre of the city. The peaceful lounge and garden decorated with orchids, candles and Asian

Cultural cooking with Lloyd

August 2004 will see the completion of the most talked-about hotel in town. An epic-scale century-old building and former youth prison on the Eastern Docklands will have been re-invented by MVRDV – those very same architectural maestros who put the Netherlands back on the map with the 'Dutch Big Mac' pavilion at Hanover's World Expo 2000 – as a light-drenched 'cultural embassy' with 120 one- to five-star 'living spaces'. These will range from inexpensive Japanese-style pods to more luxurious rooms complete with customised Atelier van Lieshout bathrooms. Groups may even opt to sleep sardine-style on mattresses on the floor. Indeed, flexibility is the name of the game here – as is providing a cultural fulcrum where artists and the art-inclined can lodge or simply drop by for the many planned events. Or to browse the library, scan for flyers or chow down in the 24-hour restaurant. Could it be that the spirit of such lost and lamented cultural squats as Silo and Vrieshuis Amerika has finally found a new (albeit more business-minded) home? Watch this space…

Lloyd Hotel

Oostelijke Handelskade 34 (419 1840/ www.lloydhotel.com). Bus 32, 39, 43. **Rates** €80-€300 doubles. **Credit** AmEx, DC, MC, V.

---

artwork make a welcome sight after a hard day's musuem exploration, as do the bedrooms decorated in classic, elegant Italian style.
Hotel services *Garden.* **Room services** *TV: cable.*

Prinsen Hotel

Vondelstraat 36-8, 1054 GE (616 2323/fax 616 6112/www.prinsenhotel.demon.nl). Tram 1, 2, 3, 5, 12. **Rates** €88-€107 single; €120-€135 double; €162-€171 triple; €185-€202 quad; €150 suite; €7 baby bed. **Credit** AmEx, DC, MC, V. **Map** p310 C6.
Gracious and friendly service is one of the good reasons to stay at this pleasant three-star hotel; its convenient location on a quiet street across from the Vondelpark and near Leidseplein is another. The place is hip and bright with sunny colours, and has a secluded garden in which to relax. Of the 45 modest rooms, four have balconies and two have terraces, both offered at no extra charge.
Hotel services *Bar. Garden. Internet (not in rooms).* **Room services** *TV: cable.*

Budget

Hotel Acro

Jan Luijkenstraat 44, 1071 CR (662 0526/fax 675 0811/www.acrohotel.nl). Tram 2, 5. **Rates** €80-€100 single; €95-€110 double; €110-€116 triple; €130-150 quad. **Credit** AmEx, DC, MC, V, JSB. **Map** p310 D6.
This comfortable, modern hotel on a leafy sidestreet is handy for the museums and Leidseplein, but if you don't want to go out, the bar – recently redone in art deco style and looking as if it's been that way forever – stays open round the clock and also serves basic snacks. Renovations have expanded Acro to 65 rooms, decking many out with wood-laminate floors and newer furnishings. They often have off-peak offers, so call ahead to check.
Hotel services *Bar. Concierge. Parking (on street). Internet (at the loby).* **Room services** *TV: cable/ pay movies.*

PC Hooft

PC Hooftstraat 63, 1071 BN (662 7107/fax 675 8961/www.pchoofthotel.nl). Tram 2, 3, 5, 12. **Rates** €35-€52 single; €55-€68 double; €75-€88 triple; €93-€100 quad. **Credit** MC, V. **Map** p310 D5.
Amsterdam addresses don't come much posher than this: PC Hooftstraat is where the city's beautiful people buy all their designer clobber. Though it's not a patch on its chic surroundings, the hotel is pleasant and clean; it's also usefully close to the museums. Three of the 16 rooms are en suite and most are modestly sized with newish furnishings (avoid the back rooms with high windows). Incidentally, Mr Hooft was a historian who hung out with friend and poet Joost van den Vondel, himself immortalised in the name of the neighbouring park.
Room services *TV: cable.*

Hostels

For **Flying Pig Hostels** and **Stayokay Hostels**, *see p55.*

Budget

Van Ostade Bicycle Hotel

Van Ostadestraat 123, 1072 SV (679 3452/fax 671 5213/www.bicyclehotel.com). Tram 3, 12, 16, 24, 25. **Rates** €75 (shared facilities), €105 (private facilities) double. **Credit** AmEx MC, V. **Map** p311 F6.
No need to worry about Van Ostade's location off the beaten path in the Pijp: it's a two-wheel-savvy hotel that has bicycles for hire. The 16 rooms are clean and basic and there's a cosy communal area with internet access. Good value all round.
Hotel services *free Internet (not in rooms). No-smoking rooms. Parking.* **Room services** *TV: cable.*

Other options

Apartment rentals

For details on how to find somewhere
permanent to live, *see p290* **Moving in**.

Amsterdam Apartments

*Kromme Waal 32, Old Centre: Old Side (626
5930/fax 622 9544/www.amsterdamapartments.nl).
Tram 4, 9, 16, 24, 25.* **Open** 9am-5pm Mon-Fri.
Credit AmEx, MC, V. **Map** p307 E2.
20-odd furnished, central, self-contained flats. Rates
start from €550 a week for a one-person studio or
flat. The minimum let is for one week.

Apartment Services AS

*Waalstraat 58, South (672 3013/672 1840/fax 676
4679/www.apartmentservices.nl). Tram 4, 12, 25.*
Open 9.30am-5pm Mon-Fri. **No credit cards.**
A wide variety of mainly furnished accommodation,
from simple short-let flats to apartments and whole
houses. Rentals start at around €1,000 per month
and a minimum let of two or three months is usual.

Bed & breakfast

B&B is catching on in the Netherlands, but
owing to restrictions on the number of rooms
and people allowed to stay – four at a time tops
– it's still not as popular as in the UK or US.
The best way to find a B&B is through **City
Mundo** or **Holiday Link**, both of which deal
with private accommodation and longer stays.

City Mundo

*Schinkelkade 47 II, 1075 VK (676 5270/fax 676
5271/www.citymundo.com).* **Open** 10am-6pm Mon-
Sat. **Credit** AmEx, MC, V.
This fine service provides visitors with short-term
private accommodation (three to 21 nights); there are
about 100 options, from B&Bs and studios to flats
on boats and even in windmills. Prices vary according to location and amenities, and there's a ten per
cent discount if you stay longer than a week. The
focus is less on budget prices and more on making
people who really relish their surroundings happy.
You can book online; everything available at a given
time is shown on the website.

Xaviera Hollander Bed & Breakfast: the Penthouse influence. *See p68.*

Holiday Link

Postbus 70.155, 9704 AD Groningen (050 313 4545/fax 050 313 3177/www.holidaylink.com).
Holiday Link is an organisation dealing with B&B and budget accommodation. Its annual guide to B&Bs is available in bookshops, tourist offices, by post or from its website for €15 (plus €2.50-€5 postage), and has stacks of information on all types of accommodation, from B&Bs to holiday home swaps. Worth investigating.

Marcel van Woerkom

Leidsestraat 87, Southern Canal Belt, 1017 NX (622 9834/fax 772 7446/www.marcelamsterdam. com). Tram 1, 2, 5. **Rates** €50-€65 per person. **Credit** V. **Map** p310 D4.
Graphic artist Marcel van Woerkom provides a creative exchange in his pristine city-centre home, where four en suite rooms are available. Van Woerkom's favourite art is on the walls; all of it by him or his friends. Guests with an appreciation of creative arts are especially welcome. Breakfast isn't included, but that's hardly the point. You're advised to book well ahead.
Hotel services *No-smoking rooms.* **Room services** *Fridge (selected rooms). TV: cable.*

Xaviera Hollander Bed & Breakfast

Stadionweg 17, Zuid, 1077 RV (673 3934/fax 664 3687/www.xavierahollander.com). Tram 5, 24. **Rates** €110 and €120 double (with breakfast) (but fluctuating based on required services). **No credit cards.**
If you want lodgings that will give you a story to tell, this is your place. Everyone calms down with age, and for Xaviera Hollander, the infamous New York madam and later *Penthouse* columnist whose 1971 book *The Happy Hooker* sold more than 17 million copies, that's meant coming home to Amsterdam. These days she's a city fixture who organises English-language dinner-theatre events (*see p240*) as well as offering B&B in two rooms in her home. The house is dense with art, musical instruments, mementoes and a steady stream of visiting friends. Whether in an upstairs bedroom – complete with terrace – or in a 'chalet' in the back garden, her accommodation can't be beaten for uniqueness. You needn't be a sexual libertine to feel at home here – though it may help.

Cake Under My Pillow

Eerste Jacob van Campenstraat 66, De Pijp, 1072 BH (751 0936/fax 776 4604/www.cakeundermy pillow.com). Tram 16, 24, 25. **Rates** €80-€150 single/double. **Credit** AmEx, DC, MC, V.
This B&B over the delightful cake shop Taart van Mijn Tante opened in August 2003. The kitsch-collecting café and B&B owners have decorated each of the three bright new rooms with a tastefully restrained handful of colourful ceramic finds (dog figurines, Delft plates). Two rooms have en suite bathrooms; all have orthopedic beds and access to a kitchen and come with a mobile phone (or two) for

a small fee. If you're lucky, breakfast (served in the upstairs kitchen) might include a little something from the café. Otherwise you get a discount.

Camping

Zeeburg is classified as a youth campsite; **Gaasper** and **Amsterdamse Bos** are more family-oriented, with separate areas for youth camping; and **Vliegenbos** is mixed.

Gaasper Camping Amsterdam

Loosdrechtdreef 7 (696 7326/fax 696 9369/www.gaaspercamping.nl). Metro 53 Gaasperplas/night bus 75. **Open** *July-Aug* 9am-10pm daily. *Sept-Nov, mid Mar-June* 9am-8pm daily. Closed Dec-mid Mar. **Rates** *Per person per night* €4.25. *Vehicles* €2.25-€7.50. **No credit cards.**
This great campsite, at the edge of the Gaasperpark, has a lake with a marina and facilities for canoeing, swimming, rowing and sailing, plus a private surf club. Ground facilities include a supermarket, bar/restaurant, terrace, launderette and camping-gas depot, and there's a service station next door.

Het Amsterdamse Bos

Kleine Noorddijk 1 (641 6868/fax 640 2378/ www.campingamsterdamsebos.nl). Bus 171, 172, 199. **Open** *Apr-mid Oct* 9am-12.30pm, 1.20-9pm daily. **Rates** *Per person per night* €5. *Vehicles* €2-€6. **Credit** MC, V.
The site is some way away, but buses for the 30-minute trip into town stop nearby hourly on the edge of Amsterdamse Bos (*see p111*). The site also has wooden cabins (€21.50 for two people; €45 for four) and six-person tents (high season only) with €18 dorm beds. Site facilities include a shop, bar and restaurant and lockers. Bikes can be hired nearby during the summer.

Vliegenbos

Meeuwenlaan 138 (636 8855/fax 632 2723/ www.vliegenbos.com). Bus 32, 36/Nightbus 73. **Open** *Apr-Sept* 9am-9pm daily. **Rates** *Per person per night* €7.60. *Vehicles* €4-€8. **Credit** MC, V.
The camping zone in 'fly forest' is close to the IJ in north Amsterdam, a mere five-minute bus journey from Centraal Station. Facilities include a bar, a restaurant, a safe at reception and a small shop (but no more currency exchange). Guests staying for fewer than three nights must pay a small supplement. Dogs are not allowed.

Zeeburg

Zuider IJdijk 20 (694 4430/fax 694 6238/ www.campingzeeburg.nl). Tram 14/bus 22, 37. **Open** *Summer* 8.30am-11pm daily. *Winter* 9am-noon, 5-8pm daily. **Rates** *Per person per night* €4.50. *Vehicles* €2.50-7.50. **Credit** AmEx, MC, V.
Facilities at these grounds, north of the IJ, include a bar, 24-hour restaurant, shop and bike hire. Log cabins sleeping two, four or six people cost €35, €70 and €105 respectively, including bedding (book during high season); the 24-bed dorm costs €8 per person.

Sightseeing

Introduction

Laces tied? Watch strap buckled? The fun starts here.

Amsterdam packs the cultural punch of a large metropolis, and yet remains a city of remarkably convenient size. Most things are within a half-hour's walk, with trams providing back-up for those low on energy. You can also take a tip from the locals and saddle up – on a bike (though beware of cycle thieves).

In the centre of town are Amsterdam's old port, its medieval buildings, the red lights that denote a hotspot of the world's oldest trade, the grand 17th-century merchants' houses, the spires of ancient religious institutions, the earliest and prettiest canals, and many of its most famous sights. Slightly further out are neighbourhoods built to house the various waves of incoming workers: the Jordaan, the Pijp, Amsterdam Oost, and suburbs further south and west.

Except to stroll Museumplein and its three major art museums, few visitors go beyond the *grachtengordel*, the calming belt of Golden Age canals – likened in Albert Camus' *The Fall* to the circles of hell – that ring the fascinating and historic Old Centre. Don't make the same mistake. While the primarily residential Jordaan and the Pijp are largely attraction-free in traditional terms, they're hugely attractive places. Further out, too, there's much to enjoy, to the north and north-east on the redeveloping Waterfront, and way down south around the idyllic Amsterdamse Bos. For more on Amsterdam's various areas, *see p71* **Neighbourhood watch**.

TICKETS AND INFORMATION

While most Amsterdam museums charge for admission, prices are reasonable: rarely more than €7. However, if you're thinking of taking in a fair few, the **Museumkaart** ('Museum Card') is a steal: €25 for adults and €12.50 for under-25s (plus a €4.95 administration fee for first-timers). The card offers free or discounted admission to over 400 attractions in the Netherlands and is valid for a year from date of purchase; discounted or free entry offered to holders of the Museumkaart is denoted in our listings by the letters 'MK'. You can buy the card at most participating museums. The Amsterdam Tourist Board (*see p290*) also sells a savings card, the **Amsterdam Pass**, that gives you free entry to major museums, free public transport and a free canal trip, along with a 25 per cent discount at participating tourist attractions and restaurants. It costs €26 for 24 hours, €36 for 48 hours and €46 for 72 hours.

The deals don't end there. On **National Museum Weekend** every April (*see p180*), some 200 small museums around the country offer free or reduced admission, though many get very busy. Also jam-packed are temporary shows at major museums on weekends, and many museums on Wednesday afternoons, when primary schools let kids out early. New website **www.amsterdammuseums.nl** lists all major Amsterdam museums and their agendas.

Two final tips. Call ahead if you plan to visit a museum on a public holiday, as many shut for the day. And don't worry about language: in Amsterdam, almost all the big museums (and many of the smaller ones) have either captions and/or guidebooks in impeccable English – or helpful English-speaking staff on hand.

Tours

For an array of non-standard excursions, *see p85* **Wacky tours**.

Bike tours

Fear not, cyclists: follow your guide's advice and you'll be fine on two wheels. Rental of a bike is included in the prices listed. For bike hire, *see p277*.

Yellow Bike

Nieuwezijds Kolk 29, Old Centre: New Side (620 6940/ www.yellowbike.nl). Tram 1, 2, 5, 13, 17. **Open** *Apr-Nov* 8.30am-5.30pm daily. **No credit cards**. **Map** p306 C2.
Of the many options, there's a three-hour City Tour (€17) that departs daily at 9.30am and 1pm; the six-hour Waterland Tour (€22.50), leaving daily at 11am, includes a visit to a pancake house.

Boat tours

There's not an awful lot of difference between the various boat tours that rove Amsterdam's waterways for an hour a time – just pick the one with the shortest queues. For longer tours, though, choose more carefully from the near-infinite possibilities. As well as day cruises, all the following firms run night cruises at 9pm daily in summer (less often in winter), costing from €20 to €25; **Lovers** and **Holland International** (for both, *see p72*) do dinner cruises for €65 to €75. Booking is vital.

Lovers also runs the **Museumboot** (Stationsplein 10, 330 1374), which runs all year generally from 9.30am to 7pm (winter times may be more restricted), for which tickets last a full day and entitle the holder to get on or off at

any of seven stops, each near several major museums. It costs €14.25, with fours to 12s paying €9.50 and under-fours riding for free. Prices drop by €2 after 1pm, and all tickets include discounts of up to 50 per cent on usual museum admission. Lovers also has a watertaxi service (535 6363/www.water-taxi.nl) for groups of one to 40; its boats also run a regular route as the **Grachtmusea Watertaxi**, daily between April and October, from Stationsplein 8, for which tickets last a full day (€25.50 adults, €12.50 children) or half day (€19.50 adults, €9.75 children), and entitle the holder to get on or off at any one of seven stops, each near one of the city's smaller canal-side museums. And for information on **St Nicolaas Boat Club**, a non-profit outfit that gives hip, toke-friendly cruises on small open-topped boats, ask **Boom**

Neighbourhood watch

THE OLD CENTRE
Amsterdam's ground zero of consumerism, vice, entertainment and history, the Old Centre is marked off by Prins Hendrikkade to the north, Oudeschans and Zwanenburgwal to the east, the Amstel to the south and Singel to the west.

Within these borders, the Old Centre is split into the **New Side** (west of Damrak and Rokin) and the **Old Side** (east of Damrak and Rokin). Within the Old Side, roughly in the triangle formed by Central Station, the Nieuwmarkt and the Dam, is the city's largest – and most famous – Red Light District.

THE CANALS
The *grachtengordel* ('girdle of canals') that guards the Old Centre is idyllic, pleasant and quintessentially Amsterdam. In the listings for shops, restaurants and the like in this guide, we've split the canals in half. **Western Canal Belt** denotes the stretch of canals to the west and north of Leidsegracht, while **Southern Canal Belt** covers the area east of here, taking in **Leidseplein** and **Rembrandtplein**.

JODENBUURT, THE PLANTAGE AND THE OOST
The area around Waterlooplein was adopted by Jews two centuries ago, and took its name – **Jodenbuurt** – from them. The **Plantage**, which lies east and south-east of Waterlooplein, holds many delights, among them the Hortus Botanicus and Artis. Further east – or **Oost** – lies the Tropenmuseum, before the city opens up and stretches out.

THE WATERFRONT
Once the gateway to the city's prosperity, Amsterdam's waterfront is now the setting for one of Europe's most exciting architectural developments. Traditional sights are few, but before long this stretch will be home to thousands of new residents.

THE JORDAAN
Bordered by Brouwersgracht, Prinsengracht, Leidsegracht and Lijnbaansgracht, the Jordaan is arguably Amsterdam's most charming neighbourhood. Working-class stalwarts rub shoulders with affluent newcomers in an area that, while lacking the grandiose architecture of the canals, wants for nothing in terms of character.

THE MUSEUM QUARTER, VONDELPARK AND THE SOUTH
Distinguished by its world-class museums and some stupendously posh fashion emporia, Amsterdam's **Museum Quarter** is a mix of culture and couture. South of Singelgracht, with blurry borders at Overtoom (west) and Hobbemakade (east), it's also home to many pleasant hotels and, at its northernmost tip, is within a stone's throw of both Leidseplein and **Vondelpark**.

THE PIJP
Against all odds, the Pijp has managed to remain a wonderful melting pot of cultures and nationalities. Located east of the Museum Quarter and south of the canals, it's an area short on traditional sights but defiantly long on character and fun.

For a religious experience...

The **Oude Kerk** (*see p82*), the **Joods Historisch Museum** (*see p96*) or the **Chinese Fo Kuang Shan Buddhist Temple** (*see p79*).

... or a trinity of Dutch clichés

A drink at the **Brouwerij 't IJ**, next to a windmill (*see p144*), shopping at cheese emporium **Wegewijs** (*see p165*), and a wander around the floating flower market **Bloemenmarkt** (*see p164*).

For art both ancient and modern

The museums on **Museumplein** (*see p106*) or the galleries in the **Jordaan** (*see p103*).

For the horny and plain curious

A walk around the **Red Light District** (*see p77*), a visit to the **Sexmuseum** (*see p77*) or an evening in the **Casa Rosso** (*see p80*).

For the longest queues in town

Anne Frankhuis (*see p89*), the **Van Gogh Museum** (*see p107*) or **boat tours** from near Centraal Station (*see p71*).

For creature comforts

Artis (*see p97*), the **Poezenboot** (*see p87*) or one of the city's **urban farms** (*see p187*).

For smoke without fire

PGC Hajenius (*see p176*) or a trip to a **coffeeshop** (*see p147*).

For the party to end all parties

The canals on **Queen's Day** (*see p179*) or **New Year's Eve** on Nieuwmarkt (*see p184*).

To step back in time...

A morning in **Amsterdams Historisch Museum** (*see p85*), an afternoon in the **Museum Amstelkring** (*see p81*) and an evening at the **Concertgebouw** (*see p217*).

... and get back to the future

A morning in **Nemo** (*see p101*), an afternoon walk round the **Eastern Docklands** (*see p100*) and a night in **Jimmie Woo's** (*see p225*).

To get away from it all

Vondelpark (*see p107*), **Hortus Botanicus** (*see p97*), or **Amsterdamse Bos** (*see p111*).

Chicago (*see p246*). For boat hire, *see p277* Head out on the waterway.

Best of Holland

Departure point at Damrak 34, by Centraal Station, Old Centre: New Side (623 1539/www.thebestof holland.nl). Tram 4, 9, 16, 24, 25. **Cruises** every 30min, 10am-5pm daily. **Tickets** €8.50; €5.50 under-13s. **Credit** AmEx, DC, MC, V. **Map** p305 D2.

Holland International

Departure point at Prins Hendrikkade 33A, by Centraal Station, Old Centre: New Side (622 7788). Tram 4, 9, 16, 24, 25. **Cruises** *Summer* every 15min, 9am-10pm daily. *Winter* every 30min, 10am-6pm daily. **Tickets** €8.50; €5 under-13s. **Credit** AmEx, MC, V. **Map** p305 D2.

Lovers

Prins Hendrikkade, opposite 25-7, nr Centraal Station, Old Centre: New Side (530 1090/www.lovers.nl). Tram 4, 9, 16, 24, 25. **Cruises** *Summer* every 30min, 9am-5pm daily. *Winter* every 30min, 10am-5pm daily. **Tickets** €8.50; €5.75 under-13s. **Credit** AmEx, MC, V. **Map** p305 D2.

Rondvaarten Rederij Kooi

Corner of Rokin and Spui, Old Centre: New Side (623 3810/www.rederijkooi.nl). Tram 4, 9, 16, 24, 25. **Cruises** *Summer* every 30min, 10am-10pm daily. *Winter* every 30min, 10am-5pm daily. **Tickets** €6.50; €3.75 under-13s. **No credit cards. Map** p306 D3.

Walking tours

Amsterdam is a great city to explore on foot, though its uneven streets and tramlines make it isn't great if you're wearing stilettos, pushing pushchairs or in a wheelchair. The Amsterdam Tourist Board (*see p290*) publishes brochures in English that suggest easy routes.

Archivisie

Postbus 14603, 1001 LC (625 9123). Tailor-made architectural tours and regular theme tours. Phone for appointments and prices.

Mee in Mokum

(625 1390). **Tours** 11am Tue-Sun. **Tickets** €3; free under-12s. **Map** p306 C3.

Locals, all over 55, give two-hour tours (in English and Dutch) of the Old Centre, Jordaan and Jewish Amsterdam. Tours leave from the Amsterdams Historisch Museum (*see p85*). Booking is required; when you call, tell them if you plan to bring children.

Urban Home & Garden Tours

(688 1243, www.uhgt.nl). **Tours** *Apr-Sep* 10.15am Mon, Fri; 11.15am Sat. **Tickets** €37.50 (includes lunch). **Map** p311 E4.

Professional garden designers and art historians give tours in English of the 17th-, 18th- and 19th-century canal houses. Tours leave from the Museum Willet-Holthuysen (*see p92*); booking is essential.

The Old Centre

History, shops, sex: the winning triple whammy of this ancient neighbourhood.

One side embraces shopping and pursuits of the mind, while the other – with the Red Light District as its red neon centrepiece – is more about sex and religion. Common feature? They both drip with history. In short: Amsterdam's compelling Old Centre (aka Oud Centrum) surfs on a wave of contradiction.

Marked off by Centraal Station, Singel and Zwanenburgwal canals, the area is bisected by Damrak, which turns into Rokin south of Dam Square. Within the Old Centre, the saucier area to the east is the ancient Old Side (Oude Zijde), while the gentler area to the west – whose most notable landmark is Spui Square – is the far-from-new New Side (Nieuwe Zijde).

The Old Side

Around the Dam

Map p308
Straight up from Centraal Station, just beyond the once-watery and now-paved and touristy strip named Damrak, lies **Dam Square**, the heart of the city since the first dam was built

across the Amstel here in 1270. Today, it's a convenient meeting point for many tourists, the majority of whom convene under its mildly phallic centrepiece, the **Nationaal Monument**. The 22-metre (70-foot) white obelisk is dedicated to the Dutch servicemen who died in World War II. Designed by JJP Oud, with sculptures by John Raedecker, it has 12 urns, 11 filled with earth collected from the (then) 11 Dutch provinces and the 12th containing soil from war cemeteries in longtime Dutch colony Indonesia.

Both the monument and the square recently had much-needed facelifts: the roughness of the new cobblestones now deters errant bikers (and wheelchairs), and their lighter colour disguises the Jackson Pollock splodges of pigeon shit. Especially in the quiet traffic-free moments of dawn, the square now reflects an elusive sense of the epic; appropriate, since the Dam has seen such singular social and political activities as nude running through the square (by Anabaptists testing the boundaries of religious freedom in 1535), chilling in the name of peace (by hippies in the '60s) and a weighty catalogue of protests, coronations and executions.

Reap the benefits of **Dam Square**.

A perfect day

If you're looking for sex, drugs and/or rock 'n' roll, you'll find your lost weekend in Amsterdam without much preparation. But for more cultural pursuits, the key is to plan ahead. You may choose to spread this timeline for an optimal Saturday over more days (but remember to catch that flight back home).

● **8am** Start the day in a healthy way: bike out of town to some flat fields of nothingness, which will serve to clear your brain– the better to soak up Amsterdam reality later on.

● **9.45am** Maintain your sense of peace by dipping into the idyllic **Begijnhof** courtyard (*see p84*).

● **10am** Visit the **Amsterdams Historisch Museum** (*see p84*) for a quick overview to enrich your later wanderings of the real thing.

● **11am** Coffee, and plenty of it. Preferably with the other coffee slurpers on the terraces of the **Spui**: this is the local ritual that holds the delicate fabric of social cosiness together.

● **11.30am** Whirlwind tour of the Red Light District, to catch its surreal blend of sex trade and locals going about their daily business. Perhaps have another coffee on **Nieuwmarkt**.

● **12.30pm** Visit a genuine temple of high culture, say, the **Rijksmuseum** (*see p106*). With the red lights still glowing in your brain,

you'll now see Rembrandt's *Nightwatch* somewhat differently: as a portrait of pirate pimps whose pallid complexions have less to do with dramatic lighting than drug addiction.

● **1.30pm** Lunch. Grab some raw herring or smoked eel from a fish stall. Trot through this bite-sized Dutch lesson: 'eet smakelijk' means bon appetit; 'lekker' means tasty; 'misselijk' means nauseous.

● **2pm** Mixing with the locals makes every vacation more memorable. So why not 'drop in' on a friendly looking houseboat owner during a scenic stroll of the **Jordaan**?

● **4.30pm:** Time to smoke that joint you bought the second you arrived. Do it in **Vondelpark**, where the paling sun makes the greenery dance like a Van Gogh painting.

● **6.30pm** Deal with hunger. Sample the heights of Amsterdam cuisine – Indonesian – with a *witbier* (a sweet, light wheat beer).

● **8pm** Take a short nap back at the hotel you booked months ago and prepare for that hot band or DJ billed at **Melkweg** (*see p213 and p225*) or **Paradiso** (*see p214 and p225*).

● **5am** On your way back to the hotel, having had the time of your life, notice how the canals of the *grachtengordel* glow purple in the last few minutes before dawn.

Sightseeing

The west side of Dam Square is flanked by the **Koninklijk Paleis** ('Royal Palace'; *see below*); next to it is the 600-year-old **Nieuwe Kerk** ('New Church', so named as it was built a century after the Oude Kerk, or 'Old Church', in the Red Light District; *see p82*). In kitsch contrast, on the south side, is **Madame Tussaud's Scenerama** (*see p75*).

Beurs van Berlage

Damrak 277, entrance at Beursplein 1 (530 4141/ Artiflex tours 620 8112/ www.beursvanberlage.nl). Tram 4, 9, 14, 16, 24, 25. **Open** *during exhibitions* 11am-5pm Tue-Sun. **Admission** varies; discount with MK. **No credit cards**. **Map** p306 D2.
Designed in 1896 by Hendrik Berlage as the city's stock exchange, the palatial Beurs, while incorporating a broad range of traditional building styles, represents an important break with 19th-century architecture and prepared the way for the modernity of the Amsterdam School (*see p32* **Back to school**). Although some jaded critics thought it 'a big block with a cigar box on top', it's now considered the country's most important piece of 20th-century architecture. By exposing the basic structures and fusing them with the stunning decorations, it celebrates the workers and artisans who built it (as

opposed to the stockbrokers who were to inhabit it). In fact, it's a solid socialist statement: much of the artwork warns against blind capitalism, and each of the nine million bricks was intended by Berlage to represent the individual; the resulting monolith stands for society at large.

Having long driven out the moneychangers, the Beurs is now all things to all other people: a conference centre, concert halls (*see p216*), a stunningly mosaic-ed café/restaurant, and an exhibition space for excellent shows that range from Harley Davidsons to Organic Architecture. In addition, 90-minute tours of the building are conducted by art historians from Artiflex, though booking is compulsory; call the number above.

Koninklijk Paleis (Royal Palace)

Dam (information 620 4060/tours 624 8698/ www.koninklijkhuis.nl). Tram 1, 2, 4, 5, 9, 13, 14, 16, 17, 24, 25. **Open** *July, Aug* 11am-5pm daily. *Sept-June* times vary. **Admission** €4.50; €3.60 5s-16s, over-65s; free under-4s. **No credit cards**. **Map** p306 C3.
Designed along classical lines by Jacob van Campen in the 17th century, built on 13,659 wooden piles that were rammed deep into the sand, the Royal Palace was originally built and used as the city hall. The poet Constantijn Huygens hyped it as 'the world's

Eighth Wonder', a monument to the cockiness Amsterdam felt at the dawn of its Golden Age. It was intended as a smug and epic 'screw you' gesture to visiting monarchs, a species that the people of Amsterdam had happily done without.

The exterior is only really impressive when viewed from the rear, where Atlas holds his 1,000-kilogram (2,205-pound) copper load at a great height. It's even grander inside than out: the Citizen's Hall, with its baroque decoration in grand marble and bronze that depicts a miniature universe (with Amsterdam as its obvious centre), is meant to make you feel about as worthy as the rats seen carved in stone over the Bankruptcy Chamber's door.

Though much of the art on display here reflects the typically jaded humour of a people who have seen it all, the overall impression is one of deadly seriousness: one screw-up and you could end up among the grotesque carvings of the Tribunal and sentenced to die in some uniquely torturous and public way. Kinder, gentler displays of creativity, though, can be seen in the chimney pieces, painted by artists such as Ferdinand Bol and Govert Flinck, both pupils of Rembrandt (who, oddly enough, had his own sketches rejected). The city hall was transformed into a royal palace in 1808, shortly after Napoleon had made his brother, Louis, King of the Netherlands, and a fine collection of furniture from this period can be viewed on a guided tour. The Palace became state property in 1936 and is still used occasionally by the royal family.

During the summer there are free guided tours (upon admission) in English on Wednesdays and Sundays at 2pm. During winter months, it's only sporadically open, so phone or surf ahead.

Madame Tussaud's Scenerama

Peek & Cloppenburg, Dam 20 (523 0623/www. madame-tussauds.nl). Tram 4, 9, 14, 16, 24, 25. **Open** *July, Aug* 10am-7.30pm daily. *Sept-June* 10am-6.30pm daily. **Admission** €18.50; €16 over-60s; €10 5s-16s; free under-5s. **Credit** AmEx, DC, MC, V. **Map** p306 D3.

A recent €4 million facelift has done nothing to dilute the queasy kitsch factor here. Waxy cheese-textured representations from Holland's own Golden Age of commerce are all depicted alongside a more contemporary golden shower of hits: the Dutch royal family, local celebs and global superstars. Some of the models look like their subjects, some don't. But while there's some campy fun to be had here, it comes at a price, and it's hard not to leave without a renewed respect for the functionality of candles.

Nieuwe Kerk (New Church)

Dam (626 8168/recorded information 638 6909/ www.nieuwekerk.nl). Tram 1, 2, 4, 5, 9, 13, 14, 16, 17, 24, 25. **Open** hours vary. **Admission** varies with exhibition. **No credit cards. Map** p306 C3.

While the 'old' Oude Kerk in the Red Light District was built in the 1300s, the sprightly 'new' Nieuwe Kerk dates from 1408. It is not known how much damage was caused by the fires of 1421 and 1452,

Regal **Koninklijk Paleis**. *See p74.*

or even how much rebuilding took place, but most of the pillars and walls were erected after that time. Iconoclasm in 1566 left the church intact, though statues and altars were removed in the Reformation. The sundial on its tower was used to set all of the city's clocks until 1890.

In 1645, the Nieuwe Kerk was gutted by the Great Fire; the ornate oak pulpit and great organ (the latter designed by Jacob van Campen) are thought to have been constructed shortly after the blaze. Also of interest here is the tomb of naval hero Admiral de Ruyter (1607-76), who initiated the ending of the Second Anglo-Dutch war – wounding British pride in the process – when he sailed up the Medway in 1667, inspiring a witness, 'I think the Devil shits Dutchmen' (*see p9* **Eejit-prop**). Behind the black marble tomb of De Ruyter is a white marble relief depicting the sea battle in which he died. Poets and Amsterdam natives PC Hooft and Joost van den Vondel are also buried here. These days, the Nieuwe Kerk hosts organ recitals (*see p219*), state occasions and consistently excellent exhibitions.

Sexmuseum Venus Tempel

Damrak 18 (622 8376). Tram 4, 9, 14, 16, 24, 25. **Open** 10am-11.30pm daily. **Admission** €2.50. **Map** p306 D2.

The Sexmuseum is one of two museums devoted to doin' the dirty in Amsterdam, and a tawdry little operation it is, too. The Damrak location, just by Centraal Station, is designed to lure in masses of passing tourists, and on this count it succeeds. But with the exception of a splendid and often hilarious collection of pornographic Victorian photographs, the exhibition is largely botched. There's a fascinating exhibition on the history of porn movies to be staged, but the all-too-brief one here ain't it. Ivory dildos, filthy porcelain, joyless cartoons, peeling pin-ups and ugly art are all shaved of any eroticism by the context and the leering gangs of gigglers that make up the majority of the punters. At least the admission price is appropriately cheap…

The Red Light District

Maps p306 & p307

The Red Light District, situated in an approximate triangle formed by Centraal Station, the Nieuwmarkt and the Dam, is at the root of Amsterdam's international notoriety. Oversexed dreamers the world over imagine breasts eagerly pancaked against red neon-framed windows and canals awash with bodily fluids; meanwhile, the postcards on sale in local shops depict a sort of small, cutesy Vegas. If truth be told, the cheesy joke shop has here been supplanted by the cheesy sex shop: instead of electric palm buzzers and comedy nose glasses, you get multi-orifice inflatables and huge dildos.

Most of the historical significance of the Red Light District – of which there is plenty, this being the oldest part of Amsterdam – has been veneered by another old and greasy trade: marketing. Although sex is the hook upon which the area hangs its reputation, it's actually secondary to window-shopping. People do buy – it's estimated to be a €500-million-per-year trade – but mostly they wander around in groups, stopping here and there to gawp at the countless live exhibits.

Most window girls are self-employed, and even though prostitution was only defined as a legal profession in 1988 and bordellos have only been officially legit since October 2000 (a tactic hoped to make taxation easier), the women have had their own union, De Rode Draad, since 1984. The prostitutes are, indeed, mostly women: despite attempts to launch male and transsexual prostitution, men have so far found it difficult to get their dicks into this particular door of opportunity. With legality has come a plethora of new rules, governing anything from the temperature at which lingerie is washed to the cleansers used to clear the adjoining showers of 'liquid-loving insects'.

As at more traditional markets like the **Albert Cuypmarkt** (*see p164*), where cheese merchants line up alongside cheese merchants and fishmongers group with fishmongers, women with specialisms also tend to clump together. Sultry Latins gather on the Molensteeg and the beginning of Oudezijds Achterburgwal, ambiguously sexed Thais on Stoofstraat, amply girthed Africans around Oude Kerk, and the model-ish and skinny on Trompettersteeg, Amsterdam's smallest street. But there is much else to absorb in this most iconoclastic of neighbourhoods. Prostitutes, clerics, schoolkids, junkies, carpenters and cops all interact with a strange brand of social cosiness, and the tourists are mere voyeurs. It's all good fun and pretty harmless, just so long as you remember that window girls do not like having their pictures taken and that drug dealers react to eye contact like dogs to bones.

Zeedijk

Facing away from Centraal Station to the left are two churches, the **St Nicolaaskerk** (whose interior of funky darkness can be viewed from Easter to mid October, and where one can hear Gregorian vespers every Sunday at 5pm from September to June) and the dome and skull-adorned exterior of the **St Olafkerk** (known locally as the 'Cheese Church', having housed the cheese exchange for many years). Between the two, you can enter Zeedijk, a street with a rich and tattered history.

Before this dyke was built some time near 1300, Amsterdam was a fishing village with barely enough bog to stand on. But by the 15th and 16th centuries, with the East India Company raking in the imperialist spoil, Zeedijk was where sailors came to catch up on their boozing, brawling and bonking – or 'doing the St Nicolaas', as it was fondly termed in those days (a tribute to their patron saint, a busy chap who also watches over children, thieves, prostitutes and the city of Amsterdam).

Sailors who had lost all their money could trade in their pet monkey for a flea-infested bed at Zeedijk 1, which still retains its old name – **In't Aepjen**, meaning 'In the Monkeys' – and is one of the oldest wooden houses and certainly the oldest bar in the city (*see p138*). Just off the street down Oudezijds Kolk, you can spot the **Schreierstoren**, aka the 'Weeping Tower' (*see p28*). It is said that wives would cry there, perhaps with relief, when husbands set off on a voyage, then cry again if the ship returned with news that the husband was lost at sea. If the latter ever happened, then – conveniently – it was but a short walk to Zeedijk, where the bereaved lady would often continue life as a 'merry widow'. Prostitution was often the female equivalent of joining the navy: the last economic option.

During the 20th century, Zeedijk has been sparked by cultural diversity. In the 1930s, the first openly gay establishments appeared, and at the now-closed – though a replica is on display in the **Amsterdams Historisch Museum** (*see p84*) – Het Mandje (Zeedijk 65), there's a window shrine to flamboyant owner Bet van Beeren (1902-67), who has gone down in local mythology as the original Lesbian Biker Chick. In the '50s, jazz greats like Chet Baker and Gerry Mulligan came to jam and hang out in the many after-hours clubs here, among them the still-functioning **Casablanca** (*see p215*).

Unfortunately, this subculture marked Zeedijk as a place where heroin could be scored with comparative ease. By the 1970s, the street had become crowded with dealers, junkies and indifferent cops, with most of the restaurants and cafés renting their tables to dealers. The junkies' magic number back then was 27: ƒ25 for the drugs themselves, and ƒ2 for the drink the owners insisted the junkies purchase to maintain the façade of legality.

Amsterdam's reputation became littered with needles and foil, never more so than when a wasted Chet Baker made his final moody decrescendo in 1988 – onto a cement parking pole – from a window (second floor on the left) of the Prins Hendrik Hotel at the entrance of the Zeedijk. A brass plaque commemorating the crooning trumpeter has been put up to the left of the hotel's entrance. But though there was a time when a German tour operator's 'criminal safari' was not even allowed on the Zeedijk, police claim to have cleaned the street up in recent years (but only after long and sustained pressure from residents); indeed, the scene is today infinitely less intimidating and packed with new-ish businesses and restaurants. The

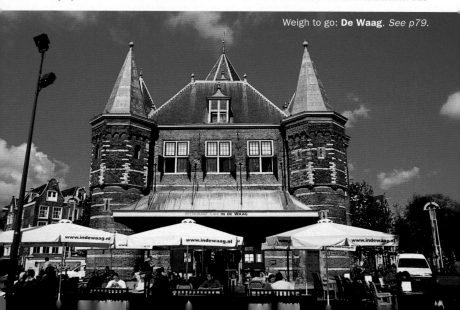

Weigh to go: **De Waag**. *See p79.*

Camouflage made easy

Amsterdam. With all the new impressions, you might feel like you're on a cloud – or, if you've inhaled some of the local greenery, inside one. Still, it's amazing how quickly a pleasant mood can evaporate when a local shouts *klootzak!* ('ball bag') or *eikel!* ('acorn') at you: cast your eye, then, over the following ways to blend in and stay out of trouble. And remember: most residents are friendly – and many began their days here as a tourist.

● **Don't stop to read your map in the middle of streets and bike paths**. It's better to get temporarily lost than become a statistic courtesy of a tram, cab or wrathful cyclist.

● **If you do get lost, only ask for directions from people over 40**. The local youngsters enjoy supplying misinformation, especially if you're travelling in a pack.

● **You are allowed to ask for directions and the like in English**. Amsterdammers always love to show off their mastery of that other Queen's tongue.

● **Don't travel in a pack**. Yes, Italians, we're talking largely to you – but Brit rugby fans come a close second. You'll notice that people get annoyed when they have to navigate through your gang. You'll also notice that few clubs will let you in.

● **Don't get high – at least, not on the street**. Amsterdammers take a dim view of roaming stoners.

● **Avoid the cool clubs**. Locals assume the doormen won't let them in, and as a newbie your chances are slimmer than theirs.

● **Only ride a bicycle if you really know how**. Stick to your right and watch out for tourists looking at maps. Ignore traffic lights if you want to blend in: local cyclists regard them as an assault on freedom of movement.

● **Be suspicious of police officers**. There are plenty of fakes around after your money. If they insist, get them to take you back to HQ to prove that your fine for ignoring the traffic lights is bona fide.

famed dance and ambient label Outland Records has its store at No.22; **Demask** offers its posh line of leathers and latexes at No.64 (*see p204*); and excellent cheap Chinese food can be found at **Nam Kee** at Zeedijk 111-13 (*see p117*). Across the street from Nam Kee, the brand spanking new **Chinese Fo Kuang Shan Buddhist Temple** (open noon-5pm Mon-Sat, 10am-5pm Sun), where monks and nuns provide a library, Internet café and vegetarian restaurant, says a lot for this street's spiritual growth.

Nieuwmarkt

At the bottom of Zeedijk, your eyes will be drawn to the huge and menacing castle-like **De Waag**, or 'the Weigh House'. The Waag, previously called St Antoniespoort, stands in the centre of the Nieuwmarkt and dates from 1488, when it was built as a gatehouse for the city defences. If you have a yen for mankind's darker traits, try to imagine the body parts that used to garnish the Waag's south-east side. The majority of Amsterdam's many public executions took place here, providing a steady supply of corpses for the medical guild to dissect in the Waag's Anatomical Theatre (and for Rembrandt to study and paint – as in his *Anatomy Lesson of Dr Nicolaes Tulp*). In the black days of the Nazi occupation, the square itself was surrounded by barbed wire and used

as one of the collection points to hold captives from the Jewish quarter who were to be shipped off to concentration camps via the **Hollandse Schouwburg** (*see p97*). More recently, in 1980, Nieuwmarkt was the site of riots when the city demolished housing to make way for the Metro. But today, de Waag is home to trendy café **In de Waag** (*see p137*) and the **Society for Old and New Media** (557 9898/www.waag.org), which surfs the radical cutting-edge between technology and culture and often organises events in the Anatomical Theatre.

The streets leading away north-east from Nieuwmarkt contain Amsterdam's small Chinatown, while the colourfully named sidestreets – among them Monnikenstraat (Monk Street), Bloedstraat (Blood Street) and Koestraat (Cow Street) – on the south-west lead into the reddest part of the Red Light District. Heading south from the Nieuwmarkt along the Kloveniersburgwal canal, though, makes for a more interesting stroll.

At Kloveniersburgwal 29 is the **Trippenhuis**, now home to the Dutch Academy of Sciences, who formerly shared it in the 18th century with the original Rijksmuseum collection. During the Golden Age, the building was owned and equally shared (witness the bisecting wall in the middle window) by the two Trip brothers and their respective families. Their fortune was made by arms dealing (witness, now, the mortar-shaped chimneys and the cannons engraved on the gable), and they could easily afford the imposing gunpowder grey exterior. They even – or so the story goes – built the **House of Mr Trip's Coachman** at No.26, in response to a one-liner the coachman reputedly made about being happy with a house as wide as the Trips' front door. He got his wish. The house, capped with golden sphinxes, is now home to a clothing store and appropriately anorexic display figures.

'De Wallen'

The canals Oudezijds Voorburgwal and Oudezijds Achterburgwal, with their interconnecting streets, are where carnal sin screams loudest. So it's with splendid irony that, right in the middle of Sin City, you'll stumble across a pair of churches. The **Oude Kerk** (*see p82*), Amsterdam's oldest building, is literally in the centre of the sleazy action, with hookers in windows ringing the mammoth church like bullies taunting the class geek. Keep your eyes peeled for the small brass bosom inlaid by a mystery artist into the pavement by the front entrance. The **Museum Amstelkring** (*see p81*), meanwhile, is tucked away a little distance from the red-lit action, but shouldn't be overlooked on your journey around the area.

The Oudezijds Voorburgwal was known as the 'Velvet Canal' in the 16th century due to the obscene wealth of its residents. Now, though, at least along its northern stretch, the velvet has been replaced by red velour, illuminated by scarlet fluorescent lighting and complemented by bored-looking girls sat in the windows of the lovely canal houses. It's incongruous, then, that this canal should be so densely populated with churches, chapels and orders. Reps from the Salvation Army lurk on many a corner, less so near the **Agnietenkapel** (*see p82*) to the quieter south end of the street, and more so around the aforementioned Oude Kerk and Museum Amstelkring to the north.

The parallel Oudezijds Achterburgwal offers some of the more 'tasteful' choices for the eroto-clubber. The **Casa Rosso** nightclub (Oudezijds Achterburgwal 106-108, 627 8954) is certainly worth a look, if only for the peculiar marble cock-and-rotary-ball water fountain at its entrance. A short walk away at No.37 is the **Bananenbar** (622 4670), where improbably dextrous female genitalia can be seen performing night after night – and, as the central part of their belief-buggering act, spitting out an average of 15 kilograms (33 pounds) of fruit every evening. A former owner of the Bananenbar once attempted to stave off the taxman – and get round the fact his drinking licence had lapsed – by picking Satan as a deity and registering the Bananenbar as a church. It was a scam that worked for years – until 1988, when the 'Church of Satan' claimed a membership of 40,000 overseen by a council of nine anonymous persons. Tax police were called in to find the loopholes and bust the joint, but the bar was tipped off just in time, and the 'church' disbanded. Now under a new owner, the Bananenbar has kept its name and returned to its roots as a purveyor of specialised sleaze.

Roll up before you roll up to the **Hash Marihuana Hemp Museum**. *See p81.*

Chinese Fo Kuang Shan Buddhist Temple. *See p79.*

If your urges are more academic, you can conduct some, ahem, research at the **Erotic Museum** (*see below*), following it in semi-traditional fashion with a smoke at the **Hash Marihuana Hemp Museum** (which doesn't actually sell dope, but you get the picture; *see below*). Other than that, sleaze and stag parties dominate this strip, with it becoming particularly unpleasant and busy on weekends.

It's a far cry from the Spinhuis, a former convent tucked away at the southern end of the canal (on Spinhuissteeg) that used to set 'wayward women' to work spinning wool. The male equivalent was at Heiligeweg 9 – now an entrance to the Kalvertoren shopping complex – where audiences used to watch the prisoners being branded and beaten with a bull's penis. In a curious foreshadowing of Amsterdam's contemporary S&M scene, the entrance gate sports a statue that bears a striking resemblance to a scolding dominatrix.

Erotic Museum

Oudezijds Achterburgwal 54 (624 7303). Tram 4, 9, 16, 24, 25/Metro Nieuwmarkt. **Open** 11am-1am Mon, Thur, Sun; 11am-2am Fri, Sat. **Admission** €5. **No credit cards. Map** p306 D2.

While the Sexmuseum (*see p77*) benefits from its Damrak location in terms of the passing trade it receives, the Erotic Museum is in the more appropriate location: slap bang in the Red Light District. That's not to say, though, that it's any more authentic or interesting. Its prize exhibits are a few of John

Lennon's erotic drawings, while lovers of Bettie Page (and there are many) will enjoy the original photos of the S&M muse on display. In general, though, the museum's name is scandalously inaccurate: despite its best intentions, it's as unsexy as can be. All in all, you're probably best off going to one of the many nearby sex shops for your kicks.

Hash Marihuana Hemp Museum

Oudezijds Achterburgwal 148 (623 5961). Tram 4, 9, 14, 16, 20, 24, 25/Metro Nieuwmarkt. **Open** 11am-10pm daily. **Admission** €5.70. **No credit cards. Map** p306 D3.

Given the decriminalised nature of dope here, it figures that Amsterdam should have a museum devoted to hash. It's just a pity that it has to be this slightly shabby, ridiculously named operation, which tries to be all things to all people and ends up being nothing to anyone, aside from a pricey way for a backpacker to waste around half an hour in the Red Light District. There's some interesting information here, sure: the display on the medical benefits of the drug is enlightening, as are a few nuggets on the history of hemp. But the small exhibition lacks cohesion and entertainment value, and comes across alternately as hippyish and – surprisingly – po-faced. Definitely a missed opportunity.

Museum Amstelkring

Oudezijds Voorburgwal 40 (624 6604/www.museum amstelkring.nl). Tram 4, 9, 14, 16, 24, 25. **Open** 10am-7pm Mon-Sat; 1-7pm Sun. **Admission** €6; €1 5s-18s; €4.50 students, over-65s; free MK, under-5s. **No credit cards. Map** p306 D2.

The Amstelkring takes its name from the group of historians who succeeded in saving it from demolition in the late 1800s. Good job they did save it, too, for what remains is one of Amsterdam's most unique spots, and one of its best kept secrets. The lower floors of the house have been wonderfully preserved since the late 17th century, and offer a look at what life might have been like back then.

The main attraction is upstairs, and goes by the name of Ons' Lieve Heer op Solder, or 'Our Sweet Lord in the Attic'. Built in 1663, this attic church was used by Catholics during the 17th century when they were banned from worshipping after the Alteration. It's been beautifully preserved, too, the altarpiece featuring a painting by 18th-century artist Jacob de Wit. The church is often used for services and a variety of other meetings. Don't miss it.

Oude Kerk (Old Church)

Oudekerksplein 1 (625 8284/www.oudekerk.nl).
Tram 4, 9, 16, 24, 25, 26. **Open** 11am-5pm Mon-Sat; 1-5pm Sun. **Admission** €4; €3 over-65s; €2 MK; free under-12s. **No credit cards. Map** p306 D2.
Originally built in 1306 as a wooden chapel, and constantly renovated and extended between 1330 and 1571, the Oude Kerk is the city's oldest and most interesting church. Its original furnishings were removed by iconoclasts during the Reformation, but the church has retained its wooden roof, which was

painted in the 15th century with figurative images. Keep your eyes peeled for the Gothic and Renaissance façade above the northern portal, and the stained-glass windows, parts of which date from the 16th and 17th centuries. Rembrandt's wife Saskia, who died in 1642, is buried under the small organ. The inscription over the bridal chamber, which translates as 'Marry in haste, mourn at leisure', is in keeping with the church's location in the heart of the Red Light District, though this is more by accident than design. The church is now as much of an exhibition centre as anything, with shows covering everything from modern art installations to the annual World Press Photo (*see p180*).

Universiteitsmuseum de Agnietenkapel

Oudezijds Voorburgwal 231 (525 3339). Tram 4, 9, 14, 16, 24, 25. **Open** 9am-5pm Mon-Fri (ring bell for entry). **Admission** free. **No credit cards. Map** p306 D3.
Of Amsterdam's 17 medieval convents, this Gothic chapel is one of a few remnants to have survived intact. Built in the 1470s and part of the university since its foundation in 1632, the chapel has an austere, Calvinistic beauty highlighted by stained-glass windows, wooden beams and benches, and a collection of portraits of humanist thinkers. The Grote Gehoorzaal ('Large Auditorium'), the country's oldest

lecture hall, is where 17th-century scholars Vossius and Barlaeus first taught; its wooden ceiling is painted with soberly ornamental Renaissance motifs including angels and flowers. Exhibitions are held here only occasionally.

Warmoesstraat & Nes

It's hard to believe that Warmoesstraat, Amsterdam's oldest street, was once the most beautiful of lanes, providing a sharp contrast to its then-evil and rowdy twin, Zeedijk. The poet Vondel ran his hosiery business at Warmoesstraat 101; Mozart's dad would try to flog tickets at the posh bars for his young son's concerts; and Marx would later come here to write in peace (or so he would claim: cynics point out that he was much more likely to be in town to borrow money from his cousin-by-marriage, the extremely wealthy Gerard Philips, founder of the globe-dominating Philips corporate machine).

But with the influx of sailors, the laws of supply and demand engineered a heavy fall from grace for Warmoesstraat. Adam and Eve in their salad days can still be seen etched in stone at Warmoesstraat 25, but for the most part, this street has fallen to accommodating only the low-end traveller. However, hip hangouts such as gay/mixed bar **Getto** (see *p208*) and the **Winston Hotel** (see *p53*), shops including the **Condomerie het Guiden Vlies** (see *p176*) and gallery **W139** (see *p196*) have ensured that the strip has retained some brighter and less commercial colours, while the council's serial clean-up operation reached the street quite recently and has at least had some of the desired cosmetic effect.

Just as Warmoesstraat stretches north from the Nationaal Monument into the Old Side, so Nes leaves the same spot to the south, parallel and to the west of Oudezijds Achterburgwal. Dating from the Middle Ages, this street was once home to the city's tobacco trade and the Jewish philosopher Spinoza (1623-77), who saw body and mind as the two aspects of a single substance. Appropriate, then, that you can now witness the alignment of body and mind on the stages of the many theatres that have long graced this street. You can also stop, recharge and realign your own essence at one of the many charming cafés hereabouts. At the end of the Nes, either take a turn left to cross a bridge where the junkies are often out making a pretty penny by selling freshly thieved bicycles for next to nothing – though be warned that buying one will have you risking jail and deportation, and in any case the bike you're purchasing has been stolen from some poor devil only a few minutes earlier – towards the

exceedingly scenic **Oudemanhuis Book Market** (where Van Gogh used to get prints to decorate his room; see *p107*) on the University of Amsterdam campus; or turn right and end up near the archaeologically inclined **Allard Pierson Museum** (see below).

Allard Pierson Museum

Oude Turfmarkt 127 (525 2556/www.uba.uva.nl/apm). Tram 4, 9, 14, 16, 24, 25. **Open** 10am-5pm Tue-Fri; 1-5pm Sat, Sun. **Admission** €4.30; €3.20 over-65s; €1.40 12s-15s; €1 4s-11s; free MK, under-4s. **No credit cards. Map** p306 D3.

Established in Amsterdam in 1934, the Allard Pierson claims to hold one of the world's richest university collections of archaeological exhibits, gathered from ancient Egypt, Greece, Rome and the Near East. So far, so good. And, if archaeological exhibits are your thing, or your children would like their names written in hieroglyphics, then it's probably a destination that will go down well. However, if you didn't spend several years at university studying stuff like this, you'll probably be bored witless. Many of the exhibits (statues, sculptures, ceramics, et cetera) are unimaginatively presented, as if aimed solely at scholars. English captions are minimal – though for the record, the Dutch ones are scarcely more helpful – and few staff are on hand to help explain exactly what you're looking at. Some items are instantly accessible and interesting – the full-size sarcophagi, the model of a Greek chariot – but otherwise this is a frustrating experience.

The New Side

Map p306

Rhyming (nearly enough) with 'cow', the Spui is the square that caps the three main arteries that start down near the west end of Centraal Station: the middle-of-the-road walking and shopping street Kalverstraat (called Nieuwendijk before it crosses the Dam), Nieuwezijds Voorburgwal and the Spuistraat.

Coming up Nieuwezijds Voorburgwal – translated literally as 'the New Side's Front of the Town Wall', to distinguish it from the Oudezijds Voorburgwal ('the Old Side's Front of the Town Wall') found in near mirror image in the Red Light District, though both city walls have long since been destroyed – the effects of tragically half-arsed urban renewal are immediately noticeable. The Crowne Plaza hotel at Nieuwezijds Voorburgwal 5 was formerly the site of the large Wyers squat, which was dramatically emptied by riot police in 1985, after a widely supported campaign by squatters against the mass conversion of residential buildings into commercial spaces (or, in the case of the domed Koepelkerk at Kattengat 1, a Lutheran church painted by Van Gogh, turned into a hotel convention centre).

Sightseeing

The multinational, perhaps predictably, proved victorious, as did the ABN-Amro Bank slightly further up, with its in-your-face glass plaza at the corner with Nieuwezijds Kolk. But urban renewal does have its benefits, in that it allows an opportunity for city archaeologists to dig down and uncover Amsterdam's sunken history (in general, every 50 centimetres downwards represents a century backwards). For instance, while the underground car park was being dug on the ABN-Amro site, researchers uncovered 13th-century wall remains which were, for a short time, surmised to be the remains of a marsh-surrounded castle belonging to the Lords of the Amstel. While this proved to be jumping the gun, it did prove that the so-called 'New Side' is not new at all.

A quiet backwater accessible via the north side of Spui square or, when that entrance is closed, via Gedempte Begijnensloot (the alternating entrances were set up to appease residents), the **Begijnhof** is a group of houses built around a secluded courtyard and garden. Established in the 14th century, it originally provided modest homes for the Beguines, a religious sisterhood of unmarried women from good families who, though not nuns, lived together in a close community and often took vows of chastity. The last sister died in 1971; one of her predecessors never left, despite dying back in 1654 – she was buried in a 'grave in the gutter' under a red granite slab that's still visible – and often still adorned with flowers – on the path. Nowadays, it's just the best-known of the city's numerous *hofjes* (almshouses); for details of others, *see p103*.

Most of the neat little houses in the courtyard were modernised in the 17th and 18th centuries. In the centre stands the **Engelsekerk** (English Reformed Church), built as a church in around 1400 and given over to Scottish (no, really) Presbyterians living in the city in 1607; many became Pilgrims when they decided to travel further to the New World in search of religious freedom. Now one of the principal places of worship for Amsterdam's English community, the church is worth a look primarily to see the pulpit panels, designed by a young Mondriaan.

Also in the courtyard is a Catholic church, secretly converted from two houses in 1665 following the banning of open Catholic worship after the Reformation. It once held the regurgitated Eucharist host that starred in the Miracle of Amsterdam (*see p179*), a story depicted in the church's beautiful stained glass windows. The wooden house at Begijnhof 34, known as the Houtenhuis, dates from as early as 1477 and is the oldest house still standing in the city, while Begijnhof 35 is an information centre. The Begijnhof is also close to one of the several entrances to **Amsterdams Historisch Museum** (*see p84*), which in turn is the starting point for the informal **Mee In Mokum** walking tours (*see p72*).

The Spui square itself plays host to many markets – the most notable being the busy book market on Fridays – and was historically an area where the intelligentsia gathered for some serious browbeating and alcohol abuse, often after an honest day's graft at one of the many newspapers that were once located on Spuistraat. The Lieverdje ('Little Darling') statue in front of the **Athenaeum Newscentrum** store (*see p154*), a small, spindly and guano-smeared statue of a boy in goofy knee socks, was the site for wacky Provo 'happenings' in the mid '60s.

You can leave the Spui by going up either the Kalverstraat, Amsterdam's main shopping street, or the Singel past Leidsestraat: both routes lead to the **Munttoren** (Mint Tower) at Muntplein. Just across from the floating flower market (the **Bloemenmarkt**; *see p164*), this medieval tower was the western corner of the Regulierspoort, a gate in the city wall in the 1480s; in 1620, a spire was added by Hendrick de Keyser, the foremost architect of the period. The tower takes its name from the time when it minted coins after Amsterdam was cut off from its money supply during a war with England, Munster and France. There's now a shop on the ground floor selling fine Dutch porcelain (**Holland Gallery de Munt**; *see p170*), but the rest of the tower is closed to visitors. The Munttoren is prettiest when floodlit at night, though daytime visitors may hear its carillon, which often plays for 15 minutes at noon.

From here, walk down Nieuwe Doelenstraat from the **Hôtel de l'Europe** (a mock-up of which featured in Hitchcock's *Foreign Correspondent*; *see p193* **Lights, camera, clog action!**). This street connects with the scenic Staalstraat – so scenic, in fact, that it's the city's most popular film location, having appeared in everything from *The Diary of Anne Frank* to *Amsterdamned*. Walk up here and you'll end up at **Waterlooplein** (*see p94 and p165*).

Amsterdams Historisch Museum

Kalverstraat 92 (523 1822/www.ahm.nl). Tram 1, 2, 4, 5, 9, 14, 16, 24, 25. **Open** 10am-5pm Mon-Fri; 11am-5pm Sat, Sun. **Admission** €6; €3 6s-16s; free MK, under-6s. **No credit cards**. **Map** p306 D3.
A note to all those historical museums around the world who struggle to present their exhibits in an engaging fashion: head here to see exactly how it's done. Amsterdam's Historical Museum is a gem: illuminating, interesting and entertaining. It starts with the buildings in which it's housed: a lovely, labyrinthine collection of 17th-century constructions built on the site of a 1414 convent. You can enter it

down Sint Luciensteeg, just off Kalverstraat, or off Spui, walking past the Begijnhof (see p84) and then through the grand Civic Guard Gallery, a small covered street hung with huge 16th- and 17th-century group portraits of wealthy burghers.

And it continues with the first exhibit, a computer-generated map of the area showing how Amsterdam has grown (and shrunk) throughout the last 800 years or so. The museum then takes a chronological trip through Amsterdam's past, using archaeological finds (love those 700-year-old shoes), works of art (by the likes of Ferdinand Bol and Jacob Corneliszoon) and plenty of quirkier displays: tone-deaf masochists may care to play the carillon in the galleried room 10A, while lesbian barflies will want to pay homage to Bet van Beeren, late owner of celebrated Het Mandje. It's all linked together with informative, multilingual captions and the occasional audio-visual exhibit. Amsterdam has a rich history, and this wonderful museum does it justice.

Wacky tours

While **Mee in Mokum** (see p72) may offer the most charming tours of Amsterdam, they are not known for their wacky factor. This market – generally only available for groups of ten or more – is stitched up by the inspired people behind **Van Aemstel Produkties** (683 2592/www.amsterdam excursies.nl), who long ago left the path trodden by the medieval guardsmen types who lead some tours. Thanks to VAP, you can learn about the world of edible flowers from a homeless man, drink tea with a transvestite, get the inside scoop on Amsterdam's most interesting toilets, or learn to use a handbow in an ancient monastery. Hell, you can even take a leather boy tour – just wait till you show Mum the snaps! These are only some of the ever-expanding list of choices – they're even looking for a Saddam Hussein look-alike to lead tours through the Torture Museum. And with tickets starting at €9 per hour, they measure up favourably, price-wise, with their less visionary competitors.

Not wacky enough for you? Then plead with **Amsterdam Backdoor** (on their informative website www.amsterdambackdoor.com) to come out of semi-retirement and take your posse on one of their three-hour tours. Priced at €15 per person, these include 'The Graffitti Scene', 'High Stone(d) Architecture', 'Second-hand Shopping', 'The Underground Party Scene' and 'Babylon by Bike'.

And if these tours sound too stressful, the **Hashtorical Daze Coffeeshop Crawl** (see p152) might be more of your cup of green tea.

Tea time! **Van Aemstel Produkties**.

Sightseeing

The Canals

Guaranteed to float your boat.

Lipsmackin' **Leidesplein**. *See p93.*

The Dutch call them *grachten*. There are 165 in Amsterdam. They stretch for 75.5 kilometres (47 miles) around the city, are crossed by 1,400 bridges and are, on average, three metres (ten feet) deep. They keep the sea and the surrounding bog at bay. Some 10,000 bicycles, 100 million litres (22 million gallons) of sludge and 50 corpses (usually of pissed tramps who trip while pissing) are dredged from their murky depths every year.

The major canals and their radial streets are where the real Amsterdam exists. What they lack in sights, they make up for as a focus for scenic coffee slurping, quirky shopping, aimless walks and meditative gable gazing. The *grachtengordel* – 'girdle of canals' – rings the centre of town, its waterways providing a trekkable border between the tourist-laden centre and the gentler, artsier and more 'local' locales of the Museum Quarter, the Jordaan and the Pijp.

The **Singel** was the original medieval moat of the city, and the other three canals that follow its line outward were part of a Golden Age urban renewal scheme; by the time building finished, Amsterdam had quadrupled in size. The **Herengracht** (named after the gentlemen who initially invested in it), the **Keizersgracht** (named after Holy Roman Emperor Maximilian I) and the **Prinsengracht** (named after William, Prince of Orange) are canals where the rich lived; but though parts are still residential, many properties now house offices, hotels and banks.

The connecting canals and streets, originally built for workers and artisans, have a higher density of cafés and shops, while the shopping stretches of **Rozengracht**, **Elandsgracht**, **Leidsestraat** and **Vijzelstraat** are all former canals, filled in to deal with the traffic. Smaller canals worth seeking out include **Leliegracht**, **Bloemgracht**, **Egelantiersgracht**, **Spiegelgracht** and **Brouwersgracht**.

In this guide, for ease of use, we've split venues on the canals into the **Western Canal Belt** (between Singel and Prinsengracht, south of Brouwersgracht, north and west of Leidsegracht) and **Southern Canal Belt** (between Singel and Prinsengracht, from Leidsegracht south-east to the Amstel). This splitting is historically justified by the fact that the Western girdle was completely finished before work began on the Eastern half.

The Western Canal Belt

Map p306

Singel

One of the few clues to Singel's past as the protective moat surrounding the city's wall is the bridge that crosses at Oude Leliestraat. It's called the **Torensluis** and did, indeed, once have a lookout tower; the space under the bridge, now ironically populated with drinkers on its terraces, was supposedly used as a lock-up for medieval drunks. The statue of Multatuli on it, depicting his head forming as smoke from a bottle, shadows the nearby **Multatuli Museum** (*see below*) and is a reference to the way he let the genie out of the bottle by questioning Dutch imperialism in such novels as *Max Havelaar* (1860), and not to the equally true fact that he was the first Dutchman to be cremated.

While you're wandering this lazy canal, you may want to join the debate on whether Singel 7 or Singel 166 is the smallest house in town. Located between them, and adored by pussy lovers, is the **Poezenboot** ('Cat Boat'; 625 8794/ www.poezenboot.nl) opposite Singel 40, home to stray and abandoned felines. Slightly further down, and always good for a snort, is the **House with Noses** at Singel 116, though arty types may be more interested in Singel 140-42, once the home of Banning Cocq – the principal figure of Rembrandt's *Night Watch*, once referred to as 'the stupidest man in Amsterdam'. A way further south, you may want to stake out the town's poshest sex club, **Yab Yum** (Singel 295, 624 9503/www.yabyum.com) to watch the country's elite enter for a good old-fashioned servicing.

Multatuli Museum

Korsjespoortsteeg 20 (638 1938/www.multatuli- museum.nl). Tram 1, 2, 5, 13, 17. **Open** 10am-5pm Tue; noon-5pm Sat, Sun; also by appointment. **Admission** free. **Map** p306 C2.
Located just off Singel in his birth house, this museum examines the life of writer Eduard Douwes-Dekker (1820-87), aka Multatuli, using by a variety of liter-

ary artefacts, and pays much respect to his credo: 'the human calling is to be human'. There's also a small library here.

Herengracht

Cross Singel at Wijde Heisteeg, and opposite you on Herengracht is the **Bijbels Museum** ('Bible Museum'; *see below*). A few doors south, at the **Netherlands Institute of War Documentation** (Herengracht 380, www.niod.nl) – whose three kilometres (1.8 miles) of archives include Anne Frank's diary, donated by her father Otto – stone masons knocked up a copy of a Loire mansion, complete with coy reclining figures on the gable and frolicking cherubs and other mythical figures around its bay window.

The northern stretch of Herengracht, from here up to Brouwersgracht, is fairly sight-free; the canal also wants for cafés and decent shops. Still, it's a very pleasant walk. Try to peek into the windows of the **Van Brienenhuis** at Herengracht 284: the excesses of bygone eras will soon become apparent. Keep walking, and you'll reach a Vingboons building at No.168, dating from 1638. Along with De Keyser's Bartolotti House, this architectural gem now houses the **Theater Instituut** (*see below*).

Bijbels Museum (Bible Museum)

Herengracht 366-8 (624 2436/www.bijbelsmuseum. nl). Tram 1, 2, 5. **Open** 10am-5pm Mon-Sat; 11am- 5pm Sun, public holidays. **Admission** €5; €2.50 13s-17s; free under-13s, MK. **No credit cards.** **Map** p310 C4.
Housed in two handsome Vingboons canal houses, Amsterdam's Bible Museum aims to illustrate life and worship in biblical times with archaeological finds from Egypt and the Middle East (including the remarkable mummy of an Israeli woman), several models of ancient temples, and a slideshow. Predictably, there's also a splendid collection of Bibles from several centuries (including a rhyming Bible from 1271). A little dry in places, this museum does attract folk merely looking to admire the restored houses, the splendid Jacob de Wit paintings, and the grand garden with biblical plants and a wild sculpture entitled *Apocalypse*.

Theater Instituut

Herengracht 168 (551 3300/www.tin.nl). Tram 13, 14, 17. **Open** 11am-5pm Mon-Fri; 1-5pm Sat, Sun. **Admission** €4.50; €2.25 students, 6s-16s, over-65s; free MK, under-6s. **Credit** AmEx, MC, V. **Map** p306 C3.
The ever-changing displays are largely drawn from the institute's collection of costumes, props, posters, memorabilia and ephemera, which will soon all be digitally catalogued. One current long-term exhibit, 'Playing Room', celebrates 1,000 years of theatre in the Netherlands: from sassy market vendors who attracted punters with their banter to the current

Mi-aow! **Poezenboot**.

fringes of the avant garde. Upstairs is a massive library; call ahead for information on hours and prices. Inside is a ceiling painting by Jacob de Wit; outside is an idyllic garden.

Keizersgracht

Walk down Keizersgracht from its northern tip (by Brouwersgracht), and you'll soon encounter the **House with the Heads** at Keizersgracht 123, a pure Dutch Renaissance classic. The official story has these finely chiselled heads representing classical gods, but according to local folklore they are the heads of burglars, chopped off by a lusty maidservant. She decapitated six and married the seventh.

Another classic is at **Keizersgracht 174**, an art nouveau masterpiece by Gerrit van Arkels and currently the headquarters of Greenpeace International (which will soon move to a harbour location). Similarly hard to ignore is the **Felix Meritis Building** at Keizersgracht 324, given that it's a neo-classical monolith with the motto 'Happiness through achievement' chiselled over its door. And achieve it did: after housing a society of arts and sciences in the 1800s, it went on to house the Communist Party and is now the European Centre for Art and Science – complete with high-minded and high-ceilinged café. Nearby is the equally epic home of the photography foundation, **Huis Marseille** (see below). This whole stretch was also the site of the Slipper Parade, where the posh-footed rich strolled

Keep it cheap

There's a wealth of, well, wealth on display in this neighbourhood, but don't think you have to spend a fortune to enjoy yourself in Amsterdam. This list of freebies shows how easily cheapskates can have fun.

- The view from **Nemo**'s roof (see p102).
- Complimentary coffee at **Albert Heijn** grocery stores (see p170).
- The **ferry trips** to the north (see p102).
- **Rijksmuseum**'s garden on its west side (see p106).
- Open air concerts and the fresh open air of **Vondelpark** (see p107).
- 'Civic Guard Gallery' at the **Amsterdams Historisch Museum** (see p85).
- **Begijnhof** (see p84).
- **Noordermarkt** flea market on Monday mornings (see p164).
- **Concertgebouw** concerts on Wednesday lunchtimes (see p217).

about every Sunday to see and be seen. From here, take a right turn down Molenpad and you'll reach Prinsengracht.

Huis Marseille

Keizersgracht 401 (531 8989/www.huismarseille.nl). Tram 1, 2, 5. **Open** *Sept-June* 11am-5pm Tue-Sun. *July, Aug* 11am-5pm Tue, Wed, Sat, Sun; 11am-8pm Thur, Fri. **No credit cards. Map** p310 C4.
Located in a monumental 17th-century house, the walls of this photography foundation might bear the corporate office imagery of Jacqueline Hassink, work by duo Teresa Hubbard and Alexander Birchler or landscapes of Amsterdam or the moon. Don't miss the videos and mags in the 'media kitchen'.

Prinsengracht

The most charming of the canals. Pompous façades have been mellowed with shady trees, cosy cafés and some of Amsterdam's funkier houseboats. The **Woonbootmuseum** ('Houseboat Museum'; see p89), one of the funkiest, is a short stroll away. Also around here are some lovely shopping thoroughfares. Working northwards, the 'Nine Streets' linking Prinsengracht, Keizersgracht, and Herengracht between Leidsestraat and Raadhuisstraat, all offer a delightfully diverse pick of smaller, artsier speciality shops that perfectly flavour a leisurely walk by the water.

On your way up Prinsengracht, the tall spire of the 375-year-old **Westerkerk** (see p89) should loom into view. Its tower is easily the tallest structure in this part of town, and if you choose to climb it, you be able to look down upon the expanded – but still modestly dimensioned – **Anne Frank Huis** (see p89). Mari Andriessen's statue of Frank (dated 1977) stands nearby, at the corner of Westermarkt and Prinsengracht. Meanwhile, any fans of René Descartes – and if you think, you therefore probably are – can pay tribute to the great thinker by casting an eye on his former house around the corner at Westermarkt 6, which looks out on the pink granite triangular slabs of the **Homomonument** (see p200), the planet's first memorial to persecuted gays and lesbians.

If it's a Monday and you find yourself at the weekly **Noordermarkt**, inside the Jordaan on the west side of Prinsengracht (see p164 **Amsterdam's markets**), make sure you stop for coffee at the **Papeneiland** (Prinsengracht 2). According to local legend, a tunnel used to run under the canal from here to a Catholic church that was located at Prinsengracht 7 at the time of the Protestant uprising. Also on this uneven numbered side of the canal, you can check to see if the doors to the courtyards of the **Van Briennen** *hofje* (No.85-133) or the **De Zon** *hofje* (No.159-71) are open.

Anne Frank Huis

*Prinsengracht 267 (556 7105/www.annefrank.nl).
Tram 13, 14, 17.* **Open** *Jan-Mar, Sept-Dec* 9am-
7pm daily. *Apr-Aug* 9am-9pm daily. **Admission**
€7.50; €3.50 10s-17s; free under-10s. **Credit** MC, V.
Map p306 C2.

Prinsengracht 263 was the 17th-century canalside
house where young Jewish girl Anne Frank and her
family hid for two years during World War II.
Today it's one of the most popular attractions in
Amsterdam, with almost a million visitors a year.

Having fled from persecution in Germany in 1933,
Anne, her sister Margot, their parents and four other
Jews went into hiding on 5 July 1942. Living in an
annexe behind Prinsengracht 263, they were sustained by friends who risked everything to help
them; a bookcase marks the entrance to the sober,
unfurnished rooms. But on 4 August 1944 the occu-
pants were arrested and transported to concentration camps, where Anne died with Margot and their
mother. Her father, Otto, survived, and decided that
Anne's diary should be published. The rest, as they
say, is history: tens of millions of copies of the diary
have been printed in a total of 55 languages.

In the new wing, there's a good exhibition about
the Jews and the persecution of them during the war,
as well as displays charting racism, neo-Fascism
and anti-Semitism, and exploring the difficulties in
fighting discrimination; all have English texts. To
avoid the famously long line-ups outside, arrive first
thing in the morning, or (in summer) after 7pm.

Westerkerk

*Prinsengracht 279 (624 7766/tower 689 2565/
www.westerkerk.nl). Tram 13, 14, 17.* **Open**
Church Apr-June 11am-3pm Mon-Fri. *July-Sept*
11am-3pm Mon-Sat. *Tower Apr-Sept* 10am-5pm Mon-
Sat. **Services** 10.30am Sun. **Admission** *Tower* €3.
No credit cards. **Map** p306 C3.

Before noise pollution, it was said that if you could
hear the bells of the Westerkerk, built in 1631 by
Hendrick de Keyser, you were in the Jordaan. These
days, its tower is just a good place from which to
view its streets and canals, provided you don't suf-
fer from vertigo: the 85m (278ft) tower sways by 3cm
(1.2in) in a good wind. Although the last tour up the
186 steps is at 5pm, and tours are only scheduled in
summer, groups may call to book for other times.

It's thought that Rembrandt is buried here, though
no one is sure where. Rembrandt died a pauper, and
is commemorated inside with a plaque. Though his
burial on 8 October 1669 was recorded in the church
register, the actual spot was not; there's a good
chance he shares a grave with his son, Titus.

From the street you can see that the tower is
emblazoned with a gaudy red, blue and gold 'XXX'
crown. Not a reference to the city's porn industry, it
is in fact the crown granted to the city in 1489 by
Maximillian, the Holy Roman Emperor, in gratitude
for medical treatment he received during a pilgrim-
age to Amsterdam. The triple-X came to be used by
local traders to denote quality. It also emblazons the
phallic (hence the confusion, perhaps) parking poles

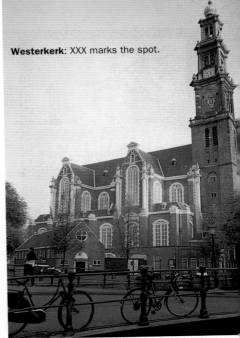

Westerkerk: XXX marks the spot.

scattered throughout the city; which incidentally can
be bought for around €50 at the city's Material depot
(Pieter Braaijweg 10, 561 2111).

Woonbootmuseum
(Houseboat Museum)

*Prinsengracht, near No.296 (427 0750/www.houseboat
museum.nl). Tram 13, 14, 17.* **Open** *Mar-Oct* 11am-
5pm Wed-Sun. *Nov-Feb* 11am-5pm Fri-Sun. Closed
last 2wks of Jan. **Admission** €3; €2.25 children
under 152cm (5ft). **No credit cards**. **Map** p310 C4.

The Houseboat Museum is not just a museum about
houseboats: it's actually one. In fact, it more or
less is one: aside from some discreet explanatory
panels, a small slide show and a ticket clerk, the
Hendrika Maria is laid out as a houseboat would be,
to help visitors imagine what it's like to live on the
water. It's more spacious than you might expect and
does a good job of selling the lifestyle afforded by
its unique comforts. Until, that is, you notice the pungent scent of piss emanating from the public 'curlie'
(as they are locally called) urinoir right by the boat.

The Southern Canal Belt

Map p310

Around Rembrandtplein

It might not be much to look at now, but way
back in the day Rembrandtplein was called
Reguliersmarkt, and it hosted Amsterdam's

butter market. In 1876, the square was renamed in honour of Rembrandt; a statue – today the oldest in the city – of the Dutch master, looking decidedly less scruffy than he does in his self-portraits, stands in the centre of the gardens, gazing in the direction of the Jewish quarter. Though there's no longer a market here, it's still the centre of probably more commercial activity than ever, with a profusion of neon and a cacophony of music blaring out from the cafés, bars and restaurants on all sides.

The area is unashamedly, unconscionably, unbearably tacky. Full of sunbathers by day and funseekers by night, the square is home to a variety of establishments, from the faded and fake elegance of the traditional striptease parlours to the seedy modern peep-show joints and nondescript cafés. That said, there are a few exceptions to the prevailing tawdriness – places like the zoological sample-filled grand café **De Kroon** and HL de Jong's insanely colourful deco masterpiece, the **Tuschinski** cinema on Reguliersbreestraat (see p192). Carry on past here and you'll end up at **Muntplein** (see p84), by the floating flower market at the southern tip of Singel (the **Bloemenmarkt**; see p164). Meanwhile, along Reguliersdwarsstraat and round the corner on the Amstel is a stretch of lively and largely popular gay cafés and bars (see p207); and on the façade of Amstel 216, the city's freakiest graffiti. This 'House with the Bloodstains' was home to former major Coenraad van Beuningen (1622-93), whose brilliance was eclipsed by insanity. After seeing visions of fireballs and fluorescent coffins above the Reguliersgracht, he scrawled the still visible graffiti of sailing ships, stars, strange symbols and his and his wife's name with his own blood. Attempts to scrub the stains off have proved futile.

From Rembrandtplein, walk south along the prime mid-range shopping and eating street Utrechtsestraat, or explore the painfully scenic **Reguliersgracht** and the grotesquely pleasant oasis of **Amstelveld**. Whichever you choose, you'll cross Herengracht as you wander.

The canals

As the first canal to be dug in the glory days, **Herengracht** attracted the richest of merchants, and this southern stretch is where you'll find the most stately and overblown houses on any of Amsterdam's canals. The **Museum Willet-Holthuysen** (see p92) is a classic example of such a 17th-century mansion.

However, it's on the stretch built later between Leidsestraat and Vijzelstraat, known as the 'Golden Bend', that things really get out of hand. By then, the rich saw the advantage of

buying two adjoining lots so they could build as wide as they built high. Excess defines the Louis XVI style of Herengracht 475, while tales of pre-rock 'n' roll excess are often told about Herengracht 527, whose interior was trashed by Peter the Great while he was here learning to be a ship's carpenter and picking up urban ideas for his dream city St Petersburg. Mischievous types, meanwhile, may relish the chance to annoy the mayor by mooring up on his personal and pleasantly scenic dock in front of his official residence at Herengracht 502. If you're caught, quickly douse your spliff and try palming off the authorities with the excuse that you're just visiting the **Kattenkabinet** ('Cat Cabinet'; see p92).

It's a similarly grand story on this southern section of **Keizersgracht**, too. For evidence, pop into the **Museum van Loon** (see p92) or the photography museum **Foam** (see p91), both on Keizersgracht just east of Vijzelstraat. But for an alternative view of this area, head half a block south to Kerkstraat, parallel to and directly between Keizersgracht and Prinsengracht. The houses here are less grand, but what they lack in swank they more than make up for in funkiness, with their galleries and shops – including smart drugs central **Conscious Dreams** (see p156) – only adding to the community feel. The pleasant oasis of Amstelveld helps, too, with the **Amstelkerk** – the white wooden church that once took a break from its holy duties to act as a stable for Napoleon's horses – worth a nose around.

Heading east along Kerkstraat will get you to the **Magerebrug** ('Skinny Bridge'), the most photographed bridge in the city and one said to have been built in the 17th century by two sisters – each living on either side of the Amstel – who wanted an easy way to get together for morning coffee (a Dutch obsession). If you cross it and go down Nieuwe Kerkstraat, you'll get to the Plantage (see p96). Alternatively, turn right at Amstel and right again down **Prinsengracht** if you can't get enough of grand canal houses, peace and general loveliness – or want to smoke your way through the 2,000-plus exhibits at the **Pijpenkabinet** ('Pipe Cabinet'; see p108).

Foam (Photography Museum Amsterdam)

Keizersgracht 609 (551 6500/www.foam.nl). Tram 16, 24, 25. **Open** *10am-5pm Mon-Wed, Sat, Sun; 10am-9pm Thur, Fri.* **Admission** *€5; free MK.* **No credit cards. Map** *p311 E4.*
This relatively new photography museum, located in a grandly renovated canal house, holds excellent exhibitions of works by shutter-button maestros like fashion guy Paul Huff and war dude Don McCullin, and shows covering local themes such as the history

Sightseeing

Foam: snap happy. *See p91.*

of Amsterdam panoramas. They also organise discussions and a variety of special events for the photographically obsessed.

Kattenkabinet (Cat Cabinet)

Herengracht 497 (626 5378/626 9040/www.katten kabinet.nl). Tram 1, 4, 9, 14, 16, 24, 25. **Open** 10am-2pm Mon-Fri; 1-5pm Sat, Sun. **Admission** €4.50; €2.25 under-12s. **No credit cards**. **Map** p310 D4.

Housed in a grand 17th-century canal house, the Cat Cabinet differs wildly from Amsterdam's more notorious pussy palaces. It's a veritable temple to the feline form: in fact, it boasts that it's the world's only museum with a permanent exhibition devoted to cats, and so far no one's come forward to disagree. Paintings, statues, posters and cattish ephemera fill the vast rooms, guarded (after a fashion) by moggies who spend the whole time lying around, cocking a silent snook at guests. Fun, especially for cat-lovers – even if the admission price seems a little steep for such a slight enterprise.

Museum van Loon

Keizersgracht 672 (624 5255/www.museum vanloon.nl). Tram 16, 24, 25. **Open** 11am-5pm Mon, Fri-Sun. **Admission** €4.50; €3 students; free MK, under-12s. **No credit cards**. **Map** p311 E4.

Amsterdam's waterways are chock-a-block with grand houses. Few of their interiors have been preserved in anything approaching their original state, but the former Van Loon residence is one that has. Designed by Adriaan Dortsman, the house was originally the home of artist Ferdinand Bol. Hendrik van Loon, after whom the museum is named, bought the house in 1884; it was opened as a museum in 1973.

The posh mid 18th century interior is terrifically grand, and admirers of Louis XV and XVI decor will find much that excites. So will art-lovers. The house holds a collection of family portraits from the 17th to the 20th century; perhaps more unexpectedly, it hosts a modern art show every two years, featuring

the likes of Steve McQueen and Richard Wright. The 18th-century, French-style garden contains Ram Katzir's striking sculpture of a headless man, *There*.

Museum Willet-Holthuysen

Herengracht 605 (523 1870/www.museumwillet holthuysen.nl). Tram 4, 9, 14. **Open** 10am-5pm Mon-Fri; 11am-5pm Sat, Sun. **Admission** €4; €3 over-65s; €2 6s-16s; free MK, under-6s. **Credit** MC, V. **Map** p311 E4.

Built in the 1680s, this mansion was purchased in the 1850s by the Willet-Holthuysen family. When Abraham died in 1889, wife Sandrina Louisa left the house and its contents to the city on the condition it was preserved and opened as a museum – a nice gesture, were it not for the fact that cats were the main residents for many years. The family had followed the fashion of the time and decorated it in the neo-Louis XVI style: it's densely furnished, with the over-embellishment extending to the collection of rare objets d'art, glassware, silver, fine china and paintings. English texts accompany the exhibits, and there's also an English-language video explaining the history of the house and the city's canal system. The view from the first floor into the recently renovated 18th-century garden almost takes you back in time, but the illusion is disturbed somewhat by the adjoining modern buildings.

Torture Museum

Singel 449 (320 6642/www.torturemuseum.nl). Tram 1, 2, 5. **Open** 10am-11pm daily. **Admission** €5; €4 students; €3.50 under-12s. **No credit cards**. **Map** p310 D4.

Tucked away on Singel, the Torture Museum is just another one of those Amsterdam tourist traps (like the Sexmuseum and Hash Marihuana Hemp Museum) that could have been a lot more informative, engaging and – most importantly – fun. Though there are a few interesting nuggets, this is mostly a frustrating experience, riddled with tattily

Susan Meiselas

Intimate Strangers

maintained exhibits and uninvolving captions. The whole place can easily be done in 20 minutes, and isn't worth the money.

Around Leidseplein

Leidseplein, which from Prinsengracht is reached via the chaotic pedestrian- and tram-packed Leidsestraat, is the tourist centre of Amsterdam. It's permanently packed with merrymakers drinking at pavement cafés, listening to buskers and soaking up the atmosphere (and the Amstel Light).

Leidseplein lies on the bottom of the 'U' made by the Canal Belt; and although it's called a square, it is, in fact, L-shaped, running south from the end of Leidsestraat to the Amsterdam School-style bridge over Singelgracht and east towards the 'pop temple' **Paradiso** (see p225) – where you can admire brass iguanas in the grass in front of an entrance made of classical columns and a chiselled Latin profundity that translates as 'Wise men don't piss into the wind' – to the Max Euweplein (a handy passage to **Vondelpark**; see p107) with its **Max Euwe Centrum** (see below) and giant chess set.

Leidseplein has always been a focal point of the town for one reason or another. Artists and writers used to congregate here in the 1920s and 1930s, when it was the scene of clashes between Communists and Fascists. In the war, protests here were ruthlessly broken up by the Nazis: there's a commemorative plaque on nearby Kerkstraat. But Leidseplein's latter-day persona is more jockstrap than political, especially when local football team Ajax wins anything and their fans take over the square. The police take the ensuing mini-riots in their stride, and so they should: they've had enough practice.

The area has more cinemas, theatres, clubs and restaurants than any other part of town. It's dominated by the **Stadsschouwburg** (the municipal theatre; see p243) and by the cafés that take over the pavements during summer; this is when fire-eaters, jugglers, musicians and small-time con-artists and pickpockets fill the square. The development of in the area in recent years has meant that there are now fast food restaurants on every corner, and many locals feel that the essential Dutch flavour of the district has been destroyed for a quick buck.

The café society associated with Leidseplein began in earnest with the opening of the city's first terraced bar, the Café du Théâtre. It was demolished in 1877, 20 years before completion of Kromhout's impressive **American Hotel** (now a meeting place for posh tourists; see p57) at the south-west end of the square. Opposite the American is a building, dating from 1882, that reflects Leidseplein's transformation: once grand, it's now illuminated by huge, vile adverts. Just off the square, in the Leidsebos, is the Adamant, a pyramid-like, hologram-effect sculpture that commemorated the 400 years of the city's diamond trade in 1986. Wittier is the sculpture of a sawing man in one of the trees.

Max Euwe Centrum

Max Euweplein 30A (625 7017/www.maxeuwe.nl). Tram 1, 2, 5, 6, 7, 10. **Open** 10.30am-4pm Tue-Fri; 10.30am-4pm first Sat of mth. **Admission** free. **No credit cards. Map** p310 D5.

Named after the only chess world champion the Netherlands has produced, occupying the city's old House of Detention – it held Resistance leaders in World War II – the Max Euwe Centrum harbours a library of works in dozens of languages, various chess artefacts, vast archives, and chess computers that visitors can use and abuse at their leisure.

Jodenbuurt, the Plantage & the Oost

The old Jewish quarter is a sampler of leafy streets, pleasant parks, singular museums and – wait for it – gay zoo animals.

Jodenbuurt

Map p307

Located south-east of the Red Light District, Amsterdam's old Jewish neighbourhood is a peculiar mix of old and new architectural styles. If you leave the Nieuwmarkt along **Sint Antoniesbreestraat**, you'll pass several bars, coffeeshops and chic clothes stores: it's a good escape route out of the throbbing sleaze of the sex quarter. The modern yet tasteful council housing that lines the street was designed by local architect Theo Bosch, while the Italian renaissance-style **Pintohuis** at No.69 was renovated by the Jewish refugee and a VOC founder, Isaac de Pinto. It now houses a public

Zuiderkerk.

library where you can browse under Jacob de Wit ceiling paintings. Pop through the skull-adorned entrance across the street between Sint Antoniesbreestraat 130 and 132, and enter the former graveyard and now restful square around **Zuiderkerk** (South Church). Designed by De Keyser and built between 1603 and 1614, it was the first Protestant church to appear after the Reformation, and is now the municipal information centre for physical planning and housing: development plans are presented as interactive scale models. But as you walk around the neighbourhood – or view it from the church's tower (689 2565, closed Mon, Tue, Sun) – it becomes obvious that shiny ideals can often create obtuse realities.

Crossing the bridge at the end of Sint Antoniesbreestraat, you'll arrive at the obtuse reality of a performing arts school, the Arts Academy (aka De Hogeschool voor de Kunsten), on the left and the **Rembrandthuis** (*see p96*) on the right, next door to the **Holland Experience** (*see p95*). Immediately before this, though, some steps will take you to **Waterlooplein Market** (*see p164* **Amsterdam's markets**). Though touristy, it can be a bargain-hunter's dream if you're a patient shopper.

Nearby is the 19th-century **Mozes en Aäronkerk**, built on Spinoza's birthplace. This former clandestine Catholic church, where Liszt reportedly played his favourite concert in 1866, is on the corner where Waterlooplein meets Mr Visserplein – the square-cum-traffic roundabout where the obtuse reality of the copper-green Film and Television Academy meets the much chirpier underground children's playground **TunFun** (*see p188*). Also near at hand is the **Joods Historisch Museum** (Jewish Historical Museum; *see p96*) and the new **Hermitage aan de Amstel** (*see p95*).

Dominating Waterlooplein is the Stadhuis-Muziektheater (the City Hall-Music Theatre). The area where it stands was once a Jewish ghetto, and later, in the 1970s, site of dozens of gorgeous 16th- and 17th-century squatters' residences, before it was decided to replace them with a €136-million civic headquarters

Waterlooplein Market: perfect for particoloured pantaloons. *See p94.*

cum opera house. The decision was controversial, as was the 'denture'-like design by Wilhelm Holtzbauer and Cees Dam, and locals showed their discontent by protesting: in 1982, a riot caused damage estimated at €450,000 to construction equipment. Such displays of displeasure are the reasons why the home to the **Nederlands Opera** and the **Nationale Ballet** (*see p248*), is still universally known as the 'Stopera'.

It's rare that science and art meet on the level, but in the passage between City Hall and the Muziektheater, the **Amsterdam Ordnance Project** includes a device showing the NAP (normal Amsterdam water level) and a cross-section of the Netherlands detailing its geological structure. Close by is the **Blauwbrug** (Blue Bridge), which links Waterlooplein with the Amstel. Years ago, it was the main route into the city from the east. The current bridge was built in 1873, but a plaque depicting the original (taken from a demolished house) has been placed at the entrance of the Muziektheater car park. Recent renovation work has returned the bridge to the same state as Dutch Impressionist painter Breitner saw it at the turn of the century. Still, you won't see much blue: that was the colour of the original wooden one…

Hermitage aan de Amstel

Gebouw Neerlandia, Nieuwe Herengracht 14 (626 8168/www.hermitage.nl). Tram 9, 14/Metro Waterlooplein. **Open** 10am-5pm daily. **Admission** €6; free under-16s, MK. **Map** p307 E3.

Set to open partially in early 2004, this outpost of the Hermitage in St Petersburg will put on two exhibitions a year, using objects and art taken from its massive, prestigious parent art collection. The projected generous exhibition space will only be completed by 2007, but meanwhile visitors can already have a look around a small part of this 19th-century building and all of its 17th-century courtyard.

The Hermitage's riches owe much to the collecting obsession of Peter the Great (1672-1725), who came to Amsterdam to learn shipbuilding and how to build a city on a bog – the latter knowledge was applied to his pet project St Petersburg. A giant of a man, Peter befriended local doctor Frederik Ruysch, perhaps the greatest ever anatomist and preserver of body bits and mutants. Not content with pickling Siamese foetuses in jars, Ruysch constructed moralistic 3D collages with gall and kidney stones piled up to suggest landscapes, dried veins weaved into lush shrubberies and testicles crafted into pottery, and he animated his scenes with dancing skeletal foetuses. After kissing the forehead of a preserved baby, Peter paid Ruysch *f*30,000 for the whole lot (much of which is still on display in St Petersburg's Kunstkammer collection). With luck, this and more of Peter's Golden Age souvenirs – including Rembrandts – will return to their hometown for a visit. So far the planned exhibits only cover Greek Jewellery (March to August 2004), Nicolas & Alexandra (September 2004 to February 2005) and Venetian painters (March to August 2005).

Holland Experience

Waterlooplein 17 (422 2233/www.holland-experience. nl). Tram 9, 14/Metro Waterlooplein. **Open** 10am-6pm daily. **Admission** €8; €6.85 over-65s, under-16s. **Credit** AmEx, DC, MC, V. **Map** p307 E3.

A monumentally peculiar attraction, this, and one hard to recommend – unless you have more money than sense and a blinkered fetish for Euro-kitsch. For your money you get to sit on an undulating platform wearing 3-D glasses and watch a half-hour film that basically acts as a roll-call of Dutch clichés. Windmills? Check. Canals? Check. Clogs? Check. Tulips? Check. Cheese? Yep, it's cheesy all right. And while children may enjoy it, and the actual technology isn't unimpressive, who needs the virtual when the actual is just outside the door?

Joods Historisch Museum (Jewish Historical Museum)

Jonas Daniël Meijerplein 2-4 (626 9945/www.jhm.nl). Tram 9, 14/Metro Waterlooplein. **Open** 11am-5pm daily. **Admission** €6.50; €4 students, over-65s; €3 13s-18s; €2 6s-12s; free MK, under-6s. **No credit cards. Map** p307 E3.

Housed since 1987 in four former synagogues in the old Jewish quarter (before that, it was housed in De Waag; *see p79*), the Jewish Historical Museum is full of religious items, photographs and paintings detailing the rich history of Jews and Judaism in the Netherlands. The interesting if unexciting permanent displays concentrate on religious practice and Dutch Jewish culture; among the more striking exhibits is the painted autobiography of artist Charlotte Salomon, killed at Auschwitz at the age of 26. An excellent new children's wing crams interactive exhibits on aspects of Jewish culture (including a nice one on music) into its galleried space. Temporary shows explore various aspects of Jewish culture; the Jonas Daniël Meijerplein site, with its *Dock Worker* statue commemorating the February Strike of 1941 in protest against Jewish deportations, sits across the street, beside the Portuguese Synagogue (*see below*).

Portuguese Synagogue

Mr Visserplein 3 (624 5351/guided tours 626 9945/ www.esnoga.com). Tram 4, 9, 14, 20. **Open** Apr-Oct 10am-4pm Mon-Fri, Sun. *Nov-Mar* 10am-4pm Mon-Thur, Sun; 10am-3pm Fri. **Admission** €5; €4 10s-15s; free under-10s. **No credit cards. Map** p307 E3.

Architect Elias Bouwman's mammoth synagogue, one of the largest in the world and reputedly inspired by the Temple of Solomon, was inaugurated in 1675. It's built on wooden piles and surrounded by smaller buildings (offices, archives, the rabbinate, and one of the oldest libraries in the world). Renovation in the late 1950s restored the synagogue nicely, and the low-key tours are informative and interesting.

Rembrandthuis

Jodenbreestraat 4 (520 0400/www.rembrandthuis.nl). Tram 9, 14/Metro Waterlooplein. **Open** 10am-5pm Mon-Sat; 1-5pm Sun. **Admission** €7; €5 students; €1.50 6s-16s; free MK, under-6s. **Credit** AmEx, DC, MC, V. **Map** p307 E3.

The renovation of Rembrandt van Rijn's old pad near Waterlooplein was a long time in coming: all in all, over 340 years. Rembrandt bought the house in 1639 for ƒ13,000 (around €6,000), a massive sum at the time. Indeed, the pressure of the mortgage payments eventually got to the free-spending artist, who went bankrupt in 1656 and was forced to move to a smaller house (Rozengracht 184). When he was

declared bankrupt, clerks inventoried the house room by room; it's these bankruptcy records that provided researchers with clues as to what the house might have looked like in Rembrandt's time.

You can't help but admire the skill and effort with which craftsmen have tried to recreate the house, nor the antiquities, objets d'art (Rembrandt was a compulsive collector) and 17th-century furniture. However, the presentation is, on the whole, dry and unengaging. Nagging at you all the time is the knowledge that this isn't really Rembrandt's house, but rather a touch-wood mock-up of it – which lends an unreal air that is only relieved when guest artists are allowed to use the studio. There's also a remarkable collection of his etchings which show him at his most experimental, and explain why this was the medium in which he gained European fame during his lifetime. But if it's his painting you're after, make for the Rijksmuseum (*see p106*).

The Plantage

Map p307 & p312

The largely residential area known as the Plantage lies south-east of Mr Visserplein and is reached via Muiderstraat. The attractive **Plantage Middenlaan** winds past the **Hortus Botanicus** (*see p97*), passes close to the **Verzetsmuseum** (Museum of the Dutch Resistance; *see p98*), runs along the edge of the zoo **Artis** (*see p97*), and heads towards the **Tropenmuseum** (*see p98*).

After a period when rich citizens populated most of the area, Jews began to settle here 200 years ago; the area was soon redeveloped on 19th-century diamond money. The headquarters of the diamond cutters' union, designed by Berlage as a more outward expression of socialism than his Stock Exchange (aka **Beurs van Berlage**; *see p74*), still exists on Henri Polaklaan as the **Vakbondsmuseum** (Trade Unions Museum; *see p98*), and other extant buildings like the Gassan, the Saskiahuis and the Coster act as reminders that the town's most profitable trade was once based here (*see p160* **A girl's best friend**). However, the spectre of World War II again raises its head at the **Hollandse Schouwburg** (*see p97*) and the **Van Eyck's Moedershuis** at Plantage Middenlaan 33 that was used as a mother and child refuge during that time.

The Plantage is still a wealthy part of town, although its charm has somewhat faded over the years. Graceful buildings and tree-lined streets provide a residential area much sought after by those who want to live centrally but still keep a safe distance away from the more touristy areas. The area has seen extensive redevelopment, and work is continuing. As one would expect, results have been mixed: while the housing association flats and houses erected where the army barracks and dockside warehouses once stood (just past Muiderpoort city gate) are unattractive, **Entrepotdok** works far better: to wander down this stretch is to admire a delicate balance between the new and the old, with docked post-hippie houseboats and the views of Artis providing a charming contrast to the apartment buildings.

Artis

Plantage Kerklaan 38-40 (523 3400/www.artis.nl). *Tram 6, 9, 14.* **Open** 9am-5pm daily. **Admission** €14; €12.50 over-65s; €10.50 4s-11s; free under-4s. **No credit cards. Map** p307 F3.

The first zoo on mainland Europe (and the third oldest in the world) provides a great day out for children and adults – as long as they don't mind crowds. Along with the usual range of animals, Artis has an indoor 'rain forest' for nocturnal creatures and a 120-year-old aquarium that includes a simulated Amsterdam canal (the main difference is the clear water that improves your chances of spotting the eels). The 160-year-old zoo expanded a couple of years ago after a long battle for extra land, and now features a mock-up of African savannah that wraps around a light-infused restaurant. Also notable – and typically Amsterdam – are the gay animal tours that introduce visitors to the zoo's resident queer elephants, monkeys and dolphins and the wonder that is flamingo same-sex orgies.

The narration in the planetarium is in Dutch, but an English translation is available. Further extras include a geological museum, a zoological museum, an aquarium and, for kids, a petting zoo and playgrounds; all this makes Artis the kind of attraction that could easily take up a whole day of your trip.

Hollandse Schouwburg

Plantage Middenlaan 24 (626 9945). Tram 7, 9, 14. **Open** 11am-4pm daily. **Admission** free. **No credit cards. Map** p307 F3.

In 1942, this grand theatre became a main point of assembly for between 60,000 and 80,000 of the city's Jews before they were transported to the transit camp Westerbork. It's now a monument with a small but very impressive exhibition and a memorial hall displaying 6,700 surnames by way of tribute to the 104,000 Dutch Jews who were exterminated. The façade has been left intact, with most of the inner structure removed to make way for a memorial.

Hortus Botanicus

Plantage Middenlaan 2A (625 9021/www.dehortus.nl). *Tram 9, 14/Metro Waterlooplein.* **Open** *Feb-Nov* 9am-5pm Mon-Fri; 11am-5pm Sat, Sun. *Jan, Dec* 9am-4pm Mon-Fri; 11am-4pm Sat, Sun. **Admission** €6; €3 5s-14s; free under-5s. **No credit cards. Map** p312 G3.

You don't have to be the green-fingered type to enjoy these beautiful gardens – although, of course, if you are, its entertainment value will be higher still. The Hortus has been at this location since 1682, although

The **Joods Historisch Museum.** *See p96.*

it was set up 50 years earlier when East India Company ships brought back tropical plants and seeds originally intended to supply doctors with medicinal herbs. Some of those specimens (which include the oldest potted plant in the world, a 300-year-old cyca) are still here in the palm greenhouse – which itself dates from 1912 – while three other greenhouses maintain desert, tropical and subtropical climates. There are also descendants of the first coffeeplant to tour the world: it was smuggled out of Ethiopia before finding its way via Hortus to Brazil, which would later become the biggest producer in the world. The terrace is one of the nicest in town: only the distant sounds of the city remind you where you are. The Hortus was part of the University of Amsterdam until 1989, when funding was tightened; now it's run by a foundation and partly supported by the city.

Vakbondsmuseum (Trade Unions Museum)

Henri Polaklaan 9 (624 1166/www.deburcht-vakbonds museum.nl). Tram 7, 9, 14. **Open** 11am-5pm Tue-Fri; 1-5pm Sun. **Admission** €2.30; €1.50 12s-18s; free under-12s. **No credit cards. Map** p307 F3.
The Trade Unions Museum offers a permanent exhibition showing the progress and history of unions in Dutch history. If you think that kind of thing sounds interesting, you'll enjoy it; if not, don't make a special trip – unless, perhaps, for the fascinating collection of posters. That said, for those whose interest in labour relations is even casual, the building itself is worth a peek: it was designed by Berlage, who looked on it as his favourite creation, to house the offices of the country's first ever trade union – that of the diamond workers.

Verzetsmuseum (Museum of the Dutch Resistance)

Plantage Kerklaan 61 (620 2535/www.verzetsmus eum.org). Tram 6, 9, 14. **Open** noon-5pm Mon, Sat, Sun; 10am-5pm Tue-Fri; **Admission** €5; €2.50 6s-16s; free MK, under-6s. **No credit cards. Map** p307 F3.
One of several addresses devoted to the trauma and tribulations of World War II, the Verzetsmuseum is also one of Amsterdam's most illuminating museums, and quite possibly its most moving. It tells the story of the Dutch Resistance through a wealth of artefacts: false ID papers, clandestine printing presses and illegal newspapers, spy gadgets and an authentic secret door behind which Jews hid. The exhibits all help to explain the ways people in the Netherlands faced up to and dealt with the Nazi occupation. The engaging presentation is enhanced by the constant use of personal testimony; indeed, the museum's disparate exhibits are linked effectively by these stories – told, by those who lived through the war, on small panels that act as adjuncts to the main displays. Regular temporary shows explore wartime themes (like the much more predominant flipside of resistance – collaboration) and modern-day forms of oppression, and there's a small research room, too. An excellent enterprise.

Map p312

South of Mauritskade is Amsterdam Oost (East), where the Arena hotel complex (*see p63 and p227*) is located along the edge of a former graveyard that was long ago transformed into **Oosterpark**. While hardly Amsterdam's most beautiful park, it's not without its charms, not least because the neighbourhood in which it sits isn't notable for much else, the **Tropenmusem** (*see below*) and the **Dappermarkt** (*see p164* **Amsterdam's markets**) excepted.

It's a similar story in the **Indische Buurt** (Indonesian neighbourhood) north-east of here, although the **Brouwerij 't IJ**, a brewery in a windmill (*see p144*), is a good place to sip on a culturally reflective beer. North and a little to the west of here are the Eastern Docklands (*see p100*), but as you head further east from the centre of Amsterdam, you'll find little of interest save for the pleasant green expanses of **Flevopark**. The peace and quiet is the main attraction here, though added bonuses come with the two open-air swimming pools. A more authentic swim can be had at the new beach further east in IJburg (*see p101*).

Tropenmuseum

Linnaeusstraat 2 (568 8215/www.tropenmuseum.nl). Tram 9, 14/bus 22. **Open** 10am-5pm daily. **Admission** €7.50; €5 students, over-65s; €3.75 6s-17s; free MK, under-6s. *Tropenmuseum Junior* €2 extra (6s-12s only). **Credit** MC, V. **Map** p312 H3.
It's a handsome and vast building, this, sitting grandly in a slightly out-of-the-way (for Amsterdam, at any rate) location. Better still: the exhibitions in the Tropical Museum are terrific. Through a series of informative and lively displays – the majority of which come with English captions – the visitor gets a vivid, interactive glimpse of daily life in the tropical and subtropical parts of the world (funny, really, given that it was originally erected in the 1920s to glorify Dutch colonialism). Exhibits – from religious items and jewellery to washing powder and vehicles – are divided by region and broad in their catchment. A musical display allows visitors to hear a variety of different instruments at the push of a button (the Tropenmuseum is also the city's leading venue for world music); walk-through environments include simulated African and South Asian villages and a Manilan street; and a Latin American exhibit is highlighted by a fun room complete with videos of sporting highlights and a jukebox. Temporary art and photography exhibitions fill a large central space on the ground floor, the shop has a good pick of books and souvenirs, and the restaurant offers fine global eats with a view-worthy terrace. Attached to the main museum is the usually all-Dutch Tropenmuseum Junior, for children aged six to 12, and a small cinema showing foreign films.

Sightseeing

The Waterfront

Ships ahoy, futurist joy.

Map p307

Amsterdam's historic wealth owes a lot to the city's waterfront, for it was here that all the goods were unloaded, weighed and prepared for storage in the warehouses still found in the area. During Amsterdam's trading heyday in the 17th century, most maritime activity was centred east of Centraal Station, along Prins Hendrikkade and on the artificial islands east of Kattenburgerstraat. At the time, the harbour and its arterial canals – many of which have been filled in since the rise of land traffic – formed a whole with the city itself. A drop in commerce slowly unbalanced this unity, and the construction of Centraal Station late in the 19th century served as the final psychological cleavage. This neo-Gothic monument to modernity – as it was seen then – blocked both the city's view of the harbour and its own past.

However, that's not to say that the harbour ever really slacked. While Rotterdam is the world's largest port, Amsterdam and the nearby North Sea Canal ports of Zaanstad, Beverwijk and IJmuiden rank among the world's top 15. Amsterdam is the centre of Nissan's European distribution, and is still the world's largest cocoa port – something that leads to week-long spewings of dark smoke whenever a storage warehouse for these most oily of nuts catches fire.

North-west of Centraal Station near the Jordaan, the **Westelijke Eilanden** (Western Islands) are artificial islands created in the 17th century for shipping-related activities. Although there are now trendy warehouse flats and a yacht basin on Realeneiland, Prinseneiland and Bickerseiland, where once shipyards, tar distillers, fish-salters and -smokers were located, the area – thanks in part to its large artist community – remains the city's best setting for a scenic stroll that hearkens back to more seafaring times.

Since 1876, access to the sea has been via the North Sea Canal. Because the working docks

Sand devils love **IJburg**. *See p101.*

Nederlands Scheepvaartmuseum.
See p102.

are also to the west, there is little activity on the IJ behind Centraal Station beyond a handful of passenger ships and the free ferry that runs across to Amsterdam Noord – an area of little interest except as a bicycling route towards the scenic fishing villages of Waterland (*see p257*) or towards the cultural breeding ground of **Kinetic Noord**, which is located in the former shipping yard **NDSM** (*see p243*). At the time of going to press, a new **Museumhaven** was due to open on NDSM's waterfront in late 2003 where vistors would be free to explore large historic boats and a Russian submarine (call the **Amsterdam Tourist Board** for details; *see p290*).

The **Schreierstoren**, or 'Weeping Tower', is the first thing you'll notice on the right if you walk east from Centraal Station, and is the most interesting relic of what's left of Amsterdam's medieval city wall. Built in 1487, it was successfully restored in 1966. In 1927, though, a bronze memorial plaque was added by the Greenwich Village Historical Society of New York: its text states that it was from this point, on 4 April 1609, that Henry Hudson departed in search of shorter trade routes to the Far East. He failed miserably in this and ended up colonising a small island in the mouth of a river in North America. The river was later named after him and the colony was called New Amsterdam, only to have its name changed by the English to New York. (Today, some of the boroughs still have a nederstamp on them: in particular, Harlem, after Haarlem, and Brooklyn, after Breukelen.) The next eye-opener you'll see is **Nemo** (*see p102*), a science museum whose stunning green building dominates the horizon and looks out over the historical boats that line Oosterdok beside it. And it positively dwarfs the nautically inclined **Nederlands Scheepvaartmuseum** (*see p102*), itself a very grand structure and a major draw for tourists, especially the Dutch.

However, the old harbour is now virtually disused and the IJ-Oevers (docklands) are undergoing massive redevelopment. Certainly, the city's subculture has lost out badly with the demise of both the sprawling Silo and Vrieshuis Amerika squats, but the city hopes that a transformed Eastern harbourfront will be as image enhancing as the one in Sydney, Australia. The water-hugging Oostelijk Handelskade and its parallel boardwalk can already be regarded as an eating and entertainment hotspot with its glass wave-shaped Passenger Terminal for luxury cruise-ships (www.pta.nl lists arrival and departure times, should you want to admire them); the new **Muziekgebouw** (www.muziekgebouw.nl), which will be home to the likes of the Bimhuis (see p215) and the IJsbreker (see p218) when it opens in late 2004 or early 2005.

But before heading further on to nightspot **Panama** (see p127 and p214), **Odessa** (see p127 and p145) and the **Lloyd Hotel** (see p66 **Cultural cooking with Lloyd**), take the spacey Jan Schaeferbrug to the left that begins by going through the de Zwijger warehouse to the tip of Java Eiland. (The less energetic can travel on the free ferry that departs every 20 minutes from Steiger 8 directly behind Centraal Station.) This is the beginning of the Eastern Docklands as showcase for the Netherlands' rather out-there experiments in residential living. At first glance, Java Eiland may look like a dense designer prison. But it's not hard to be charmed while on the island's bisecting walking street, which will have you crossing canals on funkily designed bridges and passing a startling variety of architecture. At Azartplein, the island changes its name to KNSM Eiland, named for the Royal Dutch Steam Company that was once located here. Jag north and follow Surinamekade with its houseboats on one side and the visible interiors of artists' studios on

the other. Returning on its southern parallel, Levantkade, you can pop through the abstract but strangely suggestive sculpted steel archway to Barcelonaplein, stop for refreshment at one of the waterside cafés or invest in an art coffin at the alternative burial store. Linger and look at the imposingly dark-brown residential Piraeus building by German architect Hans Kollhoff, with its eye-twisting inner courtyard.

The two peninsulas to the south are Borneo-Sporenburg, designed by the urban planners and landscape architects of West 8. The lots are all sized differently, in an attempt to inspire the many participating architects – a veritable who's who of the trade – to come up with creative solutions for low-rise living. Cross to Sporenburg via the Verbindingsdam to the building that has probably already caught your eye: the raised silver **Whale** residential complex, designed by architect Frits van Dongen, on Baron GA Tindalplein. For folksy contrast, a floating styrofoam park produced by onetime Provo Robert Jasper Grootveld has been placed in front of it on Panamakade.

From here, cross to Borneo via a very red and very swoopy bridge and you'll eventually

Smisle!

By its completion in 2012, the seven man-made islands that make up IJburg will be home to 18,000 residences (many of which will float) for 45,000 residents and be a showcase for both Dutch landscape architecture – maximised for both leisure and the attraction of wildlife – and residential architecture that will combine thrilling aesthetics with all the latest environmentally friendly mod-cons. But until then these projections of the Dutch's plucky battle with Mother Nature are really just vast canvases of sandy nothingness with just enough patches of yummy rucola for ample seating and eating. It's just a matter of laying down a towel and before you know it you'll be dreaming of the future yourself. Sure, these islands already have a few constructions suggesting stacked Little Designer Houses on the Prairie, a few pioneering homesteaders to go with them, and a school, a crèche, a supermarket and a hospital have been clumped together into a symmetrical gypsy camp of pre-fabs. But for the time being, it's the perfect surreal place to bring your homemade tumbleweeds to – so you can recreate the whistling scenes from The Good, the Bad, and the Ugly.

Forget Bloemendaal beach (see p228) and its overpriced lounging-gone-all-rigidly-uptight options; IJburg will surely be the hip star for several summers to come. In fact, since summer 2003, there's been an official swimming beach, Blijburg, complete with an official beach restaurant bar, Blijburg aan Zee. They have beanbag chairs, a generally chilled vibe, a changing roster of DJs, and food in the form of wraps, soups and salads by day and barbecues by night. Yes, folks: unlikely as it sounds, Amsterdam has become a beach town.

Should you decide to get there by bicycle, make the half-hour trek to IJburg, then head east on Zeeburgerdijk (map p303). This connects up with Zuiderzeeweg, which then bends left onto a long bridge that ends at a set of traffic lights. From here, follow the bike path to the right over the swoopy white bridge, and you've arrived. A sign indicates the left turn towards Blijburg.

Blijburg aan Zee
Bert Haanstrakade 2004, IJburg (06 460 30929/www.blijburg.nl). Bus 326/IJBurg tram (from early 2004). **Open** times vary, daily. **No credit cards**.

find Scheepstimmermanstraat, Amsterdam's most eccentric architectural street. Each façade, whether with twisting steel rods or with wilfully haphazard plywood, seems odder than the next. For more information on architectural tours of these areas, call **Arcam** (*see p198*).

In addition, a classic old ferry (423 1100) sails from Steiger 9 behind Centraal Station on Sundays and holidays between mid April and the end of October, at noon, 2pm, 4pm and 6pm; it stops at Wilhelminadok, Java Eiland, KNSM Eiland, Sporenburg, Entrepotdokhaven and Nieuwendam. The same ferry also does a tour around the residential artificial island of IJburg (*see p101* **Smisle!**) leaving from Steiger 9 behind Centraal Station at 2pm on Saturdays between mid April and the end of October; it returns around three hours later. KNSM Eiland and Java Eiland are both served by assorted buses (28, 32, 59 and 61 among them), though a tram, the IJburg Tram linking the islands with Centraal Station and IJburg, should be completed by early 2004.

Nederlands Scheepvaartmuseum (Dutch Maritime Museum)

Kattenburgerplein 1 (523 2222/www.scheepvaart museum.nl). Bus 22, 32. **Mid June-mid Sept** 10am-5pm daily. **Open** *Late Sept-early June* 10am-5pm Tue-Sun. **Admission** €7; €6 over-65s; €4 6s-17s; free MK, under-6s. **Credit** AmEx, MC, V. **Map** p307 F2.

The Dutch nautical history is a rich and fascinating one. The city's prosperity was largely built on the seas, especially back in the Golden Age of the 1600s, but the tradition encompasses more than just the East India Company. It follows, then, that the country should boast one of the world's finest nautical museums; second only, say experts, to the National Maritime Museum in London.

However, non-Dutch speakers may get a tad frustrated with the Netherlands Maritime Museum. There's no doubt as to the importance of the collection of models, portraits, boat parts and other naval ephemera; nor can there be any quibbling with the wonderful building in which it's housed (built 350 years ago by Daniel Stalpaert). But while the Dutch captions are excellent, the British, French and German ones are brief and unilluminating. For example, many of the portraits on display are captioned in Dutch with mini-biographies, or at least details of why the subjects merit inclusion in the museum; the non-Dutch captions consist only of a name and the dates the subject was alive. It's a similar deal with the objects: displaying a rudderhead from a 17th-century yacht is all very well, but without any context or explanation – in contrast to the detailed Dutch caption, the English labelling reads only 'Rudderhead from yacht, 17th century' – it's merely old junk. Only the huge replica VOC ship at the rear, complete with costumed 'sailors', really excites. Given the prevalence of full English cap-

tioning in almost all Amsterdam's other major museums, it seems fair to criticise; it's an oversight that, for the average visitor, turns a potentially fascinating museum into a largely dull one.

Nemo

Oosterdok 2 (531 3233/0900 919 1100 premium rate/www.e-nemo.nl). Bus 22. **Open** 10am-5pm Tue-Sun; during school holidays 10am-5am daily. **Admission** €10; €8 students; free under-3s. **Credit** AmEx, DC, MC, V. **Map** p307 F2.

The impossibly striking Nemo opened in 1998 and after much financial struggle has managed to survive as a kid-friendly science museum. And indeed, it's aimed squarely at children, eschewing traditional exhibits in favour of all manner of hands-on trickery, gadgetry and tomfoolery (in English and Dutch): you can mess around on a virtual stock market, play a hi-tech happy families game and use the Internet (albeit on oddly archaic gear). The museum's open-plan interior means that aside from the plush film theatre, there's no escape from the young 'uns, who run riot in hair-raising fashion. Some floors have the feel of a vast, high-budget crèche, and adults without kids should save their money. However, those with children in tow (particularly under-12s) should find their kids leave with smiles.

Childless adults, however, should at least check out the building. Renzo Piano's mammoth structure resembles a green ship rising from the water, and never fails to raise a gasp from people seeing it for the first time. Energetic types will enjoy the climb all the way to the top via the long, sloping roof, where you'll get a breathtaking view of the city and a variety of historical boats below. Best of all, it's free to get up there (although in summer 2003, they re-invented the whole roof as 'NEMO beach' and started to charge a modest entrance fee). The outdoor café at the top is as lovely a place to spend an afternoon and early evening as anywhere in town.

Persmuseum (Press Museum)

Zeeburgerkade 10 (692 8810/www.persmuseum.nl). Bus 39, 43. **Open** 10am-5pm Tue-Fri; noon-5pm Sun. **Admission** €3.50; €2.50 6s-18s; free under-6s. **No credit cards.**

This newly revamped museum covers in its permanent exhibition the 400-year history of the press in Amsterdam and the Netherlands. Temporary shows are usually focused more on graphics, cartoons, photography and magazines.

Werf 't Kromhout

Hoogte Kadijk 147 (627 6777/www.machinekamer. nl/museum/index.html). Bus 22. **Open** 10am-3pm Tue. **Admission** €4.50; €2.75 under-15s. **No credit cards.**

A nostalgic museum, full of old, silent ship engines and tools. The shipyard is proud of the fact that it's one of the few remaining original yards still in use, but its 18th-century heritage is no longer very apparent, nor is the yard especially active. Worth a peek, though, if you're in the area or are of a nautical bent.

The Jordaan

The most charming neighbourhood in town? Only one way to find out...

The Jordaan is roughly sock-shaped, with borders at Brouwersgracht, Prinsengracht, Leidsegracht and Lijnbaansgracht. The area emerged when the city was extended in the 17th century and was designated for the working classes and smelly industries; it also provided a haven for victims of religious persecution, such as Jews and Huguenots. In keeping with the residents' modest circumstances, houses are small and densely packed, at least when compared to dwellings along the swankier canals to the east.

The area is a higgledy-piggledy mixture of old buildings, bland modern social housing and the occasional eyesore. Despite its working-class associations, properties here are now highly desirable, and though the residents are mainly proud, community-spirited Jordaansers, the *nouveaux riches* have long moved in to yuppify the 'hood: once one of the most densely populated neighbourhoods in Europe with 80,000 residents at the end of the 19th century, it now houses under a fifth of that number.

There are several theories about the origin of the name 'Jordaan'. Some believe it to be a corruption of *joden*, Dutch for Jews, while others think it's from *jardin*, the French word for garden. The latter seems more plausible: the area was formerly a damp meadow, and many streets are named after flowers or plants. Other streets are named after animals whose pelts were used in tanning, one of the main – and stinkiest – industries here in the 17th century. Looiersgracht ('Tanner's Canal') sits near streets like Hazenstraat ('Hare Street'), Elandsgracht ('Elk Canal') and Wolvenstraat ('Wolf Street').

North of Rozengracht

Map p305

The Jordaan has no major sights; it's more of an area where you just stumble across things. It's also constantly surprising to wander through its streets and see hardly a soul. In general, the area north of the shopping-dense **Rozengracht**, the Jordaan's approximate mid-point, is more interesting and picturesque, with the area to the south more commercial.

Much of the area's charm comes from what's hidden from the uninformed eye. Chief among these treats are the *hofjes* or almshouses, many of which are pretty and deliciously peaceful. As long as you behave well, the residents don't

Local colour,
Noordermarkt. *See p104.*

Eel-advised?

In 1886, something happened that helped gel the Jordaan's fierce sense of community. Before Lindengracht was filled in, it was the city's premier venue for the indigenous sport of eel-pulling. The trick to this most peculiar of games was to yank a live eel from the rope which dangled it over the canal, while standing in a tipsy – an adjective that could also probably be applied to the participants – boat. The sport was banned, and on the fateful day a passing policeman elected to cut the rope from which the eel was hanging. This was, perhaps, not the wisest idea: the residents of the Jordaan had long felt hard done by, and the cop's interference was the final straw. The Eel Riot of 1886, as the incident came to be known, escalated so quickly that the army had to be called in. After a few days, it was announced that 26 Jordaansers had died and 136 were wounded. And the eel? Astonishingly, it survived the event, and its dry husk was auctioned in 1913 for the sum of ƒ1.75 (less than €1 in today's money).

Authenti-city or Amst-ersatz?

Often called the 'real Amsterdam', the Jordaan began life as a working-class slum where – if you believe the many great songs that glorify its fun-loving and colourful inhabitants – the men drank *jajum* (aka *jenever*, the Dutch gin), the women sang while doing the laundry, and kids roamed the streets stealing apples. Those were the days. Those were the people. And when Johnny Jordaan, one of their favourite singers, turned out to be gay, they threw stones at him and chased him out of town. Yup, those were the days.

But such 'real Amsterdammers' hardly live here any more. Many moved in the 1950s to satellite towns like Purmerend, Diemen and Weesp. A much larger exodus in the 1970s aimed for a Promised Land won from water: the polder of Flevoland, where a settlement called Almere ('Big Lake') was taking shape. Although the city, now home to 150,000 souls, has a rep as a boring suburb, it's really a rather sci-fi sort of town. The planned Rem Koolhaas-designed city centre will boost its modern architecture credentials still further.

It's here that you'll find the highest concentration of original Amsterdammers, with their grass-free tiled gardens and snow-white curtains through which you can admire the porcelain dog collection. And even though these Amsterdammers left 'Dam long ago, they're still fiercely proud of their capital.

In fact, Almere is now throwing its own Jordaan festival (www.jordaanfestival.nl) in July to rival the traditional one held in September every year in the Jordaan proper. In a big tent in the middle of a vast meadow,

they gather all their favourite artists to sing classic songs about life in a confined urban space. With the field awash with suntan lotion and peroxide, it's a feast for ear and eye. And the beautiful thing is, you don't have to ask a girl her name: it's probably written in 18-carat gold around her neck.

Almere is 20 minutes by rail from Amsterdam Centraal Station. For more on Almere, go to www.stadspromotie-almere.nl.

mind people admiring their garden courtyards. Best known are **Venetie** (Elandsstraat 106-36; the only one on this list south of Rozengracht), **Sint Andrieshofje** (Egelantiersgracht 107-14), **Karthuizerhof** (Karthuizerstraat 21-31), **Claes Claesz Hofje** (1e Egelantiersdwarsstraat 3), **Suyckerhofje** (Lindengracht 149-63), **Raepenhofje** (Palmgracht 28-38), and the oldest, **Lindenhofje** (Lindengracht 94-112). *Hofje*-hopping is a gamble, as entrances are sometimes locked in deference to the residents. But take a chance, and you may get lucky.

The area north of Rozengracht is easy to get pleasantly lost in. Little lanes and alleys link the already quiet main streets in a mazy haze, and it's no surprise that such a chilled atmosphere incorporates some of the city's best cafés: **'t Smalle** (Egelantiersgracht 12; *see p146*),

for example, set on a small, picturesque canal, where Peter Hoppe (of Hoppe & Jenever, the world's first makers of gin) founded his distillery in 1780. (The Japanese have built an exact replica of 't Smalle in Nagasaki's Holland Village.)

Between scenic coffees or decadent daytime beers, check out one of the many specialist shops tucked away on these adorable side streets. Some of the best of the outdoor markets are found nearby: Monday morning's bargain-packed **Noordermarkt** and Saturday's foodie paradise **Boerenmarkt** (for both, *see p164* **Amsterdam's markets**) are held around the Noorderkerk, the city's first Calvinist church, built in 1623. Adjacent to the Noordermarkt is the **Westermarkt**, while another general market fills Lindengracht on Saturdays (*see p164* **Amsterdam's markets**).

Between Brouwersgracht and the blisteringly scenic Westelijk Eilanden (*see p99*), more quirky shopping opportunities can be found on Haarlemmerstraat and its westerly extension Haarlemmerdijk. Though not officially part of the Jordaan, this strip and its alleys share an ambience. Head east towards Centraal Station past the West Indische Huis (Herenmarkt 93-7), where as home to the West Indies Trading Company (WIC), it stored the silver Piet Hein took from the Spanish after a sea battle in 1628, and was the setting for such dubious decisions as selling Manhattan for 60 guilders and running the slave trade between Africa and the Caribbean. Today you can pop your head into the courtyard to say hello to the statue of Peter Stuyvesant. Heading west, Haarlemmerdijk ends at Haarlemmerplein, where you'll see the imposing **Haarlemmerpoort** city gate, built in 1840. Behind it is wanderful Westerpark, which connects to the **Westergasfabriek** (*see p217* **It's a gas**).

(*see p217* **It's a gas**).

Rozengracht & further south

Map p305, p309 & p310

As its name suggests, **Rozengracht** was once a canal. It's now filled in, and scythes through the heart of the Jordaan in unappealing fashion. It's unlikely it was so traffic-clogged when Rembrandt lived at No.184 from 1659 until his death a decade later; all that remains of his

former home is a plaque on the first floor bearing an inscription that translates into 'Here Stood Rembrandt's Home 1410-1669'. While you're here, look up the gable of Rozengracht 204 to spy an iron stickman wall anchor. As well as serving up such folksy flourishes, the Jordaan is home to galleries and resident artists (*see p199*).

The area south of Rozengracht is notable for its shops, especially two browse-worthy antique markets; what's more, both **Rommelmarkt** and Looier (*see p164* **Amsterdam's markets**) have cafés. Nearby, Elandsgracht 71-7 is the spot where the maze-like Sjako's Fort once stood. Sjako is often referred to as the 'Robin Hood of Amsterdam', which glosses over the fact that while he was happy stealing from the rich, he usually neglected to give to the poor. Still, he had style: not many burglars go about their business dressed in white and accompanied by henchmen clad in black. His 24-year-old head ended up spiked on a pole in 1718 where the Shell Building now stands, but local band Sjako!, anarchist-oriented bookstore **Fort van Sjako** (Jodenbreestraat 24, 625 8979), and a shrine in the window of the building that replaced his fort keep his name alive. Another tribute can be paid where Elandsgracht hits Prinsengracht: here you'll find statues of Tante Leni, Johnny Jordaan and Johnny Meijer, who personified the spirit of the Jordaan by crooning of lost love and spilt beer in local cafés (*see p104* **Authenti-city or Amst-ersatz?**).

Noodermarkt. See p104.

The Museum Quarter, Vondelpark & the South

Pots of money, culture and botany.

The Museum Quarter

Map p310

Little over a century ago, the area now known as the Museum Quarter was still officially outside the city limits and consisted of little more than vegetable patches. Towards the end of the 19th century, though, the city expanded rapidly and the primarily upper-class city fathers decided to erect a swanky neighbourhood between the working-class areas to the west and south. Most of the beautiful mansions, with their art deco gateways and stained-glass windows, were built in the late 1890s and early 1900s.

The heart of the area is **Museumplein**, the city's largest square, bordered by the **Rijksmuseum** (*see below*), the **Stedelijk Museum of Modern Art**, the **Van Gogh Museum** (for both, *see p107*) and the **Concertgebouw** (*see p217*). Sadly, the heart will have a fainter beat in the coming years since the Rijksmuseum and the Stedelijk are both due to close (at least partially) in 2004 for years of extensive work. The Museumplein itself is not really an authentic Amsterdam square, its recent revamping accenting its more 'park' – or, rather, 'cow pasture' – aspects. Developed in 1872, it served as a location for the World Exhibition of 1883, and was then rented out to the Amsterdam ice-skating club between 1900 and 1936. During the Depression, the field was put to use as a sports ground, and during World War II the Germans built four bunkers and a concrete shelter on it. Further annoyance followed with the laying of the country's 'shortest motorway', Museumstraat, in 1953, which cut the *plein* in two and remained until the latter's recent resurrection with grass, wading pool, skate ramp, café and wacky new addition to the Van Gogh Museum.

As you'd expect in such high-falutin' cultural surroundings, property here doesn't come cheap, and the affluence of the residents is reflected in architecture and consumerism. **Van Baerlestraat** and, especially, **PC Hooftstraat** are as close as Amsterdam gets to Rodeo Drive, their clothing boutiques offering shopping solace to ladies who would

otherwise be lunching. It's little wonder that this neck of the woods is also where you'll find the majority of Amsterdam's diamond retailers.

Nearby **Roemer Visscherstraat**, which leads to Vondelpark, is notable not for its labels but for its buildings. The houses from Nos.20 to 30 each represent a different country and are built in the appropriate 'national' style: Russia comes with a miniature dome, Italy has been painted pastel pink, and Spain's candy stripes have made it one of the street's favourites.

Rijksmuseum

Stadhouderskade 42 (674 7047/www.rijks museum.nl). Tram 2, 5, 6, 7, 10. **Open** 10am–5pm daily. **Admission** €9; free MK, under-19s. **Credit** AmEx, MC, V. **Map** p310 D5.

Designed by PJH Cuypers and opened in 1885, the Rijksmuseum holds the largest collection of art and artefacts in the Netherlands including 40 Rembrandts and four Vermeers. However most of its million exhibits will be out of the public eye until 2008 while the Rijksmuseum gets a remarkable €200 million facelift at the able hands of Spanish architect bureau Cruz y Ortiz. For many, though, the closure may turn out to be a blessing in disguise: instead of overdosing on the vastness of the place, visitors will be able to see the 400 most masterful 'Masterpieces' in the Philips Wing. Some of the collection will be used in other exhibitions organised by museums throughout the country. In addition, the Rijksmuseum Amsterdam Schiphol (Schiphol Airport, Holland Boulevard between E and F) offers the viewing of a few choice pieces by the likes of Rembrandt, Steen and Ruysdael while travellers are waiting for their plane. In short: there will still be plenty of Golden Age art to look at, but you'd do well to check the museum's excellent website for more details on such matters before you visit.

The collection was started when William V started acquiring pieces just for the hell of it, and has been growing ever since: it includes Dutch paintings from the 15th century until 1900, as well as decorative and Asian art. The 'Masterpieces' that will almost certainly stay on display will include Rembrandt's *Night Watch*, the jewel of the collection, and Vermeer's *Kitchen Maid* and *Woman Reading a Letter*, each capturing a moment in the lives of women from different backgrounds; and a selection of the likes of Frans Hal, Jacob de Wit and

Ferdinand Bol. There should also be a wealth of decorative arts on display, including 17th-century furniture and intricate silver and porcelain, 17th- and early 18th-century dolls' houses, plus furniture to give a glimpse of how canal-house interiors looked. 18th- and 19th-century paintings; art objects from Asia, statues, lacquer work, paintings, ceramics, jewellery, weaponry and the Textile and Costume collection will also undoubtedly be visible; the freely accessible garden, filled with Golden Age gateways and construction fragments on the west side, will remain an oasis of rest.

Stedelijk Museum of Modern Art

Paulus Potterstraat 13 (573 2911/www.stedelijk.nl). **Tram** *2, 3, 5, 12, 16.* **Open** *11am-5pm daily.* **Admission** *€7; €3.50 7s-16s; free MK, under-7s.* **Credit** *Shop* AmEx, MC, V. **Map** p310 D6.

The Stedelijk offers the best collection of modern art in Amsterdam. Displays change regularly: some exhibitions are drawn from the collection, while others are made up from works loaned to the museum, but each tends to focus on a particular trend or the work of a specific artist. After occupying various locations around the city, the Stedelijk finally settled in its present neo-Renaissance abode, designed by AW Weissman, in 1895. In time, the building became too small for the ambitions of its directors and an ugly new wing was tacked on in 1954.

The museum is currently expanding still further. Although plans for the building of two grand new wings, both designed by Portuguese architect Alvaro Siza, have been scuttled by a shortage of cash, the Stedelijk is still due to close in 2004 for at least two years of massive and much-needed renovation. As of April 2004, it should have settled into the temporary space earmarked for it in the old post office building on Oosterdokseiland near Centraal Station. Be sure to call before setting out, or check the website for up-to-date information.

When it's open, though, the museum is a real winner. Pre-war highlights include works by Cézanne, Picasso, Matisse and Chagall, plus a prized collection of paintings and drawings by Malevich. Post-1945 artists represented include De Kooning, Newman, Ryman, Judd, Stella, Lichtenstein, Warhol, Nauman, Middleton, Long, Dibbets, Kiefer, Polke, Merz and Kounellis. The Nieuwe Vleugel ('New Wing') is used as a temporary space for exhibitions often focusing on design and applied art. CoBrA artist Karel Appel decorated the Appelbar and restaurant; the latter is still in use, and its picture windows make it an ace place to sit in on a sunny day.

Van Gogh Museum

Paulus Potterstraat 7 (570 5200/www.vangogh museum.nl). **Tram** *2, 3, 5, 12, 16.* **Open** *10am-6pm daily.* **Admission** *€9; €2.50 13s-17s; free MK, under-13s. Temporary exhibitions prices vary.* **Credit** MC, V. **Map** p310 D6.

As well as the bright colours of his palette, Vincent van Gogh is also known for his productivity, and both are clearly reflected in the 200 paintings and

Museumplein.
See p106.

500 drawings that form part of the permanent exhibition here. In addition to this large collection, there are also examples of his Japanese prints, and works by the likes of Toulouse-Lautrec that add perspective to Van Gogh's own efforts.

After a major and impressive refurbishment, the enlarged Rietveld building remains the home base for the permanent collection, while the new wing by Japanese architect Kisho Kurokawa is usually the home to temporary exhibitions that focus on Van Gogh's contemporaries and his influences on other artists. These shows are assembled from both the museum's own extensive archives and private collections; forthcoming exhibitions will feature Rossetti's femme fatales (Mar-May 2004), Manet's seascapes (June-Sept 2004) and Siegfried Bing's art nouveau collection (Dec 2004-Feb 2005). Do yourself a favour and get there early in the morning, though: the queues in the afternoon can get frustratingly long, and the gallery unbearably busy.

As of February 2004, the museum will stay open until 10pm every Friday; besides the museum's regular exhibitions, these late shows will also dish up lectures, concerts and films.

Vondelpark

Map p310

Amsterdam's largest green space is named after the city's most famous poet, Joost van den Vondel (1587-1679), whose controversial play *Lucifer* caused the religious powers of the time to come down hard on those who engaged in what was quaintly termed 'notorious living'. The concerted campaign by the moral majority helped bring about the downfall of Rembrandt and Vondel; the latter ended his days forlornly as a pawnshop doorman.

The collectors' collectors

Little wonder that an eclectic town like Amsterdam should have such an impressive list of eclectic collections.

For planes

Aviodome *Dakotaweg 11a, Lelystad Airport (01320 289840/www.aviodome.nl). Bus 147 from Lelystad NS station.* **Open** *Jan-June, Sept-Dec* 10am-5pm daily. *July, Aug* 10am-6pm daily. **Admission** €12.80 adults; €10.80 4s-12s; free under-4s. **No credit cards.**
Aeroplane enthusiasts will loop the loop over this aviation theme park and museum. They have a 1903 Wright Flyer, a Spider (designed by Dutch pioneer Anthony Fokker), and more recent aeronautical exhibits.

For trams

Electrische Museum Tramlijn Amsterdam *Haarlemmermeerstation, Amstelveenseweg 264 (673 7538/www.museumtram.nl). Tram 16.* **Open** *Apr-June, Sept, Oct* every 20mins, 11am-5pm Sun, public holidays. *July, Aug* every 20mins, noon-5pm Wed. **Tickets** €3 round trip; €1.50 children. **No credit cards.**
The pride and raison d'être of the Electric Tram Museum, housed in a beautiful 1915 railway station, is its rolling stock. For its one-hour round trips, colourful antique streetcars from several cities make their way along a track through the nearby Amsterdamse Bos.

For pianolas

Pianola Museum *Westerstraat 106, Jordaan (627 9624/www.pianola.nl). Tram 3, 10.* **Open** 1-5.30pm Sun. **Admission** €4. **No credit cards. Map** p305 B2.
Ever wanted the full scoop on the full history of piano-playing devices? Look no further...

For mutants

Museum Vrolik *Entrance on south side of AMC medical faculty, Meibergdreef 15 (566 9111). Metro Holendrecht.* **Open** 9am-5pm Mon-Fri. **Admission** free. **No credit cards.**

This anatomical laboratory way out in the south-east of the city contains 18th- and 19th-century specimens of human embryos and malformations collected by Professor Gerardus Vrolik and his son: clearly not recommended for those with weak stomachs. Funny fact: 'vrolik' is Dutch for cheerful.

For mini modern art

Reflex Minituur Museum voor Hedendaagse Kunst *Entrance by 'polikliniek' entrance of AMC, Meibergdreef 9 (627 2832/www.reflex-art.nl). Metro Holendrecht.* **Open** 8am-5pm daily. **Admission** free. **No credit cards.**
Some 1,500 works no larger than ten centimetres (four inches) across: artists on show include Warhol, Appel, Scholte, Beuys, Kienholz, Lichtenstein, Leibovitz and LeWitt.

For pipes

Pijpenkabinet *Prinsengracht 488, Southern Canal Ring (421 1779/www.pijpenkabinet.nl). Tram 1, 2, 5.* **Open** noon-6pm Wed-Sat. **Admission** €5. **No credit cards. Map** p310 D5.
This national pipe museum staggers mind and lungs with a vast collection: clay pipes, opium pipes and paraphernalia. Good 'Smokiana' shop for connoisseurs and souvenir hunters.

For lifts

Energetica *Hoogte Kadijk 400, Eastern Docklands (422 1277/www.energetica.nl). Tram 9, 14; bus 22, 32.* **Open** 10am-4pm Mon-Fri. **Admission** €3; free under-12s, MK. **No credit cards. Map** p307 F2.
This museum of 'energy techniques, elevators, household appliances and city gas' is a world leader among functioning lift collections; it includes the famous 'Pater Noster'.

For all and sundry

For **cats** *see p92*; for **Bibles** *see p87*; for **coffee and tea** *see p169*; for **beer** *see p136*; for **torture** *see p92*; for **drugs** *see p81 and p156*; for **sex** *see p77 and p81*.

Vondelpark is the most central of the city's major parks, its construction inspired by the development of Plantage, which had formerly provided the green background for the leisurely walks of the rich. It was designed in the 'English style' by Zocher, with the emphasis on natural landscaping; the original ten acres opened in 1865. There are several ponds and lakes in the park – no boating, though – plus a number of children's play areas and cafés; most

pleasant are **Het Blauwe Theehuis** (Round Blue Teahouse; *see p146*) and **Café Vertigo** at the **Nederlands Filmmuseum** (*see p194*). The NFM is less a museum and more a cinema with a café attached and a library nearby; local movie fans rejoiced when a recent decision to move it to Rotterdam was overturned. Around the corner – and also providing a unique place to drink a coffee – is the epic **Hollandsche Manege** (Vondelstraat 140, 618 0942), a wooden

'Spanish riding school', which was the first hall in the world to be supported by a lightweight steel construction.

Vondelpark gets fantastically busy on sunny days and Sundays, when bongos abound, dope is toked and football games take up any space that happens to be left over. The dicky-tickered would be do well to look out for rollerbladers, who meet here weekly for the Friday Night Skate (*see p237*). Films, plays and concerts are also put on here, with a festival of free open-air performances in summer (*see p214*).

Further south

The Museum Quarter is the northernmost tip of Amsterdam's **Oud Zuid** (Old South), which stretches down beyond Vondelpark. This area is defined by residential housing, with the more bohemian streets around the park contrasting nicely with their smarter equivalents by the museums and comparing favourably with the uglier modern buildings nearby.

Nieuw Zuid

Stretching out in a ring beneath Vondelpark is a fairly indeterminate region known as Nieuw Zuid (New South), bordered to the north by Vondelpark, to the east by the Amstel and to the west by the **Olympisch Stadion** (www.olympisch-stadion.net), built for the 1928 Olympics, recently renovated to its original Amsterdam School glory and now notable

primarily for its club/restaurant **Vakzuid** (*see p131*). The New South was planned by Berlage and put into action by a variety of Amsterdam School architects, who designed both private and public housing for the area. It's the former that's given the New South what character it has, most notably around the likes of Apollolaan (where you'll find the Hilton from which legendary local rocker and 'cuddle junkie' Herman Brood tossed himself in 2001) and Beethovenstraat (worth visiting simply for the **Oldenburg** bakery at No.17; *see p165*).

The few visitors this area draws are here on business, especially around the World Trade Center, witness to massive construction. The controversial Noord-Zuidlijn Metro line is set to link this district with the centre of town and Amsterdam Noord. East of here is another staple of Amsterdam business life: the ugly **RAI Exhibition and Congress Centre**, which holds numerous trade fairs, conventions and public exhibitions throughout the year.

However, in between the RAI and the WTC lies one of Amsterdam's loveliest parks. Extended and renovated in 1994, **Beatrixpark** is a wonderfully peaceful place, handy if you want to avoid the crowds in town on a summer's day. The Victorian walled garden is worth a visit, as is the pond, complete with geese, black swans and herons. Amenities include a wading pool and play area for kids; there are concerts in July and August.

Still further south, **Amstelpark** was created for a garden festival in 1972, and now offers

Tea for two hundred: **Het Blauwe Theehuis**.

It means squat

It's hard to tell what's what in the world of Amsterdam squatting these days: there are proper squats (reappropriated buildings that had been left empty for more than a year), counter-squats (buildings with temporary residents paying no rent so that squatters can't squat in them); 'bought squats' (old squats that were sold cheaply by the city to the inhabitants in the name of stress relief); and non-squats called *broedplaatsen* (government-funded 'breeding grounds').

Squatting, in this city, goes back a long way. As Amsterdam expanded, the poor got pushed outwards – outside the city gate in medieval times, outside the freshly built canal ring in the Golden Age, and completely outside the city in the 20th century. Still, it wasn't until 1965 that squatting (in the modern sense) began in earnest. The general public – not sympathetic to the way speculators held on to their (empty) properties to drive up rents and property values – began regarding it as a legitimate way of dealing with the housing shortage; the *Handbook for Squatters* even became a national best-seller in 1969. Squatting hit the headlines again in 1980, when hundreds of by now highly organised squatters captured Vondelstraat 72 and built barricades. The tanks rolled in. On 30 April, the date of Queen Beatrix's inauguration, more huge riots broke out, and tear gas was used. Squatting became yet more politicised as a result, and factions emerged.

1998 was another landmark year. Two mega-squats which epitomised the cultural/artistic side of squatting were emptied. The **Graansilo** and **Vrieshuis Amerika** had hosted artist studios, parties, festivals, restaurants and 100,000 visitors a year, and the void they left in Amsterdam's cultural life was so large that even the city council noticed it. To make amends, the authorities introduced the concept of *broedplaatsen* – 'breeding grounds' of the arts, ie buildings filled with cheap studio spaces, and tax money was found to rebuild what had grown organically. It remains to be seen if happening scenes can thrive in the new settings.

Happily, a few squat hotspots remain. While the **Westergasfabriek** (*see p217* **It's a gas**) has been scrubbed of its squat roots, **NDSM** (*see p243*) has retained some grit in its vibe and programming. The artists who have occupied the nearby village of Ruigoord (*see p229*) since the 1970s saw a long land dispute with the port authority end in a partial victory: they can keep their studio spaces, but they can't live there. **Binnenpret** has a great sauna and a squat-like sister venue in **OCCII** (*see p213*). Venerable squatters' bar **Vrankrijk** (Spuistraat 216; www.vrankrijk.org), now a 'bought squat', continues to dispense politics and cheap beer (including one from a Frisian anarchist brewery) behind its fluorescent façade. Near Vondelpark and equipped with temporary 'breeding ground'

recreation and respite to locals in the suburb of Buitenveldert, near the RAI. A formal rose garden and rhododendron walk are among the seasonal floral spectacles, and there are also a labyrinth, pony rides and a children's farm, plus tours on a miniature train. The Rosarium Restaurant serves expensive meals, though its outdoor café is less pricey. For more on parks, *see p188* **A ton of fun**. Just north of Amstel park, along the scenic banks of the Amstel, lies the city's most evocative cemetery, **Begraafplaat Zorgvlied** (Amsteldijk 273, 644 5236), which is filled with ancient and arty headstones – perfect for an introspective stroll.

Amstelveen

Of all Amsterdam's southern suburbs, Amstelveen is the most welcoming to the casual visitor. Though the **CoBrA Museum** (*see p111*)

helps, the main attraction here is the **Amsterdamse Bos**, a mammoth artificially-built wood that's treasured by locals yet neglected by visitors (which, you suspect, probably makes the locals treasure it even more). The 2,000-acre site sprawls beautifully, and comes with a great many attractions in case the tranquility isn't worthwhile enough. The man-made Bosbaan is used for boating and swimming, with canoe and pedalo rental available. Other attractions include play areas, a horticultural museum, jogging routes, a buffalo and bison reserve, a bike-hire centre (open March to October), a water sports centre, stables and a picnic area. The non-subsidised goat farm sells cheese, milk and ice-cream: you can even feed the goats while you're there. Happily, the wood feels a lot further away from Schiphol Airport than it actually is: the airport is less than a mile from the wood's western edge.

status, **Ot301** (Overtoom 301, 779 4912/
http://squat.net/overtoom301), also known
as Academie (it's housed in the old film
academy), shows quality movies on its
big screen and will hopefully soon reopen
its excellent restaurant after extensive
renovations. The **ADM**, a vast former dry
dock in the western harbour (Hornweg 6,
411 0081/www.contrast.org/adm), has
a restaurant and often holds festivals. The

CIA Infocafé (3de Oosterparkstraat 166hs,
777 4944) continues the tradition of
dispensing both activist information and
cheap beer, and the squat cum Internet
café **ASCII** (Kinkerstraat 92/http://squat.net/
ascii) provides free web access for activists.
 Anyone interested in finding out about the
ever-evolving squat scene should log on to
http://squat.net, www.vrijeruimte.nl (Dutch
only) or www.underwateramsterdam.com.

Bosmuseum

*Bosbaan, near Amstelveenseweg, Amsterdamse Bos
(676 2152). Bus 170, 171, 172.* **Open** 10am-5pm
daily. **Admission** free. **No credit cards.**
The Bosmuseum, in a swoopy new building as of
January 2004, recounts the history and use of the
Amsterdamse Bos. Its mock woodland grotto, which
turns from day to night at the flick of a switch, is
wonderful for kids.

CoBrA Museum of Modern Art

*Sandbergplein 1 (547 5050/www.cobra-museum.nl).
Tram 5/Metro 51/bus 170, 172.* **Open** 11am-5pm
Tue-Sun. **Admission** €6; €4 over-65s; €2.50 5s-16s;
free MK, under-5s. **Credit** *Shop* MC, V.
The CoBrA group (*see p39 and p195*) attempted to
radically reinvent the language of paint in 1948,
preaching an ethos of participation and believing
everyone should make art, regardless of ability or
education. Artists such as Dane Asger Jorn and
Dutchmen Karel Appel, Eugene Brands and
Corneille were once regarded as little more than

eccentric troublemakers; they've now been absorbed
into the canon .This museum provides a sympathetic environment in which to trace the development of one of the most influential Dutch art
movements of the 20th century.

Hortus Botanicus
(Vrije Universiteit)

*Van de Boechorststraat 8, Zuid (444 9390/
www.vu.nl/hortus). Tram 5/Metro 50, 51/bus 142,
170, 171, 172.* **Open** 8am-4.30pm Mon-Fri; 9am-
5pm Sat. **Admission** free Sep-June; €2 Jul-Aug. **No
credit cards.**
This small but perfectly formed garden is, rather
curiously, wedged between the high buildings of a
university and a hospital. Built in 1967, it doesn't
have the charm of its counterpart in the city centre
(*see p97*), but it's a pleasant enough place for a stroll
if you're in the neighbourhood. The fern collection
is one of the largest in the world, while the Dutch
garden next door shows the great variety of flora
found in this country.

The Pijp

Artists, hookers, cheap ethnic eats and the best market
in town: let yourself be sucked in.

Map p311

Not to be confused with the suggestive slang
in Dutch for the act of 'piping' – 'giving a blow
job' – doing the Pijp can still be a colourful
experience: the district definitely has a spunky
verve about it. It's hardly a treasure trove of
history and traditional sights, but the Pijp's
time is the present, with over 150 different
nationalities keeping its global village vibe
alive and the recent economic upturn seeing
the opening of more upmarket and trendy
eateries and bars than ever before.

The Pijp is the best known of the working-
class quarters built in the late 19th century.
Harsh economics saw the building of long,
narrow streets, which probably inspired the
change in name from the official, double-yawn-
inducing 'Area YY' to its more appropriate
nickname, 'the Pipe'. Because rents were too
high for many tenants, they were forced to let
rooms out to students, who then went on to
give the area its bohemian character.

That said, the many Dutch writers who lived
here helped add to it. Among the locals were
luminaries like Heijermans, De Haan and
Bordewijk, who famously described World
War I Amsterdam as a 'ramshackle bordello, a
wooden shoe made of stone'. Many painters had
studios here, too – people like Piet Mondriaan,
who once lived in the attic of Ruysdaelkade 75,
where he began formulating de Stijl while
enjoying a view of the decidedly old school
Golden Age depot of the Rijksmuseum.

And, of course, the area was packed with
brothels and drinking dens. In the basement
of Quellijnstraat 64, the Dutch cabaret style –
distinguished by witty songs with cutting
social commentary for lyrics – was formulated
by Eduard Jacobs and continues to live on
through the likes of Freek de Jonge, Hans
Teeuwen and Najib Amhali.

At the turn of the century, the Pijp was a
radical socialist area. The area has lost much
of its bite since those halcyon days, and many
families with children have fled to suburbia.
Still, the number of cheap one- and two-
bedroom places, combined with the reasonably
central location, makes the area very attractive
to students, young single people and couples,
and the area also has the densest gay
population in Amsterdam.

During the last 40 years, many immigrants
have found their way into the Pijp to set up
shop and inspire the general economic upswing
of the area. The Pijp now houses a mix of
nationalities, providing locals with plenty of
Islamic butchers, Surinamese, Spanish, Indian
and Turkish delicatessens, and restaurants
offering authentic Syrian, Moroccan, Thai,
Pakistani, Chinese and Indian cuisine. Thanks
to these low-priced exotic eats, the Pijp is the
best place in town for quality snacking treats,
the ingredients for which are mostly bought
fresh from the largest daily market in the
Netherlands: **Albert Cuypmarkt**, the hub
around which the Pijp turns. The market
attracts thousands of customers every day,
and spills merrily into the adjoining roads:
the junctions of Sweelinckstraat, Ferdinand
Bolstraat and 1e Van der Helststraat, north into
the lively Gerard Douplein, and south towards
Sarphatipark. The chaos will be heightened
over the next few years by the construction
of the Metro's controversial Noord–Zuidlijn,
whose route will run pretty much underneath
Ferdinand Bolstraat.

Still on Albert Cuypstraat, cross Ferdinand
Bolstraat and you'll find a cluster of fine, cheap
Chinese-Surinamese-Indonesian restaurants.
After passing the coach-party attraction of the
Van Moppes & Zoon Diamond Factory
(*see p161* **A girl's best friend**), diamond

He's bovine, fine, fine:
1e Van der Helststraat.

Albert Cuypmarkt. *See p113.*

turns to ruby around the corner along Ruysdaelkade, on the Pijp's very own mini red light district. Enjoy the sight of steaming, hooter-happy motorists caught in their own traffic gridlock while you lounge casually around an otherwise restful canal.

Close by, at Ruysdaelkade 149, is the **Jan Steen Café**. Steen (1625-79) was a barkeeper and painter of rowdy bar scenes, and this locals' hangout represents him well: the beer is cheap and the crowd is loud. And why view his subjects in the Rijksmuseum when you can see them – or descendants of them – in the flesh? The Pijp, of course, didn't even exist in Steen's day, but artists have since found it much to their liking. It's estimated that over 250 artists currently live in the area, and the current crop is gaining more status in a district where most streets are named after their illustrious forebears. Steen, Ferdinand Bol, Gerard Dou, and Frans Hal (whose street, Frans Halstraat is particularly pretty and rich with cafés and bars) are just a few of the artists honoured in this way.

Head back away from the water (and the red lights) a few blocks along 1e Jan Steenstraat, passing splendid bric-a-brac shop Nic Nic as you go, and you'll soon run across the Pijp's little green oasis: the grass-, pond- and duck-dappled **Sarphatipark**, designed and built as a mini Bois de Boulogne by the slightly mad genius Samuel Sarphati (1813-66). Aside from building the Amstel hotel and the Paleis voor Volksvlijt, Sarphati showed philanthropic tendencies as a baker of inexpensive bread for the masses, and as initiator of the city's rubbish collection. The centrepiece fountain comes complete with a statue of Sammy himself.

Edging along and beyond the south edge of Sarphatipark, Ceintuurbaan offers little of note for the visitor, with the exception of the buildings at Nos.251-5. Why? Well, there aren't many other houses in the city that incorporate giant ball-playing green gnomes with red hats in their wooden façades. The unique exterior of the **Gnome House** was inspired by the owner's name: Van Ballegooien translates (clumsily) as 'of the ball-throwing'. Around the corner from here, on the Amstel river, stands the city's archive, **Gemeentearchief Amsterdam** (Amsteldijk 67, 572 0202/ www.gemeentearchief.amsterdam.nl), where you can peruse the library or one of its excellent exhibitions (though bear in mind they plan to move in late 2004).

After a stroll through the park, wander north up 1e Van der Helststraat towards Gerard Douplein. This little square, with its cafés, coffeeshops, chip shops and authentic Italian ice-cream parlour, turns into one big terrace during the summer, and is hugely popular with

the locals. Bargain second-hand Euro knick-knacks can be bought at the nearby **Stichting Dodo** at No.21; trivia hounds should know that the Dutch – or rather their egg-eating animals – were responsible for this bird's extinction after colonising the island of Mauritius in 1598. A few streets away, overlooking Singelgracht from the decidedly unappealing Stadhouderskade, is the old **Heineken Brewery** (*see below*), now an interactive museum.

Heineken Experience

Stadhouderskade 78 (523 9666/www.heineken experience.com). Tram 6, 7, 10, 16, 24, 25. **Open** 10am-6pm (no entry after 5pm) Tue-Sun. **Admission** €10. **Credit** MC, V. **Map** p311 E5.
Once upon a time, this vast building was the main Heineken Brewery. We know this from the blurb by the entrance that hyperbolically states that the building is 'where Heineken was actually brewed'. In 1988, Heineken stopped brewing here, but kept the building open for endearingly unflashy tours: for a charitable donation of *f2* (less than €1 in today's money), you got an hour-long guided walk through the site, followed by as much Heineken as you could neck. It's safe to say that more punters were there for the free beer than the brewing education.

Unfortunately, Heineken have cottoned on to this, and recently renovated the huge building so tourists can enjoy the Heineken Experience. And while it's a lot flashier, it's a little less illuminating and a lot less fun. There's an interesting story to be told here, but this botched affair fails to narrate it. Plus points: the quasi-virtual reality ride through a brewery from the perspective of a Heineken bottle is easily the most ludicrous exhibit in Amsterdam, and you still get three free beers plus a surprise free gift (and not a bad one at that) at the end. But all in all, you're probably better off just going to a bar.

Eat, Drink, Shop

Restaurants

Glorious grub.

It's official: the term 'Dutch cuisine' is no longer a jolly knee-slapper. For sure, it's taken a few centuries, but Amsterdam has transcended its geographic setting on a land best suited to spuds, cabbages, carrots and cows. Many of the famed greenhouses now grow a stunning array of more delicate and often organic ingredients, and the city's well travelled chefs are taking full advantage of them. Of course, visitors should try the traditional grub (the carrots, in particular, taste all the better when you know that 17th-century Dutch royalists grew them for their orange colour). And you'd be silly missing out on such homegrown delicacies as herring, shrimp, cheese, asparagus or lamb. But rest assured, there's also a dizzying array of more global and globally-inspired options.

The local medieval diet began as a holy trinity of fish, gruel and beer (Yes, beer: would you want to drink the canal water?) The rich could always afford to indulge in the luxuries of taste – just look at those Golden Age paintings groaning with hogs and pheasants – but it was only with Napoleonic rule at the dawn of the 19th century that the middle-classes began to be seduced by innovations like herbs, spices

and the radical concept that over-cooking is bad culinary policy. Sadly, a century later a well-meaning section of the bourgeoisie developed simplified recipes for the working classes that instead proved popular with the next generation of the bourgeoisie; the subtleties of southern cuisine were thereby eradicated from the home and passed down via only a few of the town's top-end restaurants.

Happily, this culinary void allowed the spicy food of Indonesia to seduce the Dutch palate after World War II, when the former colony was granted independence and the Netherlands took in Indonesian immigrants. Take your pick from the various cheap Surinamese-Indonesian-Chinese snack bars or visit the purveyors of the 'rice table', where every known fish, meat and vegetable is worked into a filling extravaganza. Along with fondue – a 'national' dish stolen from the Swiss because its shared pot appealed to the Dutch sense of the democratic – Indo is the food of choice for any celebratory meals. Other waves of immigrants helped create a vortex of culinary diversity where traditional dishes from Asia, the Middle East and the Mediterranean are fully represented.

If you prefer to stroll and sniff out your own sustenance, here are a few tips. If you want to pick your own rocket salad, go to IJburg (*see p101*). Go to the Pijp if you crave econo-ethnic; cruise Haarlemmerstraat, Utrechtsestraat, Nieuwmarkt, the 'Nine Streets' area (the streets linking the canal ring between Leidsegracht and Raadhuisstraat) and Reguliersdwarsstraat if you want something posher; and only surrender to Leidseplein if you don't mind being overcharged for a cardboard steak or porridge-like pasta.

Quality snack opportunities (*see also p134* **Give grease a chance**) can be found in the form of fish (*see p128* **Tales of herring-do**), rolled 'pizzas' from Turkish bakeries, Dutch *broodjes* (sandwiches) from bakers and butchers, and nice and spicy Surinamese *broodjes* from 'Suri-Indo-Chin' snack bars. And you really should visit an **Albert Heijn** (*see p169*) grocery store to get an insight into Dutch eating habits and, more importantly, buy a box of *hagelslag* (flaked chocolate bread topping) for your emergency travel kit.

In addition to the restaurants listed below, there are many cafés and bars serving good – even inspired – food at fair prices; for these,

The best Restaurants

Blue Pepper
Designer Indo. See p122.

Hap Hmm
Affordable farmyard fare served with a grandmother's flair. See p123.

Helder
Clearly the best lunch in town. See p119.

Inez IPSC
A perfect fusion of food, décor and views. See p125.

Nam Kee
Cheap Chinese, divine oysters, central location. See p117.

Riaz
The Surinamese with the best rice and beans. See p133.

see p136. For gay-friendly and gay-owned restaurants and cafés, *see p208.* For more places to take the kids to, *see p186.*

LEISURELY DINING

Dining in Amsterdam is a laid-back affair, though the Dutch do tend to eat early: many kitchens close by 10pm. All bills should, by law, include 19 per cent tax and a 15 per cent service charge, though it's customary to leave between five and ten per cent if the service merits it. If you have any special requirements, like high chairs or disabled access, it's always best to phone the restaurant before setting out.

Since the euro was adopted in 2002, prices have shot up; prices listed here should only be used as a guideline. Go to www.dinnersite.nl/amsterdam or www.diningcity.com for online menus and, in some cases, reservations for a variety of restaurants. Local foodies weigh in at www.specialbite.nl to discuss the city's hotspots.

Fondue memory: **Café Bern**. *See p118.*

The Old Centre: Old Side

Cafés & snack stops

Brasserie Harkema

Nes 67 (428 2222/www.brasserieharkema.nl). Tram 4, 9, 14, 16, 24, 25. **Open** 1pm-1am Mon; 11am-1am Tue-Thur, Sun; 11am-3am Fri-Sat. *Kitchen* 1-11pm Mon; 11am-11pm Tue-Thur, Sun; 11am-1am Fri-Sat. **Main courses** *Lunch* €4-€6.50. *Dinner* €10-€16. **Credit** MC, V. **Map** p306 D3.

A brand new landmark has titillated the local scene with its shocking sense of designer space, excellent wines and a kitchen that stays open late pumping out reasonably priced French classics. It's hard to believe this was once a tobacco factory.

De Bakkerswinkel

Warmoesstraat 69 (489 8000/www.bakkerswinkel.nl). Tram 1, 2, 4, 5, 9, 13, 14, 16, 17, 24, 25. **Open** 8am-6pm Tue-Fri; 8am-5pm Sat; 10am-5pm Sun. **Main courses** €3-€11. **No credit cards**. **Map** p306 D3.

A bakery-tearoom where you can indulge in lovingly prepared, hearty sandwiches, soups and the most divine slabs of quiche you've ever had. For feeling civilised when the Red Lights get too bright. **Other locations**: Roelof Hartstraat 68 (662 3594).

De Jaren

Nieuwe Doelenstraat 20-22 (625 5771/www.cafe-de-jaren.nl). Tram 4, 9, 14, 16, 24, 25. **Open** *Café* 10am-1am Mon-Thur, Sun; 10am-2am Fri, Sat. *Restaurant* 5.30-10.30pm daily. **Main courses** *Café* €3-€5. **Restaurant** €11-€16. **Credit** V. **Map** p306 D3.

The grand De Jaren occupies a beautifully restored former bank, and has also absorbed the building's slightly sterile business feel. The food in the ground-floor café is OK; upstairs in the restaurant (with terrace) service can be painfully slow, but worth it.

Latei

Zeedijk 143 (625 7485). Tram 4, 9, 14, 16, 24, 25/Metro Nieuwmarkt. **Open** 8am-6pm Mon-Thur; 8am-10.30pm Fri-Sat; 11am-6pm Sun. **No credit cards**. **Map** p306 D2.

Packed with kitsch and funky Finnish wallpaper – all of which is for sale – this friendly little café serves up healthy juices and snacks all day long, plus vegetarian dinners based around couscous (after 6pm from Thursdays to Saturdays).

Tisfris

Sint Antoniesbreestraat 142 (622 0472/www.tisfris.nl). Tram 9, 14/Metro Nieuwmarkt. **Open** *Summer* 9am-8pm Mon-Sat; 10am-8pm Sun. *Winter* 9am-7pm Mon-Sat; 10am-7pm Sun. **Main courses** €4-€8. **No credit cards**. **Map** p307 E3.

A trendy but undaunting split-level café that's popular with a young and arty clientele. It's the place for a healthy breakfast or lunch (quiches, salads, soups), and the soundtrack is bang up to date.

Chinese & Japanese

Hayashi

Kloveniersburgwal 30 (320 2583). Tram 4, 9, 14, 16, 24, 25/Metro Nieuwmarkt. **Open** noon-8.30pm Mon-Wed, Sun; noon-9pm Thur-Sat. **Main courses** €5-€13. **No credit cards**. **Map** p306 D2.

This place sells the ingredients to make your own Japanese food, but why bother when both the sushi and the warm meals are such a deal?

Nam Kee

Zeedijk 111-13 (624 3470/www.namkee.nl). Tram 4, 9, 14, 16, 24, 25/Metro Nieuwmarkt. **Open** 11.30am-midnight daily. **Main courses** €6-€15. **No credit cards**. **Map** p306 D2.

Cheap and terrific food has earned this Chinese joint a devoted following: the oysters in black bean sauce have achieved classic status. If it's busy, try massive sister operation Nam Tin nearby (Jodenbreestraat 11, 428 8508) or, alternatively, neighbour New King (Zeedijk 115-17, 625 2180).

Eat, Drink, Shop

Come-to-bed look:
Supper Club. *See p121.*

See p121.

Oriental City

Oudezijds Voorburgwal 177-9 (626 8352). Tram 4, 9, 14, 16, 24, 25. **Open** 11.30am-10.30pm daily. **Main courses** €8-€23. **Credit** AmEx, DC, MC, V. **Map** p306 D2.
The views overlook Damstraat, the Royal Palace and the canals. And that's not even the best bit: they serve some of city's most authentic dim sum.

Dutch & Belgian

De Brakke Grond

Nes 43 (626 0044). Tram 4, 9, 14, 16, 24, 25. **Open** noon-1am Mon, Tue, Sun; 11am-1am Wed, Thur; 11am-2am Fri, Sat. **Main courses** €12.50-€18.50. **Credit** AmEx, DC, MC, V. **Map** p306 D3.

Though Chez Georges (Herenstraat 3, 626 3382) offers a more sophisticated take on Belgian cuisine, De Brakke Grond shows somewhat more sensitivity to those who have an abiding love for Belgian beers by recommending the best choice of beverage to accompany each dish. Great patio, too.

Café Bern

Nieuwmarkt 9 (622 0034). Tram 4, 9, 14, 16, 24, 25/Metro Nieuwmarkt. **Open** 4pm-1am daily. *Kitchen* 6-11pm daily. **Main courses** €9-€13. **No credit cards. Map** p306 D2.
Despite its Swiss origins, the Dutch adopted the cheese fondue as a 'national dish' long ago. Sample its culinary conviviality at this suitably cosy brown bar: the menu is easily affordable and the bar stocked with a variety of grease-cutting agents.

French & Mediterranean

Blauw aan de Wal
Oudezijds Achterburgwal 99 (330 2257). Tram 9, 16, 24. **Open** 6-11.30pm Mon-Sat. **Main courses** €23.50-€25. **Set menu** €37.50 (3 courses). **Credit** AmEx, MC, V. **Map** p306 D2.
Down an alley in the carnal heart of the Red Light District lies this oasis of reverence for the finer things in life. The hallmarks of this culinary landmark are tempting dishes (largely French in origin) and an inspired wine list.

Café Roux
The Grand, Oudezijds Voorburgwal 197 (555 3560/ www.thegrand.nl). Tram 4, 9, 14, 16, 24, 25. **Open** noon-3pm, 6.30-10.30pm daily. **Main courses** €22-€39. **Credit** AmEx, DC, MC, V. **Map** p306 D3.
The food here is identical to that of the Grand Hotel itself, and is overseen by Albert Roux. Despite Roux's stellar status, meals here are good value for money, especially at lunch and afternoon tea. The sommelier is excellent, too. *See also p49.*

Centra
Lange Niezel 29 (622 3050). Tram 4, 9, 14, 16, 24, 25. **Open** 1.30-11pm daily. **Main courses** €7-€22. No credit cards. **Map** p306 D2.
Good, wholesome, homely Spanish cooking with an unpretentious atmosphere to match. The tapas, lamb and fish dishes are all great.

1e Klas
Centraal Station, Line 2B (625 0131). Tram 1, 2, 4, 5, 9, 13, 16, 17, 24, 25. **Open** 8.30am-11pm daily. **Main courses** €15-€22. **Credit** AmEx, DC, MC, V. **Map** p306 D1.
This former brasserie for first-class commuters is now open to anyone who wants to kill some time in style – with a full meal or with snackier fare – while waiting for a train. The art nouveau interior will whisk you to the 1890s without stopping.

Excelsior
Hôtel de l'Europe, Nieuwe Doelenstraat 2-8 (531 1777/ www.leurope.nl). Tram 4, 9, 14, 16, 24, 25. **Open** 7-11am; 12.30-2.30pm, 7-10.30pm Mon-Fri; 7-10.30pm Sat, Sun. **Main courses** €35-€45. **Credit** AmEx, DC, MC, V. **Map** p306 D3.
Indulgently elegant with a watery view to swoon over, this purveyor of formality features the mainly classical French menu of Jean-Jacques Menanteau.

Vermeer
NH Barbizon Palace Hotel, Prins Hendrikkade 59-72 (556 4885/www.restaurantvermeer.nl). Tram 1, 2, 4, 5, 9, 13, 14, 16, 17, 24, 25. **Open** noon-3pm, 6-10pm Mon-Fri; 6-10pm Sat. **Main courses** €34-€39. **Credit** AmEx, DC, MC, V. **Map** p306 D2.
Set within the 17th-century wing of a hotel, Vermeer has so far netted two Michelin stars under young chef Pascal Jalaij, who balances texture and contrast in his French-leaning dishes. Say yes to excess by spending €100 to taste everything on the menu.

Indonesian & Thai

Raan Phad Thai
Kloveniersburgwal 18 (420 0665). Tram 4, 9, 14, 16, 24, 25/Metro Nieuwmarkt. **Open** 1-10pm daily. **Main courses** €10-€15. No credit cards. **Map** p306 D2.
A gaggle of friendly ladies cooks up a storm behind the counter, pumping out fish cakes and chicken pad thai to die for. Pretentious it ain't.

Thaise Snackbar Bird
Zeedijk 72 (snack bar 420 6289/restaurant 620 1442). Tram 1, 2, 4, 5, 9, 13, 14, 16, 17, 24, 25. **Open** *Snack bar* 3-10pm daily. *Restaurant* 5-10.30pm daily. **Main courses** €10-€17. **Credit** (restaurant only) AmEx, DC, MC, V. **Map** p306 D2.
The most authentic Thai place in town. It's also the most crowded – but worth waiting for, whether you pick tom yam soup or a full-blown meal. If you plan to linger, go to their restaurant opposite.

The Old Centre: New Side

Cafés & snack stops

Al's Plaice
Nieuwendijk 10 (427 4192). Tram 1, 2, 4, 5, 9, 14, 16, 17, 24, 25. **Open** noon-10pm daily. **Main courses** €3-€8. No credit cards. **Map** p306 D2.
Brits will spot the pun from 50 paces: yep, it's an English fish 'n' chip tent. Besides fish, there's a selection of pies, pasties, peas and downmarket tabloids.

Delores
Nieuwezijds Voorburgwal, opposite No.289 (626 5649). Tram 1, 2, 5. **Open** noon-10pm Mon-Wed, noon-1am Thur, noon-3am Fri-Sat. **Main courses** €7-€15. No credit cards. **Map** p306 C2.
Conveniently located in the hipster bar zone, this former police post is now a snack bar. Greasy fries have been replaced with healthful snacks and meals, harsh colours and neon forsaken for funky warmth.

Helder
Taksteeg 7 (320 4132). Tram 4, 9, 14, 16, 24, 25. **Open** noon-6pm Wed-Sun. **Set menu** *Lunch* €7.50. No credit cards. **Map** p306 D3.
The tiny 'Clear', in an alley off Kalverstraat, has an inspired chef who only uses the freshest ingredients in his salads, sandwiches, pastas and blinis. Groups of more than eight people can arrange a four-course dinner for €33 a head; there's a takeaway option, too.

Chinese & Japanese

Tokyo Café
Spui 15 (489 7918/www.tokyocafe.nl). Tram 1, 2, 4, 5, 9, 14, 16, 24, 25. **Open** 11am-11pm daily. **Main courses** €4-€20. **Set menu** *Lunch* €11-€14. *Dinner* €19-€26.50. **Credit** AmEx, DC, MC, V. **Map** p310 D4.

Eat, Drink, Shop

Thought to be haunted, this Jugendstil monument now hosts its umpteenth eatery in the form of a Japanese café, complete with lovely terrace, teppanyaki pyrotechnics and sushi and sashimi bar. Hopefully their high quality – and cocktail hour (from 5pm to 7pm) – will keep the ghosts at bay.

Dutch & Belgian

De Roode Leeuw

Damrak 93-4 (555 0666/www.restaurantderoode leeuw.com). Tram 4, 9, 14, 16, 24, 25. **Open** 9am-11.30pm daily. *Kitchen* 9am-10pm daily. **Main courses** *lunch* €4-€11; *dinner* €12-€20. **Credit** AmEx, DC, MC, V. **Map** p306 D2.
This brasserie, housed in the oldest covered terrace in Amsterdam, harks back to classier times. It specialises in Dutch fare – it does a 'Hotchpotch Festival' – and even has a selection of Dutch wine.

D'Vijff Vlieghen

Spuistraat 294-302 (624 8369/www.d-vijffvlieghen. com). Tram 1, 2, 5, 13, 17. **Open** 5.30-10pm daily. **Main courses** €22-€28. **Credit** AmEx, DC, MC, V. **Map** p306 C3.
'The Five Flies' tries for a Golden Age vibe – it even has a Rembrandt's Room, with etchings – but does rather better as a purveyor of kitsch. The food here is probably best described as poshed-up Dutch.

Global

Supper Club

Jonge Roelensteeg 21 (344 6400/www.supperclub.nl). Tram 1, 2, 5, 13, 17. **Open** 7.30pm-1am Mon-Thur, Sun; 7.30pm-3am Fri, Sat. **Set menu** €60 (5 courses). **Credit** AmEx, DC, MC, V. **Map** p306 D3.
With its white decor, beds for seating, irreverent food combos and acts, this arty joint is casual to the point of narcoleptic; the lounge is just as hip. Dining cruises began in October 2003; see the website for details.

Vegetarian

Green Planet

Spuistraat 122 (625 8280/www.greenplanet.nl). Tram 1, 2, 5, 13, 17. **Open** 5.30pm-midnight Mon-Sat; 5.30-10.30pm Sun. *Kitchen* 5.30-10.30pm daily. **Main courses** €13-€16. **No credit cards. Map** p306 C2.
The best veggie restaurant in town builds organic ingredients into soups, lasagne and stir fries. Finish with the house cognac and a slice of chocolate heaven.

Western Canal Belt

Cafés & snack stops

Foodism

Oude Leliestraat 8 (427 5103). Tram 1, 2, 5, 13, 17. **Open** 11am-10pm daily. **Main courses** €3-€10. **No credit cards. Map** p306 C3.

English and pan-Yugoslavian are the languages of choice here in this comfortable joint. Choose from appetising sandwiches, salads, pastas and hearty shakes; it's also good for takeaway.

Gary's Muffins

Prinsengracht 454 (420 1452/www.garys-muffins.nl). Tram 1, 2, 5. **Open** 9am-5pm Mon-Fri; 9am-6pm Sat, Sun. **Main courses** €2.30-€4.35. **No credit cards. Map** p310 C5.
One of the best snack stops in town, serving bagels, brownies and muffins. In good weather, sit outside by the canal and share your food with the sparrows. **Other locations:** Jodenbreestraat 15 (421 5930); Kinkerstraat 140 (412 3025); Raadhuisstraat 18 (638 0186).

Greenwoods

Singel 103 (623 7071). Tram 1, 2, 5. **Open** 9.30am-7pm daily. **Main courses** €3-€11.50. **No credit cards. Map** p306 C3.
Service at this teashop is friendly but can be slow. Everything is freshly made, though, so forgive them: cakes, scones and muffins are baked daily on the premises. In summer, sit on the terrace by the canal.

't Kuyltje

Gasthuismolensteeg 9 (620 1045). Tram 1, 2, 9, 24, 25. **Open** 7am-4pm Mon-Fri. **Sandwich** €1.70-€3.30. **No credit cards. Map** p306 C3.
The world of Dutch *broodjes* (sandwiches) has its greatest champion in this takeaway, one of the very few that still features home-made – as opposed to factory-prepared – meat and fish salads in your bun.

Loekie

Prinsengracht 705a (624 4230). Tram 1, 2, 5, 6, 7, 9. **Open** 9am-5pm Mon-Sat; 11am-5pm Sun. **Sandwich** €4-€8. **No credit cards. Map** p310 D4.
This *traiteur* ain't cheap, and you'll have to queue, but one of their French sticks with Italian fillings makes for a meal. Fine quiche and tapenade, too. **Other locations:** Utrechtsestraat 57 (624 3740).

Lust

Runstraat 13 (626 5791/www.lustamsterdam.nl). Tram 1, 2, 5. **Open** 9.30am-11pm daily. **Main courses** *Lunch* €4-€9. *Dinner* €8-€16. **Credit** MC, V. **Map** p310 C4.
Mmm, lust... Sadly, *lust* means 'appetite' in Dutch, though you'll soon have one at this slick trendy lunch venue. It serves a healthy and global array of lunches and – new for 2004 – dinners.

French & Mediterranean

Belhamel

Brouwersgracht 60 (622 1095/www.belhamel.nl). Tram 1, 2, 5, 13, 17. **Open** 6-10pm daily. **Main courses** €17-€21. **Credit** AmEx, MC, V. **Map** p306 C2.
The French-inspired cooking seems to have lost some zest in recent years, but the darkly evocative art nouveau interior makes it perfect if you crave some fin de siècle atmosphere.

Eat, Drink, Shop

Café Cox

*Marnixstraat 429 (620 7222). Tram 1, 2, 5, 6, 7,
10.* **Open** 5.30pm-1am Mon-Thur, Sun; 5.30pm-2am
Fri, Sat. *Kitchen* 5.30-10pm daily. **Main courses**
€13-€17. **Credit** AmEx, DC, MC. **Map** p310 C5.
Imaginative French and modern Dutch cooking in a
lively theatrical crowd environment. The prices are
eminently reasonable, especially given its proximity
to Leidseplein.

Christophe

*Leliegracht 46 (625 0807/www.christophe.nl). Tram
13, 14, 17.* **Open** 6.30-10.30pm Tue-Sat. **Main
courses** €25-€35. **Set menu** €51-€65. **Credit**
AmEx, DC, MC, V. **Map** p306 C3.
Hyper-posh and mega-expensive, Christophe serves
up inspired French cuisine with Algerian flourishes
to movers and shakers with ample expense
accounts. It straps a booster to your taste buds and
blasts you off to those Michelin stars.

Lof

*Haarlemmerstraat 62 (620 2997). Tram 1, 2, 4, 5,
9, 13, 16, 17, 24, 25.* **Open** 6.45pm-1am Tue-Sun.
Kitchen 7-11pm Tue-Sun. **Set menu** €35-€42.50.
No credit cards. **Map** p306 C2.
During the day, you could mistake Lof for a soup
kitchen. At night, though, it's a different story: the
lighting works miracles, as does the chef, who
improvises dishes drawn equally from Far Eastern
and Mediterranean repertoires.

Global

Blakes

Keizersgracht 384 (530 2010). Tram 1, 2, 5. **Open**
noon-2pm, 6.30-11pm Mon-Fri; 6.30-11pm Sat; 12.30-
2.30pm Sun. **Main courses** €24-€88. **Credit** AmEx,
DC, MC, V. **Map** p310 C4.
The critics were right to lavish praise on this elegant
restaurant in Anoushka Hempel's modish hotel (*see
p55*). The menu is East meets West, though leaning
noticeably towards Japan (as does the decor). Book
ahead, sit down and Zen out.

Indian

Himalaya

Haarlemmerstraat 11 (622 3776). Tram 1, 2, 5.
Open 5-11.30pm daily. **Main courses** €12-€22.
Credit AmEx, DC, MC, V. **Map** p306 C2.
Excellent Indian cuisine at nice prices. The staff can
make any dish more or less spicy than usual and the
service is invariably welcoming and friendly, match-
ing the wonderful art and designs on the walls.

Indonesian & Thai

Blue Pepper

Nassaukade 366 (489 7039). Tram 7, 10. **Open** 6-
10pm daily. **Main courses** €18-€23. **Credit** AmEx,
DC, MC, V. **Map** p310 C5.

A brand new Indonesian restaurant near Leidseplein
that combines a nearly unparalleled tantalising of
the tongue and a designer posh decor. Combine with
wine and you'll have the perfect romantic date.

Southern Canal Belt

Cafes & snack stops

Café Américain

Leidseplein 97 (556 3232). Tram 1, 2, 5, 6, 7, 10.
Open 7am-11pm Mon, Tue, Sun; 7am-midnight Wed-
Sat. **Main courses** €12-€18. **Credit** AmEx, DC,
MC, V. **Map** p310 C5.
Café Américain's glorious art deco interior – murals,
stained glass and marbled lampshades – is a listed
monument; Mata Hari is said to have held her wedding reception here. Now mostly tourists meet here
for a coffee and a pastry.

Chinese & Japanese

An

Weteringschans 76 (624 4672). Tram 6, 7, 10.
Open 6-10pm Tue-Sat. **Main courses** €17-€22.
No credit cards. **Map** p311 E5.
An serves some of the city's best Japanese cuisine –
sushi as well as starters and grilled dishes. Staff are
friendly and you'll have no problem getting comfy
in their oddly Mediterranean interior, but An is also
great for takeaway: weather permitting, make off
with your food to the Amstel river or Sarphati Park.

Japan Inn

*Leidsekruisstraat 4 (620 4989). Tram 1, 2, 5, 6, 7,
10.* **Open** 5-11.45pm daily. **Main courses** €8-€35.
Credit AmEx, DC, MC, V. **Map** p310 D5.
Japan Inn offers quality and quantity. The fresh sushi
and sashimi are served from the open kitchen in the
back; both are hits with students (who dig the quantity) and Japanese tourists (who come for the quality).

Shabu Shabu

Kerkstraat 47 (638 3774). Tram 1, 2, 5, 11.
Open noon-11pm daily. **Set menu** €16.50.
No credit cards. **Map** p310 C4.
'Shabu shabu' is the name of a warming winter dish.
This 'Japanese, Chinese and Korean good food grill
and fondue buffet restaurant' offers fondue pots supplied with a grill so you can also brown the meat,
fish and veg slivers. It's nothing fancy, but a good
spot for all-you-can-eat chaos.

Wagamama

*Max Euweplein 10 (528 7778/www.wagamama.
com). Tram 1, 2, 5, 6, 7, 10.* **Open** noon-10pm Mon-
Wed, Sun; noon-11pm Thur-Sat. **Main courses** €9-
€15. **Credit** AmEx, DC, MC, V. **Map** p310 D5.
Amsterdam's branch of the popular London fran-
chise of quick 'n' cheap noodle bars. You may not
fancy lingering in the minimalist canteen setting,
but you certainly can't fault the speedy service or
the tasty noodle dishes and soups.

Location, location, location…

The latest dining trend in Amsterdam is like the wind: it blows across town and stops in a field here or a squatted church there or an abandoned factory over yonder. It's all about local chefs taking their culinary show on the road to wow a lucky few in some obscure, temporary location. The roots of this trend undoubtedly lie in the fact that there are now fewer squats offering singular settings, so people have been encouraged to embrace a more guerrilla-like approach to alternative dining. Also, the squat cooks of yesterday are now the up-and-coming chefs of today who sometimes enjoy returning to their roots. Sadly, short-term visitors are very unlikely to get their finger on the ever-fleeting pulse.

Still, you can try your luck at **Buitenland** (www.buitenland.org), one of the few remaining 'free zones' on the outskirts of Amsterdam, and home to regular family affairs on summer weekends, when a changing roster of talented cooks provides the eats and a crew of DJs provides the

tunes. And if the weather permits, there's even a lake you can go swimming in.

A more trendy (and more legal) option is **Amsterdam Plage** (www.amsterdamplage.nl; pictured), which in the summer of 2003 concocted a restaurant out of tents and bean bag chairs – complete with sand to create a more beach-like vibe – to serve not only snacks but also a daily three-course Mediterranean menu prepared by two of Amsterdam's more acclaimed chefs. Its location in the Western Docklands is threatened but it aims to recreate its groovy summer paradise elsewhere if necessary.

For all of these, it's best going to the relevant website to get on the relevant mailing list; alternatively, log on to local hipster foodie website www.specialbite.com, since it does stay nicely abreast of the scene. Also check out *Shark* magazine (www.underwateramsterdam.com), which covers the ever-changing world of more traditional (read: vegetarian) squat dining.

Dutch & Belgian

Hap Hmm
1e Helmerstraat 33 (618 1884). Tram 1, 6, 7, 10.
Open 4.30-8pm Mon-Fri. **Main courses** €5-€10.
No credit cards. **Map** p310 C5.
Hungry but hard up? You need some of the Dutch grandma cooking served up in this canteen with a living-room feel. 'Bite Yum', near Leidseplein, will be pleased to pack your empty insides with meat and potatoes for a mere €5.

Fish

Le Pêcheur
Reguliersdwarsstraat 32 (624 3121). Tram 1, 2, 5.
Open noon-2.30pm, 6-10.30pm Mon-Fri; 6-10.30pm Sat. **Main courses** €21-€40. **Credit** AmEx, DC, MC, V. **Map** p310 D4.
Multilingual menus let you choose from à la carte or the menu of the day with minimal effort. The service is friendly but formal; the mussels and oysters are particularly excellent, as is the Golden Age patio.

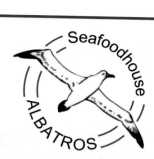

French & Mediterranean

La Rive

*Amstel Hotel, Prof Tulpplein 1 (520 3264/www.
amstelhotel.nl). Tram 6, 7, 10/Metro Weesperplein.*
Open 7-10.30am, noon-2pm, 6.30-10.30pm Mon-Fri;
7am-12.30pm, 6.30-10.30pm Sat; 7am-12.30pm Sun.
Main courses €33-€50. **Credit** AmEx, DC, MC, V.
Map p311 F4.
Holland's most famous chef Robert Kranenborg left
this elegant eaterie to open (and bankrupt) Vossius,
but his successor and rising star Edwin Kats still
produces superb regional French cuisine.

Segugio

*Utrechtsestraat 96a (330 1503/www.segugio.nl).
Tram 4, 6, 7, 10.* **Open** 6-11pm Mon-Sat. **Main
courses** €22-€28. **Set menu** (5 courses) €49.50.
Credit AmEx, MC, V. **Map** p311 E4.
Best. Risotto. Ever. In fact, this Italian has all the
ingredients to make the perfect lingering meal for
foodies and romantics alike. Bellissima!

Global

Eat at Jo's

*Marnixstraat 409 (638 3336). Tram 1, 2, 5, 6, 7,
10.* **Open** 12-9pm Wed-Sun. **Main courses** €6.50-
€14. **No credit cards**. **Map** p310 C5.
Each day brings a different fish, meat and vegetarian dish to the menu of this cheap and tasty international kitchen. Starspotters take note: whichever
act is booked to play at the Melkweg (*see p213 and
p225*) may very well chow down here beforehand.

Herengracht

*Herengracht 435 (616 2482/www.deherengracht.nl).
Tram 1, 2, 5.* **Open** noon-1am Mon-Thur, Sun; noon-
3am Fri, Sat. Kitchen noon-10.30pm Mon-Thur, Sun;
noon-10.30pm Fri, Sat. **Main courses** Lunch €4-€8.
Dinner €16-€20. **Credit** AmEx, MC, V. **Map** p310 D4.
Waving a 'food/drink/art' banner, this new lounge
doesn't rely on its trendy brown-orange interior to
attract the punters: both the service and the food –
call it sassy international – are excellent. There's a
nice canalside patio in the summer, too.

Inez IPSC

*Amstel 2 (639 2899/www.inezipsc.com). Tram 4,
9.* **Open** 7pm-1am Tue-Thur; 7pm-3am Fri, Sat.
Kitchen 7-10.30pm Tue-Sat. **Main courses** €10-
€15. **Credit** MC, V. **Map** p307 E3.
Blessed with fantastic urban views and snappy
decor (from designer Peter Giele of the late, lamented Roxy), Inez is a hotspot of the moneyed clubby and artistic set. The food matches the setting:
flavour and presentation rise to giddy heights.

Moko

*Amstelveld 12 (626 1199/www.goodfoodgroup.nl).
Tram 16, 24, 25.* **Open** 11.30am-1am Mon-Thur,
Sun; 11.30am-2am Fri, Sat. Kitchen noon-4pm, 6-
11pm daily. **Main courses** €16-€18. **Credit** AmEx,
DC, MC, V. **Map** p311 E4.

With one of the most scenic terraces in Amsterdam,
this wooden church – once the stable for Napoleon's
horses – is a lovely place at which to munch posh
sandwiches on a sunny day. Evenings see it transform into a highly regarded purveyor of fusion food.

Noa

*Leidsegracht 84 (626 0802/www.withnoa.com). Tram
1, 2, 5.* **Open** 6pm-midnight Tue, Wed; 6pm-1am Thur,
Fri; 1pm-1am Sat; 1pm-midnight Sun. **Main courses**
€14-€16. **Credit** AmEx, MC, V. **Map** p310 C4.
This lounge is geared towards the international jet-
set and their aspiring disciples. Beyond an excellent
complement of beers, wines and champagnes, you
can enjoy pan-Asian cooking (of the noodly persuasion) from their open kitchen while lounging on comfortable couches. No bookings.

Pygma-Lion

*Nieuwe Spiegelstraat 5a (420 7022/www.pygma-
lion. com). Tram 1, 2, 5.* **Open** 11am-11pm Tue-Sun.
Kitchen 11am-5pm, 6-10pm Tue-Sun. **Main courses**
lunch €5-€9; *dinner* €18-€21. **Credit** AmEX, MC, V.
Map p310 D4.
This South African restaurant is open all day for
sandwiches, but it's only at dinner that the zebra,
the croc' and other oddities get thrown in the pot.
History and geography have made this country's
food an exotic blend of African, Asian and Dutch
taste-bud sensibilities. Quite pricey but nice.

Indonesian & Thai

Bojo

*Lange Leidsedwarsstraat 51 (622 7434). Tram 1,
2, 5.* **Open** 5pm-2am Mon-Thur, Sun; 5pm-4am Fri,
Sat. **Main courses** €8-€12. **Credit** AmEx, MC, V.
Map p310 C5.
Bojo is a fine Indo-eaterie, and one of the few places
– regardless of type – that stays open into the small
hours. The price is right and the portions are large
enough to glue your insides together before or after
an evening of excess. Its sister operation at No.49
compensates for its slightly earlier closing time with
the serving of alcohol.

Puri Mas

*Lange Leidsedwarsstraat 37-41 (627 7627/www.
puri mas.nl). Tram 1, 2, 5.* **Open** 5-11pm daily.
Main courses €13-€23. **Credit** AmEx, DC, MC, V.
Map p310 C5.
Puri Mas has impeccable service and fine rice tables
(which they also offer to solo diners, unlike most
places where there's a two-diner minimum).

Tempo Doeloe

*Utrechtsestraat 75 (625 6718/www.tempodoeloe
restaurant.nl). Tram 4, 6, 7, 10.* **Open** 6-11.30pm
daily. **Main courses** €18-€44. **Credit** AmEx, DC,
MC, V. **Map** p311 E4.
This cosy and rather classy Indonesian restaurant
(heck, it even has white linen) is widely thought of
as one of the city's best and spiciest purveyors of
rice table, and not without good reason. Book ahead.

Eat, Drink, Shop

Tujuh Maret

Utrechtsestraat 73 (427 9865). Tram 4, 6, 7, 10.
Open noon-11pm Mon-Sat; 5-11pm Sun. **Main courses** €12-€23. **Credit** MC, V. **Map** p311 E4.
A relaxed and rattan-chaired Indo gaff whose champions claim is superior to posher neighbour Tempo Doeloe (*see above*). Tujuh Maret also does takeaway.

South American

Los Pilones

Kerkstraat 63 (320 4651/www.lospilones.nl). Tram 1, 2, 5, 11. **Open** 4pm-midnight Tue-Thur, Sun; 4pm-1am Fri, Sat. **Main courses** €10-€12.50. **Credit** AmEx, DC, MC, V. **Map** p310 D4.
A splendid Mexican cantina with an anarchic bent, Los Pilones is run by two young and friendly Mexican brothers; one of them does the cooking, so expect authentic grub rather than standard Tex-Mex fare. There are 35 – yes, 35 – tequilas on offer.

Jodenbuurt, the Plantage & the Oost

Global

De Kas

Kamerlingh Onneslaan 3 (462 4562/www.restaurant dekas.nl). Tram 9/bus 59, 69. **Open** noon-2pm, 6.30-10pm Mon-Fri; 6.30-10pm Sat. **Set menu** *Lunch* €31 (4 courses). *Dinner* €42 (5 courses). **Credit** AmEx, DC, MC, V.
In Frankendael Park, way out east, is a renovated 1926 greenhouse. It's now a posh and peaceful restaurant that inspires much fevered talk among local foodies. Its international menu changes daily based on what was harvested earlier in the day.

The Waterfront

French & Mediterranean

Wilhelmina-Dok

Noordwal 1 (632 3701/www.wilhelminadok.nl). Restaurant boat leaves from Pier 9, or take ferry from Pier 8 to Amsterdam Noord. **Open** noon-midnight Mon-Thur, Sun; noon-1am Fri, Sat. *Kitchen* 6-10pm daily. **Main courses** €13-€18. **Credit** AmEx, MC, V.
Through the large windows of this cubic building you get great views of the Eastern Docklands. Come for soup and sandwiches by day and a daily menu of Mediterranean dishes by night. DJs, terrace and open air cinema spice it up in summer.

Global

Kilimanjaro

Rapenburgerplein 6 (622 3485). Bus 22. **Open** 5-10pm Tue-Sun. **Main courses** €10-€18. **Credit** AmEx, MC, DC, V. **Map** p307 F2. **Map** p307 F2.

This relaxed and friendly pan-African eaterie offers an assortment of traditional recipes from Senegal, the Ivory Coast, Tanzania and Ethiopia that can be washed down with the fruitiest of cocktails and the strongest of beers.

Odessa

Veemkade 259 (419 3010/www.de-odessa.nl). Bus 28, 39. **Open** *Apr-Nov* noon-1am Mon-Thur, Sun; noon-3am Fri, Sat. *Dec-Mar* 4pm-1am Mon-Thur, Sun; 4pm-3am Fri, Sat. *Kitchen* 6-9.30pm Mon-Thur, Sun; 6-11pm Fri, Sat. **Main courses** €15-€22; **Set menu** €27.50. **Credit** AmEx, MC, V.
Hipsters come for the fusion food and the revamped interior on this Ukrainian fishing boat. The vibe is '70s Bond filtered through a modern lounge sensibility. On warmer nights, dine on the funkily lit deck; at weekends, DJs spin from 10pm.

Panama

Oostelijke Handelskade 4 (311 8686/www.panama. nl). Bus 32, 39. **Open** 4pm-1am Wed, Thur, Sun; 4pm-3am Fri, Sat. *Kitchen* 4-10.30pm Wed, Thur, Sun; 4-10.30pm Fri, Sat. **Main courses** €18-€21. **Set menu** €44.50 (3 courses with club entrance). **Credit** AmEx, DC, MC, V.
Panama's 19th-century industrial architecture has recently been updated with modern furnishings. It serves globally inspired dishes, with an emphasis on fish – not amazing food-wise but handy if you came to experience the nostalgia-free programming in their club (*see p214*).

The Jordaan

Cafés & snack stops

De Frans Kaasmakers Abraham Keff

Marnixstraat 192 (626 2210). Tram 3, 10. **Open** 10am-6pm Tue-Thur; 9am-6pm Fri; 9am-5pm Sat. **No credit cards**. **Map** p305 B3.
This charming shop offers the best French farmer-produced cheeses (st marcellin!) with wine and bread to match. A pre-picnic paradise.

Small World Catering

Binnen Oranjestraat 14 (420 2774). **Open** 10.30am-8pm Tue-Sat; noon-8pm Sunday. **Main courses** €6-€10. **No credit cards**. **Map** p305 B2.
The home base for this catering company is a tiny deli, which feels like the kitchen of the lovely proprietor. Besides superlative coffee and fresh juices, enjoy salads, lasagne and quiches.

Dutch & Belgian

Amsterdam

Watertorenplein 6 (682 2666/www.cradam.nl). Tram 10. **Open** 11am-midnight Mon-Thur, Sun; 11am-1am Fri, Sat. *Kitchen* 11.30am-10.30pm Mon-Thur, Sun; 11.30am-11.30pm Fri, Sat. **Main courses** €10-€21. **Credit** AmEx, DC, MC, V.

Eat, Drink, Shop

Tales of herring-do

You really must, yes, you really *must* try raw herring. Especially between May and July when the *nieuw* (new) catch hits the stands. These new arrivals don't need any extra garnish like onions and pickles, since their flesh is at its sweetest – thanks to the high fat content that the herring was planning to burn off in the arduous business of breeding. There's a quality fish stall or store around most corners, but here are some of the best purveyors of not only herring but also smoked eel and other – perhaps less controversial – fishes for the sandwich. And they're as cheap as chips (or at least a lot cheaper than sushi).

Altena
stall at Stadhouderskade/Jan Luijkenstraat, the Museum Quarter. Tram 2, 5, 6, 7, 10.

Huijsman
Zeedijk 129, Old Centre: New Side (624 2070). Tram 4, 9, 14, 24, 25/Metro Niewmarkt.

Kromhout
stall at Singel/Raadhuisstraat, Old Centre: New Side. Tram 13, 14, 17.

Volendammer Viswinkel
1e Van der Helststraat 60, the Pijp (676 0394). Tram 6, 7, 10.

This spacious monument to industry just west of the Jordaan pumped water from the coast's dunes for around a century. Now it pumps out honest Dutch and French dishes – from *krokets* to caviar – under a mammoth ceiling and floodlighting rescued from the old Ajax stadium. It's a truly unique – and child-friendly – experience.

Groene Lantaarn
Bloemgracht 47 (620 2088/www.fondue.nl). Tram 10, 13, 17. **Open** 6-9pm Thur-Sun. **Main courses** €14-€24. **Credit** MC, V. **Map** p305 B3.
For posh fondues, try the old-world vibe of Groene Lantaarn. Bread comes pre-chunked, the desserts are suitably and deliciously decadent, and the menu even stretches out globally to include dim sum.

Moeder's Pot
Vinkenstraat 119 (623 7643). Tram 3, 10. **Open** 5-9.30pm Mon-Sat. **Main courses** €4-€11. **No credit cards. Map** p305 B1.

Mother's Pot serves up – you guessed it – the sort of simple and honest fare a Dutchman would expect to get from his mum. The decor is woody farmer's kitsch, and the grub's not bad at all.

French & Mediterranean

Balthazar's Keuken
Elandsgracht 108 (420 21145). Tram 7, 10. **Open** 6-11pm Wed-Fri. **Set menu** €23.50. **Credit** AmEx, DC, MC, V. **Map** p310 C4.
This tiny favourite is always packed because its set menu (meat or fish) invariably induces culinary delight – as do the specially selected wines. So book ahead to be rewarded.

Bordewijk
Noordermarkt 7 (624 3899). Tram 3. **Open** 6.30-10.30pm Tue-Sun. **Set menu** €37-€49. **Credit** AmEx, DC, MC, V. **Map** p305 B2.

Ideal for sampling some of the city's finest original food and palate-tingling wines in a designery interior. The service and atmosphere are both relaxed, and Bordewijk has a very reliable kitchen. A perfectly balanced restaurant.

Cinema Paradiso
Westerstraat 186 (623 7344). Tram 10. **Open** 6-11pm Tue-Sun. **Main courses** €14-€20. **Credit** AmEx, DC, V. **Map** p305 B2.
This Italian purveyor of fine pizza and even finer antipasti is agreeably situated in a former cinema. There's a bit of an echo, and their no-reservation policy sometimes makes for a long wait by the bar.

Duende
Lindengracht 62 (420 6692/www.cafeduende.nl). Tram 3, 10. **Open** 4pm-1am Mon-Thur, Sun; 4pm-3am Fri, Sat. **Average** *Tapas* €2.50-€8.50. **No credit cards**. **Map** p305 B2.
Get a taste of Andalusia with the good tapas at Duende. Place your order at the bar and prepare to share your table with an amorous couple or a flamenco dancer who might just offer you free lessons. Performances of live flamenco every Saturday night (11pm) and Sunday afternoon (4pm).

Tapasbar a la Plancha
1e Looiersdwarsstraat 15 (420 3633). Tram 1, 2, 5, 7, 10. **Open** 2pm-1am Tue-Thur, Sun; 2pm-3am Fri, Sat. **Main courses** €3-€12. **Credit** MC, V. **Map** p310 C4.
The bull's head barely fits into this tiny spot, but the extended opening hours allow you more than enough time to squeeze in and experience the delicious flavours of some of the best tapas in town. Bring your Spanish phrasebook.

Toscanini
Lindengracht 75 (623 2813). Tram 3, 10. **Open** 6-10.30pm daily. **Main courses** €16-€18. **Credit** AmEx, DC, MC, V. **Map** p305 B2.
The authentic and invariably excellent Italian food at this bustling spot is prepared in an open kitchen. Don't go expecting pizza, but do make sure that you book early (from around 3pm) if you want to be sure of getting a table.

Yam-Yam
Frederik Hendrikstraat 90 (681 5097/www.yam yam.nl). Tram 3. **Open** 6-10pm Tue-Sun. **Main courses** €7-€15. **No credit cards**. **Map** p305 A3.
Unparalleled and shockingly inexpensive pastas and pizzas in a hip and casual atmosphere: no wonder Yam-Yam is a favourite of clubbers and locals alike. Well worth the trip.

Global

Nomads
Rozengracht 133 (344 6401/www.restaurant nomads.nl). Tram 13, 14, 17. **Open** 7pm-1am Tue-Thur, Sun; 7pm-3am Fri, Sat. **Set menu** €42.50. **Credit** AmEx, DC, MC, V. **Map** p305 B3.

With a wonderfully evocative decor of curtains, mosaics and marbles, Nomads (from the people who brought you Supper Club; *see p121*) has taken lounging back to its oriental roots. Diners sit on cushions, from where they enjoy masses of Middle Eastern delights (the mezzes range from €3 to €7.50). After 11pm, it's time for drinking, dancing or some more lounging.

Semhar
Marnixstraat 259-261 (638 1634). Tram 10. **Open** 4-10pm daily. **Main courses** €10.50-€14. **Credit** MC, V. **Map** p305 B3.
A great spot with a terrace to sample the injera pancake-based food of Ethiopia (best washed down with a calabash of beer) after a day of leisurely Jordaan wandering. Be warned: the veggie-friendly food calls for restraint since you'll want to keep eating regardless of how full you feel.

Indian

Balraj
Haarlemmerdijk 28 (625 1428). Tram 3. **Open** 5-11pm daily. **Main courses** €9-€13. **No credit cards**. **Map** p305 B2.
A small, cosy eating house with several decades of experience under its belt. The food is reasonably priced and particularly well done, with vegetarians generously catered for.

Vegetarian

De Vliegende Schotel
Nieuwe Leliestraat 162 (625 2041). Tram 13, 14, 17. **Open** 4-10.45pm daily. **Main courses** €8.50-€11.50. **Credit** AmEX, MC, V. **Map** p305 B3.
The funky and venerable 'Flying Saucer' serves up a splendid array of dishes, buffet style. If they are booked, the nearby and kitschy De Bolhoed (Prinsengracht 60-62, 626 1803) offers hearty vegan dishes as a canal-side consolation prize.

The Museum Quarter, Vondelpark & the South

Café & snack stops

Bagels & Beans
Van Baerlestraat 40 (675 7050/www.bagelsbeans.nl). Tram 3, 5, 12. **Open** 8.30am-6pm Mon-Wed, Fri; 8.30am-9pm Thur; 9.30am-6pm Sat; 10am-6pm Sun. **Main courses** €3-€5. **Credit** AmEx, DC, MC, V. **Map** p311 E6.
B&B has consolidated its position in Amsterdam, thanks in part to this success story with its astonishingly peaceful back patio. Perfect for an econo-breakfast, lunch or snack; sun-dried tomatoes are employed with particular skill.
Other locations: Ferdinand Bolstraat 70 (672 1610); Keizersgracht 504 (330 5508).

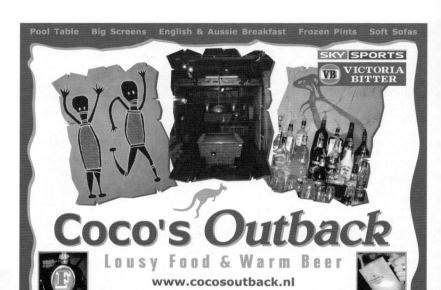

Fish

Vis aan de Schelde

Scheldeplein 4 (675 1583/www.visaandeschelde.nl).
Tram 5, 25. **Open** noon-2.30pm, 5.30-11pm Mon-Fri;
5.30-11pm Sat. **Main courses** €23.50-€38. **Credit**
AmEx, DC, MC, V.
This eaterie out near the RAI convention centre has
become a fish temple for the connoisseur. The menu
sees classy French favourites colliding with more
exotic dishes such as Thai fish fondue.

French & Mediterranean

Eetcafé I Kriti

Balthasar Floriszstraat 3 (664 1445). Tram 3, 5, 12,
16. **Open** 5pm-1am Mon-Thur, Sun; 5pm-3am Fri,
Sat. **Main courses** €11-€16. **Credit** DC, V.
Eat and party Greek style in this superior evocation
of Crete, where a standard choice of dishes is lovingly prepared. Bouzouki-picking legends drop in
on occasion and pump up the frenzied atmosphere,
further boosted by plate-lobbing antics.

Le Garage

Ruysdaelstraat 54-6 (679 7176/www.diningcity.com/
ams). Tram 3, 5, 6, 12, 16. **Open** noon-2pm, 6-11pm
Mon-Fri; 6-11pm Sat, Sun. **Set menu** €39-€48.50.
Credit AmEx, DC, MC, V. **Map** p311 E6.
Don your glad rags to blend in at this fashionable
brasserie, which is great for emptying your wallet
while watching a selection of Dutch glitterati do
exactly the same. The authentic French regional cuisine – and 'worldly' versions thereof – is pretty good.
They also have a more loungy sister establishment,
En Pluche (Ruysdaelstraat 48, 471 4695), next door:
it serves posh and global 'street food'.

Pulpo

Willemsparkweg 87 (676 0700). Tram 2.
Open noon-10pm Mon-Sat. **Main courses** €12-€17.
Set menu €25. **Credit** AmEx, DC, MC, V.
Map p310 C6.

The name of the game here is to serve original yet
nicely priced Mediterranean food – including a killer
polenta and a mighty fine selection of wines to wash
it down with – to diners who are looking for trendy
surrounds, complete with a hipster lounge soundtrack and shaggy walls.

Global

CoBrA Café

Hobbemastraat 18 (470 0111/0900 1232 6272
premium rate/www.cobracafe.com). Tram 3, 5, 12.
Open 10am-9pm Mon, Tue; 10am-midnight Wed-
Sun. *Kitchen* 10am-9pm daily. **Main courses** €12-
€19. **Credit** MC, V. **Map** p310 D6.
Named, with unintentional irony, after an art movement that worshipped spontaneity, the CoBrA Café
is a tight, hi-tech ship anchored in Museumplein. Pop
in for salads, sushi, yoghurt and snacks by day, or
indulge in the highly regarded menu by night.

Vakzuid

Olympisch Stadion 35 (570 8410/www.vakzuid.nl).
Tram 16, 24/bus 15, 63. **Open** 10am-1am Mon-
Thur; 10am-3am Fri, 4pm-3am Sat; 3pm-10pm Sun.
Kitchen noon-2.30pm, 6-10.30pm daily. **Main
courses** €14-€27. **Credit** AmEx, DC, MC, V.
Dubbed 'Fuck Zuid' by waggish locals, this lounge
restaurant, located in the revamped 1928 Olympic
Stadium, is hugely popular with working trendies.
With modish cons and views over the tracks, it's a
stunning site; hopefully the food – call it Med-
Oriental – will match its standards. *See also p109.*

Indonesian & Thai

Djago

Scheldeplein 18 (664 2013). Tram 4. **Open** 5-9.30pm
Mon-Fri, Sun. **Main courses** €7-€23. **Credit**
AmEx, DC, MC, V.
Djago's West Javanese eats are praised to the hilt by
Indo-obsessives. Set near the RAI convention cen-
tre, it's a bit out of the way, but worth the trip south.

Small World Catering. *See p127.*

noodle bar | **informal, fun and friendly atmosphere**

wagamama offer delicious noodles, fabulous rice dishes, freshly squeezed juices, wine, sake and japanese beers

wagamama amsterdam **max euweplein** 10

for menu / locations and chatroom visit: www.wagamama.com
uk | dublin | amsterdam | sydney

wagamama and positive eating positive living are registered trade marks of wagamama ltd

wagamama

Pitch camp at **De Taart van m'n Tante**.

De Orient

Van Baerlestraat 21 (673 4958). Tram 2, 3, 5, 12.
Open 5-10pm daily. **Main courses** €12.25-€19.
Credit AmEx, DC, MC, V. **Map** p310 C6.
An Indonesian restaurant with a folklore-decor and a large, vegetarian-friendly menu. 50 years of experience have taught them to mellow the spices, so this makes for a gentler introduction to the rice table.

Sama Sebo

PC Hooftstraat 27 (662 8146). Tram 2, 3, 5, 12.
Open noon-2pm, 6-10pm Mon-Sat. **Set menu** €25 (16 dishes). **Credit** AmEx, DC, MC, V. **Map** p310 D5.
Mellow out at this comfortable and spacious Indo restaurant with a brown café vibe. There's no minimum charge, so even if you just fancy a coffee and a snack between museums, it's a good bet.

Middle Eastern

Paloma Blanca

JP Heyestraat 145 (612 6485). Tram 7. **Open** 6-10pm Mon-Wed; 5pm-midnight Fri-Sun. **Main courses** €7-15. **No credit cards.**
Fans of North African cuisine: don't miss this slightly out-of-the-way treasure. The acclaim is universal: in simple surrounds (and with no alcohol), diners can scale the heights of Moroccan couscous-ology.

South American

Riaz

Bilderdijkstraat 193 (683 6453). Tram 3, 7, 12, 17.
Open noon-9pm Mon-Fri; 2-9pm Sun. **Main courses** €5-€14. **No credit cards. Map** p309 B5.

Amsterdam's finest Surinamese restaurant is where Ruud Gullit scores his rotis when he's in town. The Indian edge to the menu sees the inclusion of some curries. There's a takeaway service, too.

The Pijp

Cafés & snack stops

De Taart van m'n Tante

Ferdinand Bolstraat 10 (776 4600/www.detaart.nl).
Tram 16, 24, 25. **Open** Tue-Sat 10am-6pm; Sun noon-6pm. **Average** €2.20-€5. **No credit cards. Map** p311 E6.
'My Aunt's Tart' started life as a purveyor of over-the-top cakes (which they still make) before becoming the campest tea-room in town. In a glowing pink space filled with mismatched furniture, it's gay-friendly (note the Tom of Finland cake) and child-friendly.

Soepwinkel

1e Sweelinckstraat 19F (673 2293/www.soepwinkel.nl).
Tram 16, 24, 25. **Open** 11am-9pm Mon-Fri; 11am-6pm Sat, Sun. **Average** €3.50-€9. **No credit cards. Map** p311 F5.
'The Soup Shop' specialises in – yes – soup. On any given day, there are nine globe-embracing recipes, including veggie versions.

Chinese & Japanese

Albine

Albert Cuypstraat 69 (675 5135). Tram 16, 24, 25.
Open 10.30am-10pm Tue-Sun. **Main courses** €4-€12. **No credit cards. Map** p311 E6.

Give grease a chance

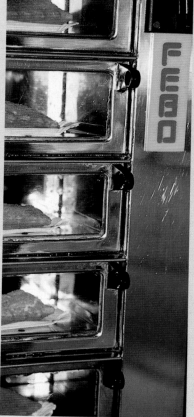

The correct local terminology for a greasy snack – *vette hap* – can be translated as 'fat bite', which says a lot for the refreshing honesty of the Dutch when it comes to the less healthy spectrum of belly-ballast foodstuffs. And honestly, why go to a multinational burger merchant in Amsterdam when there's such a rich local grease tradition to indulge in? After all, variety is not only the spice but the lubricant of life.

THE BEST CHIPS

Vleminckx *Voetboogsteeg 31, Old Centre: New Side (no phone). Tram 1, 2, 5.* **Open** 11am-6pm Mon-Sat; noon-5.30pm Sun. **No credit cards. Map** p310 D4.
Chunky Belgian ('Vlaamse') potatoey goodness served with your pick of toppings. Go for *oorlog* ('war'): chips with mayo, spicy peanut sauce and onions.

THE BEST 'BALL'

Het Koffiekeldertje *Frederiksplein 4, Southern Canal Belt (626 3424). Tram 4, 6, 7, 10.* **Open** 9.30am-5.30pm Mon-Fri. **No credit cards. Map** p311 F4.
A large melts-in-your-mouth ground beef sphere served on a bun and with a smile in a charming basement café.

THE BEST PANCAKE

Pancake Bakery *Prinsengracht 191, the Jordaan (625 1333/www.pancake.nl). Tram 13, 17.* **Open** noon-9.30pm daily. **Main courses** €5-€10. **Credit** AmEx, MC, V. **Map** p306 C2.
Dutch recipes stress the importance of sheer density so that the pancake can hold a dense array of topping choices that span from sweet to hardcore savouries like bacon and cheese. Yup, you can indeed double your pleasure at this quaint canal-side restaurant.

One in a whole row of cheap Suri-Chin-Indo spots, Albine – where a Chinese influence predominates – gets top marks for its service and its solid vegetarian or meat meals of roti, rice or noodles.

Yamazato
Okura Hotel, Ferdinand Bolstraat 333 (678 8351/ www.okura.nl). Tram 12, 25. **Open** 7.30-9.30am, noon-2pm, 6-9.30pm daily. **Main courses** €25-€37. **Credit** AmEx, DC, MC, V.
If you want class, head out here and surrender to the charming kimono-clad staff, the too-neat-to-eat presentation and the restful views over a fishpond. Lunch is priced more attractively than dinner.

Zen
Frans Halsstraat 38 (627 0607). Tram 16, 24, 25. **Open** noon-8pm Tue-Sat. **Main courses** €7-€19. **No credit cards. Map** p311 E6.
This Japanese delicatessen with limited seating lives up to its name: calm, friendly and delicious.

French & Mediterranean

L'Angoletto
Hemonystraat 18 (676 4182). Tram 3, 4, 6, 7, 10. **Open** 6-11pm Mon-Fri, Sun. **Main courses** €5-€9. **Credit** V. **Map** p311 F5.

THE BEST STEAK

Eetcafé Loetje *Johannes Vermeerstraat 52, Museum District (662 8173). Tram 16.* **Open** 11am-1am Mon-Fri; 5.30pm-1am Sat. *Kitchen* 11am-10pm Mon-Fri; 6-10pm Sat. **Main courses** €5-€16. **No credit cards. Map** p310 D6.

After a day's tourism there's nothing better than a fillet of beef steak served with fries and mayo (and maybe salad). A fine antidote to the rarefied air you may have inhaled while gazing at a Rembrandt.

THE BEST KROKET

Van Dobben *Korte Reguliersdwarsstraat 5-9, Southern Canal Belt (624 4200). Tram 4, 9, 16, 24, 25.* **Open** 9.30am-1am Mon-Thur, 9.30am-2am Fri-Sat, 11.30am-8pm Sun. **Main courses** €2-€8. **No credit cards. Map** p311 E4.

A *kroket* is a version of a croquette: a mélange of meat and potato with a crusty, deep-fried skin best served on a bun with lotsa hot mustard. And while this 1945-vintage late-nighter is the uncontested champion, you can also find a more refined shrimp *kroket* nearby at famous bakery Holtkamp (Vijzelgracht 15, 624 8757).

THE BEST ALL-ROUND GREASE MERCHANT

Febo *Venues across town (www.febo.nl).* Grease comes of space age at the Febo (pronounced 'Fay-bo') *automaats*: you put your change into a glowing hole in the wall and, in exchange, get a dollop of grease in the form of a hot(-ish) hamburger, *kroket*, *bamibal* (a deep-fried noodle-y ball of vague Indonesian origin) or a *kaas soufflé* (a cheese treat that's surprisingly tasty if eaten when still hot).

The most authentic trattoria in town has a Fellini-esque edge. It gets very busy, but the food – often hyped as the best pizza and pasta in Amsterdam – makes the wait for a table worthwhile.

District V

Van der Helstplein 17 (770 0884). Tram 12, 25. **Open** 6pm-1am daily. *Kitchen* 6-10.30pm daily. **Set menu** €28.50 (3 courses). **No credit cards. Map** p311 F6.

District V not only offers a divine and econo French-inspired, daily menu, but also sells the locally designed plates, cutlery and tables it is served on. The patio is a lovely spot to sit at in summer.

Global

Aleksandar

Ceintuurbaan 196 (676 6384). Tram 3. **Open** 5-10pm daily. **Main courses** €16-€31. **No credit cards. Map** p311 E6.

Balkan food comes in huge heaps here, as does the hospitality. Surrender to the grilled selections and the *slivovic*, a plummy and poetic hard liquor that have you hymning the excellent frog's legs and snails.

Eufraat

1e Van der Helststraat 72 (672 0579/www.eufraat.nl). Tram 3, 12, 24, 25. **Open** 3-10.30pm Tue-Sun. **Main courses** €7-€13. **Credit** AmEx, DC, MC, V. **Map** p311 E5.

This family-run restaurant is named after one of the rivers that's said to have flowed through the Garden of Eden. The ancient Assyrian recipes are brought to life with love: Eufraat even makes its own pittas and yoghurts. Don't miss the supreme Arabic coffee.

Mamouche

Quellijnstraat 104 (673 6361) Tram 3, 12, 24, 25. **Open** 6.30-10.30pm Tue-Sun. **Main courses** €15-€20. **Credit** AmEx, DC, MC, V. **Map** p311 E5.

In the heart of the multicultural Pijp is a new Moroccan restaurant with a difference: it's posh, stylish (in a sexy minimalist sort of way) and provides groovy background music that can only be described as 'North African lounge'.

Indian

Balti House

Albert Cuypstraat 41 (470 8917). Tram 6, 7, 10, 16, 24, 25. **Open** 5-11pm daily. **Main courses** €10-€21. **Credit** AmEx, MC, V. **Map** p311 E6.

Balti and tandoori dishes at Amsterdam's only balti house come in big portions, which are usually mildly seasoned to suit the average Dutch palate. If you make a special request for something hotter, however, you get the full spicy works.

Indonesian & Thai

Siriphon

1e Jacob van Campenstraat 47 (676 8072). Tram 6, 7, 10. **Open** 3-10.30pm daily. **Main courses** €8-€14. **Credit** MC, V. **Map** p311 E5.

A small comfy Thai with a green kaeng khiaw curry to die for and many other dishes worthy of a coma.

Warung Spang-Makandra

Gerard Doustraat 39 (670 5081). Tram 6, 7, 10, 16. **Open** 11am-10pm Mon, Tue, Thur-Sun. **Main courses** €2-€7. **No credit cards. Map** p311 E6.

A Java-Suri restaurant where the Indo influence always comes up trumps with the great Javanese rames. The decor is kept simple, but the relaxed vibe and beautifully presented dishes will make you want to sit down for the meal rather than take it away.

Eat, Drink, Shop

Bars

Hic, hic, hooray!

One of the first things visitors to the city may notice when they order a beer is the size of the glass it's served in. And let's face it: when it comes to beer, size matters. Not only is that thimble before you the standard glass (250ml, or 0.44pt) for a *pilsje*, but it comes with a sizeable head of froth. In fact, when beer here is served correctly, it comes topped with exactly two fingers' worth of beer-scented foam.

Another, er, quirky Dutch habit that may take visitors by suprise is the way the empties are often casually sluiced out in a sink of water at the bar during busy periods. Check the rim of the glass carefully before taking your first swig, and don't be afraid to hand it back at the slightest hint of washing-up liquid or lipstick.

All that said, once you're fully initiated to the bizarre and bubbly world of beer in Amsterdam, you'll find that the streets really are paved in gold – or at least, amber nectar: there are more bars per square foot than you could shake those two fingers at.

Most common is the old-style *bruin café* or brown bar, so called because over the years, nicotine has stained their walls. Wood, warmth and well-worn *gezelligheid* (a uniquely Dutch type of social cosiness) typify the best. Brown bars have a good range of local and national

brews, but uncompromising enthusiasts should head to specialist purveyors such as **'t Arendsnest** or **In de Wildeman** (for both, *see p140*); and for fine, locally-produced beer, take a trip to **De Bekeerde Suster** (*see below*) or **Brouwerij 't IJ** (*see p144*).

However, there's much more to Amsterdam's bars than boozing. Some simply ooze history, like **In 't Aepjen** (*see p138*) or **In de Waag** (*see p137*). Others preserve an important Dutch tradition: *proeflokaal* (tasting houses) specialise in *jenever* (a gin-like spirit made from juniper berries), *brandewijn* (literally, burnt – or distilled – wine) and other old Dutch liquors.

Recent years have seen a steady growth in lounge bars, but thankfully, other types of bar – geared towards political, literary, musical, trad or mad crowds – are still out there.

The Old Centre

The Old Side

De Bekeerde Suster
Kloveniersburgwal 6-8 (423 0112/www.beiaard groep.nl). Tram 4, 9, 14, 16, 24, 25. **Open** 10am-1am Mon-Thur, Sun; 10am-2am Fri, Sat. **Credit** AmEx, DC, MC, V. **Map** p306 D3.

In 1544, nuns began producing beer at the cloisters on this site: the drinking water was that bad. Times and standards of hygiene have changed, of course, but this address – praise the Lord – still dispenses beer, and the taps on the bar still connect directly to huge copper vats of the stuff.

De Buurvrouw
St Pieterspoortsteeg 29 (625 9654/www.debuurv rouw.nl). Tram 4, 9, 14, 16, 24, 25. **Open** 9pm-3am Mon-Thur, Sun; 9pm-4am Fri, Sat. **No credit cards.** **Map** p306 D3.
A lively, alternative and popular late-night haunt notable for its sawdust-strewn floor and quirky art. DJs spin on Saturday and there's occasional live music and offbeat performances.

Café Cuba
Nieuwmarkt 3 (627 4919). Tram 4, 9, 14, 16, 24, 25/ Metro Nieuwmarkt. **Open** 1pm-1am Mon-Thur, Sun; 1pm-3am Fri, Sat. **No credit cards.** **Map** p306 D2.
One of the Nieuwmarkt square's most beautiful cafés, Cuba is spacious with plenty of snug seating. Black and white photos of the commie country and posters of Che Guevara adorn the walls. Most importantly, they never skimp on the mint in their wicked Mojito cocktails. Hemingway would have loved it.

Café Fonteyn
Nieuwmarkt 13-15 (422 3599). Tram 4, 9, 14, 16, 24, 25/Metro Nieuwmarkt. **Open** 9.30am-1am Mon-Thur, Sun; 9.30am-3am Fri, Sat. **No credit cards.** **Map** p306 D2.
The 'Fountain' sprinkles a warm, home-from-home feel through its drawing room interior. Local customers devour the dailies and the decent cooked breakfasts; the only dampener, in fact, is the busker traffic on their doorstep – and in your face – during the summer. Still, the heated terrace allows for late-night conversations on nippy summer evenings when the noisemongers are elsewhere, drinking away their day's takings.

Café Stevens
Geldersekade 123 (620 6970). Tram 4, 9/Metro Nieuwmarkt. **Open** 11.30am-1am Mon-Thur, Sun; 11.30am-3am Fri, Sat. **No credit cards.** **Map** p306 D2.
This place stands on a corner of the Nieuwmarkt, and its huge picture windows catch the sun and look out on to the bustle of the square. It's rustic and peaceful spot with good nosh and friendly service; try to grab one of the armchairs in the corner!

De Diepte
St Pieterspoortsteeg 3-5 (06 2900 5926 mobile). Tram 4, 9, 14, 16, 24, 25. **Open** 10pm-3am Mon-Thur, Sun; 10pm-4am Fri, Sat. **Map** p306 D3.
Its name – the Depths – refers to the bowels of damnation. In this unholy hole, with its walls seemingly on fire, you can toss back beers to a soundtrack of randy rockabilly, snotty punk and filthy rock 'n' roll. Hell has never seemed so *gezellig*.

Engelbewaarder
Kloveniersburgwal 59 (625 3772). Tram 4, 9, 14, 16, 24, 25/Metro Nieuwmarkt. **Open** noon-1am Mon-Thur; noon-3am Fri, Sat; 2pm-1am Sun. **No credit cards.** **Map** p306 D3.
Engelbewaarder is popular with quasi-academics and beer lovers enjoying the fine brews. Others simply admire the views from the huge picture windows. Live jazz brightens up Sunday afternoons between 4pm and 7pm.

't Hoekje
Krom Boomssloot 47 (622 8131). Metro Nieuwmarkt. **Open** 4pm-11pm Mon-Thur, Sun; 4pm-1am Fri, Sat. **No credit cards.** **Map** p307 E2.
Five women run this charming bar, which still retains its original 1929 art deco fittings and mosaic-tiled floor. Delicious bar food (with plenty for veggies) can be washed down with a glass of vino from their eclectic wine list.

In de Olofspoort
Nieuwebrugsteeg 13 (624 3918). Tram 4, 9, 14, 16, 24, 25. **Open** 4pm-midnight Tue-Thur; 4pm-1am Fri, Sat. **Credit** MC, V. **Map** p306 D2.
Come here for *jenevers* and liquors from Oud Amsterdam. The renaissance-style building dates from the 17th century and has been granted monument status. Worth a look.

In de Waag
Nieuwmarkt 4 (422 7772/www.indewaag.nl). Tram 4, 9, 14, 16, 24, 25/Metro Nieuwmarkt. **Open** 10am-midnight daily. **Credit** AmEx, DC, MC, V. **Map** p306 D2.
The building can seem imposing and the terrace uninspiring, but walk through the doors of this former weigh house (*see p79*) and you'll be pleasantly wafted back in time: there's no music here – piped or otherwise – and candles are the only lighting. The prices on the drinks, however, will bring you back to the 21st century with a thump.

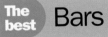

The best Bars

Brouwerij 't IJ
Serves the best local beer. *See p144.*

Het Blauwe Theehuis
For a glass in the park. *See p146.*

Moko
Cocktails on the church terrace? How divine... *See p141.*

Suite
Check in to lounge heaven. *See p140.*

Wynand Fockink
Boozer oozing old 'Dam charm. *See p139.*

In 't Aepjen

Zeedijk 1 (626 8401). Tram 4, 9, 14, 16, 24, 25.
Open *3pm-1am daily.* **No credit cards.**
Map *p306 D2.*
Located in one of the oldest wooden houses in town, this is a terrific bar. The name – 'In the Monkeys' – comes from when Zeedijk was frequented by sailors: those who couldn't pay their bills would settle up by handing over a monkey from the Dutch East Indies. (Note: apes are not legal tender now.) *See also p78.*

Kapitein Zeppos

Gebed Zonder End 5 (624 2057/www.zeppos.nl).
Tram 4, 9, 14, 16, 24, 25. **Open** *11am-1am Mon-Thur; 11am-2am Fri, Sat; noon-1am Sun.* **Credit**
AmEx, MC, V. **Map** p306 D3.
Once used for storing horse-carriages and as a cigar factory, Kapitein Zeppos has retained a seductive (and thirst-inducing) olde worlde feel. With its setting down a narrow alley, fairy-lit terrace and conservatory-style restaurant, it's quite a find. It hosts eclectic live music every Sunday.

Lime

*Zeedijk 104 (639 3020). Tram 4, 9, 14, 16, 24, 25/
Metro Nieuwmarkt.* **Open** *5pm-1am Mon-Thur, Sun; 5pm-3am Fri, Sat.* **No credit cards. Map** *p306 D2.*

Snuggling up to the Buddhist Temple next door, the minimalist Lime is the trendiest bar in this area. However, it's also surprisingly unpretentious. The music is upbeat (DJs play regularly), the cocktails are fab and it's particularly popular in the evenings as a pre-club destination.

The Tara

Rokin 89 (421 2654/www.thetara.com). Tram 4, 9, 14, 16, 24, 25. **Open** *11am-1am Mon-Thur, Sun; 11am-3am Fri, Sat. Kitchen 11am-9pm (breakfast and lunch till 4.30pm).* **Credit** AmEx, MC, V.
Map p306 D3.
This large yet cosy Irish bar has three bars, two pool tables and a couple of log fires. DJs play at weekends, there's regular live music, the food is superb, and TVs – mainly screening football – remain unobtrusive to the non-fan. The best Irish pub in town.

't Tuinfeest

Geldersekade 109 (620 8864). Tram 4, 9, 14, 16, 24, 25/Metro Nieuwmarkt. **Open** *4pm-1am Mon-Thur, Sun; 4pm-3am Fri, Sat.* **Credit** AmEx, DC, MC, V. **Map** p306 D2.
This split-level corner café serves delicious, well-presented food at decent prices. The music can be loud – though fortunately not so loud as to be intrusive

Food for drinking

Forget museums and canals: Amsterdam's sweetest pleasure is chilling in a local café. If weather permits, exploit a terrace; otherwise, pick a place with the brownest of woods and the most nicotine-stained of ceilings. Such hangouts – the likes of **Katte in 't Wijngaert** (*see p145*) and **De Prins** (Prinsengracht 124; 624 9382/www.deprins.nl) – often provide the most culturally satisfying experiences. As exhorters of excess for eons, such places have learned to offer various snacks – known as *borrel hapjes* ('booze bites') – formulated to gel the belly back together. Inevitably, the menu begins with the strongest of stereotype reinforcers: *kaas* (cheese), which can be ingested either via *tostis* (grilled cheese sandwiches) – to research the full *tosti* spectrum, head to the Spui for specialist snackbar **Cheesers** (Hiesteeg 5, 420 4098/www.cheesers.nl) – or pure in the form of a plate of young, rich gouda or edam, cut into cubes and served with a dipping bowl of mustard. (Other mustard-dipping options may include cubed salami and liverwurst.) But there are also more complex options; booze bites that even deserve the respect of being preceded by the palate-cleansing powers of *jenever* (Dutch gin). The most universal in the Netherlands are *bitterballen*

('bitter balls'), spherical deep-fried blobs of potato and meat that are – in spite of their unappetising name – very tasty and addictive. Essentially, they're the cocktail version of the *kroket* sold in every snack bar across the country. They go with any liquid, but really come into their own when washed down with dark beer (Palm, for instance, or De Koninck).

A rather rarer deep-fried snack – though it's gaining popularity almost by the second – are *vlammetjes* ('little flames'), filo-wrapped packets of spicy meat. These little tongue-scorchers are best enjoyed with tapped *witbier* ('white beer'), the ultimate summer quaff: its sweetish edge is a happy antidote to the tang of the meal. As the Dutch say, 'Eet smakelijk!'. *See also p128* **Give grease a chance.**

– and the place attracts a young crowd. A chance to sample 't Tuinfeest, though, is not guaranteed: its popularity means it can be hard to get a table.

VOC Café

Schreierstoren, Prins Hendrikkade 94-5 (428 8291/ www.schreierstoren.nl). Tram 4, 9, 14, 16, 24, 25. **Open** 10am-6pm Mon; 10am-1am Tue-Thur; 10am-3am Fri, Sat; noon-8pm Sun. **No credit cards.** **Map** p306 D2.

Housed in the city's oldest defence tower (*see p100*), the VOC Café has two terraces overlooking Geldersekade plus a good range of *jenevers* and liqueurs: try De Zeedijker Schoot An, brewed to an old VOC recipe.

Wynand Fockink

Pijlsteeg 31 (639 2695/www.wynand-fockink.nl). Tram 4, 9, 14, 16, 24, 25. **Open** 3-9pm daily. **No credit cards.** **Map** p306 D3.

Dating from 1679, this is the most charming tasting house in town. Around 50 old Dutch liquors and 20 *jenevers* are served (the former are produced just next door). Strictly no mobile phones.

The New Side

Belgique

Gravenstraat 2 (625 1974/www.xs4all.nl/~phj). Tram 1, 2, 4, 5, 9, 13, 14, 16, 17, 24, 25. **Open** 2pm-1am Mon-Thur; noon-3am Fri, Sat; noon-1am Sun. **No credit cards.** **Map** p306 C3.

As the name suggests, this little bar offers beer from Holland's neighbour. Eight Belgian brews are on tap and around 20 are served by the bottle. Trappist cheese will make you thirsty for more.

Bep

Nieuwezijds Voorburgwal 260 (626 5649). Tram 1, 2, 5. **Open** 4pm-1am Mon-Thur, Sun; 4pm-3am Fri, Sat. **No credit cards.** **Map** p306 D3.

A painfully fashionable New Side hangout that sits nicely among its similarly cool neighbours Diep (*see below*) and the Getaway (*see p140*). Go there to be seen, by all means, but don't pass up the terrific bar food and cocktails.

Café het Schuim

Spuistraat 189 (638 9357). Tram 13, 14, 17. **Open** 11am-1am Mon-Thur; 11am-3am Fri, Sat; 1pm-1am Sun. **No credit cards.** **Map** p306 C2.

An unsignposted, rustic-arty bar particularly popular with students and a creative crowd. Chilled music makes it a dreamy hangout on a rainy day.

Café Luxembourg

Spui 24 (620 6264/www.luxembourg.nl). Tram 16, 24, 25. **Open** 9am-1am Mon-Thur, Sun; 9am-2am Fri, Sat. **Credit** AmEx, DC, MC, V. **Map** p310 D4.

Ignore the aloof service and make the most of a fine people-watching vantage-point. This elegant spot – with white-aproned waiting staff and a high-ceilinged, art deco interior – has a well-placed terrace for people who need to see and be seen.

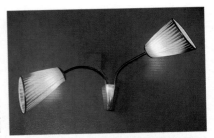

Suite dreams are made of this. *See p140.*

Diep

Nieuwezijds Voorburgwal 256 (420 2020/www.diep. tv). Tram 1, 2, 5. **Open** 5pm-1am Mon-Thur, Sun; 5pm-3am Fri, Sat. **No credit cards.** **Map** p306 D3.

Diep's brown café-meets-opulent disco palace interior should ring bells with anyone who likes their bars eclectic and camp – and a little crushed. DJs spin their wheels of steel here at weekends.

De Drie Fleschjes

Gravenstraat 18 (624 8443/www.driefleschjes.nl). Tram 1, 2, 4, 5, 9, 13, 14, 16, 17, 24, 25. **Open** noon-8.30pm Mon-Sat; 3-7pm Sun. **No credit cards.** **Map** p306 C3.

While the saints are in De Nieuwe Kerk, the sinners can be found next door in one of the oldest tasting houses in Amsterdam. Its street is calm and picturesque, and since opening in 1650 the place has specialised in *jenever*, traditional Dutch liquors and wine – one wall is lined with barrels of the stuff.

The Getaway

Nieuwezijds Voorburgwal 250 (627 1427). Tram 1, 2, 5. **Open** noon-1am Mon-Thur, Sun; noon-3am Fri, Sat. **No credit cards. Map** p306 D3.

Formerly the Seymour Likely Lounge, this place remains a very handy getaway indeed, especially if you've just been Dieply Bepped at its neighbours (*see p139*). DJs play good music and, despite the Getaway's perpetually hip reputation, the crowd here is chilled and approachable. There's a lunch and dinner menu, too.

Henri Prouvin

Gravenstraat 20 (623 9333). Tram 1, 2, 4, 5, 9, 13, 14, 16, 17, 24, 25. **Open** 3-11pm Tue-Fri; 2-9pm Sat. **Credit** MC, V. **Map** p306 C3.

This dark, elegant but slightly snooty café offers a spectacular variety of reasonably priced fine wines and champagnes – either by the bottle or the glass. If you're hungry, it serves a few meat dishes and complimentary snacks.

Hoppe

Spui 18-20 (420 4420). Tram 1, 2, 5. **Open** 8am-1am Mon-Thur, Sun; 8am-2am Fri, Sat. **Credit** AmEx, DC, MC, V. **Map** p310 D4.

This brown café is always a popular joint, though the left-hand entrance leads to the more easygoing of its two bars. A haunt of radicals in the '60s, its old pews and beer barrels make a refreshing change from the chrome fittings or generic tawdriness in most New Side haunts.

In de Wildeman

Kolksteeg 3, by Nieuwezijds Kolk (638 2348/ www.indewildeman.nl). Tram 1, 2, 5, 13, 17. **Open** noon-1am Mon-Thur; noon-2am Fri, Sat. **No credit cards. Map** p306 D2.

The Wildeman's main bar offers a selection of 200 bottled brews from around the world, as well as 18 draughts (including a monthly special). The only drawback can be noise made by some of the customers – male pissheads dribbling froth onto their beards. Happily, the small no-smoking room provides a degree of refuge from the din.

Stereo Sushi

Jonge Roelensteeg 4 (777 3010). Tram 4, 9, 14, 16, 24, 25. **Open** 9pm-1am Thur; 9pm-3am Fri, Sat. **No credit cards. Map** p306 E2.

A hip but tiny lounge bar that serves sushi snacks late into the night while DJs spin.

De Still

Spuistraat 326A (427 6809/www.destill.nl). Tram 4, 9, 14, 16, 24, 25. **Open** 5pm-1am Mon-Thur; 5pm-3am Fri; 3pm-3am Sat; 3pm-1am Sun. **No credit cards. Map** p306 D3.

De Still's defining feature is its giant range of whiskies (from bottle and vat): around 400 in total. The bar also organises tasting tours of distilleries (arrange one at the bar) and is involved with the annual whisky festival (www.whiskyfestival.nl) held in a nearby town in November.

Who's who: **Wolvenstraat 23**. *See p141.*

Suite

Sint Nicolaasstraat 43 (489 6531). Tram 1, 2, 5, 13, 17. **Open** 6pm-1am Mon-Thur, Sun; 6pm-3am Fri, Sat. **Credit** DC, MC, V **Map** p306 C2.

Advertising darlings, celebs and Amsterdam's beautiful people are all present and correct on both floors of the city's lushest lounge bar. You, too, can sip on cocktails and dine on Japanese-Mediterranean fusion tapas as DJs dish up a diverse soundscape.

The Canals

Western Canal Belt

't Arendsnest

Herengracht 90 (421 2057/www.arendsnest.nl). Tram 1, 2, 5, 13, 17. **Open** 4pm-midnight Mon-Thur, Sun; 4pm-2am Fri, Sat. **No credit cards. Map** p306 C2.

There's nothing but beer from Dutch breweries served at 'The Eagle's Nest'; around 140 bottled beers with 12 on tap (try their home-brewed 'Nest Vlieder'). €6 will get you mini-tastes of four of them.

Het Molenpad

Prinsengracht 653 (625 9680). Tram 7, 10. **Open**
noon-1am Mon-Thur, Sun; noon-2am Fri, Sat. *Kitchen*
noon-4pm, 6-10.30pm daily. **No credit cards.**
Map p310 C4.
This hangout is particularly popular with studious
literary types, who tend to pop in on their way back
from the nearby library. Het Molenpad's staff serve
delicious lunches and dinners, the artists' exhibits
rotate on a monthly basis, and there's a decent canal-
side terrace. Pull up in your boat and they'll even
come to serve you on board.

Van Puffelen

Prinsengracht 375-7 (624 6270). Tram 1, 2, 5, 7,
10. **Open** 3pm-1am Mon-Thur; 3pm-2am Fri; noon-
2am Sat; noon-1am Sun. *Kitchen* 6-10pm daily.
Credit AmEx, DC, MC, V. **Map** p306 C3.
This is the biggest brown café in Amsterdam and a
haunt of the beautiful people, especially on balmy
summer evenings. Arrive by boat if you'd really
intend to make an impression.

Wolvenstraat 23

Wolvenstraat 23 (320 0843). Tram 1, 2, 5. **Open**
8am-1am Mon-Thur; 8am-2am Fri; 9am-2am Sat;
10am-1am Sun. **No credit cards. Map** p310 C4.
This anonymous (i.e. untitled) haunt is actually a
far-from-forgettable lounge bar: affluent beings sink
into its sofas, attracted by fab music and art exhibitions. It's great for breakfast and lunch; at night,
take a culinary trek from Shanghai to Beijing.

De Zotte

Raamstraat 29 (626 8694). Tram 1, 2, 5. **Open**
4pm-1am Mon-Thur, Sun; 4pm-3am Fri, Sat. **Credit**
AmEx, MC, V. **Map** p310 C4.
De Zotte, appropriately enough, is Belgian for
'drunken fool' – a state of being that you will
inevitably come to know after sampling their giant
selection of 130 beers. As luck would have it, however, you can stave off sottishness by soaking up
some of the excess with great food from the kitchen.
Incomparably *gezelligheid*.

Southern Canal Belt

Het Land van Walem

Keizersgracht 449 (625 3544). Tram 1, 2, 5. **Open**
10am-1am daily. **Credit** AmEx, DC, MC, V. **Map**
p310 D4.
One of the first designer bars in Amsterdam, this
long, narrow and bright filling station was the work
of renowned Dutch architect Gerrit Rietveld. There
are two terraces, one out front by the canal, the other
out back in the small garden.

Moko

Amstelveld 12 (626 1199/www.moko.nl). Tram 16,
24, 25. **Open** 11.30am-1am Tue-Thur, Sun (in
summer also Mon); 11.30am-2am Fri, Sat. **Credit**
AmEx, DC, MC, V. **Map** p311 E4.
Enjoy the cocktails, lounge and terrace at this former wooden church. *See p125.*

Morlang

Keizersgracht 451 (625 2681/www.morlang.nl).
Tram 1, 2, 5. **Open** 11am-1am Tue-Sun. *Lunch*
11am-5.30pm, *dinner* 5.30pm-11pm. **Credit** AmEx,
MC, V. **Map** p310 D4.
Although it has a conveniently large canalside terrace, the two-floor Morlang lacks the bright designer
looks of Het Land van Walem next door, but it's still
a stylish hangout. The food is good, and the selection of spirits simply amazing.

Around Leidseplein

Aroma

Leidsestraat 96 (624 2941/www.cafe-aroma.nl). Tram
1, 2, 5, 6, 7, 10. **Open** 9am-1am Mon-Thur, Sun;
9am-3am Fri, Sat. **No credit cards. Map** p310 D4.
A welcome respite from the prevailing touristic area,
this spacious café-bar is done out in white '60s style.
They dish up healthy, Mediterranean-influenced
food, real fruit shakes and Chai tea. Happy hour runs
from 6pm to 7pm daily.

De Balie

*Kleine Gartmanplantsoen 10 (553 5130/restaurant
553 5131/www.balie.nl).* Tram 1, 2, 5, 6, 7, 10.
Open 11am-1am Mon-Thur, Sun; 11am-2am Fri, Sat.
No credit cards. Map p310 D5.
The café within this cultural and political centre is
always crowded with artsy types and the politically
aware. Meet here before attending a lecture or movie,
or simply enjoy the elevated view across the hectic
Leidseplein.

Boom Chicago

Leidseplein 12 (530 7307/www.boomchicago.nl).
Tram 1, 2, 5, 6, 7, 10. **Open** noon-1am Mon-Thur,
Sun; noon-3am Fri, Sat. **Credit** AmEx, MC, V.
Map p310 C5.
Comedy fans grab a drink at Boom Chicago's bar
before adjourning to its theatre out the back (*see
p246*). The pre-theatre dinner is popular, and you
can't go wrong with the pitchers of beer or cocktails.
DJs play nightly from Wednesday to Saturday, and
there are happy hours, theme or karaoke nights (first
Sunday of the month) and pub quizes (Mondays).

Café de Koe

Marnixstraat 381 (625 4482/www.cafedekoe.nl).
Tram 7, 10. **Open** 4pm-1am Mon-Thur, Sun; 4pm-
3am Fri, Sat. *Kitchen* 6-10.30pm daily. **Credit** AmEx,
DC, MC, V. **Map** p305 B2.
The decor at this lively, two-level bar-restaurant
takes its thematic lead from the name: 'Cow'.
Drinkers find their good-mooed pasture upstairs,
while diners descend to a restaurant serving appetising fodder at reasonable prices.

Hard Rock

Max Euweplein 59 (523 7625/www.hardrock.com).
Tram 1, 2, 5, 6, 7, 10. **Open** *June-Aug* 10am-
midnight Mon-Thur, Sun; 10am-1 am Fri, Sat. *Sept-
May* noon-midnight daily. **Credit** AmEx, MC,V.
Map p310 D5.

Eat, Drink, Shop

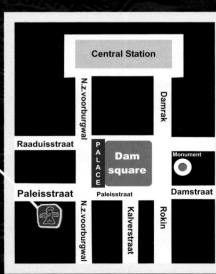

The Hard Rock formula with an Amsterdam twist – complete with a waterside terrace. Child-friendly during the day, it's food-friendly at night: the kitchen is open till 12.30am during the summer. They've also started their own canal cruise.

Joia
Korte Leidsedwarsstraat 45 (626 6769). Tram 1, 2, 5, 6, 7, 10. **Open** 6pm-1am Mon-Wed, Sun; 6pm-2am Thur; 6pm-3am Fri, Sat. **Credit** AmEx, MC, V. **Map** p310 C5.
With a lush brothel-like sensibility and tucked down a little street from the Leidseplein, this lounge bar is popular with a chic crowd heading here for cocktails or for its imaginative world menu.

Lux
Marnixstraat 403 (422 1412) Tram 1, 2, 5, 6, 7, 10. **Open** 8pm-3am Mon-Thur, Sun; 8pm-4am Fri, Sat. **No credit cards**. **Map** p310 C5.
One of the best late-opening hangouts, this split-level designer bar has DJs every night and draws an alternative and trendy crowd. Lux's owners also run the quieter Weber, at No.397.

Noa
Leidsegracht 84 (626 0802/www.withnoa.com). Tram 1, 2, 5. **Open** 6pm-midnight Tue, Wed, Sun; 6pm-1am Thur-Sat. **Credit** AmEx, MC, V. **Map** p310 C4.
A hip, jet-setty lounge bar. 'Satan doesn't drink', avers its website. *See p125.*

Van Gogh's green genie

'After the first glass, you see things as you wish they were. After the second glass, you see things as they are not. Finally you see things as they really are, and that is the most horrible thing in the world.' Thus wrote Oscar Wilde on the affects of absinthe.

Derived from the Greek word *apsinthion* (meaning 'undrinkable'), absinthe has, at various times, been blamed for falling birth rates, mental illness and murders. It was banned in Belgium in 1905, the US in 1912 and France in 1915. And it's alleged to have ruined more lives than cocaine.

It was invented in Switzerland in 1792 by French chemist Pierre Ordinaire. Originally created as a digestive, it quickly caught on as an apéritif and was popularised by Henri-Louis Pernod (yes, *that* Pernod) at the beginning of the 19th century. The drink is distilled from the leaves of wormwood (ominously called *chernobyl* in Russia), a herb originally used to treat gastrointestinal disorders such as worms (hence the name). In 17th-century England, it was used as a vermin repellent.

Its alcohol content traditionally varies from 55 per cent to 72 per cent, depending on the brand and country of origin, and in large doses its active ingredient 'alpha-Thujone' is a convulsive poison. Coincidentally, alpha-Thujone has been shown to have a remarkably similiar molecular structure to THC (tetrahydrocannabinol) – the active ingredient in cannabis.

However, despite – or because of – its on-the-edge appeal, it was particulary popular in *fin de siècle* France, and was the tipple synonymous with the Bohemian lifestyle (as romanticised in Baz Luhrmann's *Moulin Rouge*). Known as *la fée verte* ('The Green Fairy') because of its emerald green colour

(which turns a cloudy white when water is added), it was the muse of writers from Baudelaire to Hemingway and the subject of paintings by Degas (*Absinthe*, 1876), Picasso (*Woman Drinking Absinthe*, 1901) and Van Gogh (*Still Life with Absinthe*, 1887, on view at the Van Gogh Museum; *see p107*). Toulouse Lautrec even reputedly carried an emergency supply of absinthe – in a hollow cane – on his travels across the artistic Paris. Van Gogh was on the stuff for most of his artistic life: his more hallucinogenic works could well have been absinthe-inspired. And he was probably tanked up on it when he went at Gauguin with a razor and sliced off part of his own ear...

So if you still have a thirst after reading this, make for **Absinthe**, an upbeat late-opener in the heart of cool clubland: this grotto-like lounge has absinthe on tap. In fact, it's the only bar in Amsterdam with a licence to sell...

Absinthe
Nieuwezijds Voorburgwal 171 (320 6780/ www.absinthe.nl). Tram 1, 2, 5. **Open** 8pm-3am Mon-Thur, Sun; 8pm-4am Fri, Sat. **No credit cards**. **Map** p306 D3.

Heavenly drinks, angelic staff:
De Engel. *See p146*.

Twstd

Weteringschans 157 (320 7030/www.twstd.nl).
Tram 6, 7, 10, 16, 24, 25. **Open** 6pm-1am Mon-
Thur; 4pm-3am Fri, Sat; 4pm-1am Sun. **No credit
cards. Map** p311 E5.
This is Amsterdam's definitive DJ bar, and it boasts
a great sound system and eclectic nights that wel-
come both established spinners and beginners.
Anyone can play: pop along with a bag of vinyl on
Monday during their open decks night.

Around Rembrandtplein

For Irish live music bar **Mulligans**, *see p213*.

De Duivel

Reguliersdwarsstraat 87 (626 6184/www.deduivel.nl).
Tram 4, 9, 14. **Open** 8pm-3am Mon-Thur, Sun; 8pm-
4am Fri, Sat. **No credit cards. Map** p311 E4.
Cypress Hill, the Roots and Gang Starr have all
popped by this small but lively hip hop bar since it
opened a decade ago. Nowadays, DJs at 'The Devil'
mix it up with funk, rare groove and breakbeats.

Schiller

Rembrandtplein 26 (624 9846). Tram 4, 9, 14.
Open 4pm-1am Mon-Thur, Sun; 4pm-2am Fri, Sat.
Kitchen 5.30-10pm daily. **Credit** AmEx, DC, MC, V.
Map p311 E4.
An absolute godsend for anyone feeling like a fish
out of water amid Rembrandtplein's crass, packed
terraces, this renowned art deco café maintains a
highbrow sensibility on weekends.

Jodenbuurt, the Plantage & the Oost

Brouwerij 't IJ

Funenkade 7 (622 8325/www.brouwerijhetij.nl).
Tram 6, 10. **Open** 3-8pm Wed-Sun. **No credit cards.**
In the shadow of the 1814 De Gooyer windmill, this
former bathhouse is home to a micro-brewery that
turns out some of the finest beer in the country.

Unfortunately its bar often resembles a smoky working men's club, but after a couple of jars you'll be
one of the lads.

Café de Sluyswacht

Jodenbreestraat 1 (625 7611/
www.welcome.to/sluyswacht). Tram 9, 14/Metro
Waterlooplein. **Open** 11.30am-1am Mon-Thur;
11.30am-3am Fri, Sat; 11.30am-7pm Sun. **Credit** MC,
V. **Map** p307 E3.
Built in 1695, this former lock-keeper's house has
retained much of its charm, as well as its foundations: the building leans heavily. It's situated across
from the Rembrandthuis (*see p96*), and the terrace
at the back is one of the most peaceful in town.

Dantzig

Zwanenburgwal 15 (620 9039). Tram 9, 14/Metro
Waterlooplein. **Open** 9am-1am Mon-Fri; 9am-2am
Sat; 10am-1am Sun. *Kitchen* 11am-10pm daily.
Credit AmEx, MC, DC, V. **Map** p307 E3.
A Paris-style grand café frequented during the day
by visitors to the adjacent Waterlooplein market,
tourists waiting for canal boats, councillors from the
city hall and theatre-goers at night. The terrace has
great views over the Amstel.

De Ponteneur

1e van Swindenstraat 581 (668 0680). Tram 9, 14.
Open 9am-1am Mon-Thur, Sun; 9am-2am Fri, Sat.
No credit cards. Map p312 H3.
Spacious and perpetually popular. Come here for
some hearty sustenance after a browse at the local
Dappermarkt (*see p164*), or to kick back with a
newspaper or magazine from their reading table.

East of Eden

Linnaeusstraat 11a (665 0743). Tram 6, 9, 10, 14.
Open 11am-1am Mon-Thur, Sun; 11am-2am Fri, Sat.
No credit cards. Map p312 H3.
Just across from the Tropenmuseum (*see p98*), this
James Dean-inspired bar is high-ceilinged and spa-
cious. Though the fake marble walls and mural of
elephants may be a little offputting, the background
music makes up for it.

Eik & Linde

Plantage Middenlaan 22 (622 5716). Tram 7, 9, 14.
Open 11am-1am Mon-Thur; 11pm-2am Fri; 2pm-2am
Sat. **No credit cards. Map** p307 F3.
'The Oak & Lime Tree' is an old-fashioned, family-
run neighbourhood bar. Local memorabilia on the
walls, including posters from radio shows held on
the premises, give it historical appeal; low prices and
a laid-back air make it user-friendly.

Entredok

Entrepôtdok 64 (623 23 56). Tram 6. **Open** 4pm-
11pm daily. **No credit cards. Map** p307 F2.
A characterful, two-floor Dutch bar on an oft overlooked picturesque canal behind Artis Zoo, with a
quiet waterside terrace that catches the sun's last rays.

The Waterfront

Kanis & Meiland

*Levantkade 127 (418 2439/www.kanisenmeiland.nl).
Bus 28, 32, 59.* **Open** 10am-1am Mon-Thur, Sun;
10am-3am Fri, Sat. **No credit cards.**
K&M is in the middle of Amsterdam's redeveloped
Eastern Docklands. The bright and spacious café is
perfect for summer – and the food's terrific.

Odessa

*Veemkade 259 (419 3010/www.de-odessa.nl). Bus
28, 39.* **Open** 4pm-1am Mon-Thur, Sun; 4pm-3am
Fri, Sat. **Credit** AmEx, DC, MC, V.
A hip Ukrainian fishing boat with a regular bar on
deck (ideal for summer nights) and a stylish lounge
bar in its hold. *See also p127.*

The Jordaan

Café Nol

Westerstraat 109 (624 5380). Tram 10. **Open** 9pm-
3am Mon-Thur, Sun; 9pm-4am Fri, Sat. **No credit
cards. Map** p305 B2.
Kitsch doesn't come any more hardcore, and this
over-the-top Jordaan bar/institution, with red
leatherette interiors and crowds of lusty-voiced locals,

is supposed to sum up the true 'spirit' of the neighbourhood. Be warned: its brand of social cosiness
comes with much jolly spittle flying through the air.

Café Soundgarden

Marnixstraat 164-6 (620 2853). Tram 10, 13, 14, 17.
Open 1pm-1am Mon-Thur; 1pm-3am Fri; 3pm-3am
Sat; 3pm-1am Sun. **No credit cards. Map** p305 B3.
Popular with a grungy crowd, which flocks to its
garden terrace on summer days, the bar also has
plenty to while away those rainy afternoons in the
form of pool, darts, pinball and table football. If
you're drinking to forget, try the Flater's Kater.

Dulac

Haarlemmerstraat 118 (624 4265). Bus 18, 22.
Open 4pm-1am Mon-Thur, Sun; 4pm-3am Fri, Sat.
Credit AmEx, DC, MC, V. **Map** p306 C2.
A wildly OTT grand café fitted out in surreal art
deco style (stuffed alligators, mutant trees and more
besides). The cosy corners, the raised gallery and the
glass-walled conservatory pack in trendies by the
hundred. DJs spin at weekends.

Finch

*Noordermarkt 5 (626 2461). Tram 1, 2, 5, 13, 17,
20.* **Open** 7am-1am Mon; 10am-1am Tue-Thur;
10am-3am Fri, Sat; 11am-1am Sun. **No credit
cards. Map** p305 B2.
Located in one of the city's more scenic squares,
Finch attracts a hip and artistic crowd to its vaguely
Wallpaper*-like interior, whose trendiness is happily muted by the carefully cultivated, carefree vibe.
The excellent eats, grooving tunes and charming
staff make it a top hangout.

De Kat in 't Wijngaert

Lindengracht 160 (622 4554). Tram 1, 2, 5, 13, 17.
Open 10am-1am Mon-Thur, Sun; 10am-3pm Fri, Sat.
No credit cards. Map p305 B2.
From 'The Cat in the Vineyard', you can spy the site
of the infamous 1886 Eel Riot. It's a neighbourhood
café that evokes a truer image of the spirit of the
Jordaan than even Café Nol (*see p145*), with locals
drawn from every walk of life. Purrrfect.

Miss Riss

Fannius Scholtenstraat 26hs (686 8686/www.miss riss.nl). Tram 10. **Open** noon-11pm Tue-Sun. **No credit cards. Map** p305 A2.

Multi-tasking bar staff serve drinks and cook up nosh right behind the bar at this bright new café, which stands a short walk west from the Jordaan near the Westergasfabriek. Come here to mingle with some interesting locals.

't Smalle

Egelantiersgracht 12 (623 9617). Tram 13, 14, 17, 20. **Open** 10am-1am Mon-Thur, Sun; 10am-2am Fri, Sat. **No credit cards. Map** p305 B3.

In 1786 Pieter Hoppe (of Hoppe & Jenever) opened a liquor distillery here. Though a few artefacts remain – including an original *jenever* pump on the bar – the place now earns its reputation as a charming café and brown bar. You can pull your boat up to their quayside terrace in summer.

The Museum Quarter, Vondelpark & the South

Het Blauwe Theehuis

Vondelpark (662 0254/www.blauwetheehuis.nl). Tram 1, 2, 6. **Open** 9am-1am Mon-Thur, Sun; 9am-3am Fri, Sat. **No credit cards. Map** p310 B5.

Looking like a flying saucer, the 'Blue Teahouse' – a functionalist masterpiece designed by HAJ Baanders and J Baanders in 1936 – is a charming and romantic spot. There are two bars: one upstairs where DJs spin and one downstairs for those with dogs and small children in tow. Snacks are available all day. It's the place to come to in summer (when a cocktail bar is set up), though it can get very crowded. By winter 2004, the upstairs will have become a restaurant (open from 6.30pm to 10pm daily) and may become a year-round operation if successful.

Café Ebeling

Overtoom 50-52 (689 4858/www.cafeebeling.com). Tram 1, 3, 6, 12. **Open** 11am-1am Mon-Thur; 11am-3am Fri, Sat; noon-1am Sun. *Kitchen* 11am-10pm daily. **Credit** AmEx, MC, V. **Map** p310 C5.

Located in an old bank – the toilets are in the safe – Café Ebeling is a split-level bar that aims itself at the young without being snobby or needing to have the music on so loud you can't think. Another plus: it's one of the few non-Irish bars in town that serve a decent Guinness.

Toussaint

Bosboom Toussaintstraat 26 (685 0737). Tram 1, 3, 6, 7, 12, 17. **Open** 10am-midnight Mon-Thur, Sun; 10am-1am Fri, Sat. **No credit cards. Map** p310 C5.

Rustic charm abounds at this welcoming café-cum-bar. You'll find it on a quiet street a mere ten-minute walk from Leidseplein, and it's well worth the short detour. Toussaint's small, open kitchen serves up super grub all day and night, and there's even a decent selection for vegetarians. For hipper fare, you can carry on down the road to Wanka (Bosboom Toussaintstraat 70, 412 6169) – pronounced, you'll be glad to hear, 'vanker'.

The Pijp

Chocolate Bar

1e van der Helststraat 62a (675 7672). Tram 16, 24, 25. **Open** Mon-Thur, Sun 10am-1am; Fri, Sat 10am-3am. **No credit cards. Map** p311 E6.

Despite the name, its notoriously slow service won't leave your mouth watering – so only come if you have the time and inclination to lounge. The experience improves with the cool clientele and regular DJs. On Tuesdays they screen cult, rare and classic films with dinner served in the style of the movie.

De Engel

Albert Cuypstraat 182 (675 0544/www.de-engel.net). Tram 16, 24, 25. **Open** 10am-1am Mon-Thur, Sun; 10am-2am Fri, Sat. *Kitchen* 10am-10pm Mon-Thur, Sun; 10am-10.30pm Fri, Sat. **Credit** MC, V. **Map** p311 F5.

Look up for the angel to find this church turned grand café, the crowning glory of Albert Cuypmarkt (*see p113 and p164*). It's elegant and yet relaxed; it hosts regularly changing exhibitions, which is how the work of Karel Appel have come to adorn the walls. Live jazz is on Friday; more genteel classical music accompanies Sunday brunch.

Kingfisher

Ferdinand Bolstraat 24 (671 2395). Tram 16, 24, 25. **Open** 11pm-1am Mon-Thur; 11pm-3am Fri, Sat. **No credit cards. Map** p311 E6.

Of the many local-ish brown cafés that actually let in fresh light and international style, the Kingfisher does the best job, balancing impeccable and neighbourly service with inventive snacks and a daily dinner special that'll take your tastebuds on a global rollercoaster ride. The archetype of the locals' local.

Mme Jeanette

1e van der Helststraat 42 (673 3332/www.jeanette. id-t.com). Tram 16, 24, 25. **Open** 6pm-1am Mon-Thur, Sun; 6pm-3am Fri, Sat. **Credit** AmEx, DC, MC, V. **Map** p311 E5.

This large lounge bar is notable for its couches, cocktails, DJs and a terrace (thoughtfully heated in winter). The place is frequented by hip young things in profusion – but its popularity generally means you can expect a long wait before you get in. Come armed with the patience of a saint.

Wildschut

Roelof Hartplein 1-3 (676 8220/www.goodfoodgroup. nl). Tram 3, 5, 12, 24. **Open** 9am-1am Mon-Thur; 9am-3am Fri; 10am-2am Sat; 10am-1am Sun. **Credit** (over €15) AmEx, DC, MC, V.

This chic, cavernous joint is still one of Amsterdam's top places to be seen in. In the summer, try to acquire a seat on the large terrace which overlooks the Roelof Hartplein – a square surrounded by typical Amsterdam School architecture.

Coffeeshops

Blowing your mind: the hash reality.

According to the UN, some 141 million people around the world indulge in marijuana: that's roughly 2.5 per cent of the world's population. It's proven to be less harmful than alcohol and its medicinal benefits – relieving discomfort in multiple sclerosis, AIDS and chemotherapy, for example – are well documented. Yet, whether you grow it or blow it, it remains a highly controversial plant.

It was in Amsterdam, in 1972, that a bakery-turned-squat on the banks of the Amstel river sowed the first seeds for what has become one of the city's most profitable tourist draws: the coffeeshop. A mish-mash of happy hippies, students, squatters and anarchists would head to pioneer Mellow Yellow for a little recreational drug-taking. Before long, coffeeshops were popping up all over Amsterdam; the Bulldog (*see p53*), which opened in 1975, being the most famous.

As the government adopted a liberal stance, the Dutch drug policy – founded on the belief that prohibition increased hard drug use and wasted valuable police resources – was born. In 1976, Holland classified marijuana as a 'soft drug' and, in 1978, decriminalised possession of up to 30 grams (1.06 ounces) – without leading to increased use. International pressure saw this amount lowered to five grams (0.18 ounces) in 1996 – but that's still more than enough to get Patsy and Edina through an episode of *Ab Fab*.

Technically, however, cannabis remains illegal. Albeit of little concern to the average visitor, this does make for some rather potty laws. For example, coffeeshops can sell you the stuff but they are not allowed to buy it from the growers. So, it comes through the back door illegally but, seemingly lawfully, goes out

through the front. And, following New York's model, the government recently threatened to impose a ban on smoking in public places. Although the law would target tobacco and not cannabis, it was still a cause of concern for the quasi-legal coffeeshops: they would still be allowed to sell their wares but customers would have to go outside to smoke 'em.

For the first-time visitor such tolerance can, naturally, take a bit of getting used to. However, it sure as hell beats phoning your dealer on his cellphone and meeting him in some dodgy bar. And though it's tempting to make a beeline for the nearest smoking establishment as soon as you arrive, however touristy and gaudy it may be, make your first toke in Amsterdam a truly pleasurable experience by checking out one of the fine joints (pun most definitely intended) described in the chapter. For a broader survey of the Dutch drugs culture, *see p40*.

ATTENTION TO DETAIL

What all coffeeshops have in common is the manner in which hashish and marijuana are sold. Almost all coffeeshops have a menu card either on the bar or just behind it. Most hash and weed is sold in one-gram bags (about €5), though many coffeeshops will weigh your wares of choice. Quality can vary hugely and, of course, as quality goes up the price follows suit.

Good coffeeshops have a bewildering array of comestibles. Each shop stocks a number of varieties, detailed on a menu with all the plain-as-day disinterestedness you'd see on a restaurant's specials board. The hash side of things is fairly clear, as varieties are usually named after the country of origin. Weed, though, is a bit more complicated. It divides

The best Coffeeshops

Abraxas
Multi-sensory goblin heaven. *See p149.*

Barney's
Bangers and hash: they're fry high. *See p149.*

Greenhouse
For weed and seed connoisseurs. *See p148.*

High Times Cannabis Cup
Everyone's a winner. *See p183.*

La Tertulia
Smoke grass amid the greenery. *See p149.*

Yo-Yo
Quite a Pijp dream. *See p152.*

roughly into two categories: bush weeds grown naturally, such as Thai; and Nederwiet or skunk, an indigenous Dutch product grown under UV lights for maximum THC (the active ingredient). As with Guinness in Ireland – well, kinda – the skunk here is worlds away from anything available elsewhere, and caution is advised if you are at all interested in remembering anything. The same caution should be exercised when it comes to most of the spacecake on offer: effects can take an hour or longer to kick in, and the return to planet Earth can be a protracted affair.

If you're not used to it, don't drink and draw – note that the majority of coffeeshops don't sell alcohol – and, if you do overdo it, eat or drink something sweet. Tourists passed out on the street from too much spliff are an all too common sight here. Sure, it'll make for a funny story when you get back home, but at the time you'll never have felt so ill in your life.

The only 'don't' that really needs to be stressed, however, is that you should never buy anything from street dealers. Junkies proliferate in certain areas of town, and if a street deal is not a precursor to a mugging you can count yourself lucky. It's also important to bear in mind that there are places where smoking is frowned upon. Not everyone in Amsterdam is going to smile and wave a peace sign if you have a joint in your hand. If in doubt, ask: the worst you'll get is a 'No'. But in the meantime, happy smoking!

Coffeeshops

For **The Otherside**, Amsterdam's only gay coffeeshop, *see p209*. In addition, lesbian bar **Saarein II** (*see p210*) organises a home-growing contest.

The Old Centre: Old Side

Greenhouse

Oudezijds Voorburgwal 191 (627 1739/www. greenhouse.org). Tram 4, 9, 14, 16, 24, 25. **Open** 9am-1am Mon-Thur, Sun; 9am-3am Fri, Sat. **No credit cards. Map** p306 D3.
The Greenhouse has a worldwide reputation for its menu, which will bring grins of sheer delight to the faces of connoisseurs (though bear in mind it comes at a price). They also serve alcohol and their location next door to the prestigious Grand Hotel means you might spot a celeb spliffing up here.
Other locations: Waterlooplein 345 (no phone); Tolstraat 91 (673 7430).

Greenhouse

Greenhouse Effect
Warmoesstraat 53 (623 7462). Tram 4, 9, 16, 24, 25. **Open** *9am-1am Mon-Thur, Sun; 9am-3am Fri, Sat.* **No credit cards.** **Map** p306 D2.
Not to be confused with the Greenhouse (*see p148*), this is a small but hip joint that also sells alcohol. However, if you fancy a modest line-up of DJs, a bit more chill-out space and a chance to sample the dubiously named Cream In Your Pants cocktail, take a trip next door to their bar-hotel of the same name (*see p53*). On the other side is Getto, arguably the best gay/mixed bar in town (*see p208*).

The Old Centre: New Side

Abraxas
Jonge Roelensteeg 12-14 (625 5763/www.abraxas.tv). Tram 4, 9, 16, 24, 25. **Open** *10am-1am daily.* **No credit cards.** **Map** p306 D3.
Comfortable and colourful, this veritable goblin's house is located down a small alley in the heart of cool clubland. As well as alcohol, they sell cannabis-infused spacecakes, shakes, bonbons, tea… all that's missing, in fact, is a cannabis drip. And there's plenty to complement the experience: chess and internet (free to customers) or watching the grass grow (literally). DJs play from Thursday to Saturday.

Dampkring
Handboogstraat 29 (638 0705). Tram 1, 2, 5. **Open** *10am-1am Mon-Thur; 10am-2am Fri, Sat; 11am-1am Sun.* **No credit cards.** **Map** p310 D4.
Dampkring, whose name translates as both 'atmosphere' and 'circle of smoke', shares the same owners as Tweede Kamer (*see below*); both places sell around 80% organically-grown weed. The colourful, ornately-decorated coffeeshop is handily located just behind the chaotic reaches of Kalverstraat: grab your bags and head here when the crowds gets too much.

Homegrown Fantasy
Nieuwezijds Voorburgwal 87A (627 5683/ www.homegrownfantasy.com). Tram 1, 2, 5, 13, 17. **Open** *9am-midnight Mon-Thur, Sun; 9am-1am Fri, Sat.* **No credit cards.** **Map** p306 D2.
One of the widest selections of Dutch-grown weed in Weedsville. The menu and the pleasant environment make it a very popular smokers' venue. The owners also manage the spacious Tetra bar next door where you're more than welcome to spliff up: DJs also spin there and they have regular parties, including a trance night every Wednesday.

Kadinsky
Rosmarijnsteeg 9 (624 7023/www.kadinsky.nl). Tram 1, 2, 5. **Open** *10am-1am daily.* **No credit cards.** **Map** p306 D3.
Pastels, plants and sofas decorate this popular hangout. The menu lists a wide range of hash and grass, including descriptions, tastes and effects (from 'well high' to 'very stoned'). The prices are a little above average, but so is the quality; one day in eight, deals are discounted by 20%.

Tweede Kamer
Heisteeg 6 (422 2236/www.detweedekamer.nl). Tram 1, 2, 5. **Open** *10am-1am Mon-Sat; 11am-1am Sun.* **No credit cards.** **Map** p306 D3.
Smoky, poky and in old Dutch style, Tweede Kamer is frequented by locals as a result of its deserved reputation for having a wide range of imported grass. You might do well to purchase your grass here but head elsewhere to actually smoke the stuff.

Western Canal Belt

Amnesia
Herengracht 133 (638 3003). Tram 13, 14, 17. **Open** *10am-1pm daily.* **No credit cards.** **Map** p306 C2.
A fresh new addition to Amsterdam, the colourful Amnesia has a certain 'home from home' charm. The regular DJs provide a mellow soundscape, the menu is of a high standard (and the kitchen staff know their stuff), plus there's a chess table to challenge your powers of concentration. This is one coffeeshop you won't forget in a hurry.

Barney's
Haarlemmerstraat 102 (625 9761/www.barneys-amsterdam.com). Tram 13, 14, 17. **Open** *7am-1am daily.* **No credit cards.** **Map** p306 C2.
The best thing about Barney's is its early opening hours and range of international breakfasts (with vegetarian and vegan options). Come here if you arrive in Amsterdam in the morning (it's just a five-minute walk from Centraal Station) or for a civilised end to a night on the tiles.

Siberië
Brouwersgracht 11 (623 5909/www.siberie.nl). Tram 1, 2, 4, 5, 13, 17. **Open** *11am-11pm Mon-Thur, Sun; 11am-midnight Fri, Sat.* **No credit cards.** **Map** p306 C2.
The friendly and interactive Siberië has regular free horoscope readings, open mic nights and exhibitions; DJs spin at weekends, too. But if you want to chill there are also plenty of board games and on-site net access. The same owners run the small but modern De Supermarkt (Frederik Hendrikstraat 69, 486 2479, www.desupermarkt.net) and well-established neighbourhood coffeeshop De Republiek (2e Nassaustraat 1a, 682 8431, www.republiek.nl), both just west of the Jordaan.

La Tertulia
Prinsengracht 312 (no phone). Tram 7, 10, 13, 14, 17. **Open** *11am-7pm Tue-Sat.* **No credit cards.** **Map** p310 C4.
A stoned-looking Van Gogh is painted on the outer walls of this charming split-level corner coffeeshop where Michelle from *EastEnders* took her first toke years ago. Inside it's bright and airy; weed brownies are served at the sunken counter and there's a miniature garden, complete with fountain. In summer, the canalside terrace is a peaceful spot at which to spliff up and watch the passers-by.

USING OR SELLING HARD DRUGS, WILL HAVE THEIR LEGS BROKEN thank you, the managment

Get the message? **De Rokerij**.

Eat, Drink, Shop

Southern Canal Belt

De Rokerij
Lange Leidsedwarsstraat 41 (622 9442/
www.rokerij.net). Tram 1, 2, 5, 6, 7, 10. **Open**
10am-1am Mon-Thur, Sun; 10am-3am Fri, Sat.
No credit cards. **Map** p310 D5.
A marvellous discovery on an otherwise hideously
touristy street by Leidseplein, De Rokerij is a veritable Aladdin's cave: lit by wall-mounted candles
and beautiful metal lanterns, it's decorated with
colourful Indian art and a variety of seating (ranging from mats on the floors to decorative 'thrones').
In line with its central location, it gets very busy in
the evening and at the weekend.
Other locations: Amstel 8 (620 0484); Singel 8
(422 6643).

The Jordaan

Brandend Zand
Marnixstraat 92 (528 7292/www.brandendzand.nl).
Tram 3, 10. **Open** 9.30am-1am Mon-Fri; 10am-1am
Sat, Sun. **No credit cards**. **Map** p305 B2.
This friendly and spacious split-level coffeeshop is
a real find on this otherwise ugly street. Downstairs
is cushion heaven, while upstairs you'll find Internet
access, a pool table and big-screen MTV. The
upright designer aquarium may be an aesthetically
pleasing addition, but chances are the fish don't
really like having to swim vertically.

Grey Area
Oude Leliestraat 2 (420 4301/www.greyarea.nl).
Tram 1, 2, 5, 13, 14, 17. **Open** noon-8pm Tue-Sun.
No credit cards. **Map** p306 C3.
The joint venture of two wacky Americans, Grey
Area is small but super-friendly. They sell top-quality
weed (their AK-47 hits the bullseye; *see also p152*)
and offer free refills of organic coffee. Plus, while you
get high, the owners can also give you the lowdown
on parties in town. On the same street is Foodism
(*see p123*), ideal for when you get the munchies.

Paradox
1e Bloemdwarsstraat 2 (623 5639). Tram 10, 13,
14, 17. **Open** 10am-8pm daily. **No credit cards**.
Map p305 B3.
When compared to the proliferation of dingy coffeeshops that dominates much of Amsterdam,
Paradox certainly lives up to its name. A bright,
characterful contradiction, it serves healthy food,
fruit shakes and fresh fruit/vegetable juices on top
of all the usual dope (though if you're feeling peck-
ish, it's worth remembering that the kitchen
shuts at 3pm). Comfortable and cosy, it's ideal for
deep-and-meaningful and you could probably bring
your mum here, too.

Samenentereng
2e Laurierdwarsstraat 44 (624 1907). Tram 10,
13, 14, 17. **Open** *Summer* noon-midnight daily.
Winter noon-7pm Mon-Thur, Sun; noon-midnight
Fri, Sat. **No credit cards**. **Map** p309 B4.
If you're after a strange experience on a par with one
of Mr Benn's visits to the fancy dress shop, then pop
into Samenentereng, ostensibly a bric-a-brac store
crammed to the nines with both brac and bric.
However, tucked at the back is an unusual African
hut-style coffeeshop-cum-conservatory, complete
with reggae, rastas and table football. Definitely
worth a ganja.

Time Out Amsterdam **151**

High-tech tokes

Let's face it: coffeeshops can no longer be considered revolutionary after three decades of service. And it's been more than a decade since the 'Green Wave' arrived in the reddish American variety of skunk that was found to grow very nicely under artificial light. It and its sensimillian (seedless, so that more of the plant's efforts went into producing that magical ingredient THC) descendants – White Widow, Northern Light, Master Kush, AK-47, Bubblegum, Bazooka Joe (the cross between AK-47 and Bubblegum) – are now long established products with new cross-bred mutants appearing on the menu on a seemingly daily basis. Again: pretty ho-hum in the breaking news department (though be warned, these skunks remain highly relevant when it comes to melting the brains of unpractised visitors).

But there have been quieter revolutions occurring in the Weed World. Vaporisers, for instance, have come a long way since appearing about a decade ago as home-made devices that wedded a water bong to an electric paint stripper with duct tape, thereby letting the user vaporise THC at such a low temperature that the leaves remained uncombusted. In other words, with no burning of tars and carcinogens, the choke was out of the toke! Today they're available as sleekly designed, pocket-sized units from all good dope outlets (see p156). Most good coffeeshops will loan you one, and **Amnesia** (*see p147*) even hosts regular vaporiser parties.

Another life-enriching change has occurred in the world of 'space cuisine'. Gone are days of having to choke down a cardboard brownie before picking the hash out from your teeth with the edge of a pack of rolling papers. Now you just have to make sure your space baker is using 'green butter' – basically a long-boiled weed infusion – with their Jamie Oliver recipe. Of course, eating a more mouth-watering product doesn't mean you won't become a drooling shadow of a human being, courtesy of the inevitable 'creeping wave' effect.

Enthusiasts may want to peruse Ed Rosenthal's 2003 book *Ask Ed: Marijuana Gold – Trash to Stash* before their vacation to learn about the latest technologies (and how to get the most out of the plant's often neglected bits). But then again, you're only ever a short coffeeshop conversation away from the latest pot practices.

The Museum Quarter, Vondelpark & the South

Kashmir Lounge
Jan Pieter Heijestraat 85-87 (683 2268). Tram 1. **Open** 10am-1am Mon-Thur; 10am-3am Fri, Sat; 11am-1am Sun. **No credit cards**. **Map** p309 B6.
Kashmir Lounge's non-central location means cheaper drinks (including alcohol) and more flexible deals on weed. Spacey and spacious, the cushioned area is a great place for a horizontal smoke, especially with DJs playing upbeat lounge in the background (Thur-Sun) – though sometimes the volume can get a little too loud to be conducive to chilling.

The Pijp

Yo-Yo
2e Jan van der Heijdenstraat 79/entrance on Hemonystraat (664 7173). Tram 3, 4. **Open** noon-7pm daily. **No credit cards**. **Map** p311 F5.
A popular neighbourhood coffeeshop situated out in the Pijp, Yo-Yo is spacious and aesthetic. The atmosphere is intrinsically mellow all day, and the weed is organic. Don't leave without trying Helga's homemade apple pie.

Events

For details of the **High Times Cannabis Cup**, held every November in various venues around town, *see p183*.

Global Days Against the Drug War
Stichting Legalize, Postbus 225, 2300 AE Leiden (06 2077 4039 mobile/www.legalize.net).
Events are organised concurrently, usually in late May or early June, in around 30 cities worldwide in an attempt to raise awareness of drugs issues. In Amsterdam the event includes a remembrance ceremony in Dam Square for victims of drug warfare and a 'Legalize' street party, attracting both party and political animals. Check their website for details nearer the time.

Hashtorical Daze
Mobile 06 1835 4111.
An informative English-language coffeeshop crawl that offers insider information on cannabis culture, as well as tips on underground parties. Tours leave daily at 12.30pm and 4.20pm from the front desk of Cannabis College (*see p153*). Cost is €15 and includes entrance to the College's indoor garden plus a small bag of homegrown weed.

Eat, Drink, Shop

Highlife Hemp Exhibition
Highlife, Discover Publishers BV, Huygensweg 7, 5482 TH Schijndel (073 549 8112/www.highlife.nl).
Organised by *Highlife* magazine, this event celebrates the cannabis plant, with an emphasis on the industrial uses of hemp. The exhibition holds displays detailing the many uses for the plant, and there are around 100 stalls selling smart drugs, weed tea and coffee, and all sorts of soft drugs paraphernalia. The event's dates and location – it's usually held outside Amsterdam – vary each year, but you can visit their website for details.

Information

For the **Hash Marijuana Hemp Museum**, *see p81*.

BCD (Bond van Cannabis Detaillisten)
627 7050.
Not all coffeeshops belong to the BCD ('Cannabis Retailers Association'), but members can be identified by a green and white rectangular sticker usually placed near or on their door. The BCD produces a marginally useful free map, available from their members, showing the locations of member coffeeshops.

Cannabis College
Oudezijds Achterburgwal 124, Old Centre: Old Side (423 4420/www.cannabiscollege.com).
Tram 4, 9, 14, 16, 24, 25/Metro Nieuwmarkt.
Open 11am-7pm daily. **Admission** free.
Map p306 D3.
Housed over two floors in a 17th-century registered monument in the Red Light District, the Cannabis College aims to provide the public with objective information about the cannabis plant (including its medicinal use). The place is run entirely by volunteers and admission is free; however, staff so request a small €2.50 donation if you take a look at their indoor garden.

Drugs Information Line
0900 1995. **Open** 1-9pm Mon-Fri; Dutch recorded message at other times.
A national advice and information number of the Trimbos Institute (Netherlands Institute of Mental Health and Addiction). When you get through, press '0'; you'll then hear a message in Dutch. Press '4' or stay on the line and you'll be connected to an operator, many of whom speak excellent English. The DIL deals with a wide variety of enquiries, from questions concerning the law to the effects and risks of taking drugs.

Shops & Services

Or how this city can help you part with your money.

Amsterdam doesn't insist you waste your precious posturing and posing time in its museums, galleries and historical streets: the city is just as keen to please those who have come to flex their retail muscle.

The shopping scene has radically changed in the past few years. Great bargains still abound, but the Dutch capital is fast becoming one of the world's great shopping attractions. With its flat streets, few places are as well suited to movement on foot, and unlike the cloned malls you'll find all over the planet, Amsterdam's quirky neighborhood boutiques have personality by the bucketful. Many occupy superb historical canal buildings or sell fantastic art and design. In other words, you'll actually be getting a dose of culture after all.

Antiques & auctions

If you aim to tread the antiques trail, trawl the dense offerings along Spiegelgracht and Nieuwe Spiegelstraat or at the city's many markets (see p164 **Amsterdam's markets**). For a more rarified air, try **Sotheby's** (De Boelenlaan 30, 550 2200/www.sothebys.com) and **Christie's** (Cornelis Schuytstraat 57, 575 5255/www.christies.com).

Art & art supplies

For commercial galleries, see p195. In addition to these and the shops listed below, it's worth checking the shops at the major museums if it's prints and postcards you're after.

Art Multiples
Keizersgracht 510, Southern Canal Belt (624 8419/ www.artmultiples.nl). Tram 1, 2, 5. **Open** 10am-6pm Mon-Wed, Fri, Sat; 10am-5pm Sun. **Credit** AmEx, DC, MC, V. **Map** p310 C4.
The most comprehensive collection of international photographs and posters in the Netherlands, and the largest collection of postcards in Western Europe: a jaw-dropping 40,000, arranged by artist and subject.

J Vlieger
Amstel 34, Southern Canal Belt (623 5834). Tram 4, 9, 14, 16, 24, 25. **Open** noon-6pm Mon; 9am-6pm Tue-Fri; 11am-5.30pm Sat. **Credit** AmEx, DC, MC, V. **Map** p307 E3.
Papers and cards of every description monopolise the ground floor; upstairs are paints, pens and inks, as well as small easels and hobby materials.

Peter van Ginkel
Bilderdijkstraat 99, Oud West (618 9827). Tram 3, 7, 12, 17. **Open** 10am-5.30pm Mon-Fri; 10am-4pm Sat. **Credit** MC, V. **Map** p309 B5.
Heaven for creative types. Shelves groan with paints and pigments, canvas and many types of paper.

Bookshops

Dutch literature is celebrated with events and offers in the third week in March; bookshops focus on children's books during the second week in October. Note: English-language books are pricey here. For book markets, see p178.

General

American Book Center
Kalverstraat 185, Old Centre: New Side (625 5537/ www.abc.nl). Tram 1, 2, 4, 5, 9, 14, 16, 24, 25. **Open** 10am-8pm Mon-Wed, Fri, Sat; 10am-9pm Thur; 11am-6.30pm Sun. **Credit** AmEx, DC, MC, V. **Map** p306 D3.
Since 1972, this vast shop has dealt in English-language books and magazines from the UK and US.

Athenaeum Nieuwscentrum
Spui 14-16, Old Centre: New Side (bookshop 622 6248/news centre 624 2972/www.athenaeum.nl). Tram 1, 2, 5. **Open** *Bookshop* 11am-6pm Mon; 9.30am-6pm Tue, Wed, Fri, Sat; 9.30am-9pm Thur; noon-5.30pm Sun. *News centre* 8am-8pm Mon-Wed, Fri, Sat; 8am-9pm Thur; 10am-6pm Sun. **Credit** AmEx, MC, V. **Map** p310 D4.
Where Amsterdam's high-brow browsers hang out. Athenaeum stocks newspapers from all over the world, as well as a fine choice of magazines, periodicals and books in many languages.

Book Exchange
Kloveniersburgwal 58, Old Centre: Old Side (626 6266). Tram 4, 9, 14/Metro Nieuwmarkt. **Open** 10am-6pm Mon-Fri; 10am-5.30pm Sat; 11.30am-4pm Sun. **No credit cards. Map** p306 D3.
The owner of this book lovers' treasure trove is a shrewd buyer who'll do trade deals. Choose from a plethora of second-hand English and American titles (mainly paperbacks).

English Bookshop
Lauriergracht 71, the Jordaan (626 4230). Tram 7, 10, 17. **Open** 11-6:30pm Tue-Sat; 11am-6pm Sun. **No credit cards. Map** p309 B4.
Fiction, non-fiction, children's books and cookbooks. If you're after reading suggestions, try the proprietor: she knows her stuff.

Waterstone's

*Kalverstraat 152, Old Centre: New Side (638 3821/
www.waterstones.co.uk). Tram 1, 2, 4, 5, 9, 14, 16,
24, 25.* **Open** 11am-6pm Mon, Sun; 9am-6pm Tue,
Wed; 9am-9pm Thur; 9am-7pm Fri; 10am-7pm Sat.
Credit AmEx, MC, V. **Map** p306 D3.

Thousands of books, magazines and videos, all in
English. The children's section is delightful.

Specialist

Architectura & Natura

*Leliegracht 22, Western Canal Belt (623 6186/
www.architectura.nl). Tram 13, 14, 17.* **Open** noon-
6pm Mon; 9am-6pm Tue, Sat; 9am-6.30pm Wed,
Thur, Fri. **Credit** AmEx, MC, V. **Map** p306 C3.

The stock here, much in English, includes books on
architectural history, plant life, gardens and animal
studies. Leliegracht 22 is also home to Antiquariaat
Opbouw, which deals in antiquarian books on architecture and associated topics.

Au Bout du Monde

*Singel 313, Western Canal Belt (625 1397/www.au
boutdumonde.nl). Tram 1, 2, 5.* **Open** 1-6pm Mon;
10am-6pm Tue-Sat. **Credit** MC, V. **Map** p306 C3.

Au Bout du Monde specialises in Eastern philosophy and religion, and stocks a daunting selection of
titles on subjects ranging from psychology to sexu-
ality. There are also magazines, plus related paraphernalia such as incense, cards and videos.

The best Shops

For a chocolate fix
Puccini Bomboni. *See p167.*

For cheese, please
De Kaaskamer. *See p165.*

For bloomin' genius
Florists Gerda's. *See p164.*

For bygone glam
Laura Dols. *See p163.*

Where eyes glaze over
Donald E Jongejans. *See p158.*

For naughty girls' toys
Stout. *See p176.*

For classy combustibles
PGC Hajenius. *See p176.*

Shoe fetishist heaven
Paul Warmer. *See p162.*

Wooden shoe fetishist heaven
't Klompenhuisje. *See p157.*

Intertaal

*Van Baerlestraat 76, Museum Quarter (575 6756/
www.intertaal.nl). Tram 3, 5, 12, 16.* **Open** 1pm-
6pm Mon; 10am-6pm Tue-Fri; 10am-5pm Sat. **Credit**
AmEx, MC, V. **Map** p310 D6.

Dealing in language books, CDs and teaching aids,
Intertaal will be of use to all learners, whether grap-
pling with basic Dutch or advancing their English.

Lambiek

*Kerkstraat 78, Southern Canal Belt (626 7543/
www.lambiek.nl). Tram 1, 2, 5.* **Open** 11am-6pm
Mon-Fri; 11am-5pm Sat; 1-5pm Sun. **Credit** AmEx,
MC, V. **Map** p310 D4.

Lambiek, founded in 1968, claims to be the world's
oldest comic shop and has thousands of books from
around the world; its on-site cartoonists' gallery hosts
exhibitions every two months. During renovation
(till late 2004) the stock moves to nearby No.119.

Pied-à-Terre

*Singel 393, Old Centre: New Side (627 4455/
www.piedaterre.nl). Tram 1, 2, 5.* **Open** 10am-6pm
Mon-Fri; 10am-5pm Sat. *Apr-Aug* 10am-9pm Thur.
No credit cards. Map p310 D4.

Travel books, international guides and maps for
active holidays. Adventurous walkers should talk
to the helpful staff here before a trip out of town.

Department stores

De Bijenkorf

*Dam 1, Old Centre: New Side (552 1700/
www.bijenkorf.nl). Tram 1, 2, 4, 5, 9, 13, 14, 16,
17, 24, 25.* **Open** 11am-7pm Mon; 9.30am-7pm Tue,
Wed; 9.30am-9pm Thur; 9.30am-6pm Sat; noon-
6pm Sun. **Credit** AmEx, DC, MC, V. **Map** p306 D3.

Amsterdam's most notable department store has a
great household goods department and a decent mix
of clothing (designer and own-label), kidswear, jewellery, cosmetics, shoes and accessories. The Chill
Out department caters to funky youngsters in need
of streetwear, clubwear, wacky foodstuffs and kitsch
accessories, while the store's restaurant, La Ruche,
is a good lunch spot. The Sinterklaas and Christmas
displays are extravagant and hugely popular.

Maison de Bonneterie

*Rokin 140-2, Old Centre: New Side (531 3400). Tram
1, 2, 4, 5, 9, 14, 24, 25.* **Open** 1-5.30pm Mon; 10am-
5.30pm Tue, Wed, Fri, Sat; 10am-9pm Thur; noon-
5pm Sun. **Credit** AmEx, DC, MC, V. **Map** p306 D3.

This venerable institution stocks quality men's and
women's clothing 'By Appointment to Her Majesty
Queen Beatrix'. As you'd expect, it's a conservative
affair: the in-store Ralph Lauren boutique is as outlandish as it gets. There's a fine household goods
department and a small café with a scenic view.

Metz & Co

*Leidsestraat 34-6, Southern Canal Belt (520 7020).
Tram 1, 2, 5.* **Open** 11am-6pm Mon; 9.30am-6pm
Tue-Sat; noon-5pm Sun. **Credit** AmEx, DC, MC, V.
Map p310 D4.

Eat, Drink, Shop

Metz is wonderful for upmarket gifts: designer furniture, glass and Liberty-style fabrics and scarves are all available. For lunch with a terrific view of the city, make for the top-floor restaurant. At Yuletide, their Christmas shop will put the holiday spirit back into the Scroogiest customer.

Vroom & Dreesmann

Kalverstraat 203, Old Centre: New Side (0900 235 8363/www.vroomendreesmann.nl). Tram 4, 9, 14, 16, 24, 25. **Open** 11am-6:30pm Mon; 10am-6:30pm Tue, Wed, Fri; 10am-9pm Thur; 10am-6pm Sat; noon-6pm Sun. **Credit** AmEx, MC, V. **Map** p306 D3.

V&D means good quality at prices just a step up from HEMA (*see 163*). There's a staggering array of toiletries, cosmetics, leather goods and watches, clothing and underwear for the whole family, kitchen items, suitcases, CDs and videos. The bakery, Le Marché, sells delicious bread, quiches and sandwiches; there's also a restaurant.

Drugs

Chills & Thrills

Nieuwendijk 17, Old Centre: New Side (638 0015). Tram 13, 14, 17. **Open** 11am-8pm Mon-Wed; 11am-9pm Thur, Sun; 11am-10pm Fri-Sat. **Credit** V. **Map** p306 C2.

A wide selection of pipes and bongs sits alongside the likes of postcards, T-shirts, mushrooms and seeds. The staff will happily show you the portable mini-vaporizer that vaporises pure THC, giving you a clean, smokeless hit.

Conscious Dreams

Kerkstraat 93, Southern Canal Belt (626 6907/ www.consciousdreams.nl). Tram 1, 2, 5. **Open** 12am-7pm Mon-Wed; noon-9pm Thur, Fri, Sat; noon-5pm Sun. Closed Oct-Apr. **Credit** AmEx, DC, MC, V. **Map** p310 D4.

Conscious Dreams was the original proponent of the smart drugs wave in Amsterdam. The staff here really knows their stuff – the owner worked as a drugs adviser for five years – and you're more or less guaranteed to find whatever you're after. **Branch**: Kokopelli Warmoesstraat 12 (421 7000).

Head Shop

Kloveniersburgwal 39, Old Centre: Old Side (624 9061/www.headshop.nl). Tram 4, 9, 14, 16, 24, 25/Metro Nieuwmarkt. **Open** 11am-6pm Mon-Sat. AmEx, MC, V. **Map** p306 D3.

Little has changed at the Head Shop since the 1960s and the store is worth a visit for nostalgic reasons, if nothing else. There are wide selections of pipes, bongs, jewellery, incense and books, and mushrooms and spores – so greenfingered types can cultivate their own – can be had here. Like, maaan.

Hemp Works

Nieuwendijk 13, Old Centre: New Side (421 1762/ www.hempworks.nl/www.thseeds.com). Tram 1, 2, 5, 13, 17. **Open** 11am-7pm Mon-Wed, Sun; 11am-9pm Thur, Fri, Sat. **Credit** AmEx, DC, MC, V. **Map** p306 C2.

One of the first in Amsterdam, and now one of the last retailers selling hemp clothes and products, Hemp Works has had to diversify into seed sales and fresh mushrooms: it won the Cannabis Cup in 2002 with its strain of the stinky weed.

Interpolm

Prins Hendrikkade 11, Old Centre: Old Side (402 0232/www.interpolm.nl). Tram 1, 2, 4, 5, 9, 16, 17, 24, 25/Metro Centraal Station. **Open** 1-6pm Mon; 10am-6pm Tue-Fri; 9am-5pm Sat. **Credit** MC, V. **Map** p306 D2.

Everything needed to set up a grow centre at home, and not just for drugs: Interpolm carries hydroponics and organic equipment, bio-growth books and videos for green-fingered types of all stripes.

Electronics

Expert Mons

Utrechtsestraat 80-2, Southern Canal Belt (624 5082). Tram 4/Metro Waterlooplein. **Open** noon-6pm Mon; 9.30am-6pm Tue-Sat. **Credit** AmEx, MC, V. **Map** p311 E4.

Washing machines, TVs, stereos, blenders, fridges and other appliances, most at competitive prices.

Fabrics & trimmings

Capsicum

Oude Hoogstraat 1, Old Centre: Old Side (623 1016). Tram 4, 9, 14, 16, 24, 25. **Open** 11am-6pm Mon; 10am-6pm Tue, Wed, Fri, Sat; 10am-9pm Thur. **Credit** AmEx, DC, MC, V. **Map** p306 D3.

All the fabrics here are made from natural fibres, such as cotton woven in India. Staff spin the provenance of each fabric into the sale. A gem.

H J van de Kerkhof

Wolvenstraat 11, Western Canal Belt (623 4666). Tram 1, 2, 5. **Open** 11am-6pm Mon; 11am-6pm Tue-Fri; 11am-5pm Sat. **Credit** MC, V. **Map** p310 C4.

Tassel maniacs will go wild here: it's a sea of shakeable frilly things, lace and rhinestone banding.

Stoffen & Fourituren Winkel a Boeken

Nieuwe Hoogstraat 31, Old Centre: Old Side (626 7205). Tram 4, 9, 16, 24, 25. **Open** noon-6pm Mon; 10am-6pm Tue, Wed, Fri; 10am-8pm Thur; 10am-5pm Sat. **Credit** MC, V. **Map** p307 E3.

The Boeken family has been hawking fabrics since 1920. Just try to find somewhere else with this kind of variety: latex, Lycra, fake fur and sequins galore.

Fashion

Children

Shops listed below carry new kids' togs. Funky vintage clothes can be found at **Noordermarkt**; for budget garments, try **Albert Cuypmarkt** (for both, *see p164* **Amsterdam's markets**).

Where to spend it

Although reckless abandon and aimless drifting can make for some memorable shopping trips, sometimes having a plan of action doesn't hurt. So, here's a cheat sheet detailing the general characteristics of Amsterdam's main shopping districts to help make your spending spree a breeze.

DAMSTRAAT
A street at war with its former self, Damstraat is fighting to jettison the sleaze and metamorphose into a boutique-lined oasis. Alas, its proximity to the Red Light District means laddish types can impinge on this otherwise lovely neighbourhood all too easily.

MAGNA PLAZA
Right behind Dam Square, this architectural treat was once a post office. Its reincarnation as a five-floor mall is beloved by tourists, though locals are less keen.

KALVERSTRAAT AND NIEUWENDIJK
Kalverstraat and its more scruffy extension Nieuwendijk are where locals come for consumer kicks. Shops here are largely unexciting, yet they still get insanely busy on Sundays. Still, it's pedestrian-only, so you can forget the dreaded bike menace and focus on the tills.

LEIDSESTRAAT
Connecting Koningsplein and Leidseplein, Leidsestraat is peppered with fine shoe shops and boutiques but you'll still have to dodge trams to shop there. Cyclists: note that bikes aren't allowed in this part of town. And yes, police do notice.

NINE STREETS
The small streets connecting Prinsengracht, Keizersgracht and Herengracht between Raadhuisstraat and Leidsegracht offer a diverse density of boutiques, antiques and speciality stores.

THE JORDAAN
Tiny backstreets laced with twisting canals, cosy boutiques, lush markets, bakeries, galleries, restful and old fashioned cafés and bars. The Jordaan captures the spirit of Amsterdam like nowhere else.

PC HOOFTSTRAAT
Amsterdam's elite shopping strip has had a rocky ride in the last few years, but with a new infusion of designer shops embracing both established and up-and-coming names, things are looking better.

SPIEGELKWARTIER
Across from the Rijksmuseum and centred on Spiegelgracht, this area is packed with antiques shops selling authentic treasures at accordingly high prices. Dress for success and keep your nose in the air.

THE PIJP
This bustling district is notable mainly for the Albert Cuypmarkt and its ethnic food shops.

Geboortewinkel Amsterdam
Bosboom Toussaintstraat 22-4, Museum Quarter (683 1806). Tram 3, 7, 10, 12. **Open** 1-6pm Mon; 10am-6pm Tue-Fri; 10am-5pm Sat. **Credit** MC, V. **Map** p310 C5.
A beautiful range of maternity and baby clothes (including premature sizes) in cotton, wool and linen. You'll also find baby articles, cotton nappy systems and videos about childbirth.

't Klompenhuisje
Nieuwe Hoogstraat 9A, Old Centre: Old Side (622 8100). Tram 4, 9, 14/Metro Nieuwmarkt. **Open** 10am-6pm Mon-Sat. **Credit** AmEx, DC, MC, V. **Map** p307 E3.
Delightfully crafted and reasonably priced shoes, traditional clogs and handmade leather and woolen slippers from baby sizes up to size 35.

't Schooltje
Overtoom 87, Museum Quarter (683 0444). Tram 1, 2, 5, 6. **Open** 1-6pm Mon; 9am-6pm Tue, Wed, Fri; 9am-9pm Thur; 9.30am-5.30pm Sat; 9.30am-5.30pm 1st Sun of mth. **Credit** AmEx, DC, MC, V. **Map** p309 B6.

Well-heeled and well-dressed kids (babies and kids aged up to 16) are clothed and shod here. The ranges are good but costly. Party costumes are a speciality.

Clubwear

For hardcore club aficionados, life has got a whole lot easier. Not only are the number and size of Amsterdam's clubwear shops growing, but they've all gravitated to the Spuistraat.

Clubwear House
Spuistraat 242, Old Centre: New Side (622 8766/ www.clubwearhouse.com). Tram 1, 2, 5. **Open** 11am-7pm Mon-Sat; 11am-9pm Thur. **Credit** AmEx, DC, MC, V. **Map** p306 C3.
Clubby clothes from all around the world, plus from its own label, Wearhouse 2000, and an in-house designer. The staff of clubbers know their proverbial onions and will be able to help you out with flyers or pre-sale tickets. DJ tapes are also available.

Cyberdog

Spuistraat 250, Old Centre: New Side (330 6385/ www.cyberdog.net). Tram 1, 2, 5. **Open** 11am-7pm Mon-Sat; 11am-9pm Thur. *Winter closing hours may vary.* **Credit** AmEx, MC, V. **Map** p306 C3.

Their mission is 'to stay one step ahead in the future of fashion', but to infinity and beyond is more like it. Rack after rack of spacey trippy tech creations for the most dedicated clubbers.

Housewives on Fire

Spuistraat 102, Old Centre: New Side (422 1067). Tram 1, 2, 5. **Open** noon-7pm Mon;10am-7pm Tue, Wed, Fri, Sat; 10am-9pm Thur. **Credit** MC, V. **Map** p306 C3.

Club clothes and accessories, an in-house hair salon offering colours, extensions and dreads, loads o'gaudy make-up, nail polishes and body paints, club flyers... All of which can be washed down with a glass of rosé at weekends.

Designer

For local designer fashion, *see p172* **Mode in the Netherlands.**

Azurro Due

Pieter Cornelisz Hooftstraat 138, Museum Quarter (671 9708). Tram 2, 3, 5, 12. **Open** 1-6pm Mon; 10am-6pm Tue, Wed, Fri; 10am-9pm Thur; 10am-5.30pm Sat; noon-5pm Sun. **Credit** AmEx, DC, MC, V. **Map** p310 C6.

If you want to splurge on designer duds, this is as good a spot as any. Saucy picks from Anna Sui, D&G, Philosophy, Chloé, Girbaud and MiuMiu attract B-celebs, PR girls, advertising wenches, and retail babes out to make their one big buy.

Khymo

Leidsestraat 9, Southern Canal Belt (622 2137). Tram 1, 2, 5. **Open** noon-6pm Mon; 10am-6pm Tue, Wed, Fri, Sat; 10am-9pm Thur; 1-5pm Sun. **Credit** AmEx, DC, MC, V. **Map** p310 D4.

20- to 40-somethings, both male and female, come for the trendy garb here. Among the labels on offer are Plein Sud, Evisu and Amaya Arzuaga.

Local Service

Keizersgracht 400-402, Western Canal Belt (626 6840). Tram 13, 14, 17. **Open** 1-6pm Mon; 10am-6pm Tue, Wed, Fri; 10am-7.30pm Thur; 10am-5.30pm Sat; 1-5.30pm Sun. **Credit** AmEx, DC, MC, V. **Map** p310 C4.

Two tiny shops sitting like kittens on a scenic canal corner form the main distribution point for Paul Smith in Amsterdam. There are also eclectic pieces by other designers that the owner chooses for their ability to complement Paul's pieces.

Razzmatazz

Wolvenstraat 19, Western Canal Belt (420 0483/ www.razzmatazz.nl). Tram 13, 14, 17. **Open** noon-6pm Mon; 11am-6pm Tue, Wed, Fri, Sat; noon-7pm Thur; 1-5.30pm Sun. **Credit** AmEx, DC, MC, V. **Map** p310 C4.

Although the staff are sometimes a pain, Razz is still a must-see on account of its designers, from Westwood's Anglomania line to Masaki Matsushima.

Spoiled

Leidsestraat 27, Southern Canal Belt (626 3818/ www.spoiled.nl) Tram 1, 2, 5. **Open** 10am-6pm Mon-Wed, Sat; 10am-9pm Thur; noon-6pm Sun. **Credit** AmEx, MC, V. **Map** p310 D4.

A lifestyle shop along London or NY lines, with edgy designs by the likes of Duffer of St. George, Evisu and Juicy Couture, plus LA coaster bikes, a hairdresser and a selection of music and mags to make your transformation complete.

2πR

Oude Hoogstraat 10, Old Centre: Old Side (421 6329). Tram 4, 9, 14, 16, 24, 25. **Open** noon-7pm Mon; 10am-7pm Tue, Wed, Fri, Sat; 10am-9pm Thur; noon-6pm Sun. **Credit** AmEx, DC, MC, V. **Map** p306 D3.

This funky number's just for the boys. Two shops side by side on Oude Hoogstraat offer urban streetwear and killer threads from the likes of Helmut Lang, Psycho Cowboy and Anglomania. **Other locations:** Gasthuismolensteeg 12 (528 5682).

Van Ravenstein

Keizersgracht 359, Western Canal Belt (639 0067) Tram 13, 14, 17. **Open** 1-6pm Mon; 11am-6pm Tue, Wed, Fri; 11am-7pm Thur; 10.30am-5.30pm Sat. **Credit** AmEx, MC, V. **Map** p310 C4.

Superb boutique with the best from Belgian designers: Martin Margiela, Dirk Bikkembergs, Ann Demeulemeester, A.F. Vandervorst and Bernhard Willhelm, Victor & Rolf forms the Dutch contingent. Don't miss the itsy-bitsy bargain basement.

Glasses & contact lenses

Brilmuseum/Brillenwinkel

Gasthuismolensteeg 7, Western Canal Belt (421 2414/ www.brilmuseumamsterdam.nl). Tram 1, 2, 5. **Open** 11.30am-5.30pm Wed-Fri; 11.30am-5pm Sat. **No credit cards. Map** p306 C3.

Officially this 'shop' is an opticians' museum, but don't let that put you off. The fascinating exhibits are of glasses through the ages, and most of the pairs you see are also for sale.

Donald E Jongejans

Noorderkerkstraat 18, the Jordaan (624 6888). Tram 3, 10. **Open** 11am-6pm Mon-Sat. **No credit cards. Map** p305 B2.

This vintage frame specialist sells unused frames dating from the mid 1800s to the present day. Most frames are at fabulously low prices and built to last – and staff are friendly. A complete treat.

Villa Ruimzicht

Utrechtsestraat 131, Southern Canal Belt (428 2665). Tram 4. **Open** 1-6pm Mon; 9am-6pm Tue, Wed, Fri; 9am-6pm, 7-9pm Thur; 9am-5pm Sat. **Credit** AmEx, MC, V. **Map** p311 E4.

Eat, Drink, Shop

You must **Ree-member** this. *See p163.*

If you're bored of coloured contacts lenses, come here for $ signs and more. They also stock a wide range of designer specs.

Hats & handbags

Many outdoor markets have huge selections of hats and bags. For warm winter gear and knock-off bags at low prices, hit **Albert Cuypmarkt**.

Cellarrich Connexion

Haarlemmerdijk 98, the Jordaan (626 5526). Tram 1, 2, 4, 5, 13, 14, 16, 17, 24, 25. **Open** 1-6pm Mon; 11am-6pm Tue-Fri; 11am-5pm Sat. **Credit** AmEx, MC, V. **Map** p305 B2.

Nab a sophisticated Dutch handbag in materials from leather to plastic. Many (but not all) of the creations are produced locally by four Dutch designers.

De Hoed van Tijn

Nieuwe Hoogstraat 15, Old Centre: Old Side (623 2759). Tram 4, 9, 14, 16, 24, 25. **Open** 11am-6pm Mon-Sat. **Credit** AmEx, DC, MC, V. **Map** p307 E3.

Mad hatters will delight in this vast array of bonnets, Homburgs, sombreros and caps, hats from as far back as 1900, plus second-hand and handmade items.

High street

America Today

Ground floor, Magna Plaza, Spuistraat 137, Old Centre: New Side (638 8447/www.americatoday.nl). Tram 1, 2, 5, 13, 14, 17. **Open** 11am-7pm Mon; 10am-7pm Tue, Wed, Fri, Sat; 10am-9pm Thur; noon-7pm Sun. **Credit** AmEx, DC, MC, V. **Map** p306 C2.

This giant started as the tiniest of ventures; today it sells American classics (Converse, Timberland and the like) at incredibly cheap prices.
Other locations: Sarphatistraat 48 (638 9847).

Exota

Hartenstraat 10, Western Canal Belt (620 9102/www.exota.com). Tram 1, 2, 5, 13, 14, 17. **Open** 11am-6pm Mon; 10am-6pm Tue, Wed, Fri, Sat; 10am-9pm Thur; 1-5pm Sun. **Credit** AmEx, DC, MC, V. **Map** p306 C3.

Tread the fine line between high street and street fashion with this funky little shop's original selection of simple yet stylish clothes and accessories.
Other locations: Nieuwe Leliestraat 32 (420 6884).

Hennes & Mauritz

Kalverstraat 125-9, Old Centre: New Side (624 0624). Tram 1, 2, 4, 5, 9, 14, 16, 24, 25. **Open** noon-6pm Mon, Sun; 10am-6pm Tue, Wed, Fri, Sat; 10am-9pm Thur. **Credit** AmEx, DC, MC, V. **Map** p306 D3.

Prices range from reasonable to ultra low; quality, too, is variable. Clothes for men, women, teens and kids are trend-conscious, plus there are often updates of classics.
Other locations: across town; check the phone book.

Sissy Boy Homeland

Magna Plaza, Spuistraat 137, Old Centre: New Side (389 2589/www.sissy-boy.nl). Tram 1, 2, 4, 5, 9, 14, 16, 24, 25. **Open** 11am-7pm Mon; 10am-7pm Tue, Wed, Fri, Sat; 10am-9pm Thur; noon-7pm Sun. **Credit** AmEx, DC, MC, V. **Map** p306 C3.

A mixture of clothing and interior items, Sissy Boy's new lifestyle shop has a decidedly upmarket rustic-urban vibe. Expect a truly quirky jumble of labels and wares; candles from the Diptyque range, satin quilts, Sissy Boy khakis, Paul Smith accessories, deer antler chairs and much more.

Zara

Kalverstraat 67-9, Old Centre: New Side (530 4050). Tram 1, 2, 4, 5, 9, 14, 16, 24, 25. **Open** noon-6pm Mon, Sun; 10am-6pm Tue, Wed, Fri, Sat; 10am-9pm Thur. **Credit** AmEx, MC, V. **Map** p306 D3.

Eat, Drink, Shop

A girl's best friend

Amsterdam is famous for its diamond trade. Indeed, it's a heritage that's still marketed heavily to this day. To be honest, the city's sparkler shops are as much tourist attractions as they are retail outlets. Still, to experience an aspirational brush with luxury, take a tour around any one of them. Just remember: falling in love with a diamond is the easy part – working out how you're going to pay for it may prove to be a little more tricky.

Amsterdam Diamond Centre

Rokin 1-5, Old Centre: New Side (624 5787/www.amsterdamdiamondcentre.nl). Tram 4, 9, 14, 16, 20, 24, 25. **Open** 10am-6pm Mon-Wed, Fri-Sun; 10am-8.30pm Thur. **Credit** AmEx, DC, MC, V. **Map** p306 D2.

Coster Diamonds

Paulus Potterstraat 2-8, Museum Quarter (305 5555/www.costerdiamonds.com). Tram 2, 3, 5. **Open** 9am-5pm daily. **Credit** AmEx, DC, MC, V. **Map** p310 D6.

Gassan Diamond BV

Nieuwe Uilenburgerstraat 173-5, Old Centre: Old Side (622 5333/www.gassan diamond. com). Tram 9, 14, 20. **Open** 9am-5pm daily. **Credit** AmEx, DC, MC, V. **Map** p307 E2.

Van Moppes & Zoon

Albert Cuypstraat 2-6, the Pijp (676 1242). Tram 16, 24, 25. **Open** 8.45am-5.45pm daily. **Credit** AmEx, DC, MC, V. **Map** p311 E6.

Imagine you have a magnificent fashion machine that can churn out decent approximations of the latest catwalk creations; now imagine they are a fraction of the price. Oops! Too late, Zara beat you to it. The styles are hot – the quality perhaps not.

Jewellery

For diamonds, *see above* **A girl's best friend**.

Biba

Nieuwe Hoogstraat 26, Old Centre: Old Side (330 5721). Tram 4, 9, 14, 16, 24, 25. **Open** 1-6pm Mon; 11am-6pm Tue-Sat; 1-5pm Sun. **Credit** AmEx, MC, V. **Map** p307 E3.
Come here for funky jewellery designed by well-known names like Gaultier, Gem Kingdom, Vivienne Westwood and E Beamon. A selection of less exclusive but still attractive brands is also available for those on a less-than-flamboyant budget.

Grimm Sieraden

Grimburgwal 9, Old Centre: Old Side (622 0501). Tram 16, 24, 25. **Open** 11am-6pm Tue-Fri; 11am-5pm Sat. **Credit** AmEx, DC, MC, V. **Map** p306 D3.
Elize Lutz's appealing gallery shop features the freshest jewellery designers; she always makes a point of stocking the most wearable pieces from the latest cutting-edge ranges.

Jorge Cohen Edelsmid

Singel 414, Southern Canal Belt (623 8646). Tram 1, 2, 5, 10. **Open** 10am-6pm Tue-Fri; 11am-6pm Sat. **Credit** AmEx, MC, V. **Map** p310 D4.
Get your mitts on the kind of art deco-inspired jewellery you'd be proud to pass off as the real thing. The shop creates its charming pieces using a combination of salvaged jewellery, silver and antique and new stones.

Large sizes

G&G Special Sizes

Prinsengracht 514, Southern Canal Belt (622 6339). Tram 1, 2, 5. **Open** 9am-5.30pm Tue, Wed, Fri; 9am-5.30pm, 7-9pm Thur; 9am-5pm Sat. **Credit** AmEx, DC, MC, V. **Map** p310 D5.
The big news is that G&G stock a full range of men's clothing from sizes 58 to 75. Pay a bit extra and sales assistants will also tailor garments to fit.

Mateloos

Kwakarsplein 1-7, Oud West (683 2384). Tram 3, 12, 13, 14, 17. **Open** 10am-6pm Mon-Fri; 10am-5pm Sat. **Credit** AmEx, DC, MC, V. **Map** p309 B5.
Mateloos cares for curves with an enormous variety of clothing for women from sizes 44 to 60: evening-wear, sportswear, lingerie, swimwear, the works.

Lingerie

Hunkemöller

Kalverstraat 162, Old Centre: New Side (623 6032). Tram 1, 2, 5, 9, 14, 16, 24, 25. **Open** 11am-6pm Mon; 9.30am-6pm Tue, Wed, Fri, Sat; 9.30am-9pm Thur; noon-6pm Sun. **Credit** AmEx, MC, V. **Map** p306 D3.
Female fancy pants should check out this chain with six branches in and around Amsterdam (call 035 646 5413 for details of others). The undies are attractive, yet simply designed and reasonably priced.

Robin's Bodywear

Nieuwe Hoogstraat 20, Old Centre: Old Side (620 1552). Tram 4, 9, 14, 16, 24, 25. **Open** 1-6pm Mon-Wed; 11am-6pm Thur, Fri; 11am-5.30pm Sat. **Credit** AmEx, MC, V. **Map** p307 E3.
Larger than the typical women's lingerie shop, Robin's has underwear, swimwear and hosiery by Naf-Naf, Calvin Klein, Lou and others.

Eat, Drink, Shop

Tothem Underwear

Nieuwezijds Voorburgwal 149, Old Centre: New Side (623 0641). Tram 1, 2, 4, 5, 9, 13, 14, 16, 17, 24, 25. **Open** 1-5.30pm Mon; 9.45am-5.30pm Tue, Wed, Fri; 9.45am-9pm Thur; 9.45am-5pm Sat; 1-5pm Sun. **Credit** AmEx, DC, MC, V. **Map** p306 D3.

This men's underwear shop mainly sells designer items: Hom, Calvin Klein, Body Art and the like.

Repairs & cleaning

Clean Brothers

Kerkstraat 56, Southern Canal Belt (622 0273). Tram 16, 24, 25. **Open** 9am-7pm Mon-Sat. **No credit cards. Map** p311 E4.

Washing and dry-cleaning in a relatively central location. Prices are reasonable.

Luk's Schoenservice

Prinsengracht 500, Southern Canal Belt (623 1937). Tram 1, 2, 5, 6, 7, 10. **Open** 9am-5.30pm Tue-Fri; 9am-5pm Sat. **No credit cards. Map** p310 D5.

Reliable and speedy shoe repairs.

Shoes

The best pick of men's and women's shoes can be had on **Leidsestraat** or **Kalverstraat**; for second-hand bargains, go to **Waterlooplein** and **Noordermarkt** on Mondays (for both, *see p164* **Amsterdam's markets**).

Big Shoe

Leliegracht 12, Western Canal Belt (622 6645). Tram 13, 14, 17. **Open** 10am-6pm Wed, Fri; 10am-9pm Thur; 10am-5pm Sat. **Credit** AmEx, DC, MC, V. **Map** p306 C3.

Fashionable footwear for men and women in large sizes only. Every women's shoe on display is available in sizes 42 to 46, men's from 47 to 50.

Kenneth Cole

Leidsestraat 20-22, Southern Canal Belt (627 6012/ www.kennethcole.com). Tram 1, 2, 5. **Open** noon-6pm Mon, Sun; 10am-6pm Tue, Wed, Fri, Sat; 10am-9pm Thur. **Credit** AmEx, MC, V. **Map** p310 D4.

Kenneth Cole stocks its own conservatively styled quality shoes. Stock changes often and bargains can be had during the frequent sales.

Paul Warmer

Leidsestraat 41, Southern Canal Belt (427 8011). Tram 1, 2, 5. **Open** noon-6pm Mon, Sun; 10am-6pm Tue, Wed, Fri, Sat; 10am-9pm Thur. **Credit** AmEx, DC, MC, V. **Map** p310 D4.

Fashionista heaven: ultra-refined footwear for men and women. Expect to find top stuff from Gucci, YSL, Roberto Cavalli and Emillio Pucci, among others.

Seventy Five

Nieuwe Hoogstraat 24, Old Centre: Old Side (626 4611). Tram 4, 9, 14/Metro Nieuwmarkt. **Open** noon-6pm Mon; 10am-6pm Tue-Sat. **Credit** MC, V. **Map** p307 E3.

Trainers for folk who don't have sport in mind: high fashion styles from Nike, Puma, Converse, Diesel. Acupuncture and many more.

Shoe Baloo

Pieter Cornelisz Hooftstraat 80, Museum Quarter (626 7993). Tram 2, 3, 5, 12. **Open** noon-6pm Mon; 10am-6pm Tue, Wed, Fri, Sat; 10am-9pm Thur; 1-6pm Sun. **Credit** AmEx, MC, V. **Map** p310 C6.

A space age shoe shop with a glowing Barbarella-pod interior. Über cool and hence worth taking the time to pop your head in and cruise the shelves for Miu Miu, Costume Nationale, Patrick Cox, and other men's and women's footwear.

Other locations: Leidsestraat 10 (626 7993).

Street

To look good but pay less, hunt down relaxed streetwear styles in **Waterlooplein Market** (*see p165* **Amsterdam's markets**).

Diesel

Heiligeweg 11-17, Old Centre: New Side (638 4082). Tram 1, 2, 4, 5, 9, 14, 16, 24, 25. **Open** noon-6pm Mon, Sun; 10am-6pm Tue, Wed, Fri, Sat; 10am-9pm Thur. **Credit** AmEx, MC, V. **Map** p310 D4.

Three stories high, filled with Diesel and Diesel only; this shop has a retro '60s decor, rockin' tunes, and fashion for the label conscious.

Henxs

Sint Antoniesbreestraat 136, Old Centre: Old Side (638 9478/www.henxs.com). Tram 4, 9, 14/Metro Nieuwmarkt. **Open** noon-6pm Mon, Sun; 11am-6pm Tue-Sat. **Credit** AmEx, MC, V. **Map** p307 E3.

A skater's paradise of graffiti magazines and hip hop styles. DJs spin as you scan the urban gear from casual Carhartt and local label g-sus.

Independent Outlet

Vijzelstraat 77, Southern Canal Belt (421 2096/ www.outlet.nl). Tram 16, 24, 25. **Open** 1-6pm Mon; 11am-6pm Tue, Wed, Fri, Sat; 11am-9pm Thur. **Credit** AmEx, MC, V. **Map** p310 D4.

Customized boards, Vans shoes and labels like Fred Perry: just some of the things in store at this temple to street cool. Great selection of punk imports.

Men at Work

Kalverstraat 172, Old Centre: New Side (624 1000/ www.menatwork.nl). Tram 1, 2, 4, 5, 9, 14, 16, 24, 25. **Open** noon-6pm Mon, Sun; 10am-6pm Tue, Wed, Fri, Sat; 10am-9pm Thur. **Credit** AmEx, MC, V. **Map** p310 D4.

The naff name doesn't stop it being the best address for denim labels like G-Star, Evisu, Kuyichi, Pepe, Levi's, Energy, and more.

Rodolfos

Magna Plaza, Spuistraat 137, Old Centre: New Side (623 1214/www.rdlfs.nl). Tram 1, 2, 5, 13, 17. **Open** 11am-7pm Mon; 10am-7pm Tue, Wed, Fri, Sat; 10am-9pm Thur; noon-7pm Sun. **Credit** AmEx, MC, V. **Map** p306 C3.

From cut-price to cutting-edge

A quarter of the Dutch population wakes to the ring of a HEMA alarm clock, one in three men wears HEMA underwear, and one in four women wears HEMA bras. HEMA sells 506,000 kilograms of *drop* (liquorice) every year, and the cashiers of their 250 national outlets process 14 million units of *tompouce* (a pink-glazed custard cake) annually, and one smoked sausage per second. Yes, the department store chain has come a long way since 1926, when it started as a 'one price business' selling products for ten, 25 and 50 cents. It was 1969 before they stocked a product that cost more than 100 guilders – an electric drill – which wrecked havoc on their two-digit cash registers. While HEMA remains the economic place to shop for basics, it's also made a name for itself as

a source of affordable, no-nonsense design objects – even their sale flyers are graphics classics. They've had products designed by bigwigs like Piet Hein Eek, Gijs Bakke and Hella Jongerius, and had a big hit in their Le Lapia whistle kettle, selling over 250,000. Of course, they've had some flops – like their award-winning hairless toilet brush – but that's life. If you like to shop, you'll love HEMA.

HEMA
Kalvertoren, Singel 457, Southern Canal Belt (422 8988/www.hema.nl). Tram 1, 2, 4, 5, 9, 14, 16, 24, 25. **Open** 11am-6.30pm Mon; 9.30am-6.30pm Tue, Wed, Fri; 9.30am-9pm Thur; 9.30am-6pm Sat; noon-6pm Sun. **Credit** MC, V. **Map** p306 D3.
Other locations: Ferdinand Bolstraat 93A, (676 3222); Kinkerstraat 313, (683 4511); Nieuwendijk 174-6, (623 4176).

An inline skate and skateboard outlet with its ear to the street. T-shirts and trainers are mainstays among its desperately hip customers.
Other locations: Sarphatistraat 59 (622 5488).

Vintage & second-hand

Loads of fab vintage clothes and accessories can be found (and often at cheaper prices) at **Noordermarkt** and **Waterlooplein**.

Lady Day
Hartenstraat 9, Western Canal Belt (623 5820). Tram 1, 2, 5. **Open** 11am-6pm Mon-Wed, Fri, Sat; 11am-9pm Thur; 1-6pm Sun. **Credit** AmEx, MC, V. **Map** p306 C3.
Beautifully tailored second-hand and period suits, and sportswear classics. Period wedge shoes, pumps and accessories complete the stylish ensemble.

Laura Dols
Wolvenstraat 6-7, Western Canal Belt (624 9066). Tram 1, 2, 5. **Open** 11am-6pm Mon-Wed, Fri, Sat; 11am-9pm Thur; 2-6pm Sun. **Credit** MC, V. **Map** p310 C4.

Laura Dols is a treasure trove of period clothing, much of it dating from the '40s and '50s. The stock is largely for women (there are some truly sumptuous dresses), but you'll find some menswear.

Ree-member
Reestraat 26, Western Canal Belt (622 1329). Tram 1, 2, 5. **Open** 1-6pm Mon; 11am-6pm Tue-Sat. **Credit** AmEx, MC, V. **Map** p306 C3.
Ree-member stocks a terrific collection of of vintage clothes and '60s standards. Their vintage shoes are easily the best in town and are priced accordingly. If you're strapped for cash you'll be pleased to learn that they sell their less-than-perfect pieces on the Noordermarkt – by the kilo! Ain't life sweet?

Zipper
Huidenstraat 7, Western Canal Belt (623 7302). Tram 1, 2, 5. **Open** 11am-6pm Mon-Wed, Fri, Sat; 11am-9pm Thur; 1-5pm Sun. **Credit** AmEx, MC, V. **Map** p310 C4.
It's not cheap, but the jeans, cowboy shirts, '80s gear and 1970s hipsters are certainly worth a gander; with luck, you'll turn up some unusual treasures.
Other locations: Nieuwe Hoogstraat 8 (627 0353).

Amsterdam's markets

Albert Cuypmarkt

Albert Cuypstraat, the Pijp. Tram 4, 16, 24, 25. **Open** 9.30am-5pm Mon-Sat. **No credit cards. Map** p311 E5.

Amsterdam's largest general market sells everything from pillows to prawns at great prices. Clothes tend to be run-of-the-mill cheapies, with the odd bargain.

Boerenmarkt

Westerstraat/Noorderkerkstraat, the Jordaan. Tram 3, 10. **Open** 9am-3pm Sat. **No credit cards. Map** p306 B2.

Every Saturday, the Noordermarkt turns into an organic farmers' market. Groups of singers or medieval musicians sometimes make a visit feel more like a day trip than a shopping binge.

Dappermarkt

Dapperstraat, Oost. Tram 3, 6, 10, 14. **Open** 9am-5pm Mon-Sat. **No credit cards. Map** p312 H3.

Dappermarkt is a locals' market: for one thing, prices don't rise in accordance with the number of visitors. It sells all the usual market fodder, with plenty of cheap clothes and underwear.

Looier

Elandsgracht 109, the Jordaan (624 9038). Tram 7, 10, 17. **Open** 11am-5pm Mon-Thur, Sat, Sun. **Credit** AmEx, DC, MC, V. **Map** p310 C4.

Mainly antiques here, with plenty of collectors' items. It's easy to get lost in the quiet premises and find yourself standing alone by a stall crammed with antiquated clocks eerily ticking.

Noordermarkt

Noordermarkt, the Jordaan. Tram 3, 10. **Open** 7.30am-1pm Mon. **No credit cards. Map** p306 B2.

Tagged on to the end of the Westermarkt, the Noordermarkt is compact and frequented by the serious shopper. The stacks of (mainly second-hand) clothes, shoes, jewellery and hats need to be sorted with a grim determination, but there are real bargains

Flowers

It's tempting to bring home a selection of bulbs from Amsterdam. However, though travellers to the UK and Ireland will be absolutely fine, some other countries' import regulations either prohibit the entry of bulbs or, in the case of the US, require them to have a phytosanitary certificate. You'll find that some of the packaging is helpfully marked with flags indicating the countries into which the bulbs can safely be carried, but most Dutch wholesalers know the regulations and can ship bulbs to your home. In terms of cut flowers, travellers to the UK and Ireland can take an unlimited quantity, as long as none are chrysanthemums or gladioli, while US regulations vary from state to state.

Bloemenmarkt (Flower market)

Singel, between Muntplein and Koningsplein, Southern Canal Belt. **Open** 9.30am-5pm Mon-Sat. **No credit cards. Map** p310 D4.

This fascinating collage of colour is the world's only floating flower market, with 15 florists and garden shops (although many are hawking cheesy souvenirs these days) permanently ensconced on barges along the southern side of Singel. The plants and flowers usually last well and are good value.

Plantenmarkt (Plant market)

Amstelveld, Southern Canal Belt. Tram 4, 6, 7, 10. **Open** 9.30am-6pm Mon. **No credit cards. Map** p311 E4.

Despite the market's predominant emphasis on plants, pots and vases, the Plantenmarkt also has some flowers for sale. In spring, most plants are meant for the balcony or living room, while later in the year there are more garden plants and bedding plants suitable for flower boxes.

Florists Gerda's

Runstraat 16, Western Canal Belt (624 2912). Tram 1, 2, 5. **Open** 9am-6pm Mon-Fri; 9am-5pm Sat. **Credit** AmEx, DC, MC, V. **Map** p310 C4.

Amsterdam's most inspired florist, Gerda's shop while diminutive is full of fantastic blooms and sports legendary window displays. If you're lucky, you'll spy sculptural bouquets on their way out the door. Gerda's takes orders for local deliveries from anywhere in the world – pay by phone with plastic.

Jemi

Warmoesstraat 83A, Old Centre: Old Side (625 6034). Tram 4, 9, 16, 24, 25. **Open** 9am-6pm Mon-Fri. **No credit cards. Map** p306 D2.

Amsterdam's first stone-built house is now occupied by a delightfully colourful florist. Jemi puts together splendid bouquets, provides tuition in the fragrant art of flower arranging, throws floral brunches and stocks loads of pots and plants.

to be had here. Arrive early or the best stuff will probably have been nabbed.

Oudemanhuis Book Market

Oudemanhuispoort, Old Centre: Old Side. Tram 4, 9, 14, 16, 24, 25. **Open** 11am-4pm Mon-Fri. **No credit cards. Map** p306 D3.
People have been buying and selling books, prints and sheet music at this arcade since the 19th century.

Postzegelmarkt

Nieuwezijds Voorburgwal, by No.276, Old Centre: New Side. Tram 1, 2, 5, 13, 17, 20. **Open** 11am-4pm Wed, Sun. **No credit cards. Map** p306 D3.
A specialist market for collectors of stamps, coins, postcards and medals.

Rommelmarkt

Looiersgracht 38, the Jordaan. Tram 7, 10, 17, 20. **Open** 11am-5pm daily. **No credit cards. Map** p310 C4.
A flea market where, nestled among the junk, you're likely to stumble across such dubious

bargains as a boxed set of Demis Roussos records. Tempting, no?

Waterlooplein

Waterlooplein, Jodenbuurt. Tram 9, 14, 20/Metro Waterlooplein. **Open** 9am-5pm Mon-Sat. **No credit cards. Map** p307 E3.
Amsterdam's top tourist market is basically a huge flea market with the added attraction of loads of clothes stalls (though gear can be a bit pricey and, at many stalls, a bit naff). Bargains can be had, but they may be hidden under cheap 'n' nasty toasters and down-at-heel (literally) shoes.

Westermarkt

Westerstraat, the Jordaan. Tram 3, 10. **Open** 9am-1pm Mon. **No credit cards. Map** p306 B2.
A general market, selling all sorts of stuff. The amount of people packing the pavement is proof as to the entirely reasonable prices and the range of goods, which includes new watches, pretty (and not so pretty) fabrics and cheap factory reject clothes.

Food & drink

Bakeries

For bread, rolls and packaged biscuits, go to a *warmebakker*; for pastries and wickedly delicious cream cakes, you need a *banketbakker*.

Mediterrane

Haarlemmerdijk 184, the Jordaan (620 3550). Tram 3/bus 18, 22. **Open** 8am-8pm daily. **No credit cards. Map** p305 B2.
French, Moroccan and Dutch baking traditions are all practised under this one roof, with mouthwatering results. The finest croissants in town, too.

Oldenburg

Beethovenstraat 17, Zuid (662 5520). Tram 5. **Open** 9am-5.45pm Mon-Fri; 9am-5pm Sat. **No credit cards.**
Dessert cakes, *bavarois* and chocolate mousse tarts, plus great choccies, marvelous marzipan confections in winter and chocolate eggs at Easter.
Other locations: Maasstraat 84 (662 2840); Singel 184 (427 8341).

Runneboom

1e Van der Helststraat 49, the Pijp (673 5941). Tram 16, 24, 25. **Open** 7am-5pm Mon, Wed, Fri; 7am-4pm Tue, Thur, Sat. **No credit cards. Map** p311 E5.

This Pijp bakery is a staunch favorite with locals. A huge selection of French, Russian, Greek and Turkish loaves is offered, with rye bread the house speciality. Delicious cakes and pastries are also sold.

Cheese

In general, the younger (*jong*) the cheese, the creamier and milder it will be; riper (*belegen*) examples will be drier and sharper, especially the old (*oud*) cheese. Most popular are Goudse (from Gouda), Leidse (flavored with cumin seeds) and Edammer (aka Edam, with its red crust). Don't miss Leerdammer, Maaslander (both mild with holes) or Kernhem (a dessert cheese).

De Kaaskamer

Runstraat 7, Western Canal Belt (623 3483). Tram 1, 2, 5. **Open** noon-6pm Mon; 9am-6pm Tue-Fri; noon-5pm Sat, Sun. **No credit cards. Map** p310 C4.
Over 200 domestic and imported cheeses, plus pâtés, olives, pastas and wines. Have fun quizzing staff on cheese types and trivia: they know their stuff.

Wegewijs

Rozengracht 32, the Jordaan (624 4093). Tram 13, 14, 17. **Open** 8.30am-5.30pm Mon-Fri; 8.30am-4pm Sat. **No credit cards. Map** p305 B3.
The Wegewijs family started running this shop more than 100 years ago. On offer are around 50 foreign cheeses and over 100 domestic types, including

Eat, Drink, Shop

gras kaas, a grassy-tasting cheese that is available in summer. Pleasingly, you can try the Dutch varieties before you buy.

Chocolate

Australian
Leidsestraat 101, Southern Canal Belt (412 4089/ www.australianhomemade.com). Tram 1, 2, 5. **Open** noon-11pm Mon, Sun; 10am-11pm Tue-Sat. **No credit cards. Map** p310 D4.
Check out the delicious selection of bonbons, ice-cream and coffees with all natural ingredients as you ponder how the Amsterdam branch of a Belgian chain ended up with this name.
Other locations aross town; check the website.

Huize van Wely
Beethovenstraat 72, Zuid (662 2009). Tram 5. **Open** 9.30am-6pm Mon-Fri; 8.30am-5pm Sat. **Credit** AmEx, MC, V.
Since 1922, Huize van Wely has been hand-making exquisite sweet confectionery at its factory in Noordwijk, on the west coast of Holland. Indeed, so sublime are its creations that the company has been rewarded with the honour of being the sole Dutch member of the prestigious Relais Desserts and Académie Culinaire de France.

Pâtisserie Pompadour
Huidenstraat 12, Western Canal Belt (623 9554). Tram 1, 2, 5, 7. **Open** 9am-6pm Mon-Sat. **Credit** MC, V. **Map** p310 C4.
This fabulous *bonbonnerie* and tearoom – with an 18th-century interior imported from Antwerp – is likely to bring out the little old lady in anyone, even strapping lads. A new branch (Kerkstraat 148, Southern Canal Belt; 9am-6pm daily) with huge tea room is opening early in 2004.

Puccini Bomboni
Staalstraat 17, Old Centre: Old Side (626 5474/ www.puccinibomboni.com). Tram 9, 14/Metro Waterlooplein. **Open** noon-6pm Mon; 9am-6pm Tue-Sat; noon-5pm Sun. **No credit cards. Map** p307 E3.
Handmade tamarind, thyme, lemongrass, pepper or anise chocolates made on the premises without artificial ingredients.
Other locations: Singel 184 (427 8341).

Delicatessens

Eichholtz
Leidsestraat 48, Southern Canal Belt (622 0305). Tram 1, 2, 5. **Open** 10am-6.30pm Mon; 9am-6.30pm Tue, Wed, Fri; 9am-9pm Thur; 9am-6.30pm Sat; noon-6pm Sun. **Credit** (over €23 only) AmEx, MC, V. **Map** p310 D4.
Eichholtz is beloved of expats for its British and American imports. This is the place where Yanks can get their hands on chocolate chips and Brits can source Christmas puddings. They stock a range of Dutch souvenirs, too.

Ron's
Huidenstraat 26, Western Canal Belt (626 1668). Tram 1, 2, 5, 7. **Open** 9am-6pm Tue-Fri; 9am-5pm Sat. **No credit cards. Map** p310 C4.
This jewel of a greengrocer-cum-deli is frequented by the most demanding food critic in Holland, Johannes Van Damme – and hence almost everyone with cash and taste buds follows suit. Great picnic pickings in the form of pastas, tarts (asparagus and quail eggs), salads and fruits.

Uliveto
Weteringschans 118, Southern Canal Belt (423 0099). Tram 6, 7, 10. **Open** 11am-8pm Mon-Fri; noon-6pm Sat. **No credit cards. Map** p311 E5.
Uliveto is a superb, rustic Italian deli that – along with the usual wines, pastas and fruity olive oils for dipping bread – has an irresistible takeaway selection of tender roasted seasonal vegetables, grilled fish, rack of lamb and polenta, and ricotta cheese cake. You'll be crying 'mamma mia' in no time.

Ethnic & speciality

Arkwrights
Rozengracht 13, the Jordaan (320 0710). Tram 13, 14, 17. **Open** 1-8pm Mon; 11am-8pm Tue-Sun. **No credit cards. Map** p306 C3.
Britons! Stop homesickness in its tracks by stocking up on fresh sausages, bacon and puddings, Walkers crisps and more. Then wash it all down with British or Irish beers and ciders also on sale here.

Casa Molero
Gerard Doustraat 66, the Pijp (676 1707). Tram 16, 24, 25. **Open** 10am-6pm Tue-Fri; 9am-5pm Sat. **No credit cards. Map** p311 E6.
Aside from stocking cheeses, spices, sausages and hams from Spain, Casa Molero is also an exclusive distributor for some Spanish and Portuguese wines.

Olivaria
Hazenstraat 2A, the Jordaan (638 3552). Tram 7, 10. **Open** 1.30-6pm Mon; 11am-6pm Tue-Sat. **No credit cards. Map** p310 C4.
What's in a name? Quite a lot, judging by Olivaria's devotion to olive oils. There's a vast array of them from around the world, both on show and for sale.

Oriental Commodities
Nieuwmarkt 27, Old Centre: Old Side (638 6181). Tram 4, 9, 14, 16, 24, 25/Metro Nieuwmarkt. **Open** 9am-6pm Mon-Sat. **No credit cards. Map** p306 D2.
Visit Amsterdam's largest Chinese food emporium for the full spectrum of Asian foods and ingredients, from shrimp- and scallop-flavoured egg noodles to fried tofu balls and fresh veg. There's also a fine range of Chinese cooking appliances and utensils.

Waterwinkel
Roelof Hartstraat 10, Museum Quarter (675 5932/ www.springwater.nl). Tram 3, 24. **Open** 1-6pm Mon; 10am-6pm Tue-Fri; 10am-5pm Sat. **Credit** AmEx, DC, V.

Eat, Drink, Shop

Choc tactics: **Puccini Bomboni**. See p167.

Mineral water galore, both native and imported. The sheer variety may induce an emergency in the more weak-bladdered of us.

Health food

See also p164 **Amsterdam's markets.**

Delicious Food
Westerstraat 24, the Jordaan (320 3070). Tram 3. **Open** 10am-7pm Mon, Wed-Fri; 9am-6pm Sat; 11am-3pm Sun. **No credit cards. Map** p305 B2.
Organic produce has reached the pinnacle of urban rustic chic at what can only be described as a bulk food boutique. Come here for the enticing dispensers of pastas, nuts, exotic spices, plus oils and vinegars.

Deshima Freshop
Weteringschans 65, Southern Canal Belt (423 0391). Tram 6, 7, 10, 16, 24, 25. **Open** noon-7pm Mon-Fri; 10am-5pm Sat. **No credit cards. Map** p310 D5.
This basement macrobiotic shop sells foods that contain no dairy products, meat or sugar, and also offers macrobiotic cookery courses in Friesland. Above the shop is a subdued restaurant serving macrobiotic lunches (noon-2pm Mon-Fri).

De Natuurwinkel
Weteringschans 133, Southern Canal Belt (638 4083/www.denatuurwinkel.nl). Tram 6, 7, 10. **Open** 8am-8pm Mon-Sat; 11am-7pm Sun. **Credit** MC, V. **Map** p311 E5.

The largest health food supermarket in Amsterdam. You'll find everything here, from organic meat, fruit and veg (delivered fresh daily) to surprisingly tasty sugar-free chocolates and organic wine and beer. **Other locations**: across town; check the phone book.

Night shops

It's 11pm, and you're in dire need of ice-cream/cigarettes/toilet roll/condoms/beer/chocolate (delete as applicable). This is where the city's night shops come in handy. Prices are often steep.

Avondmarkt
De Wittenkade 94-6, West (686 4919). Tram 10. **Open** 4pm-midnight Mon-Fri; 3pm-midnight Sat; 2pm-midnight Sun. **No credit cards. Map** p305 A2.
The biggest and best of all night shops, this is basically a supermarket, albeit a late-opening one. Worth the trek out just west of the Jordaan.

Big Bananas
Leidsestraat 73, Southern Canal Belt (627 7040). Tram 1, 2, 5. **Open** 10am-1am Mon-Fri, Sun; 10am-2am Sat. **No credit cards. Map** p310 D4.
A passable selection of wine, some dodgy-looking canned cocktails and a variety of sandwiches are stocked here. Expensive, even for a night shop.

Dolf's Avondverkoop
Willemstraat 79, the Jordaan (625 9503). Tram 3. **Open** 4pm-1am daily. **No credit cards. Map** p306 B2.

This Shangri-la for whisky (and whiskey) lovers has a great selection of elixirs from Scotland, Ireland and America, and a nice mix of Scottish mineral waters for mixing if you're so inclined.

Supermarkets

A few tips for shopping in Dutch supermarkets. Unless a per piece (*per stuk*) price is given, fruit and veg must be weighed by the customer. Put your produce on the scale, press the picture of the item, and press the 'BON' button to get the receipt. You must pack your groceries yourself, too – and if you want a plastic bag, you'll have to ask (and pay) for it.

Albert Heijn

Nieuwezijds Voorburgwal 226, Old Centre: New Side (421 8344/www.ah.nl). Tram 1, 2, 4, 5, 9, 13, 14, 16, 17, 24, 25. **Open** 8am-10pm Mon-Sat; 11am-7pm Sun. **No credit cards. Map** p306 D3.
This massive 'Food Plaza', just behind Dam Square, is one of over 40 branches of Albert Heijn in Amsterdam. It contains virtually all the household goods you could ever need, though some of the ranges are more costly than at some of its competitors. Note: most branches do not have extended opening hours such as these.
Other locations: across town; check the phone book.

Dirk van den Broek

Marie Heinekenplein 25, the Pijp (673 9393). Tram 16, 24, 25. **Open** 8am-9pm Mon-Fri; 8am-8pm Sat. **No credit cards. Map** p311 E5.
Dirk van den Broek is decidedly unflashy, but a perfectly decent grocery store nonetheless; it's cheaper – though with less choice and less luxury – than Albert Heijn (*see p169*).
Other locations: across town; check the phone book.

Tea & coffee

Geels & Co

Warmoesstraat 67, Old Centre: Old Side (624 0683). Tram 4, 9, 14, 16, 24, 25. **Open** *Shop* 9.30am-6pm Mon-Sat. **Credit** MC. **Map** p306 D2.
Coffee beans and loose teas, plus a large range of brewing contraptions and serving utensils. Upstairs is a small museum of brewing equipment, which is open only on Saturday afternoons.
Other locations: 't Zonnetje Haarlemmerdijk 45 (623 0058).

Simon Levelt

Prinsengracht 180, Western Canal Belt (624 0823/ www.amsterdamcoffeeandtea.com). Tram 13, 14, 17. **Open** noon-6pm Mon; 10am-6pm Tue-Fri; 10am-5pm Sat. **Credit** AmEx, DC, MC, V. **Map** p305 B3.
Anything and everything to do with brewing and drinking, stocked in a remarkable old shop. The premises date from 1839 and the place is still replete with much of the original tiled decor.
Other locations: across town; check the phone book.

One of the best night shops in the Jordaan, Dolf's stocks all the urgent products you might suddenly need late at night. As pricey as most night shops.

Sterk

Waterlooplein 241, Old Centre: Old Side (626 5097). Tram 9, 14/Metro Waterlooplein. **Open** 8am-2am daily. **Credit** MC, V. **Map** p307 E3.
Less of a night shop and more of a deli: quiches, pastries and salads are made on site, and there's also fruit and veg. Be prepared to ask for what you want here – there's no self-service. Its branch is known as 'Champagne Corner', which hints at what's on offer.
Other locations: De Clercqstraat 1-7 (618 1727).

Off-licences (Slijterijen)

De Bierkoning

Paleisstraat 125, Old Centre: New Side (625 2336/ www.bierkoning.nl). Tram 1, 2, 5, 13, 14, 16, 17, 24, 25. **Open** 1-7pm Mon; 11am-7pm Tue, Wed, Fri; 11am-9pm Thur; 11am-6pm Sat; 1-5pm Sun. **Credit** AmEx, DC, MC, V. **Map** p306 C3.
Named for its location behind the Royal Palace, 'The Beer King' stocks a trifling 850 brands of beer from around the world, and a range of nice glasses.

Cadenhead's Whisky

Huidenstraat 19, Western Canal Belt (330 6287/ www.cadenhead.nl). Tram 1, 2, 5, 7. **Open** 11am-6pm Tue-Sat; 11am-9pm Thur; 1-5pm Sun. **Credit** AmEx, MC, V. **Map** p310 C4.

Eat, Drink, Shop

Furniture

For intensive browsing, don't miss the **Overtoom** (*map p310 C5-C6*), recently re-invented as a furniture boulevard, or **Pakhuis Amsterdam** (*see p199* **Living for design**).

Bebob Design Interior Add

Prinsengracht 764, Southern Canal Belt (624 5763/ www.bebob.nl). Tram 4. **Open** noon-5.30pm Tue-Fri; 11am-5pm Sat. **Credit** AmEx, DC, MC, V. **Map** p311 E4.
Bebob stocks highly sought-after vintage furnishing from the likes of Eames on up. The quality of pieces is fantastic, the selection superb and the prices accordingly high.

De Kasstoor

Rozengracht 202-210, the Jordaan (521 8112). Tram 13, 14, 17. **Open** 10am-6pm Mon-Wed, Fri; 10am-9pm Thur; 10am-5pm Sat. **Credit** AmEx, MC, V. **Map** p305 B3.
De Kasstoor is not your average stunning modern Dutch interior shop; it also has spectacular hand-picked vintage pieces from Le Corbusier, Eames, Citterio and a very extensive upholstery and fabrics library. Plan to pay for oversized luggage.

Galerie KIS

Paleisstraat 107, Old Centre: New Side (620 9760/ www.house-of-design.nl/kis/). Tram 1, 2, 4, 5, 9, 11, 13, 16, 17, 24, 25. **Open** noon-6pm Wed-Sun. **No credit cards. Map** p306 C3.
Despite stocking masses of furniture, lighting and housewares from independent designers, artists and architects, Galerie KIS goes to great lengths to always keep the numbers in each series small and therefore exclusive.

Games, models & toys

Joe's Vliegerwinkel

Nieuwe Hoogstraat 19, Old Centre: Old Side (625 0139). Tram 4, 9, 16, 24, 25/Metro Nieuwmarkt. **Open** 1-6pm Mon; 11am-6pm Tue-Fri; 11am-5pm Sat. **Credit** AmEx, DC, MC, V. **Map** p307 E3.
Kites, kites and more kites, plus a quirky array of boomerangs, yo-yos and kaleidoscopes can be found at this spectacularly colourful shop.

Kramer/Pontifex

Reestraat 18-20, Western Canal Belt (626 5274). Tram 13, 14, 17. **Open** 10am-6pm Mon-Fri; 10am-5pm Sat. **No credit cards. Map** p306 C3.
Broken Barbies and battered bears are restored to health by Mr. Kramer, a doctor for old-fashioned dolls and teddies who has practiced here for 25 years. Pontifex, at the same address, is a candle seller.

Schaak en Go het Paard

Haarlemmerdijk 147, the Jordaan (624 1171/ www.xs4all.nl/~paard/). Tram 3/bus 18, 22. **Open** 10.30am-5.30pm Tue-Wed, Fri-Sat; 10.30am-8pm Thur. **Credit** AmEx MC, V. **Map** p305 B1.

This is the place to come to for a simply glorious selection of chess sets. Encompassing the beautiful and the exotic, the choice ranges from African to ultra-modern.

Schaal Treinen Huis

Bilderdijkstraat 94, Oud West (612 2670/www.schaal treinenhuis.nl). Tram 3, 7, 12, 13, 14, 17. **Open** 1-5pm Mon; 9.30am-5.30pm Tue-Sat. **Credit** AmEx, DC, MC, V. **Map** p309 B5.
DIY kits and a ready-made parade that includes electric trains, modern and vintage vehicles and some adorable dolls' houses.

Gifts & souvenirs

Delftshop

Spiegelgracht 13, Southern Canal Belt (421 8360). Tram 4, 9, 16, 24, 25. **Open** 9.30am-6pm Mon-Sat; 11am-6pm Sun. **Credit** AmEx, DC, MC, V. **Map** p310 D5.
Souvenirs with provenance. Delftshop are the official dealers of Royal Delft and Makkum pottery, the bread and butter of the Dutch antique trade. Their stock includes pieces dating from as far back as the 17th century – for a price, of course.
Other locations: Prinsengracht 440 (627 8299); Rokin 44 (620 0000).

Holland Gallery de Munt

In the Munttoren, Muntplein 12, Old Centre: New Side (623 2271). Tram 4, 9, 14, 16, 24, 25. **Open** 10am-6pm Mon-Sat. **Credit** DC, MC, V. **Map** p310 D4.
This gallery stocks a selection of antique Royal Delft and Makkum pottery, plus other handpainted objects such as traditional tiles and decorated wooden trays and boxes. Other highlights include miniature ceramic canal houses and dolls in traditional Dutch costume.

Het Kantenhuis

Kalverstraat 124, Old Centre: New Side (624 8618/ www.kantenhuis.nl). Tram 4, 9, 14, 16, 24, 25. **Open** 11.45am-6pm Mon; 9.15am-6pm Tue, Wed, Fri, Sat; 9.15am-9pm Thur; noon-5pm Sun. **Credit** AmEx, DC, MC, V. **Map** p306 D3.
The 'Lace House' sells lace in a variety of forms. There are tablecloths, place mats, doilies and napkins that are embroidered, appliquéd or printed with Delft blue designs. You'll also find lace-curtain materials, and kits with which to cross-stitch pictures of cutesy Amsterdam canal houses.

Tesselschade: Arbeid Adelt

Leidseplein 33, Southern Canal Belt (623 6665). Tram 1, 2, 5, 6, 7, 10. **Open** 11am-6pm Tue-Fri; 10am-5pm Sat. **Credit** AmEx, MC, V. **Map** p310 D5.
Everything at this unusual operation is sold on a non-profit basis by Arbeid Adelt ('work ennobles'), an association of Dutch women. There are plenty of toys and decorations, as well as some more utilitarian household items such as tea cozies and decorated clothes hangers.

Health & beauty

Douglas
Kalvertoren, Singel 457, Southern Canal Belt (422 8036/www.douglas.nl). Tram 1, 2, 4, 5, 9, 14, 16, 24, 25. **Open** 11am-6.30pm Mon; 10am-6.30pm Tue, Wed, Fri; 10am-9pm Thur; 9am-6pm Sat; noon-6pm Sun. **Credit** AmEx, MC, V. **Map** p306 D3.
The scents and labels you'd expect from any good high street perfumery, plus special, rarer brands like La Prairie, Urban Decay and Versace.
Other locations: across town; check the website.

Lush
Kalverstraat 98, Old Centre: New Side (330 6376/ www.lush.nl). Tram 4, 9, 14, 16, 24, 25. **Open** noon-6pm Mon, Sun; 10am-6pm Tue, Wed, Fri, Sat; 9am-9pm Thur. **Credit** MC, V. **Map** p306 C3.
Lush looks lovely and smells divine. Friendly staff helps you pick which products suit you best.

Rituals
Kalverstraat 73, Old Centre: New Side (344 9222/ www.rituals.com). Tram 4, 9, 14, 16, 24, 25. **Open** 11am-6pm Mon; 9am-6pm Tue, Wed, Fri; 9am-9pm Thur; 9am-5.30pm Sat; noon-5pm Sun. **Credit** MC, V. **Map** p306 D3.
A concept shop integrating products for body and home. They reckon we all have to brush our teeth and do the dishes, so the shop is full of enticing products to turn such daily grinds into rituals.

Skins Cosmetics Lounge
Runstraat 9, Western Canal Belt (528 6922). Tram 13, 14, 17. **Open** 10am-6pm Mon-Sat. **Credit** AmEx, DC, MC, V. **Map** p310 C4.
Sleek, sexy and full of products you'll have trouble finding anywhere else in town: Benefit, Bliss, Agent Provocateur and more. The tasteful salon in the back will pamper you when the retail whirl gets too much.

De Witte Tandenwinkel
Runstraat 5, Western Canal Belt (623 3443). Tram 1, 2, 5. **Open** 1-6pm Mon; 10am-6pm Tue-Fri; 10am-5pm Sat. **Credit** AmEx, DC, MC, V. **Map** p310 C4.
The store that's armed to the teeth with brushes, pastes and other gimmickry to ensure your gnashers are whiter than white and ready to bite.

Home accessories

Kitsch Kitchen
Rozengracht 8, the Jordaan (622 8261). Tram 13, 14, 17. **Open** 10am-6pm Mon-Sat. **Credit** AmEx, DC, MC, V. **Map** p305 B3.
Mexican Mercado with a twist. Even the hardiest tat queen will love the colourful culinary and household objects here (including wacky wallpapers).

Marañón Hangmatten
Singel 488-90, Southern Canal Belt (420 7121/ www.maranon.com). Tram 1, 2, 5. **Open** 10am-5.30pm Mon-Sat; 10am-5pm Sun. **Credit** AmEx, DC, MC, V. **Map** p310 D4.

Mex textiles: **Santa Jet**.

Europe's biggest collection of hammocks. The hand-woven ones from South America are the comfiest but also the dearest. Note that closing times vary slightly (and unpredictably) by season.

Santa Jet
Prinsenstraat 7, Western Canal Belt (427 2070/ www.santajet.com). Tram 1, 2, 5. **Open** 11am-6pm Mon-Fri; 10am-5pm Sat; noon-5pm Sun. **Credit** AmEx, DC, MC, V. **Map** p306 C2.
Live *la vida loca* with Mexican housewares, mini altars and much more Mexican kitsch madness. Olé!

What's Cooking

Reestraat 16, Western Canal Belt (427 0630). Tram 13, 14, 17. **Open** 11am-6pm Tue-Sat. **Credit** AmEx, MC, V. **Map** p306 C3.

Pink salad bowls, green sauces, orange peppermills: culinary gifts don't come any more retina-searing.

Vintage

Keystone Novelty Store

Huidenstraat 28, Western Canal Ring (625 2660/ www.wenh.nl/keystone). Tram 13, 14, 17. **Open** 10am-6pm Mon-Sat. **Credit** AmEx, DC, MC, V. **Map** p310 C4.

Collectable toys, vintage furnishings and goofy games from your grandpa's day. Good stuff, all hand picked for your shopping pleasure.

Nic Nic

Gasthuismolensteeg 5, Western Canal Belt (622 8523). Tram 1, 2, 5, 13, 17. **Open** noon-6pm Mon-Fri; 10am-5pm Sat. **Credit** AmEx, MC, V. **Map** p306 C3.

The is best shop of its ilk in Amsterdam, selling '50s and '60s furniture, lamps, ashtrays and kitchenware, mostly in mint condition.

Other locations: 1e Jan Steenstraat 131 (675 6805).

Quadra Original Posters

Herengracht 383-9, Western Canal Belt (626 9472). Tram 1, 2, 4, 5, 14, 16, 24, 25. **Open** 10.30am-4.30pm Tue-Sat. **Credit** MC, V. **Map** p310 D4.

Suffering from a surfeit of bare walls in your humble abode? Why not nab yourself an original fin de siècle advertising poster, or decorate your room with a '30s circus poster? Whatever your tastes stretch to – from beer adverts to B-movies – you're sure to find the poster you want here.

Music

Vintage vinyl collectors should also head to the **Noordermarkt** and **Waterlooplein** (for both see p164 **Amsterdam's markets**).

Blue Note from Ear & Eye

Gravenstraat 12, Old Centre: New Side (428 1029). Tram 1, 2, 4, 5, 9, 13, 16, 24, 25. **Open** 11am-7pm Tue-Sat; noon-5pm Sun. **Credit** AmEx, DC, MC, V. **Map** p306 C3.

This conveniently central boutique stocks a full spectrum of jazz, from '30s stompers to mainstream, avant-garde and Afro jazz: you can almost hear the shelves groan under the weight. Niiiice.

Eat, Drink, Shop

Mode in the Netherlands

Every fashionista knows about Belgium's designers, but the other low country is also making a modish mark. The couture crown belongs to **Viktor & Rolf**, the Prins Hendrikkade-based high-conceptualists, who've straddled the art/fashion divide since 1993. Their collections have featured inflatable and barely wearable clothes, they've collaborated with novelists, and they constantly question the meaning of the fashion label: their house perfume smelled of nothing and came in an unopenable bottle. No surprise, then, that you're as likely to find them hanging in a gallery – they've exhibited at the Stedelijk Bureau (see p200), in Utrecht and Groningen – as on a clothes rack: only 80 stores stock them worldwide, and they're particular about who wears their stuff (Madonna can, Britney's a no-no). If you think you can join this exclusive club, take megabucks to **Van Ravenstein** (see p158).

In polar opposition are **Zusjes aan Zee** (www.zaz.nl), whose glam, femme designs – using diaphanous fabrics and Swarovski gems – are seen on Dutch celebrities... and Victoria Beckham. The fairytale rise of Marielle and Sharon van Vessem seems set to continue: brought up among the fabric bolts of their parents' textile shop De Kniphal on Albert Cuypstraat, they were discovered wearing their own designs in a Paris department store, exhibited at a fashion fair a few weeks later and the rest, as they say, is fashion. Catch their almost-affordable pieces before they go stellar, in their own store **ZAZ** (Govert Flinckstraat 210, 673 2902).

Lower down the price-scale – though equally high on the styl-o-meter – are Amsterdam-based **g-sus industries** (www.g-sus.nl), aka Jan Schrijver and Angelique Berkhout. They began a decade ago in a small boutique in Arnhem, and now stitch up streetwear, smart shirts and accessories. Their magpie approach means that collections may be inspired by Pacific islands and racing drivers all at once, but fluoro-colours always betray the duo's clubby roots. Fair prices mean that everyone can have a friend in g-sus: find them in the chill-out department of **De Bijenkorf** (see p155) and at **Henxs** (see p162).

But perhaps the local name to really look out for is Alexander van Slobbe and his **SO** label. He has near rock star status in Japan, where he has dozens of shops filled with his sleek minimalist threads, and his dream of opening an Amsterdam outlet may now come true since he won the prestigious Prins Bernard Cultural Fund prize in 2004.

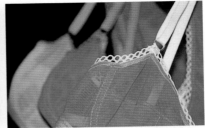

Undress to impress: seductive accessories from **Stout**. *See p176.*

Boudisque
*Haringpakkerssteeg 10-18, Old Centre: New Side
(623 2603/www.boudisque.nl). Tram 1, 2, 4, 5, 9,
13, 14, 16, 17, 24, 25.* **Open** noon-6pm Mon, Sun;
10am-6pm Tue, Wed, Fri, Sat; 10am-9pm Thur.
Credit AmEx, DC, MC, V. **Map** p306 D2.
Pop, rock, heavy metal, ambient, house, techno,
world music... the whole gamut, basically, plus T-
shirts, CD-ROMs and other malarkey.

Charles Klassiek en Folklore
*Weteringschans 193, Southern Canal Belt (626
5538). Tram 6, 7, 10, 16, 24, 25.* **Open** 1-6.30pm
Mon; 10am-6.30pm Tue, Wed, Fri; 10am-9pm Thur;
10am-5.30pm Sat.* **Credit** AmEx, DC, MC, V. **Map**
p311 E5.
Literally, 'classical and folk'. A good place for some
of the smaller German and French labels, and, buck-
ing trends, for good, old-fashioned vinyl.

Concerto
*Utrechtsestraat 54-60, Southern Canal Belt (626 6577/
624 5467). Tram 4.* **Open** 10am-6pm Mon-Wed,
Sat; 10am-9pm Thur; noon-6pm Sun. **Credit** (over
€12 only) AmEx, DC, MC, V. **Map** p311 E4.
Head here for classic Bach recordings, obscure
Beatles items, or that fave Diana Ross album that
got nicked from your party. There are also second-
hand 45s and new releases at decent prices. Massive.

Fame
*Kalverstraat 2, Old Centre: New Side (638 2525/
www.fame.nl). Tram 1, 2, 5, 13, 14, 17.* **Open**
10am-7pm Mon-Wed, Fri-Sun; 10am-9pm Thur.
Credit AmEx, DC, MC, V. **Map** p306 D3.

It comes as little surprise that the biggest record
store in Amsterdam sits bang on its busiest shopping thoroughfare. Fame offers a vast array of stock
in a variety of genres.

Fat Beats
*Singel 10, Western Canal Belt (423 0886/www.fat
beats.com). Tram 1, 2, 5.* **Open** 1-6pm Mon; 11am-
6pm Tue-Wed, Fri-Sat; 11am-9pm Thur. **Credit**
AmEx, MC, V. **Map** p306 C2.
Amsterdam's one stop hip hop shop. With its roots
in NYC, Fat Beats has all the vinyl and CDs that any
DJ (or aspiring upstart) could dream up. Staff are
seriously informed and have all the dirt on the local
party and music scene.

Get Records
*Utrechtsestraat 105, Southern Canal Belt (622 3441).
Tram 4.* **Open** 10am-6pm Mon-Wed, Fri, Sat; 10am-
9pm Thur; noon-6pm Sun. **Credit** AmEx, DC, MC, V.
Map p311 E4.
Much of the vinyl has been cleared away to make room
for a decent pick of alternative and independent CDs;
it's also good for roots, Americana and dance. Don't
miss the 'cheapies' corner at the front of the shop.

Midtown
*Nieuwendijk 104, Old Centre: New Side (638 4252).
Tram 1, 2, 5, 13, 17, 24, 25.* **Open** noon-6pm Mon;
10am-6pm Tue, Wed, Fri, Sat; 10am-9pm Thur; noon-
5pm Sun. **Credit** AmEx, DC, MC, V. **Map** p306 D2.
Dance music galore: hardcore, gabber, trance, club,
mellow house and garage are among the styles on
the shelves. Midtown is also a good source of information and tickets for hardcore parties.

Eat, Drink, Shop

Shops by area

The Old Centre: Old Side

Absolute Danny (Sex shops, *p176*); **Biba** (Fashion, *p161*); **Book Exchange** (Bookshops, *p154*); **Capsicum** (Fabrics & trimmings, *p156*); **Condomerie het Gulden Vlies** (Sex shops, *p176*); **Dam Apotheek** (Pharmacies, *p175*); **Gassan Diamond BV** (Diamonds, *p161*); **Geels & Co** (Food & drink, *p169*); **Grimm Sieraden** (Fashion, *p161*); **Head Shop** (Drugs, *p156*); **Henxs** (Fashion, *p162*); **Himalaya** (New Age & Eco, *p174*); **De Hoed van Tijn** (Fashion, *p159*); **Interpolm** (Drugs, *p156*); **Jacob Hooy & Co** (New Age & eco, *p175*); **Jemi** (Flowers, *p164*); **Joe's Vliegerwinkel** (Games, models & toys, *p170*); **'t Klompenhuisje** (Fashion, *p157*); **Oriental Commodities** (Food & drink, *p167*); **Oudemanhuis Book Market** (Markets, *p165*); **Palm Guitars** (Music, *p174*); **Puccini Bomboni** (Food & drink, *p167*); **Robin's Bodywear** (Fashion, *p161*); **Seventy Five** (Fashion, *p162*); **Sterk** (Food & drink, *p169*); **Stoffen & Fourituren Winkel** (Fabrics & trimmings, *p156*); **2πR** (Fashion, *p158*).

The Old Centre: New Side

Albert Heijn (Food & drink, *p169*); **America Today** (Fashion, *p159*); **American Book Center** (Bookshops, *p154*); **Amsterdam Diamond Centre** (Diamonds, *p161*); **Athenaeum Nieuwscentrum** (Bookshops, *p154*); **De Bierkoning** (Food & drink, *p169*); **De Bijenkorf** (Department stores, *p155*); **Blue Note from Ear & Eye** (Music, *p172*); **Boudisque** (Music, *p173*); **Chills & Thrills** (Drugs, *p156*); **Christine le Duc** (Sex shops, *p176*); **Clubwear House** (Fashion, *p157*); **Cyberdog** (Fashion, see *p158*); Diesel (Fashion, *p162*). **Fame** (Music, *p173*); **Female & Partners** (Sex shops, *p176*); **Galerie KIS** (Furniture, *p170*); **HEMA** (Department stores, *p163*); **Hemp Works** (Drugs, *p156*); **Hennes & Mauritz** (Fashion, *p159*); **Holland Gallery de Munt** (Gifts & souvenirs, *p170*); **Housewives on Fire** (Fashion, *p158*); **Hunkemöller** (Fashion, *p161*); **Het Kantenhuis** (Gifts & souvenirs, *p170*); **Lush** (Health & beauty, *p171*); **Maison de Bonneterie** (Department stores, *p155*); **Men at Work** (Fashion, *p162*); **Midtown** (Music, *p173*); **PGC Hajenius** (Tobacconists, *p176*); **Pied-à-Terre** (Bookshops, *p155*); **Postzegelmarkt** (Markets, *p165*); **Rituals** (Health & beauty, *p171*); **Rodolfos** (Fashion, *p162*); **Tothem Underwear** (Fashion, *p162*); **Vitals Vitamine-Advieswinkel** (New Age & Eco, *p175*); **Vroom & Dreesmann** (Department stores, *p156*); **Waterstone's** (Bookshops, *p155*); **Zara** (Fashion, *p159*).

Western Canal Belt

Architectura & Natura (Bookshops, *p155*); **Big Shoe** (Fashion, *p162*); **Au Bout du Monde** (Bookshops, *p155*); **Brilmuseum/ Brillenwinkel** (Fashion, *p158*); **Cadenhead's Whisky** (Food & drink, *p169*); **Exota** (Fashion, *p159*); **Fatbeat** (Music, *p173*); **Florists Gerda's** (Flowers, *p164*); **H J van de Kerkhof** (Fabrics & trimmings, *p156*); **De Kaaskamer** (Food & drink, *p165*); **Keystone Novelty** (Home accessories, *p172*); **Knopen Winkel** (Fabrics & trimmings, *p156*); **Kramer/ Pontifex** (Games, models & toys, *p170*); **Lady Day** (Fashion, *p163*); **Laura Dols** (Fashion, *p158*); **Local Service** (Fashion, *p158*); **Nic Nic** (Home accessories, *p172*); **Pâtisserie Pompadour** (Food & drink, *p167*); **Quadra Original Posters** (Home accessories, *p172*); **Razzmatazz** (Fashion, *p158*); **Ree-member** (Fashion, *p163*); **Ron's** (Food & drink, *p167*); **Santa Jet** (Home accessories, *p171*); **Simon Levelt** (Food & drink, *p169*); **Skins Cosmetics Lounge** (Health & beauty, *p171*); **Stout** (Sex shops, *p176*); **Van**

Sound of the Fifties

Prinsengracht 669, Southern Canal Belt (623 9745). Tram 6, 7, 10. **Open** 1-5pm Mon; noon-6pm Tue-Sat. **Credit** AmEx, MC, V. **Map** p310 C4.
This specialist store sells collectable vinyl from the '50s, from Liberace to Yma Sumac. Records and sleeves are in good nick, but that does mean prices are accordingly high.

Palm Guitars

's Gravelandse Veer 5, Jodenbuurt (422 0445/ www.palmguitars.nl). Tram 4, 9, 16, 24, 25. **Open** noon-6pm Wed-Sat. **Credit** AmEx, DC, MC, V. **Map** p307 E3.

Palm Guitars stocks a huge collection of new, antique, used, and rare musical instruments (and their parts). They also have an excellent website which features a calendar of upcoming local gigs, all of a worldly and rootsy nature.

New Age & Eco

Himalaya

Warmoesstraat 56, Old Centre: Old Side (626 0899/www.himalaya.nl). Tram 1, 2, 4, 5, 9, 16, 17, 24, 25/Metro Centraal Station. **Open** 1-6pm Mon; 10am-6pm Tue, Wed, Fri, Sat; 10am-8.30pm Thur; 12.30-5pm Sun. **Credit** AmEx, MC, V. **Map** p306 D2.

Ravenstein (Fashion, *p158*); **What's Cooking** (Home accessories, *p172*); **De Witte Tandenwinkel** (Health & beauty, *p171*); **Zipper** (Fashion, *p163*).

Southern Canal Belt

Art Multiples (Art & art supplies, *p154*); **Australian** (Food & drink, *p167*); **Bebob Design Interior** (Furniture, *p170*); **Big Bananas** (Food & drink, *p168*); **Bloemenmarkt** (Flowers, *p164*); **Charles Klassiek en Folklore** (Music, *p173*); **Clean Brothers** (Fashion, see *p162*); **Concerto** (Music, *p173*); **Conscious Dreams** (Drugs, *p156*); **Delftshop** (Gifts & souvenirs, *p170*); **Deshima Freshop** (Food & drink, *p168*); **Douglas** (Health & beauty, *p171*); **Eichholtz** (Food & drink, *p167*); **Expert Mons** (Electronics, *p156*); **G&G Special Sizes** (Fashion, *p161*); **Get Records** (Music, *p173*); **HEMA** (Department stores, *p163*); **Holland Gallery de Munt** (Gifts & souvenirs, *p170*); **Independent Outlet** (Fashion, *p162*); **J Vlieger** (Art & art supplies, *p154*); **Jorge Cohen Edelsmid** (Fashion, *p161*); **Kenneth Cole** (Fashion, *p162*); **Khymo** (Fashion, *p158*); **Lambiek** (Bookshops, *p155*); **Luk's Schoenservice** (Fashion, see *p162*); **Marañón Hangmatten** (Home accessories, *p171*); **Metz & Co** (Department stores, *p155*); **De Natuurwinkel** (Food & drink, *p168*); **Paul Warmer** (Fashion, *p162*); **Plantenmarkt** (Flowers, *p164*); **Sound of the Fifties** (Music, *p174*); **Spoiled** (Fashion, *p158*); **Tesselschade** (Gifts & souvenirs, *p170*); **Uliveto** (Food & drink, *p167*); **Villa Ruimzicht** (Fashion, *p158*).

Jodenbuurt, the Plantage & the Oost

Dappermarkt (Markets, *p164*); **Waterlooplein** (Markets, *p165*).

The Jordaan & Oud West

Arkwrights (Food & drink, *p167*); **Avondmarkt** (Food & drink, *p168*); **Boerenmarkt** (Markets, *p164*); **Cellarrich Connexion** (Fashion, *p159*); **Delicious Food** (Food & Drink, *p168*); **Dolf's Avondverkoop** (Food & drink, *p168*); **Donald E Jongejans** (Fashion, *p158*); **English Bookshop** (Bookshops, *p154*); **HEMA** (Department stores, *p163*); **Kasstoor** (Funiture, *p170*); **Kitsch Kitchen** (Home accessories, *p171*); **Looier** (Markets, *p164*); **Mateloos** (Fashion, *p161*); **Mediterranee** (Food & drink, *p165*); **Noordermarkt** (Markets, *p164*); **Olivaria** (Food & drink, *p167*); **Peter van Ginkel** (Art & art supplies, *p154*); **Rommelmarkt** (Markets, *p165*); **Schaak en Go de Paard** (Games, models & toys, *p170*); **Schaal Treinen Huis** (Games, models & toys, *p170*; **Wegewijs** (Food & drink, *p165*); **Westermarkt** (Markets, *p165*).

The Museum Quarter, Vondelpark & the South

Azzuro Due (Fashion, *p158*); **Coster Diamonds** (Fashion, *p161*); **Geboortewinkel Amsterdam** (Fashion, *p157*); **Huize van Wely** (Food & Drink, *p167*); **Intertaal** (Bookshops, *p155*); **Lairesse Apotheek** (Pharmacies, *p176*); **Oldenburg** (Food & Drink, *p165*); **'t Schooltje** (Fashion, *p157*); **Shoe Baloo** (Fashion, *p162*); **Waterwinkel** (Food & drink, *p167*).

The Pijp

Albert Cuypmarkt (Markets, *p164*); **Casa Molero** (Food & drink, *p167*); **Dirk van den Broek** (Food & drink, *p169*); **HEMA** (Department stores, *p163*); **Runneboom** (Food & drink, *p165*); **Van Moppes & Zoon** (Fashion, *p161*); **ZAZ** (Fashion, *p172*).

Shop-gallery-teahouse Himalaya is a haven of calm amid seedy, bustling surroundings. Come here for an extensive range of books and magazines, crystals, tarot cards and jewellery. The café at the back has a lovely view as well.

Jacob Hooy & Co

Kloveniersburgwal 12, Old Centre: Old Side (624 3041/www.jacobhooy.nl). Tram 4, 9, 14, 16, 24, 25/Metro Nieuwmarkt. **Open** 10am-6pm Mon; 9am-6pm Tue-Fri; 9am-5pm Sat. **Credit** V. **Map** p306 C3. Established in 1743, this chemist sells around 600 kitchen and medicinal herbs, spices, natural cosmetics, health foods and homeopathic remedies.

Vitals Vitamine-Advieswinkel

Nieuwe Nieuwstraat 47, Old Centre: New Side (427 4747/www.vitals.nl) Tram 1, 2, 5, 13, 17. **Open** 9.30am-6pm Mon-Fri; 11am-4.30pm Sat. **Credit** AmEx, DC, MC, V. **Map** p306 C2.
Food supplements, vitamins and friendly advice.

Pharmacies

Dam Apotheek

Damstraat 2, Old Centre: Old Side (624 4331). Tram 4, 9, 14, 16, 24, 25. **Open** 8.30am-5.30pm Mon-Sat. **No credit cards. Map** p306 D3.

The cigar's the star: **PGC Hajenus**.

This centrally located pharmacy is notable for its extended opening hours. Should you find yourself in desperate need of a pharmacy in the middle of the night, *see p283*.

Lairesse Apotheek

Lairessestraat 40, Museum Quarter (662 1022/ www.delairesseapotheek.nl). Tram 3, 5, 12, 16. **Open** 8.30am-5.30pm Mon-Fri. **Credit** AmEx, MC, V. **Map** p310 D6.

One of the largest suppliers of alternative medicines in the Netherlands, chemist Marjan Terpstra wanted her shop to reflect her speciality. Collaborating with design team Concrete, the shop is a touch out of the way if you're just popping in for haemorrhoid cream, but its award-winning interior is so inspiring it should be on any design junkie's must-see list.

Sex shops

Absolute Danny

Oudezijds Achterburgwal 78, Old Centre: Old Side (421 0915/www.absolutedanny.com). Tram 4, 9, 16, 24. **Open** 10am-9pm Mon-Thur; 10am-10pm Fri; 10am-8pm Sat; noon-8pm Sun. **Credit** AmEx, DC, MC, V. **Map** p306 D2.

Everything from rubber clothes to erotic tooth-brushes, all under one saucy roof.

Christine le Duc

Spui 6, Old Centre: New Side (624 8265/ www.christineleduc.nl). Tram 1, 2, 4, 5, 9, 14, 16, 24, 25. **Open** 10am-10pm Mon-Fri; 10am-6pm Sat; 1-6pm Sun. **Credit** AmEx, MC, V. **Map** p306 D3.

One of the more plebeian erotic shops, Christine le Duc is trashy but never seedy. Staff sell crotchless red panties in an array of synthetics, porn mags and novelties such as an elephant's head G-string.

Condomerie het Gulden Vlies

Warmoesstraat 141, Old Centre: Old Side (627 4174/www.condomerie.com). Tram 4, 9, 14, 16, 24, 25. **Open** 11am-6pm Mon-Sat. **Credit** AmEx, DC, MC, V. **Map** p306 D2.

No surprises for guessing this jolly emporium's vocation. An astounding variety of rubbers will wrap up trouser snakes of all shapes and sizes.

Female & Partners

Spuistraat 100, Old Centre: New Side (620 9152/ www.femaleandpartners.nl). Tram 1, 2, 5, 13, 17. **Open** 1-6pm Mon, Sun; 11am-6pm Tue, Wed, Fri, Sat; 11am-9pm Thur. **Credit** AmEx, DC, MC, V. **Map** p306 C2.

The polar opposite of most Red Light District enterprises, the ten-year-old Female & Partners welcomes women (and, yes, their partners) with an attractively presented array of clothes, videos and toys.

Stout

Berenstraat 9, Western Canal Belt (620 1676). Tram 13, 14, 17. **Open** noon-7pm Mon-Fri; 11am-6pm Sat; 1-5pm Sun. **Credit** AmEx, DC, MC, V. **Map** p310 C4.

This is the kind of friendly haven where women can leisurely ponder which erotic toy, video or book they'd like to buy. Fellas should also note that the staff love helping a bloke select that special present for her indoors.

Tobacconists

PGC Hajenius

Rokin 92-6, Old Centre: New Side (625 9985/ www.hajenius.com). Tram 4, 9, 14, 16, 24, 25. **Open** noon-6pm Mon; 9.30-6pm Tue, Wed, Fri, Sat; 9.30am-9pm Thur; noon-5pm Sun. **Credit** AmEx, DC, MC, V. **Map** p306 D3.

A smoker's paradise (tobacco, not dope) for well over 250 years, Hajenius offers all manner of cigarabilia, from long traditional Dutch pipes to own-brand cigars. With its stunning art deco interior, even rabid anti-smokers should pop their heads in for a whiff.

Eat, Drink, Shop

Arts & Entertainment

Features

Festivals & Events

It can't always give you sun, but Amsterdam delivers four seasons of fun.

After a good day's work keeping the sea at bay and their bellies filled, Amsterdammers of yore reaped the therapeutic benefits of letting their hair down in a pagan psychosis of song, dance and drink. These days, the relatively mellow locals now only act as if they've been 'hit on the head by a windmill blade' – as the local saying goes – on **Oudejaarsavond** (New Year's Eve; *see p184*), **Koninginnedag** (Queen's Day; *see p179* **A right royal knees-up**), and when Ajax wins an important football match. Otherwise, the year's calendar is filled with shenanigans of a more cultural bent. But happily, these events – whether focusing on art, music or theatre – often betray the kind of cutting-edge savvy usually associated with larger cities like New York and London. And this globe-embracing ambition is what makes this dinky town so special – oh, and of course, the fact that some of these events embrace such singularities as boat-bound **Gay Pride** parades and the taste-testing of bushels of weed.

The **AUB** (0900 0191; *see p279* **Tickets please**) and the **Amsterdam Tourist Board** (0900 400 4040; *see p289*) list upcoming events in *Uitkrant* and *Day by Day* respectively, and www.timeout.com/amsterdam previews the best. For a list of public holidays, *see p290*. Unless stated, all events are free.

The best Events

Koninginnedag
A right royal birthday knees-up. See p179 **Orange crush**.

Museum Night
Lounge in a synagogue or sleep in a zoo. See p183 **A night to remember**.

Open Monument Days
Access all areas: a chance to look behind the gabled façades. See p182.

Parade
Absurd theatrics meets carnival madness. See p181 and p244.

SAIL2005
A gridlock of tall ships. See p182.

Frequent events

Arts & crafts markets
Spui *Old Centre: New Side (www.artplein-spui.nl). Tram 1, 2, 4, 5, 9, 14, 16, 24, 25.* **Map** p310 D4. **Date** *Mar-Oct* 10am-5pm Sun.
Thorbeckeplein *Southern Canal Belt (www.modern-art-market.nl), Tram 4, 9, 14.* **Map** p311 E4. **Date** *Mar-Oct* 10am-5pm Sun.
Two open-air arts and crafts markets are held every Sunday for half the year, depending on weather. They're decent places to browse, but don't come here to buy elephant dung, a bovine in brine or a crucifix in urine: most of the jewellery, paintings, vases and prints are of a less radical nature. Buskers touting CDs and tapes enhance the laid-back vibe.

Rowing contests
Amsterdamse Bos, Bosbaan 6 (646 2740/ www.knrb.nl). Bus 170, 171, 172. **Date** Apr-June.
Visit this lovely green expanse to watch participants get wet. There are various rowing contests held here from April to December; check local press or phone the Amsterdam Tourist Board for details.

Book markets
Various locations (627 5794). **Date** May-Aug.
Besides the year-round Friday book stalls on the Spui, there are four more fleeting but sprawling book markets in summer: two along the Amstel (art book market, mid June; religion, mid Aug) and two on Dam (children's, mid May; mysteries, mid July).

Antiques market
Nieuwmarkt, Old Centre: Old Side. Tram 9, 14/ Metro Nieuwmarkt. **Map** p306 D2. **Date** *Mid May-Sept* 9am-5pm Sun.
Lovers of antiques and bric-a-brac should head for this small antiques market. There's a fair amount of naffness, but also a few gems, especially books, furniture and objets d'art.

Spring

Spring is when the tulips and crocuses push through the earth, and a winter's worth of dog dung defrosts: those who know about this sort of thing put the amount at 20 million kilograms (44 million pounds tons). It's also when the city shrugs off the existential gloom that defines the northern European mindset in winter. Energised by a visible sun, the city-dwellers take on the shiny *joie de vivre* that's more readily associated with southern European terrace-café cultures. Relax and enjoy the city at a time when lounging in a park or on a terrace is seen as a respectable thing to do after a long winter's cold rain and mental drain.

Stille Omgang (Silent Procession)

Starts at Spui, Begijnhof (information 023 524 6229 after 7pm/write to Gezelschap van de Stille Omgang, Zandvoorterweg 59, 2111 GS Aerdenhout). **Date** wknd after 10 Mar (20 Mar in 2004), Sat 11.30pm.

This singular annual event commemorates the 1345 'Miracle of Amsterdam': a dying man was given the viaticum, which he vomited into a fire – yet the host emerged unscathed and the man recovered. Every year since then, local Catholics make a silent nocturnal procession that begins and ends at Spui, via Kalverstraat, Nieuwendijk, Warmoesstraat and Nes. The sight of the candle-lit procession moving through the Red Light District at night is decidedly surreal.

Orange squash

Party lovers, crap collectors and students of the stupendously surreal, listen up. If you only go to Amsterdam once in your life, make sure your visit coincides with 30 April. Queen's Day, or **Koninginnedag** in the local lingo, is (in theory) a one-day celebration of Beatrix's birthday. As it happens, her birthday falls in winter, but the ever-pragmatic Dutch choose to celebrate it on her mother's birthday, when the climatic conditions are more clement.

Her Highness is soon forgotten amid the revelry. More than a million people pour into the city, making every single street and canal dense with different sounds, suspicious smells and hopeful stallholders. It's a day of excess. You might discover a leather-boy disco party on one sidestreet, boogie through and get to an old-school Jordaan crooner on another, when suddenly a boat bellows by with a heavy metal band on deck, whose amps get short-circuited at the next bridge when a gang of boys dressed in head-to-toe orange urinate on them. If nothing else, you'll come away with a few stories of debauchery derring-do to tell your grandchildren. (If you have your own offspring in tow, head straight to Vondelpark, which is dedicated to children.)

Meanwhile, the gay and lesbian festivities spread like ripples from the Homomonument (*see p202*) and the Reguliersdwaarsstraat. Dam Square becomes a fairground, and the mind gets clogged with an overdose of sensations, and pockets slowly empty as punters get tricked into buying just what they always (read: never) wanted – a pair of orange clogs, a brain implant or some processed uranium. Former Mayor Patijn played party pooper a few years ago by banning all street hawkers on Queen's Eve (29 April), but there are signs it may return in a mellower form in 2004 – stay tuned.

But regardless: with performances, markets, crowds and, of course, alcohol, the scenic streets of Amsterdam have it all, for one day only. Come and see what the fuss is about. Just don't make too many plans for 1 May.

Now that's flower power: **Bloemencorso**. *See p182.*

World Press Photo

Oude Kerk, Oudekerksplein 23, Old Centre: Old Side (625 8284/www.worldpressphoto.nl). Tram 4, 9, 16, 24, 25. **Admission** *€5; €4 concessions.* **Map** *p306 D2.* **Date** *Apr-May 10am-6pm Mon-Sat; 1-6pm Sun.*

This is the world's largest photography competition, and it lines up exhibits chosen from tens of thousands of shots taken by thousands of photojournalists. The exhibition is held in the sight-worthy confines of the Oude Kerk (*see p82*), and after kicking off in Amsterdam it goes on tour to another 70 locations around the world.

National Museum Weekend

Around the Netherlands (670 1111/www.museum weekend.nl). **Admission** *mostly free.* **Date** *mid Apr.*

Many state-funded museums offer discounted or free admission and special activities during National Museum Weekend. Opening hours are frequently extended, but most museums are still pretty busy. For more information pick up the Museum Weekend newspaper at the Amsterdam Tourist Board (*see p289*), the ANWB (auto association; *see p276*) and the museums themselves.

Koninginnedag (Queen's Day)

Around the city. **Date** *30 Apr.*

See p179 **Orange squash.**

Herdenkingsdag & Bevrijdingsdag (Remembrance Day & Liberation Day)

Remembrance Day *National Monument, Dam, Old Centre: Old Side. Tram 1, 2, 4, 5, 9, 13, 14, 16, 17, 24, 25.* **Map** *p306 D3.* **Date** *4 May.*

Liberation Day *Vondelpark (tram 1, 2, 3, 5, 6, 12) & Museumplein (tram 1, 2, 5, 6, 7, 10), Museum Quarter.* **Map** *p310 C6.* **Date** *5 May.*

Those who lost their lives during World War II are remembered at the National Monument on Dam Square on 4 May at 7.30pm. Homosexuals who died in the war are also remembered at a gay remembrance service at the Homomonument (*see p202*).

Liberation Day is celebrated on 5 May. Rokin, Vondelpark, Museumplein and Leidseplein are the best places to make for: expect live music, speeches and information stands for political groups, and a market where you can sell everything you bought in a drunken stupor on Queen's Day a week earlier.

Oosterpark Festival

Oosterpark, Oost. Tram 3, 6, 9, 14. **Map** *p312 H3.* **Date** *first wk in May.*

The culturally eclectic east of Amsterdam makes a perfect setting for this one- or two-day free festival emphasising community between nationalities. It has its own links with Remembrance Day, since many local Jews were deported during World War II, but this fact isn't commemorated here: the festival is really just a great opportunity to experience different music, customs, food, games and sports.

National Windmill Day

Around the Netherlands (075 621 5148). **Admission** *free; donations welcome.* **Date** *2nd Sat in May.*

Members of the public are welcome at about 75 watermills and 600 of the country's 1,035 windmills, including Amsterdam's half-dozen working mills. Those open to the public carry a blue banner; for full details, call the above number.

National Cycling Day
Around the Netherlands (071 560 5959). **Date** 2nd Sat in May.

National Cycling Day means the roads are even more densely packed with cyclists than usual. Upwards of 200 routes of varying lengths are marked out especially for the occasion, and if you want to saddle up for some two-wheeled action of your own – or, alternatively, avoid the event altogether – contact the Amsterdam Tourist Board (*see p289*) for details.

KunstRAI (RAI Arts Fair)
RAI Congresgebouw, Europaplein, Zuid (549 1212, www.kunstrai.nl). Tram 4, 25/NS rail RAI station. **Open** *Office* 8am-6pm Mon-Fri. **Admission** €10-€15. **No credit cards. Date** mid May-early June.

Every art form from ceramics and jewellery to paintings and sculpture are featured at this huge annual exhibition of contemporary art. In 2003 they nobly tried to shake free from its mediocre and staid image with mixed but promising results. All in all, about 100 Dutch and international galleries take part.

Open Ateliers (Open Studios): Kunstroute de Westelijke Eilanden
Prinseneiland, Bickerseiland & Realeneiland (627 1238, www.oawe.nl). **Date** late May/early June.

Many neighbourhoods with large artist populations and artists' studio complexes hold open days in spring and autumn, when, over a weekend or more, dozens of artists – the starving and the successful – open their doors to the public. The annual Westelijke Eilanden is the most popular, situated on the picturesque and peaceful islands around Prinseneiland, all connected by traditional 'skinny bridges'. Be sure, also, to check out the Jordaan event, which is usually held on the same weekend. Find out about times and venues for all the different Open Ateliers by picking up the Kunstladder (the official list), available at the Amsterdam Tourist Board (*see p289*) or from the AUB (*see p279* **Tickets please**).

Europerve
Information: Demask, Zeedijk 64, Old Centre: Old Side (620 5603/www.demask.com). **Admission** prices vary. **Date** last Sat in May.

Organised by Demask (*see p204*), Europerve brings together thousands of Europe's most sexually adventurous people – with the Germans and English seemingly the most needy of a buttock blushing – for a long evening of fashion, performance, dancing, naughty games and friction fun. Leather, latex, PVC and/or adult-sized nappies are required dress.

Summer

With the consistent sunshine that summer brings, Amsterdammers move outdoors for their leisure time. Liberally undressed bodies pack like sardines on the nearby beaches at Bloemendaal, Zandfoort and Amsterdam's new one at IJburg (*see p101*); and Vondelpark gets jammed with skaters, joggers, sun-worshippers and bongo players. Many locals depart for holiday heaven, while the city's tourist load reaches critical density.

Amsterdamse Grachtenloop (Canal Run)
Around Amsterdam (585 3203/www.amsterdamse grachtenloop.nl). **Admission** around €5 participants; free spectators. **Date** late May/early June.

Nigh on 5,000 people take part in a 5km (3.1-mile) or 9km (5.6-mile) run along the city's canals (Prinsengracht and Lijnbaansgracht). Would-be participants can sign up from mid May at VSB banks (there's one at Rozengracht 207, 638 8009) or register a mere half-hour before the 11am start at the Stadsschouwburg (*see p220*). If you'd rather – perhaps understandably – sit outside with a beer and observe the runners getting knackered, there are plenty of decent vantage points. Avoid the usually crowded Leidseplein and make, instead, for the banks of Prinsengracht.

Holland Festival
Stadsschouwburg, Leidseplein, Southern Canal Belt (530 7110/www.holndfstvl.nl). Tram 1, 2, 5, 6, 7, 10. **Admission** €8-€40. **Credit** AmEx, MC, V. **Map** p310 C5. **Date** early-mid June.

A fixture in the diaries of the Netherlands' cultured populace, the Holland Festival features art, dance, opera, theatre and a whole lot more. The programme includes both mainstream and oddball works, and is held in the Stadsschouwburg (*see p220*) and other venues – some events in the Hague. Tickets are sold from May from the AUB Ticketshop, Amsterdam Tourist Board offices and theatres.

Open Garden Days
Around Amsterdam. **Date** mid June.

Similar to the Open Monument Days (*see p182*), this weekend event sees owners of beautiful, hidden backyard gardens open their doors to the general public, who file in and emit admiring 'oohs' and 'aahs' in honour of their hosts' landscaping skills. Contact Museum van Loon (*see p92*) for details.

Kwakoe
Bijlmerpark, Bijlmer (416 0894/www.kwakoe.nl). Metro Bijlmer. **Date** mid July-mid Aug.

The name of this ever-growing, mulitcultural festival means 'slave', and alludes to the emancipation of the people of Surinam. Every weekend in summer you can drop in and find some form of theatre, music, film, literature or sport and – perhaps most enticingly – a large range of exotic food stalls.

Parade
Martin Luther Kingpark, Zuid (033 465 4577/www. mobilearts.nl). Tram 25/Metro Amstel. **Admission** free-€10. **No credit cards. Date** 1st 2wks in Aug (3pm-1am Mon-Thur, Sun; 3pm-2am Fri, Sat).

One of the highlights of the cultural year, this outdoor theatre festival (*see also p244*) comes pretty close to re-enacting the vibes of ancient carnivals. Enter into another, alcohol-fuelled world, where a

Arts & Entertainment

beer garden is surrounded by kitschily decorated tents that each feature a different cabaret, music or theatre act. Afternoons are child-friendly.

Amsterdam Gay Pride Boat Parade

Prinsengracht (620 8807/www.amsterdampride.nl). Tram 13, 14, 17. **Map** p306 C1. **Date** 1st Sat in Aug, 2-5pm.

If the weather's fine, there might be as many as 250,000 spectators lining the Prinsengracht and its bridges to watch the spectacular Gay Pride Boat Parade. 80 boats with garish decorations and loud sound systems crewed by incredibly extravagant sailors set sail at this carnivalesque climax to a whole weekend of special activities (check the website for the full array). *See also p202* **The queer year**.

Hartjesdag

Zeedijk, Old Centre: Old Side (625 8467/ www.zeedijk.nl). Tram 4, 9, 14, 16, 24, 25. **Map** p306 D2. **Date** mid Aug.

An ancient Amsterdam celebration, 'Heart Day' was traditionally held on the last Monday of August and involved a great deal of drinking, cross-dressing and firecrackers. The event wasn't held for decades, but some resourceful folk resurrected it in 1999, primarily to focus on the booze and drag side of things. Marvel at the parade of boys dressed as girls and girls dressed as boys: it's predictably popular with the city's burgeoning transvestite population, as are its associated theatrical and music events.

SAIL2005

Around Amsterdam (681 1804/www.sail-amsterdam.nl). **Date** 17-21 Aug 2005.

The history of sailing will be on full display along the waterfront of Amsterdam as 2.5 million visitors come to this, the largest nautical gathering in Europe, to stroll along Oostelijke Handelskade and admire dozens of tall ships and thousands of more modern aquatic crafts. There's an armada of related events to choose from – you can easily fill up the day. Consult the website and plan ahead.

Uitmarkt

Various locations, including Museumplein, Dam & Amstel (www.uitmarkt.nl). **Date** last wknd in Aug.

The chaotic Uitmarkt previews the coming cultural season with a fair on and around Museumplein, Leidseplein, Dam and Nes, giving foretastes of theatre, opera, dance and music. From Friday to Sunday, several outdoor stages are set up in squares around the centre of Amsterdam, presenting free music, dance, theatre and cabaret shows. Not surprisingly, it gets very crowded.

Autumn

Amsterdam has the occasional Indian summer, but otherwise this season's stormy disposition is a warning of the winter despair that is sure to follow; it's a time when Amsterdammers start storing any razor blades out of sight.

As a visitor, though, this might be just the right time to visit the city. With the tourist tide finally beginning to ebb and touring bands arriving in their droves to play the Melkweg or Paradiso, the true spirit of Amsterdam comes bubbling to the surface. Just bring a robust brolly and be prepared to duck into a pub to avoid the elements – hardly a hardship.

Bloemencorso (Flower Parade)

Around Amsterdam: route usually via Overtoom, Leidseplein, Leidsestraat, Spui, Spuistraat, Dam, Rembrandtplein, Vijzelstraat, Weteringschans (029 732 5100/www.bloemencorsoaalsmeer.nl). **Date** 1st Sat in Sept.

Since the 1950s, this spectacular parade of floats bearing all kinds of flowers – except tulips, funnily enough, as they're out of season – has made its way from Aalsmeer (*see p254*), the home of Holland's flower industry, up the waterways to Amsterdam. Crowds line the pavements to get a glimpse of the lovely, fragrant displays; then, at 4pm, the parade reaches a packed Dam to be the guest of honour at a civic reception. At 9pm, it begins an hour-long illuminated cavalcade back through Aalsmeer.

Next Five Minutes: International Festival of Tactical Media

Various locations in Amsterdam & Rotterdam (553 5171/www.next5minutes.org). **Admission** prices vary. **Date** Sept.

Theorists, artists, activists and media-makers from around the world meet to exchange ideas and strategies for social change in the digital age. Workshops, exhibitions and performances take place in a variety of locations, but most of the action is at the Paradiso (*see p214*) and De Balie (*see p241*).

Open Monument Days

Around Amsterdam (552 4888/www.openmonument endag.nl). **Date** 2nd wknd of Sept.

Every year, owners of some of Amsterdam's most historic buildings open their doors to the public, who can open their eyes to the past as they amble around behind the gabled façades and peer into lives lived and living in Golden Age grandeur. It's a national event: wherever you find yourself in the Netherlands, look out for the flying Monumenten flag.

Jordaan Festival

The Jordaan (626 5587/www.jordaanfestival.nl). **Map** p310 C4. **Date** 3rd wknd in Sept.

This annual neighbourhood festival, usually focused along Elandsgracht, features local talents following in the footsteps of Johnny Jordaan and Tante Leni. *See p104* **Authenti-city or Amst-ersatz?**

Dam tot Damloop

Prins Hendrikkade, Amsterdam, to Peperstraat, Zaandam (072 533 8136/www.damtotdamloop.nl). **Date** 3rd Sun in Sept.

The annual 'Dam to Dam Run' stretches 16.1km (ten miles) from Amsterdam to Zaandam. Up to 150,000 gather to watch 25,000 participants, many of whom are world-class athletes. Bands line the route and there's also a circus and various mini-marathons in Zaandam for children.

Chinatown Festival
Nieuwmarkt, Old Centre: Old Side (06 2476 0060/ www.zeedijk.nl). Tram 9, 14, 20/Metro Nieuwmarkt. **Map** p306 D2. **Date** mid Sept.
The ancient square of Nieuwmarkt gets covered with stalls of Chinese food and enlivened with many acts and artists in this traditional celebration.

High Times Cannabis Cup
Melkweg, Lijnbaansgracht 234A (624 1777/www. hightimes.com). **Admission** prices vary. **No credit cards. Date** Nov.
Harvest time means it's time for High Times' annual (and heavily commercialised) Cannabis Cup, where all things related to wastedness are celebrated over five days or so. There are banquets, an impressive array of bands, cultivation seminars and a competition where hundreds of judges (you too, if you wish) ascertain which of the hundreds of weeds are the wickedest, dude. The event is scattered – as are the minds – all over town, but is invariably focused around the Melkweg at night.

Crossing Border
Various locations in the Hague (www.crossing border.nl). Den Haag CS. **Date** Oct/Nov.

Sadly this unique 'literary festival that rocks' returned to its original home of the Hague in 2003. Still, even now it's but a 45-minute train trip away. Even though there will be strictly defined 'authors' present, the vast majority of the more than 120 acts come from the world of music who will perform concerts and/or spoken word. Past participants have included: Harlem Gospel Choir, David Byrne, David Sedaris, Henry Rollins, R. Crumb, Norman Mailer, Goran Bregovic, Dave Eggers and Jill Scott.

Museum Night
Around Amsterdam. **Date** 2nd Sat in Nov.
See p183 **A night to remember**.

Amsterdam Dance Event
Around Amsterdam (035 621 8748/www.amsterdam-dance-event.nl). **Admission** prices vary. **Date** mid Oct.
Schmooze by day and party by night during this annual music conference concerned with all things disco. Felix Meritis is the location for daytime convention activities and workshops where over 1,000 delegates come to discuss the business of boogie. During the evening, venues such as the Melkweg and Paradiso host DJs from around the world.

Sinterklaas Intocht
Route via Barbizon Palace on Prins Hendrikkade, Damrak, Dam, Raadhuisstraat, Rozengracht, Marnixstraat, Leidseplein. **Date** mid Nov.

A night to remember

It's a shame an occasion like this only comes round once a year: a night when the Jewish Historical museum might become a lounge bar or a recreation of 1920s Russia; a night when the Rijksmuseum might host tango dancing under a Rembrandt or play 'reverse striptease' under a Vermeer; a night when the Amsterdams Historisch Museum sparkles with a fashion show or rocks to the sound of a rapper. **Museumnacht** (Museum Night) – which involves nearly all of Amsterdam's major museums and galleries – has been providing once-in-a-lifetime enjoyment for only a few years now, but has already established itself as a solid and inspired part of this city's cultural menu. Consult the programme (widely available a month in advance; 2003 edition pictured) and see what singularities you'd like to sink your teeth into: unplugged grunge acts in the 'Our Lord in the Attic' church, or sleepovers at Artis zoo, perhaps?

Museumnacht
Around Amsterdam (0900 0190/www.n8.nl). **Admission** €12-€16. **Credit** varies. **Date** 2nd Sat in Nov.

Sinterklaas is coming to town.

In mid November, Sinterklaas (St Nicholas) marks the beginning of the Christmas season by stepping ashore from a steamboat at Centraal Station. St Nick – with his white beard, robes and staff – is every Dutch kid's favourite patron saint, and the old boy distributes sweets during this annual parade of the city. Meanwhile, his Zwarte Piet (Black Peter) helpers represent a threat to any naughty kids. Depending on which story you believe, Black Peter was originally the devil – the colour and appetite for mischief are the only leftovers of an evil vanquished by Sinterklaas – or he got his dark skin from climbing down chimneys to deliver sweets.

Winter

In the typical Amsterdam winter, with luck, the canals turn solid enough for scenic skating. Otherwise, only the two family festivals – St Nicholas's Day, as important to the Dutch as Christmas, and New Year's Eve – break up the monotony of this most sleety of seasons.

Sinterklaas

Around Amsterdam. **Date** 5, 6 Dec.
While St Nicholas, aka Sinterklaas, is directing his Black Peter helpers down chimneys on the eve of his feast day, 6 December, families celebrate by exchanging small gifts and poems. This tradition started when the Church decided to tame the wild pagan partying that had always accompanied the end of the slaughter season. It began by ruling that the traditional celebration should be based around the birthday of St Nicholas, the patron saint of children (and, curiously enough, of prostitutes, thieves and Amsterdam itself); a once violent tradition was reborn as a Christian family feast. Sinterklaas eventually emigrated to the States, changed his name to Santa Claus and moved his birthday to 25 December.

Oudejaarsavond (New Year's Eve)

Around Amsterdam. **Date** 31 Dec.
Along with Queen's Day (*see p179* **Orange crush**), New Year's Eve is Amsterdam's wildest celebration. There's happy chaos throughout the city, but the best spots are Nieuwmarkt and Dam, both of which get crowded and noisy: the ample use of firecrackers gives a fair impression of an artillery barrage. The Dutch often begin with an evening of coffee, spirits and *oliebollen* ('oil-balls', which taste better than they sound: they're deep-fried blobs of dough, apple and raisins, with a sprinkle of icing sugar) with the family; many bars don't open until the witching hour.

Chinese New Year

Nieuwmarkt, Old Centre: Old Side (mobile 06 2476 0060/www.zeedijk.nl). **Map** p306 D2. **Date** late Jan/early Feb.
Lion dances, firecrackers and Chinese drums 'n' gongs may scare away evil spirits, but your children will have a roaring good time chasing the dragon through Amsterdam's scenic Chinatown.

Children

Amsterdam likes kids – and the feeling's mutual.

Children still happy to be seen in public with mum or dad will no doubt be delighted to hear that playground Amsterdam has more to offer than just canal cruises. And parents, relax: sex and drugs are not ubiquitously in your face. As it happens, how you choose most of the activities on offer will largely depend on Mother Nature. Indoor or outdoor? This question will constantly be bouncing around any parent's mind: in Amsterdam a clear sky in the morning seems to be a reliable precursor for rain.

Whatever the weather or time of year, though, you're sure to find a variety of things to do that will keep the kids at bay and might even entertain you. After researching what's regularly on offer, march straight to Leidseplein to find out what's on for children during your stay. The **AUB Ticketshop** (0900 0191; see p279 **Tickets please**) is a great place to collect information about activities for kids. A copy of *Uitkrant* (look under 'Jeugd') can also be enlightening if you can navigate the primarily Dutch text. Note, though, that toilets are tiny – and where changing facilities are available, they're usually only in the ladies.

For kid's clothes and shoe shops, see p157; for toy shops, see p168.

The best Kids' stuff

De Blauwe Poort
Free water paradise in an idyllic setting (pray for sun). See p188 **A ton of fun**.

Canal rides
Glass-topped boats or canal bikes offer the best vantage points in town. See p187.

Efteling
You simply can't beat talking rubbish bins. See p189.

Park life
No need to be fussy – go for green and fresh air. See p188 **A ton of fun**.

TunFun
These underground playground complexes teach kids to look beneath the surface of things. See p188 **A ton of fun**.

Getting around

Few cities can match Amsterdam when it comes to public transport. Effective and cheap trams, buses and the Metro cover most of the existing city. A tram ride can also be a great way to catch your breath, entertain the kids and find your bearings, but fold pushchairs before boarding to minimise congestion. A more pleasurable ride can be taken in the antique electric tram carriages at the **Electrische Museumtramlijn Amsterdam** (see p108 **The collectors' collectors**) to Amsterdamse Bos.

Children love Amsterdam's waterways. A pricey but pleasant way of getting around is by water taxi, but a decent free alternative is to take a trip on the River IJ ferry to Amsterdam Noord; boats leave from behind Centraal Station about every ten minutes. If you have older kids, you may enjoy renting a canal bike, but remember to proceed on the right-hand side of the waterway. For more information on all transport in Amsterdam, see p274.

Indoor entertainment

For indoor park **TunFun**, see p188 **A ton of fun**.

Applied arts

Keramiekstudio Color Me Mine
Roelof Hartstraat 22, Museum Quarter (675 2987/ www.colormemine.nl). Trams 3, 5, 12, 24. **Open** Tue, Wed 11am-7pm; Thur-Sat 11am-10pm; Sun noon-6pm. **Admission** €12.50; €10 under-12s. **Credit** MC, V.
This child-friendly ceramic studio gives the whole family the chance to create custom crockery. With painting and mosaic as additional options, a session here could make a nice complement to a museum visit. Reservations essential.

Films

Most films for children are dubbed (indicated by 'Nederlands Gesproken'), though original versions are often shown at non-matinée times. The **Kriterion** (see p192), the **Rialto** (see p192) and the **Nederlands Filmmuseum** (see p194) cinemas all have screenings for kids. Check local listings for times and other information. During the autumn holidays (mid October), the **Cinekid** film festival (531 7890/www.cinekid.nl) takes place nationwide, offering quality kids' films from across the globe (including many in English).

Go-cart racing

Race Planet Amsterdam
Herwijk 10 (0900 722 3752/www.raceplanet.nl). Sloterdijk rail (direction IJmuiden), then bus 82, 182 (bus stop Herwijk), or a taxi bus from same station (call 460 5252 to book). **Open** 1-11pm Mon-Fri; noon-11pm Sat, Sun. **Admission** from €14 per person/12min. **Credit** MC, V.
In town with big kids (taller than 1.4m) and looking for something a little more exciting than a lengthy stroll along the canals? Indoor go-cart racing will pump up the adrenaline and placate any adventure-seeking young 'uns. You might ket a get kick out of it, too. For Grand Prix racing and longer activities, visit the website.

Museums

The actual announcement that you'll be visiting a museum will hopefully be the hardest part of any museum visit in the Netherlands. The Dutch pride themselves on viewing things from an off-kilter perspective, a dynamic often seen in their exhibits: look out for museums with hands-on displays or a full-immersion approach. For full details on Amsterdam's museums, *see pp70-114.*

Good bets for children include the interactive, non-Western exhibitions (mostly in Dutch) aimed at ages six to 12 at the **Tropenmuseum Junior** (part of the **Tropenmuseum**, for which *see p98*), and the interesting array of scientific activities designed to appeal to over-fours at **Nemo** (*see p102*). Any of Amsterdam's big museums should hold children's attention at least for a while, but the city's smaller, quirkier museums might prove better suited to the young concentration span: places such as the **Woonbootmuseum** (*see p89*), which reveals life on a houseboat, and the **Kattenkabinet** (*see p92*), which is cool for its cats.

Restaurants

Most restaurants and *eetcafes* in Amsterdam welcome children; however, if you're worried, it's a good idea to call ahead and check. Many eateries have special children's menus which usually offer chips or pancakes: if no one's complaining, why change the recipe? Bear in mind, though, that most Dutch restaurants and cafés do not have changing facilities, and that toilets are often in the cellar at the bottom of a steep flight of stairs. *See also p116.*

KinderKookKafé
Oudezijds Achterburgwal 193, Old Centre: Old Side (625 3257). Tram 1, 2, 4, 5, 9, 14, 17, 24, 25/Metro Nieuwmarkt. **Open** 3.30-8pm Sat, Sun. **No credit cards. Map** p306 D3.
The 'children's cooking café' runs kids' cookery courses in Dutch during the week (4.30-7pm Monday, Tuesday). But the real fun comes at weekends, with kids running the entire place: they cook, serve, present the bill and wash up – with a little help from the grown-up staff. The simple set menu includes a main course and dessert, and dishes are fresh, healthy and cheap. Book ahead.

Pizzeria Capri
Lindengracht 63, Jordaan (624 4940). Tram 3, 10/ bus 18, 22. **Open** 5-10pm daily (kitchen from 6pm). **No credit cards. Map** p305 B2.
Children are welcome at this pizzeria-cum-gelateria with a small pavement terrace. Staff and customers remain unfazed by kids dropping pasta on the floor, and there's plenty of real Italian ice-cream on hand for blackmail purposes. High chairs are available.

Restaurant David & Goliath
Amsterdams Historisch Museum, Kalverstraat 92, Old Centre: New Side (623 6736). Tram 1, 2, 4, 5, 9, 14, 16, 24, 25. **Open** 10am-5pm Mon-Fri; 11am-5pm Sat, Sun. **No credit cards. Map** p306 D3.
This museum (*see p84*) has a reasonably priced restaurant with its own entrance on a peaceful court-yard, where boisterous youngsters can play before and after their pancakes or fries.

Swimming pools & saunas

Good for kids are **De Mirandabad** (a sub-tropical pool with a wave machine, whirlpool, toddler pool and slide), the **Zuiderbad** indoor pool, and the **Brediusbad** and **Flevoparkbad** outdoor pools. For local pools, check the phone book under 'Zwembad' and call for special children's hours. Most saunas tolerate quiet children, especially at off-peak hours, and some offer family-only hours. For saunas, *see p236*; for pools, *see p238.*

Theatre & circus

The Dutch pride themselves on their cultural development, something that holds true for the way they stimulate their children's appreciation of art and entertainment. The **Children's Theatre Phoneline** (622 2999) offers recorded information in Dutch on kids' theatre, though you can also check under 'Jeugd' in *Uitkrant.* In addition to specialised children's theatre groups, many theatres and music venues hold kids' concerts and the like during the year; the Concertgebouw's *Kijk met je Oren*, for example, which combines classical music and puppetry. Check with **Uitlijn** (0900 0191) for details.

Outdoor entertainment

Amsterdam is one of the quirkiest and most beautiful cities in the world, and one whose small scale means tangible surprises at nearly every turn. Children love the variety of transportation, bridges, the crookedness of the buildings and activities as simple as scaling the steep stairways of city centre houses. While there's plenty of outdoor entertainment throughout the year, keep an eye open for impromptu performances around the main squares (Dam Square, Leidseplein and Rembrandtplein); Amsterdam's street artists can hold any crowd's attention – as long as you're not too PC for the occasional anti-Belgian joke. Also keep an eye open for Jan Klaasen performances (the equivalent of Punch and Judy) on Dam Square during the week.

The armada of flat, glass-roofed canal boats that tour the canals of Amsterdam usually keep the waters from freezing over when a truly icy winter sets in, but skating on canals can be fabulous fun (ask the locals if it's safe). When the conditions aren't right, the family can ice skate at the **Jaap Edenhal** rink (*see p237*).

Vondelpark. *See p188.*

Circustheater Elleboog

Passeerdersgracht 32, Western Canal Belt (626 9370/www.elleboog.nl). Tram 1, 2, 5, 7, 10. **Open** 9am-5pm Mon-Fri. *Bookings* 10am-2pm Mon-Fri. *Activities* times vary Sat, Sun. *Shows* times vary. **Admission** €7.50 adults; €5 under-17s. **No credit cards. Map** p310 C4.

Kids between four and 17 can learn circus and clowning tricks, make-up skills, juggling and tightrope walking. Activity days end with a performance for parents and friends. Non-member sessions are always busy, mostly with Dutch kids, but the troupe does not see language as a barrier. Children's birthday parties can also be arranged by phone. They also have a new sister theatre, Circustheater Elleboog ZO in the south-east of the city (Hoogoord 1A, 365 8313).

De Krakeling

Nieuwe Passeerdersstraat 1, Western Canal Belt (625 3284/reservations 624 5123/www.krakeling.nl). Tram 7, 10. **Shows** 2.30pm Wed, Sun; 8pm Thur-Sat. **Admission** €9; €7 adults accompanying child; €8 over-65s; €6 under-18s. **No credit cards. Map** p310 C4.

De Krakeling is the only Dutch theatre that produces programming exclusively for children. This unique venue has separate productions for over-12s and under-12s: phone to check what's going on at any given time. For non-Dutch speakers, there are puppet and mime shows and sometimes musicals. Shows are listed in a programme available from the theatre, as well as in *Uitkrant*.

Urban farms

Children's farms dot the Netherlands, and Amsterdam is no exception. **Artis** (*see p97*) is home to surprisingly tame pigs, goats, sheep and chickens, and also has great playgrounds. All Amsterdam's neighbourhoods have at least one urban farm; check the *Gouden Gids* (yellow pages) under 'Kinderboerderijen'. With the exception of Artis, admission is usually free.

Outside Amsterdam

On the beaten track but out of town, these attractions appeal to kids of all ages and are easy to reach by train or car. Check with the local **Amsterdam Tourist Board**, **ANWB** shops or the Netherlands Railways (**NS**) for ideas on day trips. The NS also has walking and cycling routes availabler; tickets for **NS Rail Idee** (*see p252*), which runs to all of the following attractions, cover the cost of transport and maps to and from the walking or cycling location. For details of other out-of-town attractions, *see pp253-272*.

Archeon

Archeonlaan 1, Alphen aan den Rijn (0172 447744/www.archeon.nl). 50km (31 miles) from Amsterdam; A4 to Leiden, then N11 to Alphen aan den Rijn. **Open** *Apr-July, Sept, Oct* 10am-5pm Tue-Sun. *Aug* 10am-5pm daily. Closed late Oct-Mar. **Admission** €13.25; €10.50 over-65s; €9.25 under-11s. **Credit** MC, V.

Arts & Entertainment

A ton of fun

Kids like to run free and parents need to recharge. So head to the great outdoors, or the next best thing: the city's parks.

Oddly enough, the newest park is to be found below ground level. **TunFun**, in the centre of the city, is a stroke of genius and another example of the creative Dutch approach to real estate: a former traffic underpass turned into 4,000 square metres (43,000 square feet) of

indoor playground, TunFun lets kids aged from one to 12 take part in activities ranging from traditional playground larks to disco dancing to indoor soccer. For parents, there's a restaurant and café.

For more traditional greenery – and dog mess – head to any of the city's parks, which offer a selection of playgrounds, child-friendly cafés and paddling pools. **Vondelpark** (*see p107*) is the most convenient and popular, with its summer programme of free afternoon entertainment, excellent playground and paddling pool. Further afield is **Amstelpark** (*see p110*) where the little ones can ride a miniature train, get lost in a maze or delegate the business of getting around to a pony. **Flevopark** (*see p98*), nicely untouched, is perfect for a peaceful picnic or a kickabout, and is near the Flevoparkbad outdoor swimming pools (*see p238*).

Plas means lake (and, interestingly, pee), and **Gasperplas Park** has a big one where one can sail, swim and sun. **Rembrandtpark** is another good patch of green, and houses **Bouwspeelplaats 't Landje** (618 3604), which organises a number of afternoon activities for kids between six and 14. **Westerpark** (*see p105*) now has a re-invented extension in the form of **Westergasfabriek** (*see p217* **It's a gas**), and though work continues, there's already a long strip of paddling pool and plans to put on lots of children's activities.

Amsterdamse Bos (*see p111*) is more than a park. It lives up to its forest name and even surpasses most forests in terms of amenities

like boating lakes, bicycle and canoe hire, open air theatre, large playgrounds, paddling pools, children's recreation island and zoos. There's also the magical **Bosmuseum** (*see p111*), which has maps of the park showing walking routes, and the **Geitenboerderij Ridammerhoeve** where kids can feed and pet more than 120 goats.

Het Twiske (Noorderlaaik 1, 075 684 4338, www.hettwiske.nl, bus 92 from CS) is a massive nature reserve just outside Amsterdam Noord/Oostzaan and is the closest example of the famous Dutch marshland polder landscape. It's named after an idyllic lake and comes with rural ambience and great bike paths. It's popular for swimming and cycling in the summer and for ice skating when winter does its stuff.

Nearby is **Waterspeelplaats De Blauwe Poort** (075 684 4338), an enormous, toddler-friendly water park. With fresh lake water continually pumped in from the Sloterplas, even the shallow water remains cool. There's an artificial beach with a fort and pirate ship in the middle of a man-made lake for bigger kids. It's only open in the warmer half of the year but is completely free.

TunFun

Mr Visserpelein, entrance by Portuguese Synagogue (689 4300/www.tunfun.nl). Tram 9, 14/Metro Waterlooplein. **Open** 10am-7pm daily (last admission 5.30pm). **Admission** €7.50 1s-12s; free under-1s, adults accompanying children. **No credit cards. Map** p307 E3.

The Archeon takes its visitors on an engaging trip through history, taking in the time of the dinosaurs, the Bronze Age and Roman era. There are loads of interactive and hands-on displays, plus an open-air plunge pool. It's all great fun.

Efteling
Europalaan 1, Kaatsheuvel, Noord Brabant (0416 288111/UK agent 01242 528877/www.efteling.nl). 110km (68 miles) from Amsterdam; take A27 to Kaatsheuvel exit, then N261. **Open** *Apr-June, Sept, Oct* 10am-6pm daily. *July-late Aug* 10am-9pm Mon-Sat; Sun 10am-midnight. Closed Nov-Mar. **Admission** €22; €10 over-65s, disabled; free under-4s. **Credit** AmEx, DC, MC, V.
Arguably better than Disney, this enormous fairy-tale forest is peopled with dwarves and witches, characters from Grimm stories and the Arabian Nights, enchanted and haunted castles, and even talking rubbish bins. The massive (and massively popular) amusement park is packed with state-of-the-art thrills, as well as more traditional fairground rides for tinies. It gets busy in summer.

Linnaeushof
Rijksstraatweg 4, Bennebroek (023 584 7624/ www.linnaeushof.nl). 20km (13 miles) from Amsterdam; take A5 to Haarlem, then head south on N208. **Open** *Apr-Sep* 10am-6pm daily. Closed Oct-Mar. **Admission** €7; €5.50 over-65s, disabled; free under-2s. **No credit cards.**
A huge leisure park near Haarlem, host to an astonishing 300 attractions: there's a Wild West train, cable cars, mini-golf, trampolines, a water play area and go-carts. Children under five are happy in the play area, and the price is most certainly right.

Madurodam
George Maduroplein 1, the Hague (070 355 3900/ 070 416 2400/www.madurodam.nl). 57km (35 miles) from Amsterdam; take A4 to the Hague. **Open** *Apr-June* 9am-8pm daily. *July, Aug* 9am-10pm daily. *Sept-Mar* 9am-6pm daily. **Admission** €11; €10 over-65s; €8 4-11s; free under-4s. **Credit** AmEx, DC, MC, V.
It claims to be the largest miniature village in the world, and we're not about to argue. Kids adore the scale models of the Netherlands' most famous sights – anything from Rotterdam's Erasmus Bridge to Schiphol Airport – all of which are built to scale on a 1:25 ratio. Go on a summer's evening, when the models are lit from the inside by over 50,000 tiny lamps.

Museum van Speelklok tot Pierement
Buurkerkhof 10, Utrecht (030 231 2789/ www.museumspeelklok.nl). 38km (24 miles) from Amsterdam; take A2 to Utrecht. **Open** 10am-5pm Tue-Sat; noon-5pm Sun. **Admission** €6; €4 4-12s; under-4s free. **Credit** MC,V.
This Utrecht attraction houses a unique collection of antique mechanical music boxes, circus, fairground and street organs and wondrous tin toys. A great day out for junior machine freaks.

Six Flags Holland
Spijkweg 30, Biddinghuizen (0321 329991/0321 329999/www.sixflags.nl). 72km (45 miles) from Amsterdam; take A1 towards Amersfoort, then A6 towards Lelystad, then follow signs for Six Flags. **Open** *Apr, May* 10am-5pm daily. *June-Aug* 10am-9pm daily. *Sept, Oct* from 10am Fri-Sun, closing times vary. **Admission** €23; €18.50 over-65s, disabled, 3s-11s; under-2s free. **Credit** AmEx, MC, V.
Opened in 2000, Six Flags Holland aims to please bigger children with the Netherlands' largest collection of rollercoasters, including one made of wood. Meanwhile, tots are sure to be entertained by the Looney Tunes characters and some tamer attractions. Opening hours are complicated and change often, so it's best to check before setting off.

Parenting

Childminders

Check the *Gouden Gids* under 'Oppascentrales' for babysitting in the suburbs.

Oppascentrale Kriterion
624 5848. **Bookings** 9-11am, 4.30-8pm daily. **Rates** from €5/hr; additional charge Fri, Sat. *Administration charge* €3.50. **No credit cards.**
This reliable service has been running for 45 years and uses male and female students aged over 18, all of whom are individually vetted. Book in advance, as the service is popular.

Children's rights

Kinder-en jeugdrechtswinkel
Staalstraat 19, Old Centre: Old Side (626 0067/ info@krwa.demon.nl). Tram 4, 9, 14, 16, 24, 25. **Open** *Walk-in consultations* 3-6pm Mon; 2-5pm Wed, Sat. **Map** p307 E3.
This children's rights office supplies under-18s with information about legal matters and the responsibilities of teachers, parents and employers. Kids may phone or visit, and while staff will answer questions from adults, they prefer dealing directly with the children involved.

Kindertelefoon (Childline)
0800 0432/office 672 2411/www.kindertelefoon.nl **Open** 2-8pm daily.
Young people from eight to 18 are welcome to phone this free line for information on bullying, sexual abuse, running away from home and so on. Staff are keen to stress that they do not give details about children's entertainment.

Toy libraries

There are several toy libraries in Amsterdam. There's a registration fee and a small borrowing charge. For details of your nearest toy library, consult the *Gouden Gids* under 'Speel-o-theek'.

Film

Dutch devotees of the silver screen keep cinemas well stocked with home-made and international fare.

Cinema's popularity in the Netherlands is still on the up: some 24 million punters went to Dutch cinemas in 2002, one million more than in 2001. Twenty- and thirtysomethings make up the bulk of the audience, and most of the tickets sold are for big-budget US blockbusters.

When it comes to home-grown films, it's usually only the trashy mainstream fare – much of which is tailor-made for a young audience – that does well at the box office, if not with critics. 2001's *Costa!*, spun around a group of youngsters living it up in Spain, was a typically unambitious crowd-pleaser, and buoyed by its cast of popular Dutch soap stars – in bikinis! – it became the biggest Dutch cinematic success since Paul Verhoeven's 1973 film *Turks Fruit*. What's more, it set the trend for a list of copycat flicks staffed by sometime soap stars and sundry TV babes. Still, there are some great Dutch movies being made (though they often disappear in weeks). Directors to watch include Jean van de Velde, Eddy Terstall, Theo van Gogh (yes, he is related), Alex van Warmerdam and Robert Jan Westdijk.

Once it seemed that every Dutch film was based on a book (often a World War II tale), but original scripts have steadily become the norm. That said, World War II and fiction are still reliable sources of inspiration: *The Discovery of Heaven* – incidentally the costliest Dutch film ever made – was based on the bestseller by Harry Mulisch and starred Stephen Fry; the critically acclaimed *Left Luggage*, from actor-turned-director Jeroen Krabbé, also dealt with World War II. More recent examples are *Phileine Zegt Sorry*, based on Ronald Giphart's bestseller, and *De Tweeling*, based on the novel by Tessa de Loo about twins separated during World War II; at the time of printing, the latter was a contender for the 2004 Best Foreign Film Oscar. Recent years have also seen a long list of family-fun films based on popular kids' books. In a trend (like so many) copied from the US, Dutch TV series from the '60s are also getting the feature film treatment. The comedy *Ja Zuster, Nee Zuster* was a huge hit, and *Floris* (based on the TV show that made Rutger Hauer famous) is due out in 2004.

Because money and fame are thin on the ground in the Netherlands – and the special tax law introduced some years ago to encourage local and international investment in Dutch film is now under threat – many Dutch film-makers aim for a career abroad. Paul Verhoeven is the most famous; others include Jan de Bont, Robby Müller (Wim Wenders' cameraman) and screenwriter Menno Meyes. Among Dutch thespian exports, Famke Janssen has made a living in the likes of *X-Men*, *X2* and *Eulogy* after her breakthrough role in *GoldenEye*. Ex-soap star Antonie Kamerling landed a part in the forthcoming *Exorcist IV* – but as a Nazi officer, a pigeonhole that many aspiring Dutch actors have occupied in non-Dutch films… when not in the one labelled 'Russian spy'.

GOING TO THE MOVIES

Amsterdam's cinemas offer as balanced and substantial a cinematic diet as any European city. Its picture palaces fall into two categories: first-run venues and *filmhuizen* (art houses). Amsterdammers have a healthy and thoroughly commendable appetite for foreign and art house fare, and the latter dish up a cosmopolitan spread of art films, documentaries and film-maker retrospectives, as well as an informed selection of more intelligent Hollywood flicks. With the exception of the **Uitkijk**, all have marvellous cafés, while **The Movies**, which is especially notable for its lavish art deco interior, also has an enchanting restaurant.

The best Cinemas

Bellevue Cinerama/Calypso
Comfy seats and wide screens. *See p192.*

Cinecenter
Laid-back lounging, hip films and an arty audience. *See p192.*

The Movies
A fine spot for food and a flick. *See p192.*

Pathé Tuschinski
Grand decor, big films. *See p192.*

Rialto
Friendly global cinema with a neighbourhood remit. *See p192.*

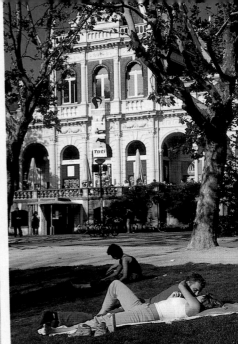

From screen kiss to green kiss: the **Nederlands Filmmuseum**. *See p194.*

Amsterdam's first multiplex, the 14-screen **Pathé ArenA** in the Bijlmer suburb, has grabbed both headlines and customers, but there are several other cinemas that prove as much of an attraction as the movies they screen. The **Pathé Tuschinski**, with its sumptuous art deco architecture and fittings, is a marvel.

TICKETS AND INFORMATION

Multiplex programmes change every Thursday. Weekly listings for all cinemas can be found in *Filmladder*, printed in the Wednesday editions of all major newspapers and displayed in many cafés, bars and cinemas. Other reliable sources of information include the Saturday 'PS' supplement of *Het Parool*; the *Amsterdams Stadsblad*; Dutch listings site www.filmfocus.nl; and, for indie and art house films, free listings mag *Shark* (www.underwateramsterdam.com). Look out, too, for fine monthly Dutch film mag *De Filmkrant*, whose movie information is in Dutch but easily understood by non-natives.

It's advisable to reserve tickets if you think the movie will be popular (opening weekends, Thursday and Friday evenings for example). Cinemas usually charge a nominal booking fee and none, except for the Pathé phone booking line, accept credit cards. Worse still for those who count English as a first language, Pathé-owned cinemas – all of those listed under **First run** below – now use a computer-operated, €0.35-per-minute telephone bookings line in Dutch only (0900 1458). If you don't speak Dutch and can't get online (you can book at www.pathe.nl), then you may have to go to the cinema itself to reserve tickets. In late 2003 Pathé introduced a new ticket price system: the newer the film, the more you have to pay for a ticket. There's also Belbios (0900 9363 premium rate/www.belbios.nl), a national ticket reservation service (Dutch only) that covers all the major cinemas in Amsterdam.

While art houses whet your appetite before the film starts by showing a few trailers of forthcoming flicks, multiplexes treat you to 15 minutes of soft drink commercials and the like. All films are shown in the original language, whether this is English or Swahili, with Dutch (and, on a few occasions, English) subtitles. Films in Dutch are indicated by the words 'Nederlands Gesproken' after the title. Some cinemas offer student discounts with ID. Purists should also note that most Dutch cinemas stick an interval in the middle of every film, even at some art house cinemas. Something to do with trying to make more money from the café? Call ahead to check if you really can't deal with such unwelcome interruptions.

Cinemas

First run

Bellevue Cinerama/Calypso

Marnixstraat 400-2, Southern Canal Belt (623 7814 after 5pm/www.filmmuseum.nl). Tram 1, 2, 5, 6, 7, 10. **Tickets** €7.20 Mon-Thur; €7.80 Fri-Sun. **Screens** 2 each. **No credit cards.** **Map** p310 C5.
Since the Filmmuseum has taken over this formerly Pathé-owned complex, the quality of films has greatly improved. Expect arty European films, plus the odd intelligent Hollywood flick.

City

Kleine Gartmanplantsoen 15-19, Southern Canal Belt (0900 9363 premium rate/www.city-bioscoop.nl). Tram 1, 2, 5, 6, 7, 10. **Tickets** €6-€8. **Screens** 7. **No credit cards.** **Map** p310 D5.
The large frontage and huge hoardings of the Pathé-owned City dominate Kleine Gartmanplantsoen. Its central location and Hollywood-or-bust policy make it hugely popular with youngsters, who talk, use their mobiles and lob popcorn during screenings.

Pathé ArenA

ArenA Boulevard 600, Bijlmermeer (0900 1458 premium rate/www.pathe.nl). Metro Bijlmer. **Tickets** €5-€9. **Screens** 14. **No credit cards.**
This glitzy multiplex next to the Ajax stadium offers 14 screens, 3,250 seats, air conditioning, digital sound and a spacious foyer. Blockbusters and other Hollywood success stories rule, drawing crowds largely from the surrounding suburbs.

Pathé de Munt

Vijzelstraat 15, Southern Canal Belt (0900 1458 premium rate/www.pathe.nl). Tram 4, 9, 14, 16, 24, 25. **Tickets** €5-€9. **Screens** 7. **No credit cards.** **Map** p310 D4.
Housed in a horrible brick edifice, this complex near the Tuschinski boasts seven screens, comfy seats and offers mainly Hollywood flicks.

Pathé Tuschinski

Reguliersbreestraat 26-8, Southern Canal Belt (0900 1458 premium rate/www.pathe.nl). Tram 4, 9, 14, 16, 24, 25. **Tickets** €5-€9. **Screens** 4. **No credit cards.** **Map** p311 E4.
Built in 1921 as a variety theatre, the Tuschinski is Amsterdam's most prestigious picture palace, which means queues at evenings and weekends. The choice of films is inspired, while the stunning design (see *p31*) looks even better since its renovation in 2002.

Pathé Tuschinski Arthouse

Reguliersbreestraat 34, Southern Canal Belt (0900 1458 premium rate/www.pathe.nl). Tram 4, 9, 14, 16, 24, 25. **Tickets** €5-€9. **Screens** 3. **No credit cards.** **Map** p310 D4.
Another Pathé cinema, neighbour to older brother Tuschinski. As the name suggests, this one offers arty films, sometimes documentaries, plus the better class of Hollywood flicks.

Art houses

Cinecenter

Lijnbaansgracht 236, the Jordaan (623 6615/0900 9363 premium rate/www.cinecenter.nl). Tram 1, 2, 5, 6, 7, 10. **Tickets** €5-€8. **Screens** 4. **No credit cards.** **Map** p310 C4.
The Cinecenter is a welcoming venue, with a hip lounge decor. Each screen has its own name – check out the 52-seat Jean Vigo room – and the programme is pleasingly international. It's popular on Sunday afternoons, though its small rooms can get stuffy.

Filmhuis Cavia

Van Hallstraat 521, West (681 1419/www.filmhuis cavia.nl). Tram 3, 10. **Tickets** €4. **Screens** 1. **No credit cards.** **Map** p305 A3.
Housed in a school that's now a squat, Cavia specialises in obscure and political pictures. It also hosts festivals covering gay and lesbian topics or religious and political themes.

Het Ketelhuis

Haarlemmerweg 8-10, the Jordaan (684 0090/www.ketelhuis.nl). Bus 18, 22. **Tickets** €7.50. **Screens** 1. **No credit cards.** **Map** p305 A1.
Devoted to Dutch films, made-for-TV films and docs (sometimes with subtitles), this brainchild of producer Marc van Warmerdam is a favourite among local buffs. It also offers lively film-related discussions and forums.

Kriterion

Roetersstraat 170, Plantage (623 1708/www.kriterion.nl). Tram 6, 7, 10/Metro Weesperplein. **Tickets** €6-€8; €5 children's matinées, previews. **Screens** 2. **No credit cards.** **Map** p312 G3.
Run by student volunteers, this popular two-screen cinema knows how to pick 'em: the intriguing programme includes European films, kids' matinées (Saturdays and Sundays), the well-regarded preview screenings (Thursdays), plus documentaries and classics. There's a large and busy bar, too.

The Movies

Haarlemmerdijk 161, the Jordaan (638 6016/www.themovies.nl). Tram 3. **Tickets** €7.50; €6.35 students. **Screens** 4. **Credit** *Restaurant* MC, V. **Map** p305 B1.
Don't be fooled by the insipid name: the Movies is a great place if you love, er, film: it offers a great pick of global flicks. The building dates from 1913, its art deco-style café is worth a visit in itself, and there's also a restaurant. Make an evening of it: if you eat here, you can slip in to the film at the last minute.

Rialto

Ceintuurbaan 338, the Pijp (676 8700/www.rialto film.nl). Tram 3, 12, 24, 25. **Tickets** €7-€8; €27.50 five-visit card; €50 ten-visit card. **Screens** 2. **No credit cards.** **Map** p311 F6.
This stylish, alternative cinema in the Pijp is one of the few with disabled access. It offers a mix of new and old international flicks and occasional European

Lights! Camera! Clog action!

With large parts of the *Ocean's Eleven* sequel – *Ocean's Twelve*, which will reconvene Pitt, Clooney and the gang – to be set and filmed in the city, the interest in Amsterdam as an international film location looks likely to rise.

Alfred Hitchcock set *Foreign Correspondent* (1940) in Amsterdam, but because World War II was raging at the time, he had to ask Hollywood set-builders to make 'a piece of Amsterdam… a few hotels, a Dutch windmill and a bit of the Dutch countryside'. The result was a huge windmill and a sprawling reconstruction of an Amsterdam square – Hôtel de l'Europe becoming 'Hotel Europe' – complete with sewer for the simulated storm scenes. The cameraman sent to get location footage lost his equipment when his ship got torpedoed but did eventually film the Jordaan for a chase scene where a jarring left-turn lands the viewer in a countryside with an oddly Spanish-styled windmill (this lack of research also flawed the windmill scene in the *South Park* movie's 'Kyle's Mom is a Bitch' segment). Still, *Foreign Correspondent* retained a realistic sense of location thanks to all the cheese references.

Another thriller that used Dutch stereotypes effectively was 1971's *Puppet on a Chain*, a tale of illicit drugs and apathetic Amsterdam cops which climaxed with traditionally dressed women doing a murderous clog dance. (For more absurd wooden shoe action, seek out Jackie Chan's *Who Am I?*) The same year brought Sean Connery to town for *Diamonds are Forever*, in which Bond fell for the charms of a typical tough and sexy Dutch chick. In fact, finding love in Amsterdam seems to be a popular theme in international productions: a feature-length *Love Boat* episode showed the long-neglected Captain Stubing finally getting some *amore* here, while Luciano Emmer's 1961 film *La Ragazza in Vetrina* ('The Girl in the Window'), partly written by Pier Paolo Pasolini, mines a similar seam of heart-warming romance – in the Red Light District, believe it or not.

Monsieur Hulot slapsticked his way through town in *Trafic* in 1971. The film was a homecoming of sorts for director/star Jacques Tati, whose grandfather was a Dutch picture-framer famed in the family for having refused to accept paintings from Van Gogh in lieu of cash payment. In addition, much of the oeuvre of art house stalwart Peter Greenaway offers an abundance of local locations.

Sadly, the film that may be the most rewarding for Amsterdam-spotters is almost impossible to find. Cheech and Chong's *Still Smokin'* (1983) sees the dopehead duo getting repeatedly mistaken for Burt Reynolds and Dolly Parton, as they participate in various local activities at places like the Tuschinski Cinema, Hotel Okura and a gay sauna. We can only hope that one day an ambitious director will be inspired to make a shot-for-shot remake, as Gus van Sant did with Hitchcock's *Psycho*.

We also hope Dutch baddie Gold Member returns in the next Austin Powers film – if only to shed light on why Austin's father hates 'two kinds of people: people who have no respect for other cultures, and the Dutch'.

premières. Themes change monthly, and classics are always on the schedule. In August Rialto screens films in the open air, on the nearby Marie Heinekenplein.

De Uitkijk
Prinsengracht 452, Southern Canal Belt (623 7460/ www.uitkijk.nl). Tram 1, 2, 5, 6, 7, 10. **Tickets** €5.50-€7. **Screens** 1. **No credit cards. Map** p310 D5.
Opened in 1929 by film-maker Mannus Franken, this converted canal house is a charming, frill-free (no café), 158-seat cinema. Purists love it and films that prove popular tend to stay put for a while.

Multimedia centres

Academie Cinema
Overtoom 301, Oud West (779 4913/squat.net/ overtoom301). Tram 1. **Tickets** €2. **Screens** 1. **No credit cards. Map** p309 B6.

Squatters moved into the former Nederlandse Filmacademie in 2000, and turned it into, among other things, an organic vegan restaurant, a club, and a cinema offering indie and experimental videos (sometimes films), plus gay and lesbian fare. After extensive work to comply with fire regulations, it reopened late in 2003. Check its website before setting out; it closes in summer.

De Balie
Kleine Gartmanplantsoen 10, Southern Canal Belt (553 5100/www.debalie.nl). Tram 1, 2, 5, 6, 7, 10. **Tickets** €5-€7. **Screens** 1. **No credit cards. Map** p310 D5.
The films shown in the cinema of this highbrow cultural centre (*see p241*) couldn't be more different from those offered opposite at City (*see p192*). Expect documentaries and obscure, frequently arty films from Europe and beyond, both old and new.

Arts & Entertainment

Pathé Tuschinski Arthouse. *See p192.*

Melkweg

Lijnbaansgracht 234A, Southern Canal Belt (531 8181/ www.melkweg.nl). Tram 1, 2, 5, 6, 7, 10. **Tickets** €6; €5 students (incl membership). **Screens** 1. **No credit cards. Map** p310 C5.
The Melkweg (*see p197, p213 and p225*) runs a consistently imaginative film programme in its cosy first-floor cinema, taking in anything from mainstream trash to cult fare and art house flicks.

Tropeninstituut

Kleine Zaal *Linnaeusstraat 2, Oost;* **Grote Zaal** *Mauritskade 63, Oost (568 8500/www.kit.nl/ tropentheater). Tram 9, 10, 14.* **Tickets** €5-€7. **Screens** 2. **Credit** MC, V. **Map** p312 H3.
Located out east by the excellent Tropenmuseum (*see p98*), this venue stages regular ethnic music and theatre performances, plus interesting documentaries and features from developing countries.

Film museum

Nederlands Filmmuseum (NFM)

Vondelpark 3, Museum Quarter (589 1400/library 589 1435/www.filmmuseum.nl). Tram 1, 2, 3, 5, 6, 12. **Open** *Library* 10am-5pm Tue-Fri; 11am-5pm Sat. **Tickets** €7.20; €7.80 weekends. **Membership** €15/yr. **Screens** 2. **No credit cards. Map** p310 C6.
Don't be fooled: this government-subsidised enterprise is as much a fine cinema as an exhibition venue. Founded in the 1940s, it now has over 35,000 films in its vaults, representing every period, cinematic style and corner of the world. Dutch films and children's matinées show on Sundays, and occasional screenings of silent movies come with piano accompaniment. Café Vertigo, in the basement, boasts one of Amsterdam's most charming terraces, home in summer to the hip and trendy and to outdoor screenings (check for details). Inside, students of cinema can be found poring over the archives.

Film festivals

Amnesty International Film Festival

626 4436/www.amnesty.nl. **Date** late Mar.
This five-day annual human rights event is held at various locations, often including De Balie (*see p193*), feature-length films, documentaries, lectures, discussions and a workshop.

Festival van de Fantastische Film

679 4875/www.filmevents.nl. **Date** Apr.
This week-long extravaganza targets lovers of horror, fantasy and SF. In 2004 it will be held at Cinerama, Melkweg and Paradiso, with premières, previews and retrospectives, and the 'Night of Terror', which spotlights some of the goriest movies imaginable. 2004's edition focuses on Japanese anime flicks.

International Documentary Filmfestival Amsterdam

627 3329/www.idfa.nl. **Date** last wk in Nov.
Documentaries are the staple of this fascinating annual festival, centred around De Balie (*see p193*). A prestigious prize named after the late documentarist Joris Ivens is awarded to the best film.

International Film Festival Rotterdam

010 890 9090 information/010 890 9000 bookings/ www.filmfestivalrotterdam.nl). **Date** late Jan.
With around 100 films in both the main programme and in retrospectives, the IFFR is the biggest event of its kind in the country. It co-opts a number of locations, all within walking distance of each other in Rotterdam. Aspiring moviemakers should visit the afternoon workshops; check out, too, the eclectic fare from Exploding Cinema, which also shows self-produced, alternative films Amsterdam.

Nederlands Film Festival

030 230 3800/030 232 2684 bookings/ www.filmfestival.nl. **Date** Sept.
An all-Dutch affair, the NFF spotlights around 100 features in a variety of venues around Utrecht, along with shorts, docs and TV shows. Every new Dutch production of the year is shown, along with flicks by students from Dutch film and art academies.

Nederlands Transgender Film Festival

636 3727/www.transgenderfilmfestival.com. **Date** May.
This five-day festival, attended by national and international guests, offers film screenings, lectures, discussions, Q&As and performance on transgender issues. *See also p205.*

World Wide Video Festival

420 7729/www.wwvf.nl. **Date** May.
Aside from videos and DVDs, the festival also features web-based projects, installations and seminars on a plethora of film- and video-related subjects. The beautiful Passenger Terminal, situated on the IJ waterfront, is the likely location for 2004.

Galleries

Display for today: how Amsterdam wears its art on its sleeve.

You see it, when descending upon Schiphol airport, in the Mondrian-like grid pattern of the landscape. You see it in the ballet-like elegance of its football players, who open space to score and close space to defend. And, of course, you see it in the art. For the Dutch have innate organisational skills, forged in the constant spring-cleaning needed to maintain a sense of space in their modestly-proportioned homeland. And when they run out of physical space, they direct their skills onto paper and canvas.

The Dutch have been famed for their depictions of reality ever since the Golden Age, when artists like Rembrandt and Vermeer were able to make a living from a large middle class that could afford to invest in its quest for status. And in Amsterdam, very little has changed: the locals still think walls are stark if they don't bear original artworks – whether figurative or painfully cutting edge – and there are plenty of galleries to meet demand.

THE 20TH CENTURY

None of the major post-photographic art movements of the 20th century grew without being absorbed by the Dutch, but two home-grown – and radically different – movements exerted an enduring influence on local and international scenes. The pristine abstraction of De Stijl ('the Style'), founded in 1917 and involving the likes of Theo van Doesburg, Piet Mondrian and Gerrit Rietveld, sought rules of equilibrium that are as useful in everyday design as in art. You just have to surf the web, leaf through Wallpaper*, visit IKEA or buy a White Stripes album to see their influence. However, some later painters chose to follow what they considered an antidotal (and much messier) muse. Under the moniker of CoBrA, such painters as Karel Appel and Eugene Brands interpreted the Liberation that ended World War II as a signal for spontaneity and the expression of immediate urges. Where their Surrealist forebears had embraced Freud, they preferred Jung's view, and sought to wire themselves into the playful unconscious of primitives, children and the mentally ill (for the **CoBrA Museum of Modern Art**, *see p112*).

Rebellion also defined the 1980s, when Amsterdam's 'After Nature' group, including Peter Klashorst and Jurriaan van Hall, decided to counter the reign of conceptual art with a renaissance of figurative work – but one marked by a spontaneous approach that betrayed their respect for CoBrA's abstract expressionism. This decade was also marked by the punk attitude of 'do-it-yourself', and squats became more cultural than political as artists sought settings for making and exhibiting new work.

THE 21ST CENTURY

The reaction against the anti-functionalism of conceptual art continues unabated – a trend that would have certainly pleased adherents of De Stijl, who hoped the future would bring a frenzy of cross-disciplinary action. Not only can photographers (Anton Corbijn, Rineke Dijkstra), VJs (Ottograph, Micha Klein) and architects (Rem Koolhaas) easily pass themselves off as 'artists', but the inspired work of John Körmeling and Atelier van Lieshout embodies a perfect fusion of function, whimsy and good old fashioned aesthetics. On the other hand, many people who would have called themselves artists in the past now proudly proclaim themselves designers (*see p198* **Living for design**).

Global acclaim has been heaped on Dutch graphic/multimedia designers for formulating a new universal visual language where stylistic simplicity (De Stijl) doesn't rule out personal expression (CoBrA). The nation's art, design

The best Galleries

Arcam
The 'silver snail' keeps up with the latest architecture. *See p198.*

Consortium
A breeding ground for the arts. *See p199.*

Frozen Fountain
Art applied right. *See p198* **Living for design**.

Stedelijk Museum Bureau Amsterdam
Often hipper than its mothership. *See p200.*

Torch
A tiny space with vast ambitions. *See p200.*

Arts & Entertainment

and architecture colleges have helped this process by making artists and designers study together and by welcoming a large number of foreign students. It's no surprise, then, that there's been a major influx of smaller, 'guerrilla' or 'viral' ad agencies who are taking full advantage of this global talent pool for their international campaigns.

However, creative Amsterdammers are not as spoiled as they once were. Generous subsidies still exist (another reason for foreign artists to visit), but things are no longer as they were in the swinging '80s. And while the government is spending millions on establishing affordable studio spaces for artists, they're just belated replacements for the organically grown squat scene (*see p110* **It means squat**), squeezed out of town in the name of commerce. As it turns out, with all its new and empty office walls, Amsterdam now needs artists more than ever.

Happily, when compared to the art factories of Paris, New York and London, which have started to play it safe in their troubled economic times, Amsterdam's galleries seem determined to remain adventurous and to welcome up-and-comers. And with the newly opened **Westergasfabriek** (*see p217* **It's a gas**), there's a brand new slew of exhibition spaces.

ON SHOW
In addition to the galleries, there are five world-famous museums of modern art in the Netherlands: the **Stedelijk Museum of Modern Art** in Amsterdam (*see p107*), the **Haags Gemeentemuseum** in the Hague (*see p265*), the wonderful **Rijksmuseum Kröller-Müller** in Otterlo, the **Groninger Museum** in Groningen and the newly expanded **Stedelijk van Abbemuseum** in Eindhoven (for all, *see pp264-265* **Beyond Holland**). All aim to showcase a mix of established international names and young, local artists.

Galleries in Amsterdam appear and vanish all the time. For the most up-to-date list, buy the monthly Alert (available at **Athenaeum Nieuwscentrum**; *see p154*); although it's in Dutch, galleries are sorted into areas and clearly marked on maps. Also, scan the flyers at the excellent art and design book store **Artbook** (Van Baerlestraat 126, Museum District, 675 6290, 10am-6pm Tue-Sat, 1-6pm Mon); check gallery shows in *Uitkrant* (www.uitkrant.nl), or the art listings pamphlet published every two months by AKKA, whose website (www.akka.nl) provides direct links to the websites of the city's more relevant galleries. Photography buffs would do well to visit **Huis Marseille** (*see p88*) and **Foam** (*see p91*).

Many galleries close during July or August and have a relaxed attitude to opening hours

Torch.
See p200.

the rest of the time, so it's best to call ahead. For **KunstRAI**, an annual art fair, and artists' **Open Studios**, *see p181*. And for more on Dutch art, *see p35*.

Galleries

The Old Centre: Old Side

Amsterdamse Centrum voor Fotographie
Bethaniënstraat 9 (622 4899). Tram 16, 24, 25. **Open** 1-5pm Wed-Fri; 11am-5pm Sat. Closed July, Aug. **No credit cards. Map** p306 D3.
Photo hounds should go directly to this sprawling space within flashing distance of the Red Light District. Besides showing photographers' work, it also has workshops and a black-and-white darkroom for hire.

Stichting Oude Kerk
Oudekerksplein 23 (625 8284/www.oudekerk.nl). Tram 4, 9, 14, 16, 24, 25. **Open** 11am-5pm Mon-Sat; 1-5pm Sun. *During World Press Photo* 10am-6pm Mon-Sat; 1-6pm Sun. **No credit cards. Map** p306 D2.
The 'Old Church', home of World Press Photo (*see p180*), exhibits everything from 'cancer art' to installations inspired by the thousands of graves (in one of which lies Saskia Rembrandt) under its stone floor. Admission shouldn't be more than €6. *See also p82.*

W139
Warmoesstraat 139 (622 9434/www.w139.nl). Tram 4, 9, 14, 16, 24, 25. **Open** 1-6pm Wed-Sun. **No credit cards. Map** p306 D2.

In its two decades of existence, W139 has never lost its squat edge. This remarkable space has room to deal with large installations, and though the work is occasionally over-conceptual, a visit is usually worthwhile. The gallery closed at the end of 2003 for renovation work that was expected to take around a year, but exhibitions will continue at other locations; check the website for details.

The Old Centre: New Side

Arti et Amicitiae
Rokin 112 (623 3508/www.arti.nl). Tram 4, 9, 14, 16, 24, 25. **Open** 1-6pm Tue-Sun. **No credit cards. Map** p306 D3.
This marvellous building houses a private artists' society, whose illustrious members gather in the first-floor bar. But members of the public can climb a Berlage-designed staircase to its large exhibition space, home to some excellent, conversation-inducing temporary shows.

Western Canal Belt

Galerie Paul Andriesse
Prinsengracht 116 (623 6237/www.galleries.nl/ andriesse). Tram 13, 14, 17. **Open** 11am-6pm Tue-Fri; 2-6pm Sat; 2-6pm 1st Sun of mth. **No credit cards. Map** p306 C2.
While perhaps no longer all that innovative, there's still a selective savvy at work that embraces both older and wiser artists (Marlene Dumas often shows new works here) and up-and-coming names such as the much-lauded Fiona Tan.

Montevideo/TBA
Keizersgracht 264 (623 7101/www.montevideo.nl). Tram 13, 14, 17. **Open** 1-6pm Tue-Sat. **No credit cards. Map** p306 C3.
Montevideo is dedicated to works that apply new technologies to visual arts, alongside photography and installations. Admire cutting-edge tech in an old world space, or read up on an assortment of topics in the reference room. There's usually a token entry fee for exhibitions.

Southern Canal Belt

De Appel
Nieuwe Spiegelstraat 10 (625 5651/www.deappel.nl). Tram 16, 24, 25. **Open** 11am-6pm Tue-Sun. **No credit cards. Map** p310 D4.
An Amsterdam institution that showed its mettle by being one of the first galleries in the country to embrace video art. It still has a nose for things modern, and gives international and rookie guest curators freedom to follow their muse.

Clement
Prinsengracht 845 (625 1656/www.gallerie-clement.nl). Tram 16, 24, 25. **Open** 11am-5.30pm Tue-Sat. **No credit cards. Map** p310 D5.

Best known as a haven for print collectors, Clement began as a printing studio in 1958 before opening its gallery a decade later. Walk your eyes through a selection that includes work by the likes of Penck, Sierhuis, Lucebert and Cremer.

Espace
Keizersgracht 548 (624 0802/www.galleries.nl/ espace). Tram 1, 2, 5. **Open** 1-6pm Wed-Sat; 2-5pm 1st Sun of mth. **No credit cards. Map** p310 C4.
Founded in 1960, Espace has an illustrious reputation. Most stories derive from a past when Dubuffet and de Kooning represented the cutting edge, but some recent exhibitions have also been known to surprise. A few doors down, Collection d'Art (Keizersgracht 516, 622 1511) mines a similar expressionist vein.

Galerie Akinci
Lijnbaansgracht 317 (638 0480/www.akinci.nl). Tram 16, 24, 25. **Open** 1-6pm Tue-Sat. **No credit cards. Map** p311 E5.
Part of a nine-gallery complex that includes Lumen Traven, Art Affair and Oele, Akinci thrives on surprising with diverse shows that employ every imaginable contemporary media: from the body-hair art of Yael Davids to the photography of Ilya Rabinovich and Juul Hondius.

Gallery Delaive
Spiegelgracht 23 (625 9087/www.delaive.com). Tram 6, 7, 10. **Open** 11am-5.30pm Mon-Sat. **No credit cards. Map** p310 D5.
An acclaimed, upmarket joint that is renowned for its over-reliance on 'names'. But, hell, it's a top one-stop shop if you're out for a collection of all your favourite CoBrA and Surrealist painters and sculptors, and you can even grab a Picasso or a Warhol while you're at it.

Gate Foundation
Lijnbaansgracht 322-3 (620 8057/www.gate foundation.nl). Tram 1, 2, 5. **Open** 10am-5pm Wed-Fri. **No credit cards. Map** p311 E4.
This 'intercultural contemporary art multicultural society' was founded in 1988 to focus on – you guessed it – the role of (multi)cultural identities in (mostly non-Western) arts. Since then it has initiated many projects and websites that promote the global exchange of ideas.

Gallery Lemaire
Reguliersgracht 80 (623 7027/www.gallery-lemaire.com). Tram 4, 16, 24, 25. **Open** 11am-5pm Tue-Fri; 11am-4pm Sat. **Credit** AmEx, MC, V. **Map** p311 E4.
In the same family for three generations now, this maze-like gallery fills a huge canal house with tribal art from around the world – in short: a heaven for collectors. Phone ahead to confirm opening times.

Melkweg
Marnixstraat 409 (531 8181/www.melkweg.nl). Tram 1, 2, 5, 6, 7, 10. **Open** 1-8pm Wed-Sun. **No credit cards. Map** p310 D5.

Arts & Entertainment

The Melkweg reflects the broad interests of director Suzanne Dechart, with quality shows of contemporary photography. Expect anything from meditative studies of the homeless to portraits of Hong Kong ravers. *See also p194, p213 and p225.*

Reflex Modern Art Gallery
Weteringschans 79A (627 2832/www.reflex-art.nl). Tram 6, 7, 10. **Open** 11am-6pm Tue-Sat. **Credit** AmEx, MC, V. **Map** p310 D5.
A New York flavour characterises Reflex, which deals with international names such as Christo and locals like Dadara and photographer Erin Olaf. They also have a gallery shop across the street at No.83, where you can get graphics and lithos by Appel and inflatable Munch Scream dolls. In 2004 a new gallery will open at No.380 to focus more on younger artists.

Jodenbuurt, the Plantage & the Oost

Arcam
Prins Hendrikkade 600 (620 4878/www.arcam.nl). Tram 9, 14/Metro Waterlooplein. **Open** 1-5pm Tue-Sat. **No credit cards**. **Map** p307 E3.

Architecture Centrum Amsterdam is obsessed with the promotion of Dutch contemporary architecture, and organises tours, forums, lectures and exhibits on the subject. Their fresh new 'silver snail' location is a monument to modernity in itself.

Mediamatic
Nieuwe Foeliestraat at the corner of Rapenburg (344 6007/www.mediamatic.net). Tram 9, 14/Metro Waterlooplein. **Open** 2-6pm Fri-Sun during exhibitions. **No credit cards**. **Map** p307 F2.
This space age construction – often enhanced by outdoor projections from the inspired likes of Nepco (www.nepco.nl) – houses an organisation dedicated to the outer reaches of technology and multimedia in art. It also organises regular exhibitions, publications, presentations, salons and events.

The Waterfront

This area of the Eastern Docklands is rapidly transforming, and many galleries should find their way here in the short term. Besides **Consortium** (*see p199*) and **Quarantine** (*see p199* **Living for design**), the former

Living for design

Droog&Co

The history of Dutch design has always fluttered between intrinsic orderliness (reinforced by Calvinism and De Stijl) and a strong desire for personal expression (perhaps an echo of the stubbornness required to battle the sea). And the fact that this design is often both ingeniously functional and downright witty has resulted in worldwide acclaim – so much so that even the tourist board has jumped on the design bandwagon at www.coolcapitals.com.

Droog&Co
Rusland 3, The Old Centre: Old Side (626 9809/www.droogdesign.nl). Tram 16, 24, 25. **Open** noon-6pm Tue-Fri; noon-5pm Sat. **Credit** MC, V. **Map** p306 D3.
This internationally acclaimed Dutch design collective now has its own shop, designed by Richard Hutten (who was wise enough to leave the 16th-century ceiling untouched).

Frozen Fountain
Prinsengracht 629, Western Canal Belt (622 9375/www.frozenfountain.nl). Tram 1, 2, 5. **Open** 1-6pm Mon; 10am-6pm Tue-Fri; 10am-5pm Sat. **Credit** V. **Map** p309 C4.
This shop on Prinsengracht is a paradise for lovers of contemporary furniture and design items. While staying abreast of

innovative young Dutch designers such as furniture god Piet Hein Eek, the 'Froz' also exhibits and sells stuff by the international likes of Marc Newsom, modern classics and even photography.

Galerie Binnen
Keizersgracht 82, Western Canal Belt (625 9603). Tram 1, 2, 5, 13, 17. **Open** noon-6pm Wed-Sat; or by appointment. **No credit cards**. **Map** p306 C2.
These industrial and interior design specialists have plenty of room in which to show work by unusual names (Sottsass, Kukkapuro, Studio Atika) and to host unusual exhibits of things like toilet brushes, Benno Primsela vases, or designers subverting Dutch cliches (www.dutch-souvenirs.org).

warehouse **Loods6** (KNSM-Laan 143, www.loods6.nl) puts on occasional exhibitions of an art/design nature, as does hip street accessory shop neighbour **90 Square Meters** (Levantplein 52, KNSM-Eiland, 419 2525/ www.90sqm.com), which also organises a variety of lectures and events that look at links between art, advertising and the street.

Consortium
Pakhuis Wilhelmina, Oostelijke Handelskade 29 (06 2611 8950 mobile/www.xs4all.nl/~conso). Bus 32. **Open** 2-6pm Fri-Sun. **No credit cards.**
Out in the Eastern Docklands, Consortium puts on exhibitions dedicated to international up-and-comers. Its warehouse home has just been renovated as a studio space for local artists and there's talk of plans for a networking-friendly bar/café.

Pakt
Zeeburgerpad 53 (06 5427 0879 mobile/ www.pakt.nu). Tram 7, 10. **Open** 2-8pm Thur-Sun. **No credit cards.**
This new, slightly out-of-the-way address will probably pick up the slack during the renovation of W139 (*see p196*). Expect the 'pure image and sound'

of Park 4DTV (www.park.nl), the mobile art/hotdog kiosks of Ki-osk, or the massive rolling printing logs of Alex Fischer. Unwind afterwards at the nearby Brouwerij 't IJ (*see p144*).

The Jordaan

Annet Gelink Gallery
Laurierstraat 187-9 (330 2066/www.annetgelink. com). Tram 13, 14, 17. **Open** 11am-6pm Tue-Fri; 1-6pm Sat. **No credit cards. Map** p309 B4.
Annet Gelink has plenty of space and light to lavish on notable names in Dutch and international art: Mat Collishaw, Harmony Korine, Alicia Framis and Kiki Lamers, among others.

Donkersloot
Leidsegracht 76 (572 2722/www.gallerydonkersloot. nl). Tram 1, 2, 5. **Open** noon-8pm daily. **Credit** AmEx, DC, MC, V. **Map** p310 C4.
Hyping itself as a 'night gallery', Donkersloot hosts 'live painting events' (such as getting 80 women together to paint each other) and works by rock 'n' roll types like the late Herman Brood. Its openings are a who's who of the city's more decadent artists.

Frozen Fountain

Pakhuis Amsterdam
Oosterdokkade 3-5, the Waterfront (421 1133/www.pakhuisamsterdam.nl). Bus 22, 32. **Map** p307 E1.
In 2003, this showroom for 30 of Europe's top interior design companies (wholesale only, but public welcome to browse), left its Eastern Docklands home. By early 2004, it should be settled in this old post office building, which will also house temporary exhibits of the Stedelijk Museum (*see p107*) during renovation work. Visit the website for details.

Quarantine
Rietlandpark 375, Eastern Docklands (419 3851/www.quarantine.nl). Bus 28, 32, 59. **Open** noon-1am Mon-Thur, Sun; noon-3am Fri, Sat. **No credit cards.**

Another cultural pioneer of the Eastern Docklands, Quarantine offers a project space for artists and designers to strut their stuff. With adjoining café De Kantine (419 4433), it's already a meeting place for the like-minded awaiting the opening of its neighbour, Lloyd Hotel (*see p66* **Cultural cooking with Lloyd**).

WonderWood
Weteringstraat 48, Southern Canal Belt (625 3738/www.wonderwood.nl). Tram 6, 7, 10. **Open** noon-6pm Wed-Sat. **No credit cards. Map** p310 D5.
The name says it all: wonderfully sculpted wood in the form of shop-made originals, re-editions of global classics and original plywood from the '40s and '50s. Wonderful.

Also...
Rozengracht and Haarlemmerstraat streets and the 'Nine Streets' (*see p157* **Where to spend it**) area are good for general design. Department store **HEMA** (*see p163*) often has cheap but savvy knock-offs. **Athenaeum Nieuwscentrum** (*see p154*) is the place for Amsterdam-centric design books and mags. And, of course, **Condomerie het Gulden Vlies** (*see p176*) remains a Valhalla for functional and whimsical designer peniswear.

Fuzzy Art

2e Tuindwarsstraat 11 (626 2780/622 2970/
www.fuzzyart.nl). Tram 13, 14, 17. **Open** 1-5.30pm
Thur-Sat; or by appointment. **No credit cards.**
Map p305 B3.

Located on one of the Jordaan's funkier streets, this
gallery appropriately dedicates itself to art with an
'unreal, non-worldly feel', which means they favour
underground comic strips (like the adventures of
local hero Gutsman) and the dizzyingly surreal.

Galerie Diana Stigter

Hazenstraat 17 (624 2361/www.dianastigter.nl).
Tram 7, 10, 13, 14, 17. **Open** 1-6pm Tue-Sat;
2-5pm 1st Sun of mth. **No credit cards.**
Map p310 C4.

The extreme and the extremely committed have
found a happy home with curator Diana Stigter: the
scary animation of Martha Colburn, the magical
videos of Baloise art prize winner Saskia Olde
Wolbers or the works of Elspeth Diederix, Tariq
Alvi and Steve McQueen.

Galerie Fons Welters

Bloemstraat 140 (423 3046/www.fonswelters.nl).
Tram 13, 14, 17. **Open** 1-6pm Tue-Sat; 2-5pm 1st
Sun of mth. **No credit cards. Map** p305 B3.
Venerable doyen of the scene Fons Welters likes
to 'discover' the latest new (and often local) talent
and has shown remarkable taste in both sculpture
and installation, having provided a home to Atelier
van Lieshout, Meirjn Bolink, Rob Birza, Jennifer
Tee and Aernout Mik. Even the entrance to the
gallery is a tour de force.

GO Gallery

Prinsengracht 64 (422 9580/www.gogallery.nl).
Tram 13, 14, 17. **Open** noon-6pm Wed-Sat;
1-5pm 1st Sun of mth. **Credit** AmEx, DC, MC, V.
Map p305 B2.

Owner Oscar van den Voorn is an energetic sup-
porter of local art that manages to display a sense
of humour. Visitors can expect themed dinners (usually served up on Thursdays), stained-glass, graffiti
or art inspired by LSD.

Serieuze Zaken

Elandsstraat 90 (427 5770). Tram 7, 10, 17.
Open noon-6pm Tue-Sat; 1-5pm 1st Sun of mth.
No credit cards. Map p310 C4.
Rob Malasch was already known as a quirky the-
atre type and journalist before opening this gallery
in the Jordaan. Shows here might feature Brit Art,
works by contemporary Chinese painters or the
'Punk Pictures' of Max Natkiel.

Stedelijk Museum
Bureau Amsterdam

Rozenstraat 59 (422 0471/www.smba.nl). Tram 13,
14, 17. **Open** 11am-5pm Tue-Sun. **Map** p309 B4.
The Stedelijk's space on Rozenstraat devoted to
younger and mostly Amsterdam-based artists has
turned out to be hipper than its mothership in recent
years, with shows including the scary styrofoam

sculptures of Folkert de Jong, the cooking-for-kids
lessons of Chiko & Toko, and the, er, sperm paintings of Arnoud Holleman.

Steendrukkerij Amsterdam

Lauriergracht 80 (624 1491/www.steen
drukkerij.com). Tram 13, 14, 17. **Open** 1-5.30pm
Wed-Sat; 2-5pm 1st Sun of mth. Closed July, Aug.
No credit cards. Map p309 B4.
This gallery and printshop specialises in hands-on
works like woodcuts and lithography. Sometimes
guest artists like Claes Oldenburg are invited to col-
laborate with the more technique-heavy printers.

Torch

Lauriergracht 94 (626 0284/www.torchgallery.com).
Tram 7, 10. **Open** 2-6pm Thur-Sat. **Credit** AmEx,
DC, MC, V. **Map** p309 D4.
If you like your art edgy you'll love Torch, which
brings the likes of Richard Kern, Annie Sprinkle,
Cindy Sherman and Anton Corbijn to Amsterdam.

The Pijp

Stip Gallery

1e Sweelinckstraat 20 (06 4143 3789 mobile/
www.stipgallery.com). Tram 4, 6, 7, 10. **Open**
1-5pm Wed-Fri; noon-4pm Sat. **Credit** AmEx, MC, V.
Map p311 F5.
Street art is the name of the game in this new gallery
in Amsterdam's ultimate street 'hood. Expect canvases from the able hands of tattoo artists like local
legend Henk Sciffmacher, or graffiti by artists such
as Ottograph.

Roving galleries

Chiellerie

www.chiellerie.nl.
Curator Chiel organises openings on Mondays from
7pm to 10pm for an 'Artist of the Week' culled from
the local scene. Fun and hip.

Jim Beard Gallery

www.jimbeard.nl.
A roving, inspired pack of artists and designers who
stage events every few months in such singular locations as storage containers and karaoke bars.

Lazy Artist

www.lazyartist.org.
A local posse out to 'creact' in the name of creative
resistance (think *Adbusters* magazine) through their
website and events.

Smart Project Space

www.smartprojectspace.net.
Though due to lose their home base in 2003, Smart
will undoubtedly remain dedicated to 'hardcore art'
and documenting the squattier side of the
Amsterdam art spectrum. But don't expect anything
low-tech: they have a snazzy website with a massive
server for artist videos.

Gay & Lesbian

Like attracts like in the Netherlands' gay capital.

With its benevolent eye to difference and diversity, Amsterdam is a magnet for gays and lesbians – indeed, it's regarded by many as the gay capital of Europe (and perhaps even the planet). Amsterdam is the capital of a country which is second-to-none for judicial equality. Holland decriminalised homosexuality as far back as 1811, lowered the age of consent for gay men to 16 in 1971, and pulled off its greatest coup in 2002, when it became the first nation to legalise same-sex marriage for nationals and residents. In the first year alone, 1339 male and 1075 female couples tied the knot.

But of course it's not just social acceptance that brings them here: it's the fun, too. For gays, the Amsterdam scene offers something to all comers, from leather-daddy to perma-tanned twink and everything in between. Alas (as is often the case elsewhere), it's hardly Sapphic heaven. There is scope to indulge everyone from separatists to S&M devotees, but lesbian opportunities tend to be restricted to a handful of venues. And it's unfortunate that such a diverse scene should be so strongly divided by gender, although girls and boys do come together for one-off club nights, for Queen's Day celebrations and – with a bang – at Gay Pride.

While **cruising** used to be broadly accepted in Amsterdam, there seems to be a relative downturn in tolerance. Vondelpark (by the rose garden; don't park your bicycle nearby at night, as slitting tyres is a popular pastime for homophobes) and the wooded De Nieuwe Meer area, in the south-west of the city, are still popular spots for sunbathing and cruising – though De Nieuwe Meer has been redesigned to make it more open, and cruising in Vondelpark is now only allowed after dusk.

The super-liberal **prostitution** laws in Amsterdam also apply to gays. The male brothels and the rent-boy bars are all legal. However, the rent-boy strip of Paardenstraat is full of exploited young men, and can be dangerous – both in terms of personal safety and unsafe sex. Proceed with caution.

Since the advent of HIV and AIDS, the Dutch have developed a responsible attitude towards the practice and promotion of **safe sex**, and condoms are available from most gay bars. The darkrooms in many of Amsterdam's gay bars and clubs are strictly regulated, and proprietors are obliged to provide safe sex information and condoms. However, STDs and HIV infections

Essential information

Amsterdam is far more tolerant of gays and lesbians than most major world cities. That said, while no one blinks an eye when two guys walk hand in hand through the centre of town, public displays of affection are viewed uneasily in the suburbs and smaller cities. **Queer-bashing** is on the up: in mid 2001, an imam from Rotterdam declared on national TV that gay people are worse than dogs (though his remarks caused an outcry); gay and lesbian teachers now often stay in the closet for fear of negative reactions from pupils and parents, though a special anti-discrimination educational campaign aimed at school children and their parents was run in 2003. What's more, the annual Gay Pride and Canal Parade are under fire for being too in-your-face – though when a boat of butt-naked men passes by, you might think the detractors have a point. Still, the Canal Parade attracts some 300,000 visitors, including whole families with kids, which makes it the second most popular event in Amsterdam after Queen's Day.

The best Hangouts

ARC
Stark design and a round-the-clock A-gay crowd. See p207.

Cockring
Sexy strippers, sleazy locals and tourists from every nation. See p206.

Club Divine
Eyeliner and electroclash. See p209.

Coffeeshop Downtown
Plenty of gossip, cakes, and a nice cup of tea. See p209.

Getto
Cocktails and Elvis the Cat. See p208.

Sappho
Girls and booze, art and film: the perfect combination. See p210.

Arts & Entertainment

are alarmingly on the rise, with bareback (unsafe) sex becoming more and more common among gay men. *See p282* for details of HIV- and AIDS-related organisations.

Homomonument

Westermarkt, Western Canal Belt. Tram 13, 14, 17. **Map** *p306 C3.*

The world's first memorial to persecuted gays and lesbians was designed by Karin Daan. Its three triangles of pink granite, recently renovated at a cost of €400,000, form a larger triangle that juts out into the Keizersgracht. Those victimised in World War II are commemorated on 4 May, but flowers are laid daily in more private acts of remembrance, and also on World AIDS Day (1 Dec).

Pink Point

Westermarkt, Western Canal Belt. Tram 13, 14, 17, 20. **Open** *daily noon-6pm. Winter noon-6pm Thur-Sat.* **Map** *p306 C3.*

Learn all about pink Amsterdam at this now year-round info kiosk near the Homomonument: it's stuffed with magazines, books, pamphlets and flyers, as well as souvenirs. The friendly staff are mines of information. Pink Point publishes a guidebook, too: the *Bent Guide To Amsterdam* (€5.99).

Publications

Gay News Amsterdam (www.gaynews.nl) and **Gay & Night**, both in Dutch and English, are published monthly. They are free in many

The queer year

Spring

Queen's Day (*see p179*), every 30 April, is a huge open-air disco plus flea-market plus almighty piss-up. Every bar in town raises a glass or several to celebrate the Queen's birthday. The special **Roze Wester** gay and lesbian festival is held on Westermarkt, with street performers, DJs and dancing.

Remembrance Day takes place on 4 May on Dam Square and commemorates victims – including gay and lesbian ones – from World War II. The **NVIH** and **COC** hold a separate tribute at the Homomonument on the same date. The following day is **Liberation Day**, with a big outdoor party for both, *see p180*).

AIDS Memorial Day is held at Dominicuskerk (Spuistraat 12, 624 2183) every last Saturday in May. Names of the dead are read out, candles are lit and commemorative white balloons are released.

Gender boundaries are crossed and blurred at the **Transgender Film Festival** held in May at De Balie (*see p192 and 194*). The wide-ranging international programme – from documentary to comedy, feature to short – is supplemented with high-calibre guests, Q&As, talks and discussion panels.

Summer

Amsterdam Diners is a huge one-day HIV and AIDS fundraiser. The date and location seem to change every year; check www.amsterdamdiners.com for details.

Gay Pride (www.amsterdampride.nl; *see also p182*) is held every first weekend in August. From Friday to Sunday Amsterdam turns pink, with street parties, performances and clubs host (expensive!) special events.

Highlights are the Canal Parade on Saturday and the grand finale party on Sunday in front of the Muziektheater.

The **Annual Drag King Contest** is strictly women-only (though, really, who'll be able to tell?) and takes place on the last Saturday in August at the COC (*see p282*). It's always packed out: expect lots of macho swaggering in fake facial fuzz and polyester suits, as a cavalcade of gender-benders attempt to out-butch each another.

The Dutch leg of femcore event **Ladyfest** (www.ladyfestamsterdam.org) shakes itself in late August; the non-profit making, socio-cultural-whatever puts the pop into politics, and serves up a roistering roster of grrrl bands, writers and performers at alternative venues all over town.

Autumn

November brings **Amsterdam Leather Pride**. Leather aficionados get greased up and chained up all over town for a whole week. The hide-bound event is mostly manly, but there are some events for women, organised by **Wild Side** (*see p206*).

Winter

On 1 December, **World AIDS Day**, there's a conference in the RAI Exhibition Centre, plus a series of fundraising events in town.

Roze Film Dagen (www.rozenfilmdagen.nl) in December brings in a veritable rainbow of celluloid from across the world. The event attracts big audiences: they're kept extra happy with themed events throughout the festival, plus DJs, VJs, parties and a fabulous opening night ball. There's a Coming Out Day special for those under 26, too.

Arts & Entertainment

Let the good times rock.

gay establishments, but also on sale in central newsagents. **sQueeze** is a Dutch glossy, a sort of gay Cosmo complete with features, fashion and beauty tips. Far more interesting is **BUTT**, a sexy/trashy/arty English quarterly (on pink paper!) that spans low and high culture. The best Dutch-language source of national and international news features is bi-weekly **De Gay Krant**, available from newsagents (www.gaykrant.nl). In addition, the freely available monthly English-language 'zine **Shark** (www.underwateramsterdam.com) includes extensive queer listings along with the best from the alternative art, film, music and squat scenes. **PS**, the Saturday supplement of newspaper **Het Parool**, also has extensive, up-to-date pink listings. Gay and lesbian health organisation **Schorerstichting** (see p283) produces a free gay tourist map and a safe sex booklet (with male bias) in English every year.

Lesbian readers are also well served. As well as a few articles in De Gay Krant and Gay and Night, there are a few dedicated dyke mags. Monthly, middle-of-the-road **Zij aan Zij** has an all-things-to-all-lesbians editorial policy, and a useful national listings section (Dutch only); go to their website at www.zijaanzij.nl. The similar, North-Holland specific **La Vita**, meanwhile, has gone totally online at www.la-vita.nl. Worth a glance is the pocket-sized, lo-fi **KUTT**, sister mag of aforementioned BUTT and full of smut, art and fashion in English and Dutch; big-name interview coups with the likes of Peaches and Chloe Sevigny make up for slightly self-indulgent articles.

Radio & TV

The stations below, both on Amsterdam cable, can be good sources of information and entertainment. Check out the gay and lesbian teletext page 447 of NOS Teletext (on Nederland 1, 2 and 3 channels), or **De Gay Krant**'s teletext service: it has pages 137, 138 and 139 on SBS6.

MVS Radio
Cable 88.1 or 106.8 FM ether (620 8866). **Times** 6-8pm daily.
Amsterdam's major gay and lesbian radio station, with news, interviews and, on Saturdays, nightlife info and the latest club sounds.

MVS TV
Salto Channel A1: S39+ or 616MHz (620 0247/ www.mvs.nl). **Times** 8-9pm Mon. **Repeats** 2am first Fri of mth.
This Dutch-language station covers gay culture, events, health, politics and more: there's even the odd item in English.

Where to Stay

It's illegal in the Netherlands for hotels to refuse accommodation to gays and lesbians, but the hotels listed below are specifically gay-run: stay at one of these and you're sure to be in good company. The **Gay & Lesbian Switchboard** (see p282) has more details of gay- and lesbian-friendly hotels. For more hotels, see p48.

Aero Hotel
Kerkstraat 45-49, Southern Canal Belt (622 7728/ www.aerohotel.nl). Tram 1, 2, 5. **Rates** €70 double. **Credit** AmEx, MC, V. **Map** p310 D4.
A small hotel conveniently situated next to Bronx sex shop, opposite Thermos Night sauna and a stone's throw away from Spijker bar, Leidseplein and Reguliersdwarsstraat. Rooms are rather blandly furnished, but the friendly staff and included breakfast make up for that.

The Amistad
Kerkstraat 42, Southern Canal Belt (624 8074/ www.amistad.nl). Tram 1, 2, 5. **Rates** €63-€99 single; €77-€128 double; €95-€139 triple. **Credit** AmEx, DC, MC. **Map** p310 D4.
The former West End hotel has been renamed and revamped: it's now a colourful IKEA-meets-Phillipe Starck stopover. After 1pm the breakfast area on the ground floor transforms into a gay internet lounge (it's also open to non-guests) where surfing explicit gay web sites is, for once, not a problem.

Black Tulip Hotel

Geldersekade 16, Old Centre: Old Side (427 0933/ www.blacktulip.nl). Tram 1, 2, 4, 5, 9, 13, 16, 17, 24, 25. **Rates** €110 single; €140-€200 double. **Credit** AmEx, DC, MC, V. **Map** p306 D2.

Housed in a 16th-century building conveniently close to the leather bars on Warmoesstraat, the men-only Black Tulip hotel targets leather aficionados with a blend of luxury and lust. S&M facilities like slings and bondage hooks are provided in all rooms, as are the more conventional TV and VCR. They also have studios and apartments.

Golden Bear

Kerkstraat 37, Southern Canal Belt (624 4785/ www.goldenbear.nl). Tram 1, 2, 5. **Rates** €55-€99 single; €70-€112 double. **Credit** AmEx, MC, V. **Map** p310 D4.

Housed in two 17th-century buildings, the Golden Bear's rooms are spacious and comfortable, though not all of them have private bathrooms. All single rooms have double beds.

Shops & services

Bookshops

The basement of the **American Book Center** (*see p154*) stocks a well-chosen, comprehensive selection of English-language lesbian and gay books, usually with much-needed bargain titles. The choice of gay men's mags is wide, the range of lesbian counterparts terrible. Otherwise, in addition to the dedicated gay stores listed here, a couple of specialist women's bookshops have sizeable lesbian stock: **Vrouwen in Druk** (Westermarkt 5, 624 5003/www.xs4all.nl/ ~vind) specialises in second-hand books, while **Xantippe Unlimited** (Prinsengracht 290, 623 5854/www.xantippe.nl) sticks to new titles.

Intermale

Spuistraat 251, Old Centre: New Side (625 0009/ www.intermale.nl). Tram 1, 2, 5, 13, 14, 17. **Open** 11am-6pm Mon; 10am-6pm Tue, Wed, Fri, Sat; 10am-9pm Thur; noon-5pm Sun. **Credit** AmEx, MC, V. **Map** p306 C3.

Books of all kinds – from downright dirty to seriously academic – from all corners of the world, as well as a selection of sexy souvenirs, fill this compact, split-level shop. Lots of magazines, too.

Vrolijk

Paleisstraat 135, Old Centre: New Side (623 5142/ www.vrolijk.nu). Tram 1, 2, 5, 13, 14, 17. **Open** 11am-6pm Mon; 10am-6pm Tue, Wed, Fri; 10am-9pm Thur; 10am-5pm Sat. **Credit** AmEx, DC, MC, V. **Map** p306 C3.

You'll find the best range of Dutch and English lesbian and gay print in town here, plus videos, postcards, CDs and a great international magazine section. They also organise occasional author appearances and book-signings.

Hairdressers

Cuts and Curls

Korte Leidsedwarsstraat 74, Southern Canal Belt (624 6881/www.cutsandcurls.nl). Tram 1, 2, 5, 6, 7, 10. **Open** 10am-8pm Mon-Thur; 10am-7pm Fri; 10am-4.30pm Sat. **Credit** AmEx, DC, MC, V. **Map** p310 D5.

Butch barbers with basic cuts: a clipper-cut costs €17.50, a head-shave €25. Handy for a 'do before hitting the scene. No appointments.

Leather-rubber/sex shops

Within the Red Light District lies the leather district, home to gay leather and rubber shops like the friendly and innovative **Mr B** (Warmoesstraat 89, 422 0003/www.mrb.nl) – that has one female staff member and is great for piercings and tattoos – and **RoB Accessories** (Warmoesstraat 32, 420 8548/ www.rob.nl). Lovers of rubber should make for the more traditional main RoB branch (Weteringschans 253, 428 3000), which sells leather and rubber, or specialist shop **Black Body** (Lijnbaansgracht 292, 626 2553) near the Rijksmuseum. Other gay sex shops include the **Bronx** (Kerkstraat 53-5, 623 1548) and **Drakes** (Damrak 61, 627 9544), both of which have a porn cinema.

Women's erotica can be had at **Female & Partners** (*see p176*), while **Demask** (Zeedijk 64, 620 5603) is popular with men and women. For erotic and fetish shops, *see p176*.

Saunas

Fenomeen

1e Schinkelstraat 14, Zuid (671 6780). Tram 1, 2. **Open** 1-11pm daily. Women's day Mon. **Admission** €8. **No credit cards**.

A relaxed squat sauna that's popular with lesbians on women-only Mondays. It's open-plan and split-level, with a sauna, steam bath, cold bath, chill-out room with mattresses, showers in the courtyard and café (non-smoking Thur-Sun). Extras include massage and a sunbed – and anyone who leaves before 6pm gets a €2 refund.

Thermos Day

Raamstraat 33, Southern Canal Belt (623 9158). Tram 1, 2, 5, 7, 10. **Open** noon-11pm Mon-Fri; noon-10pm Sat, 11am-10pm Sun. **Admission** €18; €13.50 under-24s with ID. **Credit** DC, MC, V. **Map** p310 C4.

Busy during the week and out-and-out crowded at weekends – yup, it's popular – this four-level sauna lays on the works: a tiny steam room, large dry-heat room, porn cinema, private cubicles, bar and restaurant, hairdresser, masseur, gym and roof terrace. Time is sure to fly.

Sapphic jam: **Sappho**. *See p209.*

Thermos Night

Kerkstraat 58-60, Southern Canal Belt (623 4936).
Tram 1, 2, 5. **Open** 11pm-8am Mon-Sat; 11pm-10am
Sun. Admission €18; €13.50 under-24s and over-65s
with ID. **Credit** DC, MC, V. **Map** p310 D4.
A stone's throw from De Spijker (*see p208*),
Thermos Night includes a bar, small jacuzzi, dry
sauna and steam room, darkroom and a maze of
cubicles. Packed on weekends, especially when it
hosts 'Salvation' after parties.

Tattoos

Eyegasm

Kerkstraat 113, Western Canal Belt (330 3767/
www.eyegasm.org). Tram 1, 2, 5. **Open** noon-8pm
Tue-Sat. **No credit cards. Map** p310 D4.
Owner of Europe's only lesbian-run tattoo parlour,
Roxx Mistry specialises in custom designs at this
beautiful cyber-submarine store.

Cinema

Amsterdam passes its homo screen test with
flying colours. Art-house cinemas like **Rialto**
(*see p192*), **Cinecenter** and **Filmhuis Cavia**
(for both, *see p192*) frequently screen gay and
lesbian flicks, as does **De Balie** (*see p193*).
The latter two are home in December to **De
Roze Filmdagen** ('Pink Film Days'; www.
rozefilmdagen.nl), a four-day event showing
underground gay and lesbian shorts and
documentaries, while De Balie plays host to the
Nederlands Transgender Film Festival
(www.transgender filmfestival.com) every May.
    Gay porn cinemas can be found in the city
centre: for details, check the ads in the gay
press. The **Gay & Lesbian Switchboard**
(*see p282*) has lists of cinemas and theatres
with gay and lesbian programmes.

Bars & nightclubs

The gay scene is concentrated around four
areas, each with its own identity. Clubs and
bars are listed by area below, with specialist
establishments – restaurants, cafés, coffeeshops
and lesbian bars – and the pick of one-off club
nights and sex parties listed separately, starting
on *p209*. Entry to bars and clubs listed here is
free unless stated otherwise.

Warmoesstraat

The seedy Warmoesstraat and the Zeedijk,
in the Red Light District, may have been
renovated in an attempt to smarten up the area,
but both streets still attract all sorts of lowlife.
Despite a high police profile and a nearby police
station in Beursstraat, just off Warmoesstraat,
it's advisable to take care when walking on
your own late at night: act streetwise and
avoid talking to the sleazy geezers and junkies
who hang around trying to sell dubious drugs.
    Apart from funky kitsch bar-restaurant **Getto**
(*see p208*) and trad brown bar **Casa Maria**
(No.60, 627 6848), the Warmoesstraat strip is
dominated by leather/sex bars. **The Web** (*see
below*) and **Cuckoo's Nest** (Nieuwezijds Kolk 6,
627 1752), the latter boasting Europe's largest
playroom in its cellar, are located nearby.

Argos

Warmoesstraat 95 (622 6595). Tram 4, 9, 16, 24,
25. **Open** 10pm-3am Mon-Thur, Sun; 10pm-4am Fri,
Sat. **No credit cards. Map** p306 D2.
The oldest and most famous leather bar in the city,
and a bit serious with it. Its basement darkroom with
cabins and a sling can get very crowded. Every second and last Sunday of the month it hosts SOS (aka
Sex on Sunday; *see p206* **Sex parties**).

Cockring

Warmoesstraat 96 (623 9604/www.clubcockring.com).
Tram 4, 9, 16, 24, 25. **Open** 11pm-4am Mon-Thur;
11pm-5am Fri, Sat. **No credit cards. Map** p306 D2.
This men-only club is one of a few gay venues where
you need to queue at weekends, particularly after
1am. Though situated in the leather district, the
Cockring attracts all types of gays and of all ages.
It's a cruisey place, helped by pumping hard house
from a female (!) DJ, strip shows, massages and a
darkroom. Some Sundays it hosts sex parties (*see*
p206 **Sex parties**).

Eagle

Warmoesstraat 90 (627 8634). Tram 4, 9, 16, 20,
24, 25. **Open** 10pm-4am Mon-Thur, Sun; 10pm-5am
Fri, Sat. **No credit cards. Map** p306 D2.
Order a drink the second you set foot in this cruisey,
leatherish, men-only bar, or the staff will get sniffy.
Its rude staff, over-priced drinks and facetious signs
('tipping is not a city in China') are offset by the large
downstairs darkroom and the upstairs pool table –
surely the only one in the world with an adjustable
sling above it. Eagle also co-hosts regular Rubber
Only parties with shop Black Body (*see p204*).

The Web

Sint Jacobsstraat 6 (623 6758). Tram 1, 2, 3, 5.
Open 2pm-1am Mon-Thur, Sun; 2pm-2.30am Fri,
Sat. **No credit cards. Map** p306 D2.
Another popular men-only leather/cruise bar, with
very friendly staff and cheap beer. It has a darkroom
upstairs and TV screens showing porn in the downstairs bar. Sundays from 5pm is snack afternoon,
and on Wednesdays after 10pm there's a lottery with
sex shop vouchers for prizes.

Zeedijk

This famous street in the Red Light District
recently saw the opening of two new gay
addresses. **The Cock & Feathers** bar-

Sex parties

Fun and games indeed… Just remember to
play it safe, and try to make time to indulge
in some of the other activities on offer in
Amsterdam's rich and varied gay scene.

COC

Rozenstraat 14, the Jordaan (626 3087/
www.stop.demon.nl). Tram 13, 14, 17.
Dates 10pm-4am, days vary. **Admission** €8.
The national gay organisation COC (*see*
p282) holds safe sex parties every other
month. There's a strict dress code: leather,
rubber, uniform or nude – and no jeans
or trainers.

Cockring

Warmoesstraat 96, Old Centre: Old Side
(623 9604/www.clubcockring.com). Tram 4,
9, 16, 24, 25. **Dates** 3-7pm (doors close
4pm), days vary. **Admission** €6.50.
Every first Sunday of the month, Cockring
(*see above*) hosts a nude party – the dress
code is shoes only. Every third Sunday of
the month it's Horsemen & Knights, where
the dress code is underwear or nude and
admission is free for those sporting more
than 18cm (7.2in). Both events – surprise,
surprise – are for men only; both lay on free
condoms and, er, sandwiches.

SOS

Warmoesstraat 95, Old Centre: Old Side
(622 6595). Tram 4, 9, 16, 24, 25. **Dates**
3-7pm, 2nd and 4th Sun of mth (doors close
4pm). **Admission** €5.

Argos hosts this regular men-only event,
pulling in a fun crowd with great music and
lots of action. The dress code is 'nude or
shirtless'. There are free condoms available.

Stable Master

Warmoesstraat 23, Old Centre: Old Side
(625 0148). Tram 4, 9, 16, 24, 25. **Dates**
9pm, Mon, Thur-Sun. **Admission** €6.
The intimate bar at gay hotel Stable Master
hosts safe, men-only jack-off parties five
nights of the week. They vary from dull to
wild, depending on night and crowd. Dress
code is nude or underwear.

Wild Side

Venues vary (www.wildside.dds.nl).
This lesbian leather and S&M group hosts
workshops and a varied programme of parties
at different venues around town throughout
the year. See also p210.

restaurant (No.23-25; 624 3141), purveyor of traditional Dutch food, and brown café **Barderij** (No.14; 420 5132).

Queen's Head

Zeedijk 20 (420 2475/www.queenshead.nl). Tram 4, 9, 16, 24, 25/Metro Centraal Station. **Open** 5pm-1am Mon-Thur; 4pm-3am Fri, Sat; 4pm-1am Sun. **No credit cards. Map** p306 D2.

Mondays and Wednesdays are cheap beer nights, and from 6pm on Sundays this popular '50s kitsch bar serves a free buffet of *bitterballen* (deep-fried meatballs) with classical music; it also hosts frequent 'sportswear parties'. Sadly, über-bitch drag queen Dusty no longer does her hilarious bingo nights, but sometimes shakes her wig as host for special nights.

Rembrandtplein

Amsterdam's neon-lit commercial nightlife hub is also home to the city's most diverse gay quarter. Half of Amsterdam's lesbian venues – **Vive La Vie** and **You II** – are here, while Paardenstraat a few doors down is the city's rent boy centre. In bright and breezy contrast are the bars along Halvemaansteeg: loud, entirely attitude-free and always up for a good time. This theme continues along the Amstel, where a strip of much-of-a-muchness bars, typified by **Hot Spot** and **Mix**, attract punters to their cheesy music and river views. Locals bar **Le Shako's** (Gravelandseveer 2, 624 0209) stands in cosy isolation on the other side of the Amstel.

Amstel Taveerne

Amstel 54 (623 4254) Tram 4, 9, 14, 24, 25. **Open** 4pm-1am Mon-Thur, Sun; 5pm-3am Fri-Sat. **No credit cards.**

This site has been dedicated to boozing since 1574. These days it fills (especially at weekends) with an older crowd of friendly and unpretentious guys who like their surroundings simple and their music tacky.

Entre Nous

Halvemaansteeg 14 (623 1700). Tram 1, 2, 4, 5, 9, 14, 16, 24, 25. **Open** 8pm-3am Mon-Thur, Sun; 8pm-4am Fri, Sat. **No credit cards. Map** p311 E4.

The feather boa lurking behind the bar should give an inkling of what's in store, as should yesteryear's Eurovision hits shaking the speakers. With lovely staff, the tiny Entre Nous attracts a real mixed bag of guys; after midnight on Saturdays it's so packed you can't move. You might also want to check across the street to see if Montmartre is open.

iT

Amstelstraat 24 (625 0111/www.it.nl). Tram 4, 9, 14. **Open** 11pm-4am Thur; 11pm-6am Fri, Sat. **Admission** €10-€15. **No credit cards. Map** p307 E3.

Once known the world over for its glamorous and hedonistic parties, club nights and visitors, this mixed club with gay nights in a converted cinema is now a shadow of its former self.

Lellebel

Utrechtsestraat 4 (427 5139). Tram 4, 9, 14, 20. **Open** *Jun-Sept* 8pm-3am Mon-Thur; 8pm-4am Fri, Sat; 3pm-3am Sun. *Oct-May* 9pm-3am Mon-Thur, Sun; 8pm-4am Fri, Sat. **No credit cards. Map** p311 E4.

Lellebel's transvestite staff spontaneously burst into song, and the fun really kicks off on Thursday's Hot Salsa Night and Saturday's Showtime with Desirée dello Stiletto. No need to dress up as a diva to enjoy the hedonism of this small, hectic bar.

Rouge

Amstel 60 (420 9881). Tram 4, 9, 16, 24, 25. **Open** 4pm-1am Mon, Thur, Sun; 4pm-3am Fri, Sat. Closed Tue, Wed. **No credit cards.**

Titchy, friendly bar on the area's main gay drag. When the French windows are thrown open on warm evenings and drinkers spill outside, it all gets very convivial.

Reguliersdwarsstraat

The second part of Reguliersdwarsstraat, between Vijzelstraat and Koningsplein, is a tremendously gay parade: there are more pansies here than at the flower market on Singel. A young, posey, designer-clad crowd hangs out here, and the bars and clubs reflect the trend. It's also where **The Otherside** (*see p209*) – Amsterdam's only gay coffeeshop – and multicultural gay bar **Reality** (No.129, 639 3012) can be found. Between Thursdays and Saturdays in summer the street is closed to traffic at night; sadly it was a fatal road rage shooting that made the council introduce this in 2003, after years of refusing bar and club owners' requests for the measure.

ARC

Reguliersdwarsstraat 44 (689 7070/www.bararc.com). Tram 1, 2, 4, 5, 9, 14, 16, 24, 25. **Open** 4pm-1am Mon-Thur; 4pm-3am Fri; noon-3am Sat; noon-1am Sun. **Credit** AmEx, MC, V.

A recent addition. Though not 100% gay, this *Wallpaper**-styled bar-cum-restaurant – and its clientele – have mastered the art of looking stylish. Image is everything and the food can be found lacking – assuming you ever get served.

Café April

Reguliersdwarsstraat 37 (625 9572/www.april-exit.com). Tram 1, 2, 4, 5, 9, 14, 16, 24, 25. **Open** 2pm-1am Mon-Thur, Sun; 2pm-2am Fri, Sat. **No credit cards. Map** p309 D4.

A spacious, trendy watering hole with a revolving bar at the back. It's a popular pre-club drinking spot and a pleasant place for a spot of afternoon reading.

Exit

Reguliersdwarsstraat 42 (625 8788/www.april-exit.com). Tram 1, 2, 4, 5, 9, 14, 16, 24, 25. **Open** 11pm-4am Mon-Thur, Sun; 11pm-5am Fri, Sat. **Admission** free-€5. **No credit cards. Map** p311 E4.

Arts & Entertainment

ARC. *See p207.*

The downstairs bar pumps out cheesy pop and gets crowded; upstairs, beautiful boys pose on the balcony, explore the darkroom or dance to funky beats. Women are allowed in, but only in small numbers.

Soho

Reguliersdwarsstraat 36 (no phone/www.april-exit. com). Tram 1, 2, 4, 5, 9, 14, 16, 24, 25. **Open** 8pm-3am Mon-Thur, Sun; 8pm-4am Fri, Sat; 6pm-3am Sun. **No credit cards. Map** p311 E4.
This packed, two-floor English-style boozer – complete with Chesterfields – is more attitude-free than April and Exit. It can get very crowded and a little intimidating if you're on your own.

Kerkstraat

This less obvious gay street is frequented by more unselfconscious locals and punters than most other areas. The most popular bar is **Spijker** (*see below*), but other hangouts include the **Bronx** sex shop (*see p204*), sauna **Thermos Night** (*see p205*) and the **Camp Café** (No.45, 622 1506), a part of the **Aero Hotel** (*see p203*), where attentive staff serve breakfast, lunch and dinner. Nearby is Arabian gay bar **Habibi Ana** (Lange Leidsedwarsstraat 4-6, no phone), which plays Arabian music only and attracts a mixed but mostly young international crowd.

De Spijker

Kerkstraat 4 (620 5919). Tram 1, 2, 5. **Open** 1pm-1am Mon-Thur, Sun; 1pm-3am Fri, Sat. **No credit cards. Map** p310 C4.
A friendly and delightfully seedy bar, attracting all kinds of men: old, young, trendy and leathery. Porn vids and cartoons are shown side by side, while cute, bare-chested staff serve with a smile. The pool table is very popular, and women are welcome.

Restaurants

Getto

Warmoesstraat 51, Old Centre: Old Side (421 5151/ www.getto.nl). *Tram 4, 9, 16, 24, 25.* **Open** 4pm-1am Tue-Thur; 4pm-2am Fri, Sat; 4pm-midnight Sun. *Kitchen* 6-11pm Tue-Sun. **Main courses** €9-€14. **Credit** DC, MC, V. **Map** p306 D2.
A trendy yet unpretentious spot, with a cool bar and a candlelit restaurant. It's a bit of a rarity: a place where lesbians and gay men genuinely mix. Some nights are mellow, others clubbier.

Hemelse Modder

Oude Waal 9-11, Old Centre: Old Side (624 3203). Tram 1, 2, 4, 5, 9, 13, 16, 17, 24, 25/Metro Nieuwmarkt. **Open** 6pm-midnight Tue-Sun. *Kitchen* 6-10pm Tue-Sun. **Set menu** €26 (3 courses); €32 (5 courses). **Credit** AmEx, DC, MC, V. **Map** p307 E2.
This homo-friendly restaurant has cool, bare styling and simple, classy Modern European food led by veggie and fish. It sells its own gift tokens, too, and there's a garden terrace in summer.

Raap & Peper

Peperstraat 23-5, The Waterfront (330 1716). Bus 22, 32, 33, 34, 35, 39. **Open** 6-11pm Tue-Sun. **Main courses** €6-€12. **Credit** AmEx, MC, V. **Map** p307 E2.
This lesbian-owned restaurant was once the in-house eatery of De Peper squat, but with dark wood and linen napkins now looks quite the doyenne of bourgeois respectability – with prices to match.

La Strada

Nieuwezijds Voorburgwal 93-5, Old Centre: New Side (625 0276). Tram 1, 2, 5, 13, 17, 20. **Open** 4pm-midnight Tue-Thur; 2pm-1am Fri-Sun. **Main courses** €7-€10. **Credit** AmEx, DC, MC, V. **Map** p306 D2.
La Strada is a spacious culinary café at a convenient central spot; it pulls in an arty crowd and is popular with lesbians. The fine food is a blend of French, Italian, Spanish and Indonesian; good veggie, too.

Cafés

Backstage

Utrechtsedwarsstraat 67, Southern Canal Belt (622 3638). Tram 4, 6, 7, 10. **Open** 10am-5.30pm Mon-Sat. **No credit cards. Map** p311 E4.
This multicoloured café-boutique serves almost as a museum to the half-Mohawk 'Christmas Twins'. Although Greg died in 1997, identical twin Gary con-

tinues to run the place, selling his unique crochet wear, chatting to customers and giving spontaneous horoscope readings. A fabulous place.

Coffeeshop Downtown
Reguliersdwarstraat 31 (06 5087 2220 mobile/ www.coffeeshopdowntown.nl). Tram 1, 2, 4, 5, 9, 14, 16, 24, 25. **Open** 11am-8pm daily. **No credit cards. Map** 310 D4.
Dinky, relaxed, split-level café which is also a shrine to local drag superstar Nicky Nicole. It serves – with a smile – American, English and Asian breakfasts, indulgent cakes, snacky meals and healthy juices and shakes. There's plenty of outside seating.

Huyschkaemer
Utrechtsestraat 137, Southern Canal Belt (627 0575). Tram 4, 6, 7, 10. **Open** 4pm-1am Mon-Thur, Sun; 4pm-3am Fri, Sat. *Kitchen* 5-11pm daily. **Main courses** €7-€9. **Credit** AmEx, MC, V. **Map** p311 E4.
Huyschkaemer's designer interior – with huge picture windows – attracts a mixed, mainly young and artistic gay and lesbian crowd. Staff are friendly.

Le Monde
Rembrandtplein 6, Southern Canal Belt (626 9922). Tram 4, 9, 14. **Open** 8.30am-1am Mon-Thur, Sun; 8.30am-2am Fri, Sat. *Kitchen* 8.30am-10.30pm daily. **Credit** V. **Map** p311 E4.
A popular, early-opening and late-closing café: a handy purveyor of sobering coffee or booze-absorbing snacks (including veggie options) to adventurers touring the Rembrandtplein bars.

Coffeeshop

The Otherside
Reguliersdwarsstraat 6, Southern Canal Belt (421 1014). Tram 1, 2, 5. **Open** 11am-1am daily. **No credit cards. Map** p310 D4.
Amsterdam's only gay coffeeshop is a bright and modern place. It has a good, varied menu that includes single joints, space cake and cannabis tea, and the friendly and informative staff will supply answers to all your consumption questions. For more on coffeeshops, *see p147*.

One-off club nights

Club Divine
www.euroclash.net.
Divine is an popular electroclash do dished up every Wednesday at 020 (*see p223*) by the Fierce Rulin' Divas Abraxas and Flamman, who have a long history on the Dutch dance music scene. Their latest nocturnal venture draws in a fashionable, bouncy bunch – distinguished by a healthy girl/boy ratio – with chunky, funky electro cuts.

MAF
www.artlaunch.nl.
Changing venues, different dates – but Multiple Arts Festival, organised by Art Launch, can be relied upon to offer great fashion, music and performance for forward-looking alterno-hipsters.

Strapping: **Mr B**.
See p204.

Queer Planet

www.spellbound-amsterdam.nl.
Held at OCCII (*see p213*), this popular mixed under-ground party with DJs, visuals and acts takes place about every six weeks and often sells out fast.

Salvation

www.salvation-amsterdam.nl.
Every first Friday of the month, Gesus and his dis-ciples bring their own brand of shirts-off, London-style hard house to Escape (*see p223*). Expect loads of shaved heads and rippling six-packs. Those who want the fun to run should head for the sexy Salvation after party at Thermos Night sauna.

De Trut

Bilderdijkstraat 165, Oud West (no phone). Tram 3, 7, 12, 17. **Open** 11pm-4am Sun. **Admission** €1.50. **No credit cards. Map** p309 B5.
A breath of fresh air – though it does get a bit stuffy – at this mixed, attitude-free Sunday-nighter. Cheap drinks and great music mean it's vital to start queu-ing no later than 10.40pm, as doors open at 11pm and shut when it's full. The club is held in the base-ment of a former squat, and is run on a non-profit basis: proceeds are donated to suitably PC causes.

Vrankrijk

Spuistraat, Old Centre: New Side 216 (no phone). Tram 1, 2, 4, 9, 14, 16, 24, 25. **Open** 10pm-2am Mon. **Admission** free. **No credit cards. Map** p306 C3.
This notorious squat near the Royal Palace hosts mixed-queer night Blue Monday every, er, Monday. With different DJs every time, the atmosphere and crowd levels can vary from dull and scanty to fran-tic and vast.

Lesbian Amsterdam

There's no getting around it: lesbian 'Dam is small, and the paucity of dyke venues means that permanent places (apart from shiny new **Sappho**, *see p 210*) get stale: they've cornered the market so don't need to make much effort. But there are good times to be had. If you're looking for quality fun, try the one-nighters dotted around town. Several popular gals-only events are held at **COC** (*see p282*), including weekly under-26 Saturday-nighters and over-30s nights on the second Saturday of the month (take ID to these – you may have to prove your age). To dance to DJs who have more than a nodding acquaintance with current musical fashion, first stop should be the mixed Divine (www.euroclash.net) on Wednesdays at **020** (*see p223*), whose collaborations with dyke one-nighters and DJs pull in a trendy all-girl throng. Another must is the peripatetic Venus Freaks (www.venusfreaks.nl), whose funky sounds keep a dancy crowd of girls (and their gay boyfriends) bouncing; meanwhile the quarterly Flirtation (check www.flirtation.nl for dates

and venues) attracts saucy sapphics who dance and flirt to a sexy house soundtrack. Be aware that although the dyke scene is hardly dynamic, places do move or close down, so check the pink press or **Gay and Lesbian Switchboard** (*see p282*) before you set off.

Finally, if you want to experience the best that the Amsterdam scene has to offer, don't overlook bars aimed mainly at gay men. Many, especially along Reguliersdwarsstraat, offer a slick and stylish drinking experience you won't find elsewhere in town – and even though you'll be in the minority, you certainly won't be unwelcome.

Saarein II

Elandsstraat 119, the Jordaan (623 4901). Tram 7, 10. **Open** 5pm-1am Tue-Thur, Sun; 5pm-2am Fri, Sat. **No credit cards. Map** p310 C4.
A long running dyke café (which nevertheless wel-comes everybody) arranged over three floors of an attractive brown bar, on a lovely corner spot in the Jordaan. It serves food in the evenings and pulls in an older and rather, well, sedate bunch. The base-ment boasts Amsterdam's only lesbian pool table.

Sappho

Vijzelstraat 103, Southern Canal Belt (423 1509/ www.sappho.nl). Tram 16, 24, 25. **Open** 3pm-1am Tue-Thur, Sun; 3pm-3am Fri, Sat. **No credit cards.**
This funky new kid on the lesbian block promises good things like art exhibitions, live music (Tuesdays) and film nights (Wednesdays) – all served up in a soothing blue bar by efficient and chatty staff. Sappho welcomes everyone throughout the week, with Friday designated as women's night (with men as guests).

Vive La Vie

Amstelstraat 7, Southern Canal Belt (624 0114/ www.vivelavie.net). Tram 4, 9, 14. **Open** 3pm-1am Mon-Thur, Sun; 3pm-3am Fri, Sat. **No credit cards. Map** p310 E4.
Dead during the week, this little sardine-can of a bar packs 'em in at the weekend, attracting a slightly dressier crowd of lesbians (and male friends) of every stripe and age, from flushed youth to geriatric. It's fun, lively and a little bit raucous, though the music policy is often eye-wateringly bad.

You II

Amstel 178, Southern Canal Belt (421 0900/ www.youii.nl). Tram 4, 9, 14. **Open** 10pm-4am Thur, Sun; 10pm-5am Fri, Sat. **No credit cards. Map** p307 E3.
A no-frills, chart-music club that attracts a mainly lesbian crowd with a nice racial mix. Most of the city's lesbians end up here because there's nowhere else to go on a weekend, so you can have either a real laugh or a thoroughly depressing time, depending on your mood. That said, the randomly enforced 'membership' policy means you may not get past the door in the first place – i.e. if the bouncer doesn't like the look of you (or your 'inappropriate' trainers).

Arts & Entertainment

Music

Eclectic? We'll show you eclectic.

Rock, Roots & Jazz

It's the world's smallest big city. Amsterdam allows the visitor the luxury of wandering by foot between club, bar and concert hall while soaking up pop, jazz, avant garde, disco, salsa, reggae, world, metal or – better still – some mutant musical combination. Long an attraction for foreign artists due to its liberal vibe, and a hangout for tourists who, quite frankly, don't feel like saying 'no', the city has a lot to offer music lovers. And visiting musicians – assuming they haven't puffed away their day in a coffeeshop – often get inspired by Amsterdam's rich musical past and work harder to put on a good show for the crowds.

Centred around two institutions, the **Paradiso** and the **Melkweg**, Amsterdam's club scene offers down-home roots venues (**Cruise Inn, Maloe Melo**), steaming cauldrons of world music (**Akhnaton, Badcuyp**), and legendary jazz hangouts (**Bimhuis, Alto**). In short: something for everyone. And while Dutch acts have only been moderately successful in the international arena (see p218 **Poptastic-scholastic**), smaller venues still offer a bevy of lesser-known artists well worth your time.

And a quick reminder: there's no harm in checking venue listings for other cities, since a performance by your favourite band or DJ may just be a short train trip away (see pp260-272).

TICKETS AND INFORMATION

For full listings of all musical genres, head to the AUB Ticketshop (0900 0191; see p279 **Tickets please**) on the Leidseplein or check out Ticketservice (www.ticketservice.nl), the free Dutch-language monthly *Uitkrant*, or the national music magazine *Oor* (www.oor.net). Details of the town's notable gigs are posted weekly on the Time Out website (www.timeout.com/amsterdam), and details of more alternative gigs are listed in 'zine *Shark* (www.underwateramsterdam.com). Book in advance: many venues sell out quickly.

Rock & roots

Apart from the clubs below, be sure to keep an eye out for squat happenings and concerts, always good nurseries for new talent. Details can be found at www.squat.net. For **Bitterzoet**, a multi-purpose venue that offers frequent gigs, see p223.

Akhnaton

Nieuwezijds Kolk 25, Old Centre: New Side (624 3396/www.akhnaton.nl). Tram 1, 2, 5, 13, 17. **Open** 11pm-5am Fri, Sat. **Admission** €5-€7. **No credit cards. Map** p306 D2.

Ethnic Amsterdam at its best: this intimate club, often bursting at the seams, offers a heady mix of world music, African and Turkish dance and salsa.

AMP

KNSM-Laan 13, the Waterfront (418 1111/www.ampstudios.nl). Bus 28, 32, 59. **Open** noon-1am Mon-Fri; noon-3am Sat, Sun. **No credit cards.**

AMP started life as a rehearsal space for local bands and now offers regular concerts and parties, as well as full recording facilities and a licensed café.

ArenA

ArenA Boulevard 1, Bijlmermeer (311 1333/www.amsterdamarena.nl). Metro Bijlmer. **Open** hours vary. **Admission** €18-€27. **No credit cards.**

Home to soccer heroes Ajax, this stadium hosts mega-acts that don't need to tour for the money. The annual Sensation dance event, held in July, always ensures a packed house.

The best Venues

Bimhuis
Celebrated jazz purveyor, heading for a great new location. *See p215.*

Concertgebouw
Plush extravagance combined with the best acoustics on the planet. *See p217.*

Melkweg
Milk factory turned hippie heaven turned everything for everyone. *See p213.*

Panama
Old school nightclub with decidedly new school programming. *See p214.*

Paradiso
They don't call it the pop temple for nothing. *See p214.*

Handy André

Every country has one: a superstar singer who can inspire either joy or pity depending on your mood and/or how much kitsch your constitution can stand. Canada has Céline Dion, France has Johnny Hallyday, and England has far too many to list in a guide of this modest size.

The Netherlands version is one André Hazes (www.andrehazes.nl), a 130-kilo blob who personifies heart-on-your-sleeveness. The sweaty icon goes straight for the emotional jugular as he literally drips with disaster. His personal tragedies have been obsessively documented by the nation's tabloids, and when this man sings of spilt beer and broken hearts, you know he knows what he's singing about. He's even used his obvious weight problem to earn some cash: a canned weiner commercial he recently made boosted sales by 35 per cent.

Hazes considers himself more of a bluesman, but his genre is actually called

'life songs', sing-a-long drinking songs – still to be enjoyed at such Jordaan bars as **Café Nol** (see p145) and **De Twee Zwaantjes** (Prinsengracht 114, 625 2729) – that glorify poverty, community bonds and the simple pleasures of 'issuing curses, making babies, drinking coffees, and hanging out on the front step'. So it's fitting that Hazes was born in the Pijp, a neighbourhood of equally solid working class reputation. It was here that he began his career as an eight-year-old, singing on the pool tables of brown cafés to enthusiastic audiences.

More than 40 years on, each one of his rhyming-dictionary-assisted albums goes platinum and he has no problem selling out the country's biggest arenas for week-long stretches. While Hazes may not really be a 'great' singer (his Caruso-inspired vibrato aside), he is certainly a 'big' singer – and hell, you can't help but like a guy who's willing to cry in the name of communication...

Badcuyp

1e Sweelinckstraat 10, the Pijp (675 9669/ www.badcuyp.nl). Tram 4, 16, 24, 25. **Open** 11am-1am Tue-Thur; 11am-3am Fri, Sat; 11am-1am Sun. **Admission** free-€8. **Credit** MC, V. **Map** p311 F5.
Focusing mainly on world music and jazz, this small and friendly venue in the Pijp also plays host to Tuesday's World Jam, where even you can air your musical talents.

Buurvrouw

St Pieterpoortsteeg 9, Old Centre: Old Side (625 9654/www.debuurvrouw.nl). Tram 4, 9, 14, 16, 24, 25. **Open** 9pm-3am Mon-Thur, Sun; 9pm-4am Fri, Sat. **Admission** free. **No credit cards**. **Map** p306 D2.
This cosy café presents DJs on weekends and the occasional singer/songwriter. Check out the eclectic CD collection behind the bar.

Carré

Amstel 115-25, Southern Canal Belt (0900 252 5255/ www.theatercarre.nl). Tram 4, 6, 7, 10. **Open** Box office 10am-7pm Mon-Sat; 1-7pm Sun. **Admission** €11-€100. **Credit** AmEx, DC, MC, V. **Map** p311 F4.
Built as a circus theatre in the late 19th century, this beautiful venue offers everything from opera and flamenco to musicals and artists such as Joe Jackson and Lou Reed. It will be closed for renovation between January and October 2004.

Club 3VOOR12

Studio Desmet, Plantage Middenlaan 4A, the Plantage (035 671 2222/www.3voor12.nl). Tram 9, 14. **Open** 10pm Wed. **Admission** free. **Map** p307 F3.

Every Wednesday, radio station VPRO broadcasts sets by three different bands of an alternative and often international nature from this former film house. Try to decipher the line-up from their website or call the above number between noon and 5pm on Tuesdays and Thursdays, a timed phone call you'll have to make anyway to get on the guest list (you can try reserving via club3VOOR12@vpro.nl). Yes, it's a hassle, but the gigs are free and a great chance to see decent bands in an up-close setting.

Cruise Inn

Zuiderzeeweg 29, Zeeburg (692 7188/www.cruise-inn.com). Tram 14/bus 22, 37. **Open** 9pm-1am Sat (until 3am on concert nights). **Admission** free-€7. **No credit cards**.
Grow those muttonchops and break out the pomade if you're heading to the Cruise Inn, Amsterdam's home of rockabilly and swing.

Heeren van Aemstel

Thorbeckeplein 5, Southern Canal Belt (620 2173/ www.deheerenvanaemstel.nl). Tram 4, 9, 14. **Open** 3pm-1am Mon-Thur; 3pm-3am Fri-Sun. **Admission** free-€3. **Credit** AmEx, MC, V. **Map** p311 E5.
Live music every night except Monday: cover bands and unknowns singing in Dutch. Beery, loud and – if you're that way inclined – culturally instructive.

Heineken Music Hall

ArenA Boulevard 590, Bijlmermeer (0900 300 1250/www.heineken-music-hall.nl). Metro Bijlmer. **Open** Box office from 6.30pm, concert days only. **Admission** €20-€60. **Credit** AmEx, MC, V.

Recently built on the outskirts of town, the Heineken Music Hall is the place to catch acts that have outgrown the smaller clubs downtown. It's a rather cheerless place, but the acoustics are decent.

Last Waterhole
Oudezijds Armsteeg 12, Old Centre: Old Side (624 4814/www.lastwaterhole.nl). Tram 4, 9, 16, 24, 25/ Metro Centraal Station. **Open** 11am-2am Mon-Thur, Sun; 11am-3am Fri, Sat. **Admission** free. **No credit cards. Map** p306 D2.
A solid favourite with tourists over the years, though the rock acts playing here are rather staid.

Maloe Melo
Lijnbaansgracht 163, Western Canal Belt (420 4592/ www.maloemelo.com). Tram 7, 10, 13, 14, 17. **Open** 9pm-3am Mon-Thur, Sun; 9pm-4am Fri, Sat. **Admission** free-€2. **No credit cards. Map** p311 E5.
Amsterdam's home of the blues, Maloe Melo is a small, fun juke joint. Catch quality blues, rockabilly and roots acts here, as well as bigger acts who drop in for a jam after their more official concert elsewhere. The closest thing to Texas in the Netherlands.

Meander
Voetboogstraat 3, Old Centre: New Side (625 8430/ www.cafemeander.com). Tram 1, 2, 5, 9, 14, 16, 24, 25. **Open** 8.30pm-3am Mon-Thur; 8.30pm-4am Fri-Sun. **Admission** free-€5. **No credit cards. Map** p310 D4.
A student hangout near Spui square, Meander focuses on themed dance nights, ranging from retro to standard rock and pop – nothing too exciting.

Meervaart
Meer en Vaart 300, West (410 7777/www.meervaart. nl). Tram 1, 17/bus 23, 192. **Open** Box office 10am-4pm Mon-Fri; 11am-4pm Sat. **Admission** €15-€30. **No credit cards.**
Its modern architecture and peripheral location do nothing for the ambience, but the Meervaart offers a mix of music, cabaret and theatre shows.

Melkweg
Lijnbaansgracht 234A, Southern Canal Belt (531 8181/www.melkweg.nl). Tram 1, 2, 5, 6, 7, 10, 20. **Open** Box office 1-5pm Mon-Fri; 4-6pm Sat, Sun. *Club* hours vary; usually 8pm-4am daily. **Admission** €5-€25. *Membership* (compulsory) €2.50/mth; €14/yr. **No credit cards. Map** p310 D5.
Once a dairy (the name Melkweg translates as 'Milky Way'), this, like Paradiso, is a top live music venue for rock, pop, dance, metal, roots and experimental music. Two large concert halls, a theatre, a cinema (*see p194*), an art gallery (*see p197*) and a restaurant have turned this recently renovated landmark into a true cultural complex where there's always something going on. For the building's nightclub programming, *see p225*.

Mulligans
Amstel 100, Southern Canal Belt (622 1330/ www.mulligans.nl). Tram 4, 9, 14, 16, 24, 25. **Open** 4pm-1am Mon-Thur; 4pm-2am Fri; 2pm-3am Sat; 2pm-1am Sun. **Admission** free. **No credit cards. Map** p307 E3.
You'll find Irish pubs in every major European town, but only a handful are as cosy and as fun as Mulligans. The music on offer at this excellent boozer ranges from traditional Celtic acts to modern-day rock and pop singer/songwriters. They also have an open session on Sundays and – most importantly of all – great beer and craic.

OCCII
Amstelveenseweg 134, Museum Quarter (671 7778/ www.occii.org). Tram 1, 2. **Open** 9pm-2am Mon-Thur, Sun; 10pm-3am Fri, Sat. **Admission** free-€5. **No credit cards.**
Formerly a squat, this friendly and down-to-earth bar and concert hall is tucked away at one end of the Vondelpark. If you're looking for good punk, reggae and experimental music, much of it local, this is a worthwhile place to investigate.

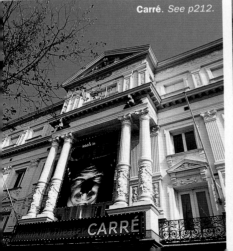

Carré. *See p212.*

Paradise lost, **Paradiso** regained.

Paleis van de Weemoed

Oudezijds Voorburgwal 15-17, Old Centre: Old Side (625 6964/www.paleis-van-de-weemoed.nl). Tram 4, 9, 16, 24, 25/Metro Centraal Station. **Open** 7pm-11pm Wed-Sun. **Admission** free. **Credit** V.

Australian-born hostess Fifi L'Amour (quite possibly not her real name) welcomes guests to her 'restaurant chantant' in the heart of the Red Light District: think Edith Piaf, Frank Sinatra and 1930s-era cabaret. Reservations are a must.

Panama

Oostelijke Handelskade 4, the Waterfront (311 8686/www.panama.nl). Bus 28, 43, 39. **Open** *Box office* 2pm-closing time. *Theatre/club* hours vary. **Admission** €8-€17. **Credit** AmEx, MC, V.

Fairly new on the scene, Panama is a music venue, restaurant and nightclub in one, offering live music, dance nights and occasional theatre events in quite relaxed and plush surroundings. *See also p127.*

Paradiso

Weteringschans 6-8, Southern Canal Belt (626 4521/www.paradiso.nl). Tram 1, 2, 5, 7, 10. **Open** hours vary. **Admission** €5-€28. *Membership* (compulsory) €2.50/mth; €18/yr. **No credit cards. Map** p310 D5.

This former church became a hippy hangout in the late '60s, turned into a punk haven towards the end of the '70s and is now one of Holland's top venues for live music. Recently renovated to accommodate a slightly larger crowd, the Paradiso remains surprisingly intimate, and the calendar bears a line-up of stellar artists. There's also a variety of club nights here, for which *see p225.*

Pepsi Stage

ArenA Boulevard 584, Bijlmermeer (0900 0194/www.pepsistage.nl). Metro Bijlmer. **Admission** €20-€50.

Built as a lower-budget reproduction of Princess Grace's Monaco palace (for a musical that quickly flopped), Pepsi Stage is not as soulless as the corporate name would imply. Opulent chandeliers, paintings on the wall and plush red seats make for comfortable concerts, with recent acts including the Isley Brothers, Elvis Costello and Brian Wilson.

Vondelpark Openluchttheater

Vondelpark, Museum Quarter (673 1499/www.openluchttheater.nl). Tram 1, 2, 3, 5, 7, 10, 12. **Open** dawn-dusk daily. **Admission** free. **No credit cards. Map** p310 C6.

On a pleasant summer day, this famous Amsterdam park can be packed. From June to September it puts on loads of music, dance, cabaret and children's activities throughout the week on this centrally located podium; from 3pm on Sundays it's usually concerts by bands.

Winston International

Warmoesstraat 129, Old Centre: Old Side (623 1380/www.winston.nl). Tram 4, 9, 16, 24, 25. **Open** 9pm-3am Mon-Thur, Sun; 9pm-4am Fri, Sat. **Admission** €3.50-€10. **No credit cards. Map** p306 D3.

Although the Winston, recently restyled, is more of a clubby affair than ever, this is a great showcase for up-and-coming acts: local, national and international. Since the shows are usually followed by a dance night, the hotel (*see p53*) upstairs might seem like a viable option. *See also p223.*

Jazz & blues

Major venues play host to big stars, with local groups and jam sessions sneaking into the early hours in snug bars most nights of the week. For **Maloe Melo**, see *p213*.

Alto

Korte Leidsedwarsstraat 115, Southern Canal Belt (626 3249/www.jazz-cafe-alto.nl). Tram 1, 2, 5, 6, 7, 10. **Open** 9pm-3am Mon-Thur, Sun; 9pm-4am Fri, Sat. **Admission** free. **No credit cards. Map** p310 D5.
Small and often quite smoky, Alto is one of the city's better jazz venues. Dutch saxophonist Hans Dulfer (Candy's dad) has a weekly Wednesday night slot.

Bimhuis

Oudeschans 73-7, Old Centre: Old Side (623 1361/ www.bimhuis.nl). Tram 9, 14/Metro Waterlooplein. **Open** Box office 8-11pm show nights. **Admission** €9-€16. **No credit cards. Map** p307 E2.
True jazz lovers don't need any explanation on hearing the name. The city's main jazz venue plays host to a multitude of well-known international artists; book in advance. At the end of 2004, they move to a new location in the Music Building (www.muziek gebouw.nl) on the Eastern Docklands.

Bourbon Street

Leidsekruisstraat 6-8, Southern Canal Belt (623 3440/ www.bourbonstreet.nl). Tram 1, 2, 5, 6, 7, 10. **Open** 10pm-4am Mon-Thur, Sun; 10pm-5am Fri, Sat. **Admission** €3-€5. **Credit** AmEx, MC, V, DC. **Map** p310 D5.
In the heart of the tourist area, this blues club has a spacious bar and a very late liquor licence that only adds to its charm.

Casablanca

Zeedijk 26, Old Centre: Old Side (625 5685/www. casablanca-amsterdam.nl). Tram 4, 9, 16, 24, 25. **Open** 8pm-4am Mon-Thur, Sun; 10pm-4am Fri, Sat. **Admission** free. **No credit cards. Map** p306 D2.
Casablanca was the city's top jazz venue in the 1950s, but nowadays often has to organise drunken karaoke evenings to pay the rent. Still, with a little luck, you'll be able to catch some talent.

Cristofori

Prinsengracht 581-83, Western Canal Belt (626 8485/ www.cristofori.nl). Tram 1, 2, 5. **Open** hours vary. **Admission** €12.50. **No credit cards. Map** p310 C4.
Worth a visit for the building alone: a beautiful canal house that doubles as a piano retailer. Be sure to drop in at the weekend, when the live entertainment ranges from jazz vocalists to chamber music.

Festivals

OK, so the weather's not always up to scratch, but Holland definitely has other charms waiting to lure the crowds to its festivals each year (and we're not just referring to the narcotics-friendly legislation). Tickets for most festivals

are available from the **AUB Ticketshop** (0900 0191) or **Ticketservice** (www.ticketservice.nl); *see p279* **Tickets please**.

Amsterdam Roots Festival

www.amsterdamroots.nl. **Date** June.
This festival, organised by the Melkweg, the Tropeninstituut and the Concertgebouw, features some of the greatest world music acts in the world. Free concerts by slightly lesser-known names in the Oosterpark add to the fun.

A Camping Flight to Lowlands

www.lowlands.nl. **Date** penultimate wknd of Aug.
The end of August is Lowlands time. Holland's largest alternative music festival takes place over the course of three days, attracting up to 60,000 young hipsters. The music, theatre acts and street performers all help to create a lively and fun atmosphere, even if the weather turns sour.

Crossing Border

www.crossingborder.nl. **Date** Nov.
Crossing Border recently downsized and moved back to its original home in the Hague. The festival offers an intellectually stimulating mix of literature and music, with many well-known international authors and artists. *Also see p183.*

North Sea Jazz

0900 300 1250/www.northseajazz.nl.
Date 2nd wknd in July.
This three-day mega-event in the Hague is a fantastic opportunity to see some bona-fide jazz legends up close and personal. Up to a thousand artists perform each year, from big names to a savvy selection of up-and-comers. Together with Switzerland's Montreux, this is where the world's best and brightest shine.

Parkpop

www.parkpop.nl. **Date** late June.
Europe's largest free festival – up to 400,000 turn up each year – is a family-friendly affair. There's nothing too challenging on offer, but Parkpop is a perfect occasion to pack a picnic basket and make off to the Hague for a (hopefully) sunny afternoon of music.

Pinkpop

www.pinkpop.nl. **Date** May/June.
Attracting a slightly younger crowd than its 'indie sister' Lowlands, Pinkpop, down in the southern tip of the country, is somewhat less adventurous and more predictable. Still, there are plenty of big names in the worlds of pop, rock, dance and metal at this three-day event.

Sonic Acts

www.sonicacts.com. **Date** varies.
Arguably Holland's most challenging festival, Sonic Acts fills the Paradiso with the sounds of new electronic and experimental music. Various workshops and an opportunity to do your own remixing attract numerous Scanner and Stockhausen fans from all over the world.

Arts & Entertainment

Classical & Opera

Although the Dutch are more known for their painters than their classical composers, the Netherlands – and Amsterdam in particular – have a lot to offer music aficionados. At a time when governments around the world are slashing arts funding in a frighteningly casual way, it's a thrill to find a city in which the arts are not only fighting back, but defiantly holding their own. The Amsterdam arts scene is on the up and up, and classical music specifically is alive and well.

Anyone with a half-decent classical CD collection owns at least one disc by the **Royal Concertgebouw Orchestra**. This famed ensemble has gone from strength to strength in recent years under Riccardo Chailly's direction. The baton has been passed on to Latvian Mariss Jansons, and guest appearances by big names like Mstislav Rostropovich, Nikolaus Harnoncourt and former chief conductor Bernard Haitink all help ensure that the name travels gracefully well into the 21st century.

Across town at the Beurs van Berlage, the **Netherlands Philharmonic**, directed by Yakov Kreizberg, plays a symphonic series alongside its regular productions at the Nederlands Opera, and is normally good value. But the other major ensembles shouldn't be forgotten: The **Rotterdam Philharmonic Orchestra** has the exceptional Valery Gergiev as its chief conductor, while the **Radio Philharmonic Orchestra**, based in Hilversum but a regular visitor to Amsterdam, continues to work at the highest levels under the skilled baton of Edo de Waart.

If you have time, try to visit Rotterdam as well for a further taste of high-quality musical accomplishment. You'll find performances and venues well worth the hour-long train trip south.

ENSEMBLES

Two types of music stand out above all others in this city of extremes. On the one hand, there's the old school: Dutch musicians were the founders of authentic performance practice – performances using authentic period instruments – and the innovation has now almost become a tradition. Ton Koopman holds the torch as harpsichordist and 'director who doesn't conduct' of the **Amsterdam Baroque Orchestra & Choir**, founded in 1979, while the **Amsterdam Bach Soloists**, formed by members of the Concertgebouw Orchestra, is led by principle violinist Henk Rubingh when it's not employing a guest conductor. Recorder-player and director Frans Brüggen extends authentic practice into the classical era with

his **Orchestra of the 18th Century**. Look out for concerts organised by **Organisatie Oude Muziek** – literally, the Organisation for Old Music – whose early music events at the **Waalse Kerk** are often unmissable.

On the flipside, there is a growing modern music scene here; **Asko Ensemble**, the **Combattimento Consort** and the **Schönberg Ensemble** are among the most notable of the city's 20-odd new music ensembles. The **Nieuw Ensemble** and the **Nieuw Sinfonietta** are also worth watching, as are minimalist eccentrics (and Louis Andriessen interpreters) **Orkest de Volharding**; contemporary music fans should check out the Proms. Kind of a down and dirty version of the British festival of the same name, it's a series of avant garde concerts held, oddly, in the **Paradiso** (*see p214*).

TICKETS AND INFORMATION

Ticket prices in Amsterdam are reasonable compared with other European cities. However, tickets for many of the larger venues are sold on a subscription system, and it can be difficult to get tickets on an ad hoc basis. For big concerts and operas, try to book as far in advance as you can, but if you're just passing through, it's always worth phoning up for returns.

For full listings information, pick up a copy of the free Dutch listings magazine *Uitkrant*, published by the **AUB** (0900 0191; *see p279* **Tickets please**), or call in at the **Amsterdam Tourist Board** (0900 400 4040; *see p290*), which has information on upcoming shows. Discounts on tickets are often available for students and over-65s.

Concert halls

Where a telephone number is given in the listings below, tickets are sold at the venue's box office. Tickets are also available from the **AUB Ticketshop** (0900 0191/www.uitlijn.nl).

Bethaniënklooster

Barndesteeg 6B, Old Centre: Old Side (625 0078/ www.bethanienklooster.nl). Tram 4, 9, 14, 16, 24, 25. Tram 4, 9, 16, 24, 25/Metro Nieuwmarkt.
Open hours vary. **Tickets** €10. **No credit cards.** **Map** p306 D2.
Hidden in a small alley between Damstraat and the Nieuwmarkt, this former monastery caters for lovers of classical music. It's a stage for promising new talents, but you might also find reputed musicians entertaining the crowds.

Beurs van Berlage

Damrak 213, Old Centre: Old Side (521 7575/ www.berlage.com). Tram 4, 9, 14, 16, 24, 25.
Open *Box office* 2.30-5pm Tue-Fri; also from 75min before performance. Closed end June-mid Aug.
Tickets €7-€16. **No credit cards.** **Map** p306 D2.

It's a gas

After years of renovation, asbestos removal and soil detoxification, the sprawling terrain of the city's century-old former gas works **Westergasfabriek** re-opened with much fanfare in 2003 as a culture and arts complex complete with acres of water and cypress-studded landscaping. With a plethora of industrial monuments being re-invented as performance, event and exhibition spaces, the Westergasfabriek will undoubtedly evolve into one of the city's premier cultural hubs (as it was through the 1990s as an ultra-happening underground squat village).

However, the 'grand opening' whiffed of jumping the gun: while the grounds are already a lovely place for a wander, and

the cinema **Ketelhuis** (see p192) and the wonderful café/restaurant **Kantine West** (488 7778) have been long fully functional, it won't be until at least the 2004/2005 season that things will truly get into full swing. But until this cultural explosion occurs, you can still probably sniff out the sporadic club night, concert, art exhibition and theatre performance. The **AUB** (0900 0191; see p279 **Tickets please**) on the Leidseplein will be handling most ticketed events.

Westergasfabriek

Haarlemmerweg 8-10, Westerpark (586 0710/www.westergasfabriek.nl). Tram 10/ bus 18, 22.

This former stock exchange is now a cultural centre, comprising a large exhibition room, two concert halls and the offices of the building's three resident orchestras: the Netherlands Philharmonic, the Netherlands Chamber Orchestra, and the very new kids on the block, the Amsterdam Symphony Orchestra. Entered from the Damrak, the medium-sized Yakult Zaal offers comfortable seating, a massive stage and controllable but not immaculate acoustics. The 200-seat Amvest Zaal is an odd-looking, free-standing glass box within the walls of a side room. *See also p74.*

Concertgebouw

Concertgebouwplein 2-6, Museum Quarter, (reservations 671 8345/24hr information in Dutch 573 0511/www.concertgebouw.nl). Tram 2, 3, 5, 12, 16, 20. **Open** *Box office* 10am-7pm; until 8.15pm for that night's concert. *By phone* 10am-5pm daily. **Tickets** €5-€114. **Credit** AmEx, DC, MC, V. **Map** p310 D6.

With its beautiful architecture (it was built in the late 19th century) and stunning acoustics, the Concertgebouw is a favourite venue of many of the world's top soloists and orchestras, including its

Poptastic-scholastic

It's an almost surreal sight: a classic 17th-century gabled house emblazoned with the words 'Nationaal Pop Instituut'. You're not dreaming: the building is indeed home to an institute dedicated to Dutch pop music. Their Multimedia Centre has a massive collection of music-related books and magazines (including English ones), press clippings and listening stations – all of which are accessible to the public. They also give advice on the full spectrum of the music business to local bands, performers and DJs, produce monthly mag *FRET*, host concerts on their in-house stage and were fundamental in establishing a 'pop professorship' at the University of Amsterdam and setting up the nation's first Pop Academy in Tilburg.

But their website can be seen as their hugest achievement. It includes links to most acts and has an almost completist encyclopaedia of Dutch pop music, with its more important entries translated into English. Here you can link to online jukeboxes and delve into such legends as the George Baker Selection (whose 'Little Green Bag' was used in Tarantino's *Reservoir Dogs*) and Shocking Blue (whose 'Venus' was resurrected by Bananarama); or immerse yourself in the snotty '60s garage of The Outsiders, the yodelling progressive rock of Focus, or the 'cuddle junkie' rock of the late Herman Brood. Or you can just play Golden Earring's 'Radar Love' over and over again...

While many acts often – understandably – sing in Dutch, don't let that stop your investigation of the deep, desperate heart of more current Nederpop: the intense Raggende Manne has a singer whose vocal chords regularly stretch beyond language, and the hiphop Osdorp Posse can be handily employed as a crash course in Amsterdam slang. Of course, many bands do opt for the more malleable and universal tongue of English; and the international respect garnered in the last decade by the more alternative likes of Urban Dance Squad, the Ex, Bettie Serveert, Junkie XL, Johan, Caesar, Solex, Zuco 103, New Cool Collective and Arling&Cameron seems to hint that there is a true – and exportable – renaissance occurring in the often slighted local music scene.

There are also the DJs. The big one is Tiësto, who was voted the world's number one spinmeister by the UK's *DJ Magazine*; young turntablists C-Mon & Kypski are also making a significant splash on the international scene. And if it's dancehall you're after, the Controverse Allstars play regularly around town and will put your finger – and your hips – on the latest bass-heavy pulses. Rich pickings indeed.

Nationaal Pop Instituut

Prins Hendrikkade 142 (428 4288/media centre 618 9217/www.popinstituut.nl). Bus 22, 23. **Open** *Media Centre 10am-5pm Mon-Fri.* **Map** p307 E2.

---

own world-renowned Concertgebouw Orchestra. The sound in the Grote Zaal (Great Hall) is second to none, while the Kleine Zaal (Recital Hall) features top-class chamber groups and soloists in its less comfortable, but nicely sized atmosphere. Visiting stars push prices up, but many of the remaining concerts are extremely affordable. Throughout July and August, tickets for the Robeco Summer Concerts, featuring high-profile artists and orchestras, are an excellent bargain. There's a lovely Christmas matinee concert every 25 December.

IJsbreker

Weesperzijde 23, the Pijp (693 9093/ www.ysbreker.nl). Tram 3, 6, 7, 10. **Admission** €6.50-€16. **Credit** MC, V. **Map** p312 G4.
Moving with its jazz sister Bimhuis (*see p215*) into the brand new harbourfront Music Building (www.muziekgebouw.nl) at the end of 2004, the IJsbreker is one of Europe's most innovative music venues, and it concentrates on contemporary classical music and experimental jazz.

Churches

Many musicians in Amsterdam take advantage of the monumental churches around the city. The bonus for concertgoers is obvious: aside from hearing largely excellent music, you also get a chance to see the interiors of these wonderful buildings. During the summer, the city's many bell-towers resonate to the intricate tinkling of their carillons. Thumping the 'keyboard' mechanism triggers a whole array of smaller bells into a clanging and barely melodious nightmare of Hunchbackian proportions. Most churches have no box office, but tickets are available from the **AUB** (0900 0191).

Dominicuskerk

Spuistraat 12, Old Centre: New Side (624 2183/ www.dominicusgemeente.nl). Tram 1, 2, 5, 14. **Open** hours vary. **Admission** varies. **No credit cards.** **Map** p306 C2.

Arts & Entertainment

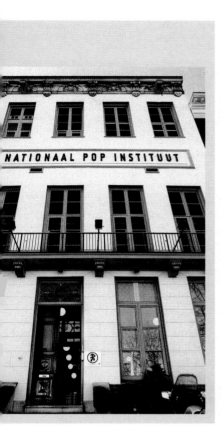

This church situated in the heart of town offers an array of evening concerts – mainly sacred and world music.

De Duif

Prinsengracht 756, Southern Canal Belt (422 0380/www.deduif.nu). Tram 4, 16, 24, 25. **Open** hours vary. **Admission** free. **No credit cards**. **Map** p311 E4.
Newly re-opened after years of renovation, the stunning 'Dove' has the perfect acoustics to enjoy classical concerts on the last Sunday of the month and at sporadic lunchtimes.

Engelse Kerk

Begijnhof 48, Old Centre: New Side (624 9665/ www.ercadam.nl). Tram 1, 2, 4, 5, 9, 14, 16, 24, 25. **Open** hours vary. **Admission** free. **No credit cards**. **Map** p310 D4.
The English Reformed Church is nestled in an idyllic courtyard, and the Academy of the Begijnhof arranges weekly concerts of baroque and classical

music here, with particular emphasis on the use of authentic period instruments. The series of free lunchtime concerts in July and August features young players and new ensembles.

Nieuwe Kerk

Dam, Old Centre: New Side (626 8168/www. nieuwekerk.nl). Tram 1, 2, 5, 9, 13, 14, 16, 17, 24, 25. **Open** during exhibitions 10am-6pm daily; 10am-10pm Thur. **Tickets** €6. **No credit cards**. **Map** p306 C3.
The Nieuwe Kerk has a magnificent 16th-century organ and hosts concerts by top Dutch and international players. Gustav Leonhardt, grandfather of baroque performance practice, is the resident organist. The church has a programme of guest organists in the summer and around Christmas. *See p75.*

Noorderkerk

Noordermarkt 48, the Jordaan (427 6163/ www.noorderkerkconcerten.nl). Tram 3, 10. **Open** 11am-1pm Sat; concerts 2-3pm Sat. **Tickets** €8. **No credit cards**. **Map** p305 B2.
Sure, the wooden benches in this early 17th-century church are a bit on the hard side, but all is soon forgotten when you're listening to the likes of cellist Pieter Wispelwey playing Bach sonatas. Reservations are recommended. They also have regular Thursday evening concerts.

Oude Kerk

Oudekerksplein 23, Old Centre: Old Side (625 8284/ www.oudekerk.nl). Tram 4, 9, 14, 16, 24, 25. **Open** 11am-5pm Mon-Sat; 1-5pm Sun. **Tickets** €4-€8. **No credit cards**. **Map** p306 D2.
Jan Sweelinck, the Netherlands' most famous 17th-century composer, was once the organist here, and concerts – running from June to August – include organ and carillon recitals, plus choral and chamber music. The Oude Kerk also holds a summer 'wandering' concert series, together with the Museum Amstelkring. *See p82.*

Waalse Kerk

Walenpleintje 159, Old Centre: Old Side (623 2074/ www.waalsekerk-amsterdam.nl). Tram 4, 9, 16, 24, 25. **Open** hours vary. **Tickets** €13.50-€25; €8 concessions. **No credit cards**. **Map** p306 D3.
Elegant, intimate and with special acoustics, concerts at the Waalse Kerk are organised by the Organisatie Oude Muziek (030 236 2236), a group devoted to early music played on period instruments. Musicians from the Netherlands and abroad perform here on a relatively regular basis.

Westerkerk

Prinsengracht 281, Western Canal Belt (624 7766/ www.westerkerk.nl). Tram 13, 14, 17. **Open** Apr-Sept 11am-3pm Mon-Fri. **Tickets** free-€10; €6-€8 concessions. **No credit cards**. **Map** p306 C3.
The Jordaan's most famous landmark features a wide range of lunch and evening concerts, many of them free of charge. Also keep in mind that cantatas are performed during church services. *See p89.*

Opera

Hungry opera fans! Staff at **Pasta E Basta** (Nieuwe Spiegelstraat 8, Southern Canal Belt, 422 2229) serve fine Italian grub while singing arias.

Muziektheater

Waterlooplein 22, Old Centre: Old Side (625 5455/ www.muziektheater.nl). Tram 9, 14/Metro Waterlooplein. **Open** *Box office* 10am-6pm Mon-Sat; 11.30am-6pm Sun; or until start of performance. **Tickets** €30-€70. **Credit** AmEx, DC, MC, V. **Map** p307 E3.

Situated in the architecturally controversial Stopera complex, the Muziektheater is home to the National Ballet and the Netherlands Opera, as well as visiting guest productions. The emphasis is on high-quality opera and dance performances at reasonable prices. The stage's generous dimensions invites particularly ambitious ideas from world-famous directors like Peter Sellars and also attracts respected artists with roots in rock and pop music, among them Björk and Marianne Faithfull.

Stadsschouwburg

Leidseplein 26, Southern Canal Belt (624 2311/ www.stadsschouwburgamsterdam.nl). Tram 1, 2, 5, 6, 7, 10. **Open** *Box office* 10am-6pm or until start of performance Mon-Sat; from 12hrs before start of performance Sun. **Tickets** €9-€35. **Credit** AmEx, MC, V. **Map** p310 C5.

This magnificent venue, situated right on the Leidseplein, is known for its theatre and opera productions. Recently, the new management has been trying to reach out – with some success – to a younger crowd, inviting artists from fields such as rock and pop music to DJs and modern dance troupes. The grand surroundings definitely lend a touch of splendour to the proceedings.

Out of town

Doelen

Kruisstraat 2, Rotterdam (010 217 1717/ www.dedoelen.nl). NS rail Rotterdam Centraal Station. **Open** *Box office by phone* 10am-6pm Mon-Thur, Sat, Sun; 10am-9pm Fri *(in person* from noon). **Tickets** €7-€35. **Credit** AmEx, MC, V.

The Doelen, best known as home to the Rotterdam Philharmonic Orchestra (RPO), contains both a large and small concert hall. The building hosts roughly two dozen series a year, ranging from contemporary orchestral work to jazz and almost everything in between, including the RPO's own season.

Vredenburg

Vredenburgpassage 77, Utrecht (box office 030 231 4544/www.vredenburg.nl). NS rail Utrecht. **Open** *Box office* noon-7pm Mon; 10am-7pm Tue-Sat; also from 45min before performance. **Tickets** €16-€35. **Credit** AmEx, MC, V.

Located in the labyrinthine Utrecht train station and shopping complex, Vredenburg offers an innovative mix of classical music, jazz, pop, rock and singer/songwriters. The setting is ugly, but the acoustics are one in a million.

Festivals & events

Further details on all the events listed below can be obtained from the **AUB** (0900 0191) and the **Amsterdam Tourist Board** (0900 400 4040). Another festival that features a whole range of arts, including classical music, is the **Uitmarkt** *(see p182).*

Grachtenfestival

Various venues (421 4542/www.grachtenfestival.nl). **Date** mid Aug. **Tickets** free-€20. **Credit** varies.

What started out life as a single free concert from an orchestra floating on a pontoon in front of the Hotel Pulitzer *(see p56)* has become the 'Canal Festival', involving over 70 chamber concerts in 20 different canal-side locations. The line-up balances international names with national talent, and the setting – especially in clement weather – couldn't be grander.

Holland Festival Oude Muziek Utrecht

Various venues in Utrecht. Box office at VVV Utrecht, Vinkenburgstraat 19 (030 230 3838/ www.oudemuziek.nl). **Date** late Aug-early Sept. **Tickets** €7-€31. **No credit cards**.

Top baroque and classical artists and ensembles converge on Utrecht each year, where they perform in churches and concert halls throughout the city. The festival is a highly popular staple of the classical season in the Netherlands, partly owing to the use of period instruments in most performances.

International Gaudeamus Music Week

Various venues (694 7349/www.gaudeamus.nl). **Date** early Sept. **Tickets** free-€10. **Credit** varies.

An international competition for young composers organised by the Centre for Contemporary Music, the week includes intense discussion of the state of the art plus performances of selected works by established composers. Contemporary music devotees shouldn't miss it – though more traditional classicists may want to plug their ears and run away.

Other organisations

STEIM (Stichting for Electro-Instrumental Music)

622 8690/www.steim.org.

Amsterdam's electronic music institution is a unique research team examining the interface between man and music: prototype MIDI controllers, novel sensors and hard- and software packages to convert any manner of signals into MIDI data. The intimate concerts and workshops they organise in different locations offer both technophobes and technophiles an intriguing glimpse into the future.

Nightclubs

Whether you want to be chilled out, mad for it or slumped in a gutter at 6am, the 'Dam's clubbing scene won't disappoint.

Clubs and drugs – an inseparable partnership, right? And Amsterdam – the most drug-friendly city in the world, right? Well, don't get complacent. Though soft on soft drugs, the Dutch authorities don't have the same easy-going take on Class As. In a 2003 raid at Escape, although people found with three ecstasy pills or fewer were let off, those with four to ten pills were warned and fined – and those with more than ten were given a gaol sentence. Cautionary tales don't come more straightforward than that.

A word of advice on getting through the door: the days of political correctness and we-don't-dare-discriminate are gone. Many larger clubs tend not to welcome groups of men – straight or otherwise – and some even insist on men being accompanied by the same number of women. Sexist? Unfair? Perhaps, but them's the breaks. As you can imagine, a degree in social etiquette is not part of the door staff job requirements. It's all about skimming off the cream, so make sure you're creamy.

Tipping the door staff as you leave is customary, especially if you hope to return to the same club on another occasion. Another little extra cost comes when you visit the powder room: you have to pay at least €0.50 to pee. But on the upside, the 'toilet ladies' do normally keep the facilities fairly clean and equipped with toilet paper, and also offer free sweets (though often touched by a series of unwashed hands) on your way out.

Apart from these anomalies, Amsterdam's clubbing scene has experienced many of the same changes as the rest of Europe. Drink prices are now on a par with London, and the days seem numbered for mega-clubs – long live the more intimate club night organisers! – as more and more people start to go in search of the personal touch.

Club venues

Particular attention has been given to the most popular club nights held at each venue. For clubs and venues where the majority of nights are aimed at the gay community (such as hetero-friendly **Exit**, and **iT** where straights are allowed in on most nights), see p205. For the **Westergasfabriek**, see p217 **It's a gas**.

The best Club nights

Advanced Party
Prime UK export. See p223 **Amuse Bouche**.

Appelsap
Fresh, fruity and funky. See p227 **Club Arena**.

Club Vegas
Still crazy after all these years. See p223 **Winston International**.

Electronation
Electroclash bash. See p223 **Amuse Bouche** and **Winston International**.

Noodlanding
For the alternative you. See p225 **Paradiso**.

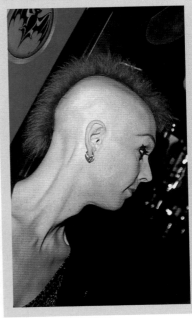

Arts & Entertainment

Viva Club Vegas:
Winston International. *See p223*.

And don't forget the city's clutch of smaller, DJ-friendly bars: among the best of them are **Twstd** (*see p144*) and **DJ Café Vaaghuijzen** (Nieuwe Nieuwstraat 17, 420 1751/www.vaaghuyzen.nl).

The Old Centre: Old Side

Winston International

Warmoesstraat 129 (623 1380/www.winston.nl). *Tram 9, 14, 25.* **Open** 10pm-3am Mon-Thur, Sun; 11pm-4am Fri, Sat. **Admission** €5-€10. **No credit cards**. Map p306 D2.
An intimate venue that attracts a mixed crowd with eclectic programming. Tuesday brings the popular hip hop/R&B night Live on the Low. Sunday's Club Vegas (www.clubvegas.nl) has been keeping the artsy, cheesy-listening crowd smiling for over five years. Freestone's Retro Sessions, on the third Thursday of the month are geared towards punk, indie or Madchester nostalgia. *See also p214.*

The Old Centre: New Side

020

Nieuwezijds Voorburgwal 163-5 (428 4418/ www.020ams.nl). Tram 1, 2, 5. **Open** midnight-4am Mon, Wed; 11pm-4am Thur, Sun; 11pm-5am Fri; midnight-5am Sat. **Admission** €5-€12. **No credit cards**. Map p306 C3.

Re-opened in 2003 with a low-key PR non-frenzy, 020 (named after the local telephone prefix) has a wonderful open-plan layout that could use some new sound and light equipment. Sunday nights are the reliable Wicked Jazz Sounds that won a 'Golden Gnome' club award for Best New Initiative in 2003. Wednesday nights are dedicated to the queer-electro of Divine.

Bitterzoet

Spuistraat 2 (521 3001/www.bitterzoet.com). Tram 1, 2, 5. **Open** 8pm-3am Mon-Thur, Sun; 8pm-4am Fri, Sat. **Admission** €5-€12. **No credit cards**. Map p306 C2.
This new bar is also a venue for theatre and music. The interior is comfortable and loungy, and there's some kind of band or DJ activity every night. Though there's a variety of musical genres on offer, most of the fare tends to be on the jazzy, world music, laid-back side.

Dansen bij Jansen

Handboogstraat 11 (620 1779/www.dansen bijjansen.nl). Tram 1, 2, 4, 5, 9, 14, 16, 24, 25. **Open** 11pm-4am Mon-Thur, Sun; 11pm-5am Fri, Sat. **Admission** €2-€4. **No credit cards**. Map p310 D4.
It's a club Jim, but not as we know it: you'll need valid student ID to get in. DJs spin sing-along Top 40 tunes and the drink prices are cheerfully affordable (for example, €1 beers on Thursdays). But if you're over 25, you'll feel like a pensioner.

Southern Canal Belt

Amuse Bouche

Lijnbaansgracht 238 (428 9380). Tram 1, 2, 5, 7, 10. **Open** hours vary. **Admission** €7-€15. **No credit cards**. Map p310 C5.
This place isn't open regularly as a club but rents itself out to some superb club organisers. The top three: Advanced Party (www.advancedparty.com), a top-notch monthly dance night; Electronation (www.electronation.nl), electro chaos at its best; and Gonzo (www.gonzone.com), a fabulous bi-monthly Hunter S Thompson-inspired dress-up party.

Escape

Rembrandtplein 11 (622 1111/www.escape.nl). Tram 4, 9, 14. **Open** 11pm-4am Thur, Sun; 11pm-7am Fri, Sat. **Admission** €10-€20. **No credit cards**. Map p311 E4.
With a capacity of 2,000, this is about as big as it gets in central Amsterdam. After a drugs bust shutdown in 2003, the shady underworld characters have gone and the arms-in-the-air Euro-house fun can continue. The bouncers are slightly wary of groups of tourists (they were voted Worst Bouncers in 2003's Golden Gnome club awards), so squeeze into a slinky T, slap on some hair product and get in line early. Thursday brings stylish RUSH (Raw Urban Sexy House), while Saturday brings the deeply popular Chemisty (www.chemistry.nl) with DJ Marcello.

Sinners in Heaven: does the devil really have all the best tunes? *See p227.*

Jimmy Woo's

Korte Leidsedwarsstraat 18 (626 3150/www.jimmy woo.nl) Tram 1, 2, 5, 6, 7, 10. **Open** 8pm-3am Wed, Thur, Sun; 8pm-4am Fri, Sat. **Admission** €7.50. **No credit cards. Map** p310 C5.

Amsterdam has never seen anything quite so luxuriously cosmopolitan as Jimmy Woo's. The key word here is quality: the sound system is the best money can buy, and the lounge area is filled with a mixture of modern and antique furniture (including a real opium bed from 1860). The urban soundtrack ranges from hip hop to garage. There's no dress code, but with a capacity of only 600, the bouncers can afford to be picky.

Melkweg

Lijnbaansgracht 234A (531 8181/www.melkweg.nl). Tram 1, 2, 5, 6, 7, 10. **Open** hours vary. **Admission** free-€20. **Membership** €2.50/mth (compulsory). **No credit cards. Map** p310 C5.

'The Milky Way' can sure feel heavenly thanks to its wonderful programming: fancy it ain't, but great value and down to earth, with a little bit of everything, it absolutely is. Thursday's Latin-flavoured Que Pasa has built up quite a following; and Fridays and Saturdays have consistently good club nights, particularly Earth on the second Friday of the month. The building also hosts movies, exhibitions and concerts; for these, *see also p194, p197 and p213* respectively.

Ministry

Reguliersdwarsstraat 12 (623 3981/www.ministry.nl). Tram 16, 24, 25. **Open** 11pm-4am Mon, Sun; 11pm-5am Fri, Sat. **Admission** €5-€12. **No credit cards. Map** p310 D4.

Ministry is a small and stylish club; its music tends towards the funky and soulful. But the door policy is not overly welcoming, so don't bother coming unless you look like you've walked off the set of a Beyoncé video.

Odeon

Singel 460 (624 9711/www.odeontheater.nl). Tram 1, 2, 5. **Open** 11pm-4am Fri, Sat; 11pm-4am Sun. **Admission** €3.50-€7. **No credit cards. Map** p310 D4.

This elegant three-storey venue on Singel offers three different styles of music for up to 800 punters. It's perfect for posses of bachelors or bachelorettes (the door people may even offer you a group discount). When the extensive renovations are complete – hopefully some time in 2004 – they'll be able to serve up old-fashioned, uncomplicated fun every night of the week.

Paradiso

Weteringschans 6-8 (626 4521/www.paradiso.nl). Tram 1, 2, 5, 6, 7, 10. **Open** 8pm-4am Wed-Fri, Sun; 8pm-5am Sat. **Admission** €5-€20 (incl membership). **No credit cards. Map** p310 D5.

Nomads is an exclusive restaurant in Amsterdam that is inspired by the Arabian Nomad culture. Lying down on an original Egyptian kelim, you find yourself in a surrealistic oasis where you can enjoy a wide variety of authentic Arabian 'mezzes', being offered a large choice in hot and cold small dishes to enjoy at any time between 7 pm and 1 am. For a small bite or extensive dinner, for a drink or just a moment to relax, Nomads welcomes you for a self-made evening out while taking in the exotic and warm interior, enjoying the entertainment and listening to the inspiring sounds of DJ Jimmy. A guest at Nomads will be guaranteed a feast for all senses and an authentic and completely unforgettable experience.

Nomads, located right above club More…, is open from Wednesday to Sunday and is an initiative from the people of the famous Supperclub.

Nomads
Rozengracht 133 I
1016lv
Amsterdam

T. 020-3446401
F. 020-3446405
info@restaurantnomads.nl
reservations@restaurantnomads.nl

www.restaurantnomads.nl

Paradiso is an Amsterdam institution and a safe clubbing bet. It's a large ex-church with the tried and tested formula of live shows followed by a DJ or club night. Saturday's Paradisco pulls in a youngish, up-for-it crowd; Noodlanding ('Emergency Landing') on a Wednesday or Thursday is particularly good if you're after a more alternative, indie feel. Door staff are thorough but friendly. For the venue's live music programming, *see p214*.

Sinners in Heaven

Wagenstraat 3-7 (620 1375/www.sinners.nl). Tram 4, 9, 14. **Open** 11pm-4am Thur; 11pm-5am Fri, Sat. **Admission** free-€11.50. **No credit cards. Map** p307 E3.

The Sinners people are boo-tiful, well groomed, and well funded – some of them are even famous, albeit in a 'big in Hollandwood' sort of way. Think *Sex in the City* meets the Fresh Prince. Saturday's FAME is pretty rocking (www.fameonline.nl).

Jodenbuurt, the Plantage & the Oost

Club Arena

's Gravesandestraat 51 (850 2420/www.hotel arena.nl). Tram 3, 6, 7, 10. **Open** 10pm-4am Fri-Sun. **Admission** €6-€20. **No credit cards. Map** p312 G3.

Another multi-purpose venue, this ex-convent also has an adjoining hotel, bar and restaurant. People from big cities will laugh at how accessible the Arena is, but Amsterdammers are less inclined to take a small detour eastwards, which makes it hard for this place to really kick clubbing butt. Appelsap (or 'Apple juice') is the exception – an excellent, friendly hip-hop/funk night every month or two on a Saturday. On Sundays (5-7pm) there are free disco and lounge afternoons. *See p63*.

The Jordaan

Korsakoff

Lijnbaansgracht 161 (625 7854/www.korsakoff.nl). Tram 10, 13, 14, 17. **Open** 11pm-3am Mon-Thur, Sun; 11pm-4am Fri, Sat. **Admission** usually free. **No credit cards. Map** p310 C4.

Korsakoff makes 'alternative' feel normal: the venue's hard rock/indie/metal/goth sounds reach the parts Kylie and Justin have never even heard about. Though the decor is rough 'n' ready, the crowd is relaxed and friendly. Low drinks prices mean you can knock 'em back all night long with little damage to the wallet (but perhaps some to the liver).

Mazzo

Rozengracht 114 (626 7500/www.mazzo.nl). Tram 13, 14, 17. **Open** 11pm-4am Thur, Sun; 11pm-5am Fri, Sat. **Admission** €7.50-€10. **No credit cards. Map** p309 B4.

One of Amsterdam's oldest clubs, Mazzo until recently offered top-quality, cutting-edge dance music. Sadly, this smallish venue is now playing

it safe to attract a better class of clubber. On the up side, service has been improved with an eye to people who like to sit and be served rather than get up and get down. DJ b-Art spins deep, sexy house on Friday and Saturday. Joints aren't allowed in here (because if they were, then, maybe, you'd spend less money on drinks).

More

Rozengracht 133 (528 7459/www.expectmore.nl). Tram 13, 14, 17. **Open** 11pm-4am Thur; 11pm-5am Fri, Sat; 5pm-midnight Sun. **Admission** €8-€12.50. **No credit cards. Map** p309 B4.

The interior looks like it was designed by someone obsessed with Lennon's 'Imagine' videoclip; some of the people on the door seem obsessed with the line 'Imagine there's no people'. Don't be put off: the bar staff are friendly and quick. Risk, on Saturday, is quite popular with a fashionable, though unspectacular crowd. On Sunday afternoons, Paleis Soestdijk attracts older punters who have to turn in early to be fresh for their media jobs on Monday.

The South

Vakzuid

Olympisch Stadion 35 (570 8400/www.vakzuid.nl). Tram 6, 16, 24, 50/bus 23, 63, 170, 171, 172. **Open** 10pm-1am Mon-Thur; 10pm-3am Fri; 4pm-3am Sat; 3-10pm Sun. **Admission** free-€12. **No credit cards.**

This chic, LA-meets-Zen hangout sits snugly under the old Olympic grandstands with a terrace overlooking the track. This is lounging in style. Vakzuid is predominantly a restaurant/bar, but the chairs and tables are pushed back from Thursday to Sunday and a dancefloor is born. The TriBeCa Lounge on a Sunday afternoon is très chilled. *See p133*.

Powerzone

Daniel Goedkoopstraat 1-3 (0900 769 379 663/ www.thepowerzone.nl). Metro Spaklerweg. **Open** 10pm-5am Fri; 11pm-5am Sat; 10pm-7am 1st Sat of mth. **Admission** €45. **VIP** membership €450/yr. **Credit** *VIPs* AmEx, MC, V.

Packing in as many as 5,000 clubbers, the cavernous Powerzone is more like an outdoor dance party that has come indoors. The staff are not particularly welcoming to gangs of tourists, so look pretty and feign a Swedish accent if you don't want to waste a taxi fare to this non-central venue. Once inside, tipping is banned – even your trip to the toilet will be gratis. But you'll need to buy tokens to purchase a beverage… unless you're a VIP, honey. Waterbeds in the lounge area? Oh, my!

Outside Amsterdam

'What other place in the world could you find, where all of life's comforts, and all novelties that man could want, are so easy to obtain as here – and where you can enjoy such a feeling

Arts & Entertainment

Hope springs nocturnal

In February 2003, Amsterdam got itself a new mayor: a 'night mayor' – not, in fact, a person, but a collective of eight prominent DJs and party organisers. Under the label **Nachtwacht** ('Night Watch'; www.nachtwachtamsterdam.nl), they aim to 'stop the frumpification' (www.stop devertrutting.nl) of the city's nightlife.

For the city is not as happening as it once was. So much so – and thanks to the 'zero tolerance' attitude of Amsterdam's daytime powers-that-be – that many believe Rotterdam has taken over as the country's nightlife capital. Indeed, the 'night mayor' concept was inspired by Amsterdam's eternal rival, the city

of freedom?' So wrote Descartes of Amsterdam in 1628. The same is still true today, but that doesn't stop a goodly number of Amsterdam clubbers from making the trip out of town, particularly for extra-late events or harder musical styles. The majority of out-of-town venues expect men to be in the company of women and not to be wearing sportswear; and yes, that includes trainers. For venues yet further out of town, *see pp260-272*.

Bloemendaal beach cafés

Beach pavilions, Bloemendaal aan Zee (023 573 2152/www.beachbop.info). NS rail to Haarlem or Zandvoort, then taxi (€12.50) or Bus 81 or train taxi to Bloemendaal aan Zee (order train taxi when buying train ticket). **Open** *May-Oct times vary.* **Admission** free-€5. **No credit cards.**
A decade ago these beach cafés were a wonderful secret. Now, some might say that they've become a victim of their own popularity, though the thousands who come here every weekend wouldn't see

where poet and Bohemian incarnate Jules Deelder has long ruled supreme.

Still, it's good news that the inspired Nightwatchers have taken their jobs so seriously. Every Thursday from 9pm, they busily indulge in the age-old Dutch ritual of endless consensus-seeking meetings upstairs at Inez IPSC (*see p125*). All are welcome to put in their two cents, at least until 11pm, when the mood lightens with an open podium and DJs. These brainstorming sessions have already produced a lengthy 'bill' (a 15-page English summary can be downloaded from the Nachtwacht website, www.nacht wachtamsterdam.nl) that they presented to the official mayor Job Cohen and is filled with ideas of how to re-pump Amsterdam's once unparalleled nightlife with more allure and freedom.

Their ideas – to name but a few – range from lowering drinks prices, making toilets and condoms free, and re-introducing drug purity tests at larger parties to re-inventing unused spaces both in and outside the city limits as one-off party locations, and getting the city to ease up on the current tactic of making club owners responsible for policing drugs. They've also helped organise related activities such as having their role-model, 'living artwork' Fabiola, lead Saturday's Mary of the Night tours (www.mariedelanuit.nl) to already inspired hotspots like the world's first and only Arabic gay bar, **Habibi Ana** (Lange Leidsedwarsstraat 4-6, www.habibiana.nl) and roots venue **Maloe Melo** (*see p213*).

While few short-term visitors will actually notice any lack of happeningness during their stay, they can be reassured that there are some Amsterdammers hard at work to make any future visits yet more happening. Bless 'em.

this as a bad thing. There are seven different cafés lined up with music, fashion and decor to suit everyone – from kooky Woodstock to chic Bloomingdale to Ibiza-esque Republiek. For Beachbop in August and September, all the cafés join forces to put on what is said to be the biggest beach festival in the world: with 23,000 visitors in 2003, the claim could be true. Great programming makes these events well worth the trip, and with reasonable weather you'll feel more like you've been to Copacabana than to the North Sea.

De Hemkade

Hemkade 48, Zaandam (075 614 8154/ www.hemkade.nl). NS rail Zaandam. **Open** 10pm-6am Sat. **Admission** €10-€20. **No credit cards**.
De Hemkade, north of Amsterdam, is a huge hall with adjoining rooms hosting music of the house/techno variety. It's usually open late on Saturday.

Lexion

Overtoom 65, Westzaan (075 612 3999/ www.lexion.nl). NS rail Zaandam. **Open** 9.30pm-6am Sat. **Admission** €10-€30. **No credit cards**.
Freshly refurbished and raring to be part of the scene again, Lexion expects you to be over 21, *sans* jeans or sports gear but accompanied by a lot of laydeez. Worth checking out for extra-late events.

De Waakzaamheid

Hoogstraat 4, Koog aan de Zaan (075 628 5829/ www.waakzaamheid.com). NS rail Koogzanddijk. **Open** 11pm-5am Sat. **Admission** €10-€20. **No credit cards**.
A cosy club whose DJ line-up often includes top names. The club opens most Saturdays and some Fridays. There's a separate bar area, and in warm weather you can sit outside. 'I Hate Trance' is held on the last Saturday of the month (www.ihatetrance.nl).

Underground scene

The powers-that-be have tried to rid the city of its alternative lifestylers, but underground culture is still blossoming. However, the best thing about it is that it doesn't exclude ordinary folk: if you're up for it, they're up for you. Should you visit around a full moon or solstice there'll be some sort of mad shindig going on. Information on events is hard to come by: look for flyers in coffeeshops, eavesdrop on the conversations of dreadlocked people, or see www.underwateramsterdam.com. For more on squats, *see p110* **It means squat**.

ADM

Hornweg 6, Westhaven (411 0081/www.contrast. org/adm). Tram 3/bus 35.
Huge parties are staged every couple of months in this out-of-town squat. Events are often held around the dates of pagan rituals: expect outdoor fires, performances, a dizzying array of music and people your mother warned you about.

Ruigoord

Ruigoord church, Ruigoord 15, Ruigoord (497 5702/ www.ruigoord.nl). Bus 82.
'Empower the Imagination,' commands their website. This long established artists' colony will bring out the crusty/shaman/fire-breather in you, and their full-moon parties are hard to beat. Ruigoord is about 15km from central Amsterdam and home to the wacky Balloon Company crew (who also throw a not-to-be missed bash at the Paradiso once a year in December). Check out their website for the full scoop.

Arts & Entertainment

After-hours venues

A Giuliani-esque former mayor made sure that it's not as easy to stay out around the clock as it used to be. There's talk of throwing away the rulebook for bar and club opening times, but that may take a little more negotiation and time. Clubs in the centre of Amsterdam usually have to close by 5am, but there are some super-late events to keep insomniacs happy. Most clubs have permission to hold about five after-hours parties every year, so there's normally at least one late knees-up going on: look out for flyers and ask people with wide pupils for advice.

Club night organisers

Look out for one-off events organised by the following companies. Flyers can be picked up and tickets bought in the stores under **Tickets & information** (*see below*). Free English 'zine *Shark* (www.underwateramsterdam.com) lists many big underground events, as does www.urbanguide.nl. The most extensive party listing is www.partyscene.nl: it's in Dutch, but not impossible to decipher.

B2S
www.b2s.nl.
It's all about hardcore, and it's all about liking it loud. B2S organise about four parties a year, including Hard Bass and Decibel Outdoor near Rotterdam.

Beat Club
www.underthehat.net/beatclub.
A little more small-time than the other organisers listed here, but if it's the Northern Soul and groovy twist a-go-go sounds you're hankering after, look no further than Beat Club, held about once a month at various Amsterdam locations.

Club Risk
www.clubrisk.nl.
Risk's resident DJs are Eric de Man and the seemingly ubiquitous Dimitri, with international guests completing the bill. Check them out at More (*see p227*) every Saturday or see the website.

Dance Valley
Spaarnwoude Recreation Area (0900 300 1250/ www.dancevalley.nl). NS rail to Sloterdijk, then free buses to Spaarnwoude.
Conceived in 1995, Dance Valley is now the biggest dance festival in Holland. On a Saturday in August, up to 30,000 people gather in a field outside Amsterdam to listen to everything from techno and hard house to speed garage, supplied by over 100 DJs and bands. DV also organises the monthly HQ (High Quality) at the Melkweg and occasional parties at other venues. Check their site for details on travel, camping and tickets.

Ex Porn Star
www.expornstar.com.
These sleazefests are held about four times a year, and have featured acts such as Ron Jeremy and go-go Grannies. No dress code equals no entry.

Extrema
www.extrema.nl.
These party organisers from the south of Holland are also active in Ibiza, and responsible for at least a couple of big techno and hard dance events a year.

Getaway
This gang throws excellent indoor parties a couple of times a year for the fah-shion crowd. No website yet, but check their latest concept www.opium.nl or visit the Getaway (*see p140*) for hip tips.

ID&T
www.id&t.com.
Apart from being behind chic cocktail bar Mme Jeanette and Bloomingdale beach café, are also responsible for humungous commercial hardhouse parties Sensation, Innercity and outdoor festival, Mysteryland. They pull top DJ names like Sven Vath, Paul van Dyk and Ferry Corsten.

Impulz
www.impulz.nl.
With high-gloss flyers/booklets and ticket sales from Germany to the UK, Impulz makes dance music lovers happy twice a year.

Monumental
0900 300 1250/www.awakenings.nl.
Monumental hosts the popular Awakenings outdoor party on the first Saturday of July, where DJs play techno until the early hours. There is usually also an indoor winter version in North Amsterdam.

Q-dance
www.q-dance.nl.
Any dance event with a 'Q' in it is probably organised by Q-dance – take the huge Houseqlassics and Qontact at the Heineken Music Hall, or Qlub-tempo in De Hemkade (*see p229*). They're also behind Q-beach on Bloemendaal beach (*see p229*).

Tickets & information

Flyers and club tickets can be acquired at a variety of city venues. Chief among them are **451F** (Leidsestraat 19, 423 4068), **Clubwear House** (*see p157*), **Conscious Dreams** (*see p156*), **Cyberdog**, **Housewives on Fire** (for both, *see p158*), hardcore and gabber specialist **Midtown**, **Boudisque** (for both, *see p173*), hardcore house specialist **Dance Tracks** (Nieuwe Nieuwstraat 69, 639 0853) and underground record store **Groove Connection** (Sint Nicolaasstraat 41, 624 7234). As well as flyers, a good many of the above sell tickets for a variety of events.

Arts & Entertainment

Sport & Fitness

Small city, huge choice of physical fun.

The Dutch are not an excessively nationalistic bunch, but they do flaunt a lot of orange in the name of supporting their teams and stars – as witnessed at the 2003 Roland Garros tennis tournament, when unknown player Martin Verkerk unexpectedly finished second. Tennis, darts, swimming, cycling, skating, field hockey and, of course, football are all sports in which the Dutch have made a considerable reputation for themselves.

However, once they've proved themselves on the home front, professional athletes tend to go abroad to attain superstardom before returning occasionally as ambassadors for Dutch sport. The chances of seeing today's stars in Holland are slim, and even securing tickets for most high profile sporting events can be more of a feat than what the athletes are up to. But still, tomorrow's stars are playing at home right now.

For those of you out to play rather than watch, the Netherlands encourages physical fitness in nearly every sport imaginable: just seize the opportunity and exploit the facilities. Most sports operate under the guidance of a national organisation; an overview of sports is given in this chapter, along with the contact numbers and web sites.

For further information on sport in the city, contact the **Municipal Sport and Recreation Department** at 552 2490, or see www.sport.amsterdam.nl (mostly in Dutch) for maps, schedules and links for almost every sport imaginable. The *Gouden Gids* (yellow pages, again mostly in Dutch) can also help you find out what's on where.

Museums

Ajax Museum
ArenA Boulevard 29, Bijlmermeer (311 1444/ www.ajax.nl). Metro Bijlmer. **Open** 10am-5pm daily. Opening hours on match days vary. **Admission** museum €3.50; with stadium tour, from €8.20. **Credit** MC, V.
A great outing for footie fans, the Ajax Museum – located way out in the South-East – covers the rich and long history of this legendary club with photographs, memorabilia, trophies and an eight-minute film showing the greatest goals of the last 25 years. A visit to the museum is also included in the stadium tours (which you can reserve by calling 311 1336 between 9am and 5.30pm, Monday to Friday).

Nederlands Sportmuseum
Museumweg 10, Lelystad (0320 261010/ www.olympion.nl). NS rail Lelystad. **Open** 10am-5pm Tue-Fri; noon-5pm Sat, Sun. **Admission** €4.50; €3.50 under-12s. **No credit cards.**
Aside from all the usual exhibits, the Sportmuseum holds comprehensive archives of books, cuttings and photos, all of which are accessible by appointment.

Orange Football Museum
Kalverstraat 236 at Muntplein, Old Centre: New Side (589 8989/www.supportersclub-oranje.nl). Tram 4, 9, 16, 24, 25. **Open** 11am-5pm Sat, Sun. **Admission** €7. **No credit cards. Map** p310 D4.
This brand new museum has packed four floors with photos, paintings, songs, videos and relics relating to the 'Orange Experience' (ie the national football team). Obsession at its purest.

Spectator sports

American football

American football is taking root in the Dutch sporting psyche. The **Admirals** are the city's pro team, while the **Amsterdam Crusaders** represent the city in the amateur league, and can be reached on 617 7450. Full details of American football are available from governing body **NAFF** (0229 214 801/www.afbn.nl).

The best Sports

Cycling and skating
It's exercise and transportation.
See p232 and p237.

Football
The country's undisputed passion.
See p232.

Hockey
The other Dutch pastime. *See p233.*

Korfball
Keeping Dutch kids off the streets for over 100 years. *See p234.*

Saunas
Why go to Finland when you can sweat it out here? *See p236.*

Arts & Entertainment

Amsterdam Admirals

*Amsterdam ArenA, Arena Boulevard 1, Bijlmermeer
(465 0550/tickets 465 4545/www.admirals.nl).*
Metro Strandvliet or Metro/NS rail Bijlmer.
Admission €13.50-€37.50. **Season** Apr-June.
Credit AmEx, DC, MC, V.

Amsterdam's representatives in the European NFL
seem to win about as many games as they lose, and
attract 15,000-plus spectators in the process.
Attending an Admirals match is one of the easier
ways to get inside the ArenA.

Baseball

Baseball and softball clubs of a variety of
standards compete between April and October.
For details, contact the regional **KNBSB** (030
607 6070/www.knbsb.nl).

Cricket

While the 2003 World Cup didn't produce a
surprise Dutch victory, Dutch cricket teams
have proven themselves worthy opponents in
several contests. There are over 100 men's and
women's teams affiliated to the **KNCB** ('Royal
Dutch Cricket Board', 645 1705/www.kncb.nl),
including several clubs in Amsterdam – the
best of which is the **VRA** (645 9816 or 641
8525). Most clubs have allied junior, veteran
and women's teams, and welcome new players.

Cycling

The Dutch would be quite different people if
it weren't for the *fiets*. Cyclists rarely manage
more than 20 kilometres (about 12.5 miles) per
hour within city limits, but set loose on the
polder, they go like the wind – except, of
course, when riding into it. The Netherlands
has produced many world class sprinters and
climbers; the Dutch still talk with awe about
Joop Zoetemelk who, after finishing second six
times, finally won the Tour de France in 1985.
There's still hope for a future champion.

Fans turn out almost every weekend of the
year for stage, *criterium* (road circuit) and one-
day road races, plus track, field, cyclo-cross and
mountain biking. The biggest Dutch races are
the **Amstel Gold Race** around Limburg in late
April; the **RAI Derny Race**, held at the RAI in
Amsterdam in mid-May; the popular **Acht van
Chaam**, a 100-kilometre (62-mile) *criterium* held
in Noord Brabant on the first Wednesday after
the Tour de France (late July/early August); and
the **Tour de Nederland**, a five-day race that
passes through Amsterdam in August. For more
details, contact the **KNWU** (Dutch Cycle Racing
Association) at Postbus 136, 3440 AC Woerden
(0348 484 084/www.knwu.nl).

If you have a racing bike yourself, head for
Sportpark Sloten. Two cycle clubs are based
here: **ASC Olympia** (617 7510/secretary 617
3057/www.ascolympia.nl), the oldest cycling
club in Europe, and **WV Amsterdam**
(secretary 619 3314). There's a 22-kilometre (12-
mile) circuit round the park, and the 200-metre
(183-yard) track is now a modern velodrome.

For a more leisurely yet organised approach,
try the **NTFU** ('Dutch Tour Bike Association',
Postbus 326, 3900 AH Veenendaal, 0318 581 300/
www.ntfu.nl), which offers members advice on
routes and groups. Their activities take place
mostly at weekends, both by day and night.

Darts

Enthusiasm for darts as a spectator sport
skyrocketed when Amsterdam native Raymond
'Barney' van Barneveld won the Embassy
world title in 1998 and 1999. Dutch fans remain
loyal and most competitions are televised.

Amsterdam has 180 teams and 1,300 members
affiliated to **DORA** (408 4184/www.dora.nl),
which organises leagues from September to
May plus smaller summer competitions. The
ADB (682 1970) is smaller, but still has 400
members who play in cafés in and around
the city. It's usually easy to find a venue in
which to play, but if you're serious, try **De
Vluchtheuvel** (Van Woustraat 174; 662 5665) or
Matchroom Sloten (Slimmeweg 8; 617 7062).

Football

The outstanding reputation Dutch football
enjoys is still warranted, though Dutch clubs
have found it hard to hold on to star players in
recent years; many prime players have been
lured to south European and English clubs. This
dynamic doesn't sit well with Dutch fans, and
they're not appeased by the argument that Dutch
training is still superior and offers an excellent
preview of up-and-comers. Disappointment is an
inevitability, as is an unpredictability that forces
football enthusiasts to keep their eyes on Dutch
leagues – last year's losers are this year's stars.

There's a huge gap between the big Dutch
clubs and the smaller ones. After Ajax, PSV
and Feyenoord, it's a long way down. The
Dutch season runs from late August until late
May, with a break from Christmas until early
February. Buying tickets for matches is still a
challenge (for agendas see www.ticketbox.nl/
voetbal); having a 'personal club card' helps,
but the waiting lists are discouragingly long.
But you can still watch the big games on
network TV, and following them at a local café
can be a viable and exciting alternative if you
can peer over the heads of partisan supporters.

Arts & Entertainment

Trams? Who needs trams? On yer bike! *See p232*.

Ajax

Amsterdam ArenA, Arena Boulevard 29,
Bijlmermeer (311 1444/www.ajax.nl). Metro
Strandvliet or Metro/NS rail Bijlmer.
Tickets €15-€40. **Credit** AmEx, DC, MC, V.
The most closely watched club in the Netherlands.
Excellent training guarantees a worthy competitor
for virtually any opponent – especially PSV. But the
future of key players always seems to be under nego-
tiation, so fans are left to speculate how they can
ever hope to win the next match.

Feyenoord

De Kuip, Van Zandvlietplein 3, Rotterdam (010
292 6888/tickets 010 292 3888/www.feyenoord.nl).
NS rail Rotterdam Centraal Station, then bus 46.
Tickets €13.75-€31. **Credit** AmEx, DC, MC, V.
This former underdog team will hopefully pick itself
out of its current dip to give its peers a run for their
money. Rotterdammers are unswayingly loyal to
everything Rotterdam, and Feyenoord fans epito-
mise this loyalty.

PSV

Philips Stadium, Frederiklaan 10A, Eindhoven
(040 250 5501/tickets 040 250 5505/www.psv.nl).
NS rail Eindhoven, then bus 4, 13. **Tickets** €16-€40.
Credit AmEx, DC, MC, V.
While PSV delivered stellar results in 2003, its
finances are a shambles. Perversely, making the
country's most winning team profitable may under-
mine the club's future.

Other teams

When Premier League games are sold out, try
the First Division… And failing that, some of
the top amateur clubs in the city – Blauw Wit,
DGC and Elinkwijk among them – play decent
football. For information, or if you fancy a
game, contact Amsterdam's KNVB (487 9130/
www.knvb.nl).

Hockey

The Dutch who play hockey (of the non-ice
variety) and the fans who support them are a
breed apart. Hockey is hugely popular, and with
good reason: the Dutch – especially the ladies'
team – have a reputation for kicking some
serious butt. The **KNHB** ('Dutch Hockey
Association') boasts the largest number of
affiliated teams of any equivalent association in
the world. The 7,000-capacity Wagener Stadium
in Amstelveen is used for club games and
internationals. The season runs from September
until May. The many clubs in the area welcome
players and spectators; details of the local
teams are available from the **KNHB Bunnik**
(030 656 6444/www.knhb.nl).

Ever heard of hockey variations like
salibandy, innebandy or stockey? These are
all legitimate hockey-style games, with
some Dutch men's teams even competing
internationally. For further information, contact
the **Netherlands Floorball and Unihockey
Federation** (053 476 0566/www.nefub.nl).

The **Jaap Edenhal** (Radioweg 64, 694 9652/
www.jaapeden.nl) is Amsterdam's home to all
things ice – including ice hockey. Contact the
rink for information on when Amsterdam's
own Amstel Tigers are playing.

Kaatsen

A forerunner to tennis, but using the hands to
hit the ball, *kaatsen* was banned between 1500
and 1750 because of the nuisance it caused.
However, this authentic Dutch sport – played
on a field 60 metres by 32 metres (197 feet by
105 feet) with two teams of three players – is

still popular in Friesland, where many contests are held. Contact governing body the **KNKB** (0517 397 300/www.knkb.nl) or the **KC Amsterdam Kaatsclub** (613 5679) for details.

Korfball

Developed by an Amsterdam teacher in 1902, *korfball* is best described as a quirky form of basketball. Its appeal has always been strong in the Netherlands and has grown considerably abroad. The season has three stages: from September to mid-November and from April to June, games are played outdoors, while from mid-November to March, it heads indoors. Contact the Amsterdam **KNKV** (471 3236/ www.noordwest.knkv.nl) for more details.

Motor sport

TT Races

TT Circuit Assen (0592 321 321/www.tt-assen.com/ advance tickets from TT Assen, Postbus 150, 9400 AD Assen, fax 0592 356 911). Exit Assen south off A28, then follow signs. **Date** *Grand Prix late June.* **Tickets** €40-€70. **No credit cards**.
Book tickets in time for when Grand Prix mania takes over the recently renovated Assen in late June.

Zandvoort

Circuit Park Zandvoort, Burgermeester Van Alphenstraat 108, Zandvoort (023 574 0750/ www.circuit-zandvoort.nl). NS rail Zandvoort. **Tickets** €7-€21. **No credit cards**.
This track, 40 minutes' drive from Amsterdam, was once a venue for Formula One racing. A programme of international races runs roughly every other weekend from March to October, with tickets available from 8am on the day.

Rugby

More than 100 clubs, both men's and women's, take part in various competitions throughout the country, with four clubs active in Amsterdam. The season runs September to May. For information on the Heineken Rugby Sevens tournament, matches or clubs that welcome new members, contact the **National Rugby Board** (480 8100/info@rugby.nl).

Volleyball

Thanks to the success of both men's and women's national teams, volleyball's popularity continues to rise in Holland. For details of events and local clubs, contact the national office of **NeVoBo** (0348 411 994/www. volleybal.nl) or its Amsterdam office (693 6458/www.holland.nevobo.nl).

Fitness & leisure

Athletics

Amsterdam boasts four athletic tracks: Elzenhagen, Olympiaplein, Ookmeer and Chris Bergerbaan. *Trimloopboekje*, published every August, lists all running events in the Netherlands. The four major events in Amsterdam are the **Vondelparkloop** in January; June's **Grachtenloop** around the city's canals (*see p181*); September's **Dam tot Damloop** from Amsterdam to Zaandam (*see p182*); and the **Amsterdam Marathon** in October. Further details on athletics in Holland are available from the **KNAU** (030 608 7300/ www.knau.nl).

Keep on runnin': **Olympisch Stadion**. *See p109.*

The word of the Redeemer

The attitudes of Dutch philosophy's major figures can often be summed up in pithy one-liners. Erasmus has his 'In the land of the blind, the one-eyed man is king', Descartes his 'Cogito ergo sum', and Spinoza his 'We are a part of nature as a whole, whose order we follow'. But Johan Cruijff is a case apart.

First, of course, he was a footballer. But he was a great footballer, and perhaps the most famous living Dutchman. As a member of Ajax and the Dutch national team in the 1960s and '70s, he personified 'total football', which he later fine-tuned as coach of Barcelona and applied at his Johan Cruijff University, where players learn to deal with life after retirement.

Cruijff, though, also commentates for big games on TV, where he has become a legend all over again. His sayings, which have been collected into best-selling books, invoke wonder by the way they make perfect sense in a strangely nonsensical way. After meditating deeply on the following shafts of insight, you'll see why it's not just his initials that earned him the nickname 'the Redeemer'.

'Football should always be played beautifully.'

'If you don't score, you don't win.'

'You should put the point on the 'i' where it belongs.'

'Every disadvantage has its advantage.'

'Coincidence is logical.'

'You should never cheer before the bear is shot.'

'The game always begins afterwards.'

'He heard the clock strike but didn't know what time it was.'

'A balloon keeps going deeper into the water until it bursts. Whenever things do not work, you realise the importance of details (details that have gone wrong in the detail).'

'A mistake begins where it's supposed to begin.'

'Either you are on time or late; therefore if you are late you must make sure you leave on time.'

'If I wanted you to understand it, I would have explained it better.'

Badminton

Contact the **Amsterdam Badminton Union** (697 3758) for more details on the sport in the city. On the national level the **NBB** (030 604 7496/www.badminton.nl) handles matters.

Basketball

While public basketball courts are a rarity in the city centre, there are several clubs in Amsterdam that welcome players: contact the **NBB** Amsterdam office (0251 272 417/ www.dunk.nl) for details.

Golf

Golf, anyone? Golf, everyone! The popularity now enjoyed by this once-exclusive sport is remarkable. During the week, things are quite comfortable, but the local courses fill up quickly during weekends with players of all standards. A safety certificate is required for private courses, but public courses are open to all, with many offering driving ranges if you want to tune up your game before you head out on the course. You can play at a private club if introduced by a member, or if you belong to a British club. For details, see the *Gouden Gids* or contact the Amsterdam Golf Club (497 7866).

Golfbaan Sloten

Sloterweg 1045, Sloten (614 2402). Bus 145. **Open** *Mid June-mid Aug* 8.30am-dusk daily. *Mid Aug-mid June* 8.30am-6pm Mon-Fri. **Rates** €13. **No credit cards.**
A nine-hole public course, with a driving range and practice green. Booking is advisable on weekends.

Golfbaan Spaarnwoude

Het Hogeland 2, Velsen-Zuid, Spaarnwoude (023 538 5599/www.golfbaanspaarnwoude.nl). Bus 82. **Open** *Summer* 6.30am-8.30pm daily. *Winter* 8.30am-3.30pm daily. **Rates** *18-hole courses* €8-12; *pitch & putt* €5. **No credit cards.**
An 18-hole course, plus nine-holers and a pitch and putt. Bookings can be made up to three days ahead.

De Hoge Dijk

Abcouderstraatweg 46, Zuid-Oost (0294 281 241/ 0294 285 313). Metro Nieuw Gein; from Holendrecht stop, take bus 120, 126 to Abcoude. **Open** dawn-dusk daily. **Rates** *18-hole* €37, €42 wknd. *9-hole* €21; €25 wknd. *Short course* €16; €19 wknd. **Credit** AmEx, DC, MC, V.
A public 18-hole polder course on the edge of Amsterdam. Reservations are required.

Health & fitness

Amsterdam has an interesting collection of health clubs thanks to proprietors' willingness to set up shop in the Dutch capital's quirky old

Amsterdam Arena vs Mount Zion

It's a funny thing, but Amsterdam's long Jewish history seems to have its greatest champions in Ajax's 'F-side' football hooligans. They often wear Stars of David around their necks, call themselves 'Super Jews', wave Israeli flags in the stadium and chant 'we are the Jews, we are the Jews' (to which fans of the opposing team reply with a chant that would make Hamas proud). Perhaps football is indeed war...

Though it originated in 1900 as a middle-class club in Amsterdam East, where the many resident Jews provided its fan base, Ajax is not a particularly Jewish club. As the club president once said, 'These fans are about as Jewish as I am Chinese.' But there's no denying the fundamental influence Jews have had here since the 17th century, when Amsterdam was the only city in Europe in which Jews were free to settle. Yiddish-derived words still pepper Amsterdam slang;

even the city's nickname, *Mokum*, means 'the place'. The standard farewell remains *mazzel* (from *mazeltov*); a close friend is a *gabber*, a word that evolved from being an F-side favourite to becoming the global name for hardcore techno music. Sadly, World War II showed another side to Amsterdammers' feelings about their Jewish neighbours. Over 75,000 local Jews were deported and never came home, and, by Nazi request, Ajax axed all their Jewish members.

So why the 'Jewish pride' among Ajax hooligans? Well, it all began as a response to the anti-Semitic chants of hooligans from competing teams; and it has to be said that many hooligans have no clue that their 'Star of Ajax' is in fact the Star of David. But rest assured: this is all just a curious footnote to the full Ajax story of football glory. That said, if you do go to see Ajax play, best leave your Palestinian shawl at home.

Arts & Entertainment

houses. Look under 'Fitnesscentra' in the *Gouden Gids* for a full listing of health centres. If you are coming for a longer stay, check out Amsterdam's hippest health club, **Shape All-In** (2e Hugo de Grootstraat 2-6, 684 5857/ www.shape-all-in.nl) which, alas, only offers long-term memberships.

Barry's Fitness Centre
Lijnbaansgracht 350, Southern Canal Belt (626 1036). *Tram 16, 24, 25.* **Open** 7am-11pm Mon-Fri; 8am-8pm Sat; 9am-6pm Sun. **Admission** €10/day; €23/wk; €60/mth. **No credit cards. Map** p311 E5.
This excellent club earned a stellar ranking from *Men's Health.* You'll find free weights and machines, cardio-vascular equipment, aerobics, massage and sauna. Individual trainers can help if required (by appointment).

The Garden
Jodenbreestraat 158, Jodenbuurt (626 8772). Tram 9, 14/Metro Waterlooplein. **Open** 9am-11pm Mon, Wed, Fri; noon-11pm Tue; noon-10pm Thur; 9am-2pm Sat, Sun. **Admission** €11.50/day; €45-€60/mth; €77/10 visits. **No credit cards. Map** p307 E3.
The cheapest all-in-one price in town gives you the choice of high- and low-impact and step aerobics, bodyshape, callisthenics and stretching. There's also a sun studio, hairdressers, and masseurs.

Horse riding

The two main centres – **De Amsterdamse Manege** (643 1342) and **Nieuw Amstelland Manege** (643 2468) – both offer rides daily in

the Amsterdam Bos for about €15/hour; lessons are available for kids. For more details, see 'Maneges' in the *Gouden Gids.*

Saunas

Leave your modesty in the changing room when visiting a sauna in Amsterdam: covering up is frowned upon in most places. Unless stated otherwise, saunas are mixed, but most do offer women-only sessions. See also the *Gouden Gids* under 'Sauna's'. For **Sauna Fenomeen**, *see p204.*

Deco Sauna
Herengracht 115, Western Canal Belt (623 8215/ www.saunadeco.nl). Tram 1, 2, 5, 13, 17. **Open** noon-11pm Mon-Sat; 1-6pm Sun. **Admission** from €12.50. **No credit cards. Map** p306 C2.
The most beautiful sauna in town has art deco glass panels and murals. Facilities include a Turkish bath, a Finnish sauna, a cold plunge bath and a solarium. Massages, shiatsu, and skin and beauty care are all available by appointment.

De Keizer
Keizersgracht 124, Western Canal Belt (622 7504). Tram 1, 2, 5, 13, 17. **Open** noon-11pm Mon, Wed, Fri, Sat; 10am-11pm Tue, Thur; noon-8pm Sun. **Admission** from €12.50. **No credit cards. Map** p306 C2.
Tucked away in the servants' quarters of an 18th-century canal house is a full sauna that conjures up Hollywood interpretations of ancient Rome.

Skateboarding, rollerblading & rollerskating

Skater dudes and dudettes flaunt their skills on the half-pipe at **Museumplein** (*see p106*) and in parks elsewhere in the city. Rollerblading is hugely popular as a sport and mode of transport, with bike paths doubling as skating paths (be wary of irritated cyclists). **Vondelpark** (*see p107*) is heaven for skaters. If it's dry, check out the informal and popular tour around Amsterdam that is **Friday Night Skate** (www.fridaynightskate.nl). Wearing protective gear and blinkers is strongly encouraged, and you must be able to stop at intersections.

Consult the *Gouden Gids* under 'Sport en Spelartikelen' for a complete list of specialist shops and rental locations.

Vondeltuin/Rent A Skate

Vondelpark 7; entrance at Amstelveenseweg, Museum Quarter (664 5091/www.vondeltuin.nl). Tram 1, 2, 3, 5, 6, 12. **Open** *Apr* 11am-9pm daily. *May* 11am-11pm daily. *Jun-Aug* 10am-11pm daily. *Sep* 11am-10pm daily. Closed Oct-Mar. **Rates** from €5. **No credit cards. Map** p310 C6.

There are two branches in Vondelpark: one at the café by the Amstelveenseweg, the other over at the Melkgroothuis.

Skate Zone

Ceintuurbaan 57-59 (662 2822/www.skatezone.nl). Tram 12, 24, 25. **Open** 1-6pm Mon; 10am-6pm Tue, Wed, Fri; 10am-9pm Thur; 10am-5pm Sun. **No credit cards. Map** p311 E6.

This shop stocks a huge supply of skates and accessories in a wide range of sizes. They also rent skates and give lessons.

Skating

The Dutch need no convincing about the Greenhouse Effect. Many remember learning to skate by pushing an old wooden chair across a frozen pond or canal, but these days conditions are rarely right – the ice must be very thick, which is why the **Elfstedentocht** – a 200-kilometre (124-mile) race round Friesland – hasn't been held since 1997. With up to 10,000 people taking part – starting early and finishing by dusk – it's a massive national event. You must be a member of the Elfstedenvereniging association to compete and, even then, lots are drawn as numbers are limited. However, exceptions are sometimes made for foreigners.

If the canals freeze over in Amsterdam and you fancy a skate, be careful: the ice is often weak. If in doubt, ask one of the locals. The reflection pool at Museumplein is meant to accommodate ice skaters who can't wait for frozen canals. If winter's just too balmy for ice, head to the **Jaap Edenhal** 400-metre (437-yard) ice track at Radioweg 64 (694 9652/ www.jaapeden.nl). Some of the ponds and lakes in and around Amsterdam may also offer safe opportunities: contact the **KNSB** in Amersfoort (0334 621 784/www.knsb.nl) for details on conditions and organised events.

Snooker & carambole

There are several halls in Amsterdam where you can play snooker or pool fairly cheaply. Carambole, played on a table without pockets, is a popular variation. Traditionally, billiards (*biljart*) has been associated with cafés: outside

Roll play: **Vondelpark**.

Strip off, dive in: **Zuiderbad**. *See p239.*

the centre of town, there are many cafés with billiards and pool tables. In town, many bars have pool tables, though they're often scruffy. For a full listing of clubs look in the *Gouden Gids* under 'Biljartzalen'.

De Keizer
Keizersgracht 256, Western Canal Belt (623 1586). Tram 13, 14, 17. **Open** 1pm-1am Mon-Thur, Sun; 1pm-2am Fri, Sat. **Rates** €5-€7 pool; €6-€8 snooker. **No credit cards. Map** p306 C3.
The most civilised club in town has two pro-sized pool tables and seven snooker tables, all in separate rooms. Players can phone orders down to the bar and have drinks or sandwiches sent up. Members pay less for tables, but all are welcome.

Snookercentre Bavaria
Van Ostadestraat 97, the Pijp (676 4059). Tram 3, 12, 24, 25. **Open** 2pm-1am Mon-Thur, Sun; 2pm-2am Fri, Sat. **Rates** €7.30/hr pool; €7.80/hr snooker. **No credit cards. Map** p311 F6.
Occupying four floors, the Bavaria boasts one carambole table, 26 billiards tables and seven snooker tables, with the first floor a pool hall. Some nights are reserved for members only.

Snooker & Poolclub Oud-West
Overtoom 209, Museum Quarter (618 8019). Tram 1/bus 171, 172. **Open** 10am-1am Mon-Tue, Sun; 10am-2am Fri, Sat. **Rates** €8. **No credit cards. Map** p309 B6.
The atmosphere in this former church is quiet, making it a club for the serious snooker player. Members pay less per hour.

Squash

For information on local clubs, phone the **Amsterdam Squash Rackets Club** on 662 8767. Details of squash courts can be found in the *Gouden Gids* under 'Squashbanen'.

Squash City
Ketelmakerstraat 6, Westerpark (626 7883). Bus 18, 22. **Open** 8.45am-midnight Mon-Fri; 8.45am-9pm Sat, Sun. **Rates** €6.80/45min before 5pm; €9/45min after 5pm. **Credit** MC, V.
Squash City is the place to come to if you see squash as more of a hobby than a form of warfare. There are 12 courts, a sauna, a weights room and two aerobics rooms.

Swimming

Public pools in Amsterdam usually have rigidly scheduled programmes for babies, toddlers, women, families, nude swimmers and those who want to swim lengths. Opening times vary for both indoor and outdoor pools; some indoor pools close during the summer holidays. While it's best to phone ahead, most pools set aside lanes for swimming lengths in the early morning, mid-afternoon and evening. Look in the *Gouden Gids* under 'Zwembaden' for a full list of pools.

Brediusbad (outdoor)
Spaarndammerdijk 306, Westerpark (684 7172). Bus 22, 55. **Open** May-Aug 7-9am, 10am-6pm Mon-Fri; 10am-6pm Sat, Sun. **Admission** €1.20. **No credit cards.**
Kiddie pools and high diving boards make this a delightful swimming pool to visit when the weather's good. Nude swimming is allowed during early weekday sessions.

Flevoparkbad (outdoor)
Zeeburgerdijk 630, Oost (692 5030). Tram 14. **Open** May-early Sept 10am-5.30pm (10am-7pm in hotter weather) daily. **Admission** from €2. **No credit cards.**
This outdoor set-up near to Flevopark has two huge pools with kids' areas, a playground and a sunbathing area. A charming spot.

Amstelpark

*Koenenkade 8, Amstelveen (301 0700/
www.amstelpark.nl). Bus 170, 171, 172 from
Amsterdam Centraal Station; 169 from Amstel
Station.* **Open** *Apr-Oct* 8am-11pm Mon-Fri; 8am-9pm
Sat, Sun. *Nov-Mar* 8am-midnight Mon-Fri; 8am-11pm
Sat, Sun. **Rates** outdoor court €20/hr; indoor €25/hr.
Credit AmEx, DC, MC, V.
All in all, 42 courts: during the summer, there are
ten indoor courts, and in the winter six of the out-
door courts are covered over. There are also 12
squash courts, a Turkish bath, a sauna, a swimming
pool and a shop. Racket hire is €3.

Tennishal Kadoelen

*Sportpark Kadoelen 5, Kadoelenweg, Noord (631
3194). Bus 92.* **Open** 9am-11pm daily. **Rates** €14-
€19/hr. **No credit cards.**
Kadoelen is subsidised by the local council, so the
nine indoor courts cost less to hire than elsewhere.
Tennis lessons can be arranged in advance.

Ten-pin bowling

There are a fair few bowling lanes in
Amsterdam; see the *Gouden Gids* under
'Bowlingbanen'. Phone the **Nederlandse
Bowling Federatie** on 010 473 5581 for more
details on all aspects of the sport, including
competitions and leagues.

Knijn Bowling

*Scheldeplein 3, Zuid (664 2211/www.knijnbowling.
nl). Tram 4.* **Open** 10am-1am Mon-Fri; noon-1am
Sat; noon-midnight Sun. **Rates** €15.80/lane before
5pm; €21.50/lane after 5pm; Sun €24.50/lane; twilight
bowl (Fri 11pm-12.30am; Sat 11.30pm-1am) €11/
person. **No credit cards.**

Watersports

The Dutch are very good at making do with
what they've got, which is one of the reasons
why watersports are very popular here. If
you want to go sailing, visit Loosdrecht (25
kilometres/15 miles south-east of Amsterdam)
or go to the IJsselmeer. Catamarans can be
rented in Muiden (20 kilometres/12 miles
east of Amsterdam). For details on canoeing,
phone the **NKB** (033 462 2341/www.nkb.nl).
Most watersports schools ask for a deposit
and ID when you rent a boat.
There are rowing clubs on the Amstel and
at the Bosbaan (the former Olympic rowing
course) in the Amsterdam Bos. For further
information, call the **KNRB** ('Dutch Rowing
Union') on 646 2740.

Gaasperplas Park

*Gaasperplas Park, South-East. Metro Gaasperplas/
bus 59, 60, 174.* **Open** 24hrs daily.
This park's large lake is a centre for watersports and
windsurfing. There's also a campsite.

Mirandabad (indoor & outdoor)

*De Mirandalaan 9, Zuid (622 8080/644 6637/
www.mirandabad.nl). Tram 25/bus 15, 169.*
Open 7am-10pm Mon-Fri; 10am-5pm Sat, Sun.
Admission €3.50. **No credit cards.**
The only sub-tropical pool in Amsterdam, De
Mirandabad is very clean, with a stone beach and a
wave machine. It's not good for swimming lengths,
but there's fun to be had on the waterslide and in the
whirlpool and outdoor pool. There are also squash
courts and a restaurant.

Zuiderbad (indoor)

*Hobbemastraat 26, Museum Quarter (678 1390).
Tram 2, 16, 24, 25.* **Open** 7am-6pm Mon, Thur;
7am-10pm Tue, Wed, Fri; 8am-3.30pm Sat; 10am-
3.30pm Sun. **Admission** from €2.80. **No credit
cards. Map** p310 D6.
One of the country's oldest pools, the beautifully
mosaic-rich Zuiderbad was built in 1912. Nude
swimming on Sundays, 4.30-5.30pm.

Table tennis

For details of clubs, contact the **Nederlandse
Tafeltennis Bond** on 079 341 4811.

Amsterdam 78

*Schoolstraat 2, Museum Quarter (683 7829). Tram
1, 6.* **Open** 7-11am Mon, Tue, Thur-Sat; 2-7pm Wed,
Sun. **Rates** €2.50/per person (incl bats and balls).
No credit cards.
One of the few places where you can both ping and
pong in town. Booking is recommended.

Tennis

For details on competitions – including
August's **Dutch Open** – and clubs, call the
national **KNLTB** office on 033 454 2600. For
a full listing of courts see the *Gouden Gids*
under 'Tennisparken en-hallen'.

Arts & Entertainment

Theatre, Comedy & Dance

There's some tradition, but Amsterdam's performers mostly enter stage left.

Theatre

Boundaries, on the Dutch theatre scene, are things to be crossed, stretched, transgressed – or forgotten altogether. This forthright way of working makes for some vibrant theatre – even as many of the larger Amsterdam venues still make a good living supplying straightforward plays and musicals.

In linguistic terms, too, there's a good mix. Plenty of productions are in English, some from start to finish, some in parallel with a number of other tongues. And then there are the shows that jettison language entirely. We're not talking hokey mime shows: some of the city's wordless performances have been regarded as the pinnacles of Dutch theatrical achievement. Dogtroep's recent international production in Moscow (*see p249* **Over the edge**) is a case in point. English-language theatre also has a very happy booker in Xaviera 'Happy Hooker' Hollander (673 3934/www.xavierahollander. com/booker; *see also p68*), who regularly brings Edinburgh Festival talent to a variety of venues around town.

Faced with dismal economic forecasts and a centre-right coalition that aims to cut arts funding, culture officials are now looking for commercial sponsorship to finance significant productions. The severe reduction in funds has had the effect of forcing smaller outfits to pool resources and look for alternative venues. Happily, this has led to some interesting partnerships in unconventional places – say, the NDSM Shipyard (*see p243*) in Amsterdam Noord, a complex intended to accommodate many small groups. A goodly number of performances take place out of doors, especially in the squares. Open-air theatre fosters a circus-meets-carnival atmosphere – or it does when the weather cooperates. Keep your eyes open for festivals such as **Parade** and **Boulevard** (for both, *see p244*).

Most of Amsterdam's non-itinerant theatres are distributed around two main areas. Around Leidseplein, the **Stadschouwburg** and the **Bellevue** (for both, *see p243*) are the most established and noteworthy. Meanwhile, the fabulously narrow Nes is the address of some truly innovative (but mostly Dutch) theatres that settled there in the heady 1960s. There are also three main theatres which hold their own regardless of their location: the **Muziektheater** on Waterlooplein (*see p248*), **De Kleine Komedie** on the Amstel (*see p241*) and **Koninklijk Theater Carré** on the Amsteldijk (*see p243*).

TICKETS AND INFORMATION

For further information about what's on in Amsterdam, call or visit the **Uitburo** on Leidseplein (*see p279* **Tickets please**) or the **Amsterdam Tourist Board** (*see p289*). Browsing through the former's free monthly *Uitkrant* will give a sound idea of programming in and around the city.

The four Nes theatres – **De Brakke Grond, Cosmic, De Engelenbak** and **Frascati** (for all, *see p241*) – now all have a central box office (Nes 45, 626 6866/www.nestheaters.nl, 1-7.30pm Mon-Sat). Only between 7.30pm and the start of the performance do the theatres open their own box offices.

Theatres

Azart Ship of Fools

Azartplein, Eastern Docklands (06 1790 0252 mobile/ www.azart.org). Bus 32, 59/Nightbus 79. **Tickets** free-€7. **No credit cards.**
The wackiest news first: this 'sailing artists collective' is based in a large and happily apocalyptic boat docked amid some decidedly unchaotic architecture. In the summer, they put on performances that combine cabaret, over-the-top costumes, music, and slapstick. They also host a free nightclub every Friday night from 11pm.

Badhuis Theater de Bochel

Boerhaaveplein 28, Oost (668 5102). Tram 3, 6, 7, 10. **Box office** 30min before performance. **Tickets** €4-€6. **No credit cards. Map** p312 G4.
A bathhouse turned cultural centre, the Badhuis Theater de Bochel stages a variety of productions that tackle multicultural and non-western themes. Performance parties dominate Saturday evenings, but other activities such as workshops and children's theatre are held regularly.

De Balie

Kleine Gartmanplantsoen 10, Southern Canal Belt (553 5100/www.balie.nl). Tram 1, 2, 5, 6, 7, 10. **Box office** 1-6pm or until start of performance Mon-Fri; 5pm-start of performance Sat; 90min before performance Sun. **Tickets** €5-€8. **No credit cards.** **Map** p310 D5.

Theatre, new media, cinema (*see p193*) and literary events sit alongside lectures, debates, discussions and political projects at this cultural centre; all informally influence the intelligentsia. There's a café, too.

De Brakke Grond

Nes 45, Old Centre: Old Side (622 9014/www.brakke grond.nl). Tram 4, 9, 14, 16, 24, 25. **Box office** *see p240.* **Tickets** €10. **No credit cards.** **Map** p306 D3. De Brakke Grond aims to spread the word about progressive theatre and Flemish culture in an intimate setting. Expect, though, rather more of the former than the latter.

Cosmic Theater

Nes 75, Old Centre: Old Side (622 8858/www.cosmic theater.nl). Tram 4, 9, 14, 16, 24, 25. **Box office** *see p240.* **Tickets** €10. **No credit cards.** **Map** p306 D3.

Cosmic formed 20 years ago in the Caribbean and, after a spell in New York, ended up here. The company has toured widely and developed an international reputation for its productions, which address the multicultural realities of the modern world.

De Engelenbak

Nes 71, Old Centre: Old Side (information 625 9375/ www.engelenbak.nl). Tram 4, 9, 14, 16, 24, 25. **Box office** *see p240.* **Tickets** €10. **No credit cards.** **Map** p306 D3.

The famous draw here is Open Bak, an open-stage event (Tuesdays at 10.30pm) where virtually anything goes. It's the longest-running theatre

The best Venues

Boom Chicago
It's just fun. *See p246.*

Danceworks Rotterdam
Leave the modern dance to the kids from the modern city. *See p250.*

Nederlands Dans Theater
Sometimes no introduction is necessary. *See p250.*

Nes Theatres
Less than conventional. *See p241.*

Parade
A proven mix of the performing arts and carnival-like wackiness. *See p244.*

programme in the Netherlands, where everybody gets their 15 minutes of potential fame; arrive at least half an hour early to get a ticket (€6.50). Otherwise, the best amateur groups in the country perform between Thursday and Saturday.

Felix Meritis

Keizersgracht 324, Western Canal Belt (623 1311/www.felixmeritis.nl). Tram 1, 2, 5, 13, 17. **Box office** 9am-7pm Mon-Fri, or until start of performance; 90min before start of performance Sat, Sun. **Tickets** prices vary. **No credit cards.** **Map** p310 C4.

The Felix Meritis stages a variety of international dance and theatre performances alongside its noted programme of discussions, lectures and courses about Europe and other subjects. Worth visiting, if just to see the building: built in 1787, it's a handsome structure overlooking the Keizersgracht.

Frascati

Nes 63, Old Centre: Old Side (626 6866/www.nes theaters.nl). Tram 4, 9, 14, 16, 24, 25. **Box office** *see p240.* **Tickets** €10. **No credit cards.** **Map** p306 D3.

Forming a true cornerstone of the Dutch theatre scene since the 1960s, Frascati gives promising writers the chance to stage their productions on one of its three stages. Programming is varied throughout the week and Sundays feature established artists (not necessarily thespians) who put on both improvised and rehearsed events. Check out the 250 Kuub, a freestyle production that lets actors make up their act as they go along, albeit within certain constraints. Members of the audience are free to come and go as they please, and there's no cover charge.

Gasthuis Werkplaats & Theater

Marius van Bouwdijk Bastiaansestraat 54, entrance opposite 1e Helmerstraat 115, Museum Quarter (616 8942/www.theatergasthuis.nl). Tram 1, 3, 6, 12. **Box office** *By phone* noon-5pm Mon-Fri. *In person* 1hr before performance. **Tickets** €8. **No credit cards.** **Map** p305 B6.

Gasthuis emerged from a group of squatters who managed to become the critics' darling in just a few years. Even when their home, a former hospital, was threatened with demolition, their activities contributed towards the building's salvation. Young theatre students trying out their talent and smaller productions often use Gasthuis. The programme is mainly experimental; check beforehand whether the production is in English.

De Kleine Komedie

Amstel 56, Southern Canal Belt (624 0534/ www.dekleinekomedie.nl). Tram 4, 9, 14, 16, 24, 25. **Box office** noon-6pm Mon-Sat; noon-performance on performance days. **Tickets** €10-€15. **No credit cards.** **Map** p307 E3.

One of Amsterdam's oldest and most important theatres, De Kleine Komedie is the country's premier cabaret stage, though it also offers a wide range of musical acts. Wildly popular among locals, it's one of the more characterful Amsterdam venues.

Arts & Entertainment

Dance festivals

In July every year, the **Stadsschouwburg** (pictured; *see p243*) hosts Julidans (www.julidans.nl), a month-long showcase of international dance. The International Concours for Choreographers in Groningen, meanwhile, is a competition event at which prizes are awarded for ensemble choreographies. Details about the events' various festivals, competitions, performances, courses and workshops are available from the **Theater Instituut** (*see p87*).

For details of the Holland Festival and Uitmarkt, two multicultural festivals that include a number of noteworthy dance performances from around the world in their pleasingly eclectic calendars, *see p181* and *p182* respectively.

Cadans

Korzo Theater, The Hague (070 363 7540/www.korzo.nl/Postbus 13407, 2501 EK, Den Haag). **Dates** Nov 2004.
The Hague's exciting international festival of contemporary dance takes place every other winter in the Hague (it alternates yearly with the Holland Dance Festival). Each work is choreographed specifically for the festival.

Holland Dance Festival

Nobelstraat 21, 2513 BC The Hague (070 361 6142/www.hollanddancefestival.com). **Date** biennial; next held in Nov 2005.
Held every two years in November, the Holland Dance Festival takes place at three different venues, including the Hague's Lucent Danstheater (*see p248*), and is easily the biggest and most important festival on the Dutch dance calendar. Many of the world's larger companies are attracted to the event – 2003's festival featured companies from almost 20 countries – and the quality of the work is consistently high. Though a variety of Dutch acts usually perform at the event, Nederlands Dans Theater (*see p250*) is invariably the country's main representative.

Spring Dance

Postbus 111, 3500 AC Utrecht (030 230 3880/www.springdance.nl). **Dates** Apr-May.
Spring Dance, held annually in Utrecht in late April and early May, attempts to give an overview of recent developments in contemporary dance, film and music from around the world.

Koninklijk Theater Carré

Amstel 115-25, Southern Canal Belt (622 5225/ 0900 252 5255 premium rate/www.theatercarre.nl). Tram 4, 6, 7, 10/Metro Weesperplein. **Box office** 10am-7pm Mon-Sat; 1-7pm Sun. **Tickets** €12-€16. **Credit** AmEx, MC, V. **Map** p311 F4.

Formerly home to a circus, the Carré now hosts some of the best Dutch comedians and cabaret artists around, and also stages opera. However, if mainstream theatre is more your thing, look out for Dutch versions of popular musicals such as *Mamma Mia*, *Cats* and *Oliver*, which usually end up here.

De Nieuw Amsterdam

Grote Bickersstraat 2/4, Westerdok, the Waterfront (627 8672/www.denieuwamsterdam.nl). Bus 18, 22. **Box office** 10am-5pm Mon-Fri; also 7.30pm-start of performance. **Tickets** €7; €6 students. **No credit cards. Map** p305 B1.

The brainchild of director Rufus Collins, De Nieuw Amsterdam is the leading socially aware theatre company in the Netherlands, and in fact usually performs at other venues such as Bellevue and Cosmic. It also runs a programme for young people set on becoming the next big thing, known as ITS DNA.

Het Rozentheater & Het Compagnietheater

Het Rozentheater *Rozengracht 117, the Jordaan (620 7953/www.rozentheater.nl). Tram 13, 17.* **Box office** 10am-5pm Mon-Sat, and 1hr before start of performance. **Performances** 8.30pm. **Tickets** €8-€10. **No credit cards. Map** p305 B3.

Het Compagnietheater *Kloveniersburgwal 50, Old Centre: Old Side (520 5320/www.theater compagnie.nl). Tram 4, 9, 14, 16, 24, 25.* **Box office** 10am-5.30pm Mon-Sat, and from 1hr before start of performance. **Performances** 8pm. **Tickets** €8-€10. **No credit cards. Map** p306 D3.

A few years ago, two production companies – De Trust and Art & Pro – allied themselves in a bid to increase their profile. Now working under the name De Theatercompagnie, they produce culturally and politically aware work for three theatres: Het Rozentheater (closed for renovation until September 2004), where the shows address themes popular amongst 15- to 30-year-olds; Het Compagnietheater, where the focus is on the work of modern Dutch writers; and a touring group, who aren't bound to one type of production or site; De Stadsschouwburg (*see below*) is home to most of their premieres.

De Stadsschouwburg

Leidseplein 26, Southern Canal Belt (624 2311/ www.stadsschouwburgamsterdam.nl). Tram 1, 2, 5, 6, 7, 10. **Box office** 10am-6pm or until start of performance Mon-Sat; from noon to before start of performance Sun. **Tickets** €8-€18. **Credit** AmEx, MC, V. **Map** p310 C5.

The Stadsschouwburg (or Municipal Theatre) is into its third incarnation, the first two buildings having been destroyed by fire in the 17th and 18th centuries. The present theatre, which opened in 1894, is a beautiful and impressive baroque building, built in the traditional horseshoe shape and seating about 950. Apart from nurturing traditional Dutch theatre, it also stages a decent variety of contemporary national and international productions. The programme consists chiefly of theatre but there's also dance, modern music and light opera. The theatre's Bovenzaal space plays host to small-scale productions that are often in English.

Theater Bellevue & Nieuwe de la Mar Theater

Theater Bellevue *Leidsekade 90, Southern Canal Belt (530 5301/www.theaterbellevue.nl). Tram 1, 2, 5, 6, 7, 10.* **Box office** 11am-start of performance daily. **Tickets** prices vary. **Credit** AmEx, DC, MC, V. **Map** p310 C5.

Nieuwe de la Mar Theater *Marnixstraat 404, Western Canal Belt (530 5302/www.nieuwedelamar theater.nl). Tram 1, 2, 5, 6, 7, 10.* **Box office** 6pm-start of performance daily. **Tickets** prices vary. **Credit** AmEx, DC, MC, V. **Map** p310 C5.

They may have fused in 1987, but these two theatres close to Leidseplein have distinct histories and specialities. The Bellevue dates from 1840 and presents popular theatre on its three stages: one for modern theatre, dance and music, one devoted to cabaret and a third for literary events. The younger Nieuwe de la Mar, which was founded in 1947, offers dance, serious spoken theatre, cabaret and an increasing number of musical productions, all performed by a mix of hot Dutch talent and imported international artists.

Theater de Cameleon

3e Kostverlorenkade 35, West (489 4656/www.de cameleon.nl). Tram 1. **Box office** noon-6pm daily. **Tickets** €3-€10. **No credit cards. Map** p305 A3.

A relatively new theatre in the old western part of town, De Cameleon, besides a wide variety of theatre performances (often in English), also offers theatre and voice workshops for children and adults.

Zaal 100

De Wittenstraat 100, Westerpark (688 0127). Tram 3, 10/bus 18, 22. **Box office** from 1hr before start of performance. **Tickets** prices vary. **No credit cards. Map** p305 A2.

This neighbourhood cultural centre, in an ex-squat building, offers a sporadic programme in its small but cosy theatre space. The in-house group, Sub Theatre, usually performs one show a month. There are live jazz nights on Tuesdays, a big band gig every third Wednesday of the month, and performance poetry every third Thursday of the month.

Cultural complexes

Kinetic Noord at the NDSM Shipyard

TT Neveritaweg 15, Noord (330 5480/www.ndsm. nl). Ferry from Centraal Station/bus 35, 94.

NDSM was a shipbuilding yard at the beginning of the last century. Today it's a cultural complex that has yet to be completed, a fact that is in step with

Arts & Entertainment

the changing needs of Amsterdam's vibrant artistic community. It already stages some of the most provocative dance, mime and theatre productions in Amsterdam and its future looks bright. Apart from two stages (one of which is to be made completely of recycled materials), it serves as a 'breeding ground' for artists. Small-scale workshops and performances are held almost daily in its labyrinth of studios and performance areas. There are plans for a skate park and a sculpture garden as well as a cinema, gallery, art market and café. The large outdoor area, meanwhile, will afford spectacular views over the IJ river of Amsterdam.

Westergasfabriek

Haarlemmerweg 8-10, West (586 0710/www.wester gasfabriek.nl). Tram 10/Bus 18, 22.
Located in the newly inaugurated Culture Park Westerpark, the Westergasfabriek, the city's former gas works, is to be a unique home to cultural events of all shapes and sizes – both indoor and outdoor. However the main performance spaces for theatre will only open sometime in 2004. For details and tickets contact the Uitburo on 0900 0191. *See also p217* **It's a gas.**

Theatre festivals

For **Over het IJ**, *see p249* **Over the edge.**

Boulevard

's Hertogenbosch (073 613 7671/www.bossenova.nl). Date mid-Aug.
In an effort to promote the arts in Brabant, Boulevard is an initiative that turns the medieval town of Den Bosch ('s Hertogenbosch) into a summer of theatre and dance – with plenty of children's activities thrown into the mix. The main festival venues are tents erected in the square next to St Jan Cathedral, though performances are also staged in theatres and other, more unlikely locations. Among the companies who've taken part in recent years are Warner en Consorten, Hans Hof Ensemble and Australia's Snuff Puppets.

ITs Festival

Around Amsterdam (527 7613/www.its.ahk.nl). Date June.
Something of a theatrical talent-spotter's dream, the International Theaterschool Festival is where students from all over the world show what they can do. A mix of cabaret, dance, mime and drama takes place in the Theaterschool (*see p247*) and at several other venues in town. During the festival, many congregate at the ITs lounge in the Theaterschool building.

Oerol

PO Box 327, 8890 AA Midsland, Terschelling (0562 448448/www.oerol.nl). Date June.
Terschelling, one of the five Frisian islands that sit off the north coast of Holland, has a unique landscape shaped by wind dunes, dykes and woodlands.

A popular holiday destination among teenagers and bird lovers (more than half the island is a bird sanctuary), it becomes a bohemian haven during the Oerol festival. Around 200 acts perform: there might be international theatre groups creating their own environments, world music events on the beaches, theatre expeditions through the woods or bicycle tours. There's a regular ferry service to the island.

Parade

Martin Luther Kingpark, Zuid (033 465 4577/ www.mobilearts.nl). Date Aug.
This unique event has captured the essence of the old circus/sideshow atmosphere that's so conspicuously absent at today's commercial fairgrounds. Parade offers a plentiful selection of bizarre shows, many in beautiful circus tents; spread between them are cafés, bars and restaurants, as well as the odd roving performer. The event has become very popular, and many shows sell out quickly: go early, have dinner and book your tickets at the Parade Kiosk for the night (some smaller shows, however, sell their own tickets separately). For more, *see p181.*

Vondelpark Openluchttheater

Vondelpark (673 1499/www.openluchttheater.nl). Tram 1, 2, 3. Date late May-Aug.
Theatrical events have been held in Vondelpark since 1865, and the tradition continues each summer with a variety of free shows. Wednesdays offer a lunchtime concert and a mid-afternoon children's show; Thursday nights find a concert on the bandstand; there's a theatre show every Friday night; various events (including another theatre show) take place on Saturdays; and theatre events and pop concerts are held on Sunday afternoons. 2004 marks its 30th anniversary and there should be plenty in store.

Bookshop

International Theatre & Film Books

Leidseplein 26, in the Stadsschouwburg building, Southern Canal Belt (622 6489). Tram 1, 2, 5, 7, 10. **Open** noon-6pm Mon; 10am-6pm Tue, Wed, Fri, Sat; 10am-7pm Thur. **Credit** (min €45) AmEx, DC, MC, V. **Map** p310 C5.
This shop caters to the theatre and film enthusiast... and how. It's the largest store of its kind in Europe, offering everything from books on circuses and musicals to production and technical manuals. If it takes place on stage, this shop is sure to carry a book on it. There's plenty of stock in English.

Museum

For the **Theater Instituut**, *see p87.*

Comedy

While the Dutch have their own background and history in hilarity, thanks chiefly to their extremely singular take on cabaret, stand-up

Azart Ship of Fools. *See p240.*

comedy is a fairly recent import to the Netherlands in general and Amsterdam in particular. However, the last few years have seen it become popular in the city, and it continues to grow. Shows often feature a mix of foreign and local acts that may or may not do their schtick in English (call ahead to check).

Boom Chicago

Leidseplein Theater, Leidseplein 12, Southern Canal Belt (423 0101/www.boomchicago.nl). Tram 1, 2, 5, 6, 7, 10. **Box office** *noon-8.30pm Mon-Sun; noon-11.30pm Fri, Sat.* **Shows** *8.15pm Mon-Fri, Sun. Heineken Late Nite 11.30pm Fri.* **Tickets** *€17-€19. Heineken Late Nite €11.* **Credit** *AmEx, MC, V.* **Map** *p310 C5.*

American improv troupe Boom Chicago is one of Amsterdam's biggest success stories. With several different shows running seven nights a week (except Sundays in winter), all in English, the group offers a mix of rehearsed sketches and audience-prompted improvisation. Audiences are an eclectic mix of Dutch and international travellers; it's a potent mix that always delivers a memorable night. New show *Boom Chicago Saves the World (Sorry About the Mess)* opened in 2003; new shows usually launch every spring. The bar offers cocktails and DJs (*see also p141*) and is something of an unofficial meeting point for wayward Americans; a restaurant serves noon-9pm daily; and they even publish a free magazine for visitors to the city. A winner.

Boom Chicago.

Comedy Café Amsterdam

*Max Euweplein 43-5, Southern Canal Belt
(638 3971/24hr bookings 639 1165/www.comedy
cafe.nl). Tram 1, 2, 5, 6, 7, 10.* **Shows** 9pm
Wed-Sun; 9pm and 11.30pm Sat. **Tickets** €5 Wed;
€14 Thur-Sat; €11 Sun. **Credit** AmEx, MC, V.
Map p310 C5.

The Comedy Café has been doing a decent job of
bringing the art of stand-up to a wider audience.
From Thursday to Saturday, there's a stand-up
show in a heady blend of Dutch and English. On
Wednesdays, comics try out new material at the
venue's open mic night, while Sundays offer improv
show *Off Your Head*.

Toomler

*Breitnerstraat 2, Zuid (670 7400/www.toomler.nl).
Tram 2, 5, 16, 24.* **Box office** from 7pm (phone
reservations 5-10pm) Wed-Sat. **Shows** 8.30pm.
Tickets €11.50. **No credit cards.**

Located next to the Hilton, this café puts something
on four nights a week. Most programming is stand-
up in Dutch, but it's the Comedy Train International
in January, July and August, when English takes
over, that has come to be most closely associated
with the venue. They also serve up live music.

Dance

Dance is a speciality in Amsterdam. The
Nationale Ballet and Nederlands Dans Theater
are international legends. Their status draws
from renewal strategies inspired by the truly
rich productions put on throughout the country.
From classical to modern as well as events that
may not necessarily be classified as dance,
companies reinvent and hone dancing into
delightful productions.

This stimulating environment draws talent
from near and far. Choreographers, dancers
and trainers flock to Amsterdam especially
to discover a niche and perhaps break out of
it. Dutch dance companies regularly import
shows, challenging dancers to interpret and
audiences to receive messages that may not
have the intended cultural resonance. There
are even a number of troupes that specialise
in non-Western productions.

The conditions under which Dutch dance
has blossomed is not only attractive to dancers,
trainers and choreographers. Also audiences
stand to benefit. Big productions are easy
to spot, but some of the most interesting
performances may be taking place in a lesser-
known venue close to you. Many dance events
take place in fringe theatres, and local festivals
are great opportunities to get a taste of what
dance companies – or collaborations – offer.

To stray from the beaten path of the
Nationale Ballet and Nederlands Dans Theater,
you almost have to be an insider to know

exactly where to go or who to look out for. It's
impossible to give a full list here, but among
the Amsterdam-based choreographers worth
checking out are Krisztina de Châtel, Beppie
Blankert, Truus Bronkhorst, Shusaku
Takeuchi, Andrea Leine and Harijono Roebana,
Marcello Evelin and Katie Duck.

TICKETS AND INFORMATION

Tickets for the majority of performances can be
bought at the venues themselves, or from any
of the various phone, online or drop-in **AUB**
operations (*see p279* **Tickets please**); their
Uitkrant offers information on dance in the city.

Venues

Dance is performed at a variety of venues in
Amsterdam, the biggest of which are detailed
below. Other primarily theatrical venues also
stage some dance, such as the **Theater
Bellevue**, the **Stadsschouwburg** (for both,
see p243), the **Cosmic Theater** (*see p241*)
and **Kinetic Noord** (*see p243*).

Danswerkplaats Amsterdam

*Arie Biemondstraat 107B, Museum Quarter
(689 1789/www.danswerkplaats.nl). Tram 1, 11.*
Open *By phone* 10am-5pm Mon-Fri. *In person*
7.30pm-15min before start of performance.
Tickets €5.50-€7. **No credit cards.**

Danswerkplaats' dance studio has been staging performances once a month, both here and elsewhere in
the city or country, since 1993. Contemporary Dance
in Evolution is its motto and it hosts a variety of
performances throughout the year. For further
details, consult their website, which has basic information in English.

Het Veem Theater

*Van Diemenstraat 401 (626 9291/www.hetveem
theater.nl). Bus 35.* **Box office** 1hr before
performance. **Tickets** €9; €8 try-out; €3.50 dance
students. **No credit cards.**

A homophone for 'fame', Veem occupies the third
floor of a renovated warehouse and hosts modern
dance and media productions from home and
around the world. Performances usually take place
at 9pm; between October and March there's also a
Sunday slot at 4pm.

International Theaterschool

*Jodenbreestraat 3, Old Centre: Old Side (527 7700/
527 7620/www.its.ahk.nl). Tram 4, 9, 14, 16, 24,
25/Metro Waterlooplein.* **Box office** times vary.
Tickets free-€10. **No credit cards. Map** p307 E3.

International Theaterschool brings together students and teachers from all over the world to learn
and create in the fields of dance and theatre.
Performances – some of which are announced in
Uitkrant – vary from studio shots to evening-long
events in the Philip Morris Dans Zaal. An annual
showcase of talent is usually planned in June.

Melkweg

Lijnbaansgracht 234A, Western Canal Belt (531 8181/www.melkweg.nl). Tram 1, 2, 5, 6, 7, 10.
Box office 1-5pm Mon-Fri; 4-6pm Sat, Sun; also 7.30pm-start of performance. **Performances** usually at 8.30pm. **Tickets** €5-€10. *Membership* (compulsory) €2.50/mth. **No credit cards.** **Map** p310 C5.

This multidisciplinary venue (*see also p194, p197, p213 and p225*) opened its doors to national and international dance and theatre groups in 1973. For many years, the small stage hosted mainly dancers and choreographers at the start of their careers. Its renovated theatre lives up to tradition, as many of the country's hottest new companies perform here – scheduled between the higher profile mainstays. There's a café, too. As befits its one-stop eclecticism, special focus is placed on multimedia performances.

Muiderpoorttheater

2e Van Swindenstraat 26, Oost (668 1313/ www.muiderpoorttheater.nl). Tram 3, 9, 10, 14.
Tickets €8. **No credit cards. Map** p312 H2.
Muiderpoorttheater is known primarily for its performances by international acts. After a brief renovation in 2003, the theatre is set to reopen its doors in January 2004. The bi-weekly Mad Sunday will then resume, combining music, dance and improvisation. There are plenty of other activities planned in between; check the theatre's website or call for details.

Muziektheater

Amstel 3, Old Centre: Old Side (625 5455/www. muziektheater.nl). Tram 9, 14/Metro Waterlooplein.
Box office 10am-6pm or until start of performance Mon-Sat; 11.30am-6pm or until start of performance Sun. **Tickets** €17-€63. **Credit** AmEx, DC, MC, V. **Map** p307 E3.
The Muziektheater is Amsterdam at its most ambitious. This plush, crescent-shaped building, which opened in 1986, has room for 1,596 people and is home to both the Nationale Ballet (*see p250*) and the Nederlands Opera (*see p220*), though the stage is also used by visiting companies such as the Nederlands Dans Theater (*see p250*), the Royal Ballet and the Martha Graham Company. On top of that, the lobby's panoramic glass walls offer impressive views of the Amstel.

Tropeninstituut Theater

Kleine Zaal Linnaeusstraat 2, Oost; Grote Zaal Mauritskade 63, Oost (568 8500/www.kit.nl/theater). Tram 9, 10, 14. **Box office** noon-6pm, and 1hr before start of performance Mon-Sat. *Phone reservations* 10am-6pm Mon-Fri; noon-6pm Sat. Tickets €12-€20. **Credit** MC, V. **Map** p312 H3.
The Tropeninstituut, just by the Tropenmuseum (*see p98*), organises performances in music, dance and, occasionally, theatre that are related to or drawn from non-Western cultures. The dance programme varies from classical Indian to South African and from Indonesian to Argentinian.

Out of town venues

Lucent Danstheater

Spuiplein 152, the Hague (box office 070 880 0333/ www.ldt.nl). NS rail Den Haag Centraal Station.
Box office noon-6pm Mon-Sat; 1hr before performance. *Phone reservations* 10am-6pm Mon-Fri; noon-6pm Sat. **Tickets** €14-€30. **Credit** AmEx, DC, MC, V.
The Lucent Danstheater, located in the centre of the Hague, is the home of the world-famous Nederlands Dans Theater (*see p250*). As well as staging high-quality Dutch productions in both dance and opera, it's also become one of the country's most important venues in which to see touring international companies. Its fine points include excellent acoustics, fine visibility and a stage that compares favourably in size to the Metropolitan in New York. In fact, this theatre is a real treat.

Rotterdamse Schouwburg

Schouwburgplein 25, Rotterdam (010 411 8110/ www.schouwburg.rotterdam.nl). NS rail Rotterdam Centraal Station. **Box office** 11am-7pm Mon-Sat; Sun 1hr before performance. Closed July-mid Aug. **Tickets** €10-€18. **Credit** AmEx, DC, MC, V.
This large, square-shaped theatre opened in 1988 and quickly became known by the waggish moniker Kist van Quist (Quist's Coffin; Mr Quist was its architect). Rotterdamse Schouwburg serves up a generous variety of classical ballet and modern dance, from both Dutch and international troupes, in its two auditoriums – one has 900 seats, the other 150 seats. There's also a bar, a café and a shop.

Toneelschuur

Lange Begijnestraat 9, Haarlem (023 517 3910/ www.toneelschuur.nl). NS rail Haarlem Centraal Station. **Box office** 2-9.45pm Mon-Sat; 1.30-9.45pm Sun. **Tickets** €10-€14. **No credit cards.**
With two stages and two cinemas in its hypermodern new home designed by cartoonist Joost Swarte, Haarlem's Toneelschuur has every reason to be proud right now. There's something going on here almost every night of the week; indeed, many dance and theatre lovers from Amsterdam come to Haarlem for the nationally renowned programme of theatre and modern dance.

Companies

The following dance companies are all based in Amsterdam. Their performances can be rather sporadic and no one company is necessarily tied to a particular venue. For details on shows, call the numbers listed, check online or pick up a copy of *Uitkrant*.

Dance Company Leine & Roebana

489 3820/www.leineroebana.com.
Harijono Roebana and Andrea Leine's company performs its exciting, inventive modern dance works at various venues across Amsterdam.

Over the edge

A summer feast of large theatrical projects and avant-garde mayhem, **Over het IJ** (www.ijfestival.nl) is usually interesting and frequently compelling. The festival of performance, set in the appropriately apocalyptic setting of former shipping yard **NDSM** (*see p243*), brings together international troupes united by a love of absurdity, spectacle and the latest multimedia technology – concepts invariably linked to more exportable Dutch theatre groups Iis Warner & Consorten and Vis a Vis (both festival favourites). Regardless of which company is in residence on any given evening, though, Over het IJ usually offers an entertaining night that could be best described as a circus-opera enacted by hallucinating cartoonists, or guerrilla street theatre evolved to its subsidised limits.

The now venerable Dogtroep, who wowed Over het IJ audiences in 2001, can be considered the spiritual forebears of this particular school of theatre. Seeing themselves more as laboratory than theatre troupe, Dogtroep have a huge output of sculpted dreamscape happenings rich in colour, technical wizardry, alien costumes and random exploding bits, all of which have evolved organically in response to the performance's site and context – be it Moscow's Red Square or Belgium's highest security prison.

If Over het IJ yanks your chain, then the still more radical **Robodock** festival (www.robodock.org), which recently moved from Amsterdam to the Rotterdam docklands, is worth investigating. Taking place on a weekend in September, the festival's line-up usually involves battling robots, orchestral pyrotechnics, brain-melting video projections, and frolicking mutants. As with Over het IJ, one of the aims of Robodock is to free theatre from the theatre, thereby liberating it from a lot of pretentious baggage and resulting in a more pure (and fun) form of entertainment. Tickets for Over Het IJ can be bought from the **AUB** (*see p279* **Tickets please**), those for Robodock on the door only.

Arts & Entertainment

Dansgroep Krisztina de Châtel

669 5755/www.dechatel.nl.
Over 25 years, Hungarian Krisztina de Châtel's company has grown into an internationally recognised dance group. Most productions last an entire evening, and combine elements of dance, music and visual art. She draws increasingly on life in the information age.

Het Internationaal Danstheater

Box office 623 5359/company 623 9112/
www.intdanstheater.nl.
This Amsterdam company has been performing since 1961. Their aim is to give traditional dance a theatrical form without compromising its music, costumes or choreography. The corps of 24 dancers works with guest choreographers on a regular basis and prides itself on being the only professional dance company that is not bound by a particular culture or tradition.

Magpie Music Dance Company

616 4794/www.magpiemusicdance.com.
Founded by dancer Katie Duck and musician Michael Vatcher in 1994, Magpie uses improvisation to mix up a remarkable blend of dance, music and text into surprising all-night events. The company has toured extensively, though it maintains a season of performances at the Melkweg (*see p248*).

Nationale Ballet

Muziektheater box office 551 8225/
www.het-nationale-ballet.nl.
Amsterdam's premier dance company calls the Muziektheater home. Seventy seems to be their magic number: there are that many productions each year, performed by a selection of as many dancers (the largest ensemble outside New York). Toer van Schayk and Rudi van Dantzig have been instrumental in developing its distinctive style. Current repetoire consists chiefly of works written exclusively for Het Nationale Ballet or ones that have made them particularly famous.

Stichting Colors Amsterdam Dance Theatre

662 7310/www.cadt.nl.
This dance troupe aims to make dance as accessible as possible without selling out. Productions largely target the young and address universal themes such as fear. 2003's *House of Fear* was well received.

Companies out of town

Amsterdam performances by the companies below are usually held in the Stadsschouwburg.

Danceworks Rotterdam

010 436 4511/www.danceworksrotterdam.nl.
An ambitious modern dance troupe under the guidance of Ton Simons and visiting choreographers. Liveliness and modern, creative technique contribute to the purity of its productions. It's considered one of the most vigorous exponents of New York modern dance in the Netherlands.

Nederlands Dans Theater

Lucent Danstheater box office 070 360 9931/
070 880 0100/www.ndt.nl.
Nederlands Dans Theater was founded in 1959 and is the country's most high-profile company. With two world-famous choreographers leading it – Jiri Kylian and Hans van Manen – the company has a firm foundation and has toured the world extensively. Apart from the main company, look out for NDt2, made up of novices and up-and-coming dancers, and NDt3, which comprises veterans. They usually perform at the Muziektheater (*see p248*).

RAZ/Hans Tuerlings

013 583 5929/www.raz.nl.
Hans Tuerlings conceives his performances as narratives without a set story, told with nonchalant, yet pure and especially well-timed movement. The RAZ company, meanwhile, consists of international dancers and performs regularly at the Bellevue.

Scapino Ballet

010 414 2414/www.scapinoballet.nl.
Scapino is the oldest dance company in the country and used to be a bit stuffy. In the 1990s attention shifted from convention to innovation (without losing sight of profits).

Movement theatre groups

Griftheater

419 3088/www.grif.nl.
Griftheater is a giant on the international mime scene. The company produces movement theatre productions for existing theatre spaces and special locations. An excellent combination of plastic arts and modern mime.

Courses & workshops

Dansstudio Cascade

Koestraat 5, Old Centre: Old Side (689 0565
information/623 0597 studio). Tram 4, 9, 14, 16,
24/Metro Nieuwmarkt. **Classes** 6-10.30pm Mon-Fri.
Cost varies. **Map** p306 D3.
Modern dance technique, capoeira, contact improvisation and Pentjak Silat are all taught here. Most teachers work within the new dance technique.

Henny Jurriens Foundation

Gerard Brandtstraat 26-8, Museum Quarter (412
1510/www.euronet.nl/~hjs). Tram 1. **Classes**
9.30am, 11am, 12.30pm Mon-Fri; 11am Sat. **Cost** €7
per class; €55 for 10 classes. **Map** p309 B3.
The Henny Jurriens Foundation provides open training for professional dancers in both classical and modern dance techniques throughout the year, with modern classes taking place at Danswerkplaats Amsterdam (*see p247*). Teachers are a mix of locals and guest teachers from abroad, and the foundation also offers workshops (pre-registration is necessary); phone for more information.

Trips Out of Town

Introduction

Urban hip to cheesy cliché: Holland's best is just a tiptoe through the tulips away.

Amsterdam is special. But before you can say you've truly visited the Netherlands, you must escape that city's suction and get to 'the real country'. Not that hard: it's a small place where most of the towns and cities worth visiting are under an hour away. Even the country's remotest corners are accessible within a half-day drive or train ride. And be careful not to fall asleep: you might wake up in Belgium or Germany.

TRAVEL INFORMATION
The **Netherlands Board of Tourism** or VVV (Vlietweg 15, 2266 KA Leidschendam, 070 370 5705/www.visitholland.com) can help with general information and accommodation, as can the **Netherlands Reserverings Centrum** (*see p48*). For national transport information and timetables (trains, buses and the Metro), call the **OV Reisinformatie** information line (0900 9292, premium rate); to use website www.ov9292.nl, *see p274* – or get train information at www.ns.nl, in Dutch but decipherable.

Getting around

Driving
The Netherlands' road system is extensive, well maintained and clearly signposted. For driving advice and details of the motoring organisation **ANWB**, *see p276*.

Buses & coaches
The national bus service is reasonably priced, but not as easy to negotiate as the railway. For information and timetables, phone **OV Reisinformatie** (*see above*).

Cycling
The Netherlands is flat (though windy); little wonder the bike is the country's favourite mode of transport. Cycle paths are abundant and the ANWB and VVV offices sell cycle maps. Most major railway stations have bike depots and offer discounts to rail ticket holders. Road bikes cost around €7 per day and €25 per week; mountain bikes about twice that. Both are in short supply in summer; book at least a day ahead. You'll need proof of identity and a cash deposit (ranging from €50 to €200). For bike hire in Amsterdam, *see p277*.

Rail

Nederlandse Spoorwegen (aka NS, translatable as Netherlands Railway) offers an excellent service in terms of cost, punctuality and cleanliness. Aside from singles and returns, you can also buy family and group passes, tickets that entitle you to unlimited travel on any given day (Dagkaarten), one that also entitles you to use buses, trams and the Metro (OV Dagkaarten) and, for selected places, NS Rail Idee tickets, all-in-one tickets that'll get you to a destination and also include the admission fee to one or more of the local sights. Services are frequent, and reservations are unnecessary.

As a rule, tickets are valid for one day only: if you make a return journey spanning more than one day you need two singles. A weekend return ticket is the exception to the rule: it's valid from Friday night until Sunday night. Credit cards are rarely accepted at ticket offices.

With a rail ticket, you can avail yourself of **Treintaxi**, a special cab that takes you to any destination within a fixed distance of 110 stations for under €5.

DISABLED TRAVELLERS
NS produces a booklet in English called *Rail Travel for the Disabled*, available from all main stations or from the above number. There is disabled access to refreshment rooms and toilets at all stations. For special assistance, call 030 235 7822 at least a day in advance.

Centraal Station Information Desk
Stationsplein 15, Old Centre: New Side (0900 9292/ www.ns.nl). Tram 1, 2, 4, 5, 9, 13, 16, 17, 24, 25. **Open** *Information desk* 6.30am-10pm daily. *Bookings* 24hrs daily. **Credit** MC, V. **Map** p306 D1.

Trips
The best

For bright-lights-big-city vibe
Rotterdam (*see p268*).

For small fortified town charm
Naarden (*see p259*).

For very small town charm
Madurodam (*see p266*).

Excursions in Holland

Pay homage to the holy Dutch trinity of cheese, tulips and windmills.

Stereotypes: you know you love 'em. Happily for visitors to the nation's capital, the majority of the most enduring and popular Dutch sights are concentrated conveniently close to Amsterdam in Noord and Zuid Holland, and readily accessible by public transport. Note that none of the establishments listed in this chapter takes credit cards.

Charming Clichés

Cheese

Ah, yes. Cheese. It gives you strange dreams, apparently. Not that the 'cheeseheads' – a name for the Dutch that dates from medieval times, when they sported wooden cheese moulds on their heads in battle – seem to mind. When they're not munching it or exporting more than 400,000 tonnes of it every year, they're making a tourist industry of it.

One ritual for both tourists and members of the cheese porters' guild is the **Alkmaar Cheese Market** – the oldest and biggest cheese market in the world – which runs from 10am to noon every Friday between April and mid September. Pristinely dressed porters, wearing straw hats with coloured ribbons denoting their competing guilds, weigh the cheeses and carry them on wooden trays hung from their shoulders. Then buyers test a core of cheese from each lot before the ceremony, which takes place at the Waag (weighhouse); here you can also find a variety of craft stalls and a **Cheese Museum**. Yet Alkmaar has a little more than cheese to offer the visitor. The VVV provides a written walking tour of the medieval centre, which dates from 935. Among the attractions at the **Biermuseum** is a cellar in which to taste various beers; the **Stedelijk Museum**, meanwhile, has impressive art and toy collections.

The Netherlands' famous indigenous red-skinned cheese is sold at **Edam**'s cheese market, held every Wednesday in July and August from 10am until noon. Though the town, a prosperous port during the Golden Age, tells many stories through its exquisite façades and bridges, they can't compete with the cheese. In 1840, Edams were used as cannon ammunition in Uruguay to repel seaborne attackers (imagine, if you can, the humiliation of dying from a cheese injury). And in 1956 a canned Edam, a relic of a 1912 expedition, was found in the South Pole – and when opened proved to be merely a trifle 'sharp'. The town itself added to this lore in 2003 by building a colossal cheese cathedral from 10,000 of the unholey orbs to raise repair funds for their ancient Grote Kerk (Big Church).

Meanwhile, over in **Gouda**, golden wheels of cheese go on sale at the cheese market every Thursday from 10am in July and August in front of the Gothic city hall of 1450 and the 1668 Waag, whose gablestone depicts cheese-weighing. There are also many thatched-roof *kaasboerderijen* (cheese farms) near Gouda, several of which are on the picturesque River Vlist. Look for signs that indicate a farm shop: see *kaas te koop* (cheese for sale) and you may well be able to peer behind the scenes as well as buy freshly made Gouda.

Still, even though its cheese is justifiably famed the world over, Gouda does have other things to recommend it beside the yellow stuff. Its other famous products include clay pipes and pottery, which can be seen in the **De Moriaan Museum**; there's also an annual pottery festival in the second week of May. Gouda's candles are another city classic: 20,000 of them illuminate the square during the Christmas tree ceremony.

Alkmaar Biermuseum

Houttil 1, Alkmaar (072 511 3801/www.bier museum.nl). **Open** *Apr-Nov* 10am-4pm Tue-Fri; 1-4pm Sat; 1.30-4pm Sun. *Nov-Apr* 1-4pm Tue-Fri; 1-4pm Sat; 1.30-4pm Sun. **Admission** €3; €1.50 concessions.

Alkmaar Cheese Museum

De Waag, Waagplein 2, Alkmaar (072 511 4284). **Open** *Mid Apr-mid Sept* 10am-4pm Mon-Thur, Sat; 9am-4pm Fri. **Admission** €2.50; €1.50 under-11s.

De Moriaan Museum

Westhaven 29, Gouda (0182 588444). **Open** 10am-5pm Mon-Sat; noon-5pm Sun. **Admission** €3.60; €2.90 over-65s; free children.

Stedelijk Museum, Alkmaar

Canadaplein 1, Alkmaar (072 511 0737/ www.stedelijkmuseumalkmaar.nl). **Open** 10am-5pm Tue-Fri; 1-5pm Sat, Sun. **Admission** €3.40; €1.70 4-13s; free MK.

Mmm. Cheese.

auctions and parades all year round. They're also, of course, a popular gift for tourists to take; for the current export rules on bulbs and flowers, *see p163*.

The world's biggest flower auction is in the world's biggest trading building (120 football fields' worth, to be precise) in Aalsmeer. The **Verenigde Bloemenveilingen** handles more than 18 million cut flowers and 2 million pot plants each day, mostly for export. Its unusual sales method gave rise to the phrase 'Dutch auction'. Basically, dealers bid by pushing a button to stop a 'clock' that counts from 100 down to one; thus, the price is lowered – rather than raised – until a buyer is found. Bidders risk either overpaying for the good or not getting them if time runs out too soon. The best action here is usually before 9am, except on Thursdays.

The 'countdown' bidding style was invented at **Broeker Veiling**, the oldest flower and vegetable auction in the world. It's a bit of a tourist trap these days, but nonetheless includes a museum of old farming artefacts, and – for a small fee – a boat trip.

There have been flowers everywhere at the **Keukenhof Bulb Gardens** since 1949. This former royal 'kitchen garden' dates from the 14th century, and contains 500 types of tulip and over six million bulbs in 1.25 square miles (over three square kilometres). The glass flower pavilion, all 6,500 square metres (70,480 square feet) of it – is just as interesting. Follow a VVV map and tour the bulb district (in bloom from March to late May), from which over half the world's cut flowers and pot plants originate. Arrive early, as the gardens get packed. For more on the bulb district's history, visit the **Museum de Zwarte Tulp**.

Getting there

Alkmaar

By car 37km (22 miles) north-west. *By train* direct from Amsterdam Centraal Station.

Edam

By car 10km (5 miles) north. *By bus* 110, 112, 114 from Amsterdam Centraal Station.

Gouda

By car 29km (18 miles) south-west. *By train* direct from Amsterdam Centraal Station.

Tourist information

Alkmaar VVV

Waagplein 2, Alkmaar (072 511 4284/www.vvvweb. nl). **Open** *Apr-Sept* 10am-5.30pm Mon-Wed; 10am-9pm Thur; 9am-6pm Fri; 9.30am-5pm Sat. *Oct-Mar* 10am-5.30pm Mon-Wed; 10am-5.30pm Thur; 10am-5.30pm Fri; 9.30am-5pm Sat.

Edam VVV

Stadhuis, Damplein 1, Edam (0299 315125/ www.vvv-edam.nl). **Open** *Nov-Mar* 10am-3pm Mon-Sat. *Apr-June, Sept, Oct* 10am-5pm Mon-Sat. *Jul, Aug* 10am-5pm Mon-Sat; 1-4.30pm Sun.

Gouda VVV

Markt 27, Gouda (0900 4683 2888 premium rate/www.vvvgouda.nl). **Open** *Apr, May, Sept, Oct* 9am-5pm Mon-Sat. *Jun-Aug* 9am-5pm Mon-Sat; noon-3pm Sun. *Nov-Mar* 9am-5pm Mon-Fri; 10am-4pm Sat.

Flowers

Want a statistic that boggles the mind? Try this: the Netherlands produces a staggering 70 per cent of all the world's commercial flower output, and still has more than enough left over to fill its own markets, botanical gardens,

Broeker Veiling

Museumweg 2, Broek-op-Langerdijk (0226 313807/www.broekerveiling.nl). **Open** *1 Apr-1 Nov* 10am-5pm Mon-Fri; 11am-5pm Sat, Sun. **Admission** *Auction & museum* €5.65; €3.25 under-15s. *Auction, museum & boat trip* €8.95; €4.95 under-15s.

Keukenhof Bulb Gardens

Keukenhof, near Lisse (0252 465555/ www.keukenhof.nl). **Open** *Mid Mar-mid May* 8am-7.30pm daily (ticket box closes 6pm). **Admission** €12; €5.50 4-11s.

Museum de Zwarte Tulp

Grachtweg 2A, Lisse (0252 417900). **Open** 1-5pm Tue-Sun. **Admission** €3; €2 under-12s.

Verenigde Bloemenveilingen

Legmeerdijk 313, Aalsmeer (0297 392185/ www.bloemenveiling-aalsmeer.nl). **Open** 7.30-11am Mon-Fri. **Admission** €4; €2 under-12s.

Getting there

Aalsmeer
By car 15km (9 miles) south-west. *By bus* 172 from Amsterdam Centraal Station.

Broek-op-Langerdijk
By car 36km (22 miles) north. *By train* from Amsterdam Centraal Station to Alkmaar, then bus 155; from Amsterdam Centraal Station to Heerhugowaard, then taxi.

Keukenhof/Lisse
By car 27km (17 miles) south-west. *By train* from Amsterdam Centraal Station to Leiden, then bus 54.

Dutch Traditions

Small historic towns in the Netherlands – the ones that depend on the tourist business – have become expert at capitalising on their traditions, right down to the lace caps, wooden shoes and working windmills that churn out souvenirs like flour and mustard. Authentic they ain't, but connoisseurs of kitsch should set course for them immediately.

Zuid-Holland & Utrecht

It's hardly catwalk glamour, but a sizeable minority of **Bunschoten-Spakenburg** residents still strut – or, rather, klog – their stuff in traditional dress on midsummer market Wednesdays between mid July and mid August; some older people wear it every day. Costumes are also worn at the summer markets in Hoorn, Medemblik (for both, *see p258*) and Schagen, and on folkloric festival days in Middelburg.

An amazing sight can be seen over in Alblasserdam, where a posse of 19 **Kinderdijk Windmills** form a group called a *gang*. Although they were originally clustered in order to drain water from reclaimed land, they are now under sail specifically for the benefit of tourists (from 2pm to 5pm on Saturdays in July and August, and on the first Saturday in May and June). During the second week in September you'll find them illuminated, and a spectacular sight it is, too; from April to September, you can take a €2.50 boat trip to see them.

Schoonhoven has been famous since the 17th century for its silversmiths, who crafted items to be worn with traditional costume.

Floral calendar

Spring
The flower trade's year kicks off in mid to late February with the indoor **Westfriese Flora** (0228 511644) at Bovenkarspel, near Enkhuizen. From late March to late May, the bulb district from Den Helder to Den Haag is carpeted with blooms of the principal crops: daffodils, crocuses, gladioli, hyacinths, narcissi and – of course – tulips.

The **Noordwijk-Haarlem Flower Parade** (0252 428237) takes place on the first Saturday after 19 April, departing from Noordwijk at 10am and arriving in Haarlem (via Sassenheim) at 7pm. The florid floats are on show in Lisse and Hobahohallen for the two days prior to the parade.

Summer
In mid to late May, golden fields of rapeseed brighten Flevoland, Friesland and Groningen. In the Hague, the Japanese Garden at **Clingendael Gardens** is in full flower from early May to mid June, while the rose garden in Westbroek Park, containing 350 varieties, bursts into colour during July and August.

In late June, there's the Floralia exhibition at the Zuider Zee Museum in **Enkhuizen**. And on the third weekend in August, it's the

Rijnsburg Parade (071 409 4444). The floats leave Rijnsburg at 11am on Saturday, reach Leiden at 1pm and journey to Nordwijk by 4pm, where they show at the Boulevard that evening and the next day.

Autumn
Heather purples the landscape – especially in **Veluwe**, in the province of Gelderland – during August and September, when greenhouse flowers also emerge. The **Bloemencorso** (0297 325100), Europe's biggest flower parade, winds from Aalsmeer to Amsterdam and back on the first Saturday in September, with float viewing taking place the day before and after the parade in Aalsmeer.

On the fourth Sunday in September, a still wackier flower parade takes place in the small West Frisian town of Winkel, the **Bloemencorso Winkel** (0224 541907), and comes complete with street theatre.

Winter
In November, the public and florists from all over the world view new varieties at the Professional Flower Exhibition at **Aalsmeer Flower Auction**. At Christmas, there's the Kerstflora show at Hillegom near Lisse.

Trips Out of Town

The fishermen may have gone, but the boats stay on in **Marken**. *See p257.*

You can see antique pieces in the **Nederlands Goud-, Zilver- en Klokkenmuseum** and the former synagogue **Edelambachtshuis** (Museum of Antique Silverware). Olivier van Noort, the first Dutchman to sail around the world, and Claes Louwerenz Blom, who locals believe introduced the windmill to Spain in 1549, are buried in the 14th-century **Bartholomeuskerk**, the tower of which leans 1.6 metres (five feet). Not buried here is Marrigje Ariens, the last woman to be burned as a witch in the country – but a circle of coloured stones by the city hall marks the spot where she died in 1591.

Dating from the 11th century, **Oudewater** (north of Schoonhoven), once famed for its rope-making, also has a rich witch-hunting past. Reaching its peak in the 1480s, the fashion didn't die out until the beginning of the 17th century, and Oudewater achieved fame for its weighing of suspected witches and warlocks in the **Heksenwaag** ('Witches' Weigh House'); today, swarms of tourists step on to the scales.

Edelambachtshuis

Haven 13, Schoonhoven (0182 382614). **Open** 10am-5pm Tue-Sat. **Admission** €1.

Heksenwaag

Leeuweringerstraat 2, Oudewater (0348 563400/ www.heksenwaag.nl). **Open** *Apr-Oct* 10am-5pm Tue-Sat; noon-5pm Sun. **Admission** €1.50; €0.25 MK, over-65s; €0.75 4-12s; free under-4s.

Kinderdijk Windmills

Molenkade, Alblasserdam (078 692 1355/ www.kinderdijk.nl). **Open** *Apr-Sept* 9.30am-5.30pm daily. **Admission** *Windmills* €2.50; €1.50 under-16s.

Nederlands Goud-, Zilver- en Klokkenmuseum

Kazerneplein 4, Schoonhoven (0182 385612). **Open** noon-5pm Tue-Sun. **Admission** €4; €2 under-12s.

Getting there

Alblasserdam

By car 55km (34 miles) south-west. *By train* from Amsterdam Centraal Station to Utrecht, then bus 154.

Bunschoten-Spakenburg

By car 35km (22 miles) south-east. *By train* from Amsterdam Centraal Station to Amersfoort, then bus 116.

Oudewater

By car 40km (25 miles) south. *By train* from Amsterdam Centraal Station to Utrecht, then bus 180.

Schoonhoven

By car 50km (31 miles) south. *By train* from Amsterdam Centraal Station to Utrecht, then bus 195.

Tourist information

Alblasserdam VVV

Cortgene 2, inside City Hall, Alblasserdam (078 692 1355). **Open** 9am-4pm Mon-Fri.

Bunschoten-Spakenburg VVV

Oude Schans 90, Spakenburg (033 298 2156/ www.vvvspakenburg.nl). **Open** *Apr-Sept* 1pm-5pm Mon; 10am-5pm Tue-Fri; 10am-4pm Sat. *Oct-Mar* 1-5pm Mon-Fri; 10am-3pm Sat.

Oudewater VVV

Kapellestraat 2, Oudewater (0348 564636/www.vvv hetgroenehart.nl). **Open** *Apr-Oct* 10am-4pm Tue-Sat; 11am-3pm Sun. *Nov-Mar* 10am-3pm Tue-Sat.

Schoonhoven VVV

Stadhuisstraat 1, Schoonhoven (0182 385009).
Open *May-Sept* 1.30-4.30pm Mon; 9am-4.30pm
Tue-Fri; 10am-3pm Sat. *Oct-Apr* 9am-4pm Tue-Fri;
10.30am-3pm Sat.

Waterland

Until the IJ Tunnel opened in 1956, the canal-
laced peat meadows of Waterland north of
Amsterdam were accessible mainly by ferry
and steam railway. This isolation preserved
much of the area's heritage; for a prime
example, look around the old wooden buildings
at **Broek in Waterland**. This area is best
explored by bike before switching over to a
canoe or electric motor boat, both of which
can be rented from Zeilkamp Waterland
(403 3209/www.kano-electroboot.nl).

Marken, reached via a causeway, was once
full of fishermen (some of whom give excellent
boat tours), but is now awash only with
tourists. Visit off-season, however, and you'll
likely find it quieter and more authentic than
Volendam (*see below*). To protect against
flooding, many houses are built on mounds
or poles. The **Marker Museum** offers a tour
of the island's history.

The number of preserved ancient buildings,
from Golden Age merchants' houses to the
famous herring smokehouses, is what makes
Monnickendam special. There's also a
kitschy collection of music boxes at the
Stuttenburgh fish restaurant (Haringburgwal
3-4, 0299 651869), and a fine antique carillon
on the bell-tower of the old town hall.

Such is **Volendam**'s runaway success
as a fishing village that it's said the town flag
was flown at half-mast when the Zuider Zee
was enclosed in 1932, cutting off access to the
sea. The village's enterprise was soon applied
to devising a theme park from its fascinating
historic features, but, sadly, the cheerily garbed
locals can barely be seen for the coachloads
of tourists dumped there every day – and
invariably pointed to the world's biggest
collection of cigar bands (11 million in all) on
view at the **Volendams Museum** (Zeestraat
37, 0299 369258).

De Zaanse Schans is not your typical
museum village: people still live here. One
of the world's first industrial zones, the Zaan
district was once crowded with 800 windmills
that powered the production of paint, flour and
lumber. Today, amid the gabled green and white
houses, attractions include an old-fashioned
Albert Heijn store. Nearby in Zaandam, you
can visit the Czaar Peterhuisje, the tiny wooden
house where Peter the Great stayed in 1697
while honing his ship-building skills.

Czaar Peterhuisje

Het Krimp 23, Zaandam (075 616 0390).
Open *May-Oct* 10am-1pm, 2pm-5pm Tue-Fri;
1-5pm Sat, Sun. *Nov-Apr* 1-5pm Sat, Sun.
Admission €2; €1 under-12s; free MK.

Marker Museum

Kerkbuurt 44-7, Marken (0299 601904).
Open *Apr-Oct* 10am-5pm Mon-Sat; noon-4pm Sun.
Admission €2; €0.75 under-12s.

De Zaanse Schans

*Information from Zaandam VVV; see below
(www.zaanseschans.nl).* **Open** times vary, generally:
Museums 10am-5pm Tue-Sun. *Shops & windmills*
9am-5pm Tue-Sun. **Admission** free-€10; free-€4
under-13s.

Getting there

Broek in Waterland

By car 10km (6 miles) north-east. *By bus* 110, 111, 114
or 116 from Amsterdam Centraal Station.

Marken

By car 20km (12 miles) north-east. *By bus* 111 from
Amsterdam Centraal Station to Marken, or 110, 114
or 116 to Monnickendam, then boat to Marken.

Monnickendam

By car 15km (9 miles) north-east. *By bus* 110, 114 or
116 from Amsterdam Centraal Station.

Volendam

By car 20km (12 miles) north-east. *By bus* 110 from
Amsterdam Centraal Station.

De Zaanse Schans

By car 15km (9 miles) north-west. *By train* to Koog-
Zaandijk. By bus 89 from Marnixstraat.

Tourist information

Waterland VVV (Marken, Broek in Waterland and Monnickendam)

*Nieuwpoortslaan 15, Monnickendam (0299 651998/
www.infowaterland.nl).* **Open** 9am-5pm Mon-Fri.

Volendam VVV

*Zeestraat 37, Volendam (0299 363747/www.vvv-
volendam.nl).* **Open** *Mid Mar-Oct* 10am-5pm daily.
Nov-mid Mar 10am-3pm Mon-Sat.

Zaandam VVV

Gedempte Gracht 76, Zaandam (075 616 2221).
Open 9am-5.30pm Mon-Fri; 9am-4pm Sat.

West Friesland

West Friesland faces Friesland across the
northern IJsselmeer. Despite being a part of
Noord Holland for centuries, it has its own
customs, and fewer visitors than its near-
neighbour. One scenic way to get there is to take

Trips Out of Town

a train to Enkhuizen, then a boat to Medemblik. From here, take the **Museumstoomtram** (Steam Railway Museum) to Hoorn.

The once-powerful fishing and whaling port of **Enkhuizen** has many relics of its past, but most people come here for the **Zuider Zee Museum**. Wander either the indoor Binnenmuseum, which has exhibits on seven centuries of seafaring life around the IJsselmeer, or the open-air Buitenmuseum, a reconstructed village (complete with 'villagers') of 130 authentic late 19th- and early 20th-century buildings transplanted from nearby towns.

The Gothic Bonifaciuskerk and Kasteel Radboud dominate **Medemblik**, a port which dates from the early Middle Ages. The 13th-century castle is smaller than it was when it defended Floris V's realm, but retains its knights' hall and towers. Glassblowers and leatherworkers show off their skills at the Saturday market in July and August. Nearby is the 'long village' of Twisk, with its pyramid-roofed farm buildings, and the circular village of Opperdoes, built on a mound.

The pretty port of **Hoorn**, which dates from around 1310, grew rich on the Dutch East Indies trade; its success is reflected in its grand and ancient architecture. Local costumes and crafts can be seen at the weekly historic market, Hartje Hoorn (10am-5pm Wednesdays in July and August only), and the **Museum van de Twintigste Eeuw** (Museum of the 20th Century), while hardly living up to its unsuitably grand name, does have plenty of interest in its permanent exhibit. The Statencollege (council building), built in 1632, houses the **Westfries Museum**, which focuses on art, decor and the region's past.

Museum van de Twintigste Eeuw

Bierkade 4, Hoorn (0229 214001/www.museum hoorn.nl). **Open** *10am-5pm Tue-Thur; noon-5pm Sat, Sun*. **Admission** €3.50; €2 4s-16s and concessions.

Museumstoomtram Hoorn-Medemblik

Hoorn-Medemblik; tickets behind the station at Van Dedemstraat 8, Hoorn (0229 214862/ www.museumstoomtram.nl), or **Hoorn VVV** *below.* **Admission** (with boat trip) *Single* €9.20; €7 *4s-11s.* *Return* €15.15; €11.50 *4s-11s.*

Westfries Museum

Rode Steen 1, Hoorn (0229 280028/www.wfm.nl). **Open** *11am-5pm Mon-Fri; 2-5pm Sat, Sun.* **Admission** €2.50; €1.25 4s-16s, family with kids €6; free MK.

Zuider Zee Museum

Wierdijk 12-22, Enkhuizen (0228 351111/ www.zuiderzeemuseum.nl). **Open** *10am-5pm daily (indoor museum only Nov-Apr).* **Admission** *May-Oct* €9.50; €7.50 *4s-12s.* *Nov-Apr* €5; €4.50 *4s-12s.*

Getting there

Enkhuizen

By car 55km (34 miles) north-east. *By train* direct from Amsterdam Centraal Station.

Hoorn

By car 35km (22 miles) north-east. *By train* direct from Amsterdam Centraal Station.

Medemblik

By car 50km (31 miles) north. *By train* direct from Amsterdam Centraal Station.

Tourist information

Enkhuizen VVV

Tussen Twee Havens 1, Enkhuizen (0228 313164/ www.vvvweb.nl). **Open** *Apr-Nov* 9am-5pm daily. *Nov-Apr* 1-5pm Mon; 10am-5pm Tue-Fri; 10am-3pm Sat.

Hoorn VVV

Veemarkt 4, Hoorn (072 511 4284/www.vvvweb.nl). **Open** *May-Aug* 1-6pm Mon; 9.30am-6pm Tue, Wed, Fri; 9.30am-9pm Thur; 9.30am-7pm Sat, 1-5pm Sun. *Sept-Apr* 1pm-5pm Mon, 9.30am-5pm Tue-Sat.

Medemblik VVV

Kaasmarkt 1, Medemblik (072 511 4284). **Open** *Apr-Oct* 9.30am-5pm Mon-Sat.

Ancient Castles

What Amsterdam lacks in palaces and castles, the rest of Holland makes up for in spades. The Netherlands is studded with 400 castles, and many fortress towns retain large parts of their defences. Some of the best are in the province of Utrecht, within half an hour of Amsterdam. Almost 100 of the castles are open for tourists or business conferences: the 15th-century **Stayokay Heemskerk**, between Haarlem and Alkmaar, is a hostel (025 123 2288/www. stayokay.com), while the ultimate power lunch can be had at **Château Neercanne** in Maastricht (043 325 1359) or **Kasteel Erenstein** in Kerkrade (045 546 1333/ www.erenstein.com).

The fairy-tale splendour of **De Haar** is appealing but misleading. Though it looks like the quintessential medieval castle, its ornate embellishments are actually relatively recent recreations. In 1892, the baron who inherited the ruins of De Haar (dating from 1391) recreated the original building on a majestic scale, moving the entire village of Haarzuilens 850 metres (259 feet) to make room for Versailles-styled gardens. The mind-blowingly lavish interior is visible only on one of the informative guided tours.

Volendam. *See p257.*

in 1752. The collections of furniture, tapestries and objets d'art displayed here gives insight into the lives of the residents. The local tour boat company, **Rondvaartbedrijf Rederij Schuttevaer**, can arrange an English guide with advance notice. Another boat drops passengers in the charming town of Loenen, which has the restored castle of Loenersloot; sadly, it's not open to the public.

De Haar

Kasteellaan 1, Haarzuilens, Utrecht (030 677 8515/ www.kasteeldehaar.nl). **Open** *June-Sept* 11am-4pm Mon-Fri; 1-4pm Sat, Sun. *Mid Mar-May, Oct-mid Nov* 1-4pm Tue-Sun. *Jan-mid Mar, late Nov* 1-4pm Sun. *Dec* groups only. *Grounds* 10am-5pm daily. **Admission** *Castle & grounds* €7.50; €5 5s-12s (no under-5s); free MK. *Grounds only* €2.25; €1.25 5s-12s; free MK, under-5s.

Muiderslot

Herengracht 1, Muiden (0294 261325/ www.muiderslot.demon.nl). **Open** *Apr-Oct* 10am-5pm Mon-Fri; 1-5pm Sat, Sun. *Nov-Mar* 1-4pm Sat, Sun. **Admission** €6; €4.50 4s-12s; free MK.

Rondvaartbedrijf Rederij Schuttevaer

Oudegracht, opposite No.85, Utrecht (030 272 0111/ 030 231 9377/www.schuttevaer.com). **Times** *June-Sept to Slot Zuylen* 10.30am Tue, 11.30am Thur, returning 4pm. *June-Sept to Loenen* 10.30am Wed (*July, Aug* also Fri), returning 6pm. **Tickets** €16-€22; €15-€21 under-13s; reservations essential.

Vestingmuseum Turfpoortbastion

Westvalstraat 6, Naarden (035 694 5459/ www.vestingmuseum.nl). **Open** *Mar-Oct* 10.30am-5pm Tue-Fri; noon-5pm Sat, Sun. *Nov-Feb* noon-5pm Sun. **Admission** €5; €3-€4 concessions; free MK, under-4s.

Many important events in Dutch history took place in the legendary **Muiderslot**. This moated castle, situated at the mouth of the River Vecht, was originally built in 1280 for Count Floris V, who was murdered nearby in Muiderberg all the way back in 1296. Rebuilt in the 14th century, the fortress has been through many sieges and frequent renovations. The 17th-century furnishings originate from the period of another illustrious occupant, PC Hooft, who entertained in the castle's splendid halls. Between April and October you can take a boat from the dock here to the medieval fort island of Pampus.

The star-shaped stronghold of **Naarden** is not only moated, but also has arrowhead-shaped bastions and a very well-preserved fortified town; it was in active service as recently as 1926. All is explained in the **Vestingmuseum**, set partly underground in the Turfpoortbastion (Peat Gate). The fortifications date from 1675, after the inhabitants were massacred by the Duke of Alva's son in 1572; the slaughter is depicted above the door of the Spaanse Huis (Spanish House), now a conference venue. Today, however, Naarden is the perfect setting for a leisurely Sunday stroll.

Meandering up the River Vecht into **Utrecht**, boat passengers can glimpse some of the plush country homes built in the 17th and 18th centuries by rich Amsterdam merchants. Two of the trips afford close-up views of castles, the first stopping on the way back downriver for a one-hour tour of Slot Zuylen, a 16th-century castle that was renovated

Getting there

De Haar

By car 30km (19 miles) south. *By train* Amsterdam Centraal Station to Utrecht, then bus 127.

Muiderslot

By car 12km (7.5 miles) south-east. *By bus* 136 from Amstel Station.

Naarden

By car 20km (12 miles) south-east. *By train* direct from Amsterdam Centraal Station. *By bus* 136 from Amstel Station.

Tourist information

Naarden VVV

Adriaan Dortsmanplein 1B, Naarden (035 694 2836). **Open** *May-Oct* 10am-5pm Mon-Fri; 10am-3pm Sat. *Nov-Apr* 10am-2pm Mon-Sat.

Trips Out of Town

City Breaks

The rest of the Randstad delivers history and on-the-edge urban appeal.

The Randstad – or 'Edge City', named for its coastal location on the Netherlands' western edge – is a loop bounded by Amsterdam, Delft, Haarlem, the Hague, Leiden, Rotterdam and Utrecht. In recent years, Gouda (*see p253*) and Dordrecht have come to be considered part of it. Though separately administered and fiercely independent, the individual towns work together for their common good. Surprisingly, it's also one of the most densely populated areas in the world: no fewer than 40 per cent of the Dutch population inhabit this urban sprawl.

The road, rail and waterway networks are impressive, and the area's economy is strong. The Randstad's importance is based on several factors: Rotterdam's huge port; Schiphol Airport and Amsterdam's role as financial and banking centre; the seats of government and royalty at the Hague; and a huge agricultural belt.

Regarded with a mix of awe, indifference and resentment by the outlying provinces, the Randstad is often accused of monopolising government attention and funds. However, it has no formally defined status and is still prone to bitter rivalry between cities and municipalities – Amsterdam and Rotterdam in particular (a feud that's only growing sharper as Amsterdam gets ever more Disneyfied and Rotterdam grows more individual). The smaller cities in the Randstad can be exploited as peaceful day-trip escapes from the swirling vortex of Amsterdam.

Delft

Imagine a miniaturised Amsterdam – canals reduced to dinky proportions, bridges narrowed down, merchants' houses shrunken – and you have the essence of Delft. However, though it's small, scoffed at for its seeming sleepiness, Delft is also a student town with social carryings-on if you care to look for them.

Everything you're likely to want to see is in the old centre. As soon as you cross the road from the station towards the city centre, you encounter the first introduction to Delft's past: a modern representation of Vermeer's *Milkmaid* in stone on the junction of Phoenixstraat and Binnen Watersloot.

Delft, though, is of course most famous for its blue and white tiles and pottery, known as Delft Blue (or internationally as Royal Blue). There are still a few factories open to visitors – among them **De Delftse Pauw** and **De Porceleyne Fles** – but for a historical overview of the industry, make for the **Museum Lambert van Meerten**. The huge range of tiles, depicting everything from battling warships to randy rabbits, contrasts dramatically with today's mass-produced trinkets.

Delft was traditionally a centre for trade, producing and exporting butter, cloth, Delft beer – at one point in the past, almost 200 breweries could be found beside the canals – and, later, pottery. Its subsequent loss in trade has been Rotterdam's gain, but the aesthetic benefits can be seen in the city's centuries-old gables, hump-backed bridges and shady canals. To appreciate how little has changed, walk to the end of Oude Delft, the oldest canal in Delft (it narrowly escaped being drained in the 1920s to become a sunken tram-line), which has some impressive mansions incorporated into its terrace. Cross the busy road to the harbour, for it was on the far side of this canal that Johannes Vermeer (1632-75) stood when painting his famous *View of Delft*, now on display in the Mauritshuis in the Hague (*see p264*).

Delft also has two spectacular churches. The first, the Nieuwe Kerk (New Church), stands in the Markt (Market) and contains the mausoleums of lawyer-philosopher Hugo de Groot and William of Orange (alongside his dog, who faithfully followed him to death by refusing food and water). It took almost 15 years to construct and was finished in 1396. Across the Markt is Hendrick de Keyser's 1620 Stadhuis (or City Hall); De Keyser also designed Prince William's black and white marble mausoleum. Not to be outdone, the town's other splendid house of worship, the Gothic Oude Kerk (c1200), is known as 'Leaning Jan' because its tower stands two metres (over six feet) off-kilter. Art-lovers should note that it's the final resting place of Vermeer.

Museums in Delft have the air of private residences and are pretty much crowd-free. **Het Prinsenhof Municipal Museum**, located in the former convent of St Agatha, holds ancient and modern art exhibitions along with the permanent displays about Prince William of Orange, who was assassinated in 1584 by one of many keen to earn the price put on his head by Philip II of Spain during Holland's 80-year fight

Stuck for gift ideas for the folks at home? You'll find them in **Delft**. *See p260.*

for independence. The bullet holes are still clearly visible on the stairs.

But though the museums are grand, it's fun to simply stroll around town. The historic centre has more than 600 national monuments in and around the preserved merchants' houses. Pick up a walk guide from the VVV and see what the town has to offer: the country's largest military collection at the **Legermuseum** (Army Museum), for example, or western Europe's largest collection of poisonous snakes at the **Reptielenzoo Serpo**. One of the many places that may draw you in is the Oostpoort (East Gate), dating from 1394. And while at the VVV, ask if you can visit the Windmill de Roos and the torture chamber in Het Steen, the 13th-century tower of the historic city hall in the market square – they're both fascinating.

De Delftse Pauw

Delftweg 133 (015 212 4920/www.delftsepauw.com). **Open** *Apr-Oct* 9am-4.30pm daily. *Nov-Mar* 9am-4.30pm Mon-Fri; 11am-1pm Sat, Sun. **Admission** free. **Credit** AmEx, DC, MC, V.

Legermuseum

Korte Geer 1 (015 215 0500/www.legermuseum.nl). **Open** 10am-5pm Mon-Fri; noon-5pm Sat, Sun. **Admission** €5; €2.50 4s-12s; free MK, under-4s. **Credit** MC, V.

Museum Lambert van Meerten

Oude Delft 199 (015 260 2358). **Open** 10am-5pm Tue-Sat; 1-5pm Sun. **Admission** €5; €4 12s-16s; free under-12s. **Credit** AmEx, MC, V.

De Porceleyne Fles

Rotterdamseweg 196 (015 251 2030/www.royal delft.com). **Open** *Apr-Oct* 9am-5pm Mon-Sat; 9.30am-5pm Sun. *Nov-Mar* 9am-5pm Mon-Sat. **Admission** €3.50. **Credit** AmEx, DC, MC, V.

Het Prinsenhof Municipal Museum

Sint Agathaplein 1 (015 260 2358). **Open** 10am-5pm Tue-Sat; 1-5pm Sun. **Admission** €5; €4 12s-16s; free under-12s. **Credit** AmEx, MC, V.

Reptielenzoo Serpo

Stationsplein 8 (015 212 2184/www.serpo.nl). **Open** 10am-6pm Mon-Sat; 1-6pm Sun. **Admission** €6; €4 4s-12s; free under-4s. **Credit** MC, V.

Where to eat & drink

Though many bars and cafés may appear to outsiders as survivors of a bygone era – white-aproned waiters and high-ceilinged interiors and all – it's the norm in Delft. Other cities offer hot chocolate finished with whipped cream; cafés here use real cream and accompany it with a fancier brand of biscuit.

Don't miss local institution **Kleyweg's Stads Koffyhuis** (Oude Delft 133, 015 212 4625), which has a terrace barge in the summer and serves Knollaert beer, a local brew made to a medieval recipe. **De Wijnhaven** (Wijnhaven 22, 015 214 1460) and **The V** (Voorstraat 11, 015 214 0916) provide delicious meals at nice prices.

Where to stay

De Ark (Koornmarkt 65, 015 215 7999/ www.deark.nl) is upmarket, with rooms priced from €95 for single and from €120 for a double. **De Plataan** (Doelenplein 10, 015 212 6046/www.hoteldeplataan.nl) is more reasonable, costing €82 for a single, €92 for a double. Budget travellers should try the campsite at **Delftse Hout** (Korftlaan 5, 015 213 0040/www.tours.nl/delftsehout), where a site for two costs €22. During colder weather,

Haarlem days: eat al fresco...

try **De Kok** (Houttuinen 14, 015 212 2125/
www.hoteldekok.nl), where singles cost from
€61 to €76 and doubles go for €71 to €115.

Getting there

By car

60km (37 miles) south-west on A4, then A13.

By train

1hr from Amsterdam Centraal Station, changing at
the Hague if necessary.

Tourist information

Toeristische Informatie Punt
(Tourist Information Point)

Hippolytusbuurt 4 (0900 515 1555/www.delft.nl).
Open 11am-4pm Mon; 10am-4pm Tue-Sat; 10am-
3pm Sun.

Haarlem

Lying between Amsterdam and the beaches
of Zandvoort and Bloemendaal, Haarlem – a
kinder, gentler and older Amsterdam – is a
stone's throw from the dunes and the sea, and
attracts flocks of beach-going Amsterdammers
and Germans every summer. All trace of
Haarlem's origins as a 10th-century settlement
on a choppy inland sea disappeared with the
draining of the Haarlemmermeer in the mid-
19th century. But the town hasn't lost its
appeal: the historic centre, with its lively main
square, canals and some of the country's most
charming almshouse courtyards, is beautiful.

To catch up with Haarlem's history, head to
St Bavo's Church, which dominates the main
square. It was built around 1313 but suffered

fire damage in 1328; rebuilding and expansion
lasted another 150 years. It's surprisingly
bright inside: cavernous white transepts stand
as high as the nave and are a stunning sight.
The floor is made up of 1,350 graves, including
one featuring only the word 'Me' and another
long enough to hold a famed local giant, plus
a dedication to a local midget who died of
injuries from a game he himself invented:
dwarf-tossing. Music buffs will swoon at the
sight of the famed Müller organ (1738): boasting
an amazing 5,068 pipes, it's been played by
Handel and the young Mozart.

Haarlem's cosy but spacious Grote Markt is
one of the loveliest squares in the Netherlands.
A few blocks away is the former old men's
almshouse and orphanage that currently houses
the **Frans Halsmuseum**. Though it holds
a magnificent collection of 16th- and 17th-
century portraits, still lifes, genre paintings
and landscapes, the highlights are eight group
portraits of militia companies and regents by
Frans Hals (who's buried in St Bavo's). The
museum also has collections of period furniture,
Haarlem silver and ceramics and an 18th-
century apothecary with Delftware pottery.
Nearby is **De Hallen**, whose two buildings, the
Verweyhal and the Vleeshal, house modern art.

Though it's rather in the shadow of the Frans
Halsmuseum, the **Teylers Museum** is equally
excellent. Founded in 1784, it's the country's
oldest museum; fossils and minerals sit beside
antique scientific instruments, and there's also a
superb 16th- to 19th-century collection of 10,000
drawings by masters including Rembrandt,
Michelangelo and Raphael. However, Haarlem
is more than just a city of nostalgia: it's one of
vision. Local illustrator/cartoonist Joost Swarte,
for example, has spread his wings and designed
the Tonelschuur theatre in the town.

... or take to the water.

Frans Halsmuseum

Groot Heiligland 62 (023 511 5775). **Open** 11am-5pm Mon-Sat; noon-5pm Sun. **Admission** €7.90; €2.50 13s-18s; €6.50 over-65s; free under-13s. **No credit cards.**

De Hallen

Grote Markt 16 (023 511 5840). **Open** 11am-5pm Mon-Sat; noon-5pm Sun. **Admission** €4; €2.70 over-65s; free MK, under-19s. **No credit cards.**

Teylers Museum

Spaarne 16 (023 531 9010). **Open** 10am-5pm Tue-Sat; noon-5pm Sun. **Admission** €5.50; €1 5s-18s; free MK, under-5s. **No credit cards.**

Where to eat & drink

The pick of the many eating spots on Groot Markt is the **Loft** (Grote Markt 8, 023 551 1350). Cosier is **Jacobus Pieck Drink & Eetlokaal** (Warmoesstraat 18, 023 532 6144), while the riverside **Eclectic Bar Restaurant Willendorf** (Bakenessergracht 109, 023 531 1970/www.willendorf.nl) is a hip space with regular DJs. Hotspot **Lambermons** (Spaarne 96, 023 542 7804/www.lambermons.nl) is in an epic industrial building where you get a different French-inspired €8 course put in front of you every half hour from 6.30pm to 11pm; stay until you're full.

If you're into wooden panelling, leather wallpaper, chaotic conviviality and infinite beer choices, head to **In Den Uiver** (Riviervismarkt 13, 023 532 5399). For bands and/or DJs, check out the **Patronaat** (Oostvest 54, 023 532 6010/www.patronaat.nl), Haarlem's answer to Amsterdam's Melkweg. Nightclub **Stalker** (Kromme Elleeboogsteeg 20, 023 531 4652/www.clubstalker.nl) specalises in upfront dance music blasted through a surround sound system.

Where to stay

The beautiful **Carlton Square Hotel** (Baan 7, 023 531 9091/www.carlton.nl) is posh and pricey, with rooms for €190 to €205. For a real splurge, however, book one of the two mind-blowingly sumptuous suites – one at €295, the other €375 – at design hotel **Spaarne 8** (Spaarne 8, 023 551 1544/www.spaarne8.com). The **Carillon** (Grote Markt 27, 023 531 0591/www.hotelcarillon.com) has doubles for €51.60, while outside the centre, the hostel **Stayokay Haarlem** (Jan Gijzenpad 3, 023 537 3793/www.stayokay.com) offers B&B for €21 to €24.

Getting there

By car

10km (6 miles) west on A5.

By train

15min, direct from Amsterdam Centraal Station.

Tourist information

VVV

Stationsplein 1 (0900 616 1600 premium rate/www.vvvzk.nl). **Open** *Oct-Mar* 9.30am-5.30pm Mon-Fri; 10am-2pm Sat. *Apr-Sep* 9am-5.30pm Mon-Fri; 9.30am-3.30pm Sat.

The Hague

While never officially a city – in days of yore, powers-that-be did not want to offend its more ancient neighbours, Leiden and Utrecht – the Hague (aka Den Haag) is the nation's power hub and centre for international justice. It began life as the hunting ground of the Counts of Holland before being officially founded in 1248, when

Beyond Holland

The country's attractions don't begin and end with the province of Holland and the cities of the Randstad. The other provinces offer a variety of attractions that provide a cultural education for those looking to explore the Netherlands beyond the usual stops. The official tourism website www.holland.com is a handy resource. Bear in mind that 0900 phone numbers are charged at premium rate.

Drenthe

Fens, moors and forests highlight this historical province: humans have lived here for some 50,000 years. The **Drents Museum** in Assen (Brink 1, Assen, 0592 377773) offers a glimpse of the area's past with its terrific prehistoric artefacts; while those bored of Rembrandts will treasure the **Museum of Fake Art** (Brink 1, Vledder, Westerveld Drenthe, 052 138 3352/ www.museums-vledder.nl).

For information on attractions in Drenthe, call the **Provincial VVV** (0900 202 2393) or visit the **Assen VVV** (Marktstraat 8-10).

Friesland

The main attraction in Friesland, once an independent tribal nation located along the coast from North Holland to East Germany, is its network of waterways; boating, still a popular pursuit, is now focused around the town of **Sneek**. To the north and west of Friesland are the desolate **Frisian Islands** with their nature and bird reserves.

The **Provincial VVV** is at Sophialaan 4 in Leeuwarden (0900 202 4060). The **Sneek VVV** can be found at Markstraat 18. For information on the Frisian Islands, visit the **VVV Waddeneilanden** (Willem Barentzskade 19a, Terschelling, 0562 443000); the largest island, **Texel**, has its own VVV (Emmelaan 66, 0222 312847).

Gelderland

The largest of the Dutch provinces, Gelderland is dominated by the **Veluwe**, a massive stretch of forest and moorland. It's here you'll find the country's biggest national park, the **Hoge Veluwe** (entrances at Otterlo, Schaarsbergen and Hoenderloo, visitors' centre 0318 591627), and the terrific outdoor **Rijksmuseum Kröller-Müller** (near Otterlo entrance of Hoge Veluwe, 0318 591041/www.kmm.nl).

The **Provincial VVV** can be reached on 0570 680700, and offers full information on the area's attractions.

Groningen

Arguably the most staid and conservative of the Dutch provinces, Groningen does nevertheless sport a studenty and scenic capital, which in turn sports an epic church (the **Martinikerk**), a smattering of notorious nightlife and a globally renowned modern art gallery. Towns such as **Ten Boer**, **Garmerwold**, **Stedum**, **Appingedam** and **Uithuizen** are all graced with ancient and wonderful rural churches.

William II built a castle on the site of the present parliament buildings, the **Binnenhof**. It was here that the De Witt brothers were lynched after being accused of conspiring to kill William of Orange; they were brutalised nearby in what is now the most evocatively grim torture museum in the country: **Gevangenpoort**.

Queen Beatrix arrives at the Binnenhof in a golden coach every Prinsjesdag (third Tuesday in September) for the annual state opening of parliament. Guided tours are organised daily to the Knights' Hall, where the ceremony takes place. The **Mauritshuis**, a former regal home, is open to the public with one of the most famous collections in the world: works by the likes of Rubens, Rembrandt and Vermeer.

The Hague's city centre is lively, with a good selection of shops lining the streets and squares around the palaces and along the lovely and more upmarket Denneweg. Architects have

worked to bring the city into a bigger and brighter cultural sphere – with mixed success – yet the Hague is also one of the greenest cities in Europe, and has a number of lovely parks. Clingendael has a Japanese garden; Meijendael, further out, is part of an ancient forest; and the Scheveningse Bosje is big enough to occupy an entire day. Between the Bosje and the city is Vredes Paleis (the Peace Palace), a gift from Andrew Carnegie that is now the UN's Court of International Justice. (Meanwhile, on Churchillplein, the International Criminal Tribunal for the former Yugoslavia is the setting for Milosevic's ongoing sulky theatrics.)

Beyond Scheveningse Bosje is Scheveningen, a former fishing village and now a huge resort. The architectural highlight is the Steigenberger Kurhaus Hotel: built in 1887, it's a legacy of Scheveningen's days as a bathing place for European high society. The town's history as a

The **Provincial VVV** and the **Groningen VVV** are housed in the same building at Gedempte Kattendiep 6 in Groningen (0900 202 3050).

Limburg

Limburg is arguably most notable – besides, of course, for their frolicsome Carnival celebrations – for the town of **Maastricht**, a lovely spot to explore, for all its somewhat unexciting European political ties. The **Maastricht VVV** can be found at Kleine Straat 1 (043 325 2121) – it also deals with the whole province.

Noord Brabant

Bordering Belgium to the south, Noord Brabant's main attractions are the **Safaripark Beekse Bergen** in Hilvarenbeek (0900 233 5732) and **De Efteling Theme Park** in Kaatsheuvel (0416 288111). However, it's also home to the city of **Eindhoven**, which offers a fine football team (PSV) and an even better modern art museum: the **Stedelijk van Abbemuseum** (Bilderdijklaan 10, 040 238 1000/www.vanabbemuseum.nl).

The **Provincial VVV** can be found in the town of Tilburg (spoorlaan 364/0900 202 0815); the **Eindhoven VVV** is at Stationsplein 17 (0900 112 2363).

Overijssel

Known as the 'Garden of the Netherlands', Overijssel is criss-crossed by long, winding rivers and 400 kilometres (249 miles) of canoe routes. Among its attractions are the

Hellendoorn Adventure Park (0548 655555), the splendid modern art museum, the **Rijksmuseum Twenthe** in Enschede (Lasondersingel 129-31, 053 435 8675) and the summer carnivals that are held in almost every town in the province.

For more information, contact the **Enschede VVV** (Oude Markt 31, 053 432 3200) or the **Provincial VVV** (0570 680700).

Utrecht

Utrecht's main attractions – the province's capital (*see p270*) and the assorted castles (*see p272*) – have been covered elsewhere in this chapter. The beautiful medieval town of **Amersfoot** is also well worth a look; its VVV can be found at Stationsplein 9-11 (0900 112 2364).

Zeeland

A large number of old buildings and farms in Zeeland were swept away in the floods of 1953. The locals learned the lesson well: the province is now home to the world's biggest flood barrier: the monumental Delta Works was completed in 1986 at an eye-watering cost of f14 billion (now €6.4 billion). Among the province's less useful but more entertaining attractions are the **Stedelijk Museum**, in the town of Vlissingen (Bellamypark 19, 0118 412498) and the historical **Zeeuws Museum**, situated in Middelburg (Abdij 3, 0118 626655).

The **Provincial VVV** is at Nieuwe Burg 42 in Middelburg (0118 659965).

---

spa has been resurrected with the opening of Kuur Thermen Vitalizee (Strandweg 13F, 070 416 6500/www.vitalizee.nl), a spa bath that offers a range of treatments. Also here is the 'Sculptures by the Sea' exhibition, a multi-dimensional collection of statues at the **Museum Beelden aan Zee**. The renovated **Panorama Mesdag** houses not only the largest painting in the country – from which it takes its name – but also works from the Hague (marine style) and Barbizon (peasant life and landscape) schools.

None, though, is worth as much as *Victory Boogie Woogie*, Piet Mondriaan's last work, which sold for a cool f80 million (€36 million) in 1998. It's now at the **Gemeentemuseum**, which holds the world's largest collections of works by Mondriaan and MC Escher in newly restored buildings. The Gemeentemuseum is next door to the excellent **Museum of Photography** (Stadhouderslaan 43, 070 338

1144/www.fotomuseumdenhaag.nl) and linked to the **Museon**, an excellent science museum that induces wonder in both kids and adults, and the Omniversum IMAX Theatre, a state-of-the-art planetarium. Gemeente's brand new sister museum, **Escher in het Paleis** on the Lange Voorhout, is a filled with the mind-melting art of MC Escher and supplemented with much interactive multimedia. One way of exploring Holland speedily is by visiting **Madurodam**, an insanely detailed miniature city that dishes up every Dutch cliché in the book. Windmills turn, ships sail and modern trains speed around on the world's largest model railway.

The Hague offers a decent calendar of events, the most entertaining of which is Queen's Day on 30 April (though it's not as wild as Amsterdam's celebrations). The North Sea Regatta is held at the end of May, falling in the middle of the International Sand Sculpture

Trips Out of Town

Festival (early May to early June). Add to this the Hague Horse Days, equestrian displays held in the Lange Voorhout (late May), Parkpop, Europe's largest free pop festival (June), the mammoth North Sea Jazz Festival (July), and the rocking literary festival Crossing Border (November; see p183), and the old cliché about there being something for everyone rears its ugly but apposite head.

Binnenhof
Binnenhof 8A (070 364 6144). **Open** 10am-3.45pm Mon-Sat. **Admission** €5; €4.30 under-13s. **No credit cards.**

Escher in Het Paleis
Lange Voorhout 74 (070 42 77730/www.escherin hetpaleis.nl). **Open** 11am-5pm Tue-Sun. **Admission** €7.50; €5 7s-15s; free MK. **No credit cards.**

Gemeentemuseum
Stadhouderslaan 41 (070 338 1111/ www.gemeentemuseum.nl). **Open** 11am-5pm Tue-Sun. **Admission** €7.50; free MK, under-18s. **No credit cards.**

Gevangenpoort Museum
Buitenhof 33 (070 346 0861/www.gevangenpoort.nl). **Open** *Tours* 11am, noon, 1pm, 2pm, 3pm, 4pm Tue-Fri; noon, 1pm, 2pm, 3pm, 4pm Sat, Sun. **Admission** €3.60; €2.70 under-13s. **No credit cards.**

Madurodam
George Maduroplein 1 (070 355 3900/www.maduro dam.nl). **Open** *Mid Mar-June* 9am- 8pm daily. *July, Aug* 9am-10pm daily. *Sept-mid Mar* 9am-6pm daily. **Admission** €11; €10 over-60s; €8 4s-11s; free under-4s. **No credit cards.**

Mauritshuis
Korte Vijverberg 8 (070 302 3456/www.maurits huis.nl). **Open** 10am-5pm Tue-Sat; 11am-5pm Sun. **Admission** €12.50; €5.50 MK; free under-18s. **No credit cards.**

Museum Beelden aan Zee
Harteveltstraat 1 (070 358 5857/www.beelden aanzee.nl). **Open** 11am-5pm Tue-Sun. **Admission** €6; €3 5s-12s; free under-5s. **No credit cards.**

Panorama Mesdag
Zeestraat 65 (070 310 6665/www.mesdag.nl). **Open** 10am-5pm Mon-Sat; noon-5pm Sun. **Admission** €4; €3 over-65s; €2 4s-13s; free under-4s. **No credit cards.**

Where to eat & drink

Juliana's (Plaats 11, 070 365 0235) is where the beautiful people enjoy lunch and dinner, whereas **De Klap** (Koningin Emmakade 118A, 070 345 4060) is a more down-to-earth café with cheap meals. For inspired Indonesian cuisine in a swish setting, try **Surakarta Indonesische Brasserie** (Prinsestraat 13, 070 346 6999/

www.surakarta.nl); for inspired Indo in a living room setting try **Bogor** (Van Swietenstraat 2, 070 346 1628). In the remarkably atmospheric catacombs underneath the old City Hall, **Catacomben** (Grote Halstraat 3, 070 302 3060) offers reasonably priced Caribbean, French, Asian and Middle Eastern eats, while **WOX** (Buitenhof 36, 070 365 3754) is the latest chic address to eat at.

Beer fans should try **De Paas** (Dunne Bierkade 16A, 070 360 0019/www.depaas.nl), while the living-room feel at **Murphy's Law** (Dr Kuyperstraat 7, 070 427 2507) attracts an odd but friendly mix of vaguely alternative folk and drunk diplomats. **De Zwart Ruiter** (Grote Markt 27, 070 364 9549), a revamped brown café with stylish décor whose regulars often head on to **Jetlag** (Kettingstraat 12B, www.jetlag-lounge.nl) for dancing. Coffeeshop connoisseurs should try **Cremers** (Prinsestraat 84, 070 346 2346), which attracts a diverse crowd with its fully stocked bar – it even has absinthe.

Where to stay

Des Indes InterContinental (Lange Voorhout 54-6, 070 361 2345/www.desindes. com) is arguably the most luxurious hotel in town, with prices to match its facilities: singles cost €230, doubles €295. The hostel **Stayokay Den Haag** (Scheepmakersstraat 27, 070 315 7888/www.stayokay.com) charges around €25 for a dorm bed and €65 to €70 for doubles.

Getting there

By car
50km (31 miles) south-west on A4, then A44.

By train
50min from Amsterdam Centraal Station to Den Haag Centraal Station; change at Leiden if necessary.

Tourist information

VVV
Koningin Julianaplein 30, outside Centraal Station (0900 340 3505 premium rate/www.denhaag.nl). **Open** *Apr-Sep* 10am-6pm Mon; 9am-6pm Tue-Fri; 10am-5pm Sat. *Oct-Mar* 10am-5.30pm Mon; 9am-5.30pm Tue-Fri; 10am-5pm Sat.

Leiden

Canal-laced Leiden derives a good deal of its charm from the Netherlands' oldest university, which was founded here in 1575 and which boasts alumni such as Descartes, US president John Quincy Adams and many a Dutch royal. The old town teems with bikes and bars, boasts the most historic monuments per square metre in the country, and is, accordingly, a rewarding place for a stroll and a short weekend away from the relative madness of Amsterdam.

In the Dutch Golden Age of the late 16th and 17th centuries, Leiden grew fat on the textile trade. It also spawned three great painters of the time: Rembrandt, Jan van Goyen and Jan Steen. Although few works by these three masters remain on display in Leiden today, the **Stedelijk Museum de Lakenhal** (Lakenhal Municipal Museum), where the Golden Age clothmakers met, does have a Rembrandt, as well as other Old Masters and collections of pewter, tiles, silver and glass. Perhaps Leiden's most notable museum, though, is the **Rijksmuseum van Oudheden** (National Museum of Antiquities), which houses the largest archaeological collection in the country: the Egyptian mummies should not be missed. The **Rijksmuseum voor Volkenkunde** (National Museum of Ethnology), meanwhile, showcases the cultures of Africa, Oceania, Asia, the Americas and the Arctic.

The ten million fossils, minerals and stuffed animals exhibited at the **Naturalis** (Natural History Museum) make it the country's largest museum collection, while the 6,000 species at the **Hortus Botanicus**, one of the world's oldest botanical gardens, include descendants of the country's first tulips. If Dutch clichés are your schtick, head to the **Molenmuseum de Valk** (the Falcon Windmill Museum), a windmill-turned-museum where you can see living quarters, machinery and a picturesque view of Leiden. An even better view can be had from the top of the Burcht, a 12th-century fort on an ancient artificial mound in the city centre.

Hortus Botanicus Leiden

Rapenburg 73 (071 527 7249/www.hortusleiden.nl). **Open** *Apr-Oct* 10am-6pm daily. *Nov-Mar* 10am-4pm Mon-Fri, Sun. **Admission** €4; €2 concessions; free MK. **Credit** AmEx, MC, V.

Molenmuseum de Valk

2e Binnenvestgracht 1 (071 516 5353/www.molen museum.nl). **Open** 10am-5pm Tue-Sat; 1-5pm Sun. **Admission** €2.50; €1.50 concessions; free MK, under-6s. **No credit cards.**

Naturalis, Nationaal Natuurhistorisch Museum

Darwinweg (071 568 7600). **Open** 10am-6pm Tue-Sun. **Admission** €8; €4.50 4s-17s; free under-4s. **No credit cards.**

Rijksmuseum van Oudheden

Rapenburg 28 (0900 6 600600/www.rmo.nl). **Open** 10am-5pm Tue-Fri; noon-5pm Sat, Sun. **Admission** €6; €5.50 6s-18s; €5 over-65s; free MK. **Credit** AmEx, DC, MC, V.

Rijksmuseum voor Volkenkunde

Steenstraat 1 (071 516 8800). **Open** 10am-5pm Tue-Sun. **Admission** €6.50; €3.50 concessions; free MK. **No credit cards.**

Stedelijk Museum de Lakenhal

Oude Singel 28-32 (071 516 55360/www.laken hal.nl). **Open** 10am-5pm Tue-Fri; noon-5pm Sat, Sun. **Admission** €4; €2.50 over-65s; free MK, under-18s. **No credit cards.**

Where to eat & drink

A trad cosy atmosphere is to be had at **De Hooykist** (Hooigracht 49, 071 512 5809) and **In Den Bierbengel** (Langebrug 71, 071 514 8056), which specialises in meat, fish and wines. Bar-restaurant **Annie's Verjaardag** (Hoogstraat 1A, 071 512 5737) occupies eight candlelit cellars underneath a bridge in the centre of town: its main selling point is the canal barge terrace.

Another unique location is **Restaurant City Hall** (Stadhuisplein 3, 071 514 4055/ www.restaurantcityhall.nl), a budget hotspot in the city's ancient – you guessed it – City Hall. For something ultra-cheap and cheerful, try **La Bota** (Herensteeg 9, 071 514 6340) near the Pieterskerk. It's really a fun studenty bar that does home-style meat and veggie dishes, salads and snacks for around €8. Excellent tapas in lounge surrounds can be had at **Oloroso** (Breestraat 49, 071 514 6633).

For a walk on the grungey side, try another student standby, **WW** (Wolsteeg 4-6, 071 512 5900/www.deww.nl), which has bands, dartboards and graffiti. **The Duke** (Oude Singel 2, 071 512 1972) offers live jazz, and **LVC** (Breestraat 66, 071 566 1059/www.lvc.nl) hosts smaller touring acts. Traditional bars are dotted along Nieuwe Beestenmarkt, Nieuwstraat and Breestraat.

Where to stay

The **Golden Tulip** (Schipholweg 3, 071 522 1121/www.goldentulip.nl) is the town's poshest hotel, with rooms between €80 and €174. Rather cheaper is the **Mayflower** (Beestenmarkt 2, 071 514 2641), where rooms cost €75 to €125, while the **Pension De Witte Singel** (Witte Singel 80, 071 512 4592) is cheaper still, at €36 to €66.

Getting there

By car

40km (24 miles) south-west on A4.

By train

35min from Amsterdam Centraal Station, direct.

Tourist information

VVV

Stationsweg 2D (0900 222 2333 premium rate/www.leidenpromotie.nl). **Open** 11am-5.30pm Mon; 9.30am-5.30pm Tue-Fri; 10am-4.30pm Sat.

Rotterdam

A skate city, a harbour city; a multicultural fusion, an artists' haven; hometown to humanism, an architectural inspiration; a Cultural Capital of Europe, a historical museum centre, a jazz-lover's dream... There's no pinning Rotterdam down.

You could argue that Rotterdam is the Netherlands' only real city, but don't say as much to an Amsterdammer. Neither should you hint at the possibility that Rotterdam may soon surpass the 'Dam in sheer happeningness. This 'Manhattan on the Maas' had a clean slate to play with after its almost complete destruction in World War II, and has recently managed to fill in the massive and long-standing gaps in both its urban and cultural landscape. Rotterdam is a city to watch, so go to the VVV for a complete overview of its offerings, including excellent architectural, harbour and industry tours.

The imposing, futuristic skyline along the banks of the River Maas is certainly a success story, with the Oude Haven (Old Harbour) now a work of imaginative modernism, the pinnacle of which is Piet Blom's witty **Kijk-Kubus**. These bright yellow cubic houses are tilted cater-corner and stand, a little goofily, on stilts. Of the houses, No.70 is open to visitors. Across the epic bridge **Erasmusbrug** (named after famous local boy, the humanist Erasmus) the renovation of the old harbour districts of Kop van Zuid and Entrepot is pretty much complete. Don't miss the cutting-edge cultural activities going down in the Las Palmas (Willeminakade 66,www.laspalmas rotterdam.nl) warehouse complex.

Across town, architectural wizard Rem Koolhaas designed Rotterdam's cultural heart, the Museum Park, where you'll find outdoor sculptures and five museums. The three best are the **Netherlands Architecture Institute**, which gives an overview of the history and development of architecture, especially in Rotterdam; the **Museum Boijmans-Van Beuningen**, with a beautiful collection of traditional and contemporary art (including works by Van Eyck and Rembrandt) and a sizeable design collection; and the **Kunsthal**, which deals with art, design and photography of a more modern persuasion. The enjoining street Witte de Withstraat has

many smaller but no less cutting-edge galleries along with some excellent restaurants and bars. A bird's eye view of all the modern development can be had from the nearby **Euromast**, if you can handle the height (185 metres, or 607 feet). The park at its base is where many locals meet when weather permits.

The sprawling **Historical Museum Rotterdam** includes the Dubbelde Palmboom (Double Palm Tree), housed in an old granary in Delfshaven and featuring life and work in the Meuse delta from 8000 BC to the present, and the **Het Schielandshuis**, a 17th-century palatial mansion and another of the few buildings spared in the bombing. Now placed in bizarre juxtaposition to Quist's 1992 Robeco Tower and the giant Hollandse Bank Unie, it displays rooms and clothing from the 18th century to the present. Old world charm also abounds at the neighbouring village of Schiedam (VVV 010 473 3000), which sports both the world's tallest windmill and the planet's largest collection of Dutch gins and liqueurs in the tasting house of its museum.

One of the shopping areas, Beurstraverse, is a modern development itself; it has the usual bright international chains along with the Bijenkorf department store. At the base of the oval World Trade Center on Coolsingel is the Koopgoot – 'the buying gutter', as it was dubbed by the playful local tongue – which was the country's first underground shopping mall. Nieuwe Binnenweg is a shopping paradise for clubbers, Van Oldenbarneveltstraat offers more upmarket fare, and Jan Evertsenplaats is a green square where you can take a rest from all that spending.

One can perhaps best experience Rotterdam as the only city in the Netherlands that is experiencing a growth in youth population by renting inline skates or roller-skates and trying out the largest outdoor skate park in the country on West-Blank; get your skates on at Rotterdam Sport Import (Witte de Withstraat 57, 010 461 0066). Where Amsterdam has bikes, Rotterdam seems to prefer smaller wheels.

If you're a backpacker, take advantage of Use-it (Conradstraat 2, 010 240 9158/ www.jip.org/use-it), located outside the station on an island surrounded by Eurolines bus bays. Rather like a young person's VVV, it offers a feast of ideas for stuff to do in the city, as well as free lockers if you want to ditch your backpack and roam unburdened for a while.

Besides the terrific **International Film Festival Rotterdam** (www.iffr.com; *see p194*) that starts at the end of January, it's one festival after another from the beginning of June until late September. The summer carnival, Streetlife, a sporty lifestyle event for young people, takes place at Blaak in late June (029 734 444). Don't miss the Dunya Festival (World Festival), with music, poetry, stories and street theatre, held at the Park (near the Euromast) in June. For Parade (033 465 4577; *see p181*), the Museumpark is taken over by a travelling theatre, and on the occasion of the Fast Forward Dance Parade in mid-August, nearly the while city becomes one massive street party.

Euromast
Parkhaven 20 (010 436 4811/www.euromast.nl). **Open** *Apr-Sept* 10am-7pm daily. *July, Aug* 10am-10.30pm Tue-Sat; 10am-7pm Mon, Sun. *Oct-Mar* 10am-5pm daily. **Admission** €7.75; €5 4s-11s. **Credit** AmEx, DC, MC, V.

Historical Museum Rotterdam
Korte Hoogstraat 31 (010 217 6767/www.hmr. rotterdam.nl). **Open** 10am-5pm Tue-Fri; 11am-5pm Sat, Sun. **Admission** €3; €1.50 4s-16s; free under-4s. **No credit cards**.

Kunsthal
Westzeedijk 341 (010 440 0301/www.kunsthal.nl). **Open** 10am-5pm Tue-Sat; 11am-5pm Sun. **Admission** €7.50; €2.50 6s-18s; free under-5s. **No credit cards**.

Kijk-Kubus
Overblaak 70 (010 414 2285/www.cubehouse.nl). **Open** *Jan, Feb* 11am-5pm Fri-Sun. *Mar-Dec* 11am-5pm daily. **Admission** €1.75; €1.25 concessions; free under-4s. **No credit cards**.

Museum Boijmans-Van Beuningen
Museumpark 18-20 (010 441 9400/ www.boijmans.rotterdam.nl). **Open** 10am-5pm Tue-Sat; 11am-5pm Sun. **Admission** free-€6; free-€2 4s-16s; free MK, under-4s. **No credit cards**.

Netherlands Architecture Institute
Museumpark 25 (010 440 1200/www.nai.nl). **Open** 10am-5pm Tue-Sat; 11am-5pm Sun. **Admission** €5; €3 4s-16s; free MK, under-4s. **No credit cards**.

Where to eat & drink

Oude Haven, the **Entrepot** district and **Delfshaven** all offer a wide choice of (grand) cafés and restaurants. For veggies, **Bla Bla** (Piet Heynsplein 35, 010 477 4448) is expensive but busy, so book ahead. **Foody's** (Nieuwe Binnenweg 151, 010 436 5163) is the latest in fine international eateries; **Colosseo** (Rodezand 36, 010 414 7030) is a fine and cheap purveyor of Indonesian cuisine; **El Faro Analuz** (Leuvenhaven 73-4, 010 414 6213) serves stellar Spanish tapas; while the best Chinese in town can be found by cruising the **Katendrecht**. Also the hotels Bazar and New York (*see 270*) both serve excellent food in singular settings. The website www.specialbite.com is a good place to check out the latest offerings.

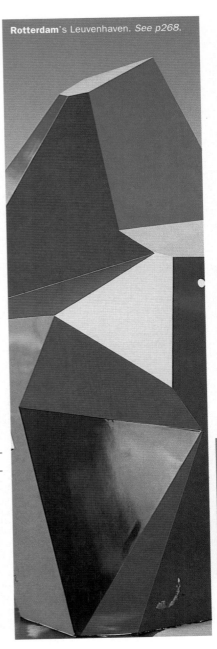

Rotterdam's Leuvenhaven. *See p268.*

Trips Out of Town

Bars-wise, **De Schouw** (Witte de Withstraat 80, 010 412 4253) is a stylish brown café, a former journalists' haunt that now attracts a mix of artists and students. Lofty ceilings give **Café Dudok** (Meent 88, 010 433 3102) an artsy feel, making it a mellow spot for lunch. Jazz fiends should try **Dizzy** ('s Gravendijkwal 129, 010 477 3014), one of the best jazz venues in the country; for bands and club nights, venture to **Nighttown** (West-Kruiskade 26-8, 010 436 1210/www.nighttown.nl), located on a multicultural road filled with inexpensive global eating treats. The similarly named but considerably smaller **Rotown** (Nieuwe Binnenweg 19, 010 436 2669/www2.rotown.nl) focuses on indie and has a fine bar/restaurant (open 11am-9.30pm). The squattier side of after-dark culture here is currently covered by **Poortgebouw** (Stieltjesstraat 27-38, www.poortgebouw.nl).

Of the vast number of clubbing options, **Now&Wow** (www.now-wow.com), long held to be one of the best dance clubs in Benelux, is reopening in a new location in early 2004; the excellent **Off Corso** (Kruiskade 22, 010 411 3897/www.off-corso.nl) has won the prestigious 'Golden Gnome' award; and **Club Las Palmas** (Wilhelminakade 66, 010 890 1075/www.club-laspalmas.nl) finds big-name DJs for its hip, up-for-it crowd.

Where to stay

Housed in the former Holland-American Line offices, the **Hotel New York** is one of the most luxurious places in town (Koninginnenhoofd 1, 010 439 0500/www.hotelnewyork.nl), but not unreasonably priced: doubles start at €90. Even if you don't stay here, pop in for a coffee or a full-blown plate of *fruits de mer*. One unusual way to spend the night is on **De Clipper** (Scheepmakershaven, 06 5331 4244/www.hostelboat.nl), a boat moored in the centre of the city. It'll set you back €22.50 a night with breakfast.

Hotel Bazar (Witte de Withstraat 16, 010 206 5151/www.hotelbazar.nl) is a little out of the ordinary, too: it sports an Arabian Nights decor and an excellent Middle Eastern restaurant. Their prices for a double range from around €75 to €125. For budget travellers, there's the hostel **Stayokay Rotterdam** (Rochussenstraat 107-9, 010 436 5763/www.stayokay.com); for about €20, you also get the use of a kitchen.

Getting there

By car

73km (45 miles) south on A4, then A13.

By train

1hr from Amsterdam Centraal Station, direct.

Tourist information

VVV

Coolsingel 67 (0900 403 4065 premium rate/ www.vvv.rotterdam.nl). **Open** *Apr-Sept* 9.30am-6pm Mon-Thur; 9.30am-9pm Fri; 9.30am-5pm Sat; noon-5pm Sun. *Oct-Mar* 9.30am-6pm Mon-Thur; 9.30am-9pm Fri; 9.30am-5pm Sat.

Utrecht

One of the oldest cities in the Netherlands, Utrecht was also, in the Middle Ages, its biggest, and was a religious and political centre for centuries. At one point, there were around 40 houses of worship in the city, all with towers and spires. From a distance, Utrecht must have looked like a giant pincushion.

However, there's more to Utrecht than history and scenery. Utrecht University is one of the largest in the Netherlands – continuing to expand and provide work for cutting-edge architects like Rem Koolhaas (who designed the Educatorium) – and the city centre is bustling with trendy shops and relaxed cafés. Happily, too, the Hoog Catharijne, the country's biggest shopping mall but also one of the biggest eyesores, is soon to be destroyed. But for some time yet, you'll have to wander its labyrinthine layout following signs to 'Centrum' in order to leave Central Station. Lovers of luxury should instead head for the boutiques and galleries tucked down the streets along the canals. Linger especially on Oudkerkhof, where there's a concentration of designer shops; La Vie, the shopping centre on Lange Viestraat; and the flower and plant markets along Janskerkhof and Oudegracht on Saturdays.

Though bikes can be hired from Rijwiel Shop (Sijpesteijnkade 40, 030 296 7287), the city is so compact that practically everything is within walking distance. A good place to start a stroll around town from is the Domtoren (the French gothic-style cathedral tower). At over 112 metres (367 feet), not only is it the highest tower in the country, but with over 50 bells it's also the largest musical instrument in the Netherlands. Visitors are allowed to climb the tower. The panoramic view is worth the effort expended on climbing its 465 steps: vistas stretch 40 kilometres (25 miles) to Amsterdam on a clear day. Buy tickets across the square at the Information Center for the Cultural History of Utrecht (Domplein 9, 030 233 3036) where you can also get details on the rest of the city and the castles located on its outskirts.

Erasmusbrug, **Rotterdam**. See p268.

Highrise **Rotterdam**. See p268.

The space between the tower and the Domkerk was originally occupied by the nave of the huge church, which was destroyed by a freak tornado in 1674. Many other buildings were damaged, and the exhibition inside the Domkerk shows interesting 'before' and 'after' sketches. Outside is the Pandhof, a cloister garden planted with many medicinal herbs. The garden, with its beautiful statuette of a canon hunched over his writing, is a tranquil spot for a breather.

Another fascinating place to explore is the Oudegracht, the canal that runs through the centre of the city. Unlike Amsterdam, where the water sits at or near street level, the people of Utrecht have been blessed with waterside footpaths and cellars, which allow them to use the basements of their canalside houses. Many of those cellars now house cafés and shops, and are excellent places for snacks and watching boats navigate their way under the narrow bridges.

Of Utrecht's several museums, the **Museum Catharijneconvent** (St Catharine Convent Museum) is located in a beautiful late medieval building and gives an account of the country's religious history, while the excellent and sprawling **Centraal Museum** harbours not only paintings by 17th-century masters but also the largest Rietveld collection in the world. The **Nationaal Museum van Speelklok tot Pierement** has the world's biggest collection of automated musical instruments, and the **Universiteitsmuseum** (University Museum) focuses on the interaction between science and education. Meanwhile the country's biggest rock garden is a striking part of **Fort Hoofddijk**; on a cold day, the tropical greenhouse is a perfect place for thawing out and absorbing themes like 'plants as clocks' or 'magic and religion'. Look out, too, for the few special days in the year when monuments and museums open their doors to the public for free (check with the VVV); also, during July and August, there are informative walking tours through the city.

Utrecht is located in an area rich with castles, forests and arboretums. In the outskirts of the city, **Slot Zuylen** (Zuylen Castle, Tournooiveld 1, Oud Zuilen, 030 244 0255) presides over exquisite ornamental waterfalls and gardens. Check the concerts and shows in **Kasteel Groeneveld**'s gorgeous gardens (Groeneveld Castle, Groeneveld 2, Baarn, 035 542 0446/www.kasteelgroeneveld.nl), just north-east of Utrecht. Take a stroll in the lovely, unique **Arboretum von Gimborn** (Vossensteinsesteeg 8, 030 253 1826) in Doorne, then pop across the town to **Kasteel Huis Doorn** (Doorn Castle, Langbroekerweg 10, 0343 421020/www.huisdoorn.nl); Kaiser Wilhelm II lived here in exile for 20 years before his death in 1941.

Centraal Museum
Nicolaaskerkhof 10 (030 236 2362/ www.centraal museum.nl). **Open** 11am-5pm Tue-Sun. **Admission** €8; €4 concessions. **No credit cards.**

Fort Hoofddijk
Budapestlaan 17, De Uithof (030 253 5455/030 2531890). **Open** *Mar-Dec* 10am-4pm daily. *May-Sept* 10am-5pm daily. **Admission** €4.50; €1.50 4s-12s; €3.50 over-65s; free MK. **No credit cards.**

Museum Catharijneconvent
Lange Nieuwstraat 38 (031 231 3835/7296/ www.catharijneconvent.nl). **Open** 10am-5pm Tue-Fri; 11am-5pm Sat, Sun. **Admission** €6; €3-€5 concessions; free MK, under-6s. **No credit cards.**

Nationaal Museum van Speelklok tot Pierement
Buurkerkhof 10 (030 231 2789/www.museum speelklok.nl). **Open** 10am-5pm Tue-Sat; noon-5pm Sun. **Admission** €6; €4-€5 concessions. **No credit cards.**

Universiteitsmuseum
Lange Nieuwstraat 106 (030 253 8008/ www.museum.ruu.nl). **Open** 11am-5pm Tue-Sun. **Admission** €4; €2-€3 concessions; free MK. **No credit cards.**

Where to eat & drink
De Winkel van Sinkel (Oudegracht 158, 030 251 0693/www.dewinkelvansinkel.nl), located in a former department store, is a grand setting for a coffee or a meal – especially at night, when its canal-level catacombs open for club nights and to act as a late-night restaurant. **Stadskasteel Oudaen** (Oudegracht 99, 030 231 1864/www. oudaen.nl), the only existing urban medieval castle left in the country, is even posher. **Casas Sanchez** (Springweg 64, 030 231 9566) serves tapas, while top Japanese sushi can be munched at **Konnichi Wa** (Mariaplaats 9, 030 241 6388). If you want a local speciality, try the **Pancake Bakery de Oude Munt Kelder** (Oudegracht aan de Wer, 030 231 6773).

Most bars in the city centre are busy with students. **ACU** (Voorstraat 71, 030 231 4590) is a superstar among squats, with cheap eats and some of the city's edgier musical events; **Belgie** (Oudegracht 196, 030 231 2666) serves over 300 types of beer; and 't **Hart van Utrecht** (Voorstraat 10, no phone) has the coolest crowd of all. The **Tivoli** (Oudegracht 245, 030 231 1491/www.tivoli.nl) – REM's choosen rehearsal space for their 2003 tour – is the best place to check for club nights and touring bands of every imaginable genre; while student favourite **Ekko** (Bemuurde Weerd Westzijde 3, 030 231 7457/ www.ekko.nl) focuses on indie rock and pop.

Where to stay
The four-star **Malie Hotel** (Maliestraat 2, 030 231 6424/www.hotelmalie.nl) is a beautiful old merchant's house: if you really want to pamper yourself, a double costs €115 to €130; singles from €94.50. Those on a tighter budget should take a ten-minute bus ride out from the city centre to Bunnik, where the **Stayokay Bunnik** (Rhijnauwenselaan 14, 030 656 1277/www.stayokay.com) offers a night in a shared room for €22 to €25.

Getting there
By car
40km (25 miles) south-east.

By rail
30min from Amsterdam Centraal Station, direct.

Tourist information
VVV
Vinkenburgstraat 19 (0900 128 873248 premium rate/www.utrechtstad.com). **Open** 9.30am-6.30pm Mon-Wed, Fri; 9.30am-9pm Thur; 9.30am-5pm Sat; 10am-2pm Sun.

Directory

Features

Directory

Getting Around

Getting around Amsterdam is easy. The city has efficient and cheap trams and buses, though if you're staying in the centre, most places are reachable on foot. Locals tend to get around by bike: the streets are busy with cycles all day and most of the evening. There are also pleasure boats, commercial barges and water taxis.

If you were thinking of bringing a car, don't. The roads aren't designed for them, and parking places are elusive. Alas, public transport provision for those with disabilities is dire. There are lifts at all Metro stations, staff can't always help people in wheelchairs.

Handy new service **9292ov** (0900 9292/www.9292ov.nl) groups national bus, train, taxi, tram and ferry information; besides phoning, you can use their Dutch language website for 'door to door' advice. Under *van* (from), type in the *straat* (street), *huisnummer* (house number) and *plaats* (town) you want to start at; then, under *naar* (to), the corresponding details for your destination; select the date and time, then select *aankomst* if that's your ideal arrival time or *vertrek* if that's your ideal departure time; then press *geef reisadvies* (get travel advice).

Arriving & leaving

By air

For general airport enquiries, ring Schiphol Airport on 0900 0141 (costs €0.10/min) or go to www.schiphol.nl.
British Airways
346 9559/www.britishairways.nl.
British Midland
346 9211/www.britishmidland.com.

EasyJet
023 568 4880/www.easyjet.co.uk.
KLM
474 7747/www.klm.com.

Connexxion Airport Hotel Shuttle

Connexxion counter, Section A7, Schiphol Airport, Arrivals (653 4975/www.airporthotelshuttle.com). **Times** every 30min 7am-1pm, every 60min 1-9pm. **Tickets** Single €10.50. *Open return* €18.
This bus service from Schiphol Airport to Amsterdam is available to anyone prepared to pay, not just hotel guests. However, to get door-to-door service and the return pick-up, you'll have to be staying at one of the over 50 allied hotels (but with buses stopping at each of these, it's easy to get off very near your destination). Schedules and the expanding list of allied hotels are on their website (which also has a booking service).

Schiphol Airport Rail Service

Schiphol Airport/Centraal Station (information 0900 9292/www.9292 ov.nl). **Times** Every 10min 4am-midnight, then every hr. **Tickets** Single €3.10; €1.80 under-12s; free under-4s. **Return** €5.50; €3.30 under-12s with adult; free under-4s.
The journey to Centraal Station takes about 20 minutes. Note that a return ticket is valid only for that day.

Taxis

There are always plenty of taxis outside the main exit. They're pricey, however: from the airport to the South and West of the city is about €25, and to the city centre is about €35.

Public transport

For information, tickets, maps and an English-language guide to the city's tickets, visit the GVB, Amsterdam's municipal transport authority, in person (the main branch is opposite Centraal Station) or at their useful website. A basic map of the tram network is on *p316*.
See p252 for details of NS, the Netherlands' rail network.

GVB

Prins Hendrikkade 108-14, Old Centre: New Side (0900 9292/ www.gvb.nl). Tram 1, 2, 4, 5, 9, 13, 16, 17, 24, 25. **Open** Telephone *enquiries* 6am-midnight Mon-Fri; 7am-midnight Sat, Sun. *Personal callers* 7am-9pm Mon-Fri; 8am-9pm Sat, Sun. **Map** p306 D1.
The GVB runs Amsterdam's Metro, bus and tram services, and can provide information on all.
Other locations: Amstel Railway Station, Julianaplein; Rembrandtplein (night buses only, 11pm-5am Thur, Fri, 11pm-6am Sat).

Fares & tickets

Don't travel on a bus or tram without a ticket. Uniformed inspectors make regular checks and passengers without a valid ticket will be fined €29.40 on the spot. Playing the ignorant foreigner won't work.

Strippenkaarten

A 'strip ticket' system operates on trams, buses and the Metro. It's initially confusing, but ultimately good value for money. Prices range from €1.60 for a strip of two units to €6.20 for 15 units and €18.30 for 45 units; children under four travel free, and older children (4s-18s) pay reduced fares (€3.90 for a 15-strip card). Prices increase annually.

Tickets can be bought at GVB offices, post offices, train stations, major supermarkets and many tobacconists. Tickets must be stamped on boarding a tram or bus and on entering a Metro station. The city is divided into five zones: Noord (north), West, Centrum, Oost (east) and Zuid (south); most of central Amsterdam falls within the Centrum zone. Strip tickets are also valid on trains that stop at Amsterdam stations, with the exception of Schiphol.

For travel in a single zone, two units must be stamped, while three are stamped for two zones, four for three zones and so on. On trams, you can stamp your own tickets in the yellow box-like contraption near the doors: fold the ticket so that the unit you need to stamp is at the end. Many trams, though, will now only allow passengers to enter at the rear, where a conductor will stamp the ticket for you. On buses, drivers stamp the tickets, and on the Metro there are stamping machines located at the entrance to stations.

More than one person can travel on one card, but the correct number of units must be stamped for each person. Stamps are valid for one hour; during this time you can transfer to other buses and trams without having to stamp your card again. If your journey takes more than an hour, you have to stamp more units, but no single tram journey within central Amsterdam should take that long. Strippenkaarten remain valid for one year from the date of the first stamp.

Dagkaarten

A cheap option for unlimited travel in Amsterdam, a 'day ticket' costs €5.50. Dutch pensioners, the unwaged and children (4s-18s) pay €3.80. Child day tickets are valid on night buses. A day ticket is valid on trams, buses and the Metro on the day it is stamped until the last bus or tram runs. You need to buy a new ticket for night buses. Only the one-day ticket can be bought from drivers on trams and buses. After you've stamped the day ticket on your first journey, you don't need to stamp it again. You can buy tickets for two days (€8.80), three days (€11.30) and nine days (€26.40).

The extended form of the day ticket is now the Amsterdam Pass (see p70), sold by the Amsterdam Tourist Board (see p290).

And if you only want to make one journey, you can get a single ticket (€2) valid for an hour or a return (€3.50), valid for an hour each way.

Sterabonnement

'Season tickets' can be bought at GVB offices, tobacconists and post offices, and are valid for a week, a month or a year. A weekly pass for the central zone (Centrum) costs €9.30, a monthly one €30.75 and a yearly one €307.50. Children (4s-18s) get cheaper season tickets: €5.90 for a day, €19.50 for a month and €195 for a year. You'll need a passport photo to get a season ticket.

Trams & buses

Buses and trams are a very good way to get around the city centre. Tram services run from 6am Monday to Friday, 6.30am on Saturday and 7.30am on Sunday, with a special night bus service taking over late in the evening. Night buses are numbered from 71 to 79; all go to Centraal Station, except 79.

Night bus stops are indicated by a black square at the stop with the bus number printed on it. Night buses run from 1am to 5.30am from Monday to Friday, and until 6.30am on weekends.

Yellow signs at tram and bus stops indicate the name of the stop and further stops. There are usually maps of the entire network in the shelters and route maps on the trams and buses. The city's bus and tram drivers are courteous and will give directions if asked; most can do so in English.

The yellow and decorated trams are synonymous with Amsterdam, but newer, bluer and higher-windowed ones are becoming more common. Other road users should be warned that they will only stop if absolutely necessary. Cyclists should listen for tram warning bells and be careful to cross tramlines at an angle that avoids the front wheel getting stuck; motorists should avoid blocking tramlines: cars are allowed to venture on to them only if they're turning right.

To get on or off a tram, wait until it has halted at a stop and press the yellow button by the doors, which will then open. On some trams you can buy a ticket from the driver at the front; on others from either a machine in the middle, or a conductor at the back.

Note that Metro 51, 53 and 54 are, confusingly, fast trams that run on Metro lines. This is not the same as the number 5 tram, actually called a *sneltram* ('fast tram').

Metro

The Metro uses the same ticket system as trams and buses (see p274), and serves suburbs to the south and east. There are three lines, all terminating at Centraal Station (which is sometimes abbreviated to CS). Trains run from 6am Monday to Friday (6.30am Sat, 7.30am Sun) to around 12.15am daily.

You can order a cab by calling the central taxi switchboard on 677 7777. The line is often busy on Friday and Saturday nights: expect a phone queuing system.

Be sure to check that the meter initially shows no more than the minimum charge (€2.90). Always ask the driver to tell you the rough cost of the journey before setting out. Even short journeys are expensive: on top of €2.90, you will be expected to pay €1.80 per kilometre for the first 25 kilometres, then €1.40 per kilometre thereafter.

If you feel you've been ripped off, ask for a receipt, which you are entitled to see before handing over cash. If the charge is extortionate, phone the TCA, the central taxi office (650 6506; 9am-5pm Mon-Fri) or contact the police. Rip-offs are relatively rare but it's always a good idea to check that the cab you are getting into has the 'TCA' sign.

Sometimes it's very hard to hail a taxi in the street, but ranks are dotted around the city. The best central ones are found outside Centraal Station, by the bus station at the junction of Kinkerstraat and Marnixstraat, Rembrandtplein and Leidseplein.

Wheelchairs will only fit in taxis if they're folded. If you're in a wheelchair, phone the car transport service for wheelchair users (633 3943 9am-5pm, Mon-Fri). You'll need to book your journey one or two days in advance and it costs around €2 per kilometre.

Driving

If you absolutely must bring a car to the Netherlands, join a national motoring organisation beforehand. This should issue you with booklets that explain what to do in the event of a breakdown in Europe. To drive in the Netherlands you'll need a valid national driving licence, although **ANWB** (*see below*) and many car hire firms favour photocard licences (Brits need the paper version as well for this to be legal; the photocard takes a couple of weeks to come through if you're applying from scratch). You'll need an international identification disk, a registration certificate, proof that the vehicle has passed a road safety test in its country of origin and insurance documents.

Major roads are usually well maintained and clearly signposted. Motorways are labelled 'A'; major roads 'N'; and European routes 'E'. Brits in particular should note that the Dutch drive on the right. Drivers and front-seat passengers must always wear seatbelts. Speed limits are 50kmph (31mph) within cities, 70kmph (43mph) outside, and 100kmph (62mph) on motorways. If you're driving in Amsterdam, look out for cyclists, who'll come at you from all directions. Many streets in Amsterdam are now one-way.

Royal Dutch Automobile Club (ANWB)

Museumplein 5, Museum Quarter (673 0844/head office 070 314 1414/customer services 0800 0503/24hr emergency line 0800 0888/www.anwb.nl). Tram 2, 3, 5, 12, 16. **Open** *Customer services* 9.30am-6pm Mon-Fri; 9.30am-9pm Thur; 9.30am-5pm Sat. **Credit** MC, V. **Map** p310 D6.
If you haven't joined a motoring organisation, enrol here for an annual €48-€74, which covers the cost of assistance if your vehicle breaks down. Members of a foreign motoring organisation may be entitled to free help. Crews may not accept credit cards or cheques at the scene.

Car hire

Dutch car hire (*autoverhuur*) firms generally expect at least one year's driving experience and will want to see a valid national driving licence (with photo) and passport. All will require you to pay a deposit by credit card, and you generally

need to be over 21. Prices given below are for one day's hire of the cheapest car available excluding insurance and VAT.

Adam's Rent-a-Car
Nassaukade 344-6, Oud West (685 0111). Tram 7, 10, 17. **Open** 8am-6pm Mon-Fri; 8am-8pm Sat. **Credit** AmEx, MC, V. **Map** p310 C5.
One-day hire costs from €32; the first 100km (62 miles) are free, and after that the charge is €0.14/km. Branch at Middenweg 51.

Dik's Autoverhuur
Van Ostadestraat 278-80, the Pijp (662 3366/ www.diks.net). Tram 3, 4. **Open** 8am-7.30pm Mon-Sat; 9am-12.30pm, 8-10.30pm Sun. **Credit** AmEx, DC, MC, V. **Map** p311 F6.
Prices start at €32 per day. The first 100km are free, then it's €0.10/km.

Hertz
Overtoom 333, Oud West (612 2441/ www.hertz.nl). Tram 1, 6. **Open** 8am-6pm Mon-Fri; 8am-2pm Sat; 9am-2pm Sun, public holidays. **Credit** AmEx, DC, MC, V. **Map** p309 B6.
Prices start at €125 per day (including insurance and mileage).

Clamping & fines

Wheel-clamp (*wielklem*) teams are swift and merciless if they see a car parked illegally. A sticker on your windscreen tells you where to pay the fine (just over €60); once you've paid, return to the car and wait for traffic police to remove the clamp. Luckily, the declampers normally arrive promptly.

If you fail to pay the fine within 24 hours, your car will be towed away. It will cost around €135, plus parking fine, plus a tariff per kilometre to reclaim it from the pound if you do so within 24 hours, and around €45 for every 12 hours thereafter. The pound is at Daniel Goedkoopstraat 7-9. Take your passport, licence number and cash, travellers' cheques or a major credit card. If your car has been clamped or towed away, go to any of the following Stadstoezicht (parking service) offices to pay.

Head office
Weesperstraat 105A, Old Centre: Old Side (553 0300). Tram 6, 7, 10.

Open 8am-6pm Mon-Fri; 8am-3.30pm Sat. **Map** p307 F3.

Branches
Weesperstraat 105A, Old Centre: Old Side (553 0333). Tram 6, 7, 9, 10, 14. **Open** 8am-6pm Mon-Fri; 8am-3.30pm Sat. **Map** p307 F3.
Beukenplein 50, Oost (553 0333). Tram 3, 9, 10, 14. **Open** 8am-6pm Mon-Fri; 8am-3pm Sat. **Map** p312 H4.
Jan Pieter Heijestraat 94, Oud West (553 0333). Tram 1, 7, 17. **Open** 8am-3.30pm Mon-Fri.
Daniel Goedkoopstraat 7-9, Oost (553 0333). Metro 51, 53, 54. **Open** 24hrs daily.

Parking

Parking in central Amsterdam is a nightmare: the whole of the town centre is metered from 9am until at least 7pm – and in many places up to midnight – and meters are difficult to find. Meters will set you back up to €3 an hour. You can buy passes for one day (€16.20), three days (€48.60) or a week (€162) – from Stadstoezicht offices (*see above*). Car parks (*parkeren*) are indicated by a white 'P' on a blue square. After controlled hours, parking at meters is free. Below is a list of central car parks where you're more likely to find a space at peak times. Empty your car of valuables: cars with foreign number plates are vulnerable to break-ins.

ANWB Parking Amsterdam Centraal
Prins Hendrikkade 20A, Old Centre: New Side (638 5330). **Open** 24hrs daily. **Rates** €3/hr; €32/day. **Credit** AmEx, DC, MC, V. **Map** p306 D2.
Many nearby hotels offer a 10% discount on parking here.

Europarking
Marnixstraat 250, Oud West (623 6694). **Open** 6.30am-1am Mon-Thur; 6.30am-2am Fri, Sat; 7am-1am Sun. **Rates** €2/53min, then €1 per 26min; €26/24hrs; €109.70/7 days. **Credit** MC, V. **Map** p309 B4.
Ticket machines take cash and cards.

De Kolk Parking
Nieuwezijds Voorburgwal 12, Old Centre: New Side (427 1449). **Open** 24hrs daily. **Rates** €3/hr; €32/24hrs. **Credit** MC, V. **Map** p306 C2.
Ticket machines take cash and cards.

Head out on the waterway

Amsterdam is best seen – and understood (*see p45*) – from the water. Sadly, Amsterdam no longer allows motorised boat rental: your options, unless you try to bond with a local boat owner, are limited to the pedal-powered 'canal bike'. While certainly not the most macho of craft, at least their current versions actually allow for forward motion without too much vein popping. Don't ignore the introductory summary of the rules of the road (put very basically: stick to the right and steer clear of canal cruisers).

If you do manage to beg, borrow or steal a proper boat, the *Amsterdamse Vaargids* (www.amsterdamsevaargids.nl), in Dutch and available at Athenaeum Newcentrum (*see p154*) is a good investment, filled with maps, routes, rules as well as recommended bars and restaurants to dock at. We recommend 't Smalle (*see p146*), Café Soundgarden, Entredok (for both, *see p145*) or any bar whose street name ends with -gracht (canal).

Canal Bike

Weteringschans 24, Southern Canal Belt (626 5574/www.canal.nl). Moorings at Leidsekade on Leidseplein; Stadhouderskade, opposite Rijksmuseum; Prinsengracht, by Westerkerk; Keizersgracht, on corner of Leidsestraat.
Open *Summer* 10am-6pm (in good weather until 9.30pm) daily. *Winter* (Rijksmuseum only) 10am-5.30pm Mon-Fri; (at Rijksmuseum, Westerkerk & Leidseplein) 10am-5.30pm Sat, Sun. **Rates** *1-2 people* €8/person/hr. *3-4 people* €7/person/hr. **Deposit** €50/ canal bike. **No credit cards. Map** p310 D5.

Petrol

There are 24-hour petrol stations (*benzinestations*) at Gooiseweg 10-11, Sarphatistraat 225, Marnixstraat 250 and Spaarndammerdijk 218.

Water transport

Boats to rent

See above **Head out on the waterway.**

Canal buses

Canal Bus
Weteringschans 24, Southern Canal Belt (623 9886/www.canal.nl). Tram 6, 10. **Open** 10am-7pm daily. **Tickets** *1 day* €15; €10.50 under-12s. *1 day incl entrance to Rijksmuseum* €20 (not available during special exhibitions). *All Amsterdam Transport Pass* €17. **Credit** AmEx, MC, V. **Map** p310 D5. The All Amsterdam Transport Pass is valid for one day plus the morning of the following day.

Water taxis

Water Taxi Centrale
Stationsplein 8, Old Centre: New Side (535 6363/www.water-taxi.nl). Tram 1, 2, 4, 5, 9, 13, 16, 17, 24, 25. **Open** 8am-midnight daily. **Rates**

1-8 person boat €75 for first 30min, then €60/30min. *9-12 person boat* €110 for first 30min, then €65/30min. *13-25 person boat* €145 for first 30min, then €95/30min. *26-44 person boat* €190 for first 30min, then €110/30min. **Credit** AmEx, MC, V (accepted only prior to boarding). **Map** p305 D1.
Try to book in advance.

Cycling

Cycling is the most convenient means of getting from A to B: there are bike lanes on most roads, marked by white lines and bike symbols. Cycling two abreast is illegal, as is going without reflectors on the wheels. Watch out for pedestrians stepping into your path.

Never leave a bike unlocked: it will get stolen. Attach the bike to something immovable, preferably using two locks: around the frame and through a wheel. If someone in the street offers you a bike for sale ('fiets te koop'), don't be tempted: it's almost certainly stolen, and there are plenty of good and cheap bike hire companies. Apart from the firms listed below, check the *Gouden Gids* (yellow pages) under 'Fietsen en Bromfietsen Verhuur'.

You can also call a 'bicycle cab' (06 282 47550/www.wieler taxi.nl) – basically a high-tech rickshaw that charges about the same as a regular cab.

Bike City
Bloemgracht 68-70, the Jordaan (626 3721/www.bikecity.nl). Tram 10, 13, 14, 17. **Open** 9am-6pm daily. **Rates** from €6.75/day. **Deposit** €25. **Credit** AmEx, DC, MC, V. **Map** p305 B3.
Opening times may vary in winter.

Mac Bike
Centraal Station, Stationsplein 12, Old Centre: New Side (620 0985/ www.macbike.nl). Tram 1, 2, 4, 5, 9, 13, 16, 17, 24, 25. **Open** 9am-5.45pm daily. **Rates** €6.50-€9.75/day. **Deposit** €50. **Credit** AmEx, MC, V. **Map** p306 D1.

Mike's Bike Tours
Kerkstraat 134, Southern Canal Belt (622 7970/www.mikesbiketours.com). Tram 1, 2, 5. **Open** 9am-6pm daily. **Rates** from €7/day. **No credit cards. Map** p310 D4.
Guided tours available.

Rent-A-Bike
Damstraat 20-22, Old Centre: Old Side (625 5029/www.bikes.nl). Tram 4, 9, 14, 16, 24, 25. **Open** 9am-6pm daily. **Rates** €9.50-€18/day; €23 deposit and passport/ID card or credit card imprint. **Credit** AmEx, DC, MC, V. **Map** p306 D3.
A 10% discount (excluding deposit) on bike hire if you mention *Time Out*.

Directory

What Londoners take when they go out.

Time Out
London
EVERY WEEK

Resources A-Z

Addresses

Amsterdam addresses take the form of street then house number, such as Damrak 1.

Age restrictions

In the Netherlands, only those over the age of 16 can purchase alcohol (over 18 for spirits), while you have to be 16 to buy cigarettes (18 to smoke dope). Driving is limited to over-18s.

Attitude & etiquette

Amsterdam is a relaxed city. However, while some assume anything goes, not everything does. Smoking dope, though decriminalised, is not accepted everywhere: spliffing up in restaurants is usually frowned upon. And while restaurants don't usually have a dress code, many nightclubs do, with sportswear and trainers banned.

Business

The forthcoming construction of a new Metro line linking north and south Amsterdam – the Noord–Zuidlijn – is indicative of the city's status as a business centre. The south of Amsterdam is where most of the action is, with corporate hotels such as the Hilton rubbing shoulders with the World Trade Center and the RAI convention centre.

The excellent website www.amsterdampromotion.nl is a mine of useful information.

Banking

The branches listed below are head offices. Most do not have general banking facilities, but staff will be able to provide a list of branches that do. For information about currency exchanges, *see p286*.

ABN-Amro

Vijzelstraat 68, Southern Canal Belt (628 9393/0900 0024/www.abn amro.nl). Tram 6, 7, 10, 16, 24, 25. **Open** 9am-5pm Mon-Fri. **Map** p310 D4.
ABN-AMRO has other locations all over Amsterdam.

Fortis Bank

Singel 548, Old Centre: New Side (624 9340/www.fortisbank.com). Tram 4, 9, 14, 16, 24, 25. **Open** 1-5pm Mon; 9.30am-5pm Tue-Fri. **Map** p310 D4.
Full banking facilities in 50 other locations.

ING Group

Bijlmerplein 888, Bijlmermeer (563 9111/0800 7011/www.ing. com). Metro Bijlmer/bus 59, 60, 62, 137. **Open** 9am-4pm Mon-Fri.
ING incorporates the 50 Amsterdam branches of the Postbank (*see below*). For more information about ING House, *see p32*.

Postbank

Postbus 94780, 1090 GT (565 5010/ www.postbank.nl). **Open** *Enquiries* 8.30am-5pm Mon-Fri.
One in every Amsterdam post office.

Rabobank

Dam 16, Old Centre: New Side (777 8899/www.rabobank.nl). Tram 1, 2, 5, 9, 13, 14, 16, 17, 24, 25. **Open** 9.30am-5pm Mon-Wed, Fri; 9.30am-6pm Thur. **Map** p306 D2.
Some 30 locations in Amsterdam.

Conventions & conferences

Most major hotels offer full conference facilities, with the Krasnapolsky's the best in town. The World Trade Center (*see p280*) will offer fine facilities when renovations are completed in 2004.

Congrex Convention Services

AJ Ernststraat 595K, Southern Canal Belt (504 0200/www.congrex.nl).

Tickets please

Though the Amsterdam Tourist board and the GWK sell tickets for concerts, plays and other events, the main ticket retailer in Amsterdam is the **AUB**. Its services run from online sales to personal service at its Leidseplein shop.

Before you go about buying tickets, it helps to know what's on when. For this, pick up the AUB's free monthly magazine *Uitkrant*, available in many theatres and bookshops (as is *Uitgids*, an annual publication offering details of subscription series and the like). It's only in Dutch – as is the online version (*see below*) – but it's easy to decipher. *Uitkrant* (pronounced 'out-krant') can also

be had at the **AUB Ticketshop** in Leidseplein, which is open from 10am to 6pm daily except Thursday, when it closes at 9pm. Expect to pay around €2 commission per ticket. It's also the place to come to if you want to browse through the different flyers and listings mags.

You can also buy tickets by phone, though the commission is about 50 per cent higher and you'll also be paying premium phone rates. The Uitlijn ('out-line') service is on 0900 0191 (+31 20 621 1288 from abroad), and is open 9am to 9pm daily. Finally, for a commission of around €3 per ticket, you can book online at www.uitlijn.nl.

Tram 5/Metro 51. **Open** 9am-5.30pm Mon-Thur, 9am-5pm Fri. **Credit** AmEx, DC, MC, V. **Map** p311 E4. Specialists in teleconferencing.

RAI Congresgebouw

Europaplein 8-22, Zuid (549 1212/ www.rai.nl). Tram 4, 25/NS rail RAI Station. **Open** *Office* 9am-5.30pm Mon-Fri.
A self-contained congress and trade fair centre in the south of the city. The building contains 11 halls and 22 conference rooms that can seat up to 1,750 people.

Stichting de Beurs van Berlage

Damrak 277, Old Centre: Old Side (530 4141/www.beursvanberlage.nl). Tram 4, 9, 14, 16, 24, 25. **Open** 9am-5pm Mon-Fri. **Map** p306 D2.
Used for cultural events and smaller trade fairs. Berlage Hall is a conference venue for between 50 and 2,000 people.

Couriers & shippers

FedEx

0800 022 2333 freephone/500 5699/www.fedex.com/nl_english). **Open** *Customer services* 8am-6.30pm Mon-Fri. **Credit** AmEx, DC, MC, V.

TNT

0800 1234/www.tnt.com. **Open** 24hrs daily. **Credit** AmEx, DC, MC, V.

Office hire & business services

Many tobacconists and copy shops also have fax facilities.

Avisco

Stadhouderskade 156, the Pijp (671 9909/www.acsavcompany.com). Tram 3, 4, 16, 24, 25. **Open** 8am-5pm Mon-Fri. **Map** p311 F5.
Slide projectors, video equipment, screens, cameras, overhead projectors, microphones and tape decks hired out or sold.

Euro Business Center

Keizersgracht 62, Western Canal Belt (520 7500/www.eurobuinesscenter.nl). Tram 1, 2, 5, 13, 14, 17. **Open** 8.30am-5.30pm Mon-Fri. **Credit** AmEx, DC, MC, V. **Map** p306 C2.
Fully equipped offices for hire (long or short term) including the use of fax, photocopier, phone and mailbox services plus multilingual secretaries.

World Trade Center

Strawinskylaan 1, Zuid (575 9111/ www.wtcamsterdam.com). Tram

5/NS rail RAI Station. **Open** *Office & enquiries* 9am-5pm Mon-Fri.
Offices here are let for long or short term; call 575 2044 for details. Assorted business services are also offered here. After renovation is completed end of 2004, there will be an additional 400 companies and 4000 people working here.

Translators & interpreters

Amstelveens Vertaalburo

Ouderkerkerlaan 50, Amstelveen (645 6610/www.avb.nl). Bus 65, 170, 172. **Open** 9am-5pm Mon-Fri. .
Translation and interpreter service for most languages.

Mac Bay Consultants

PC Hooftstraat 15, Museum Quarter (24hr phoneline 662 0501/fax 662 6299/www.macbay.nl). Tram 2, 3, 5, 12. **Open** 9am-7pm Mon-Fri. **Map** p310 C6.
Specialists in financial documents.

Useful organisations

Many of the agencies below are in The Hague, though they can deal with basic enquiries on the telephone or by post. For full information on embassies and consulates, see p282.

American Chamber of Commerce

Scheveningseweg 58, 2517 KW The Hague (070 365 9808/ www.am cham.nl). **Open** 9am-5pm Mon-Fri.

British Embassy

Commercial Department, Lange Voorhout 10, 2514 ED The Hague (070 427 0427/fax 070 427 0345/www.britain.nl). **Open** 9am-1pm, 2-5.30pm Mon-Fri.
There's also a consulate in Amsterdam; *see p282.*

Commissariaat voor Buitenlandse Investeringen Nederland

Bezuidenhoutseweg 2, 2500 EC The Hague (070 379 8818/fax 070 379 6322/www.nfia.nl). **Open** 8am-6pm Mon-Fri.
The Netherlands Foreign Investment Agency is probably the most useful first port of call for business people wishing to relocate to Holland.

Effectenbeurs (Stock Exchange)

Beursplein 5, Old Centre: New Side (550 4444/www.euronext.com). Tram 4, 9, 14, 16, 24, 25. **Open** for free tours. **Map** p306 D2.
Stock for listed Dutch companies is traded here, and for Nederlandse Termijnhandel, the commodity exchange for trading futures, and Optiebeurs, the largest options exchange in Europe.

EVD: Economische Voorlichtingsdienst

Bezuidenhoutseweg 181, 2594 AH The Hague (070 7788888/www. hollandtrade.com). **Open** 8am-5pm Mon-Fri.
The Netherlands Foreign Trade Agency incorporates the Netherlands Council for Trade Promotion (NCH), both handy sources of information. You need to make an appointment in advance; don't turn up on spec.

Travel advice

For up-to-date information on travel to a specific country – including the latest news on safety and security, health issues, local laws and customs – contact your home country government's department of foreign affairs. Most have websites packed with useful advice for would-be travellers.

Australia
www.dfat.gov.au/travel

New Zealand
www.mft.govt.nz/travel

UK
www.fco.gov.uk/travel

Canada
www.voyage.gc.ca

Republic of Ireland
www.irlgov.ie/iveagh

USA
http://travel.state.gov

Home Abroad

Weteringschans 28, Southern Canal Belt (625 5195/fax 624 7902/www. homeabroad.nl). Tram 6, 7, 10. **Open** 10am-5.30pm Mon-Fri. **Map** p311 E5. Assistance in all aspects of life and business in the Netherlands.

Kamer van Koophandel

De Ruijterkade 5, the Waterfront (531 4000/fax 531 4799/www.kvk.nl). Tram 1, 2, 4, 5, 9, 13, 16, 17, 24, 25. **Open** 8.30am-5pm Mon, Tue, Thur, Fri; 8.30am-8pm Wed. **Map** p306 C1. Amsterdam's Chamber of Commerce has lists of import/export agencies, government trade representatives and companies by sector.

Ministerie van Buitenlandse Zaken

Bezuidenhoutseweg 67, Postbus 20061, 2500 EB The Hague (070 348 6486/fax 070 348 4848/ www.bz.minbuza.nl). **Open** 9am-5pm Mon-Fri. The Ministry of Foreign Affairs. Detailed enquiries may be referred to the EVD *(see above)*.

Ministerie van Economische Zaken

Bezuidenhoutseweg 30, 2594 AV The Hague (070 379 8911/fax 070 379 4081/www.minez.nl). **Open** 8am-5.30pm Mon-Fri. The Ministry of Economic Affairs can provide answers to general queries concerning the Dutch economy. Detailed enquiries tend to be referred to the EVD *(see above)*.

Netherlands–British Chamber of Commerce

Oxford House, Nieuwezijds Voorburgwal 328L, Old Centre: New Side (421 7040/fax 421 7003/ www. nbcc.co.uk). Tram 1, 2, 5, 13, 14, 17. **Open** 9am-5pm Mon-Fri. Map p306 D3.

Consumer

If you have any complaints about the service you received from Dutch businesses that you were not able to resolve with the establishment, call the National Consumentenbond on 070 445 4000 (in Dutch only).

Customs

EU nationals over the age of 17 may import limitless goods into the Netherlands for their personal use. Other EU countries may still have limits on the quantity of goods they permit on entry. For citizens of non-EU countries, the old limits still apply. These are:

● 200 cigarettes or 50 cigars or 250g (8.82oz) tobacco;

● 2 litres of non-sparkling wine plus 1 litre of spirits (over 22 per cent alcohol) or 2 litres of fortified wine (under 22 per cent alcohol);

● 60cc/ml of perfume;

● other goods to the value of €167.

The import of meat or meat products, fruit, plants, flowers and protected animals to the Netherlands is illegal.

Disabled

The most obvious difficulty people with mobility problems face here is negotiating the winding cobbled streets of the older areas. Poorly maintained pavements are widespread, and steep canal house steps can present problems. But the pragmatic Dutch can generally solve any problems quickly.

Most large museums have facilities for disabled users but little for the partially sighted and hard of hearing. Most cinemas and theatres have an enlightened attitude and are accessible. However, it's advisable to check in advance.

The Metro is accessible to wheelchair users who 'have normal arm function'. There is a taxi service for wheelchair users *(see p275)*. Most trams are inaccessible to wheelchair users due to their high steps.

The AUB *(see p279* **Tickets please)** and the Amsterdam Tourist Board *(see p290)* produce brochures on accommodation, restaurants, museums, tourist attractions and boat excursions with facilities for the disabled.

Drugs

The locals have a relaxed attitude to soft drugs, but smoking isn't acceptable everywhere, so use discretion. Outside Amsterdam, public consumption of cannabis is largely unacceptable. For more information, *see p43*.

Foreigners found with harder drugs should expect prosecution. Organisations offering advice can do little to assist foreigners with drug-related problems, though the Drugs Prevention Centre is happy to provide help in several languages, including English. Its helpline (626 7176/408 7774, 3-5pm Mon-Thur) offers advice and information on drugs and alcohol abuse. There's also a 24-hour Crisis/Detox emergency number: 408 7777.

Electricity

The voltage here is 220, 50-cycle AC and compatible with British equipment, but because the Netherlands uses two-pin continental plugs you'll need an adaptor. American visitors may need to buy a transformer for use with larger appliances.

Embassies & consulates

American Consulate General

Museumplein 19, 1071 DJ (664 5661/visas 0900 872 8472 premium rate/www.usemb.nl). Tram 3, 5, 12, 16. **Open** *US citizens & visa applications* 8.30am-11.30 Mon-Fri. **Map** p310 D6.

Australian Embassy

Carnegielaan 4, 2517 KH The Hague (070 310 8200/ 0800 0224 794 Australian citizen emergency phone/www. australian-embassy.nl). **Open** 8.30am-4.55pm Mon-Fri. *Visa enquiries* 10am-12.30pm, 3-4.30pm Mon-Fri.

British Consulate General

Koningslaan 44, 1075 AE (676 4343/ www.britain.nl). Tram 2. **Open** *British citizens* 9am-noon, 2-3.30pm Mon-Fri. *Visa enquiries* 9am-noon Mon-Fri.

Directory

British Embassy

Lange Voorhout 10, 2514 ED The Hague (070 364 5800/www. britain.nl). **Open** 9am-5.30pm Mon-Fri.
For visa and tourist information, contact the Consulate General (*see above*).

Canadian Embassy

Sophialaan 7, 2514 JP The Hague (070 311 1600/www. dfait-maeci.gc.ca/canadaeuropa/ netherlands). **Open** 10am-noon Mon-Fri. *Canadian nationals 2.30-4pm Mon-Fri.*

Irish Embassy

Dr Kuyperstraat 9, 2514 BA The Hague (070 363 0993). **Open** 10am-12.30pm, 2.30-5pm Mon-Fri. *Visa enquiries 10am-noon Mon-Fri.*

New Zealand Embassy

Carnegielaan 10, 2517 KH The Hague (070 346 9324/visas 070 365 8037/www.immigration. govt.nz). **Open** 9am-12.30pm, 1.30-5.30pm Mon-Thur; 9am-12.30pm, 1.30-5pm Fri.

Emergencies

In an emergency, call 112, free from any phone (mobiles included), and specify if you need ambulance, fire service or police. For helplines, *see p284*; for hospitals, *see p283*; for addresses of police stations, *see p286*.

Gay & lesbian

Help & information

COC Amsterdam

Rozenstraat 14, the Jordaan (626 3087/www.cocamsterdam. nl). Tram 13, 14, 17. **Open** *Telephone enquiries 10am-5pm Mon-Fri. Info-Coffeeshop 1-5pm Sat.* **Map** p305 B3.
The Amsterdam branch of the COC deals largely with the social side of gay life. The Info-Coffeeshop is a useful place to make enquiries about the COC or the gay scene in general.

COC National

Rozenstraat 8, the Jordaan (623 4596/textphone 620 7541/www. coc.nl). Tram 13, 14, 17. **Open** 9am-5pm Mon-Fri. **Map** p306 C3.
COC's head office deals with all matters relating to gays and lesbians; the organisation has strong social and activist tendencies.

Gay & Lesbian Switchboard

Postbus 11573, 1001 GN (623 6565/ www.switchboard.nl). **Open** 2-10pm daily.
Whether it's information on the scene or safe-sex advice you're after, the friendly English-speakers here are well informed.

Homodok-Lesbisch Archief Amsterdam

Nieuwpoortkade 2A, Westerpark (606 0712/fax 606 0713/www.ihia.nl). Tram 10, 12, 14. **Open** 10am-4pm Mon-Fri.
Books, journals, articles and theses are housed here, as is a large video collection. However, the location is by no means permanent; call or check the website before visiting.

IIAV

Obiplein 4, Oost (665 0820/ www. iiav.nl). Tram 3, 6, 10, 14/ bus 15, 22. **Open** noon-5pm Mon; 10am-5pm Tue-Fri.
This women's archive was confiscated during World War II and removed to Berlin, where it vanished. In 1992, it was found in Moscow, but the Russians are still refusing to return it. The current collection, started after the war, is officially an archive, but there are a lot of other resources, including several online databases.

Het Vrouwenhuis (the Women's House)

Nieuwe Herengracht 95, Southern Canal Belt (625 2066/ fax 538 9185/www.akantes.nl). Tram 7, 9, 14/Metro Waterlooplein. **Open** *Office 10am-5pm Mon-Fri. Info-Café, library, internet café noon-5pm Wed, Thur.* **Map** p307 F3.
There's a well-stocked library here (around 4,000 books; membership is €9 a year) plus free Internet facilities (noon-5pm Wed, Thur). Most classes are held in Dutch.

Other groups & organisations

Dikke Maatjes

Kantershof 583, 1104 HG (www.dikkemaatjes.nl).
'Dikke Maatjes' means 'close friends', though its literal translation is 'fat friends'. That's exactly what this gay club is for: chubbies and admirers. English/Dutch website lists all the upcoming events.

Long Yang Club

PO Box 15871, 1001 NJ (06 228 003 202/www.longyangclub.nl).

The Dutch branch of this worldwide organisation for Asian and oriental gays and their friends meets often.

Mama Cash

PO Box 15686, 1001 ND (689 3634/fax 683 4647/www. mama cash.nl). **Open** 9am-5pm Mon-Fri.
This group supplies funding for women-run businesses, and has sponsored many lesbian organisations and events in the city.

Netherbears

c/o Le Shako, Postbus 15495, 1001 ML (www.netherbears.nl).
This hairy men's club meets at Le Shako (Gravelanderseveer 2, Rembrandtplein, 624 0209) every second and fourth Sunday of the month from 5pm.

Sjalhomo

Postbus 2536, 1000 CM (023 531 2318 evenings only).
This national organisation for Jewish gays, lesbians and bisexuals organises regular activities on and around Jewish feast days.

Sportclub Tijgertje

Postbus 10521, 1001 EM (673 2458/664 3922/www.tijgertje.nl).
Tijgertje organises a wide variety of sports activities, from yoga to wrestling, for gays and lesbians, including an HIV swimming group.

Wild Side, Women to Women SM Group

c/o COC Amsterdam, Rozenstraat 14, the Jordaan (070 346 4767/ www.wildside.dds.nl).
A group for woman-to-woman SM, which holds workshops, meetings and parties, and publishes a free bi-monthly, bilingual newsletter available from the COC Amsterdam (*see p282*) and the Vrolijk (*see p204*).

Health

As with any trip abroad, it's advisable to take out medical insurance before you leave. If you're a UK citizen, you should also get hold of an E111 (*see p284*) to facilitate reciprocal cover. For emergency services, medical or dental referral agencies and AIDS/HIV information, *see p283*.

Afdeling Inlichtingen Apotheken

694 8709.
A 24-hour service that can direct you to your nearest chemist.

Centraal Doktorsdienst/Atacom

*592 3434/592 3809/592 3333/
www.atacom.nl.*
A 24-hour English-speaking line for
advice about medical symptoms.

Accident & emergency

In the case of minor accidents,
try the outpatient departments
at the following hospitals
(*ziekenhuis*), all open 24 hours
a day year-round.

Academisch Medisch Centrum

*Meibergdreef 9, Zuid (switchboard
566 9111/first aid 566 3333). Bus
59, 60, 120, 126, 158/Metro
Holendreschp.*

Boven IJ Ziekenhuis

*Statenjachtstraat 1, Noord (634
6346). Bus 34, 36, 37, 39, 171, 172.*

Onze Lieve Vrouwe Gasthuis

*'s Gravesandeplein 16, Oost
(switchboard 599 9111/first aid
599 3016). Tram 3, 6, 10/Metro
Weesperplein or Wibautstraat.*
Map p312 G4.

St Lucas Andreas Ziekenhuis

*Jan Tooropstraat 164, West
(switchboard 510 8911/first aid
510 8161). Tram 13/bus 19, 47,
80, 82, 97.*

VU Ziekenhuis

*De Boelelaan 1117, Zuid
(switchboard 444 4444/first aid 444
3636). Bus 142, 147, 148, 149, 170,
171, 172/Metro Amstelveenseweg.*

Contraception & abortion

Amsterdams Centrum voor seksueele gezondheid

*Sarphatistraat 618-26, the Plantage
(624 5426). Tram 6, 9, 10, 14/
bus 22.* **Open** 9am-4pm Mon-Fri.
Map p312 G3.
An abortion clinic that offers help
and advice. Besides giving
information on health issues, the
staff at this family planning centre
can help visitors with prescriptions
for contraceptive pills, morning-after
pills and condoms, IUD fitting and
cervical smear tests. Prescription
charges vary.

Polikliniek Oosterpark

*Oosterpark 59, Oost (693
2151). Tram 3, 6, 9.* **Open**
Advice services 9am-5pm daily.
Map p312 H4.
Advice on contraception and
abortion. Non-residents without
appropriate insurance will be
charged from €330 for an abortion.
The process is prompt and backed
up by sympathetic counselling.

Dentists

For a dentist (*tandarts*), call
the dentist administration
bureau on 0900 821 2230.
Operators can put you in
touch with your nearest
dentist; lines are open 24
hours. Alternatively, make
an appointment at one of the
clinics listed below.

AOC

*Wilhelmina Gasthuisplein 167,
Oud West (616 1234). Tram 1, 2,
3, 5, 6, 12.* **Open** 9am-4pm Mon-Fri.
Map p309 B5.
Emergency dental treatment. They
also have a Dutch language recorded
service at 686 1109 that tells you
where a walk-in clinic will be open
12.30-1.30pm and 9.30-10.30pm
that day. Ask staff at your hotel
to call if you're not confident of
understanding Dutch.

TBB

570 9595.
A 24-hour service that can refer
callers to a dentist. Operators can
also give details of chemists open
outside normal hours.

Opticians

For details of opticians and
optometrists in Amsterdam,
see p158 or look under
'Opticiens' in the *Gouden Gids*.

Pharmacies

For pharmacy hours, *see
below* **Prescriptions**. For
pharmacies, *see p175*.

Prescriptions

Chemists (*drogists*) sell
toiletries and non-prescription
drugs and are usually open
from 9.30am to 5.30pm,
Monday to Saturday. For
prescription drugs, go to a

pharmacy (*apotheek*), usually
open from 9.30am to 5.30pm
Monday to Friday.
    Outside these hours, phone
the Afdeling Inlichtingen
Apotheken (see p282) or
consult the daily newspaper
Het Parool, which publishes
details of which apotheken are
open late that week. Details are
also posted at local *apotheken*.

STDs, HIV & AIDS

The Netherlands was one of
the first countries to pour
money into research once the
HIV virus was recognised. But
though the country was swift
to take action and promote safe
sex, condoms are still not
distributed free in clubs and
bars as they are in the UK.
    As well as the groups listed
below, the AIDS Helpline 689
2577; open 2-10pm Mon-Fri),
which is part of the Stichting
AIDS Fonds (*see below*), offers
advice and can you bring
in contact with every
departement you need.

HIV Vereniging

*1E Helmersstraat 17, Oud West
(689 3915/www.hivnet.org). Tram
1, 2, 3, 5, 6, 12.* **Open** 9am-5pm
Mon-Fri. **Map** p310 C5.
The Netherlands HIV Association
supports the interests of all those
who are HIV positive, including
offering legal help, and produces a
bi-monthly Dutch magazine, *HIV
Nieuws* (€38 per year). There's an
HIV Cafe every Tuesday lunch
(noon-2pm); Wed dinner (from 5pm)
and Sunday (4pm-9pm). You can
also call 689 2577 to make an Friday
appointment for a speedy (within
1-hour) HIV test for €15.

SAD-Schorerstichting

*PC Hooftstraat 5, Museum
Quarter (662 4206/www.
schorer.nl). Tram 2, 3, 5, 6,
7, 10, 12.* **Open** 10am-4pm
Mon-Fri. **Map** p310 D5.
This state-funded agency offers
psycho-social support, education
and HIV prevention advice for gays
and lesbians. Examinations and
treatment of sexually transmitted
diseases, including an HIV test, are
free. The clinic is held at the city's
health department, the GG&GD
(Groenburgwal 44); call ahead to
make an appointment. Staff here
speak English.

Directory

Stichting AIDS Fonds

Keizersgracht 390, Western Canal Belt (626 2669/fax 627 5221/ www.aidsfonds.nl). Tram 1, 2, 5. **Open** 9am-5pm Mon-Fri. **Map** p310 C4.

This group, which runs fundraisers such as the Amsterdam Diners (*see p202* **The queer year**), channels money into research and safe sex promotion. It also runs a helpline for gay and lesbian-specific health questions (0900 204 2040, 2-10pm Mon-Fri) and organises workshops such as F*CKSH*P, on anal sex. Parts of its website are in English.

Helplines

Alcoholics Anonymous

625 6057. **Open** 24hr answerphone. A lengthy but informative message details times and dates of meetings, and contact numbers for counsellors.

Narcotics Anonymous

662 6307. **Open** 24hr answerphone with phone numbers of counsellors.

SOS Telephone Helpline

675 7575. **Open** 24hrs daily. A counselling service – comparable to the Samaritans in the UK and Lifeline in the US – for anyone with emotional problems, run by volunteers. English isn't always understood at first, but keep trying and someone will be able to help you.

ID

Regulations concerning identification require that everyone carries some form of ID when opening accounts at banks or other financial institutions, when looking for work, when applying for benefits, when found on public transport without a ticket and when going to a professional football match. You then have to register with the local council, which is in the same building as the Aliens' Police (*see p290*).

Insurance

EU countries have reciprocal medical arrangements with the Netherlands. British citizens will need form E111, obtained by filling in the application form in leaflet SA30, available from the Post Office. Read the small print so you know how to get treatment at a reduced charge: you may have to explain this to the Dutch doctor or dentist who treats you. If you need treatment, photocopy your insurance form and leave it with the doctor or dentist concerned. Not all treatments are covered by the E111, so take out private travel insurance covering both health and personal belongings. Citizens of other EU countries should make sure they have obtained one of the forms E110, E111 or E112; citizens of almost all other countries should take out insurance before their visit.

Internet

Among Amsterdam's ISPs are Xs4all (www.xs4all.nl), and Chello (www.chello.nl). All of the main global ISPs, such as Planet, AOL and Compuserve, have a presence here (check websites for a local number). Local hotels are increasingly well equipped for surfing, whether with dataports in the rooms or a terminal in the lobby. For a selection of good websites, *see p293*.

Internet cafes

Easy Internet Café

Reguliersbreestraat 22, Southern Canal Belt (no phone/www.easy everything.com). Tram 16, 24, 25. **Open** 9am-10pm daily. **Rates** from €2.50/unit. **Map** p311 D4.

The amount of time one unit buys you depends on how busy the place is: it can be as little as a half-hour or as much as six hours. There are also branches at Damrak 33 and Leidsestraat 24.

Freeworld

Nieuwendijk 30, Old Centre: New Side (620 0902/www. freeworld-internetcafe.nl). Tram 1, 2, 5, 13, 17, 20. **Open** 9am-1am Mon-Thur, Sun; 9am-3am Fri, Sat. **Rates** €1/30min. **Map** p306 D2.

If you want to surf here, you'll have to buy a drink: refreshments are compulsory.

Internet Cafe

Martelaarsgracht 11, Old Centre: New Side (627 1052/www.internet cafe.nl). Tram 4, 9, 16, 20, 24, 25. **Open** 9am-1am Mon-Thur, Sun; 9am-3am Fri, Sat. **Rates** around €0.50/20min. **Map** p306 D2.

Funky spotlighting and speedy connections, but compulsory drinks: beware of staff offering refills.

Left luggage

There is a staffed left-luggage counter at Schiphol Airport, open from 7am to 10.45pm daily. There are also lockers in the arrival and departure halls, while in Amsterdam there are lockers at Centraal Station with 24-hour access. Expect to pay €2.70-€6 per item per day.

Legal help

ACCESS

Plein 24, 2511 CS The Hague (070 346 2525/www.euronet.nl/users/ access). **Open** 10am-4pm Mon-Fri. The Administrative Committee to Coordinate English Speaking Services is a non-profit organisation, which provides assistance in English through a telephone information line, workshops and counselling.

Bureau Voor Rechtshulp

Spuistraat 10, Old Centre: New Side (520 5100/ http://www.bureau rechtshulp.nl). Tram 1, 2, 5. **Open** *Telephone enquiries* 9am-1pm; 2-5pm Mon-Fri. *By appointment* 9am-1pm Mon-Fri. **Map** p306 C3.

Qualified lawyers who give free legal advice on a variety of matters.

Legal Advice Line

444 6333. **Open** *Telephone enquiries* 9pm-5pm Mon-Thur. Free advice from student lawyers.

Libraries

You'll need to show proof of residence in Amsterdam and ID to join a library (*bibliotheek*) and borrow books. It costs €20 (23s-64s) or €12 (18s-22s, over-65s) per year and is free for under-18s. However, in public libraries (*openbare bibliotheek*) you can read books, papers and magazines without taking out membership. For university libraries, *see p288*.

British Council Education Centre

Oxford House, Nieuwezijds Voorburgwal 328L, Old Centre: New Side (421 7040/fax 421 7003/ www.nbcc.co.uk). Tram 1, 2, 5, 13, 14, 17. **Open** *9am-5pm Mon-Fri.* **Map** p306 D3.

Centrale Bibliotheek

Prinsengracht 587, Western Canal Belt (523 0900/www.oba.nl). Tram 1, 2, 5. **Open** *1-9pm Mon; 10am-9pm Tue-Thur; 10am-5pm Fri, Sat.* **Map** p310 C4.
Anyone is welcome to use this, the main public library, for reference purposes. There is a variety of English-language books.

Lost property

For the sake of insurance, report lost property to the police immediately; *see p286*. If you lose your passport, inform your embassy or consulate as well. For anything lost at the Hoek van Holland ferry terminal or Schiphol Airport, contact the company you're travelling with. For lost credit cards, *see p286*.

Centraal Station

Stationsplein 15, Old Centre: Old Side (customer service 0900 202 1163). Tram 1, 2, 4, 5, 9, 13, 16, 17, 24, 25. **Open** *8am-8pm Mon-Fri, 9am-5pm Sat.* **Map** p306 D1.
Items found on trains are kept here for four days (it's easiest to just go in person to any locket and ask) and then sent to NS Afdeling Verloren Voorwerpen, 2e Daalsedijk 4, 3500 HA Utrecht (030 235 3923, 8am-8pm Mon-Fri, 8.30am-5pm Sat).

GVB Lost Property

Prins Hendrikkade 108-14, Old Centre: New Side (460 5858). Tram 1, 2, 4, 5, 9, 13, 16, 17, 24, 25. **Open** *9am-4pm Mon-Fri.* **Map** p306 C1.
Where to head for items lost on a bus, metro or tram. If you're reporting a loss from the previous day, phone after 2pm to allow time for the property to be sorted.

Police Lost Property

Stephensonstraat 18, Zuid (559 3005). Tram 12/Metro Amstel Station/bus 14. **Open** *In person 9.30am-3.30pm Mon-Fri. By phone noon-3.30pm Mon-Fri.*
Report any loss to the police station in the same district: it holds items for a day or so before sending them here for up to three months.

Media

Newspapers & magazines

De Telegraaf, a one-time collaborationist and still right-wing daily, is the Netherlands' biggest-selling paper, the nearest the country has to a tabloid press. *Het Parool* was the main underground wartime journal, but is now a hip afternoon rag and rates as *the* Amsterdam paper (its Saturday *PS* supplement also has easily decipherable entertainment listings). The national *De Volkskrant* also enjoys a relatively young, progressive readership. While *NRC Handelsblad* is the national choice of the yet more highbrow.

For Anglophones, the Amsterdam Tourist Board publishes the monthly *Day by Day*, a basic listings guide. However, *Shark*, an alternative freesheet found in bars and clubs, does a fine job of picking up the slack with round-ups of films and music, as well as a section for gay and lesbian events. For more, check www.underwateramsterdam. com. And a promising new English-language arts and culture weekly, *Amsterdam Weekly* (www.amsterdam weekly.nl) is set to start publishing in Autumn 2003.

Foreign magazines and papers are widely available, but pricey; British papers are around €2 for a daily, €4 for a Sunday. Athenaeum is a browser's dream; 100 metres away, Waterstone's stocks UK publications, and the American Book Center nearby has plenty of American mags. For all, *see p154*.

Broadcast media

Besides the national basics (Ned 1, Ned 2 and Ned 3, the latter being by far the hippest),

Amsterdam also has its own 'city CNN' – the really quite cool AT5 (its site www.at5.nl has some English) – as well as Salto, that broadcasts typically local and low budget culture/cult stuff. There's also about a dozen national commercial stations, most of which are as short on viewers as they are on style; they include Yorin and Veronica (both painfully commercial); and NET5, RTL4 and RTL5 (mostly series and films from the US). There are now about 30 extra channels on cable, including non-commercial stations in German, French, Italian and Belgian, various local channels, and English-language multinationals such as Nickelodeon, BBC World, CNN and National Geographic. The basic deal also includes BBC1 and 2, so there's no need to miss out on *EastEnders*. The wall-to-wall porn is largely an urban myth, so don't expect any late-night thrills unless your hotel has the 'extended service', which usually also features film channels, Discovery, Eurosport and others. Dutch radio is generally as bland as the TV, but Radio Netherlands (www.rnw.nl) often has some interesting stuff in English.

Money

Since January 2002, the Dutch currency has been the euro.

ATMs

Cash machines are only found at banks here: as yet, no bank has been resourceful enough to set any up in shops or bars, as is increasingly the case in the UK and parts of the US. If your cashcard carries the Maestro or Cirrus symbols, you should be able to withdraw cash from ATMs here, though it's worth checking with your bank a) that it's possible and b) what the charging structure is.

Banks

There's usually little difference between the rates of exchange offered by banks and bureaux de change, but banks tend to charge less commission. Most banks are open from 9am to 5pm from Monday to Friday, with the Postbank opening up on Saturday mornings as well. Dutch banks will buy and sell foreign currency and exchange travellers' cheques, but few of them will give cash advances against credit cards. For a list of banks, *see p279*, or check the Amsterdam *Gouden Gids* under 'Banken'.

Bureaux de change

A number of bureaux de change can be found in convenient locations in the city centre, especially on Leidseplein, Damrak and Rokin. The ones listed below offer reasonable rates, though they usually charge more commission than banks. Hotel and tourist bureau exchange facilities generally cost more.

American Express

Damrak 66, Old Centre: New Side (504 8777). Tram 4, 9, 14, 16, 24, 25. **Open** 9am-5pm Mon-Fri; 9am-noon Sat.
Map p306 D2.
A number of facilities here.

GWK

Centraal Station, Old Centre: Old Side (627 2731). Tram 1, 2, 4, 5, 9, 13, 16, 17, 24, 25. **Open** 7am-10.30pm daily (Sun from 9am).
Map p306 D1.
Other locations: Leidseplein 123 (622 1425); Schiphol Airport (in the railway station; 653 5121); Damrak 86 (624 6681/624 6682).

Thomas Cook Travelex

Dam 23-5, Old Centre: New Side (625 0922). Tram 4, 9, 14, 16, 24, 25. **Open** 9.15am-7.15pm daily.
Map p306 D3.
Other locations: Damrak 1-5 (620 3236), 9.15am-9pm daily); Leidseplein 31A (9.45am-6.15pm Mon-Thur; 9.45am-8.15pm Fri, Sat).

Credit cards

Credit cards are widely used here, but not every establishment accepts them. The majority of restaurants will take at least one type of card; they're less popular in bars and shops, so always carry some cash. The most popular cards, in descending order, are Visa, Mastercard (aka Eurocard), American Express and Diners Club. If you lose your cards, call the following relevant 24-hour numbers immediately.
American Express 504 8666.
Diners Club 654 5511.
Mastercard/Eurocard 030 283 5555 if card was issued in the Netherlands; otherwise, freephone 0800 022 5821.
Visa 660 0611 if card was issued in the Netherlands; otherwise, freephone 0800 022 4176.

Tax

Sales tax (aka BTW) – 19 per cent on most items, six per cent on goods such as books and food, more on alcohol, tobacco and petrol – will be included in the prices quoted in shops. If you live outside the EU, you are entitled to a tax refund on purchases of up to €150 from one shop on any one day. Get the clerk to give you an export certificate, and then present it to a customs official as you leave the country, who'll stamp it; you can then collect your cash at the ABN-AMRO bank at Schiphol Airport or via post at a later date (ask the official for information).

There's an additional tourist tax of five per cent levied on hotels, though in all but the priciest spots, this will be included in the prices quoted.

Opening hours

For all our listings in this Guide we give full opening times, but as a general rule, shops are open from 1pm to 6pm on Monday (if they're open at all; many shops are closed Mondays); 10am to 6pm Tuesday to Friday, with some staying open until 9pm on Thursdays; and 9am to 5pm on Saturdays. Smaller shops tend to open at varying times; if in doubt, phone first. For shops that open late, *see p168*.

The city's bars open at various times during the day and close at around 1am throughout the week, except for Fridays and Saturdays, when they stay open until 2am or 3am. Restaurants are generally open in the evening from 5pm until 11pm (though some close as early as 9pm); many are closed on Sunday and Monday.

Police stations

The Dutch police are under no obligation to grant a phone call to those they detain – they can hold people for up to six hours for questioning if the alleged crime is not serious, 24 hours for major matters – but they'll phone the relevant consulate on behalf of a foreign detainee. If you are a victim of theft or assault, report it to the nearest police station. For emergencies, *see p282*. There is also a 24-hour police service line 0900 8844 for the Amsterdam area.

Hoofdbureau van Politie (Police Headquarters)

Elandsgracht 117, the Jordaan (559 9111). Tram 7, 10. **Open** 24hrs daily. **Map** p310 C4.

Postal services

For post destined for outside Amsterdam, use the overige bestemmingen slot in letter boxes. The logo for the national postal service is ptt post (white letters on a red oblong). Most post offices – recognisable by their red and blue signs – are open 9am to 5pm, Monday to Friday. The postal information phoneline is 058 233 3333. Housed in every

The euro files

As of 1 January 2002, Europe has had a new currency. It's certainly handy for European travellers: gone are the days of changing money whenever they cross a border. Even though it has resulted in skyrocketing prices in the Netherlands, the Euro can be rated a success: within seven months of its launch over 90 per cent of the circulating bills were found to have traces of cocaine on them.

One euro is made up of 100 cents. The euro symbol is €. There are eight coins (€2, €1, 50 cents, 20 cents, 10 cents, 5 cents, 2 cents, 1 cents) and seven banknotes. The notes are of differing colours and sizes (€5

is the smallest, €500 the largest). They were designed by Austrian artist Robert Kalina and can be used as primers for the different periods and styles of European architecture.

€5 (grey; classical)
€10 (red; Romanesque)
€20 (blue; Gothic)
€50 (orange; Renaissance)
€100 (green; baroque and rococo)
€200 (yellow-brown; iron and glass)
€500 (purple; 20th century)

For more information on the euro and all that it entails, check online at www.euro.ecb.int.

post office is the Postbank, a money-changing facility. It costs €0.59 to send a postcard from Amsterdam to anywhere in Europe, and €0.75 outside Europe. Stamps (postzegels) can be bought with postcards from postoffice, tobacconists and souvenir shops.

Post offices

For all the post offices in the region, look in the *Gouden Gids* under 'postkantoren'. Two handy branches are at Waterlooplein 10 (Jodenbuurt, 620 3081, 9am-6pm Mon-Fri, 10am-1.30pm Sat) and Albert Cuypstraat 151/155 (the Pijp, 662 2635, 9am-5pm Mon-Fri, 10am-1.30pm Sat).

Main Post Office
Singel 250, Old Centre: New Side (330 0555). Tram 1, 2, 5, 13, 14, 17. **Open** 9am-6pm Mon-Wed, Fri; 9am-8pm Thur; 10am-1.30pm Sat. **Map** p306 C3.

Post restante/ general delivery

Post Restante
Hoofdpostkantoor, Singel 250, 1016 AB Amsterdam. **Map** p306 C3. If you're not sure where you'll be staying in Amsterdam, people can send your post to the above address. You'll be able to collect it from the main post office (*see above*); take along some picture ID.

Religion
Catholic
St John and St Ursula *Begijnhof 30, Old Centre: New Side (622 1918). Tram 1, 2, 4, 5, 16, 24, 25.* **Open** 1-6.30pm Mon; 8.30am-6.30pm Tue-Sat; 9am-6.30pm (10am Dutch; 11.15am French service) Sun. **Services** in Dutch and French; phone for details. **Map** p306 D3.

Dutch Reformed Church
Oude Kerk *Oudekerksplein 33, Old Centre: Old Side (625 8284). Tram 4, 9, 16, 24, 25.* **Open** 11am-5pm Mon-Sat; 1-5pm Sun. **Services** in Dutch; 11am Sun. **Map** p306 D2.

Jewish
Liberal Jewish Community Amsterdam *Jacob Soetendorpstraat 8, Zuid (642 3562/office rabbinate 644 2619). Tram 4.* **Open** *Rabbi's office* 10am-3pm Mon-Thur. **Services** 8pm Fri; 10am Sat.
Orthodox Jewish Community Amsterdam *Postbus 7967, Van der Boechorststraat 26, Zuid (646 0046). Bus 69, 169.* **Open** 9am-5pm Mon-Fri by appointment only. Information on orthodox synagogues and Jewish facilities.

Muslim
THAIBA Islamic Cultural Centre *Kraaiennest 125, Zuid (698 2526). Metro Gaasperplas.* Phone for details of mosques, prayer times and cultural activities.

Reformed Church
English Reformed Church *Begijnhof 48, Old Centre: New Side (624 9665/www.ercadam.nl). Tram*

1, 2, 4, 5, 9, 16, 24, 25. **Services** in English 10.30am Sun. **Map** p306 D3. The main place of worship for the local English-speaking community.

Safety & security

Amsterdam is a relatively safe city, but that's not to say you shouldn't take care when walking through it. The Red Light District is rife with undesirables who, if not necessarily violent, are expert pickpockets; be vigilant, especially on or around bridges, and try to avoid making eye contact with anyone who looks like they may be up to no good (a relative term in the Red Light District, but the point stands).

Take care on the train to Schiphol, where there has been a recent spate of thefts, and, if you cycle in town, lock your bike super-securely. Otherwise, just use your common sense, keeping valuables in a safe place, not leaving bags unattended, and so on.

Smoking

Smoking is widely tolerated in Amsterdam though an impending law that aims to guarantee a smoke-free work environment may change that. But meanwhile, you'll have no

Directory

problems sparking up in a bar or most restaurants. For smoking dope, *see p147*.

Study

Amsterdam's two major universities are the UvA (Universiteit van Amsterdam), which has around 27,000 students, and the VU (Vrije Universiteit), with about half that (14.000). Many UvA buildings across town are historic and listed (recognise them by their red and black plaques), whereas the VU has just one big building at de Boelelaan, in the south of Amsterdam.

Students are often entitled to discounts at assorted shops, attractions and entertainment venues; presenting an ISIC card is usually enough.

Courses

A number of UvA departments offer international courses and programmes at all levels. Details are available from the Foreign Relations Office (Spui 25, 1012 SR). Most postgraduate institutes of the UvA also take foreign students.

Amsterdam Summer University

Felix Meritis Building, Keizersgracht 324, Southern Canal Belt (620 0225/ www.amsu.edu). Tram 1, 2, 5. **Courses** mid July-early Sept. **Map** p310 C4.
The ASU offers an annual summer programme of courses, workshops, training and seminars in the arts, economics, politics, european studies, sciences, plus international classes in both Amsterdam and Maastricht.

Crea

Turfdraagsterpad 17, Old Centre: Old Side (525 1400/www.crea. uva.nl). Tram 4, 9, 14, 16, 24, 25. **Open** 10am-11pm Mon-Fri; 10am-5pm Sat; 11am-5pm Sun. Closed July-Aug (phone to check). **Map** p306 D3.
Inexpensive creative courses, lectures and performances, covering theatre, radio, video, media, dance, music, photography and fine art. Courses are not in English. They've also got a new second branch, Crea II, to expand their offerings.

UvA Service & Information Centre

Binnengasthuisstraat 9, Old Centre: Old Side (525 8080). Tram 4, 9, 16, 24, 25. **Open** *In person* 10am-5pm Mon-Wed, Fri; 10am-7pm Thur. *Telephone enquiries* 9am-10amTue-Thur; free appintement 11am-noon Tue-Thur. **Map** p306 D3.
Personal advice on studying and everything that goes with it.

VU Student Information

Office 444 7777/direct line 444 5000. **Open** 9am-5pm Mon-Fri.
The VU's helpline provides advice on courses and accommodation. International students should call 444 5030.

Student bookshop

VU Boekhandel

De Boelelaan 1105, Zuid (644 4355). Tram 5/Metro 51. **Open** 9am-7pm Mon-Fri; 10am-3.30pm Sat. **Credit** AmEx, MC, V.

Students' unions

AEGEE

Vendelsstraat 2, Old Centre: Old Side (525 2496/www.aegee-amsterdam.nl). Tram 4, 6, 9, 24, 25. **Open** 2-5pm Mon-Fri. **Map** p306 D3.
The Association des Etats Généraux des Etudiants de l'Europe basically organises seminars, workshops, summer courses and sporting events in Amsterdam and around 170 other European university cities.

SRVU

De Boelelaan 1083A, Zuid (444 9424/www.srvu.org)). Tram 5/Metro 51. **Open** 11am-4pm Mon-Fri.
SRVU is the union for VU students. Its accommodation service can also help foreign students find a place to stay, and offer general advice. Membership is €10 per year.

University libraries

Both libraries below hold many academic titles and also provide access to the Internet. There is a Adam Net-pas that you can use for Uva, VU libraries and Public Libraries of Amsterdam (Openbare bibliotheek) €32.50 a year.

UvA Main Library

Singel 425, Old Centre: New Side (525 2326/www.uba.uva.nl). Tram 1,
2, 5. **Open** *Study* 8.30am-midnight Mon-Fri; 9.30am-5pm Sat; 11am-5pm Sun. *Borrowing* 9.30am-5pm Mon-Thur; 9.30am-5pm Fri; 9.30am-1pm Sat. **Map** p310 D4.
To borrow books you need a UB (Universiteit Bibliotheek-University Library) card (€22.50): foreign students can get one if they're in Amsterdam for three months or more. Cards can be issued for one day, one month or one year. Day €3 and week €7.50 cards enable you to read books there, but not to withdraw them.

VU Main Library

De Boelelaan 1105, Zuid (444 5200/ www.ubvu.vu.nl). Tram 5/Metro 51. **Open** *Study* 7am-11pm Mon-Fri; 8.15-4pm Sat; July-Aug 8.15am-11pm Mon-Fri. *Borrowing* 9am-6pm Mon-Thur; 9am-5pm Fri. **Membership** €20/yr.
Not one big library, but several small ones. Membership is open to foreign students.

Telephones

All Amsterdam numbers within this book are listed without the city code, which is 020. To call Amsterdam from within the city, you don't need the code: just dial the seven-digit number. To call an Amsterdam number from elsewhere in the Netherlands, add 020 at the start of the listed number. Numbers in the Netherlands outside of Amsterdam are listed with their code in this Guide.

In addition to the standard city codes, three other types of numbers appear from time to time in this book. 0800 numbers are freephone numbers; those prefixed 0900 are charged at premium rates (€0.20 a minute or more); and 06 numbers are for mobile phones. If you're in doubt, call directory enquiries (0900 8008).

Dialling & codes

From the Netherlands

Dial the following code, then the number:
To Australia: 00 61
To Irish Republic: 00 353
To UK: 00 44, plus number (drop first '0' from area code)
To USA & Canada: 00 1

To the Netherlands

Dial the relevant international access code listed below, then the Dutch country code 31, then the number; drop the first '0' of the area code, so for Amsterdam use 20 rather than 020. To call 06 (mobile) numbers from abroad, there is no city code: just drop the first '0' from the 06 and dial the number as it appears. However, 0800 (freephone) and 0900 (premium rate) numbers cannot be reached from abroad.

From Australia: 00 11
From Irish Republic: 00
From UK: 00
From USA: 011

Within the Netherlands

National directory enquiries: 0900 8008
International directory enquiries: 0900 8418
Local operator: 0800 0101
International operator: 0800 0410

Making a call

Listen for the dialling tone (a hum), insert a phonecard or money, dial the code (none for calls within Amsterdam), then the number. A digital display on public phones shows credit remaining, but only wholly unused coins are returned. Phoning from a hotel is pricey.

International calls

International calls can be made from all phone boxes. Off-peak rates apply 8pm to 8am Monday to Friday and all weekend. For more information on rates, phone international directory enquiries (costs €1.15) 0900 8418.

Telephone directories

Found in post offices (see p287). When phoning information services, taxis or train stations you may hear the recorded message, 'Er zijn nog drie [3]/twee [2]/een [1] wachtende(n) voor u.' This tells you how many people are ahead of you in the telephone queuing system.

Public phones

Public phone boxes are mainly glass with a green trim. There are also telephone 'poles', identifiable by the KPN logo. Most phones take cards rather than coins, available from the Amsterdam Tourist Board, stations, post offices and tobacconists. You can use credit cards in many phones.

Mobile phones

Amsterdam's mobile network is run on a mix of the 900 and 1800 GSM bands, which means all dual-band UK handsets should work here. However, it's always best to check with your service provider that it has an arrangement with a Dutch provider. US phone users should always contact their provider before departure to check compatibility.

Time

Amsterdam is an hour ahead of Greenwich Mean Time (GMT). All clocks on Central European Time (CET) now go back and forward on the same spring and autumn dates as GMT.

Tipping

Though a service charge will be included in hotel, taxi, bar, cafe and restaurant bills, it's polite to round your payment up to the nearest euro for small bills and to the nearest five euros for larger sums, leaving the extra in change rather than filling in the blank on a credit card slip. In taxis, the most common tip is around ten per cent for short journeys.

Moving in

Expats moving to Amsterdam have **Access** (Herengracht 472, 421 8445/www.access-nl.org), a new, volunteer-driven organisation founded to answer questions about life in the Netherlands. But to find a flat, you will also need friends, money and loads of luck.

There are two main price bands: below €450 per month, and above €450 per month. Anything above €450 is considered free sector housing and can be found through agencies or in newspapers (in particular, the Wednesday, Thursday and Saturday editions of De Telegraaf and De Volkskrant) and every Tuesday and Thursday in the ads paper Via Via. Unfortunately, flatsharing is not common, and agency commissions are high.

If you're looking for properties under the €450 mark, you have two main choices. Both require a residents' permit (see above). If you're studying here, register with one of the three big housing co-ops: **Woning Net** (0900 8210 premium rate), **Archipel** (511 8911) and **Spectrum** (489 0085). For a charge of around €16 (registration is an extra €11 with Archipel), these agencies supply information on available accommodation. However, this method can take forever given the shortage of properties and surfeit of clients.

The other alternative is to register with one of the many non-profit agencies that hold property lotteries among would-be tenants. This may seem bizarre, but they do at least give you a chance of eventually getting a room. Call **ASW Kamerbureau** on 523 0130. Holders of residents' permits can also apply for council (public) housing. Alternatively, register with the **Stedelijke Woning Dienst** ('City Housing Service'; Stadhuis, Waterlooplein; 552 7511/www.swd. amsterdam.nl). Bank on a very long wait.

Directory

Weather report

Average daytime temperatures, rainfall and hours of sunshine in Amsterdam

	Temp (°C/°F)	Rainfall (mm/in)	Sunshine (hrs/dy)
Jan	4/39	68/2.7	1.8
Feb	6/43	48/1.9	2.8
Mar	9/48	66/2.6	3.7
Apr	13/55	53/2.1	5.5
May	17/63	61/2.4	7.2
June	20/68	71/2.8	6.6
July	22/72	76/3.0	6.9
Aug	22/72	71/2.8	6.7
Sept	19/66	66/2.6	4.4
Oct	14/57	73/2.9	3.3
Nov	9/48	81/3.2	1.9
Dec	6/43	84/3.3	1.5

Toilets

Using Amsterdam's historic green metal urinals should be a part of any visiting boy's agenda. On weekends, the city also places 'grey rocket' urinals on nightlife-oriented squares such as Leidseplein. If you choose to ignore these options you could get a €40 ticket for *wildplassen* ('wild pissing'). For the ladies, it's a sadder story: public loos are rare, and you may be forced to buy something in a bar or a café.

Tourist information

Amsterdam Tourist Board (VVV)

Stationsplein 10, Old Centre: New Side (0900 400 4040/www.visit amsterdam.nl). Tram 1, 2, 4, 5, 9, 13, 16, 17, 24, 25. **Open** 9am-5pm daily. **Map** p306 D1.
The main office of the VVV is right outside Centraal Station. English-speaking staff can change money and provide details on transport, entertainment, exhibitions and day-trips in the Netherlands. They also arrange hotel bookings for a fee of €2.75, and excursions and car hire for free. There is a good range of brochures for sale detailing walks and cycling tours, as well as cassette tours, maps and, for €1.50, a monthly listings magazine *Day by Day*. The info line features an English-language service (premium rate).
Other locations: Leidseplein 1 (9am-5pm Sun-Wed; 9am-7pm Thur-Sat); Centraal Station, platform 2B 15 (8am-8pm Mon-Sat; 9am-5pm Sun); Schiphol Airport, arrivals hall 40 (7am-10pm daily).

Visas & immigration

A valid passport is all that is required for a stay in the Netherlands of up to three months if you're from the EU, the USA, Canada, Australia or New Zealand. Citizens of other countries should apply in advance for a tourist visa. As with any trip, confirm visa requirements well before you plan to travel, with your local Dutch embassy or consulate or on www.immigratiedienst.nl.

For stays longer than three months, apply for a residents' permit (MVV visa), generally easier to get if you're from one of the countries listed above. (Technically, EU citizens don't need a residents' permit, but they will be required for all sorts of bureaucratic functions.)

When you have a fixed address, take your birth certificate to the Dienst Vreemdelingenpolitie (Aliens' Police; Johan Huizingalaan 757, Slotervaart; 559 6300/ www.immigratiedienst.nl), pick up a form and wait to hear if you've got an interview.

When to go

CLIMATE

Amsterdam's climate is very changeable, and often wet and windy. January and February are coldest, with summer often humid. If you can understand Dutch, try calling the weather line on 0900 8003 (€0.60/min).

PUBLIC HOLIDAYS

Called 'Nationale Feestdagen' in Dutch, they are as follows: New Year's Day; Good Friday; Easter Sunday and Monday; Koninginnedag (Queen's Day, 30 April); Remembrance Day (4 May); Liberation Day (5 May); Ascension Day; Whit (Pentecost) Sunday and Monday; Christmas Day, and the day after Christmas.

Women

Aside from some pockets of the Red Light District late at night, central Amsterdam is fairly safe for women, as long as usual common-sense safety precautions are observed.

De Eerstelijn

613 0245. **Open** 10.30am-11pm Mon-Fri; 3-11pm Sat, Sun.
A helpline for victims of rape, assault, sexual harassment or threats.

Meldpunt Vrouwenopvang

611 6022. **Open** 9am-11pm Mon-Fri; 3-11pm Sat, Sun.
Victims of abuse will be referred to a safe house or safe address.

Working in Amsterdam

EU nationals with a residents' permit (*see above*) can work here; non-EU citizens will find it difficult to get a visa without a job in place. Jobs are hard to come by; more so with no visa.

Vocabulary

The vast majority of people you'll meet in Amsterdam will speak good English, and you'll probably be able to get by without a word of Dutch during your stay. However, a little effort goes a long way, and the locals are appreciative of those visitors polite enough to take five minutes and learn some basic phrases. Here are a few that might help.

PRONUNCIATION GUIDE

ch – as in 'lo**ch**'
ee – as in 'h**ay**'
g – similar to '**ch**'
ie – as in 'l**ea**n'
ei – as in 'l**i**ne'
j – as in '**y**es' except when preceded by 'i', when it should be said as a 'y'
oe – as in 'l**oo**n'
oo – as in 'n**o**'
ou, au, ui – as in 'c**ow**'
tie – as in 'i**tsy** bi**tsy**'
tje – as in '**ch**urch'
v – as in 'f**or**'
w – as in '**w**hich', with a hint of 'v'
y, ij – a cross between 'i' (as in 'h**i**de') and 'ay' (as in 'w**ay**')

WORDS

hello – hallo (*hullo*) or dag (*daarg*)
goodbye – tot ziens (*tot zeens*)
bye – dag (*daarg*)
yes – ja (*yah*)
yes please – ja, graag
no – nee (*nay*)
no thanks – nee, dank je (*nay, dank ye*)
please – alstublieft (*als-too-bleeft*); also used to mean 'there you are' when exchanging items with others
thank you – dank u (*dank-oo*)
thanks – bedankt
excuse me – pardon
good – goed
bad – slecht
big – groot
small – klein (*kline*)
waiter – ober
nice – mooi (*moy*)
tasty – lekker (*lecker*)
open – open
closed – gesloten/dicht
inside – binnen
outside – buiten (*bowten*)
left – links
right – rechts (*reks*)
straight on – rechtdoor
far – ver (*fair*)
near – dichtbij (*dikt-bye*)
entrance – ingang
exit – uitgang (*owtgang*)

car – auto
bus – bus
train – trein
ticket/s – kaart/kaarten
postcard – briefkaart
stamp – postzegel
glass – glas
coffee – koffie
tea – thee
water – water
wine – wijn
beer – bier
booking – reservering
the bill – rekening

PLACES

street – straat (*straart*)
square – plein (*pline*)
canal – gracht
shop – winkel
bank – bank
post office – postkantoor
pharmacy – apotheek
hotel – hotel
hotel room – hotelkamer
single/twin/double bedroom – eenpersoonskamer/tweepersoons-kamer met aparte bedden/tweepersoonskamer
bar – bar
restaurant – restaurant
hospital – ziekenhuis
bus stop – bushalte
station – station

DAYS

Monday – Maandag
Tuesday – Dinsdag
Wednesday – Woensdag
Thursday – Donderdag
Friday – Vrijdag
Saturday – Zaterdag
Sunday – Zondag
today – vandaag
yesterday – gisteren
tomorrow – morgen
morning – ochtend
afternoon – middag
evening – avond
night – nacht
weekend – weekeinde

PHRASES

excuse me, do you speak English?
– sorry, spreekt u Engels? (*sorry, spraykt oo Engels?*)
sorry, I don't speak Dutch
– het spijt me, ik spreek geen Nederlands (*et spite meh, ik spraykhane nayderlants*)
I don't understand
– Ik begrijp het niet (*ik begripe et neet*)
what is that?
– wat is dat? (*vot is dat?*)
where is...?
– waar is...?
what's the time?
– hoe laat is het?

my name is...
– mijn naam is... (*mine naam is...*)
I want...
– Ik wil graag...
how much is...?
– wat kost...?
could I have a receipt?
– mag ik een bonnetje alstublieft?
Do you accept credit cards?
– Nemen jullie/u krediet kaarten?
how far is it to...?
– hoe ver is het naar...?
I would like a ticket to...
– Ik wil graag een kaart naar...
Do you have a light?
– Hebt je/u een vuurtje?
What's your name?
– Hoe heet jij/u?
Would you like a drink?
– Wil je/u iets te drinken?
I don't smoke
– Ik rook niet
I'm tired
– Ik ben moe
I disapprove of drugs
– Ik heb een afkeur voor drugs
I am sick
– Ik ben ziek
I think I ate too much spacecake
– Ik denk dat ik te veel spacecake heb opgegeten

INSULTS

fuck! – kut (female private parts)
bloody lunatic! – boer (literally 'farmer' – used by cyclists against car drivers)
arsehole! – lul (male private parts)
motherfucker! – moederneuker
beanpole! – volgescheten palingvel (literally 'shit-filled eel-skin' – directed towards skinny person)

NUMBERS

0 nul
1 een
2 twee
3 drie
4 vier
5 vijf
6 zes
7 zeven
8 acht
9 negen
10 tien
11 elf; **12** twaalf; **13** dertien; **14** veertien; **15** vijftien; **16** zestien; **17** zeventien; **18** achttien; **19** negentien; **20** twintig; **21** eenentwintig; **22** twee'ntwintig; **30** dertig; **31** eenendertig; **32** twee'ndertig; **40** veertig; **50** vijftig; **60** zestig; **70** zeventig; **80** tachtig; **90** negentig; 100 honderd; **101** honderd een; **200** tweehonderd; **1,000** duizend; **2,000** twee duizend; **100,000** honderd duizend; **1,000,000** een miljoen.

Further Reference

Books

Fiction

Baantjer *De Cock* series
This ex-Amsterdam cop used his experiences to write a series of crime novels set in town. Also a great TV series.

Albert Camus *The Fall*
Man recalls his Parisian past while in Amsterdam's 'circles of hell'.

Arnon Grunberg *Blue Mondays*
Philip Roth's *Goodbye Columbus* goes Dutch in this cathartic 1994 bestseller.

John Irving
A Widow for One Year
Classic Irving, partly set in the Red Light District.

Tim Krabbé *The Vanishing*
A man's search for his vanished lover. Twice made into a feature film (the first is the best).

Marga Minco *Bitter Herbs*
An autobiographical masterpiece about a Jewish family falling apart during and after the war.

John David Morley
The Anatomy Lesson
Morley's novel is about two very different American brothers growing up in Amsterdam.

Harry Mulisch *The Assault*
A boy's perspective on World War II. Also classic film.

Multatuli *Max Havelaar or the Coffee Auctions of the Dutch Trading Company*
The story of a colonial officer and his clash with the corrupt government.

Cees Nooteboom *The Following Story*
An exploration of the differences between platonic and physical love.

Heleen van Royen
The Happy Housewife
A fine debut from this Dutch writer, about a woman coming to terms with having a baby.

Renate Rubinstein
Take It or Leave It
Diary of one of the Netherlands' most renowned journalists and her battle against MS.

Irvine Welsh *The Acid House*
Short stories, one set – perhaps predictably – in Amsterdam's druggy underworld.

Janwillem van der Wetering
The Japanese Corpse
An off-the-wall police procedural set in Amsterdam, and one of an excellent series.

Manfred Wolf (ed) *Amsterdam: A Traveller's Literary Companion*
The country's best writers tell tales of the city.

Non-fiction

Rudy B Andeweg & Galen A Irwin
Dutch Government & Politics
An introduction to Dutch politics that assumes no prior knowledge.

Kathy Batista & Florian Migsch
A Guide to Recent Architecture: The Netherlands
Part of the excellent pocket series, with great pictures.

Derek Blyth *Amsterdam Explored*
Nine walks around the city.

Matthijs van Boxsel
The Encyclopeadia of Stupidity
Impressive global survey that suffers fools gladly.

CR Boxer
The Dutch Seaborne Empire
The Netherlands' wealth and where it went.

Peter Burke *Venice & Amsterdam*
A succinct comparative history of these two watery cities.

Simon Carmiggelt *I'm Just Kidding: More of a Dutchman's Slight Adventures*
A collection from an Amsterdam columnist famous for sucking his readers in to take a closer look at Amsterdam.

Sean Condon *My 'Dam Life*
Offbeat Amster-insights by Australian wit.

Anne Frank
The Diary of Anne Frank
The still-shocking wartime diary of the young Frank.

RH Fuchs *Dutch Painting*
A comprehensive guide.

Miep Gies & Alison Leslie Gold
Anne Frank Remembered
The story of the woman who helped the Frank family during the war.

Paul Groenendijk
Guide to Modern Architecture in Amsterdam
What the title suggests.

Zbigniew Herbert
Still Life with a Bridle
The Polish poet and essayist meditates on the Golden Age.

Etty Hillesum
An Interrupted Life: The Diaries and Letters 1941-1943
The moving wartime experiences of a young Amsterdam Jewish woman who died in Auschwitz.

Jonathan I Israel
The Dutch Republic and the Hispanic World 1606-1661
How the Dutch Republic broke free.

EH Kussmann
The Low Countries 1780-1940
Good background reading.

Geert Mak *Amsterdam: A Brief Life of the City*
The city's history told through the stories of its people, both acclaimed and plain.

Paul Overy *De Stijl*
Modern art examined.

Simon Schama
The Embarassment of Riches
A lively social and cultural history of the Netherlands. His biography of sorts, Rembrandt's Eyes, is also well worth a look.

William Z Schetter
The Netherlands in Perspective
An essential book that goes beyond the usual stereotypes.

Peter van Straaten
This Literary Life
A highly amusing collection of one of the Netherlands' most popular cartoonist's works.

Jacob Vossestein
Dealing with the Dutch
Netherlanders explained in fascinating fashion.

David Winners *Brilliant Orange: the Neurotic Genius of Dutch Football*
Excellent delve into the Dutch pysche that takes in much more than just football.

Wim de Wit
The Amsterdam School: Dutch Expressionist Architecture
Early 20th-century architecture.

Music

Albums

Arling & Cameron
Music for Imaginary Films (2000)
Showered with acclaim, eclectic duo reinvent the history of film soundtracks.

Chet Baker *Live at Nick's* (1978)
Accompanied by his favorite rhythm section, Chet soars in one of his best live recordings.

The Beach Boys *Holland* (1973)
Californians hole up in Holland and start recording.

Bettie Serveert *Palomine* (1993)
Alt.rock guitar with perfect pop songs and angelic vocals.

Herman Brood & His Wild Romance *Shpritsz* (1978)
The nation's cuddle junkie rocker scored international hit with 'Saturday Night'.

The Ex *Starters Alternators* (1998)
Anarcho squat punks/improv-jazzsters team up with Steve Albini.

Focus *Hocus Pocus: the Best of Focus* (1975)
Prog rock – with yodelling!

George Baker Selection
Little Green Bag (1970)
Part of the 'Dutch Invasion', who exchanged the rocking riffs of this album for softer moods a few years

later with the somewhat icky 'Una Paloma Blanca'.

Golden Earring *Moontan* (1974)
The Hague's answer to The Who; includes hit 'Radar Love'.

The Herb Spectacles
The Incredible World of... (2003)
Alpert meets Surf meets Middle East.

Human Alert *Dirty Dancing* (2002)
Hysterically funny punk legends go orchestral.

Junkie XL *Radio JXL* (2003)
The Lowlands' answer to the Chemical Brothers.

Osdorp Posse
Origineel Amsterdams (2000)
Nederhop maestros offer a primer in local street talk for 'moederneukers'.

Outsiders
Capital Collectors Series (1996)
Dutch take on '60s beat and garage punk whose legend goes beyond their four-year existence.

Lee 'Scratch' Perry *The Return of Pipecock Jackxon* (1980)
Godfather of dub burns down studio and comes to Amsterdam to drop acid and record this brain-melter.

Oscar Peterson
Trio At Concertgebouw (1958)
One of many jazz legends who've taken advantage of the ace acoustics to record a live set.

Shocking Blue
The Best of... (1994)
Killer bubblegum riffs in songs like 'Send Me a Postcard'. Bananarama covered 'Venus'.

Solex *Pick Up* (1999)
Amsterdam record-store owner and sample impresario turns dance music on its head.

Urban Dance Squad *Mental Floss for the Globe* (1990)
Rude Boy and gang produce influential crossover album.

Various *Als Je Haar Maar Goed Zit, Vols 1 & 2* (1982/1983)
Documents Amsterdam's early '80s hardcore scene with tracks recorded by the likes of BGK, Amsterdamned, Null, Frites Moderns and Nitwitz.

Various *Amsterdammers* (1996)
Local bands of every genre, including Solid Ground, pay tribute to their hometown.

Songs

assorted singers
'Aan de Amsterdamse Grachten'
Bone Thugs-N-Harmony
'The Weed Song'
Bertus Borgers 'Red Red Lebanon'
Brainbox 'Amsterdam, the First Days'
Jacques Brel 'Amsterdam'
John Cale 'Amsterdam'
Coldplay 'Amsterdam'
Kevin Coyne 'Amsterdam'
Cypress Hill 'Spark Another Owl'
Dorus 'Het Mooiste van Mokum'; 'Hij Vindt Amsterdam wel Aardig'
Drukwerk 'Hey Amsterdam'
Eminem 'Under the Influence'
Herman Emmink 'Tulpen uit Amsterdam'
Ruud Gullit & Revelation Time 'Not the Dancing Kind'
The Streets 'Too much Brandy'
Tol Hansse 'Big City'
Ronnie Hilton 'A Windmill in Old Amsterdam'
Rika Jansen 'Amsterdam Huilt (Waar het Eens Heeft Gelachen)'
Jesus & the Gospelfuckers 'Amsterdam'
Jasperina de Jong 'De Rosse Buurt'
Johnny Jordaan 'Geef Mj Maar Amsterdam'; 'Bij Ons in de Jordaan'
Kirsty MacColl 'Here Comes That Man Again'
NRA 'Amsterdam Surf Song'
Mojo Nixon 'Amsterdam Dogshit Blues'
Porn Kings 'Amsterdam XXX'
Willem Breuker Kollectief meets Djazzex 'Amsterdam Thoroughfare'
Van Halen 'Amsterdam'

Films

Amsterdam Global Village
dir. Johan van der Keuken (1996)
A meditative and very long arty cruise through Amsterdam's streets and peoples.

Amsterdamned
dir. Dick Maas (1987)
Thriller with psychotic frogman and lots of canal chase scenes, made only slightly worse by continuity problems that result in characters turning an Amsterdam corner and ending up in Utrecht.

Foreign Correspondent
dir. Alfred Hitchcock (1940)
The perfect lesson in creating a sense of location from a film made almost entirely in Hollywood. But then nothing is as it seems in this (anti-Nazi) propagandist thriller.

The Fourth Man
dir. Paul Verhoeven (1983)
Mr *Basic Instinct* films Gerard Reve novel with Jeroen Krabbe seething with homoerotic desire. Better than it might sound.

Hufters en Hofdames (Bastards and Bridesmaids)
dir. Eddy Terstall (1997)
Twentysomethings use Amsterdam as backdrop against which to have relationship trouble.

Karacter (Character)
dir. Mike van Diem (1997)
Oscar winner for Best Foreign Language film: an impeccably scripted father-son drama.

Naar de Klote! (Wasted!)
dir. Ian Kerkhof (1996)
An appropriately hallucinogenic trip through Amsterdam's techno clubland. This was the first feature film to be made on DV.

De Noorderlingen (The Northerners)
dir. Alex van Warmerdam (1992)
Absurdity and angst in a lonely Dutch subdivision.

Turks Fruit (Turkish Delight)
dir. Paul Verhoeven (1973)
Sculptor Rutger Hauer witnesses the brain tumour of his babe.

Zusje (Little Sister)
dir. Robert Jan Westdijk (1995)
A family affair with voyeuristic overtones.

Websites

www.amsterdam.nl
An accessible site with advice on living in, as well as visiting, Amsterdam. The searchable maps are terrific.

www.amsterdamhotspots.nl
An upbeat review-based site of, er, Amsterdam hotspots.

www.amsterdam-webcams.com
Some personal, some public, all in Amsterdam.

www.archined.nl
News and reviews of Dutch architecture, in both Dutch and English. Informative and interesting.

www.bmz.amsterdam.nl/adam
Fantastically detailed site devoted to Amsterdam's architectural heritage. Some pages in English.

www.channels.nl
Takes you, virtually, through Amsterdam's streets with reviews of their hotels, restaurants and clubs.

www.expatica.com
English news and reviews aimed at the Expat in the Netherlands.

www.gayamsterdamlinks.com
What you'd expect.

gemeentearchief.amsterdam.nl
Dutch-only site of city archive packed with a billion things Amsterdam.

www.nobodyhere.com
Winner of the 2003 Webby Award for best personal website. Wierd and beautiful.

www.simplyamsterdam.nl
Aimed at the 'independent traveller'.

www.uitlijn.nl
Event listings for Amsterdam, in Dutch but fairly easy to navigate.

www.underwateramsterdam.com
The web home of alternative listings mag Shark, in whose shallows several Time Out writers lurk.

www.urbanguide.nl
A guide to clubs, restaurants etc. geared to the urban trendy hipster.

www.visitamsterdam.nl
The tourist board site which has gotten a tad hipper recently.

www.xs4all.nl/~4david
An anatomy of the mind, Amsterdam-style (ie left brain). Drug techniques you never knew existed.

Directory

Index

Index

Advertisers' Index

Please refer to the relevant sections for addresses/telephone numbers

PIC Answer Key

Answers to common queries

1. Be polite and make clear arrangements about your desires.
2. Expect to pay €35-€50 for around 20 minutes.
3. No, but prostitutes do visit clinics and will insist on condoms.
4. Each sexworker has her own personal reasons for choosing prostitution.
5. Legalisation recognises prostitution as work and thereby allows prostitutes to demand better working conditions, health care, protection, and benefits.

Answers to queerer queries

1. Perhaps you should look for an S&M studio or individuals who specialise in fetishes and fantasies.
2. No, they all dye their pubes purple and shave in political statements for clients to read. Next!
3. Probably yes, if you are looking particularly sore. So give it a rest for a while.
4. That's why lube was invented.
5. Sorry, but test-driving prostitutes is not part of PIC's mission statement.

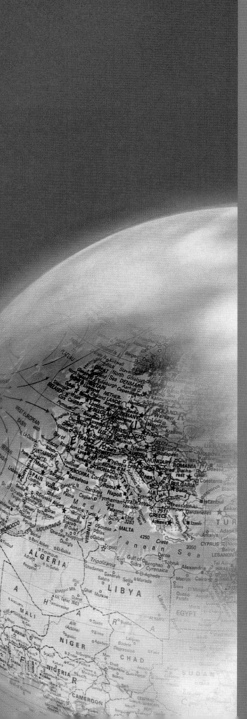

Maps

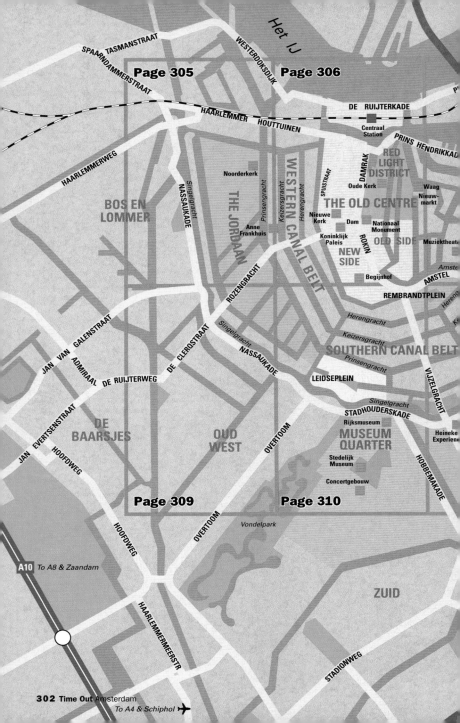

Page 305

Page 306

Page 309

Page 310

Het IJ

SPAARNDAMMERSTRAAT

TASMANSTRAAT

WESTERDOKSDIJK

HAARLEMMER HOUTTUINEN

DE RUIJTERKADE

Centraal
Station

PRINS HENDRIKKADE

HAARLEMMERWEG

Noorderkerk

WESTERN CANAL BELT

SPUISTRAAT

DAMRAK

RED
LIGHT
DISTRICT

Oude Kerk

Waag
Nieuw-
markt

BOS EN
LOMMER

Singelgracht

Nassaukade

THE JORDAAN

Prinsengracht

Keizersgracht

Herengracht

THE OLD CENTRE

Anne
Frankhuis

Nieuwe
Kerk

Dam

Koninklijk
Paleis

Nationaal
Monument

OLD SIDE

Muziektheat

ROKIN

NEW
SIDE

Amste

ROZENGRACHT

Begijnhof

AMSTEL

REMBRANDTPLEIN

Herengi

JAN VAN GALENSTRAAT

Singelgracht

NASSAUKADE

Herengracht

Keizersgracht

SOUTHERN CANAL BELT

ADMIRAAL DE RUIJTERWEG

DE CLERQSTRAAT

Prinsengracht

LEIDSEPLEIN

VIJZELGRACHT

JAN EVERTSENSTRAAT

HOOFDWEG

DE
BAARSJES

OUD
WEST

OVERTOOM

Singelgracht

STADHOUDERSKADE

Rijksmuseum

MUSEUM
QUARTER

Heinek
Experien

Stedelijk
Museum

HOBBEMAKADE

Concertgebouw

OVERTOOM

Vondelpark

HOOFDWEG

A10 To A8 & Zaandam

ZUID

HAARLEMMERMEERSTR.

STADIONWEG

To A4 & Schiphol ✈

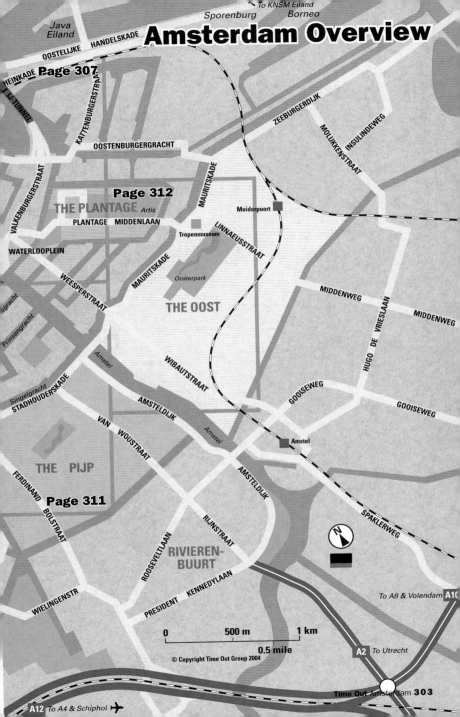

The Netherlands

0 25 50 km

30 miles

Schiermonnikoog
Borkum
Ameland
Terschelling
Hoogebeintum
Uithuizermeeden
Uithuizen
Warffum Kantens Spijk Bierum
Middlestum Stedum Loppersum Appingedam
Dokkum
GRONINGEN Garmerwolde
Vlieland
WADDEN ISLANDS
LEEUWARDEN
GRONINGEN
Harlingen
Grouw Drachten
Veendam
Winschoten
Bellingwolde
Texel
Sneek FRIESLAND
Fochteloöerveen
Assen
Stadskanaal
Terherne
Heeg Heerenveen
DRENTHE Borger
Den Helder
Sloten Lemmer
Ellertsveld
Uffelter Westerbork Orvelte
Anna Veen
Paulowna IJSSELMEER
Schagen Opperdoes Medemblick
Steenwijk Dwingeloose
Giethoorn Heide
Hoogeveen
Emmen
Broek-op-
Langedijk Twisk Enkhuizen
Emmeloord
Uffelte
Wanneperveen Meppel
Heiloo Alkmaar Hoorn
Urk
Vollenhove Staphorst
Zwartsluis
Limmen
NOORD MARKERMEER Kampen
HOLLAND Ketelhaven ZWOLLE
Beverwijk Pumerend
Edam Lelystad
Ommen
Lemelerveld
IJmuiden Zaanstad Volendam Oostvaarders- Flevohof
OVERIJSSEL Oothaarsum
Kennemer Monnickendam plassen Denekamp
Duinen Nat.Pk. Broek in W Hellendoorn
Zandvoort AMSTERDAM FLEVOLAND Raalte Nijverdal Almelo Oldenzaal
Benneboek Almerestad Harderwijk Deventer Holterberg Hengelo
Keukenhof Muiden 81m
Bussum APELDOORN Zutphen ENSCHEDE
Lisse Hillegom Naarden Laren Bunschoten-
Noordwijk Vogelenzang Fort Spakenburg
Katwijk Rijnsburg Breukelen Soestdijk Hoge Veluwe
Aalsmeer Vreeland Siostelh Amersfoort Nat. Park
LEIDEN Loenen Winterswijk
Scheveningen De Haar Austerlitz Ede
ZUID Alphen UTRECHT Oosterbeek
DEN HAAG HOLLAND Gouda Castle UTRECHT Wijkbij
Naaldwijk Zoetermeer Oudewater Duurstede GELDERLAND
DELFT Cujlemborg Rhenen ARNHEM Doetinchem
Hoek van Holland Schoonhoven
Europoort Tiel
ROTTERDAM NIJMEGEN
Vlaardingen Gorinchem
Voorne Alblasserdam Oss
Stellendam Putten De Biesbosch 'S-HERTOGENBOSCH
DORDRECHT Nat. Park
Schouwen Hoekse-Waard Geertruidenberg Drunen Overloon
Brouwershaven Waalwijk De Groote Peel Uden
Oosterhout Kaatsheuvel Nat. Reserve
Oosterscheldedam Goeree- Oudenbosch BREDA
Delta Expo Overflakkee NOORD - BRABANT Nuenen
Zierikzee TILBURG Helmond
Middelburg Noord Roosendaal
Veere Beveland Tholen EINDHOVEN Venlo
Zoutelande Goes Bergen op
Vlissingen Kapelle Zoom Kruiningen LIMBURG
Yerseke
ZEELAND Weert Thorn
Zeebrugge Zeeuws - Vlaanderen Terneuzen Roermond
BRUGGE Sittard
BRUGES ANTWERPEN Geleen
ANVERS Valkenburg Heerlen
GENT Schin
GAND MAASTRICHT AACHEN

NORTH SEA

BELGIUM

GERMANY

1. Oud-Loosdrecht
2. Breukeleveen
3. Westbroek

© Copyright Time Out Group 20

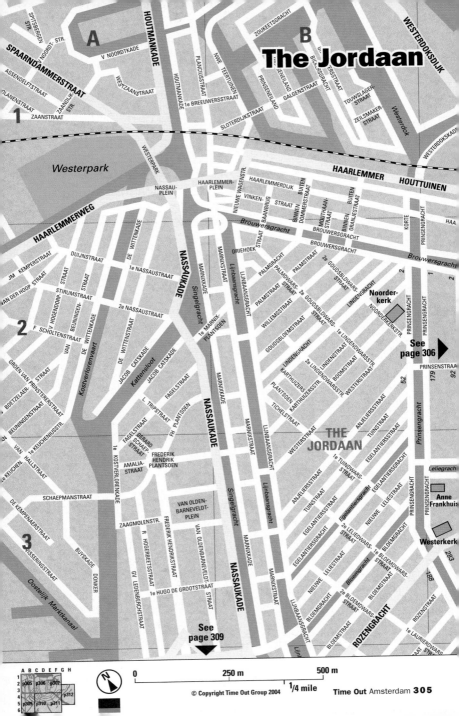

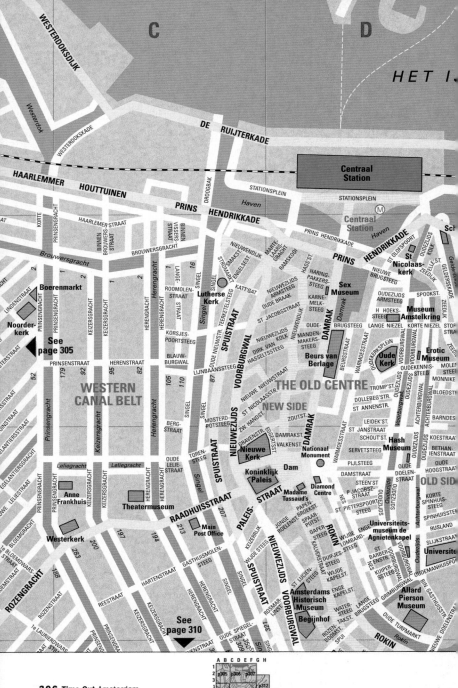

WESTERDOKSDIJK

Westerdok

C

D

HET IJ.

DE RUIJTERKADE

WESTERDOKSKADE

HAARLEMMER HOUTTUINEN

DROOGBAK

STATIONSPLEIN

Haven

Centraal
Station

STATIONSPLEIN

PRINS HENDRIKKADE

Centraal
Station

Haven

PRINS HENDRIKKADE

Sch

KORTE PRINSENGRACHT

HAARLEMER STRAAT

BINNEN VISSERS-STRAAT

BINNEN BROUWERS-STRAAT

NIEUWENDIJK

MARTE LANRS-GRACHT

RAMSKOOI

St OLOFSPOORT

OUDEZIJDS KOLK

St
Nicolaas-
kerk

ZEEDIJK

GELDERSEKADE

Brouwersgracht

PRINSENGRACHT

HERENGRACHT

KEIZERSGRACHT

ROOMOLEN-STRAAT

LANGE-STRAAT

Singel

TEERKETELSTEEG

KATT'GAT

NIEUWENDIJK

HARING-PACKERS-STEEG

Sex
Museum

NIEUWE BRUGSTEEG

PRINS HENDRIKKADE

OUDEZIJDS ARMSTEEG

SPOOKST.

ZEEDIJK

Boerenmarkt

Lutherse
Kerk

STROMARKT

TENGELSSTEEG

OUDE BRAAK

NIEUWEZIJDS ARMSTEEG

Museum
Amstelkring

KORTE NIEZEL

Noorder-
kerk

LINDENSTRAAT

PRINSENGRACHT

KEIZERSGRACHT

KORSJES-POORTSTEEG

ST JACOBSSTR.

NIEUWEZIJDS KOLK

KARNE-MELK-STEEG

H HOEKS-STEEG

LANGE NIEZEL

STOF STRA

See
page 305

Singel

NIEUWEZIJDS

DIRK VAN HASSELTSSTEEG

MANDEN-MAKERS-STEEG

OUDE-

BRUGSTEEG

Oude
Kerk

Erotic
Museum

MOLEN

PRINSENSTRAAT

179

92

HERENSTRAAT

95

82

BLAUW-BURGWAL

LIJNBAANSSTEEG

Beurs van
Berlage

BEURSSTRAAT

WARMOESSTRAAT

OUDEKERKSPLEIN

OUDEKENNIS-STEEG

MONNIKE

WESTERN
CANAL BELT

Prinsengracht

Keizersgracht

Herengracht

105

110

Singel

NIEUWE NIEUWSTRAAT

ST. NICOLAASTR.

THE OLD CENTRE

TROMP'ST.N

OUDEZIJDS VOORBURGWAL

BLOEDSTH

52

BERG-STRAAT

MOSTERD-POTSTEEG

NEW SIDE

DOLLEBEG'STR.

ST ANNENSTR.

ACHTERBURGWAL

BARNDES

Leliegracht

Leliegracht

TOREN-STEEG

Singel

ZW. HANDST.

ZOUTST.

LEIDEK'ST.

ST JANSTRAAT

SCHOUT'ST.

DAMRAK

OUDEZIJDS

KOESTRAA

Anne
Frankhuis

Nieuwe
Kerk

GRAVENSTR.

EGGERTSST.

DAMRAKST.

VALKENST.

SERVETSTEEG

Hash
Museum

OUDEZIJDS

BETHAN-IENSTRAAT

Theatermuseum

Dam

Nationaal
Monument

WARMOESSTRAAT

PIJLSTEEG

OUDE DOELEN-STRAAT

OLD SID

Westerkek

Koninklijk
Paleis

DAMSTRAAT

STEEN'ST

J PACOBSZ-STRAAT

Madame
Tussaud's

Diamond
Centre

Universiteits-
museum de
Agnietenkapel

Main
Post Office

PAPEL BROEKST.

SPAAR-POTST.

NES

ST PIETERSPOORT-STEEG

OUDEZIJDS

KORTE SPINHUIS-STEEG

SPINHUISSTEEG

RAADHUISSTRAAT

207

PALEIS-STRAAT

KEIZERSRIJK

GAPER-STEEG

JONGE ROELENSTRAAT

DUIFJES-STEEG

ROKIN

LOMBARD-STEEG

RUSLAND

ST BARBER-STEEG

SLIJKSTRAAT

197

194

213

Singel

WIJDE KAPELST.

KALVERSTRAAT

ST LUCIEN STEEG

KUIPER-STEEG

VOORBURGWAL

OUDEMANHUISPOORT

Universite

200

283

GASTHUISMOLEN-STEEG

NIEUWEZIJDS VOORBURGWAL

WIJDE STEEG

WATER-STEEG

ENGE KAPELST.

LANGE BRUGSTEEG

GRIMBURGWAL

OUDEZIJDS VOORBURGWAL

Allard
Pierson
Museum

ROZENGRACHT

HARTENSTRAAT

REESTRAAT

HERENGRACHT

ROSMAR-LIJNST.

ST LUCIEN STEEG

Amsterdams
Historisch
Museum

Begijnhof

TAKST.

ROZEN-BOOMST.

SPUI

ROKIN

OUDE TURFMARKT

Rokin

ROKIN

1e LAURIERDWARS-STRAAT

PRINSENGRACHT

KEIZERSGRACHT

OUDE SPIEGEL-STRAAT

NIEUWEZIJDS VOORBURGWAL

Singel

OUDE DOELENSTRA

See
page 310

A B C D E F G H

1 p305 p306 p307

2

3   p312

4

5

6 p309 p316 p311

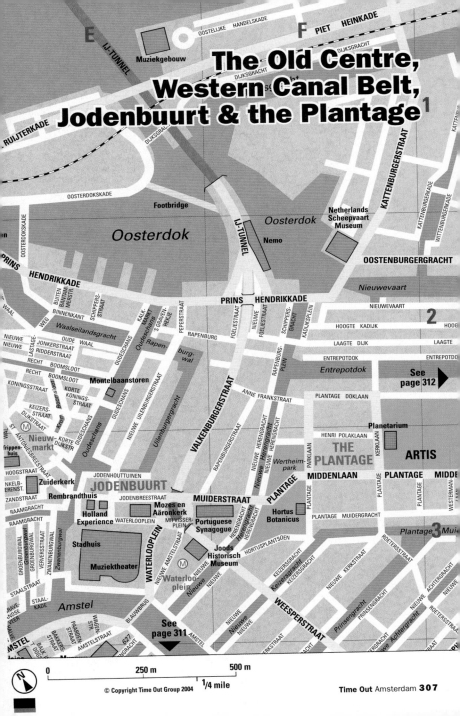

A taste of Time Out City Guides

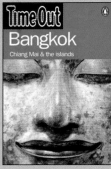

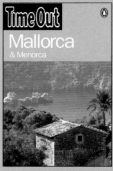

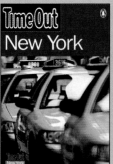

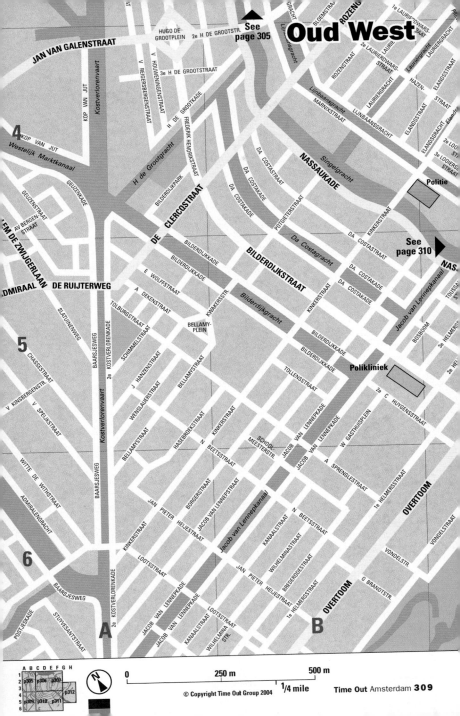

Oud West

See page 305

See page 310

4

5

6

JAN VAN GALENSTRAAT

HUGO DE GROOTPLEIN

2e H DE GROOTSTR.

3e DE GROOTSTRAAT

KOP VAN JUT

Kostverlorenvaart

Westelijk Marktkanaal

V HOUWENINGENSTRAAT

V REIGERSBERGENSTRAAT

H DE GROOTKADE

FREDERIK HENDRIKSTRAAT

H de Grootgracht

BILDERDIJKPARK

DE CLERCQSTRAAT

Geuzenkade

GEUZENSTRAAT

AV BERGEN STRAAT

'M DE ZWIJGERLAAN

ADMIRAAL DE RUIJTERWEG

SLATUINENWEG

BAARSJESWEG

KOSTVERLORENKADE

Kostverlorenvaart

BAARSJESWEG

CHASSÉSTRAAT

V KINSBERGENSTR.

V SPELJKSTRAAT

WITTE DE WITHSTRAAT

ADMIRALENGRACHT

BAARSJESWEG

POSTJESKADE

STUYVESANTSTRAAT

BILDERDIJKKADE

BILDERDIJKKADE

E WOLFFSTRAAT

A DEKENSTRAAT

TOLBURGSTRAAT

SCHIMMELSTRAAT

J HANZENSTRAAT

WENSLAUERSTRAAT

HASEBROEKSTRAAT

BELLAMYSTRAAT

BELLAMY-PLEIN

KWAKERSSTR.

N BEETSSTRAAT

KINKERSTRAAT

BELLAMYSTRAAT

BORGERSTRAAT

JAN PIETER HEIJESTRAAT

JACOB VAN LENNEPSTRAAT

KINKERSTRAAT

LOOTSSTRAAT

2e KOSTVERLORENKADE

JACOB VAN LENNEPKADE

KANAALSTRAAT

JACOB VAN LENNEPKADE

WILHELMINA STR.

Jacob van Lennepkanaal

BILDERDIJKSTRAAT

Bilderdijkgracht

BILDERDIJKKADE

BILDERDIJKKADE

TOLLENSSTRAAT

SCHOOLMEESTERSTR.

JACOB VAN LENNEPKADE

JACOB VAN LENNEPKADE

JAN PIETER HEIJESTRAAT

KANAALSTRAAT

WILHELMINASTRAAT

N BEETSSTRAAT

BREDERODESTRAAT

1e HELMERSSTRAAT

DA COSTASTRAAT

DA COSTAKADE

DA COSTAKADE

POTGIETERSTRAAT

Da Costagracht

DA COSTASTRAAT

DA COSTAKADE

DA COSTAKADE

NASSAUKADE

Singelgracht

NASSAU

KINKERSTRAAT

Jacob van Lennepkanaal

A SPRENGLESTRAAT

W GASTHUISPLEIN

2e C HUYGENSSTRAAT

1e HELMERSSTRAAT

VONDELSTR.

VONDELSTR.

G BRANDTSTR.

OVERTOOM

OVERTOOM

BOSBOOM

3e HELMERSSTR.

2e HE

TOUSSA

ST

ROZENG

ROZENG

1e LAURIERDWARS-STRAAT

BLOEMSTRAAT

Lijnbaansgracht

ROZENSTRAAT

2e LAURIERDWARS STRAAT

LAURIERGRACHT

LAURIERGRACHT

2e LAURIERDWARS-STRAAT

HAZEN-

ELANDSGRACHT

ELANDSSTRAAT

Lijnbaansgracht

MARNIXSTRAAT

LIJNBAANSGRACHT

ELANDSSTRAAT

STRAAT

2e LOO

3e LOOIERS

STRAAT

Politie

Polikliniek

A

B

| A B C D E F G H |
| 1 p305 p306 p307 |
| 2 |
| 3 p312 |
| 4 |
| 5 p309 p310 p311 |
| 6 |

0   250 m   500 m

1/4 mile

© Copyright Time Out Group 2004

Time Out Amsterdam **309**

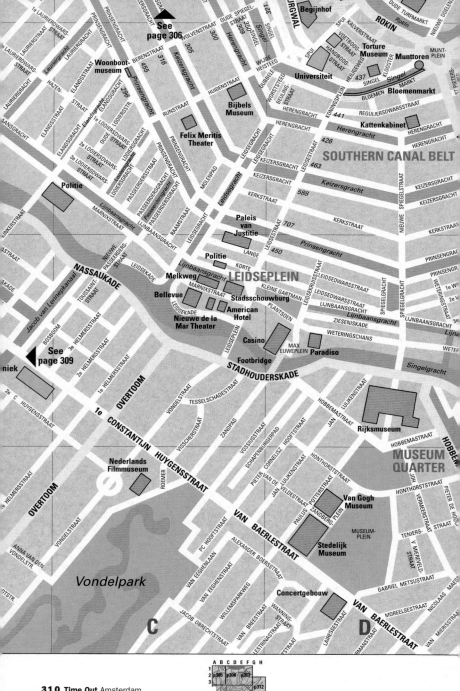

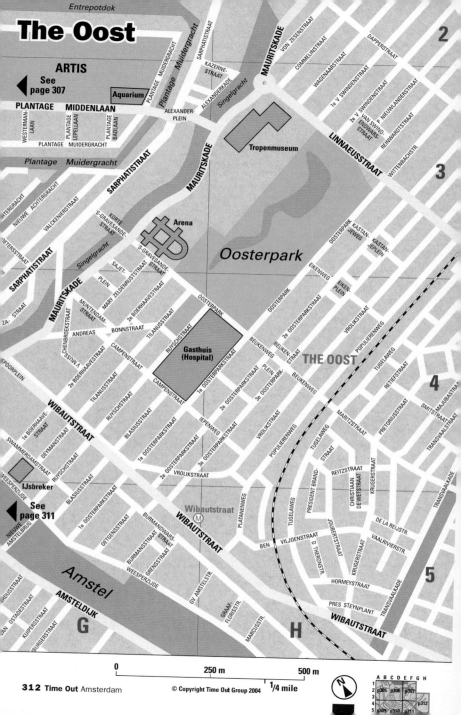

The Oost

Entrepotdok

ARTIS

See page 307

PLANTAGE MIDDENLAAN

Aquarium

Plantage Muidergracht

Tropenmuseum

Oosterpark

Arena

Gasthuis
(Hospital)

THE OOST

IJsbreker

See
page 311

Amstel

AMSTELDIJK

G

Wibautstraat

WIBAUTSTRAAT

H

0   250 m   500 m
1/4 mile

© Copyright Time Out Group 2004

2

3

4

5

Street Index

About the maps

This index has been designed to tie in with other available maps of Amsterdam, and certain principles of the Dutch language have been followed for reasons of consistency and ease of use:

● Where a street is named after a person – Albert Cuypstraat, for example – it is alphabetised by surname. Albert Cuypstraat, therefore, is listed under 'C'.

● Where a street takes a number as a prefix, it has been listed under the name of the street, rather than the number. 1e Bloemdwarsstraat, then, is alphabetised under 'B'.

● The following prefixes have been ignored for the purposes of alphabetisation: Da, De, Den, 's, Sint (St), 't, Van, Van der. Where street names contain one of these prefixes, they have been alphabetised under the subsequent word. For example, Da Costakade can be found under 'C', and Van Breestraat is listed under 'B'.

● In Dutch, 'ij' is essentially the same as 'y'. Street names containing 'ij' – Vijzelstraat, for example – have been alphabetised as if 'ij' were a 'y'.

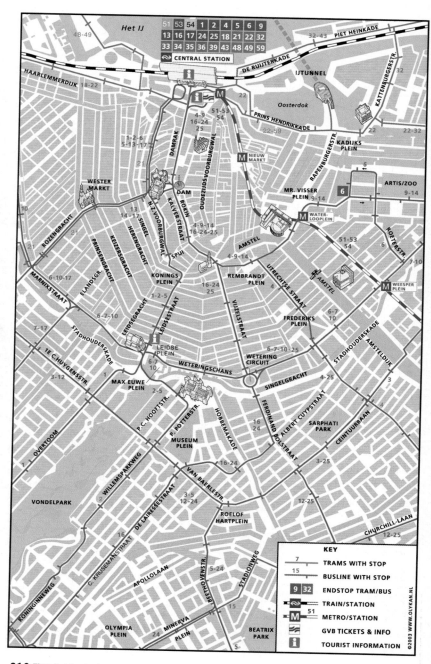

TimeOut

Amsterdam Please let us know what you think

(EIGHTH EDITION)

About this guide...

1. How useful did you find the following sections?

	Very	Fairly	Not very
In Context	☐	☐	☐
Where to Stay	☐	☐	☐
Sightseeing	☐	☐	☐
Eat, Drink, Shop	☐	☐	☐
Arts & Entertainment	☐	☐	☐
Trips Out of Town	☐	☐	☐
Directory	☐	☐	☐
Maps	☐	☐	☐

2. Did you travel to Amsterdam...?

Alone ☐   With children ☐
As part of a group ☐   On vacation ☐
On business ☐   To study ☐
With a partner ☐   I live here ☐

3. How long was your trip to Amsterdam? (write in)

_____ days

4. Where did you book your trip?

Time Out Classifieds ☐
On the Internet ☐
With a travel agent ☐
Other (write in) ☐
_____

5. Where did you first hear about this guide?

Advertising in Time Out magazine ☐
On the Internet ☐
From a travel agent ☐
Other (write in) ☐

6. Is there anything you'd like us to cover in greater depth?

_____
_____
_____

7. Are there any places that should/ should not* be included in the guide?
(*delete as necessary)

_____
_____
_____

8. How many other people have used this guide?

none ☐ 1 ☐ 2 ☐ 3 ☐ 4 ☐ 5+ ☐

9. What city or country would you like to visit next? (write in)

_____
_____

About other Time Out publications...

10. Have you ever bought/used Time Out magazine?

Yes ☐   No ☐

11. Do you subscribe to Time Out London?

Yes ☐   No ☐

12. Have you ever bought/used any other Time Out City Guides?

Yes ☐   No ☐

If yes, which ones?
_____

13. Have you ever bought/used other Time Out publications?

Yes ☐   No ☐

If yes, which ones?
_____

About you...

13. Title (Mr, Ms etc):

First name:
Surname:
Address:

Postcode:
Email:
Nationality:

14. Date of birth: ☐☐/☐☐/☐☐

15. Sex: male ☐   female ☐

16. Are you...?

Single ☐
Married/Living with partner ☐

17. What is your occupation?

18. At the moment do you earn...?

under £15,000 ☐
over £15,000 and up to £19,999 ☐
over £20,000 and up to £24,999 ☐
over £25,000 and up to £39,999 ☐
over £40,000 and up to £49,999 ☐
over £50,000 ☐

☐ Please tick here if you'd like to hear about offers and discounts from Time Out and relevant companies.

Time Out Guides

FREEPOST 20 (WC3187)
LONDON
W1E 0DQ